For The School
of Notre Dame

THROUGH A
GLASS DARKLY

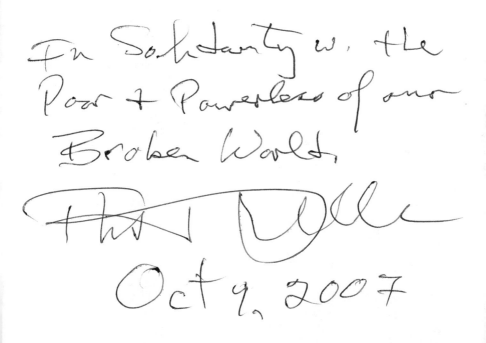

In Solidarity w. the
Poor + Powerless of our
Broken World,

[signature]

Oct 9, 2007

Rev. Ronald W. Hennessey, M.M. (Credit: Maryknoll)

THROUGH A GLASS DARKLY

THE U.S. HOLOCAUST IN CENTRAL AMERICA

Thomas R. Melville

To order additional copies of this book, contact:
Xlibris Corporation
1-888-795-4274
www.Xlibris.com
Orders@Xlibris.com
19742

CONTENTS

List of Illustrations

Following Chapter 25

Following Chapter 29

Following Chapter 31

Following Chapter 36

"For now we see through a glass, darkly; but then, face to face; now I know in part; but then I shall know even as also I am known."—St. Paul, 1 Corinthians, 13:8.

"(T)he management of foreign relations appears to be the most susceptible of abuse, of all the trusts committed to a Government because they can be concealed or disclosed, or disclosed in such parts and at such times as will best suit particular views; . . . the prerogative that superintends all foreign dangers and designs exhibit and vary the picture of them at its pleasure."—James Madison writing to Thomas Jefferson in 1798. Quoted in Emma Rothschild, "Empire Beware," *New York Review of Books,* 25 March 2004, 38.

"I helped make Mexico . . . safe for American oil interests in 1914. I helped make Haiti and Cuba a decent place for the National City Bank boys to collect revenues in. I helped in the raping of a half dozen Central American republics for the benefit of Wall Street . . . . I helped purify Nicaragua for the international banking house of Brown Brothers in 1909-1912. I brought light to the Dominican Republic for American sugar interests in 1916. I helped make Honduras 'right' for American fruit companies in 1903. In China in 1927 I helped see to it that Standard Oil went its way unmolested. In short, I was a racketeer for capitalism."—General Smedley Butler, Commandant of the U.S. Marine Corps. Quoted in Holly Sklar, *Washington's War on Nicaragua* (Boston: South End Press, 1988)

Introduction

Through a Glass Darkly is the story of a regime change executed in Guatemala by the Republican occupant of the White House some forty-nine years ago and its consequences. That act, accomplished in secret by President Dwight D. Eisenhower at a time when it was still important to the political leaders of the United States to protect the undeserved reputation of our country as a nation respectful of international law, proved to be a short-term political success in the narrowest sense of the term. But the aftermath of the installation of a puppet regime in Guatemala in 1954 has proven to be an economic, political, and social disaster for the Guatemalan people, the results of which remain to this day. If the effects of what the overthrow of a democratically elected president has meant to the Guatemalan people—and to the standing of the United States among the peoples of Latin America—were known, perhaps we would have been a bit more hesitant about letting George W. Bush lead us into war in Iraq. A closer look at what the gods and the United States hath wrought in Guatemala in 1954 and during the intervening years should provide the readers of this volume some small insight into what in all probability awaits the Iraqi, American, and Middle Eastern peoples in the years to come, though I fear the results of Hussein's disappearance will vastly overshadow the tragedy that is Guatemala's American-engineered patrimony.

The present volume is the result of efforts I began in earnest some eighteen years ago, while George Bush Sr. was Ronald Reagan's vice president covering for his boss's criminal policies in Central America.[1] The reasons for the long delay in publishing this effort are several. Among the contributing factors have been the emotional content of the material; the complex personality of the principal character through whose eyes, ears, emotions, and activities the narrative comes to light; the exotic nature of the story's historical and cultural background; the sense of moral obligation that I have felt as I try to make this story as believable as it is real; and the discouraging awareness that a large percentage of the American reading public seems to choose its recreational literature not with a view to enlightenment but for the confirmation of their nationalistic prejudices with fanciful Tom Clancy-type novels or right-wing hit pieces à la Sean Hannity. All of these factors have made the public telling of this story a steep mountain to climb.

This story, in a special way, is about a farm boy of Irish-Swiss descent, Ronald William Hennessey, born and bred in the corn and oat fields of eastern Iowa during the Depression. He was drafted into military service some years after high school and sent off to war in Korea, where the reality of war made him feel a call from God to become a missionary. He returned home, farmed a bit more, entered a Roman Catholic seminary, and was ordained a priest in 1964. That same year he was missioned to Guatemala.

Over the next thirty-five years, Hennessey witnessed up close the effects of U.S. foreign policy on the Guatemalan people. That experience turned a rural, conservative American patriot, pacifist by nature if not by ideology, into a severe critic of the ethnocentric, arrogant foreign policy so prevalent in the Reagan and first Bush administrations. He lived through many life-threatening situations only to have death sneak up on him in his sleep on 29 April 1999 in Iowa, where he had gone to celebrate the funeral mass for an older sister.

Ronald W. Hennessey was a hero in my estimation and in that of the thousands of folks he befriended, pleaded for, hid, and protected. He is sorely missed. My most acute disappointment is that he did not live to see this story published. He had hoped that it would cast light on the hidden premises of U.S. foreign policies. He had not the slightest desire to be recognized as the moral and courageous giant that he was.

Ron Hennessey arrived in Guatemala in August 1964. When I first planned to write his story, I thought to begin with that event. However, it became ever more clear to me as I proceeded that the incredible experiences, activities, and responses of Hennessey and his Guatemalan Mayan parishioners and those of their oppressors could only be understood in the context of a knowledge, albeit skimpy, of a series of prior histories. I then decided to begin my account with Hennessey's boyhood and parallel it with events occurring in Guatemala at approximately the same time. I quickly recognized that I had to go still deeper, centuries back, to explain Latin American propensities for benign and murderous dictatorships and the reasonable anticlerical inclinations of Catholic nationalists. This led to discontinuities of place and characters, which at first sight, the reader might find disconcerting. I believe, however, that with a minimum of patience one can quickly attune oneself to the back and forth nature of the narrative and grasp its explanatory power. For it is essential that I present the reader with explanations, with the opportunity to understand. To describe the events chronicled herein without offering some sort of explanation would probably lead to much disbelief and would defeat my purpose in writing this story.

Many books have been written about Guatemala and its last five decades of history, about the destructive role played by the United States in channeling that history. I quote these books throughout my narrative in order to demonstrate historical details of Guatemala's national tragedy and to show that others such as Schlesinger and Kinzer's classic, *Bitter Fruit,* and Gleijeses's *Shattered Hope* have presented the same analysis you'll find in this book. However, most of these books were written by and for the edification of academics, or at least intellectuals. Such narratives do not ably convey the intimacies of implementing, or being subjected to, state-sponsored terrorist activities. *Through a Glass Darkly* is intended to fill this void.

My purpose, then, is to try to break the intellectual and emotional isolation of a nonacademic American readership historically protected from the anger, agony, and enervating powerlessness that flow from living at the receiving end of U.S. ahistorical foreign policies undertaken in the name of an ethnocentric and quasi-religious nationalism. Is it too much to expect that some readers of Hennessey's story might come away with the conviction that a citizen's decision to go to war at the request/order of one's president is always and everywhere a moral decision before it is a patriotic duty? To listen to the rationales provided on the evening news by soldier after sailor going off to war in Iraq sounding like puppets of George W. Bush is to recognize that the "orchestrated" goose-stepping of North Korean "patriots" echoing their maximum leader's call to defend the fatherland is a dark mirror image of American behavior. The underpinnings of such behavior can only be that of might—not morality—makes right and that religion is not only another way of doing politics but it is a way of enlisting the divinity in war.

To this end I have used quotes extensively in order to give life and vividness to scenes in which real people make decisions to take concrete actions with life and death consequences. I want the reader to be present, looking on and listening in, when those decisions and consequences take place. Participants have verified the facts behind the quotes, the dialogue conforming to their memories, letters, and diaries of what was said at the time.

In other words, the use of quotation marks is not meant to claim a verbatim repetition of the syntax and vocabulary employed at a given moment when agreements, discussions, arguments, and judgments were actually made. All scenes in which Hennessey appears have dialogue that has been reconstructed from his diaries and memory, and from the hundreds of letters he wrote to his family members (and which they saved) during his thirty-five years of residency in Central America. All of this material proved to be an invaluable source of information for me. Some readers may wonder how much of what I attribute to Hennessey is a true reflection of what he said and how much of the dialogue is made up of words that I have put into his mouth. The question is valid and one I cannot easily answer. All I can say is that Ron and I talked for hours, days, weeks, and years, going over this manuscript time and again as I tried to pull from a very modest and self-deprecating individual the words, reactions, and emotions that he experienced in the situations described. Often, he would say to me, "What do you think I felt?" or "What would you have said?" Whatever I answered, albeit hesitatingly, he would smile and respond, "Right! That's it! Put it down!" So that is what I often had to do.

For reasons that should be obvious to the reader, I have used a number of pseudonyms for Mayan actors who appear in this book. The Guatemalan Army has a history of kidnapping, torturing, and killing family members of individuals whom they are not able to reach, either because the target is already dead or because he/she has gone underground or abroad. I want this story told like few things I've desired in life, but certainly not at the expense of the health, sanity, and life of the helpless relatives of protagonists. I have also used pseudonyms for three Maryknoll missionaries whose stories are anything but edifying; they have since passed away.

I have used a fractured idiom when quoting most of Ron's Mayan interlocutors in order to underline their lack of native proficiency in Spanish. Since my quotes are in English, not Spanish, the idiom I use for them is not entirely faithful to their on-the-ground expressions. Though Hennessey also lacked a native speaker's facility in Spanish, I quote him in English, and therefore was not able to modify his speech to show his grammatical and accentual inaccuracies without making him sound like a bumpkin, something he decidedly was not.

I first met Ron Hennessey in September 1964 at the Maryknoll Fathers language school in Huehuetenango (pronounced way-way-ten-ahngo). He had arrived a week or two earlier to begin a six-month intensive course in Spanish, Guatemalan history, and some basic acquaintance with Mayan culture and that of the Mayans' Hispanicized fellow citizens, popularly known as "ladinos." We were both Roman Catholic priests, members of the Catholic Foreign Mission Society of America, a.k.a. Maryknoll. I had been in Guatemala seven years at the time.

The following February, Ron arrived in Cabricán, the Mayan parish in Quezaltenango of which I was pastor, to serve as my assistant. A friendly relationship quickly developed between us. The personality of this slow-talking, self-contained, wisecracking priest from Iowa was most notably expressed in his calm and steady demeanor in the face of highly charged, emotional, sometimes depressing situations. I attributed this almost fatalistic attitude to his rural upbringing as the eleventh of fourteen children whose farming parents waged a constant struggle in search of financial stability in the face of the fickleness of Iowa's weather, the hard-nosed business practices of Iowa's bankers, and the nation's depressed agricultural economy prevalent during the 1920s and 30s.

In December 1967, Maryknoll, the papal nuncio, the archbishop of Guatemala City, the Guatemalan president and his defense minister, and the U.S. ambassador to Guatemala all agreed that I and several other Maryknollers (including Margarita Bradford, the Maryknoll Sister who would later become my wife) should immediately leave Guatemala because we participated in a secret meeting—revealed by one of the participants, a Spanish priest, Luis

Gurriarán—with a guerrilla leader to discuss our role as Christians living under a terrorist government supported by the United States. Our intentions were to join the guerrilla movement in some undefined capacity, perhaps initiate our own revolutionary organization.[2]

When the Maryknoll regional superior, responding to our expulsion, appointed Ron Hennessey to replace me as councilor and chaplain to a resettlement project in the northern Petén jungle, Ron knew nothing of that meeting other than that it had taken place. He had to face alone the vicissitudes of that assignment with a minimum of preparation, but he proved equal to the task. When I left Guatemala, I also left behind the priesthood, Maryknoll, and Ron Hennessey.

December 1967 was the last time I saw or heard from Ron until we met again in Houston in December 1985. All Maryknollers in Guatemala had been forbidden by their superior to contact any of us exiles lest knowledge of such contacts prejudice the Maryknoll Society in official Guatemalan and Church eyes. I had read some of Ron's letters to his family in the intervening years, letters that detailed his experiences, joys, and anguish as he witnessed the heroics, missteps, intrigues, crimes, and massacres of the people around him. These were letters Ron had written to his mother, brothers, and sisters— his dad had died a few short months after his arrival in Guatemala. His three sisters—all nuns[3]—mimeographed the letters and distributed them to people interested in the Central American conflict. I was eager to ask Ron a hundred questions about the incidents he had described, to sound out his feelings and perspectives regarding the atrocities both committed and endured by the people we had both known, respected, and in many cases had learned to love. Ron spoke in his usual hesitant way, without passion, without condemnation.

As Ron was leaving our home that December evening, I told him that his story had to be told, that the American people had to hear it. "You alone, Ron," I told him, "can make the unbelievable believable."

He shrugged his shoulders and replied in his laconic way, "I've been assigned to El Salvador. I won't have time to write anything beyond a few letters. Maybe you could write it for me?"

A few months later, with much misgiving, I began the project that became a source of joy and horror for me. Joy that I had the opportunity, the privilege, to associate with and plumb the spiritual depths of an individual whom I felt and still feel represented the finest of the American and Christian traditions; horror at the tales he had to tell. I also felt excitement, perhaps misplaced, at the prospect of playing a role in getting this important story out to those with the will to read and understand it. The pages that follow are the result of our years of collaboration.

I now wish to indulge myself in the little ritual that is so much a part of publishing, though in my case, after eighteen years of trying to get this story into readable and understandable form, it has a weight that goes far beyond what I can express in a few lines: thanking those who have persevered in their encouragement and help. Obviously, in a category by himself, stands Ronald William Hennessey. We spent countless hours together, in the United States and in Guatemala, most of them trying to figure out how to say what needed to be said, what had to be dropped of the literally hundreds of dramatic incidents that would have shown different angles to his character and the nature of the conflict, as well as the hours of comradely exchange regarding our personal spiritualities, Maryknoll, Guatemala, the priesthood, and the present state of Roman Catholicism.

Of a second order are Ron's three sisters, Dorothy Marie, Miriam (now deceased), and Gwen. They provided me with all of Ron's correspondence covering his years in Guatemala and El Salvador and with clippings, memories, documentation, and advice. Ron's ten other siblings, particularly Maurice (known to family and friends as "Junior") and Dave, the closest to Ron in age, also shared memories of childhood incidents that gave me insight into Ron's character.

Thanks also to my many coaches, not named in any hierarchical order that might indicate the importance of their contributions, among them Estar Baur, Roger Bunch, Charlie Kelleher, Terry Mason, Stuart Miller, Greg Rienzo, Loretta Strharsky, Pravin and Ruth Varaiya, Leon and Roz Wofsy, Fred Zierten, and others I'm sure to have forgotten over these many intervening years. To the latter I owe a sincere apology. Special thanks have to include Tom Fenton and Mary Heffron, my editors, colleagues, and friends, who struggled with me to make this effort a readable whole, and Nicole Hayward, who contributed her expert services in designing the book's cover. Also in a sui generis category resides Jane Staw, who gave more time and effort to this work than one should expect from a teacher and friend and to whom I am extremely grateful. There are also a couple of Ron's clerical colleagues who have been very helpful but who would probably prefer their names not be mentioned due to the critical nature of some things I say about Maryknoll and a few Maryknollers.

Most important of all, I take this opportunity to express my heartfelt gratitude to my loving helpmate and benignly biased critic, Margarita Bradford Melville, who pushed me again and again to keep going, who read, corrected, and critiqued every last word more times than I or she care to count, and who sometimes cried over the manuscript's emotional content, but who persevered through seven complete drafts and innumerable partial rewritings with patience and equanimity. There is no question that this project would never have been completed without her unselfish support, encouragement, and arm-twisting.

Of course, there is the usual caveat: no one but myself is responsible for what appears in these pages. It is a responsibility that weighs heavily on my mind. I pray that none of those mentioned above experience any regrets for having their names associated with this project.

Thomas R. Melville
Philadelphia, Pennsylvania
April 2004

List of Abbreviations

AID   (U.S.) Agency for International Development
ASC   Asamblea de la Sociedad Civil
CACIF   Coordinating Committee of Agricultural, Commercial, Industrial, and Financial Associations
CCL   Clandestine Local Committees (guerrilla support networks)
CEG   Comité Episcopal de Guatemala (Guatemalan Episcopal Conference)
CEH   Historical Clarification Commission, established by the United Nations
CELAM   Latin American Episcopal Conference
CIA   U.S. Central Intelligence Agency
CIC   Inter-Institutional Coordination Committees (government structure to control rural communities)
CNUS   National Committee for Trade Union Unity
CORDS   Civil Operations and Revolutionary Development Support Program (Vietnam)*
CPP   Chief of Psychological and Paramilitary Warfare (CIA)
CRN   Committee for National Reconstruction (after the 1976 earthquake), Government of Guatemala
CRT   Regional Telecommunications Center
CUC   Committee of Peasant Unity
DC   Partido Democracia Cristiana
DCI   Director of Central Intelligence (CIA)
DD/P   Deputy Director of Plans (CIA)
EGP   Ejercito Guerrillero de los Pobres (Guerrilla Army of the Poor; one of four groups composing URNG)

---

*   References to Vietnamese organizations are meant to show tactics used in Vietnam that were later utilized in Guatemala.

ESA	Secret anti-Communist Army (death squad)
FAR	Fuerzas Armadas Rebeldes (Rebel Armed Forces; one of four groups composing URNG)
FMLN	Farabundo Martí National Liberation Front (El Salvador)
FRG	Frente Republicano de Guatemala (Ríos Montt's political party)
FTN	Northern Transversal Strip (virgin land in the Ixcán claimed by army generals)
FYDEP	Fomento y Desarrollo de El Petén, or Promotion and Development of El Petén
GANA	Gran Alianza Nacional (winner of the 2003 presidential elections)
GOG	Government of Guatemala
IAC	Intelligence Advisory Committee (U.S. government)
INTA	National Institute for Agrarian Development, also Agrarian Institute (the government agency in charge of legalizing the Ixcán land grants)
IOB	Intelligence Oversight Board (named by President Clinton)
IRCA	International Railroads of Central America, a UFCO subsidiary
JCMM	Julio Cesar Méndez Montenegro (president of Guatemala, 1966-70)
LADC	Latin American division chief (CIA)
LOG	La Liga de Obreros Guatemaltecos (workers' union founded by Archbishop Rossell)
MAG	U.S. Military Assistance Group
MAP	Military Assistance Program (U.S. government)
MINUGUA	UN mission in Guatemala
MITFCA	Marin Interfaith Task Force (Marin, California)
MLN	National Liberation Movement (Movimiento de Liberación Nacional, remnants of Castillo Armas's political followers)
MMM	Mario Méndez Montengro (brother of JCMM and leader of a revolutionary party)
OAS	Organization of American States
OCS	Officer Candidate School (U.S. Army)
ODHAG	Guatemalan Archdiocesan Office on Human Rights
ORPA	Revolutionary Organization of an Armed People (one of four groups composing URNG)
PAC	Patrulla de Autodefensa Civil (Civil Defense Patrol)

PDC	Christian Democrats (same as DC)
PGT	Guatemalan Workers Party (the Communist Party; member of the URNG)
PID	Partido Institucional Democrático (founded by dictator Peralta Azurdia, 1963-66)
PMA	Policia Militar Ambulante (rural military police)
PR	Partido Revolucionario (drifted rightward after its founding)
PRU	Provincial Reconnaissance Units (Vietnam)
REMHI	The Project for the Recovery of Historical Memory, sponsored by the Guatemalan Episcopal Conference
SA/D	Special Assistant to the DCI (CIA)
UFCO	United Fruit Company
UMP	Permanent Military Units
UNE	Unidad Nacional de Esperanza (participant in runoff presidential election, December 2003)
URNG	Unidad Revolucionaria Nacional de Guatemalteca (organization that united the four guerrilla organizations)
USAID	U.S. Agency for International Development
USCC	U.S. Catholic Conference
USIA	U.S. Information Agency

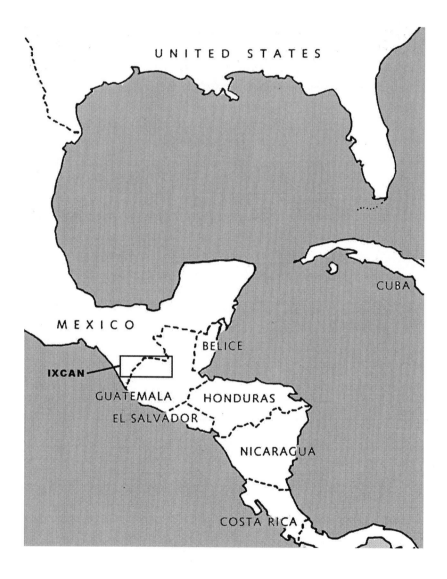

Guatemala and Its Departments

1. PETEN
2. HUEHUETENANGO
3. QUICHE
4. ALTA VERAPAZ
5. IZABAL
6. ZACAPA
7. EL PROGRESO
8. BAJA VERAPAZ
9. TOTONICAPAN
10. QUEZALTENANGO
11. SAN MARCOS
12. RETALHULEU
13. SUCHITEPEQUEZ
14. SOLOLA
15. CHIMALTENANGO
16. GUATEMALA
17. SACATEPEQUEZ
18. JALAPA
19. CHIQUIMULA
20. ESCUINTLA
21. SANTA ROSA
22. JUTIAPA

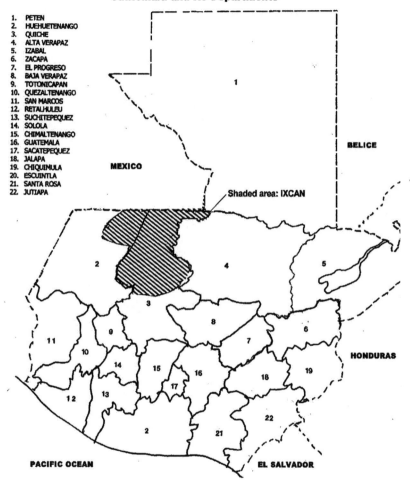

Shaded area: IXCAN

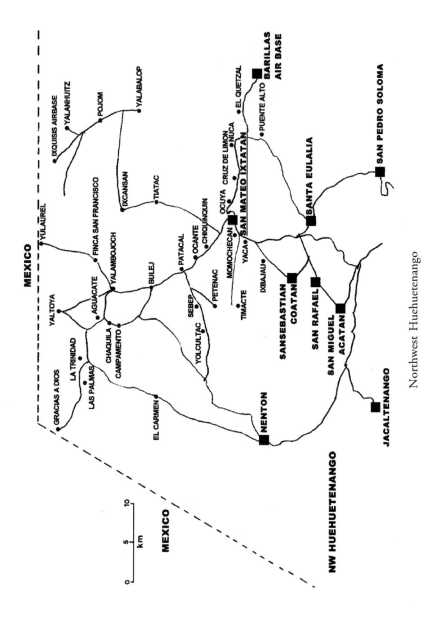

Northwest Huehuetenango

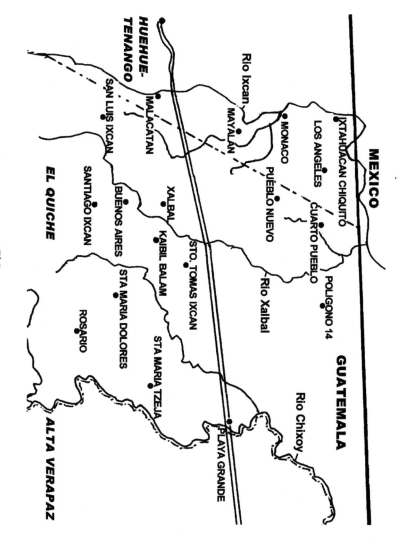

El Ixcan

PART I

Chapter 1

God's Avenging Angels

17 July 1982

The priest sat on the edge of his bed, bent over, head in his hands, eyes squeezed shut, a chunk of ice where his stomach should have been. He felt cold all over, shivered a bit every few seconds. His legs and feet didn't want to move, feeling like they were nailed to the floor, paralyzed. He couldn't stop the series of gruesome scenes that flashed over and over behind his eyes: blood and flesh splattered on the ground, slit throats, burning children and women, headless bodies, crushed skulls. Ron Hennessey rocked back and forth, slowly at first, trying to slip in thoughts of Iowa, the farm, the faces of his sisters and brothers. But they wouldn't come, not clearly. More blood, more screams. He rocked a little faster. Finally, with a push that seemed to take all his strength and not a little courage, he was on his feet.

> *Move! You've got to get dressed! Pull on your pants! Now your shirt!*
> *Arms in! Button up! Put your slippers on! You don't need to sit! You've*
> *got to write it all down. For Diego! For Ambrosia! For all of them!*
> *God, where are You?*

The priest was Ronald W. Hennessey of Ryan, Iowa, a veteran missionary with eighteen years in Central America, now living in the small Mayan town of San Mateo Ixtatán, in northwest Guatemala. Before him, he knew, lay one of the most wrenching days of his eventful missionary career, the long hours needed to record the details of the beastly rituals performed by a company of Guatemalan soldiers as they massacred scores of his parishioners in three different villages. It had all happened over the three preceding days while Hennessey was out of town.

The priest had returned to his rectory dusty and tired two nights earlier, Thursday, after several days of pastoral meetings in Huehuetenango, the provincial capital (population: 25,000) of Guatemala's northwestern state bearing the same name. It had been a five-hour drive over a twisting dirt and gravel, one-lane mountain road, climbing from 5,400 feet at Huehuetenango out through Chiantla into a series of switchbacks and hairpin turns to an altitude of just over 10,000 feet at Paquix. The road then continued across an 11-mile-wide quasi-moonscape of volcanic rock outcroppings and patches of grass nibbled by a few scrawny sheep here and there, past Capzín and its 800-foot sheer drop-off, down through another series of switchbacks to tiny San Juan Ixcoy. Then came a straight (almost) run to the ring of mountains around San Pedro Soloma, up through the pass, down into the San Pedro, across and up into Santa Eulalia, and finally on into the pine forest marking the beginning of San Mateo Ixtatán's territory, climbing, climbing, and then down into the cloud-shrouded valley of San Mateo at 8,700 feet and home.

Hennessey's absence from San Mateo had coincided—not coincidentally—with the three massacres that had occurred in villages four to five hours walk north of town. A few minutes after his arrival, having washed the road dust from his face, arms, and hair, he was sitting at a small table in the adobe convent dining room, picking slowly at his black bean, rice, and corn tortilla supper, served up by the two Mayan nuns who staffed the parish clinic and conducted catechetical classes. While he ate, the priest listened wordlessly as the two women recounted in typical Mayan fashion, devoid of emotion, the sparse details of what they had learned of the killings.

"They forced the people in Yolcultac to beat seven men to death using clubs or else face the same punishment themselves. They accused the victims of being guerrillas."

Sister Francisca spoke softly, reverently. She waited for her companion, Sister Justa, the more articulate of the two, to continue the account.

"They killed everyone in Petenac, men, women, children, babies. They tied them all together, in three groups, doused them with gasoline and burnt them alive. They are all with God."

Sister Justa nodded, signaling she had finished her account.

The two nuns waited a moment or two to see if Hennessey had anything to say. He did not.

Finally, Sister Francisca continued: "They made the civil patrol members club to death four men in Bulej whom they said were communists. The captain himself hacked off the head of your chief catechist, Diego Pérez. He said that Diego's brother was a guerrilla leader. Only five dead."

The priest nodded almost imperceptibly. In an incremental way, his eighteen years in Central America, mostly in Guatemala, had prepared him to accept the nuns' account without question, if not without hurt. He had known for over a year, since that night when three pickup loads of men had slipped into town and randomly shot to death thirty-eight people, including children, that his town appeared on somebody's hit list, probably powerful and respected somebodies living in Huehuetenango.

Two weeks before that slaughter, an entourage of army vehicles and soldiers had rolled into San Mateo to invite forty of the town's most prominent Mayans to accompany them to their base in neighboring Barillas to train as core members of the town's civil patrol. Only ten of the forty were present in the crowded square. These, after being treated courteously by the officer in charge and given some food and drink, had been driven away, fear written in their eyes, members of their families crying softly nearby. Outside town, after the thumbs of the ten had been bound together, their throats were slit from ear to ear, their bodies thrown from a nearby cliff in pantomime of the ritualistic expulsion from Mayan society.

Hennessey, in an act of defiance that risked a similar death, had helped recover the bodies and transport them back to town for religious burial. But while listening to the nuns on that Thursday night, he had experienced a visceral sadness like none he recalled having felt since the murder of Archbishop Romero in El Salvador in March 1980. But like the nuns, no trace of emotion could be read from his hooded eyes or seemingly relaxed, lanky body.

A few minutes more were spent in muted conversation. They asked themselves the unanswerable: What to do? The Sisters hesitated to teach the priest, but Justa finally broke the silence: "We must pray for them, padre, both victims and killers. What they have done is God's will . . . . Otherwise, it wouldn't have happened."

In those simple words, the nun had expressed and solved to her own satisfaction the major problem of Judeo-Christianity, how an all-powerful, all-knowing, all-loving God could first create and then permit his handiwork to indulge themselves in such barbarity. It was a Mayan answer, whose antiquity predated John Calvin's predestination theory by a millennium or more, as logical and valid as the contrary "orthodox" version.

Hennessey shook his head, stood up, and bid the nuns goodnight. He had decided to sleep before pursuing the matter—and the trail of the killers—the following day, Friday.

Hennessey was a native son of the black fertile soils of eastern Iowa, the eleventh of fourteen children born to tenant farmers, Ana and Maurice Hennessey, on 12 October 1929, in Rowley, Iowa. Brought up on one farm after another owned by people other than his sharecropping parents, he knew farming and poverty as a way of life like that experienced by so many of Iowa's population during the depression years. Farming was a family enterprise from which no one but infants was excused, where the sharing of hard work and the table provided by it created a family structure of deep affection, natural religiosity, and psychological security.

Hennessey's appearance was not one that would recommend him for the role of a Catholic priest in any Hollywood production. He looked more like the Iowa farmer he was, a Gary Cooper type at best, certainly not a Bing Crosby. He was lanky and lean, with a body lacking in fat tissue, perhaps 160 pounds on his six-foot, muscled frame, looking like a scarecrow in his loose-fitting khaki clothes. Under an ever-present canary yellow cap with a Caterpillar logo, his sandy-colored hair framed a leathered and freckled face that had seen too many suns, and which came together in a series of angles and planes. His pointed nose seemed to support a pair of light blue eyes set deep in their sockets, with lids that often fluttered and sometimes closed, giving an onlooker the impression that an attack of somnolence was imminent. His firm chin formed a chiseled boundary between his big teeth and prominent Adam's apple. His was an unimpressive appearance for those who looked for physical beauty, but one, coupled with a consistently relaxed air, that hid a sharp mind, a prodigious memory, and an iron will.

The preceding day, Friday, had not seen the priest take to the trail to find the killers and do what, he knew not. Instead, he spent the day bottled up in his office for fourteen hours, receiving one furtive survivor after another from Yolcultac and Bulej, wives, relatives, *compadres*, and friends of the victims, noting the names of the dead and other vital information, including the manner in which they were killed, the threats and curses of the killers, and any pieces of information, including conversations and distinctive clothing, that might identify the executioners.

Residents of a village neighboring Petenac came in with information they had gleaned after nightfall when they crept into the burned-out hamlet to bury the dead, in itself a subversive act according to army edicts. Even as the Iowan transcribed the information, the killers were slaughtering more than a score of residents of another village, Sebep, close by the first three, but no word of these latest killings had yet filtered into town.

All day long Hennessey wrote, sipping the watered-down coffee the nuns brought him periodically. Numerous times during the day he had felt the urge to flee the office and search out the killers to confront them, suspecting that they might still be on their murderous path. But each time he was dissuaded by the realization of a confrontation's futility. What could he say or do to change things? Ride in on the killers wearing his cassock while holding aloft a crucifix and yelling, *"In the name of the crucified Christ, stop this madness!"*?

No! The theatricality of such a thought repelled him. He knew what their response would be. They would laugh at him, take pleasure in shooting him, then blame the murder on their enemies. This, he knew he could accept if it would stop the killing. But he knew it would not. One hundred fifty thousand innocents had already been murdered and another forty thousand had been "disappeared" since the beginning of this conflict almost three decades earlier, and the totals were rising every day.[1]

At the same time, Hennessey felt the need to document as completely and faithfully as possible all the information he could gather regarding the names of the victims and the identity of the killers. He knew that powerful people who had a stake in hiding an account of these barbarous attacks would challenge his report. Among them, he was sure, were some very powerful countrymen of his own.

One item the priest decided to leave out of his report, however, was the suspected identity of an individual who had apparently played a key role in the killings. From the survivors' description, Hennessey thought the man must have been the same person who had given an impassioned speech on behalf of the guerrillas and revolution eighteen months earlier, Miguel de San Miguel Acatán. His was a nickname, given at the time when the guerrillas made their first public appearance in San Mateo. But of those who had been present in the plaza that day a year-and-a-half earlier, few could now agree that this was the same man. Their confusion arose from the fact that the individual involved in the massacres had covered his nose and lips with a ski mask during the time he remained in each village, identifying alleged guerrilla collaborators. The possibility that this man was the same Miguel de San Miguel, a Mayan guerrilla leader, intrigued the Iowan, but he believed that if, in fact, that were his true identity, the man must have been acting under extreme duress. Furthermore, Hennessey's primary interest was in publicizing a pattern of near genocide that was sweeping the whole northwest countryside and those who were directing it, before trying to identify any individuals on the ground.

Now, on Saturday morning, as he prepared to continue Friday's task, Hennessey had no indication that his decision not to pursue and confront the killers would remain one of the deepest regrets of his long and surreal priestly career.

For Francisco Paiz García and his wife, Matilde, close personal friends of Ron Hennessey and residents of San Francisco, a Mayan peasant village just north of Yolcultac, Petenac, Bulej, and Sebep, where the massacres had taken place, Saturday, 17 July 1982 began just as had thousands of days before that date—perhaps tens of thousands if one included untold generations of their ancestors—except for the garbled reports and speculative rumors of savage killings that had occurred during the preceding days in the four neighboring villages.

San Francisco, like so many other Mayan villages that dotted the landscape of northwest Guatemala and southern Mexico, was peopled by dirt farmers like Francisco and Matilde who saw salvation—both transcendental and physical—in doing things exactly as their forebears had done for centuries, a people who saw time as circular, not linear and progressive, as what goes around comes around again and again and again, in recurring mathematical sequences, a prehistoric, astronomical, and religious harbinger of Einstein's theory of relativity.

If time had forgotten the inhabitants of San Francisco, or they time, their enemies had not. By sundown of that fatal day, more than 350 San Franciscans, men, women, and children, would be dead, murdered in the most macabre way. The killers would leave a grotesque scene that had no other possible meaning nor explanation for surviving relatives and friends from surrounding villages than that they, for unknown reasons, had been spared the wrath of a paradoxical God, at once both terrifyingly vengeful and munificently benevolent, a God egotistically concerned that he be appropriately honored for his creative, albeit defective, wisdom, a composite of Mayan and Roman Catholic beliefs.

Matilde, Francisco's wife, like the other married women of San Francisco, rose about 3:00 a.m. from her woven sleeping mat spread on the dirt floor of their one-room, wattle-and-daub home and dressed quietly to the cadence of a whispered, ancient Mayan prayer. She clothed herself in traditional San Mateo dress, a red, wraparound, ankle-length, handwoven skirt and a brightly embroidered, knee-length, Mother Hubbard blouse. She then began her main task of the day: grinding lime-softened, boiled corn between two stones, one flat, the other round like a rolling pin, in order to make the main—and sometimes only—staple of her family's daily diet, an ample supply of corn tortillas.

Matilde's husband, Francisco Paiz García, the wise and much beloved, natural leader of San Francisco's populace, like his adult male neighbors, rose about 4:00 a.m., ate in silence a breakfast of tortillas, black, syrup-like coffee, and, since he considered Saturday his heavy workday, an egg fried in an inch of sizzling pig fat. Before attending to a few community problems and heading out to his cornfield, he sat and cared for his most prized and utilitarian possession, honing his machete to a razor-like sharpness, testing the edge periodically with a spittle-wetted fingertip. When Padre Ronaldo came to San Francisco once a month to hear confessions and to celebrate Mass, Francisco and Matilde would host him in their small home, providing him with room for his cot under their roof and a hearty breakfast (that he could never quite finish) the following day. At the table, while playing peeka-boo with his hosts' handsome four-year-old granddaughter, Juanita, Ron would tell stories and sometimes a slightly bawdy joke at the expense of the Guatemalan military. His intention was to match Francisco's mood, calling forth gales of laughter from his host, a laughter that was matched by Matilde's beautiful, toothless smile, though she understood not a word of the two men's Spanish.

San Francisco was located in the lowland, rolling hill country that stretches north from Huehuetenango's Cuchumatán Mountain Range out to and beyond the Mexican border. The scrubby fields in the area were even poorer than the over-cultivated mountain lands to the south where most of the Mayan inhabitants of the parish of San Mateo Ixtatán lived. The general area of San Francisco was called *tierra caliente* by the local inhabitants, "hot land," where one could watch the heat waves bend the distant landscape all year round and send little rivulets of perspiration cascading down one's face, chest, and back until challenged by an article of clothing. It was a climate quite different from that of San Mateo, 8,000 feet higher in the mountains, often clouded over in a misty fog for weeks at a time.

San Francisco cannot be found on any official geographic map of Guatemala, even those printed before 17 July 1982. Its 60-plus families never warranted any such recognition from the national government. No one who didn't live in San Francisco or in the neighboring villages of Bulej, Petenac, or Yalanbajoch—except those with a moral mandate like Hennessey—would ever want to go there anyway. Even the census takers would skip San Francisco when they made their rounds every ten to twelve years. It was easier to ask the mayor of San Mateo Ixtatán how many people he thought lived in the little village than to make the six-hour hike up and down rock-strewn mountain trails to get there.

And for those who did make the trip, there wasn't much to see once they arrived, just a haphazard series of fragile, reed-and-mud houses with huge, overhanging straw roofs, surrounded by dwarfed *palo blanco* trees, struggling coffee plants, and sad-looking corn fields that any Iowa farmer would plow under without a second thought.

The houses were divided from one another by a 150-meter-long "street," not much wider than a horse trail, which ran down the center of the village and changed from baked clay to a wet, gum-like mud during the rainy season, making travel difficult. But the rainy season, from May to November, was the "sacred corn" growing season, and its rain, mud and all, was considered a manifest gift from God, a sign of divine affection for lives well lived, both ritually and morally.

The village stretched from a footbridge at the stream on the southern end of the settlement to the jail, school, and Catholic church on the north side. All three constructions were made of the same unstable materials as the houses, except for sporting a thin, corrugated zinc roof to indicate their superior status as public buildings.

The reed-and-mud jail, besides satisfying the need to occasionally dampen the drunken anger of a jealous spouse or to punish a careless villager whose unattended scrawny mule had feasted in a neighbor's corn field, also served as the office of the village's only official, the auxiliary mayor. This official, appointed by the mayor of San Mateo Ixtatán and answerable to him, settled according to the dictates of Mayan tradition and a dose of Guatemalan law—sometimes with more than a pinch of personal whim disguised as a legal obligation—those domestic and interfamilial disputes that had escaped the hermetic boundaries of familial and neighborly loyalties. Nor had the flimsy construction of the jail ever been intended to detain a serious offender, since the village inhabitants themselves formed a prison without walls, sentencing miscreants to various degrees of social marginalization, including expulsion.

Few got beyond the second grade in San Francisco's one-room school house—most taking several years to get that far—due to the enculturated hostility of the ladino *(mestizo)* instructors to the thought of educating Mayan children, as well as their unhappiness at being assigned to work in such a forsaken locale. Prejudice against educated Mayans, especially women, permeated all levels of ladino society, as well as the government. Teaching Mayan children to read and write was perceived as a danger to the prevailing social structure and national economy, built as they were on the backs of uneducated Mayan laborers. The teaching profession where it was aimed at the Mayans, therefore—and this was especially true in San Francisco—was often little more than a government make-work program for young ladinos who had finished the equivalent of high school plus an additional year of teacher certification.

The Catholic church was small, not big enough to accommodate more than seventy-five to one hundred faithful. On religious feast days, many would stand outside and watch the liturgy through the cracked walls where the mud had peeled away from the reeds, or stand jammed together inside should a mid-afternoon, rainy-season downpour arrive while the priest was still celebrating Mass. On such occasions, a healthy sneeze could set off a wave of movement that looked like it might endanger the entire structure.

Other landmarks of note in the little village were the crumbling remains of an ancient, 1,200-year-old Mayan temple next to the church, twenty-five feet high, made of rocks the size of cement blocks, with narrow, dizzying steps wide enough only for a toe-hold running up its facade to where an altar once stood to receive the hearts of sacrificed war captives demanded by an Old Testament-like, anthropomorphic God, Vucub Caquix; a small, grassless soccer field in front of the school and jail, where the village adolescents got their only taste of competitive sports; and the remains of *la casa del patrón,* what had been a five-room, single story, wooden house with a corrugated zinc roof belonging to an absentee landlord, Army Colonel Victor Manuel Bolaños (ret.). The house had been torched some months earlier by a band of guerrillas belonging to the Ejercito Guerrillero de los Pobres (EGP), the Guerrilla Army of the Poor.

The guerrillas' arson was a political mistake that alienated the local, unpoliticized populace. San Franciscans held Colonel Bolaños, a shadowy figure, in high regard as a consequence of his successful efforts to obtain a government grant of lands for establishing a daughter village a short distance to the north to accommodate San Francisco's expanding population. Prior to its blazing demise, the colonel's house had generally remained empty except on those scheduled occasions when his representative came from Guatemala City to check on the colonel's 300-plus head of cattle.

San Francisco itself sat on land owned by Colonel Bolaños. The sixty families living there were sharecroppers who took care of the colonel's cattle in return for being allowed to sow a half-acre each of corn and beans, the main staples of their ancient Mesoamerican diet. Francisco Paiz García served as their foreman, the colonel's alter ego, making sure that the cattle were duly cared for. With the appearance of guerrillas in the area a little more than a year earlier, however, care of the colonel's cattle had become a difficult, even dangerous, enterprise. The guerrillas were ideologically opposed to all large landowners, classifying them as land thieves and exploiters, claiming that the animals that grazed such lands really belonged to "the people." In this case, "the people" meant the guerrillas themselves, giving them the perceived right to slaughter and consume a young steer any time they passed through the area. Francisco's objections, as well as his position, made him the main target of their verbal assaults, and more than once they threatened him with death if he continued to take the colonel's side against them.

The villagers, however, not only respected Colonel Bolaños, they often referred metaphorically to his cattle as their children, reflecting an almost parental pride exhibited by their conscientious care. At one point, some ten months earlier, the villagers had sent Milenario Pérez, the village health promoter—who was to become a close friend of Hennessey—to visit the newly arrived priest in San Mateo Ixtatán and seek his advice in combating the guerrillas' design on their bovine charges. Of equal concern was the need to avoid any conflict with the colonel, as well as to prevent an inevitable "police action" against the village by the Guatemalan Army if it harbored any suspicion of collusion between the villagers and the guerrillas. The San Franciscans felt that if Hennessey used his influence to convince San Mateo's townspeople to hide the cattle in the municipal seat, the guerrillas would be stymied in their desire to feed on the colonel's animals.

"Do you think that the guerrillas won't learn where the cattle are located?" the priest had asked the health promoter on that occasion. "They have sympathizers here in town. Moving the cattle here would only antagonize them and then they'd blame Francisco and might make good their threat against him . . . . What about moving them deep into Mexico?"

Milenario took this idea back to San Francisco. After some discussion, the villagers rejected Hennessey's suggestion as a logistical impossibility. But the priest and the health promoter had become good friends during the process of discussion and negotiation.

At about 7:00 a.m. on that fateful 17 of July, Milenario was just beginning to make his weekly public health rounds, trudging over mud paths to give vitamin pills to pregnant women, antidiuretics to newborns, aspirins and antimalarial medicines to those who needed them, encouraging one and all to boil their drinking water, especially for the many dehydrating, diarrhetic infants, and to build privies some distance behind their homes.

Francisco Paiz García, for his part, was advising a newly married couple how the *antepasados,* their Mayan ancestors, handled housekeeping differences and antagonisms that arose between a young wife and her husband's mother with whom the couple lived. As usual, Francisco hoped to resolve the marital dispute by emphasizing the authority of both the mother-in-law and the husband before the problem became public knowledge and ended up in the hands of the auxiliary mayor.

Francisco's position as the recognized leader and peacemaker of the village, his 60-plus years, his large girth, his intelligence and integrity, and especially his sense of humor, were what had first brought the man to Hennessey's attention and had cemented a respectful, even affectionate, friendship between the two shortly after the American's arrival in the village twenty months earlier.

About 11:00 a.m., men dressed in camouflaged field uniforms and mud-caked field boots began arriving at the village from several directions. Each carried an Israeli-manufactured Galil assault rifle cradled in the crook of his arms. They made no attempt to sneak up on the population, though their eerie silence and hostile looks indicated that they regarded the inhabitants as something other than friendly allies.

It was difficult to tell how many visitors—which is how the inhabitants regarded the intruders—there were, maybe three hundred, perhaps as many as five hundred. Everyone they encountered on the trails, paths, or working in the fields, they ordered with a wordless, upward thrust of the chin, a grunt, or a sweeping motion of their assault rifles to march in front of them to the vicinity of the soccer field. Other villagers saw the newcomers from a distance and returned to their homes with a sense of curious foreboding and the need to be with their families.

Shortly after the arrival of the uniformed men, a U.S.-made HU-1B Huey helicopter, painted deceptively with the browns and greens of nature, circled the village before landing on the soccer field. Five men dressed in camouflaged field uniforms, four of them ladinos, descended. The first led another, a Mayan, tall and lanky, his nose and lips covered with a ski mask, tied "like a dog" to his captor's belt with a rope. The leader was of medium build, perhaps five and a half feet tall, light skin, clean shaven, black hair, and dark brown penetrating eyes that refused to blink. His standing was evidenced by his commanding presence, ramrod posture, the fearful respect of his troops, and mode of transportation, though he wore neither insignia nor name tag. Several of the villagers thought they recognized the man, but his identity would remain hidden until some months later.[2] As soon as his feet touched the ground, he began shouting orders, breaking the eerie silence that had begun to envelop the scene except for the whooshing sound of the slowing rotor blades. "You fucking excuses for soldiers," he yelled at the Mayan troops, "round up all the women and children and bring them here to the center. Get some *indio* shit over here to unload the helicopter."

Although the total scene disturbed the locals, no one seemed to feel anything more threatening than a beating or two, perhaps of the village leaders. As Mayans, they accepted ladino abuse with submissive behavior in order to shorten humiliating, sometimes dangerous, encounters. And although those issuing commands were ladinos, those carrying out their orders were Mayans, some from neighboring municipalities like Todos Santos and Jacaltenango, identified by their distinct Mayan languages and dialects, "brothers" who could be trusted to ameliorate harsh ladino commands. Furthermore, army soldiers dressed exactly like the troops now present had passed through their village a month earlier and had expressed no hostility toward the San Franciscans at that time, even promising to send chemical fertilizer to the village to help bolster the sad-looking corn seedlings.

Following that June visit and fearful that the army might misunderstand the village's antagonistic relationship with the guerrillas and the disappearance of Colonel Bolaños's calves, Milenario Pérez had been delegated by his neighbors to go to Huehuetenango's military base to proclaim the entire village's loyalty to the army and to make a request for community amnesty. The quasi-mystical, self-anointed president, General José Efraín Ríos Montt, had made the offer of generalized amnesty shortly after he took power in a military coup some four months earlier. The promised amnesty was aimed at all guerrillas, their supporters and sympathizers, and anyone accused or suspected of same, who dared ask for the president's indulgence.

Now, however, the villagers' confidence began to drain away as the commanding officer demanded that a local be brought to him, an individual at the front of the crowd who had caught the officer's eye. With only a curse at the man's ancestry by way of explanation, the *comandante* whipped out a ten-inch blade and slashed it across the unsuspecting man's face. As the victim fell to his knees with his butchered features buried in his hands, blood flowing between his fingers, a chorus of muffled gasps escaped the startled onlookers. Still, Mayan culture and practice counseled collective silence, and no one protested.

Meanwhile, up in the mountains at San Mateo Ixtatán some six hours away and 8,000 feet higher, Ron Hennessey sat at the table in his adobe rectory now well into a new round of interviews with dozens of neighbors from Sebep, eyewitnesses to a fourth massacre, one that had occurred only the day before.

"Are the killers still out there, *don* Santiago?" the priest asked the parish's venerable sacristan in his soft, hesitant way, the pain hidden in his shuttered eyes. "Do you think that if I go out there I might be able to halt this madness?" Hennessey's hesitant way of speaking, a life-long characteristic, gave interlocutors the impression that he would never finish his sentence, often forcing listeners to provide the words they incorrectly judged him to be seeking.

The old man shook his head slowly. "You know they won't stop, *padrecito!* They are like mad dogs and they will tear off your arms and legs before you can speak . . . . Please, *padrecito,* do not think of it!"

The sacristan was present at the priest's side to act as an interpreter for those who did not speak Spanish, or for those who simply preferred to express their emotion in the local Mayan language, Chuj.

Hennessey rubbed his eyes, yawned, and shook his head. Something— or someone—was urging him to go, despite similar warnings from the nuns and several catechists, the parish's lay teachers of Catholic doctrine. He was not afraid of death and would gladly go if he thought he could save but one life. After all, martyrdom was a higher calling than the priesthood, and if the occasion presented itself, it was to be embraced, but never sought out. At the same time, his self-contained, farm-bred personality and conservativeness would not allow an inchoate emotion to push him into making dangerous, more than likely idle, gestures. He also felt that he might save many other lives by staying alive and telling "the world"—though that be only his own community back in Iowa—of what was happening to the Maya.

It is doubtful, however, that had Hennessey known what was happening even then to his friends, Francisco Paiz García, Matilde, his wife, their lovely four-year-old granddaughter, Juanita, and to Milenario Pérez and his neighbors, his farmer's calm disposition and Santiago Quot's advice would have dissuaded him from borrowing a parishioner's horse and heading for San Francisco as fast as the animal could take him.

At that very moment, Francisco Paiz García stood inside the jail/auxiliary mayor's office with the commandant's .45 caliber pistol pressed to his ear. The still furious officer was yelling at the ranch foreman to either divulge the location of an alleged secret guerrilla base and field hospital, or he would watch his family, friends, and neighbors die horrible deaths, only then to join them. Francisco shook his head, replying over and over, *"Yo no sé nada, mi colonel. No hay tal cosa en este lugar.* There is no guerrilla base here."

As a group of neighbors were herded into the auxiliary mayor's office beside him, Francisco's face reflected a troubled resignation to the impending disaster that he alone seemed to recognize as inevitable. Now, watching the officer closely, he addressed his companions softly, in Chuj: "My friends, it be time for us to pray . . . . We be finished . . . . We work our fields no more. God calls."

Although the San Franciscans held the ranch foreman in highest regard, his words did not convey the finality he intended. The villagers still believed the anger of the Mayan troops and their ladino officers could be assuaged by giving them two of the settlement's best young bulls to feast on, a demand that had been made by the commandant almost as soon as his helicopter had landed.

As the men dressed in camouflage went from house to house to round up any and all women and children who remained hiding there and to herd them into the church twenty-five meters across the plaza from the jail, a sense of fear gradually began to pervade the men. Ladino authorities never bothered with monolingual Mayan women for whom they had little patience and less regard. So why were they now being herded into the church?

Once all the men had been pushed into the jail, several soldiers, their Galils at ready, closed the door behind them while the commandant surveyed the scene around him. The officer's gaze quickly fell on a group of five men standing behind a desk at the back of the room. "Who are you?" he demanded of the tallest.

"Rogelio Cruz, auxiliary mayor, *mi colonel*," the man responded stiffly.

"Rogelio *mierda!* Auxiliary mayor shit! *Mierda comunista!*" the commandant shouted as he walked toward the man. "I am the only authority here!" Then, about two feet distance, the officer raised his .45 and shot the man fully in the face, splattering cerebral matter and blood on the wall behind.

"And who are you, you communist sons-of-whores?" he asked the four men standing over Rogelio's almost headless body.

For a moment, none of the men answered, not wanting to hasten the end they now recognized as close at hand. Then, as the menacing officer's pistol shifted from face to face, one of them responded, "We are all volunteer policemen, *mi colonel.*"

"Volunteer policemen, shit! You are all communist guerrillas. Traitors to Guatemala! You all die!"

Four more point blank rounds pounded the ears of the stricken onlookers while four more patterns of blood and cerebral matter painted the back wall, a prophetic montage of San Francisco's impending demise. Five slaughtered San Franciscans lay together in a bloody heap on the floor as many lips began to move in silent prayer. At the same time, a chorus of children's desperate cries escaped their mothers' control and the church's reed walls to ricochet across the plaza, announcing that even the most innocent were no longer immune.

Late that afternoon, just before sunset, the still unidentified commandant took off from San Francisco in his helicopter, its rotor blades flashing in the setting sun like a fistful of giant machetes swung by a diabolical robot. He left behind the dismembered and ritually butchered bodies of over 350 of San Francisco's inhabitants—children, women, and men—their corpses and members strewn around the village center and among the ashes of the burned-out church like so many pieces of half-consumed firewood. Three bodies, those of the village's oldest male inhabitants, men who had been the most revered and honored for their age, experience, and wisdom, lay together in the dust where they had been murdered, their throats slit in a ritual that their Mayan killers laughingly compared to the butchering of sheep. Nearby lay the bodies of two infants. One exhibited a gaping hole in its chest where a butcher had dug out its baby heart in a grotesque attempt to reenact an ancient Mayan rite, perhaps inspired by the ageless temple at his back, and with burlesque bravado, had smeared his lips, teeth, and tongue with the infant's bloody organ. The other tiny body, a mash of flesh where its head had been, had suffered the fate of many Mayan infants during troubled times in the past, its killer having swung the child by its feet against a nearby tree, shattering its head like a ripe melon. Only sixteen villagers, all men, were still alive at the time, fifteen of whom, Milenario Pérez among them, were shut up in the jail, praying for strength and awaiting their fate. Francisco Paiz García, the sixteenth, a stake hammered into his rectum, was being herded like a tortured animal along a path in the direction of Bulej, accompanied by the hysterical laughter of his captors and their increasingly ineffective proddings.

Many executioners sat around the village center eating, singing, and joking, some playing music from stolen transistor radios. Meanwhile, the ladino officers choked off what little ripples of guilt might have touched their charges' already benumbed consciences by sharing a prized find, dozens of stored bottles of the Mayans' favored social and religious drink, fermented corn alcohol. As they drank, they savored the approaching deaths of the fifteen men they still had cornered in the jail. Of the fifteen, three would miraculously survive.[3]

A few days later in his office in the national palace in Guatemala City, General Ríos Montt was preparing another presidential sermon for the following Sunday's television and radio address to the nation. When he took power in late March, he proclaimed "neither votes nor bullets gave me this position of authority; neither votes nor bullets. God placed me here."[4] And while he decried the political violence that had wracked Guatemala for more than a generation and pleaded for peace in God's name, he had added, "Subversives, hear me well. We are able to speak politically, but we also have the ability to defend ourselves with weapons, to work with weapons, to fulfill our duty with weapons . . . . Father, Lord, I beg you to bring peace to the hearts of Guatemalans, to bring confidence to the people and to consolidate your family. Thank you, God, in the name of Jesus Christ. Amen."[5]

Now it was time to warn the nation once again what would happen to the subversives who worked against his government, especially those in Huehuetenango, his home province.

Three weeks earlier, in the Washington, D.C., home of William Middendorf, President Reagan's ambassador to the Organization of American States, a group of prominent U.S. religious and political leaders met to discuss how they could support General Ríos Montt, Latin America's first openly evangelical president, to combat the negative press he was receiving in some American newspapers. They claimed the stories filtering out of Guatemala describing in detail massacres committed by Ríos Montt's army to be vicious propaganda generated by his political enemies, especially sympathizers of the communist guerrillas. Among those present at the meeting, besides Middendorf, were the Reverends Pat Robertson of the Christian Broadcasting Company and Jerry Falwell of the Moral Majority, ultra-fundamentalist Christian James Watt, secretary of the interior, U.S. ambassador to Guatemala Frederic L. Chapin, Edwin Meese, personal friend of and advisor to President Reagan, and Francisco Bianchi, spiritual mentor of President Ríos Montt.[6]

Chapter 2

To Carry a Bucket of . . .

29 September 1982

Ron Hennessey eased himself into the passenger seat of an all-terrain Suzuki driven by Bill Mullan, the Central American Superior for the Maryknoll Society and Hennessey's boss. The two men were heading for the American Embassy on Avenida La Reforma on the outskirts of Guatemala City's commercial zone. Hennessey had replaced his normal attire of khaki pants and open-collared work shirt for a black suit and roman collar at Mullan's suggestion in order to emphasize the formality of their visit and conform to their hosts' expectations. Mullan had arranged the appointment for this interview two weeks earlier at the insistence of the embassy's political officer.

"You ready for a confrontation, Ron?" Mullan asked his passenger, a concerned look on his sharply featured face, reflecting his doubt that Hennessey shared his view of the conflictual nature of the impending meeting.

Hennessey, relaxed, grunted by way of reply.

"I'm told the ambassador is pretty upset with the publicity you've gotten his embassy. I'm almost positive that he's going to try to force you out of the country."

Mullan glanced vainly at his passenger for an answer as he eased his vehicle through the big iron gates of the Maryknoll Center House in the southeast suburbs of Guatemala City. The Maryknoll superior quickly jockeyed his vehicle into the honking traffic of buses, trucks, and cars on 20th Street and then made a sharp left on 12th Avenue, cutting in front of a wheezing No. 14 bus whose driver raised the middle finger of his right hand in an international gesture of injured pride.

"Anticlerical!" muttered Mullan. Hennessey smiled.

The two men were en route to a meeting with Harold Baum, the political officer, and Philip Taylor, the consul general at the U.S. Embassy. Baum had contacted Mullan to request the meeting because of pressure coming from the U.S. Congress to the ambassador, Frederic Lincoln Chapin, demanding that the embassy protect Hennessey from a possible death-squad attempt on his life. The threat was considered serious by more than two-score U.S. congressional representatives, led by Congressmen Tom Harkin (Democrat) and Jim Leach (Republican), both of Iowa, as well as by Hennessey's own religious superiors. Their agreement on the threat, however, did not mean they were of one mind as to the source of the danger.

If the provenance of the threat on Hennessey's life was in doubt, the cause was not. In late July 1982, after two days of soul searching, the priest had smuggled a letter to his family in Iowa accusing the Guatemalan Army of committing murderous atrocities in his parish. At Hennessey's request, his sister Dorothy made the letter public, sending it to the *Des Moines Register* where it appeared on the front page of the Sunday edition of 12 September 1982. Among other things, the Iowan had stated, "I cannot tell if (President) Ríos Montt is truly a mystic elevated beyond the cruel reality imposed on the people by his subordinate military officers, or if he is a genocidist in the guise of a Christian prophet."

The priest was sure he knew which of the two alternatives suggested in his letter was actually true, but in his usual forgiving manner he looked for an escape from responsibility for Ríos Montt . . . just in case. He also did not want to sound unnecessarily antagonistic to the Central American foreign policy of a very popular president, Ronald Reagan, who had repeatedly shown his support for Ríos Montt. To do otherwise would close the minds of many fellow citizens whom he knew he had to reach to be effective.

The particulars of the "cruel reality" that Hennessey described had created an uproar in Washington, D.C. The priest's letter had contradicted the claim of Ambassador Chapin and that of the U.S. State Department that the Guatemalan government under Ríos Montt, as distinct from its predecessors, was showing increasing respect for its citizens' human rights.

The Reagan administration was piggybacking its Central American policy of overthrowing the Marxist-led government of Nicaragua on the preachings of televangelists Pat Robertson and Jerry Falwell, and those of other New Right Religious leaders. And because the Religious Right saw Ríos Montt as he saw himself, as God's chosen instrument of righteous anger against the Guatemalan—and hopefully, the Nicaraguan and El Salvadoran—apostles of Marx, Engels, and Lenin, the Reagan administration viewed the new Guatemalan president as political manna from heaven.

Reagan had been pushing vigorously to increase congressional support for renewed military aid to Guatemala since his inauguration, aid that had been terminated in 1977 by the Carter administration because of the Guatemalan Army's dismal human rights record. Hennessey's accusations of a wave of murderous assaults in his parish had undercut the Reagan administration's efforts, angering not only Ambassador Chapin and the State Department, but more importantly, as far as Hennessey's health was concerned, the Guatemalan recipients of the proposed assistance.

Some of Hennessey's colleagues said that the Iowan's accusations, whether accurate or mistaken, were a virtual invitation to right-wing military elements in Guatemala to eliminate him. Others, with connections to embassy personnel or to Guatemala's political and economic elite, claimed that Hennessey had provided the Marxist guerrillas active in his area with a convenient cover for doing the same thing while blaming it on the army, thereby undermining U.S. public support for Ríos Montt and the Guatemalan government.

The day following the publication of Hennessey's letter, congressional opponents of Reagan's Central American policies latched on to the Iowan's statements to mount a new offensive against the administration's plans. Forty-two representatives wrote to Secretary of State George Shultz asking for an investigation of Hennessey's accusations and requesting embassy protection for the priest. At the height of this commotion Harold Baum, the embassy's political officer, acting on the ambassador's orders, requested that Hennessey come in from his parish to consult with embassy personnel and defuse the anger of the Guatemalan government.

"What do you think Baum wants to tell me besides the need to get out of the country for my own good?" Hennessey asked in his hesitant, nasal twang.

"Well," replied Mullan slowly, "if Baum's perspective is anything like that of the two State Department human rights investigators who came to see me two weeks ago, he's going to insist that communist guerrillas disguised as soldiers are committing the killings, and that we're almost criminally naive to think the Guatemalan government and army is at fault. And, like you say, he's going to ask you to leave the country for your own good. A suggestion that I tend to agree with."

The two human rights investigators mentioned by Mullan, Melvyn Levitsky and L. Craig Johnstone, had visited the Maryknoll superior and his assistant, Father Ron Michels, two weeks earlier, having made a special trip to Guatemala—prompted by the wide publicity Hennessey's letter continued to receive—to sound out the Iowan's superiors on their views of the priest's statements and their assessment of the local political situation. Neither man had inspired much confidence in Mullan.

Melvyn Levitsky, himself a product of Des Moines, had been named political officer at the U.S. Embassy in Moscow early in his diplomatic career, and later, officer in charge of U.S.-Soviet bilateral affairs. Because of such experience and similar positions in Eastern Europe during the heyday of the cold war, Levitsky was considered to be one of the State Department's premier experts on international communism. His arrogance and sarcasm, honed by the maneuvering and infighting that characterized Washington's bureaucracy, only contributed to his reputation as a baptized cold warrior, a true believer, and professional anticommunist tactician. These qualities now recommended Levitsky to the Reagan administration, given its belief that all Central America was in danger of falling into the Soviet Union's orbit, earning him the post of deputy assistant secretary for human rights.

Craig Johnstone had served in Vietnam where he was listed as the State Department's contact with the CIA. In view of his work there, evaluating the effectiveness of the agency's Phoenix Program, which aimed at assassinating suspected leaders of the Viet Cong's underground supply and training network, his primary loyalty was more probably to Langley, Virginia. The program was effective enough, resulting in the killing of perhaps twenty thousand or more suspected guerrillas and their supporters, but not so effective as to prevent the fall of Saigon. Johnstone was a disciplined and brave man, one who risked his life numerous times in the days preceding the collapse of the Saigon regime to smuggle out of the country one after another of his Vietnamese Phoenix operatives. His skills as a counterinsurgency expert were noted by the administration when it appointed him deputy secretary for Central American and Panamanian affairs.

Neither Levitsky nor Johnstone had prior Latin American or human rights experience.

"Well, Bill," Hennessey finally replied, "you're the boss, though I hate to say so. But I don't think I'm in any more danger now than I have been for years . . . . Hepatitis, dysentery, dehydration, amoebas, jungle cats, and poisonous snakes have all had shots at me . . . . So who's going to come after me now that I'm supposed to be a national icon?"

"Your newfound enemies are more powerful than a few microbes or jungle cats, Ron. Don't joke about your situation."

Mullan, as Hennessey's superior, did have the authority "to call Hennessey's shots," but he knew that no one could fill the post in San Mateo as could his passenger. Furthermore, the two men were good friends.

As a native of New York City, Mullan was in many ways the polar opposite of the farmer from Iowa, exhibiting an intensity of purpose that sometimes showed up in an impatience that the priest struggled to control. Where Hennessey seemed to flow with the human tide around him, Mullan followed a strict schedule to accomplish a series of daily goals. While the Iowan eschewed intellectuality, the New Yorker was academic and analytical. But while other characteristics and idiosyncrasies may have differentiated the two men, they shared an unselfish affection for the Mayan people of Guatemala and, unlike some of their Maryknoll colleagues, a profound respect for Mayan communitarian culture and the remnants of Mayan pre-Christian beliefs and rituals.

A few seconds later, Hennessey spoke again. "Do you know who these newly found enemies of mine are?"

"I think you will have a good idea very shortly. But I also suspect you know already."

The Iowan nodded. "And what did the two State Department types think of my letter?"

Mullan glanced furtively at his friend. "I tried to read it to them," he answered sheepishly, "but halfway through, . . . I choked up. Ron Michels had to finish . . . . What you described . . . was too much for me! . . . Those Mateanos were my friends! I still can't believe so many are gone!"

Mullan had been pastor of San Mateo Ixtatán until his election as regional superior in September 1980, taking over the position from Hennessey who had held it for the previous five-and-three-quarters years. The Iowan then exchanged places with the New Yorker as pastor of San Mateo Ixtatán.

Now, as Mullan pulled up on a side street adjacent to the U.S. Embassy, he remarked in a clipped tone, "Come on, Ron, let's get this over with."

"I've heard from my sister," the Iowan responded as he exited the jeep. "She said that a Melvyn Levitsky from the State Department had told the *Des Moines Register* that no one can believe us because we always take the side of the guerrillas. He also said that he had helicoptered over the destroyed villages but couldn't tell who had burned them."

Mullan shook his head. "Well I'll be . . . ! Levitsky was one of the two so-called human rights investigators sent down from Washington. So that's the impression I gave him? . . . And how the devil can you tell from a helicopter who burned a village? He tried to tell me that those killings were the work of guerrillas. The other guy, Johnstone, was more interested in what we knew about the strength of the guerrillas than in the massacres."

The two priests walked past a pair of indifferent Guatemalan police officers standing guard at the embassy gate and approached the building. The embassy was a fortress-like, three-story, granite building, surrounded by a 15-foot-high iron fence, situated on Guatemala's most beautiful and frequented thoroughfare, La Reforma. At the building's entrance, two marine guards gave the priests only a cursory glance as they passed, indicating that they were not expecting any trouble despite the high level of violence throughout the country.

Once inside, Mullan asked the bilingual Guatemalan receptionist to announce their presence to the political officer and waited while her manicured fingers manipulated a long pencil to punch in the appropriate number on her console. With a gracious smile, she waved the two men toward the reception area.

The two priests took seats on one of several unoccupied sofas. In front of them sat another marine guard enclosed in a small, bulletproof glass booth watching everyone who came through the front door. At his fingertips were two telephones and a console of buttons, presumably to signal the embassy's various occupants at the first sign of trouble. Up on the wall, to either side of his booth, hung portraits of the smiling, fatherly figure of Ronald Reagan and what looked like an almost impishly grinning visage of Vice President George Bush.

Within a few minutes, Harold Baum came through a side door. He was of medium build, a bit prim, hardly the type one would associate with international politics. After introductions, Baum escorted the two priests to a small, cramped room on the second floor in what he explained was the political section of the embassy. Books and papers were piled high in seeming disarray on a table, giving Hennessey a feeling that the occupant was both studious and overworked.

The two Maryknollers accepted the diplomat's invitation to sit on a brown leather couch, while he occupied one of two overstuffed armchairs placed strategically a few feet in front of them.

"Mr. Philip Taylor, the consul general," Baum's voice broke in, "wants to participate in our conference. He should be here any moment."

A few moments later, the consul general came into the room. As the diplomat approached, the priests stood to receive his outstretched hand. Taylor gestured toward the couch in peremptory fashion, indicating that he was in charge and that the meeting was not to his liking.

Baum, uncomfortable, cleared his throat and went directly to the subject at hand: "I have here two letters. One is from Congressman Jim Leach of Iowa requesting protection for you," nodding toward Hennessey and giving a little shake to the paper in his hand. "The second is a copy of your statement of the killings in your parish. As you can see from the letterhead [he handed the copy to Hennessey], a radical left-wing group in the United States is distributing your report . . . . You may not know it, Father Hennessey, but you are being used by the radical left."

Hennessey sat quietly, hands folded in his lap, legs crossed at the knees, looking at Baum. Mullan was sitting semi-sideways on the couch, watching his companion, trying to signal him with a muffled cough that he was expected to answer.

"I merely wrote the truth of what happened as I heard and saw it," Hennessey finally responded in his laconic way. "You know that I also said that the guerrillas have been guilty of killing some of our parishioners . . . . I'm not hiding the atrocities of either side."

"That's not my point," Baum responded. "The U.S. left has selectively quoted your letter to make it look as if only the Guatemalan Army is doing the killing. Now, since you've been used by the left, I'm sure you'd like to balance the picture by giving us written permission to isolate those parts of your letter that refer to the guerrillas' atrocities and quote you."

As he spoke, Baum handed the priest a document he had drawn up for Hennessey to sign, a memorandum that indicated the Iowan's approval of his suggestion.

Hennessey took the paper, glanced at it, a puzzled look crossing his face. "I can understand your wish to have me back away from my accusations against the army," Hennessey replied, "believing that I am either misinformed or do not understand the situation in San Mateo . . . . But what you are asking for is permission to take out of context what I have said, to manipulate the facts I have presented. I . . . ."

"Manipulation, no! Balance, yes!" Baum broke in, his face flushing slightly.

"The entire letter has already been published," Hennessey replied with a shrug. "You can't isolate parts of it now without doing what you say the left is doing . . . . And since the *Des Moines Register* has already published it, you really don't need my okay."

As the priest finished, Baum reached over to reclaim his document, traces of frustration noticeable in the tensing of his jaw.

Consul General Taylor had not moved nor altered his stony expression during the exchange. Now, he broke in, leaning forward: "Your statements decrying the alleged activities of the Guatemalan Army have some people worried that you have put your life in danger, Father Hennessey. There are many who believe that the brutal attacks you attribute to the army were really committed by communist guerrillas disguised as soldiers. They have done that before, you know."

Again, Hennessey paused before answering. "I don't know who these people are who believe the killings I attribute to the army were really committed by communist guerrillas . . . . Where do they get their information? . . . When the soldiers come disguised as guerrillas, which they have done in the past, the people know who they are. And there's no way for the guerrillas to look like well-fed, well-armed, disciplined troops . . . . The guerrillas look like peasants, think like peasants, and carry decrepit arms that no self-respecting army would bear. They are who they seem to be— peasants—with some exceptions in their leadership! . . . Furthermore, the guerrillas don't have helicopters."

Taylor sucked in a short breath before answering. "How many of the killings you detail were due to troops landing in helicopters?" the consul general asked with studied politeness. "And how many helicopters were there and did you see them?"

"Just one helicopter! Its occupants participated in the murders only at San Francisco where the worst massacre occurred. But they used the helicopter to service the troops who had committed the earlier massacres . . . . And I did not see it myself. Our parishioners told me about it."

"Don't you think they could have made it up? Maybe threatened by the guerrillas to tell that story?"

"The various stories were all quite consistent . . . . The guerrillas don't have that kind of hold over the people. There are plenty of parishioners who oppose them, and blame them for bringing the army down on them."

During the exchange with Taylor, Baum had been busy taking notes. At this point, he broke in and asked, "What we can't figure out, Father Hennessey, is your motive for making such inflammatory statements, just when our government's relationship with the Guatemalan government is improving and some needed headway is being made against those communist guerrillas. I thought the Catholic Church stood four-square against communism."

Hennessey sat looking at Baum. "What was my motive?" the priest repeated slowly. "Can you think of a reason why a priest or clergyman of any faith should not denounce these killings and the killers, Mr. Baum?"

Hennessey went on: "It wasn't until July, when things went from terrible to disastrous, and Ray Bonner of the *New York Times* told me the only way I could get the story out was to give dates, places, and names, . . . especially my own. That's when I decided to write this letter and ask my sisters to get it published . . . . My motive was to try to stop the Guatemalan government from killing more innocent people, and . . . to stop U.S. support for the killers."

"Let's get something clear," responded Taylor forcefully, sitting forward in his chair. "The United States has not and will not participate in the murders of innocent Guatemalan citizens! If it had, I would be among the first to stand up and condemn my own government . . . . You talk like I'm some sort of right-wing nut. I'll have you know that I publicly protested the Vietnam War and later worked in the Dominican Republic as a Peace Corps volunteer.

I'm surprised that a Catholic priest and U.S. citizen could entertain the idea, even for a moment, that our government supports repression. You've chosen the wrong side to take a stand on, my friend!"

Hennessey's head jerked ever so slightly. "I have never sided with the guerrillas. Nor am I in favor of overthrowing the present regime. What would come after it? I, too, love my country, if not its government, and I served in the army in Korea during the war there, fighting what I thought was international communism . . . . My only motive here has been to stop both the government and the guerrillas from killing innocent people . . . . What I can't figure out is your motive for wanting to cover up the source of these atrocities."

"I'll tell you one thing," responded Taylor as he slapped the armrest of his stuffed chair, "your accusations are sometimes way out of line. I resent your public statement that we embrace governmental genocide as an alternative to an ineffective AID [U.S. Agency for International Development] birth control program for the Indians."

The consul's display of temper brought an apologetic smile to Hennessey's lips. Taylor was referring to a facetious remark that the Iowan had made that was then quoted by those whom Baum had referred to as "that radical leftist group."

"I agree with you, Mr. Taylor . . . . I was merely trying to startle people to make them look at what's going on in this country . . . . But you still haven't explained why you won't admit to the identity of the killers."

"First of all," Taylor responded in a calmer voice, "we have only your unfounded accusation against the Guatemalan Army. On the other hand, we have credible information, the sources of which I can't reveal, that point to communist guerrillas as the perpetrators of most of these killings. I admit, however, that a company of renegade soldiers acting on their own behalf might have committed some of the killings. But if you were only trying to get attention with that inflammatory remark about our birth control program, you certainly got mine! By making such statements, you bring into disrepute your other accusations."

Up to this point, Mullan had been content to let Hennessey defend himself. Now he broke in: "We agree that Father Hennessey's remark was inappropriate. We apologize for his words about the AID birth control program. But you should apologize for statements made by Undersecretary of State Levitsky about us always being on the side of the guerrillas."

"We didn't make that remark," volunteered Baum, "so there's no need for us to apologize. If the observation is not true, it would be best for you to address that request to Undersecretary Levitsky."

"You must know," Taylor continued, "that you, Father Hennessey, have put your life in danger by making these statements. And it is our job to see that nothing happens to you insofar as we can. You are a U.S. citizen and our primary duty is to protect our citizenry."

"And where might this danger be coming from, Mr. Taylor?" the priest asked pointedly.

"We don't believe you have anything to fear from the Guatemalan Army. However, if some rich landowner's daughter studying in Iowa sees your statements and sends the clippings to her father, he could get some hired killer, even a military man, to go to San Mateo to kill you. It would be the work of an individual, not the Guatemalan Army. And there's nothing we could do to stop it! So it's our opinion and especially that of Ambassador Chapin that you, for your own safety should leave Guatemala immediately."

Baum nodded his head as Taylor spoke. "You not only face danger from some misguided landowner, but from the communist guerrillas, as well. You'll recall that your letter also attributes many of the murders to the guerrillas."

Hennessey muffled a sigh. "I am familiar with what is going on in San Mateo and what I am facing there. And if there is any danger to me, it comes from the Guatemalan Army, not from some faceless landowner . . . and not from our local guerrillas . . . few of whom are communists, as far as I can tell."

"Oh!" exclaimed Baum, a look of intrigue and triumph lighting up his features. "So you do have firsthand contact with these guerrillas, I take it, Father Hennessey?"

"If someone were to ask me," the priest continued in an attempt to be evenhanded while ignoring the implication of Baum's question, "who killed the most people in San Mateo Ixtatán this week, I would have to say that the guerrillas did, since they killed three people, while the army, fortunately, has killed none. But the guerrilla killings are almost always selective and of individuals, and they have never posed a threat to me . . . . Besides," the priest added with more than a trace of irony, "if I were in danger from the guerrillas, I could always seek protection from President Ríos Montt's civil patrols, now couldn't I?"

The priest's obvious sarcasm in reference to the civil patrols was not lost on the two diplomats, drawing a grimace from the consul general. These patrols, another tactic of Ríos Montt's government, were locally conscripted, paramilitary forces under strict army control, most often armed with nothing more that their personal machetes. They served two functions. In the hunt for guerrillas, they were forced to march ahead of the soldiers in case of a guerrilla ambush, drawing fire and serving as cannon fodder. Their other duty was to arrest and kill a given quota of guerrilla supporters from their area. Failure to do so brought them under official suspicion of being supporters themselves, incurring army wrath, possibly resulting in execution. To avoid such a consequence, the civil patrols sometimes engaged in settling personal feuds and land disputes that benefited their ladino leaders under the guise of eliminating guerrilla supporters. For the most part, the Mayan patrollers served the army unwillingly, but they had no choice in the matter.

"What we have to do is to assure that you are safe wherever the threat comes from," Taylor replied. "If you get killed, no matter who does it, we're going to be accused of not performing our duty . . . . Why is it that we seem more concerned for your safety, Father Hennessey, than either of you two?"

Once again, Mullan stepped into the discussion: "Look, we appreciate your concern, Mr. Taylor, but you must understand that Father Hennessey is a priest. If he risks his life denouncing these murders, that's a demand made on him by his vocation and his conscience. That's not to say that we're not concerned for his safety. But his departure from Guatemala is a decision that must be made in conjunction with the papal nuncio, the bishop of Huehuetenango, by my counselors, and myself. Give us a week and I'll get back to you."

Taylor was already standing when Mullan finished speaking, signaling that the meeting was over. The consul shook hands with the two priests in much the same perfunctory manner he had used when he introduced himself, saying that Baum would show them to the front door.[1]

As the political officer escorted the two Maryknollers back the way they had come in, none of the three made any attempt at small talk or any effort to pretend that the encounter had been a pleasant one.

Leaving the embassy, Hennessey and Mullan walked down the splendidly florid Avenida de La Reforma toward their jeep. As he approached the vehicle, the Iowan stopped. "Wait a second, Bill," he uttered softly.

Mullan halted, looked quizzically at Hennessey, but said nothing.

"It's difficult for me to make quick shifts between fantasy and the real world we live in here," Hennessey said quietly. "After eighteen years in Guatemala, you'd think magical realism would come easy for me . . . . Most of the time, it does . . . . But not now, coming from the U.S. Embassy."

Mullan looked sheepishly at his friend as he formulated a question he thought might bring a guffaw from the Iowan. "Do you think that either Taylor or Baum is CIA? This country must be crawling with spies and some are always posted to the embassy. Those guys live in a fantasy world of white hats and black hats."

"The political officer is a natural cover for the CIA," responded the Iowan. "I knew the guy who preceded Baum in the job, Ray Gonzalez, and he had to be a white hat. He was on a first-name basis with every commandant in the country. But Baum seems too naive to be a professional sneak. I think he must have been a priest in a past life."

"What?" Mullan nearly choked. "You do deal in magical realism, don't you?"

Then, with his sad eyes mirroring his thoughts, Mullan muttered, "Ron, you've got to be more careful . . . . We can't afford to lose you!"

The two priests were silent as they drove back to the Maryknoll Center House. Mullan looked out at the volcanoes surrounding the city, stretching their perfectly symmetrical peaks in apparent geological tranquility toward the clear blue sky, with no indication of the brooding fires bubbling below, impatient to spew once again their destructive force on the innocents who farmed their slopes. "What a metaphor," the New Yorker murmured.

Hennessey didn't answer—he was asleep at the superior's side.

After leaving Hennessey and Mullan, Baum and Taylor met with Ambassador Chapin and detailed their conversation with the two priests. By the end of their session, they had decided which of Hennessey's remarks the ambassador might use to calm congressional concern for the priest's safety and to bolster the administration's case for increased military aid to the Guatemalan government. It meant a bit of subterfuge but Chapin—like any good ambassador, a team player—was up to it.

Frederic Lincoln Chapin, known around the State Department as "somewhat of a Democrat," a pin-striped traditionalist, and a buff of European history, was an odd choice to serve as President Reagan's ambassador to Guatemala at such a critical and tumultuous juncture. His receding hair parted in the middle, a jowly, almost pudgy face, an indecisive chin, and jug-handle ears that gave him the appearance of having been the loser in one too many wrestling matches, did not contribute to the command persona that one would expect of a State Department troubleshooter.

Chapin had been chargé d'affaires in the U.S. Embassy in El Salvador in December 1980 when three American nuns—two of them Maryknollers and personal friends of Hennessey—and a lay missioner were raped and murdered by members of El Salvador's National Guard. When U.S. ambassador Robert White, an appointee of the Carter administration and a man who sometimes put conscience above teamwork, insisted that the top echelons of the National Guard and the El Salvadoran government were responsible for the murders, President Reagan's newly appointed secretary of state, Alexander Haig, fired White and put Chapin in charge. Haig's understanding was that Chapin would not climb the ladder of military rank looking for culprits above the lowest levels of guardsmen. The rationale for Haig's action was one that he had stated at congressional hearings at the time of his appointment, that is, that the El Salvadoran National Guard was one of the few remaining bastions of freedom in Central America protecting U.S. interests on the Isthmus against inroads from Soviet imperialism. It was Haig's version of the domino theory transposed from Southeast Asia to Central America, and one amply supported by Reagan appointees.

Chapin fulfilled Haig's expectations and was rewarded with the ambassadorship to Guatemala. In his parting remarks to the embassy corps in El Salvador, Chapin told his listeners he "felt like he had been running a police station rather than a U.S. embassy." He also confided to a friend that he didn't consider his assignment to Guatemala a reward for his work in El Salvador: "You carry a bucket for just so long, and all they do is hand you another bucket."[2] It was a bucket that Ambassador Chapin, suffering pangs of conscience, would spill and then drop almost two years later with unforeseen consequences for his diplomatic career.

At the time of Ronald Hennessey's visit to the U.S. Embassy in late September 1982, Ambassador Frederick L. Chapin was acting as if he did not mind carrying another bucket for his bosses. As a result of Hennessey's meeting with Chapin's underlings, Taylor and Baum, the ambassador was able to send a reassuring telegram to Senator Roger Jepsen of Iowa in late October, stating the following:

> With regard to Father Hennessey's personal safety, officers of the embassy met with him . . . [and] pointed out that . . . [he] had placed himself in a position [of] . . . advocacy of one side or another in the Guatemalan conflict . . . [and] it would appear prudent for him to leave Guatemala to assure his safety . . . . [since we] could not guarantee him protection from the guerrillas should he decide to return to his parish . . . . Father Hennessey . . . stated that he felt well protected from leftist threats by the government's civil defense patrol system presently operating in Huehuetenango.[3]

On 1 October 1982, Bill Mullan informed the embassy that he, along with Pope John Paul's newly appointed nuncio, Archbishop Quilici, and Bishop Victor Hugo Martínez of Huehuetenango had all agreed that Hennessey should remain in his parish in San Mateo Ixtatán as a witness to the culpability of the parties in conflict, a source of moral support for his parishioners, and a symbol of perseverance in the face of possible death.

When Hennessey got the news, he was delighted. He knew that the decision was primarily that of Nuncio Quilici who had recently replaced the ambitious and often devious Archbishop Emmanuel Gerarda, and wondered how a man like Quilici, who put pastoral considerations ahead of political ones, could climb to such heights in the highly politicized Vatican curia of Pope John Paul II.

Chapter 3

GUERRILLAS MAKE THEIR PITCH

After getting a pat on the back and word from Bill Mullan that he was to stay at his post, Hennessey hurried back to San Mateo Ixtatán in a cautious, albeit cheerful, mood. He was pleased that a member of the Church's hierarchy, Nuncio Quilici, had taken a stand—implicit though it was— against the Guatemalan government and its army. It was not a common occurrence in Guatemala where the Cross, as in colonial times, generally stood side-by-side with the Sword. He knew for certain that if Cardinal Mario Casariego, the archbishop of Guatemala City, had anything to say about the matter, his departure for Iowa would have already occurred. The priest's many confrontations with the cardinal over the years had been harsher than any he had experienced with several U.S. diplomats, but only because he expected morality among hierarchs of the Church to take precedence over religious and civil politics.

Now, as he drove distractedly toward San Mateo Ixtatán, he almost missed a hairpin turn at Capzín above San Juan Ixcoy with its 800-foot drop-off. Despite his feelings of joy at being allowed to return to his parish, the Iowan had become more conscious of the new difficulties, perhaps dangers, he faced as a public antagonist of the Guatemalan Army and the U.S. Embassy.

Hennessey's belief, expressed to Taylor and Baum at the embassy, that he remained safe from any attempt on his life by the guerrillas, was well founded. It was the result of several encounters he had had with members of the Guerrilla Army of the Poor (Ejercito Guerrillero de los Pobres, or EGP) during the eighteen months he had been serving as Catholic pastor in San Mateo. The first of such had occurred 30 November 1980, less than a month after his arrival in San Mateo, on a sunny Sunday morning.

30 November 1980

As the priest was removing his liturgical vestments in the church sacristy after celebrating Mass, a breathless Santiago Quot came through the door with an uncharacteristic burst of energy.

"Padre! Did you see them? The five armed men in the back of church? They were there during the last part of Mass."

The priest turned to look at the speaker, trying to discern whether the emotion in his sacristan's hoarse whisper was excitement or fear. As he spoke, the normally reserved old man laid his shaking hand on the priest's arm.

"Yes, *don* Santiago, . . . I saw them," the priest responded in his usual hesitant way, as if he had to think of the words before uttering them. As he spoke, he covered the sacristan's wrinkled, brown hand with his own to reassure his friend.

"I heard a helicopter land on the soccer field yesterday afternoon. It probably left them here then . . . . They must have gotten word that there are guerrillas in the area and want to investigate . . . . I wouldn't worry about them."

"*Padrecito,* these weren't soldiers," the old man responded with a trace of assertiveness, letting his hand slip from the priest's arm. "They took off their caps during Mass and seemed very respectful."

Then whispering again, although they were alone, he continued, "I think they must be *los muchachos,* the *guerrilleros.*"

Before Hennessey had a chance to question the logic of Santiago's identification of the armed visitors, the two men were interrupted by a woman's voice booming from the plaza, broadcasting over a squealing public address system. The speaker alternated between Spanish and Q'anjob'al, a local Mayan language spoken in several neighboring municipalities understood by the Mateanos but not spoken by them: "Brothers and sisters! *Compañeros!* We have an important message for you. *Titanej!* Come! Hear us out! *Todos! Maasanil!* We want to talk to you! This is important!" She repeated her invitation a second, then a third time.

That a woman would take the initiative to organize a public meeting in patriarchal San Mateo was not just an extraordinary event, it was unheard of. And she was not a Mateana. Judging from her language and accent, she was a Migueleña from San Miguel Acatán.

The two men looked at each other, recognizing at the same time that this strange invitation had something to do with the five armed men in church. "What do you say, *don* Santiago? Let's see what this is all about," the priest prompted.

The old man nodded as he turned and walked toward the door, his head bobbing slightly with each step, giving him a look of dogged determination. Hennessey had never seen the sacristan move so fast. He was halfway up the short hill to the plaza before the priest caught up with him.

This day, like every Sunday, was the weekly market day, when local *comerciantes* and many from neighboring towns—San Miguel Acatán, San Rafael La Independencia, Santa Eulalia, San Pedro Soloma, Santa Cruz Barillas, all Q'anjob'al-speaking enclaves—spread their wares before the multitudes who came in from San Mateo's surrounding villages to make their purchases.

San Mateo Ixtatán is a small town of 5,000 to 6,000 Chuj-speaking Mayans nestled in the Cuchumatán Mountains of northwest Guatemala. The parish not only embraced the town of San Mateo, but also more than two score of smaller, associated villages, called *aldeas,* inhabited almost exclusively by perhaps another 20,000 Chuj speakers.

When the Iowan arrived, the plaza looked like it did every Sunday. Colorful blankets and baskets were spread in quilted fashion over the cobblestone square, displaying black, purple, and yellow corn, black beans, pea potatoes, coffee-colored canela sugar, locally mined black salt, and dozens of other staples and spices. Ceramic jugs and bowls, colorfully embroidered blouses and hand-woven skirts, onions and garlic, cheap sugar alcohol, inexpensive Mexican cutlery, and watches and other simple necessities of Mayan village life were all on display. Interspersed among this collage of edibles and culinary utensils were hastily constructed open stalls exhibiting cafeteria-green cotton pants and white cotton shirts, made by the many male and female tailors of San Miguel Acatán from the bales of monocolored cloth smuggled from Mexico under the protection of the Virgin.

It looked as if there were well over fifteen hundred people, mostly Mateanos, already present, milling about, stepping over displays on the ground, brushing past each other, laughing, greeting friends. The women were dressed in their finely embroidered *huipiles* (thigh-length blouses) billowing out over their handwoven, cochineal-colored, ankle-length, wraparound skirts, many of them balancing baskets of foodstuff on their heads with one hand, dragging one or more uncooperative offspring by the other. The men wore the area's typical Mayan pullover, a chocolate-colored, coarsely woven, woolen *capixay*, with slits on the underside of the elbow-length sleeves to facilitate arm movements in raising and lowering the hundred-pound loads of corn or wares that they carried on their backs, held there by a hemp rope tied to a two-inch-wide leather band called a *mecapal* that was anchored across the bearer's forehead. Male heads were covered with a distinctly Mateano felt hat, rather than the typical woven straw hats that surrounding Mayan populations exhibited.

Most of those present would have been in the plaza or its immediate vicinity when the first invitation to the public meeting was made. Among them, close to the center, in front of the mayor's office, were twenty-five or so men and women dressed in khaki military fatigues. The shoulder-length hair of the men, the participation of the women, the grayish depressions around the eyes on many of their faces emphasizing more than the usual degree of Mayan undernourishment, and the unaffected manner with which they moved among the Mayan peasants, all evidenced that these were not members of Guatemala's armed forces.

So the guerrillas have finally made their public appearance in San Mateo, the priest thought to himself.

"They must be members of the EGP!" Hennessey whispered to the sacristan. "The five in church were probably sent to monitor our Mass so that this meeting wouldn't start before we had finished. That's smart politics! . . . What are they going to tell us?"

Santiago shrugged.

As if in answer to the priest's identification, two of the visitors began to unroll a large image of Che Guevara's face and nail it to a post directly behind them. At the bottom of the panel were the initials, "EGP."

How many of these people recognize a likeness of Che Guevara? the priest thought. Why not the image of Tecún Umán, the legendary leader of the Quiché who died fighting the Spanish invaders? Or even their *patrón*, San Mateo, believed by the Mateanos to possess miraculous powers while on 24-hour daily duty looking out for the needs of his ritual clients.

Many of the bystanders, gathered in groups of from five to ten, were talking and laughing with the guerrillas. Others crowded around the young female announcer as she repeated her invitation. No one seemed afraid of the visitors nor concerned with the possibility of being surprised by soldiers while attending a forbidden meeting. There was the usual degree of market-day festivity in the air. Market day in San Mateo, as in all Guatemalan Mayan towns, was a day not only to buy and sell the necessities of life, but a day to meet distant relatives, to see friends and be seen, to renew acquaintances, solidify friendships, to swap news and gossip, and for young men and women to smile coyly at each other suggesting better days ahead. It also was an occasion to drink, and for too many, to take a religious journey into a drunken stupor. The guerrillas' presence had done nothing to dampen the spirit of the occasion.

Yet, in spite of the apparent normalcy of the event and the presence of many of his parishioners, Hennessey decided to remain twenty to twenty-five feet from the edge of the crowd. To mingle with the others, the Iowan thought, would be taken as a sign of support for what was about to happen. He had been in Guatemala long enough to know that things are never what they seem, that one should walk slowly, tread lightly, and be ready to shift gears at any moment. He was not about to send a message that he supported the guerrillas or what they might say, at least not until they laid out a map of the road they intended to travel, one that paralleled his own.

As the priest watched, an armed young man in his middle twenties—obviously Mayan—dressed in dirty army fatigues and wearing a black beret, made his way through the onlookers to the side of the female announcer. The two guerrillas whispered together for a moment. Then, taking the microphone, the man turned toward the assembled audience and waited. He was tall and thin, with a sharp nose and chin, and just the semblance of a beard. His Mayan genes did not encourage the production of the prolific facial hair that his few ladino companions exhibited. The man maintained a steady gaze, waiting for silence, holding his rifle by the barrel, the butt resting easily on the ground. He looked totally at ease, relishing his moment in the sun.

After a few minutes, he cleared his throat and, speaking in Spanish with a Migueleño Q'anjob'al accent, addressed his audience, identifying himself and his companions as members of the EGP, and the EGP as the Mateanos's army. There was no hesitancy in the man's voice, no indication of nervousness, making Hennessey think that the speaker at one time might have been a schoolteacher, or even a catechist.

"We have declared war on the murderous army of General Romero Lucas García and the blood-sucking large landowners," the man stated forcefully. "We must fight to take back our lands, the lands of our ancestors, stolen from us by one murderous government after another."

His pause was met with a thunderous response of clapping and shouting, prompting a broad grin on the face of the speaker.

"Many of us will die so that our brothers, sisters, and children can live in peace, with their own lands to grow enough food, and not be forced to work for the criminal *finca* owners . . . . But as we must sacrifice our family life, and many of us our lives, so you must also make sacrifices. We don't have the liberty to grow our corn and beans, so you must supply us with food . . . . We are now the government here in San Mateo. We are going to appoint people in each town and village to serve as our representatives, to collect food and money in our name . . . . And if any of them abuse their authority, we will punish them. In this way, we will be very different from any government Guatemala has ever known. We will form a truly revolutionary, democratic government."

Heads were nodding agreement and apparent approval on all sides. Only the town's ladinos seemed to withhold their assent, pretending not to listen while occupied with the purchase or sale of market wares. Hennessey shook his head, thinking to himself that a revolution would go hard on the local ladinos, the majority of whom made their living by exploiting and lording it over the illiterate Mayans, acting as middlemen in the sale or purchase of every item exported from San Mateo to the provincial capital or imported therefrom, or while acting as government appointees, demanding bribes at every turn. This denial of an unjust situation, even though a central characteristic of ladino culture, was a submerged, inchoate fear of touching off just such a Mayan uprising.

The speaker was again addressing his audience, making a strong statement intended to emphasize his and his companions' religious beliefs to counter the government's claims that they were all God-hating, atheistic communists. He looked in the Iowan's direction as he made his statement of faith, but if he expected a reaction from the priest, he didn't get it.

He added that he expected every one of his listeners to be on the side of the EGP and then closed with a veiled threat: "Anyone suspected of serving the interests of the assassin army or the blood-sucking landowners will be dealt with justly by a people's court made up of his or her fellow citizens."

With raised fist in the air, he led the crowd in shouting, *"Qué viva El Ejercito Guerrillero de los Pobres! Qué viva Che Guevara!* Until the final victory! *Qué viva!"*

Hennessey was well aware of what seemed to be unanimous *"qué vivas"* echoing across the plaza. Clearly, the crowd gave a lot of public support to what the speaker had said, a man quickly nicknamed *Miguel de San Miguel* by his listeners because of his particular Q'anjob'al accent. Still, the priest did not doubt that there must have been some—perhaps many—Mayans present who opposed the idea of taxes being levied and vague punishments being promised for noncompliance. But any opposition they felt would remain unarticulated, at least in the present circumstances.

Some of the "orthodox" Catholics, those who had exchanged *la costumbre*—the amalgam of traditional Mayan folk beliefs that carried a façade of Catholicism forced on them by the Spanish conquest—for the American Roman version Hennessey and his Maryknoll colleagues preached, looked furtively at the priest each time a particularly revolutionary statement was made. They did not want to be seen as approving something that the padre did not, while at the same time wishing to participate in the seemingly unanimous spirit of the event.

The Iowan smiled each time one of his parishioners caught his eye, to reassure them. Always careful not to impose his ideas or will, he wanted them to know that he had confidence in their judgment as to what was appropriate under the circumstances. Furthermore, more time, more watching and listening, more prayer had to go into any personal decision of his as to the rights and wrongs of the complex scenario beginning to unfold before his eyes. Pope Paul VI had stated the conditions under which a revolutionary movement was morally justified and Guatemala certainly seemed to fit his terms.[1] But Pope John Paul II—Paul's successor (elected in 1979)—was adamantly opposed to any such activity, convinced by his Polish background that revolution was always communist inspired, directed, and evil. His turn to the administrative and ideological right was in many cases extreme, mirroring Pius XII's preference for fascism over communism.[2]

Even with his doubts, Hennessey couldn't help but be struck by the guerrillas' boldness. They seemed confident that they would encounter broadbased support from the town and its villages and meet no organized opposition from the army, based only twenty kilometers away down the road in Santa Cruz Barillas.

The guerrillas had posted contingents of guards at the points where the roads from Barillas on the east and Santa Eulalia on the south entered town. At both positions, they stopped all buses and trucks to ask the drivers and passengers for "war taxes." And with little cans of red and black spray paint, they emblazoned their revolutionary message on the sides of the vehicles: "Death to Lucas García!" "Agrarian Reform, Sí!" "Agrarian Theft, No!" The truckers and bus owners were generally ladinos, opposed to the pro-Mayan and anticapitalist ideology of the EGP, but in no position to deny the guerrillas the use of their vehicles as circulating advertisements for the EGP cause.

The majority of the two hundred or more guerrillas were young Mayan men in their late teens and early twenties. Perhaps 5 percent were young Mayan women. A good number of middle-aged and older Mayan men were also among them, as were a scattering of young, urbanized ladino men, probably university students from the capital. Many of the guerrillas were armed only with 30-inch machetes, a tool possessed by all rural males for cutting corn stalks, sugarcane, and firewood, for killing snakes, and for personal protection. Some carried old single-shot .22 caliber rifles, and a few possessed pistols. Some few, the leaders, had Galil automatic rifles, taken— as Hennessey later found out—from dead or wounded soldiers or purchased on the black market, probably smuggled there by officers interested in supplementing their salaries. But a lack of adequate armaments to meet a challenge from the army, should it have occurred, did not seem to dampen the festive atmosphere as the relaxed guerrillas swapped small talk with groups of townsfolk and villagers.

The second speaker, a self-assured attractive Mayan woman, somewhat younger than the speaker who preceded her, made an electrifying presentation. Dressed in patched but clean army fatigues belted at the waist, emphasizing her femininity, with black rubber boots like her companions, she spoke in what Hennessey considered flawless Spanish. She knew exactly what she was trying to accomplish, carrying on a dialogue with her audience, using gestures and cadences like an orchestra leader. The Iowan decided that the woman— quickly nicknamed Comandante María by her audience—must have had a university education.

But Comandante María did not talk about grand schemes, or brotherhood, or sacrifice. She confined her remarks to a single subject, one that was bound to strike a responsive chord in every Mateano present, no matter their religious affiliation, political orientation, or economic status: "La Cuchumadera."

Hennessey's eyes opened wide when he heard the name "La Cuchumadera." Although at this point he had been in San Mateo less than a month, he was well acquainted with the significance of that name. In his previous position as Maryknoll's regional superior, the prior pastor of San Mateo, Bill Mullan, had sought Hennessey's advice several times regarding how to handle the problems created for his parishioners by La Cuchumadera. At one point, it meant inviting U.S. Ambassador Frank Ortiz to Thanksgiving dinner at the Maryknoll Center House in Guatemala City to discuss the problems with Mullan. The ambassador lent a sympathetic ear and gave a promise to look into the matter of La Cuchumadera. But as far as Hennessey could determine, he never did.

La Cuchumadera was a powerful lumber company created in mid-1977 by President/General Romeo Lucas García, General Otto Spiegler, his minister of defense, Adolfo Spiegler, brother of the minister of defense and head of the government's Forestry Institute, Colonel Rodolfo Lobos Zamora, commandant of the Huehuetenango military zone, and Francisco Ovalle, the military-appointed, civilian governor of the province of Huehuetenango. The company's one purpose was to purchase and mill Mayan community-owned timber holdings throughout the province of Huehuetenango. San Mateo's rain forest was high on their list of desirable targets. However, the Mateanos, like their Mayan cousins throughout the country, considered such property to be their community's sacred and exclusive patrimony, left by their ancestors to provide timber for house construction and firewood for cooking and warmth. For people who would not cut down a single tree without first asking permission from their ancestral spirits and the spirits of the forest, it was blasphemy to talk about wiping out the whole stand, to say nothing about the ecological devastation such a measure would inflict on the Mateano environment and the local economy.

The Mateanos had been discussing what to do to stop La Cuchumadera for almost three years, long before Hennessey's arrival on the scene. The problem had erupted when a former Mayan mayor, prodded by the town's ladino secretary, talked up the benefits of selling "a few trees" to a sawmill in Huehuetenango in order to get ten thousand quetzales[3] for civic improvements in town.

Profound, broad-based opposition to the plan surfaced immediately. The Mayans in nearby Paquix had made just such an agreement with La Cuchumadera and had seen their forest turned into a rock-strewn wasteland. Furthermore, a general distrust of any agreement made with ladinos, particularly with powerful ladinos in the government or military, permeated Mayan culture. The mayor, intimidated by the town's opposition, backed away from closing the deal.

Opposition to the proposed contract grew exponentially when the town treasurer, Octavio Hernández Gómez, publicly declared his support for the sale of the trees. Hernández Gómez was universally detested by the Mateano Mayans. He carried a small .22 caliber pistol inside his shirt, conspicuously caressing it when he wanted to intimidate anyone opposing his decisions. He cultivated his reputation as the town's number one stud by using his position as town treasurer to force sexual favors from those Mayan women who needed his official services. His support for the sale of the trees was not necessary to guarantee universal Mateano opposition to the agreement, but the mention of his backing did serve as a convenient shorthand for expressing deep-felt bitterness toward the proposed contract.

When a new mayor, also a Mayan, was elected in 1978, Hernández Gómez used the man's naïveté and insecurity to threaten and then convince him to sign the contract with La Cuchumadera. Word leaked out quickly that the contract called for the harvest of the entire pine forest, calculated at a value of six million quetzales, for the price of only ten thousand quetzales. The Mateanos, furious, literally cried in frustration.

The Mateanos responded by organizing a committee to visit the Catholic bishop of Huehuetenango, Víctor Hugo Martínez, in order to publicize their plight and obtain advice on hiring a lawyer. The committee did not trust the honesty quotient of Huehuetenango's legal establishment, made up exclusively of ladinos, a problem they sought to obviate by requesting the bishop's intervention. The lawyer, a ladino recommended by the prelate, said he would take the case as a work of charity, as a favor to Bishop Martínez.

Meanwhile, the owners of La Cuchumadera tried to outflank the Mateanos by sending a company representative to town shortly before Christmas to distribute toys to the children. He went first to the rectory to ask Bill Mullan if the priest would distribute the gifts. Mullan quickly deduced from the man's remarks that his intention was to conceal the donor's identity, while publicly establishing the Mateanos's indebtedness to the bogus philanthropists. Mullan refused the request.

Not getting the pastor's cooperation, the emissary went to the municipal offices and, with the unsuspecting approbation of the mayor, began the distribution himself. When Mullan heard what was happening, he asked Santiago Quot to warn the people that if they accepted the toys, the donors would claim that the trees had been paid for, at least in part, thereby demonstrating the recipients' acceptance of the contract.

When the Mateanos heard that the toys were from the lumber company and that what seemed like Christmas magnanimity was, in reality, a trick, they appealed to traditional Mayan justice. After a quick, informal poll of the approving onlookers, a few men grabbed the bags of toys, took them outside and threw them over a nearby embankment. Others began pushing the company's representative around the mayor's office, threatening him. The mayor looked on in silent anguish.

Finally, the frightened toy-man was able to tear himself free with the tacit consent of his adversaries, escape to his car, and lock the doors. Six or seven menacing men followed him and put on a good show of trying to tip over his vehicle. La Cuchumadera's emissary lost no time in taking his leave, throwing up a torrent of mud and gravel as he slid around the several curves on his way out of town, accompanied by cries of delight from the assembled audience.

In attacking the lumber company's representative, the people had reacted according to a time-honored political tradition among the Maya. Most Mayan towns in Guatemala have no trained, salaried police force, no canonically controlled judicial system to pretend that the rule of coded laws held sway. They could not afford the expense. Mayors appointed unpaid aldermen to function as police, while they themselves, although sometimes illiterate, acted as justices-of-the-peace in the name of the national government and were expected to uphold the national government's laws. Nevertheless, a mayor could not act against community consensus unless he was prepared to call on the national police or army in Huehuetenango to back him up. In doing so, he would irreparably damage his political standing and destroy any moral authority he might otherwise possess within the community, perhaps becoming a social outcast.

Community order was basically maintained by dependence upon a series of recognized traditional values and close personal relationships. Social ostracism, or more serious punishments, could be meted out by means of a community consensus, reached with a large input from the elderly, both men and women. Sometimes this consensus was obtained in a formal meeting. More often, there was an unspoken sense of the community, understood by all, flowing from the near unanimous attachment to traditional values and procedures. Such were the dynamics of the confrontation between the Mateanos, the mayor, and the representative of La Cuchumadera.

Two days after the confrontation with the toy-man, a telegram came to San Mateo's mayor from Colonel Rodolfo Lobos Zamora, one of La Cuchumadera's principal owners, demanding that all those opposed to the lumber contract report immediately to the main army base in Huehuetenango.

When word got out about the order, anxiety washed over the town, silencing all but muttered opposition. No one wanted to go to Huehuetenango to represent the community's interests, since it was common knowledge that many people had gone through the gates of Lobos Zamora's army base never to be seen again. When the Mateanos sought the advice of their pastor, Bill Mullan, he recommended they curtail their opposition to the contract lest they lose their lives as well as their trees.

The townspeople did not want to accept the priest's suggestion, but they saw no alternative. That is, not until Tomás Acún spoke up.

Tomás was a Protestant fundamentalist accustomed to disagreeing with the padre on many subjects. Confined to a wheelchair since childhood, due to polio, he expressed his combative energy verbally. "We can't allow them to take our trees," Tomás protested. "We must leave them for our children and their children. If we give up our trees now, they'll take all our lands tomorrow. If we die in the struggle, we die! But at least we'll go to live with our ancestors in peace, not in disgrace. I'm going to Huehuetenango to talk to Colonel Lobos Zamora."

Tomás's short, brave speech was like a communal shot of adrenaline. Agape Toltz, the oldest elder present, was the first to speak up, exclaiming: "If Tomás is going to speak up for all of us, I can do no less. I'm going too."

Agape's declaration was quickly echoed by Santiago Quot, and then by three more catechists. Within thirty seconds, a score of men had raised their voices to announce that they too would go to the army base to defend their ancestral rights.

At 5:30 a.m. the following day, twenty men set off on a battered, produce-packed bus for Huehuetenango, hoping there would be safety in numbers. Despite the early hour, a sizable crowd of relatives and neighbors assembled to see them off and wish them Godspeed. The mood of the well-wishers was one of anxiety, knowing the men were heading off on a dangerous journey. But everyone realized that the trip had to be made. As the bus pulled out, several wives brushed tears from their eyes.

When the Mateanos arrived in Huehuetenango, they walked directly to the army base, their air of resolution somewhat dissipated. After a short discussion explaining their presence to a guard at the gate, an orderly ushered them into a small office where a husky major, a ladino—like the entire commissioned officer corps of the Guatemalan Army—stared at them for a few moments. Finally, the officer pushed back his chair, stood up, and demanded, "What are you *muchachos* [boys/guerrillas] doing here?"

Tomás and Agape began a courageous attempt to give reasons for the town's opposition to the sale of their trees to La Cuchumadera. They tripped over each other's words in their haste to complete their presentations before the officer cut them off—as they knew he would. But the major would hear none of it, launching into a diatribe laced with the favorite expletives used by powerful ladinos when attempting to intimidate Mayans. "You have no right to speak here about matters that I have not introduced. You are *indio* shit! What are your names? I want all your names!"

The major glared at Tomás, standing over him with head thrust forward. Tomás stared back and responded aggressively, "My name is not important and I am not shit! I came representing my people. We are all opposed to this sale. It will leave us without firewood and building timbers. We cannot permit the destruction of our trees."

"Look," the major shot back, "I can throw all of you Indian shit in jail right now and let you rot there, if you don't starve to death first. Who do you Indian sons-of-whores think you are, opposing the Guatemalan government? Give me your names right now."

The major's tone and threat did just what he intended. The men, sensibly, backed down. Tomás gave his name first, then Agape, Santiago and the others, one by one, while the major's secretary recorded them.

When the Mateanos finished giving their names, the major spoke once more: "You sons-of-whores ought to be grateful that I am letting you go. If I ever see you in here again, I won't be as gentle as I have been today."

Over the next two years, the same twenty men were called again and again to the army base to determine if there had been a change of mind in the town. Each trip began with the foreboding thought that it might be the men's last. Each return was greeted with jubilation, even though the basic problem remained unsolved. Each trip meant two days of work lost, sometimes three. The round-trip bus fare cost another two days' income. At each encounter, the men were treated to a venomous harangue by the major—later by his replacement—insulting their ancestry, questioning their intelligence, and threatening them with dire consequences.

But the men held fast while the legal charade regarding the validity of the contract was pushed from one bureaucratic hand to another. Finally, four weeks before Ronald Hennessey arrived in San Mateo, the judge handed down his ruling: "The contract is valid and La Cuchumadera has full legal right to harvest the San Mateo forest." One of the arguments made by the lumber company and used by the judge to justify his recognition of the company's claim was "the lawless behavior" employed by the Mateanos when they expelled the company's toy-bearing representative.

Their lawyer, recommended by Bishop Martínez, had not only lost the case, he then surprised his clients with a substantial 3,000-quetzal fee for his services. The Mateanos, for their part, were totally convinced that the lawyer and the judge had been paid off—or threatened!—by La Cuchumadera's principals. When the Mateanos reported back to Bishop Martínez the outcome of their efforts, he shrugged his shoulders, held out his hands, and replied, "What can I do, my sons?"

It was now two months after the court's decision, and a very effective orator for the Guerrilla Army of the Poor, Comandante María, stood with outstretched arms, before fifteen hundred people in the town plaza asking,

"Brothers and sisters, are you ready to give up your patrimony to feed the greed of Colonel Lobos Zamora and those military *cabrones* that work with him?"

With the movement of her hands, the speaker urged fifteen hundred voices to yell back a resounding and prolonged "Nooooo!"

"And do you think," said the woman, shaking her head to signal the answer she knew they all wanted to hear even as she asked the question, "and do you think that your trees will be protected by the judges in Huehuetenango, by the courts that are owned by the rich and powerful?"

"Nooooo!" came back the animated cry.

Then, in what was a stroke of experienced oratory and political skill, the speaker asked her final question: "And how do we get justice from the government? By asking for it, or by taking it by force?"

"*Por la fuerza! La fuerza!*" thundered the crowd, almost in a frenzy of excitement.

When the cries had died down, the woman waited another full minute until there was almost total silence, broken only by the cries of a half-dozen babies and the smoker's cough of several old men. Then, in a whisper that the loudspeaker carried across the plaza, she swore a solemn oath: "We, the Guerrilla Army of the Poor, today, promise you, our brothers and sisters of San Mateo, that we will give our lives before we let La Cuchumadera thieves take a single tree from your forest. You have my promise as a member of the leadership of the EGP, as a Maya, as a Guatemalan, and as a woman!"

When the speaker finished, the wild cheers and enthusiastic applause told Hennessey that the woman had the total approval of every man, woman, and child present. The few ladinos had long since slipped away.

The Iowan stood transfixed. If he could only preach like that, he thought, he'd have a parish of sober saints.

After hearing the closing remarks and seeing that the meeting was over, Hennessey turned back toward his rectory. Only then, as he descended the short hill from the plaza, did he see the graffiti that some EGP members—or their supporters—had painted on the front wall of his residence: "Let's do away with the assassin government of President Romeo Lucas García." He paused for just a second to read the inscription again and then continued on into his house, knowing there were many pairs of eyes waiting to see his reaction.

Inside, Hennessey poured himself a cup of warm water and sat at his table, trying to measure the consequences of leaving in place the graffiti on his wall or painting over it. Personally, he was not at all antagonistic toward the sentiments expressed. It was only a question of the means to that end. He had developed a profound distrust of the army, but this had not translated into unambiguous support for the guerrillas. President/General Romeo Lucas García, the army's commander in chief, was a special object of the Iowan's mistrust, having been the minister of defense and the general most vehement in wanting Maryknoll Father Bill Woods out of the country shortly before the Texan's untimely death in what was more than likely a murder arranged by the army's top brass. But those sentiments he preferred to keep to himself. He knew that the guerrillas had targeted him intentionally in order to test his loyalties. His instincts were to not satisfy them. But how did that translate into action—or lack thereof—without getting caught between the two enemy forces?

The priest's first thought was to paint over the graffiti, but he recognized immediately that any such act could be misinterpreted by the townspeople as opposition to the guerrillas' offer of protection, thereby aligning himself with the army and La Cuchumadera. Better to wait and watch and not send any ambiguous messages. It was like dealing with a bull in the pasture: no move is the best move! If the soldiers came to town and asked him about the slogan, he could invite them to erase it themselves.

By early afternoon, the more than two hundred guerrillas had faded back into the mountains. But they left behind a flood of rumors, conjectures, questions, animation, and proffered support. The insurgency had arrived in San Mateo Ixtatán. And Hennessey knew that his sixteen years of hard-earned understanding of Guatemala's political culture would be thoroughly tested in the weeks and months to come. It made him wonder at how far he had come from the idyllic cornfields of eastern Iowa, where politics consisted of nothing more than going to the local schoolhouse once every two years to vote the straight Democratic Party ticket, particularly when the name of a Hennessey clan member appeared in the ballot's slot for Buchanan County sheriff.

Now, twenty-two months later, Ambassador Frederick Chapin, Consul Philip Taylor, and Political Attaché Harold Baum, were trying to convince Hennessey that his life was in danger from these same "communist hordes" and were trying to convey that information to the U.S. Congress.

San Mateo (Credit: Maryknoll)

Fr. Ron and parishioners in San Mateo Ixtatán (Credit: Maryknoll)

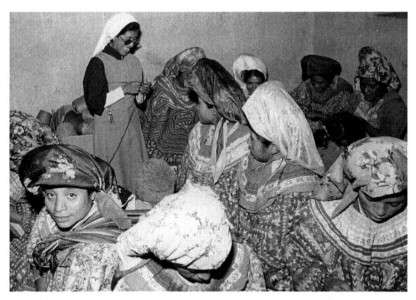

Sr. Francisca in sewing class with Mateana women (Credit: Maryknoll)

Graduation ceremony at the army's elite Kaibil counterinsurgency unit; graduate receiving his machete from Gen. Rodolfo Lobos Zamora (© Jean-Marie Simon 2003)

PART II

Chapter 4

Some Pertinent Histories

Hennessey's long and innocent march along the road that years later was to lead into the black hole that is Guatemala's Byzantine politics began in another age, in a different culture. But that long road, in one of those inexplicable ways that Fate, Mother Nature, or God deals us our cards, prepared him to make the adaptations necessary to survive and blossom in the strange surroundings that Latin American authors and artists have utilized to communicate their views of social reality, the world of "magical realism."

Magical realism is a genre of literature that mirrors Latin Americans' ability to move from the cares of everyday life to levels of fantasy that make such cares, if not understandable, at least bearable. In this environment little is what it seems and what seems to be is only a shadow of what is; dreams, beliefs, and thoughts blend together in an ever-shifting kaleidoscope of interpretations; souls/spirits and angels, good and bad, flit about, some on miraculous contracts of love and devotion, others doing the diabolical work of their malevolent patrons, making the actual seem frivolously supernatural, all overseen and apparently approved by a nitpicking God. In other words, Latin Americans in the literature they produce and in the culture they live are eminently religious, overwhelmingly folk Roman Catholic.

Ronald W. Hennessey was born into a different brand of devout Roman Catholicism in a rented, clapboard farmhouse outside the little town of Rowley, Iowa, on 11 October 1929, his arrival preceding by two weeks "Black Thursday," the day the New York Stock Exchange collapsed. The resulting economic disaster for the United States, Iowa, and the Hennessey family was an experience that would contribute in the years to come to the future missionary's gut-understanding of poverty and powerlessness and to his unspoken determination never to allow either condition to influence his life choices.

Thirty-two hundred miles south of Rowley, in the capital city of the province of Huehuetenango, Guatemala, a small boy by the name of José Efraín Ríos Montt, the third of what would eventually be twelve children born to Antonio Ríos and Consuelo Montt, also Roman Catholics, had just turned three years old. His father's business, a small store that sold everything from fruits and vegetables to flashlights and doorknobs, began to collapse. And like Ronald W. Hennessey, José Efraín Ríos Montt would begin to feel the sting of want, against which his boyhood struggle would produce an implacable determination to survive and overcome, a determination like that found in saints, CEOs, militarists, and tyrants.

Decades later, Ronald W. Hennessey would discover how José Efraín Ríos Montt's upbringing would in important ways parallel his own, producing deeply religious similarities in the two self-contained men, but with cultural and characterological differences that would have them understand God's will for them and their world in ways that were diametrically opposed.

Thirteen days after Ronald's birth, life in the Hennessey household returned to its normal routine. These two events, the stock market crash and their eleventh child's arrival, became sources of additional anxiety for the parents of baby Ronald. Maurice and Anna Killias-Spescha Hennessey were not stock investors. They had invested all their resources and sweat in the black, fertile soils of east central Iowa. But as the confusing news out of Wall Street spread westward, the Rowley street-corner and feed-store economists chomped nervously on their oat stems and opined that a gut-wrenching situation was bound to get worse, with even small bank credits drying up, grain brokers and railroad spurs shutting down, and the sale prices of their grain and hogs hitting rock bottom.

The stock market crash began a process that was to squeeze the smokestack industries and banking system of the United States for a decade or more. However, proto-depression forces had already been creeping across America's farmlands for eight years by the time Ronald put in his appearance on Earth. As prices for farm products fell year by year, beginning in 1921, more and more farmers were unable to make the scheduled payments on their bank loans. Maurice Hennessey was no exception. In 1924, Irish tears in his eyes and Gaelic frustration in his heart, he had stood at the edge of a crowd of neighbors and land speculators in Oneida, Iowa, watching his life's earnings slip away with the sale of his 160-acre farm, a sale executed by a gesticulating auctioneer hollering out a sing-song of indecipherable phrases in the name of Oneida's only bank and of Adam Smith's invisible, idealistic hand, the Anglo version of magical realism.

The farm near Rowley on which Ronald was born was the fifth his parents had sharecropped since losing their own land. Each first of March saw them pack their bedding, kitchen wares, clothes, and farming tools in their all-purpose, horse-drawn wagon, gather their few head of livestock, bundle up their growing brood of offspring, and set out with an uneasy sense of hope for new acreage, praying their rosaries as they went. There, as tenant farmers, they had the fragile security of their faith in a loving but mysteriously capricious God and a one-year contract to eke out a living for their expanding family.

The migrating Hennesseys were not alone in making this annual pilgrimage. During the depression years, all rental contracts were for one year only, with the understanding that a likely looking prospect received possession of a farm in exchange for one-half the corn, one-third the oats, and a negotiated share of any other harvested crops or animals born during the term of the lease. So, on 1 March, tenant farmers all over Iowa moved as coordinated pawns on a giant chessboard, with owners searching for more productive renters and tenants looking for more generous landlords. The lucky ones, those who managed to receive a second or third one-year lease to remain on the same farm, could claim a match made in heaven.

Over the years, Mom and Pop Hennessey had grown stubbornly determined to bear the burden of feeding and clothing their brood by becoming increasingly dependent upon their religious faith. As devout Roman Catholics, they had never considered birth control measures a moral alternative. Furthermore, as professional farmers in a pre-mechanized environment, they believed that limiting the number of family farm hands did not make long-term, economic sense. But in the short-term, another child often meant the threat of additional hunger, when, as Pop once told his parish priest, "feeding my family often depends upon whether my hens lay before noon."[1]

But even as the Hennesseys were feeling the feverish pressures of an economic system that had lost what little, if any, immunological strength its asocial free market structure possessed, the Great Depression was spreading its sickness across the globe. Nation after nation saw its foreign trade shrivel, its numbers of unemployed mushroom, its incidence of crime skyrocket. And the five small nations of Central America that depended so much on trade with the United States were hardly an exception. Four of the five, Guatemala, El Salvador, Nicaragua, and Honduras responded according to a firmly established political tradition born in ancient Spanish history by accepting a military strong man, a dictatorial *caudillo,* as the sole arbiter of their political and economic fortunes.

The Latin American dictatorial tradition, especially that of Central America— the hand of God, and the fingers of the Virgin and patron saints are seen in such traditions—is one whose origins are thought to be based in a disciplined, heroic past, perhaps in the persons of a King David or an unnamed Spanish/ Roman Emperor, but ultimately attributable to the will of God. It is one of historical fascination with the "virtues" of the unbending *caudillo* who rides to the rescue on a white stallion, sent to save God's children from anarchy and madness. This the *caudillo* does by embodying such supposedly divine characteristics as biological, culturological, and class prejudices, vindictiveness, and demands for eternal gratitude, obsequious adoration, and unquestioning obedience, despite the pain he inflicts.

The truth is that Latin America's succession of messianic *caudillos,* still very much in evidence today in the top ranks of its military establishments, including those of its so-called developing democracies, became a cultural tradition a millennium ago through the efforts of a hodgepodge of competing kingdoms and principalities on the Iberian Peninsula trying to drive from their lands the Islamic Moors who had invaded from North Africa five hundred years earlier.

The final victory over the Moors occurred in Granada in 1492 after four hundred years of on-and-off-again warfare. Those four centuries of struggle and war proved to be the birth pains of a nation, España, born of numerous fractionalized principalities and kingdoms brought together under the leadership of the houses of Castile and Aragón. Their military/political union had been strengthened in 1469 with the marriage of Prince Ferdinand of Aragón and Princess Isabella of Castile. It was sealed when Ferdinand and

Isabella ascended their respective regal thrones during the decade that followed and were blessed with the title "the Catholic Monarchs."

The ideology and glue of the new nation, as it had been of its fractionalized parts, remained Roman Catholicism. Roman Catholicism had become synonymous with Hispanic nationalism. Those who did not embrace Catholicism, such as the Jews and Moors still on the peninsula, were obliged, according to a 1492 regal edict, to convert—which many did by going through the motions—or leave Iberia or suffer imprisonment and possible execution as traitors. This edict, not the first nor last example of religio-ethnic cleansing, was carried out in the name of a discriminating, political/militaristic, Old Testament, Hebraic God who used warfare as a major instrument of his reign, but who now had switched sides. It was the beginning of the Spanish Inquisition and its consequences, the deaths of perhaps thousands of Moors and Jews, some legal (i.e., sanctioned by the Church and Crown), others summary, at the hands of mobs and soldiers of fortune.

In 1493, the year following the establishment of the Spanish Inquisition, a Borgia pope, Alexander VI, "by divine right" declared all peoples 475 kilometers west of the Azores to be in sanctified territory, subject to the rule of the Catholic Monarchs. Thus, when Hernán Cortés, Pedro de Alvarado, Francisco Pizarro, and their cohorts arrived in Nueva España and points south, they considered themselves the enforcers of a divine legacy. When entering a hitherto pristine town or coming face to face with a potential enemy force, they began the encounter by reading a proclamation in Spanish requiring an oath of obedience to the Crowns of Aragón and Castile. If the uncomprehending audience did not issue such an oath by word or deed, a holy war was declared and executed.

A lieutenant of Hernán Cortés, Pedro de Alvarado, the conqueror of what is today Guatemala, may have been stretching the boundaries of theological orthodoxy when he and his men massacred Mayan men, women, and children in the name of the Catholic Monarchs, but not by much. Fray Bartolomé de Las Casas, later Bishop of Chiapas, a contemporary of Alvarado, wrote that the latter "had massacred one group of Indians after another . . . killing, ravaging, burning, robbing and destroying all the country, wherever he came . . . in the name of an unknown king of Spain of whom they had never heard."[2] Las Casas further accused Alvarado of having killed more than 4 million "Indians" between 1524 and 1540.[3]

Although the Holy Office of the Inquisition was not formally established in the Americas until the 1540s, its practices were common long before that time. Even the tortures to which the Inquisitors subjected their unfaithful and idolatrous prisoners—suspension by the wrists with weights attached to dangling feet ("the queen of tortures"), dousings with boiling water, large quantities of water forced down the throat with pressure applied to the swollen stomach until blood came from the nose and mouth, cutting off circulation in arms and legs by twisting cords tighter and tighter, use of the rack—were standard Inquisitorial practices sanctioned by the Church to obtain confessions ("the queen of proofs") of heresy,[4] confessions often followed by execution.

In 1562, the head of the Franciscan Order in Yucatán, Mexico, Fray Diego de Landa, questioned his Mayan converts regarding reports that some still practiced idolatry. When the accused refused to confess their guilt, he stated that he "chose the remedy of hanging them by the hands with a rope, arms stretched out and turned forward, rather than torment [sic]."[5] During one three-month investigation in 1563, de Landa supervised the questioning and torture of 4,500 suspected idolaters, of whom 158 were said to have died during the interrogation.[6] In recognition of his zeal, de Landa was awarded the episcopal miter by the papacy in 1570.

Theological orthodoxy, furthermore, included the Roman Catholic Church's claim to be a monotheistic God's exclusive vehicle for attaining eternal salvation. A corollary of that doctrine, one that held sway during the Middle Ages and retains today much of its potency in the thinking of numerous hierarchs throughout Latin America and in Rome, is that "errors" and "purveyors of errors" have no rights.[7] Just as some governments today reserve the right to execute those guilty of physical murder or treason, so the Church in centuries past has maintained that death was a reasonable punishment for murderers of the life of divine grace in the soul, an act of eternal treason.

The discovery, invasion, and conquest of the Americas begun by the Spaniards in the year of the expulsion of the Moors from Iberia and the establishment of the Inquisition, meant that the tactics, strategies, and goals of the wars against the infidel Moors would be replicated against the newly encountered and equally nonbelieving, dark-skinned Native Americans. The consequence was military subjugation with the loss of health, lands, freedom, and substantial elements of their cultures, as well as their lives. Their reward for accepting subjugation was slavery, the imposition of the Spanish language and civilization, an infusion of "white" blood, baptism, and possible eternal salvation.

This, in essence, is the cultural inheritance of the "Reconquest" of the Iberian Peninsula and the "Conquest" of the Americas, molded by the passage of time and the hand of God that is still embraced today by the ruling elite of Guatemala. It was God's will then; it is still largely God's will now. And any loosening of the iron grip on the throat of Mayan subjugated status is to court Mayan rebellion, Mayan idolatry and barbarism, and the death of Western (ladino) civilization.

In Guatemala, the richest and most populous of the Central American nations, the onslaught of the Great Depression ushered Jorge Ubico into the presidency in 1931. He was a despotic, cruel, paranoid, sexually impotent but politically astute army general, son of a wealthy landowning family. Ubico was the fourth *caudillo* to take the reins of Guatemala's government since the country had gained its political independence from Spain in 1821 and—supposedly— its ideological, political, and economic independence from the Catholic Church. By the end of Ubico's tenure, Guatemala had been under dictatorial rule for 75 of the 123 years of its "independence." The other forty-eight years were generally ones of turbulence and fractionalization as short-term, less successful *caudillos* pushed, and were pushed by, would-be *caudillos,* all of whom occasionally used civilian puppets to further their poorly disguised ambitions.

The independence movements throughout Hispanic America were roundly condemned as heretical and treasonous by the Catholic bishops of each geographical region, the members of which all made valid claims to titles of Spanish nobility and received generous stipends from the Spanish crown. These bishops had been named to their episcopal sees by the pope only after the Spanish monarchs had exercised their right, called the *Patronato Real,* granted by Pope Julius II in 1504, to vet and approve—or veto—the episcopal candidates' loyalty to the throne. The monarchs' rights included all decisions on where to establish cathedrals, churches, monasteries, convents, and benefices, as well as the granting of permissions to enlarge or move them once established. These rights were granted with the proviso that the Catholic Monarchs would send their crusaders not only to conquer the heathen but also to take responsibility to see that they learned Catholic doctrine and accepted baptism. Conquest and conversion were seen as a single undertaking, the marriage of the Cross and the Sword that remained the exclusive ideological current of the ruling elite of the various Latin American ecclesial political jurisdictions until Independence. It remains that of a multitude of prelates to the present day.[8]

The Church and its bishops, both as an institution and as individuals, were the single largest group of landowners in the New World and Spanish America's primary money lenders.[9] As such it and they were the prime targets of independence leaders, not a few of whom were themselves priests. Thirteen of twenty-nine signatories of Guatemala's Declaration of Independence were minor clerics, as both sides claimed the Christian God as their champion.

So it was that although independence raised anticlericalism to an official dogma of the new regimes, the grip of a folk Catholicism concentrating on the pre-Columbian worship of the spirits of the dead, appeals to the motherly concern of the Virgin Goddess—whether Mary, Tonantzin, or Coatlicue— and the strength and suffering of the Crucified Christ were embedded in the hearts of most Latin Americans. And it is by means of this folk Catholicism that the hierarchical Church in the persons of the bishops—although they had received a humiliating social demotion as a result of the independence movements—has managed, as the recognized broker of religious mysteries, to retain at least a modicum of political power. It is a power that all postindependence *caudillos* have had to take into consideration if they wished to maintain a degree of civil tranquility, either by isolating the bishops and their most determined followers by deportation and repression—the favored choice, as, until recently, in Mexico—or by a subtle accommodation that benefits both the bishops and the *caudillos*. Jorge Ubico chose a mild form of the latter course for Guatemala in 1931.

The Hennessey household attained a quotient of stability with the election of President Franklin Delano Roosevelt in 1932 and his repeat victories in 1936 and 1940, instilling in Mom and Pop Hennessey a life-long commitment to the Democratic Party. That stability came as a result of FDR's Farm Credit Administration (FCA), established to make long-term loans at low interest rates, and the Agricultural Adjustment Administration (AAA), to regulate agricultural production and stabilize prices. An AAA program that was especially beneficial to Pop Hennessey was one that he called "the corn and hog plan," mandating that farmers take only limited amounts of corn to market, storing the remainder, and that they respect a ceiling on the number of pigs they raised.

When word went around that a government inspector was in the area checking that excess corn was sealed in cribs or bins and that the hog limit had not been exceeded, Pop would employ his "impression-making" technique. He'd call his five oldest boys together to help hide their extra pigs in the hayloft. The exercise often tried Pop's patience to the limit as Ron, the family clown, made acrobatic but intentionally futile dives to catch a squealing piglet he had purposely let slip from his arms, accompanied by a chorus of side-splitting laughter from his brothers.

Afterwards, Maurice Sr. would caution his sons to stay away from the inspector "so he don't get a chance to ask if the penned hogs are the only ones we've got. If he asks me, I'll tell him to look around. That way, we don't get into telling him lies." It was a lesson in political morality that Ron learned well.

Roosevelt's farm policies, Pop's energy and dedication, Mom's determination and management abilities, a considerate landowner, and the developing maturity of the Hennessey children all contributed to the family's increasing productive capabilities, which enabled them to remain stable on the Diemer farm in Brandon, six miles west of Rowley, from 1933 to 1938. Mom's childbearing years were over by 1937, having delivered fifteen children in all (John, number eight, died shortly after birth due to a bowel obstruction). Two of the older girls, Dorothy and Miriam, had entered the convent, Tom and Jack, the two oldest boys, were Pop's full-time helpers on the land, another seven were either attending the nearest one-room schoolhouse or studying their books under Mom's unflinching gaze; only baby Mary June was exempt from performing barnyard chores.

Meanwhile, Mom and Pop had taught all their children by word and example that their ability to accept hardship and suffering without complaint and their willingness to share their time and possessions with those in need was the essence of their Roman Catholic faith, which some day would earn them bountiful, heavenly rewards. Theirs was a strict Irish-American version (Pop's) of Roman Catholicism with a healthy dash of Swiss pragmatism (Mom's). It was a worldview that assimilated Northern Europe's Calvinistic "Protestant ethic" of cleanliness and hard work, combined with Manichean, dualistic forces that held that one's body was of the earth, earthy, and that human sexuality in thought, word, and deed was intended by an unsympathetic Creator to be employed only for sacramentalized reproduction, and as such was the primary source of hedonistic temptation and eternal damnation.

Motivated by her immigrant Swiss parents, who kept one foot in the old country where they had left two of Mom's brothers—hoping to the end to bring them to the United States—one of Mom Hennessey's principal intellectual goals was to understand other peoples, their cultures, their values. As a former school teacher, she never tired of using her pedagogical skills to teach her children to "take care not to judge others. You can never tell how they have been brought up, their history, their culture."

Ronald developed into the family's number one practical joker, the first to grasp any opportunity to provoke laughter, often, but not always, at his own expense. When he wasn't tricking brother Dave into dating an aggressive or unattractive female, or jerry-rigging the cars of his sisters' boyfriends, he was embarrassing Mom when their parish priest came to dine by deliberately ignoring proper table manners and then pretending she had kicked him under the table.

Afterwards, Ron never failed to apologize, his eyes fluttering, the corners of his mouth twitching with a smothered smile. It was a trait that he would carry into adult life—one that often left his friends and close associates laughing gleefully, but also in wonder. His humor seemed to serve him as a bridge for establishing friendly relationships with whomever he came in contact, and as a foil to ward off potential conflict. Perhaps, some colleagues would later think, it was a way of denying that such conflict of opinions or mores even existed.

During the late thirties and early forties, letters from two uncles and aunts and several cousins in Switzerland assured an above-average understanding among the Hennessey children of political happenings in both Europe and the United States. Mom led discussions at the dinner table on the characteristics of fascism, communism, and democracy, and their mutually destructive wars. She questioned the morality of the opposition of many

Irish American bishops—including the Bishop of Dubuque—to the United States' evolving support of the hated British in their war against Hitler, as well as the saturation bombing of Dresden and President Truman's decision to drop atomic bombs on civilian populations in Japan. At one point, Mom had forbidden her offspring to bring books or papers to the table that one or another sought to use to support a position or to frame a complex question.

The marriage of Roman Catholic values and patriotic emotions, plus the table discussions on international events fed off one another to the point that it was difficult to discover what provided the most persuasive power. But in principle, there was no mistake that God came before country, religion before patriotism, and that all political/military decisions had to be made in the light of a well-formed, Catholic moral conscience. As a result, sons Tom and Jack, and then daughter Catherine, signed up for military service shortly after the United States entered World War II, Tom joining the navy, Jack the army air corps, and Catherine enlisting as an army nurse. Neither they, nor any other member of the clan, perceived any moral reason to oppose the war against Hitler and fascism.

General Jorge Ubico, astute politician that he was, gained the presidency of Guatemala in a time-honored tradition, by going through the motions of a rigged election in which he ran unopposed. This was not an easy accomplishment for someone who had lost his sexual potency in a boyhood riding accident in a culture where male, heterosexual aggressiveness and marital infidelity are, among others, defining characteristics of *caudillismo*. Ubico accomplished this feat by demonstrating adolescent acts of *caudillo* bravado—breakneck horseback and motorcycle acrobatics, climbing into the lions' cage at Guatemala City's zoo and kicking its occupants into a state of cowering confusion—as well as implacable cruelty. Further, he enlisted the political support of two of the three most powerful institutions in Guatemala: the hierarchy of the Catholic Church and the on-scene representatives of the U.S. government. As an army general, he already possessed and maintained by force of character the third leg of Guatemala's power tripod, the temporary loyalty of his military officer corps.

Ubico played to the weakness of President Herbert Hoover's ambassador to Guatemala, Sheldon Whitehouse, a confirmed tennis enthusiast, letting the diplomat occasionally win a set or two. The general would follow up such flattering encounters by outlining the favors he would do for U.S. business interests once he became president, particularly for the state within a state, the well-connected, all-powerful United Fruit Company (UFCO), known in Guatemala as "the Octopus."

The U.S. State Department accepted the word of Whitehouse that "Ubico is the best friend the United States has in Latin America,"[10] and orchestrated the general's march to the presidency by employing a tactic that had become the hallmark of American diplomacy in Latin America over the preceding three-quarters of a century: insisting that candidates considered less friendly to the United States not be allowed to run against the chosen candidate. The request in this case was backed by the threat of nonrecognition of any government led by undesirable individuals, a move that would cancel all U.S.-Guatemalan trade agreements.

Ubico demonstrated the accuracy of Ambassador Whitehouse's assessment when the new president granted the Boston-based United Fruit Company an exemption from all property taxes, duty-free importation of goods and equipment, no limits on remittance of profits, and a salary limit of fifty cents per day for UFCO workers. He also gave the company a 99-year lease on 200,000 acres of land on the country's Pacific coastal plain in exchange for a promise to build a port on the Pacific coast, a promise that the dictator later canceled in exchange for $50,000. This grant mirrored a similar concession made by dictator Estrada Cabrera to UFCO at the turn of the century with lands on the Atlantic piedmont.

Ubico also took care to grant generous concessions to other U.S. firms, such as International Railroads of Central America (IRCA, the railroad monopoly and an UFCO subsidiary), Electric Bond and Share (the country's electricity monopoly), the Rockefellers' Standard Oil, and any U.S. investor who cared to knock on his door.

The Catholic Church was a more accommodating and a less expensive target of the general's political legerdemain than was the U.S. government. Ubico explained to the archbishop of Guatemala City, Monseñor Luis Durou, that he was willing to reestablish diplomatic relations with the Vatican after a reasonable amount of time, ties that had been broken sixty years earlier by the then anticlerical dictator General Justo Rufino Barrios.

Archbishop Durou was an understanding man, a Frenchman who had been archbishop of Havana and who carried no legacy of Spanish noble pretensions. His predecessor, Monseñor Muñoz y Capurón (the custom of joining the two family names with the connective "y" was a subtle claim to such pretensions) had been expelled in 1922 by the government of General José Maria Orellana. When Durou was finally admitted into the country in 1928, he prevailed upon Orellana's successor to allow Bishop Mariano Rossell y Arellano to accompany him as his auxiliary bishop with the promise of keeping his assistant "out of politics." Rossell y Arellano had been expelled in 1922 along with Archbishop Muñoz y Capurón.

In 1932, the Little Dictator—who fancied himself the political reincarnation of Napoleon—signed into law a blanket permission to exempt all landowners from the legal consequences of any action taken in defense of their goods and property. It legalized what had always been the practice: murder with impunity by large landowners of any Mayans suspected of organizing strikes intended to hinder the landowners right to exploit his farm hands even unto death. Two years later he outlawed debt-peonage, the inheritance of debt, the mechanism by which owners of extensive land holdings ensured a slave-like work force generation after generation. He replaced debt-peonage with a government controlled system of Vagrancy Laws, mandating under penalty of imprisonment that all Mayans work from 100 to 150 days a year on large plantations, including those of the dictator himself (who became the country's largest private landowner during his tenure), as well as those of the United Fruit Company.

Despite Ubico's concessions to private American corporations, the Guatemalan strongman walked a political tightrope during the decade of the 1930s. J. Edgar Hoover, the FBI director and a man of some influence in Washington, hated the Little Dictator, who looked and acted so much like himself. Hoover had sent his agents to comb Guatemala from the Atlantic to the Pacific, looking for Nazi sympathizers, especially among the country's large and wealthy German landowners—immigrants during the previous sixty years—and the small, equally wealthy, pro-Franco, proto-fascist Hispanic community. Hoover's suspicions were not a product of his customary paranoia. In addition to Ubico's open expressions of admiration during the first half of his "presidency" for Europe's three fascist dictators—Franco, Mussolini, and Hitler—he had also allowed German submarines to refuel at Puerto Barrios.

To calm Hoover's suspicions of divided loyalties, Ubico appointed a series of U.S. army officers as commanders of Guatemala's military academy, the Politécnica. Others were appointed academy instructors. The *caudillo* also allowed U.S. troops to be stationed at the capital's La Aurora Airport, the only paved landing field in the country.

After the U.S. entrance into World War II and at the suggestion of Nelson Rockefeller, FDR's coordinator of inter-American affairs, Ubico acquiesced to Washington's request that he expropriate the property of German-Guatemalans and send their owners to prison camps in Texas.

Also in 1942, at the behest of then-reigning archbishop Mariano Rossell y Arellano (Durou had died in 1938), the dictator invited a group of American priests to establish themselves in Guatemala, a play for both U.S. and Catholic Church support. The following year, the Maryknoll Society of Ossining, New York, sent their first two priests to "The Land of Eternal Spring," after first agreeing to Ubico's demands to avoid all political activity, as well as to abstain from all pronouncements on political matters and social problems.

The two Maryknoll priests knew little of the history and culture of Guatemala, including the background of Archbishop Rossell y Arellano. And because they had spent their early missionary years in disciplined Asian countries (one in Japan, the other in Korea) they had a difficult time adapting to the rambunctious Guatemalan scene, particularly in backward Huehuetenango, the province they chose for their missionary activity. Recognizing their inadequacies, Fathers Arthur Allie and Clarence Witte asked Archbishop Rossell y Arellano to serve as their mentor. This was a smart political move, but it carried some racist, anti-Mayan baggage.

In Huehuetenango, one of the first programs undertaken by the Maryknollers was the formation of a boys club in hopes of fostering among its young members an interest in attending the archbishop's seminary and eventually to embrace a priestly vocation. The club was a cross between a Boy Scout troop and an altar boys' sodality. Overnight camping trips, soccer matches and raffles, marches with the boys clothed in donated uniforms and stepping to the beat of small snare drums while carrying aloft Guatemalan and U.S. flags were some of the major attractions of the association. Assisting the priest at Mass dressed in liturgical garments while proud parents and relatives looked on was another benefit.

The first lads to enlist were two brothers, one, a very ambitious, disciplined, 16-year-old by the name of José Efraín Ríos Montt, and the other, his younger sibling, Mario.

For Efraín, membership in the club meant an opportunity to develop and demonstrate leadership abilities in preparation for a life in the military; evidence of these was already present in the boy. But membership also gave him the chance to bend moral imperatives to meet the needs of an overriding personal ambition, a characteristic that would later carry him to a *caudillo* presidency. As a member of the boys club, his rationalizations for pilfering the church's poor box resulted in a profoundly unpleasant confrontation with Father Allie and his expulsion from the club. It was an incident that would midwife a bitter, lifelong, though largely unarticulated, anticlerical bias.

For the younger boy, Mario, membership led to the archbishop's seminary and the priesthood, and eventually to the Guatemalan episcopacy.

Meanwhile, the Maryknollers seemed totally unaware of Archbishop Rossell's social views. The prelate had become a strong supporter of Ubico early on when the dictator fulfilled his promise of diplomatic recognition of the Vatican. On numerous occasions, the archbishop had exhorted the faithful to respect all authority, however gained and whatever its demands, "to give unto Caesar [Ubico] that which is Caesar's, and to God [the Church] that which is God's."[11] At other times, his theme was to justify the oppressive nature of Guatemala's social structure, stating that "the Church sees in human inequality a divine permission for the wealthy to be masters and fathers of the less fortunate," and that teaching the Catholic catechism is an "eminently patriotic work" since it "makes people hard-working and obedient, and the wealthy magnanimous and generous."[12]

Ubico and Rossell saw eye-to-eye on many issues, not the least of which was their low opinion of the Maya. In a pastoral letter of 1939, the archbishop made reference to the "glory of the Catholic Spanish conquest which brought civilization to a savage land."[13] In another such letter, the prelate exclaimed that "the disorganized tribes which inhabited our America would have caused themselves to become extinct had not the Spanish conquest arrived so providentially which united them and gave them their triple gifts of religion, blood, and language."[14]

Writing back to their headquarters in Ossining, the Maryknoll pioneers praised Rossell as a "splendid churchman and gentleman," and "deeply spiritual with an understanding heart, well chosen to lead his people in these troubled days."

Archbishop Rossell's unquestioning support for Ubico's dictatorship allowed the prelate to publicly express his anti-independence, pro-Spanish perspectives without offending the dictator. The prelate's esteem for Ubico's European soul mates, Franco, Mussolini, and Hitler, also strengthened the relationship between the two men. On special occasions, the archbishop allowed the flags of Nazi and phalange youth organizations to be hoisted in sanctuaries of the archdiocese's churches. And these men—Rossell y Arellano, Ubico, Franco, Mussolini, and Hitler—all agreed, though it was never publicly acknowledged,—that the "International Communist Conspiracy" was a growing and implacable threat to an ill-defined "Western Civilization," a sacred biology and culture that each of them felt they represented in its purest and highest form.

The infidel and heathen hordes were now seen to respond to a new, more insidious foreign ideology, one that worshipped no gods, and as such, was more threatening than Islamic, Jewish, and Native American beliefs had ever been. After more than a century of distrust and antagonism, the Guatemalan Cross in Archbishop Rossell y Arellano's hands and the Guatemalan Sword in Ubico's would again work together to protect a singular sacred tradition: the social inferiority of the Mayan people.

Despite all Ubico's political maneuvers, including the murders of over one hundred of his political opponents, the imprisonment and/or exile of thousands of others, the dictator's unbroken, 14-year, despotic, paranoid reign was slowly coming unglued. The *caudillo's* ever-escalating repression, as well as the Allies' pro-democracy political propaganda and the influence of U.S. military instructors at the Politécnica on young, impressionistic, military minds, sowed the seeds of Ubico's demise.

Democratic ideals and a thirst for electoral freedom ultimately led to a middle-class work stoppage championed by schoolteachers in early July 1944. When the little dictator ordered his troops to move against the demonstrators, he detected resistance among younger officers creeping up the ranks to their superiors. Professional paranoia took over. Hadn't the red stain of communism first infected the czar's army? Or was this a mad rush to so-called democracy, which invariably glorified ignorance and disorder, where manipulation of slogans like "freedom," "voting and human rights," and "autonomy" would replace—hopefully for a short time only—the disciplined use of divine justice undergirded by organized force?

The Guatemalan Napoleon appealed to the sense of discipline and order of his U.S. military advisors but received no encouragement. Ubico's usefulness to his patron, the "Colossus of the North," had apparently evaporated. The Age of Colonialism was dying with the end of World War II, not because the United States and Western Europe necessarily wanted it so, but because fascism had made it unpalatable. Furthermore, the Soviet Union was also a major victor and ally in the war, and Stalin was more than ready to denounce economic colonialism even while establishing his own version of political and military neocolonialism across Eastern Europe.

The United States would always prefer an electoral democracy—no matter how the votes were counted—to a dictatorship, as long as it remained within the economic framework set for it by the sages of Washington, Boston, and New York. The idealistic, democratic theme of the great American experiment had always been basically economic, as in Secretary of State James G. Blaine's words, "Our great demand is expansion," but only in trade, for "we do not seek annexation of territory."[15] America's aboriginals might wonder at such a claim, as might the peoples of Puerto Rico, Cuba, Panama, the Philippines, Hawaii, and Guam, but such acquisitions were always intended to bring progress to the natives, as well as enrich the liberators. In 1944, however, Guatemala proved to be a singular, though short-lived, foreign example of America's embrace of its own ideals, forced on it by the triumph of its wartime propaganda. Elections were to be held and an elected president, hopefully sympathetic to the United States, would be allowed to take power. This page of history, truncated though it would prove to be, was, in 1944, on the side of the Guatemalan teachers and their allies.

Now that the *caudillo* could no longer muster support from the American Embassy, his flamboyant courage deserted him and he suddenly resigned. To take his place, he appointed a triumvirate of trusted generals, men whom he thought he could manipulate from behind the scene. One of the three, Federico Ponce, an alcoholic with his own aspirations to be Guatemala's next *caudillo* but without the necessary inspirational qualities, grabbed the government's reins at the point of a gun aimed at the heads of his two less bellicose but equally alcoholic colleagues, as well as at members of Ubico's rubber-stamp and cowed legislative assembly. The move resulted in a further escalation of civil unrest. Ponce tried to calm the storm with promises of future, free elections, an old tune that even his own partisans discounted. Finally, in late October, after the murder of a crusading, anti-Ponce newspaper editor, popular anger and frustration pushed some younger members of the officer corps backed by their troops and more than two thousand armed civilians to move against Ponce. About one hundred died in the conflict.

From the ashes, a new day came aborning in Guatemala. But the new era, foreign to Guatemalan traditions, would have a short life of only ten years, and would end in shame. Its death throes propelled the nation back to the sixteenth century, recreating the brutality of the Conquest. Now, however, modern weapons and a modern anti-ideology ideology were being used to repel the infidels and heathen at the gate. The demise of those "Ten Years of Spring" would go on to create a scenario that few outside Guatemala and Latin America would fully understand, while making philosophers out of those who tried. Ronald W. Hennessey spent many of his years in Guatemala wrestling with the ghosts of "The Ten Years of Spring."

Engraving from Bartolomé de las Casas, *Narratio Regiorum Indicarum per Hispanos quosdam devastatarum verissima* (Frankfurt: DeBry and Sauri, 1598). The Spanish invaders and their Maya foes. Reproduced by permission of the Huntington Library, San Marino, California.

Father Ron and some small friends. (Credit: Maryknoll)

Backyard of cattle breeder Manuel Ralda, La Máquina, Suchitepequez. Not seen are dozens of his workers' homes/shacks—without plumbing, without privacy, without any of the minimal necessities, because "[my father] cannot pay more than the minimum wage [$1 a day] or he would go broke." (© Jean-Marie Simon 2003)

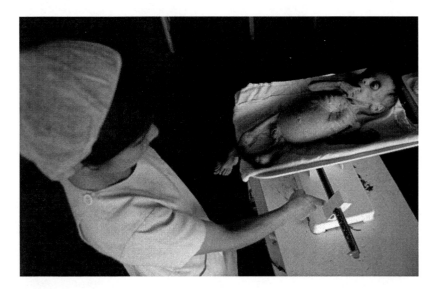

A not-untypical case of malnutrition in Guatemala. There is one soldier for every 213 Guatemalans, one doctor for every 2,000 Guatemalans, the majority of them in urban, non-Mayan areas. (© Jean-Marie Simon 2003)

Man carrying firewood using the Mayan *mecapal* braced across his forehead. A father uses the *mecapal* to carry his sick son to the local health clinic—five miles distant. (© Jean-Marie Simon 2003)

PART III

Chapter 5

WHOSE SIDE, PADRE?

By the time Ronald Hennessey arrived in San Mateo Ixtatán on 30 October 1980, sixteen years into his Guatemalan mission, he no longer was the political innocent who had stepped off a Delta Airlines flight from New Orleans back in September 1964.

Hennessey now knew that Guatemala was not a proto-democracy struggling to follow the example of early American experiments in limited electoral democracy as he had first believed. He had also learned the difference between a government of laws and a government of men (the question of justice and access to power is simply a question of whom you know), between British Common Law and Napoleonic Law (guilty until proven innocent, except for military personnel and those wealthy enough to pay "court costs"). He had discovered that progressive social legislation can be enacted to present a modern façade to the world-at-large and yet have nothing to do with domestic, regional, and national relations between individuals, institutions, and the state. And most important of all, he now understood the consequences of the *fuero militar,* mandating that all accusations against and crimes committed by military personnel were to be investigated and tried by their peers, without any civilian input.

Hennessey definitely was no longer the 1964 Iowa version of Johnny Appleseed, all shiny and polished, a political neophyte in the field of international intrigue and relations. The preceding five-and-three-quarters years as Maryknoll's regional superior for Central America had seen to that.

When Father Ronald Hennessey arrived as pastor of San Mateo Ixtatán, he knew that he would find a more tenacious traditional mind-set than that encountered in more open neighboring parishes, a version of ancient Mayan cosmology that resisted, often with violence, intrusions from outsiders with new ideas. A crowd of machete wielders drove Father Edmund McClear, an early predecessor of Hennessey, from a San Mateo village in the early 1960s when the priest tried to say Mass among them. The early chronicles of Spanish invaders also singled out the inhabitants of San Mateo as more hostile, aggressive, and devious than any of their Mayan neighbors. Knowing this, the priest believed that the guerrillas would encounter more difficulties making inroads among the Mateanos than they might experience in surrounding towns and municipalities. He was both right and wrong.

When the Iowan made his first five-hour jeep ride from Huehuetenango to San Mateo as the new pastor, he found a welcoming committee of four to meet him: two Mayan Catholic nuns, their cook, and the church/rectory caretaker. It was not an auspicious beginning, but that did not concern him. He had come back to his first love, pastoring, far from the intrigues of Church and State politics in Guatemala City. Swapping his stiff roman collar and the ritualistic courtesies of the capital for an open-necked shirt and the unaffected simplicities of San Mateo Ixtatán's inhabitants had been like a gift from on High.

By early February 1981, almost three months after the Iowan had taken over San Mateo's pastorate and two months since the EGP's public meeting in the town square, it had become evident to the Iowan that the guerrillas' politicizing efforts were producing tangible results in several Mateano villages. One such village was Yolcultac.

In late December 1980, Hennessey had visited Yolcultac to introduce himself to the residents and celebrate Mass. The village was situated a grueling three-hour walk west-northwest of town, out toward the Mexican border, reachable only by a narrow trail over rugged mountain terrain. It was big by San Mateo standards, encompassing 350 single-room, mud-and-reed houses topped with straw roofs. It was also a relatively poor village with no water system, a situation that forced the inhabitants to collect runoff from the mountains during the rainy winter season and to depend during the dry season on the shallow, hand-dug cisterns that harbored and oozed the muddy remains of captured winter water.

The majority of Yolcultac's residents were practitioners of the traditional Mayan religion, which also reflected the impact of five hundred years of Roman Catholic power and indoctrination. Their religion, the *costumbre*, was constructed on the base of calendrical calculations of appropriate days for particular gods to be honored and propitiated, sacred places and stone formations that served as sites for community and personal rituals, ancestral propitiation, and cosmological determination of recurring cycles of life and death, rebirth and catastrophe.

The numerous statues lined up along the parish church walls served as the traditionalists' idols, each thought to possess an individualistic spirit and power, members of the Mateanos' own pantheon. The rite of baptism, a sine qua non of Mayan social and religious life with no relation to the Catholic doctrine of original sin, provided the *costumbristas* with their only claim to the label "Catholic."

Only about 50 of the 350 Yolcultac families were orthodox Catholics, a number, nevertheless, sufficient to necessitate the construction of a village chapel where the padre could hear confessions and celebrate Mass on his bimonthly visits.

The first resident there to outwardly embrace the Roman Curia's version of orthodox Catholicism as filtered through American minds and culture was a respected elder of the village named Diego Cristobal. He, his wife, and three sons had converted in the early 1960s. Since then, another son had appeared on the scene and the three eldest had married and fathered numerous children, forming among themselves the nucleus of a strong, albeit small, orthodox Catholic community.

When old Diego broke ranks with the traditionalists in Yolcultac, he had not been simply indulging his own private religious beliefs. Many *costumbre* rituals, led by the elders, involved the whole community and were performed for the community's benefit. Held on special feast days, the rituals were selected on the basis of either the Mayan or Gregorian calendars, sometimes when the two coincided, and involved public prayers and offerings at selected holy sites. A procession through the village with a statue of the *santo patrón*— the major local god for whom the town was named, Saint Matthew—accompanied hundreds of determined vocalists singing dirges and hymns. No fiesta was complete without the sharing of alcohol-induced expressions of trust and love between relatives, *compadres* and neighbors, and much drunken dancing accompanied by the monotonous, repetitive beat of an inebriated marimba combo.

Diego's conversion represented a public rejection of the belief system that had sustained community solidarity over centuries, perhaps millennia. As a trusted elder, his sin was doubly serious, a grave threat to the well-being of the entire village. It was feared that his renunciation of the *costumbre* would bring down the displeasure of ancestral spirits and their metaphysical allies upon all villagers, causing irreparable harm to the community's public health and economy. As a result, some elders made threats against Diego's life, family, and property.

But when no dire consequences came to pass, other families, some simply wanting to escape the financial burdens of rituals whose efficacy they had begun to doubt, followed his example. As the ranks of the orthodox Catholic community grew, the animosity of the traditionalist leaders toward old Diego and his family became more intense, though less outspoken.

A few weeks after the EGP had issued its call for volunteers to represent the guerrilla organization in the villages, Miguel Cristobal, Diego Cristobal's second son and a Church catechist trained to teach his neighbors their God-given rights as human beings as well as about the road to eternal salvation, sought out the EGP to proffer his services. Miguel's offer was accepted and his appointment made public.

Now, in early February, prompted as much by reports of the growth of revolutionary fervor in Yolcultac as by ordinary pastoral concerns, Hennessey decided to make a return visit to the village with hopes of talking to Miguel Cristobal and sounding out other leaders of the orthodox Catholic community regarding their political concerns and perspectives. His intention was realized when Miguel took the initiative and approached the priest after Mass, expressing a need to talk.

"Padre, you be recent in San Mateo," began the catechist, speaking in the fractured syntax common to the Mayan version of Spanish, "but you be in Guatemala a long time and know how it be for us *indios*. You be present in plaza when EGP say itself our government. In Yolcultac, we be with EGP."

Miguel waited for Hennessey to answer. A minute passed and the priest said nothing. Miguel took a deep breath and continued. "The Lucas García government be army government for rich people, . . . rich ladino government.

He want to make us work in their plantations, steal our lands, our trees, our sons, make us *burros* to serve them."

The two men had exited the chapel together and were now sitting on a couple of logs nearby. A small group of worshippers gathered around to listen, anxious to hear how the padre would respond to Miguel's ideas. They had heard Miguel's ideas over the previous two months and, judging from their nods, apparently agreed with him. Among Mayans, all open-air conversations are considered of public interest with no cultural prohibition against approaching and listening to the conversing individuals.

Miguel spoke slowly, showing no expression on his face, carefully watching the Iowan's eyes. He waited for the priest to reply. Hennessey returned the man's steady gaze, blinking as he often did. He admired the catechist's strength. Mayans seldom look into the eyes of one whom they consider a social superior, . having been taught that such a look indicated equality and could mean a rebuke or more severe consequences.

Finally, Miguel spoke again, still more slowly, interpreting Hennessey's failure to answer as disapproval. "It be a sin for us to . . . fight, . . . protect ourselves, our trees, . . . take back our stolen land, . . . save our children, our *siembras,* animals, our lives?" he asked.

The mention of the theft of Mayan lands was a refrain that Hennessey had heard almost daily during his many years in Guatemala, but never before linked to a suggestion of resistance. The Mayans were accustomed to voicing their protests with one another in terms of the inevitability of oppression and repression, often seen as divine punishment for mythical sins committed by some ancestor too evil to have a name, or simply the working out of the Mayans' cosmological destiny. Generally, such a cry would tumble from the drunken lips of someone celebrating a religious fiesta, often in the local Mayan language, sometimes in Spanish: "Ay! Ay! I be son of my people! My people be of this land! I not be ladino! This land be my mother! Ay!"

The frustration, anger, and despair contained in the cry were something its author in more temperate moments would not dare express publicly, particularly in Spanish.

The priest waited a few more moments, not entirely sure how he should answer. Finally, he responded sympathetically, telling Miguel and the small group of listeners that God's authority rested with those who had been chosen by the people to rule over them—a decidedly non-Catholic version of political authority—a Hennessey interpretation of the Second Vatican Council's statement on the subject. "But you must first think of how much it will cost you in blood and destruction to defeat a military government . . . . And how can you be sure that an EGP government will serve your interests more than the present regime? It could be worse!"

Miguel squirmed a bit as he listened, hunching his shoulders, obviously wanting the priest's approval of his yet unexpressed intentions. "Padre, no government be worse than military. If we *indios* fight, we be part of new government, we make laws to protect all *indios,* all *indio* lands and trees."

Miguel had again used the term "indios"—a disparaging epithet used by ladinos—to underscore his recognition of his people's inferior status, as well as a bit of pride in the singularity that the term gave his people. "How can EGP government be worse than military? We not torture, not murder! We be needing you, padre, your thoughts, blessing!"

The priest suddenly realized that Miguel was unequivocally identifying himself with the EGP and that the catechist was not just asking an ethical question; he was delivering a subtle invitation to the Iowan that he, too, become a member of the EGP, their counselor and chaplain.

It was an invitation that Hennessey instinctively wanted to refuse, recalling the fate of a former Maryknoller and friend who, along with several priests and nuns, had accepted just such an invitation thirteen years earlier.[1] That acceptance had soon become public knowledge resulting in a nationwide uproar, with the near expulsion of all Maryknollers from Guatemala. Since then, other priests and some nuns—no Maryknollers among them—had opted for the same clandestine route, seeing the Mayan's status and conditions of life as ones properly described as "slavery," and the apparatus built around it to maintain the status quo as "state terrorism."

Still, an unsettled battle continued to rage behind closed rectory and convent doors as to the morality of revolutionary movements in general and of the Guatemalan movement in particular. All the discussants knew the conditions of the Church's just war theory, but it was simply that, a *theory;* it had no concrete moorings that would enable one to clearly discern the existence of all necessary qualifying conditions. Furthermore, the Catholic hierarchy never applied the theory to revolutionary movements unless such revolutions tended to support the episcopacy's concepts of its rights, privileges, and power. Pope Pius IX during the 1860s granted indulgences to all who enrolled in his war against the Italian government in order to maintain papal control over central Italy. The Mexican Catholic hierarchy was instrumental in inciting the Cristero rebellion against the Obregón government during the late 1920s. Latin American history is replete with examples of high churchmen standing beside dictatorial and repressive governments that acknowledged Church (i.e., hierarchical) rights granted on the backs of the poorest of their faithful.[2] Archbishop Rossell was neither the first nor the last of that genre.

Hennessey, however, like a sizable minority of religious in Guatemala, was a convert to the Second Vatican Council's efforts (1961-65) to open itself to the modern world, and an admirer of Popes John XXIII (the council's initiator) and Paul VI (its valedictorian), both of whom upheld the rights of the oppressed to take up arms against a dictatorial government to defend themselves. It was a Catholic version of Thomas Jefferson's "Declaration of Independence." As such, the Iowan was sympathetic to the guerrillas' expressed goals of democracy, education, health, and land, and he believed that aiding them was not wrong. But the methods of obtaining those goals were a stumbling block. At the same time, he felt that to hope for a successful struggle against a military government armed to the teeth and willing to use torture and bizarre executions of innocents to terrorize the population in order to remain in power was to fly away on the wings of suicidal fantasy. Now, he hesitated to answer his guerrilla-in-the-making catechist.

Hennessey answered slowly, enumerating a litany of questions regarding the EGP's respect for the lives of innocents; asking whether every member of the Guatemalan Army was fair game for the EGP, even the Mayan recruits who had been dragged from their homes and villages and then beaten and starved into behaving like murderous automatons; the fate of captured soldiers; of neighbors suspected of informing.

"Padre," the man responded with a note of satisfaction in his voice, "this is why we be needing your help. You understand many things. We be fooled. We not trust everybody in EGP. We be trusting you! You be a padre!" Then, softening his tone and speaking with some hesitation: "You be on our side, padre?"

Hennessey bent forward, propped a fist under his chin, and fell silent. He looked steadily at Miguel, then shifted his gaze to the eyes of the men gathered around them. The group had grown to about twenty, both young and old, listening intently to everything said, edging ever closer until they formed a tight circle around the priest and catechist. Although this audience refrained from any verbal interventions, their smiles, nods, and eye-squints indicated to Hennessey that most had already formed an opinion on the subject under discussion—and seemed to come down on Miguel's side. All of them now looked to the Iowan for his answer.

Hennessey knew his words would be repeated in every home in the village before the day was out, and in some neighboring villages as well. He also knew the question led into a bed of quicksand from which there would be no easy exit, that whatever he said would be repeated over and over again, passing through various permutations, like a shaman's cure for fright or impotence. He'd have to frame his answer in the clearest, but most general, terms possible.

"Miguel," the priest finally responded, "I'm on your side and the side of all Mateanos. But not all Mateanos agree that your course is the best course of action. What do the *costumbristas* think?"

Miguel shrugged his shoulders to indicate that either he did not know or that he did not care.

The Iowan continued his train of reason and doubt: "The Catholic Church doesn't have moral answers necessary to take sides in every political or social conflict . . . . The Lucas García government is patently unjust, even insanely murderous . . . but that doesn't necessarily mean that the EGP is to be trusted to come up with something better . . . . You have to decide how you should do this. I can't give clear answers to every problem that comes up! . . . You know God's laws and you've always respected them. Just try to continue that way."

Miguel Cristobal sat looking at the priest, biting his bottom lip, a look of frustration on his face. He had not received the unequivocal answers he had hoped for, a catechetical map to help navigate the ethical minefield in front of him, or even the Iowan's promise to be there to analyze the problems as they arose. The majority of the bystanders also seemed to harbor expressions of discontent, although Hennessey hoped he saw some heads nodding in agreement with him.

By the time the priest said good-bye, he knew he had not given the guidance that Miguel Cristobal and his neighbors had been looking for and deserved. He also realized that his answers had not satisfied his own desire for clarity and that he was not apt to come by a more categorical position any time soon. Now he wondered if he hadn't confused the issue, leaving himself open to be interpreted as counseling both support and opposition to the EGP. He wondered how many more discussions like this he could participate in and still be considered a reliable moral guide by his parishioners.

In any case, the EGP had already accepted Miguel Cristobal's offer to serve as their representative in Yolcultac and Hennessey made no attempt to dissuade him. This, despite the fact that Miguel's position as Yolcultac's head catechist would probably link the Church and Hennessey to the guerrilla organization in many people's minds. The EGP had given Miguel an old .22 caliber, single-shot rifle and told the residents assembled at the time that the catechist would henceforth collect taxes in the EGP's name and serve as auxiliary mayor in place of the one appointed by San Mateo's mayor. Unfortunately, Miguel's interpretation of his new authority went beyond what the village residents, especially the *costumbristas,* thought appropriate.

Miguel fulfilled his revolutionary duties by collecting corn and money from his neighbors and storing it in his house to await the next visit of EGP troops. By mid-February, there was a substantial amount of goodwill in Yolcultac toward the EGP and its professed program, although their newly appointed representative—as son of the first orthodox Catholic convert in Yolcultac—had continued to be a source of religious conflict that rubbed off on the EGP.

Two weeks after the collections began, in early March, some men broke into Miguel Cristobal's house and stole the tax money and much of the collected corn. It was not difficult in such an intimate community to discover who the culprits were and for whom they were acting. Miguel decided that they must be taught a lesson. He talked it over with his father and brothers and decided that the point man, Felipe Mateo, a young apprentice shaman aspiring to ingratiate himself with the traditionalist elders, should be arrested and turned over to the EGP for punishment. With that decision, the struggle was no longer—if it ever had been—one between the EGP and the Lucas García government, but a continuation of a conflict born two decades earlier, that between the *costumbristas* and orthodox Catholics.

Accompanied by his two brothers, Miguel challenged Felipe near the chapel and attempted to arrest him. Felipe resisted and, in the ensuing struggle, Miguel shot and killed him. Knowing that the dead man's coreligionists would be infuriated by the death and would invoke self-help justice, the three brothers scattered.

Felipe Mateo's relatives and friends, as well as members of his traditionalist religious network, were outraged. Neighbors urged that according to tradition the killing must be avenged. In response, four elders, accompanied by a group of angry supporters, headed for Diego Cristobal's house.

When the group arrived at the old man's compound, only Diego and his fourth son, Tomás, a teenager, were present. There was little discussion about what self-help justice demanded, given the common belief that Diego Cristobal and his sons were responsible for much of the sickness and death that had occurred in the village over the preceding twenty years, a result of ancestral spirits' displeasure. Frustration and anger quickly deteriorated into uncontrollable rage.

"The ancestors say they die!" an anonymous voice yelled from the support group. A machete was shoved into the trembling hand of the elder standing closest to old Diego. As the old man raised the weapon, hesitating to strike, perhaps hoping to hear a voice of caution, the same voice came slicing through again, "He die! Kill him! The ancient ones say he die! Kill him!"

Old Diego did not budge as a chorus of voices, shouting the same refrain, picked up the cry. The elder's arm came down with the full force of tradition, energized by neighbors who harbored twenty years of resentment that fed on old Diego Cristobal's religious betrayal.

No one saw the old man wince nor heard him cry as he went to his knees, the machete buried beneath his shattered collarbone. At that moment, young Tomás broke loose from the grasp of several participants and ran to the side of his quivering father. A half-dozen more machetes were already hacking away before the two men sprawled face forward in the dirt. Finally, as angry passions gave way to a feeling of justice satisfied, the two mutilated bodies were dragged to a nearby cliff and, in a traditional gesture of community excommunication, thrown over.

Hennessey received the news of the Yolcultac tragedy piecemeal, as witnesses relayed their perspectives, painting a muddled picture of the sequence of events. Part of the confusion resided in the witnesses' fear of talking in front of each other, making it difficult to confront conflicting versions. But as the Iowan put each piece of the puzzle in place, he shook his head in sorrow. The very thing about which he had tried to caution Miguel Cristobal was now coming to pass.

When the regional EGP directorate heard about the murders, they sent a contingent of about fifteen well-armed men to Yolcultac to demand a public trial for the four offending elders. The leader of the guerrilla group, himself a Mayan, explained in a calm voice that revolutionary justice demanded the deaths of the four men, and that anyone else working against the revolution would suffer the same fate. No one dared to speak out to exonerate the elders or justify the killings of old Diego Cristobal and his son.

The sentence was carried out the same day when each of the four was shot once in the back of the neck. The EGP judges and jury had made no serious attempt to determine greater or lesser individual culpability, to determine the identities of the faceless individual inciting death, or the names of the machete-wielders. Collective guilt, it seemed, could function as a working principle of revolutionary justice, as well as of traditional Mayan cosmology.

When word of this further bloodshed reached Hennessey, he recalled the conversation he had had with Miguel Cristobal a little over a month earlier and wondered if there was anything he could have said at that time that could have averted the tragedy. He had a feeling in his stomach that this was the first of many abuses and crimes to come in the names of religion and revolution.

Yolcultac's was a tragedy that would buffet the Iowan's soul, confirm his pacifist inclinations, and test his belief in the righteousness of the Mayan revolt. And as he tried to unravel the intricacies of the conflict in Yolcultac and separate out errors from bad intentions, traditions from game plans, factoring in his own inability to lay down clear ethical guidelines, he reflected once again on the meaning of the "Ten Years of Spring." What might have been, except for the historical and cultural ignorance of a distinguished American war hero? He also could have increased his understanding of the religious roots of earlier pan-Mayan rebellions had he read the histories of such revolts, those that occurred in Chiapas in 1712 and 1867, in Yucatán in 1761 and 1847, and in Totonicapán, Guatemala, in 1820.

Chapter 6

A Contest for Loyalty

March 1981

If Hennessey had hoped to have breathing room to bring together the disparate, not to say contradictory, pieces of his social theology and the roles revolutionary and governmental violence could morally play therein, he was quickly disillusioned. One week after the executions of the Yolcultac elders, he had gone with three catechists to several small villages northeast of town, a trip that would keep him on the road for three or four days. The purpose of the trip was to celebrate Mass in each village, give catechetical instructions, administer the sacraments of reconciliation (confession) and Eucharist to orthodox Catholics and, possibly, to officiate at a few marriages of *costumbrista* couples converting to Roman orthodoxy.

Early in the evening of his first day out, while in Pojom, a village four hours walk from town, the Iowan noticed his catechists talking agitatedly with a passing peddler. The priest feigned indifference, but wondered whether they wished to share their concern with him. The three quickly approached with the news. A confrontation between a squad of soldiers and a troop of EGP guerrillas had occurred earlier in the day in San Mateo and had resulted in the deaths of fifteen innocent bystanders. The three men all lived in town and were obviously shaken by the information, fearful that members of their families might have been victims. They wanted to cut their trip short and return to town that same night.

After talking it over, Hennessey agreed that his assistants should leave immediately for San Mateo while he remained in Pojom to celebrate Mass for the locals the following day. He would then head back to town.

When Hennessey arrived at the rectory the next day, he was somewhat relieved—but only momentarily—to hear Sister Justa report that the killings had not occurred in San Mateo but in El Quetzal, a small town ten kilometers down the road toward Santa Cruz Barillas. She recounted in her patient, controlled way that thirty or so EGP guerrillas, armed only with machetes, with maybe a rifle or two among them, had suddenly appeared in El Quetzal in mid-morning the preceding day and had forced every adult male they had encountered to accompany them to the town hall. Fortunately for most villagers, the EGP timing was a political mistake since 98 percent of the town's male population was absent, working in their cornfields to prepare for late April and early May plantings.

The guerrillas' intention was to hold a meeting, what they called "armed propaganda," to detail the generalizations they had enunciated in San Mateo's . plaza in late November. They forced all whom they encountered, on this occasion sixteen men, including the town's Mayan mayor, its ladino secretary, three Mayans from San Miguel Acatán and another from Todos Santos passing through on a bus, the ladino bus driver, and nine Mayan locals. The obligatory attendance was meant to give everyone cover so that no one could thereafter accuse another of voluntary participation.

About thirty minutes into the meeting, an EGP lookout spotted two truckloads of soldiers coming up the road from Barillas and ran to warn his companions. The town's ladino telegrapher had tipped off the army. The guerrilla leader abruptly declared the meeting over and climbed out a back window, his comrades pushing and shoving to do likewise. In a matter of seconds, all had disappeared into a pine grove a short distance behind the town hall.

The assembled townspeople and visitors stayed where they were, knowing that to be seen fleeing would suggest guilt and subject them to the *Ley de Fuga*. They believed that their only defense was to stay put and explain that they had no choice but to attend the meeting. But it was no defense at all. Mayan destiny would rule.

The first truckload of soldiers took up positions near the town center to prevent any escape, apparently realizing they would not encounter armed resistance. A second group advanced on the municipal offices and town hall.

The commanding officer, a lieutenant, first assured himself that no guerrillas were hiding nearby. He then led a squad of ten to the town hall and paused. On signal, the men burst through the door with maniacal screams sounding like a troop of rabid rhesus monkeys. Inside, ten Galils began sweeping the room, back and forth, a giant threshing machine, cutting bodies in half, turning heads to a fleshy pulp, splattering blood everywhere. The shooting continued long after it was necessary, giving the soldiers ample opportunity to exhaust the effects of their pounding adrenaline, their momentary collective madness.

Finally, the lieutenant raised his arm and the shooting stopped. Silence . . . for thirty seconds, or perhaps a full minute . . . then a soldier giggled . . . then another . . . finally the whole room was engulfed in laughter.

No one had been given a chance to explain. No one had been asked a single question, why he/they had attended. Instant death was their pitiless sentence. Except, that is, for one person: the ladino bus driver. "A miracle!" he would later claim, invoking the classic Christian claim that a loving God interferes in the affairs of humankind to help the few while abandoning the many to their terrible temporal fates.

The bus from Huehuetenango had pulled into El Quetzal shortly before 10:00 a.m., just in time for the driver and his four passengers to fall into the embrace of the EGP roundup. As the soldiers approached and the guerrillas scattered, the bus driver was apparently the only one to recognize the improbability of being given time to explain his presence at the meeting. As soon as the would-be warriors burst into the room, he dove for the floor. His quick reaction saved his life.

The soldiers, still giddy, went laughing among the dead taking anything of value they could find: money, watches, boots, wallets. When one spotted the bus driver's wrist adorned with a watch of imitation gold, he grabbed for it. The driver came upright with a scream. The soldier, frightened out of his wits, dropped what he probably thought was the arm of an awakened spirit reaching out to him from the pits of hell, and fell backwards. It gave the driver just enough time to again scream, this time his identity, and that he had been forced to attend the meeting.

The lieutenant, regaining his composure, intervened. "Let him go. You can see he is an educated man, not a dumb *indio*. He speaks the truth . . . . Give me his watch! You are too stupid to know how to use it."

"He's the one who described what happened after the soldiers left," Sister Justa continued.

Hennessey thought he noticed a hitch in the nun's voice, a trace of emotion he had never heard before. "Are you all right, *hermana?*"

"*Sí,* padre. It is what we expect."

The priest watched the young woman and marveled at her strength, her ability to share the details of the butchery, repeat the humiliating insults employed by the officer when speaking of her people, and still maintain a calm exterior demeanor. His admiration and affection for the woman shone in his eyes.

Twenty-nine-year-old Sister Justa was one of two nuns of Mayan descent who staffed the parish. Both were among the first fruits of the parochial school system that had been set up in several dioceses to remedy the government's indifference, not to say opposition, to Mayan education. Justa was a plain woman, with a toothy smile, high, rounded cheekbones, and almond-shaped black eyes. She possessed the quiet depth of character and deep reservoir of emotional strength that Hennessey felt to be the outstanding cultural characteristic of all Mayan women, something he had often seen in his mother's female friends.

"When they left," the nun continued, "the officer noticed a few men in the fields and called them over. He said that in the future the townspeople had better kill any guerrillas they encountered. Otherwise, he would return and kill every man, woman, and child in town as guerrilla collaborators."

As Justa finished, Hennessey remained quiet, lost in his own thoughts. The nun waited, not because she expected the priest to say anything, but out of courtesy. After a proper moment or two, she stood up and excused herself. As she turned to leave, the Iowan nodded. "They said they were the people's army and would protect them," he repeated, shaking his head, talking more to himself than to Justa.

The nun stopped and waited, but Hennessey said no more. She left him alone.

The moral confusion in the parish continued. The majority of those who sided with the guerrillas did so tentatively, not sure that their priest stood with them. Those who hoped the army would prevail, especially the *costumbristas,* were sure he leaned toward the guerrillas. It was a condition Hennessey felt helpless to remedy without creating more confusion and misunderstanding, especially since there was more than a grain of truth in both positions.

The lack of clear-cut answers, however, did not slow the procession of perplexed parishioners seeking their empathetic pastor's categorical advice. And Hennessey knew that if he couldn't find more satisfactory answers for them, they would find them for themselves. And now he was beginning to think, that might be the best alternative altogether. But his conscience nudged him into recognizing that such an idea merely obscured the desire to escape his pastoral responsibility.

The frustration Hennessey felt over the moral dilemma he faced began to manifest itself in the Iowan's correspondence with family members in Dubuque, Monti and Ryan. He had just finished one such letter to his sister, Dorothy Marie, describing the killings in Yolcultac and El Quetzal and sharing his misgivings, when Santiago Quot shuffled into his office and dropped another basket of cracked eggs in his lap: Juan Silvestre, the father of the only orthodox Roman Catholic family in the village of Yacá, had been shot and needed medical attention. "The *muchachos* did it, padre."

The Iowan sighed, hesitated a moment, then pulled his lanky frame from the hemp-woven chair, went outside, and walked toward the garage. He knew the victim to be a practicing Catholic, a bit better off financially than the average Mateano, but he couldn't imagine what the guerrillas—if, indeed, it had been the guerrillas—had against the man.

Accompanied by Santiago Quot and two catechists, the priest drove his jeep the eight kilometers—twenty-five minutes—back along the road toward Santa Eulalia to a small grassy plain called Momoxchecán, in the middle of San Mateo's pine forest. There, he pulled the vehicle off the road and left it under the watchful eyes of his two catechists while he and his sacristan walked the one-and-a-half hours to Yacá. Santiago was to serve as the priest's translator since most of the people in Yacá spoke only Chuj.

When the two men reached the Silvestre compound—consisting of three adobe houses with corrugated metal roofs, two of which belonged to married sons—they found no one. All three dwellings had been abandoned, their doors open wide to reveal their empty interiors to any passerby who might be tempted to break down boarded doors. A neighbor who recognized the priest said she was sworn to secrecy, but told him he could find Juan's wife at a relative's house nearby.

The padre found Magdalena Mateo in a state of stark terror, shaking from head to toe. At first, she refused to answer Santiago's translation of the priest's inquiry, taking cover behind the droopy sleeve of her brightly embroidered *huipil,* leaving only a slit for her fear-hooded eyes. It occurred to Hennessey that Magdalena must be one of those who felt that he had unequivocally sided with the guerrillas and it pained him.

Magdalena needed much reassurance from Santiago that their pastor was not taking sides, but was attempting to help all Mateanos and finding it difficult. Finally, the woman revealed that her husband was hiding in the mountains, afraid for his life. The guerrillas, she said, had threatened Juan, but had not shot him. He'd been strung up for several hours with a nonslip noose around his neck, a punishment intended to inflict pain, not death.

After several minutes of soft-spoken remarks funneled through Santiago, Hennessey was able to convince Magdalena to send one of her sons, hidden with other relatives, to invite her husband to talk to him.

An hour later, Juan Silvestre appeared. Hennessey had met the man during an earlier trip to Yacá and was prepared for what stood before him. Juan was a short man even for a Mayan, about five feet, one inch tall, who walked with his upper torso inclined forward as if he were pushing a wheelbarrow, a posture that made him look even smaller. He was about fifty-five years old and positively homely, presenting an almost porcine look, with his short, heavy bull neck, broad nose with upturned nostrils, and thick lips that refused to hide a mouthful of crooked, discolored teeth.

On the occasion of that earlier visit, Hennessey passed the night in Juan's house and had engaged him in a long discussion regarding the local political situation. Juan was of the opinion that the guerrillas were going to bring much animosity and suffering to the town and villages of San Mateo, without accomplishing any noticeable good.

Despite Juan's unattractive appearance, or perhaps because of it and his self-deprecating sense of humor, Hennessey had taken an instant liking to the man. Juan had laughed at himself several times that first evening due to his poor command of Spanish, resulting in several misunderstandings. When a mistake was obvious, he would slap his knee and throw his head back in laughter, looking homelier than ever. Even while enjoying his laughter, Hennessey couldn't help but feel sorry for the man. The Iowan was sure that Juan's looks must have provided his neighbors with plenty of ammunition for offensive remarks, particularly where his was the only orthodox Catholic family in Yacá.

Now, six weeks after that first visit, as the priest rose to shake Juan's hand, the homely little man could only groan a greeting. Hanging by the neck for almost four hours had injured his vocal cords. The guttural noises issuing from his throat were mostly unintelligible and the pain that his effort caused was evident. The rope burns were still clearly visible on his neck.

After Magdalena had arranged three, three-legged, twelve-inch-high stools for Hennessey, Santiago, and her husband, the two sons sat down on a nearby log and the older of the two recounted the details of the guerrillas' visit. Magdalena stood unobtrusively to one side.

"The boys, they be angry at papá. He be labor contractor in Yacá for coffee farms. Army make him military commissioner in Yacá," the oldest son explained. "They say he be traitor to Maya, serve criminal *finca* owners and help army kidnap *indios* for army. Now EGP be government here. Papá must be loyal to Maya, no to *fincas,* no to army."

The younger son continued the account. "They hang papá from rafters. A *Migueleña* girl laugh, shoot between papá's legs. She boys' boss. We afraid she shoot knees or cut *huevos!*"

Hennessey listened quietly. He had had the desire for some time now to meet the local leaders of the EGP. Silvestre Juan's recitation of his father's encounter with the guerrillas only convinced the priest that his own meeting with them should take place as soon as possible.

At this point, Magdalena, surprisingly, broke in, speaking in little more than a whisper, directing herself in Chuj to her husband. Santiago Quot listened closely, waiting for her to finish and then translated for Hennessey. "Magdalena says that everyone in Yacá hate the Silvestre family because they not practice *costumbre* and have gone over to *el padre.* Everyone who owes Juan money help *los muchachos* make a list of how much each owes. How else could the guerrilla woman know?"

Now it was Juan's turn to try to speak, energized by his wife's contribution. In a barely audible whisper that caused obvious pain, he asked the priest, "What . . . you think padre . . . moving . . . family . . . to town? The boys . . . say . . . they ask me . . . be their tax-collector . . . for Yacá . . . . I can't!"

Juan's last words burst out with a cough that twisted his face in pain.

Hennessey saw a pleading look in the man's eyes. But what was the priest to counsel him? He knew that there was no way to hide from the guerrillas within the township. "I think you should stay in Yacá, Juan," he told the man. "It'll be easy for the guerrillas to find you in San Mateo, and they might go harder on you if they think you are trying to put something over on them . . . . I think they might leave you alone if you stop contracting workers for the *finca* owners . . . . Tell them you can't be their tax-collector because nobody here trusts you."

Juan nodded his head, recognizing the sense of the padre's observation, that either he stay in Yacá or move out of the area entirely. But this latter course was unthinkable, since it meant abandoning his lands, his ancestors' graves, and his Mateano identity. His shoulders slouched in resignation.

A few moments later, the priest stood to give his friend an *abrazo* of encouragement. "If I run across any guerrilla leaders or anyone who can carry a message to them, I will try to explain your situation, Juan. Things have to change, . . . but they're not going about it in the right way."

As the Iowan walked back to his jeep, he questioned the advice he had given to Juan, to stay put. Was it the best thing to tell him? That question would have an answer some months later when the priest found his friend's butchered body covered by a blanket in the town hall, under circumstances he could not have then imagined.

When Hennessey returned to his jeep at Momoxchecán in mid-afternoon, he found that the two catechists who were supposed to be guarding his jeep had disappeared. After several calls directed into the woods at different compass points, the two men emerged, somewhat shaken.

"We hear bomb go off, padre, two hours past. You hear?"

"I didn't hear it. But then, maybe I'm going deaf. What direction did the noise come from?"

"It be like thunderclap, padre. We know it be bomb, big bomb! We not know where it come from or who shoot it. We hide."

An inconclusive discussion followed as to which direction the sound might have come from. It was obvious that their location in the forest, surrounded on all sides by pine trees, had made pinpointing the direction impossible.

"If it was somewhere here in the forest, it might have been a mine or an ambush, . . . but there's no way of knowing where," the priest offered. "We can discount the direction of Juan Silvestre's village . . . . Let's go back to San Mateo and see if anything has happened along the road, or in San Mateo itself. Somebody else must have heard the noise."

It was another decision for which Hennessey would second-guess himself, but not until the next day.

The four men piled into the jeep and returned to town, seeing nothing out of the ordinary on the way. Back in San Mateo, no one could be found who had heard anything sounding like an explosion. But an explosion it was; one with serious consequences.

The following day, about 9:30 a.m., a 20-year-old bus lumbered into San Mateo from Huehuetenango with six bloodied and somewhat broken passengers, two propped up in their seats by others, four lying in the aisle, fading in and out of consciousness, mumbling incoherent prayers to their ancestors.

The bus driver explained to the mayor that his injured Mayan passengers were the victims of a remote controlled bomb set off on the Santa Eulalia road just before it entered San Mateo's forest, a place where the stake truck carrying them had to slow down on a prolonged incline. The bomb had been planted in the upper embankment alongside the road, about four feet high, intended to expend its force against the passengers of whatever unlucky vehicle was chosen as its target.

Four passengers in the truck had been killed instantly, their torn bodies left at the site so that San Mateo's mayor could make his required investigation and draw up a report. Five others were capable of limping or crawling away from the scene and escape into the woods nearby, not knowing who their attackers were or if more danger awaited them. The six who came in on the bus had spent almost twenty-four hours at the side of the road, incapacitated, awaiting the arrival of a Good Samaritan.

The mayor sent a volunteer police officer to advise Hennessey of the bombing and to ask if the parish hospital—more a four-bed clinic than a hospital—was equipped to care for the victims. The priest recognized from the messenger's account that the parish did not have the resources to tend to the needs of the four more seriously wounded and told the officer to advise the mayor that he, Hennessey, would drive the four to the public hospital in Huehuetenango. He also learned in the exchange, much to his chagrin, that the site of the explosion had been only four kilometers farther up the road from where he had parked the previous day.

When the priest arrived at the mayor's office some minutes later, he discovered that the town secretary had decided that his official report of the tragedy needed input from all six victims. Over the next hour, as Hennessey waited patiently—not without expressing his concern for the survival of the four he wanted to take to Huehuetenango—the secretary struggled with long periods of silence punctuated by low, painful moans and the breathless recitation of incomprehensible details before pressing the inked thumbs of his four barely conscious witnesses to the bottom of his chronicle. What that report contained by way of information gleaned from the four, the priest could not imagine.

Hennessey then accommodated the four men as best he could on mattresses spread on the floor of his jeep. The ladino student doctor doing his required fieldwork in San Mateo declined the priest's request to accompany him, afraid of being captured by the assailants and made to suffer the consequences of aiding their enemies. The Iowan shrugged. Sister Justa, hearing the exchange, offered to go to maintain the proper flow of the intravenous solutions that she had rigged up earlier.

Once everyone was jammed into place, the makeshift ambulance set out for Huehuetenango. As they passed Momoxchecán, the priest shook his head and mentally chastised himself for not having driven a few kilometers more after his catechists had reported hearing an explosion the day before. As they came up to the site of the attack, he carefully skirted the battered truck pushed off to one side by the bus. As they passed the grotesque memorial, he whispered a silent prayer for the nameless dead whose blood could still be seen staining the roadway.

They were nearly halfway to Huehuetenango when the jeep engine coughed and died. It didn't take long for the former Iowa farmer and natural born mechanic to discover water in the fuel line. The inflated price of Huehuetenango's gasoline, brought to San Mateo in 55-gallon drums, was no guarantee that it would be moisture-free.

Over the next one hundred kilometers the engine quit fifteen different times. Sister Justa faithfully counted each stall as if she intended to hold someone—maybe God—accountable. Each time, even before the jeep had stopped rolling, Hennessey would be out of the vehicle with the hood up, dismantling the fuel pump. The patience he had cultivated three decades earlier, going through the same motions with his family's first tractor—an old second-hand Ford—did not desert him. But now, the stakes were much higher. He was certain they would lose one or more of their passengers before their arrival at the hospital.

Ten hours after leaving San Mateo and thirty-six hours after the bombing, Hennessey was able to turn over his four, barely alive passengers to the bleary-eyed doctor in charge of the emergency room at Huehuetenango Hospital. It was nearly midnight.

By 8:00 a.m., the Maryknoll Center House mechanic had drained the jeep's gas tank and fuel line, refilled the tank with what the priest hoped to be uncontaminated gasoline, and then he and Sister Justa were off on their five-hour return trip to San Mateo.

On the last day of March, 1981, the EGP hoisted their red and black flag over San Mateo's plaza and let everyone know that if it were removed, they would hold the individuals who took it down responsible for a hostile act. For two days, the flag floated over the town. Then, about 7:00 a.m. on the third day, two pickup loads of heavily armed men dressed in civilian clothes arrived. Hennessey was sitting in the Sisters' convent eating breakfast when he spotted the men through the window.

A group of six ladinos stood on the embankment overlooking the church, staring down the hill at the convent one moment, seeming to argue among themselves the next. Finally, after five minutes or so, they walked down the hill and into the church. The priest could tell by their neat dress and ramrod bearing they were professional soldiers, probably an elite patrol.

Knowing they had not gone into church to pray, Hennessey decided to go out to meet them. Just as he was about to open the convent door, they knocked heavily. Remembering how quick the soldiers were to use their guns at El Quetzal, he rattled the latch as he slowly opened the door so as not to startle them or provoke any precipitous action.

"*Qué es su gracia, señor?*" was the leader's curt introduction, indicating his desire to show his education by his choice of a very formal expression.

"Ronaldo Hennessey, Catholic priest and pastor of the parish of San Mateo Ixtatán, *señor*," the priest replied in the same tone of voice, a barely concealed attempt at mimicry. "Is there something wrong?"

The question went unanswered as the officer made sure the priest understood who was in charge of the interrogation by asking in a firmer voice, "How long have you been in San Mateo?"

"Not quite four months," was the reply.

"Where were you before you came to San Mateo?"

Each question was delivered in a tone of voice intended to intimidate. But the intention went unrewarded. "I lived in Guatemala City in zone 10 for almost six years. Before coming to Guatemala I lived in the United States, and before that I served in the U.S. Army in Korea."

Hennessey hoped that mentioning zone 10, his U.S. citizenship, and his army service in Korea would give him some stature in the officer's eyes. All Guatemalans familiar with the capital knew that zone 10 was a pleasant, upper-middle-class and wealthy residential section, an area where priests sympathetic to guerrilla movements were not apt to be stationed. The priest also felt that U.S. support for Guatemala's counterinsurgency program and military government, plus his own military background, would provoke some feelings of synthetic brotherhood between them. In this, he was mistaken.

"You attended the subversives' meeting in the plaza back in November! No?"

Hennessey felt a slight tightening of his stomach muscles, like that which he'd felt on occasion as he turned to find the family bull, watching, raking the turf with his front hoof. So they're watching me, he thought. I wonder who in town is keeping an eye on me and reporting to them.

"I was interested in what the guerrillas had to say," the priest responded slowly. "I am the Catholic pastor here. I have to know what is going on in town and what people are saying."

A slight narrowing of the leader's eyes told Hennessey that his answer was not entirely satisfactory. The Iowan was convinced, however, that the officer knew that he had stayed beyond the edge of the plaza crowd and had not participated in the festive nature of that meeting.

After a few other questions regarding the priest's background, the leader turned on his heel and waved to his companions to follow. He had not inquired about guerrilla activity in the area, nor had he attempted to sound out the priest's feelings on the struggle taking place for the loyalties of the people of San Mateo Ixtatán. Also, he had ignored the remains of the EGP antigovernment graffiti still somewhat visible on the front wall of the rectory.

At 9:00 a.m., after talking to and threatening town officials, and having removed the EGP flag, the men piled into their pickups, and headed for Barillas. At 9:20, they were all dead, ambushed by a guerrilla patrol about five kilometers down the road. By 2:30 p.m., the EGP's red and black flag was again flying over San Mateo's plaza.

PART IV

Chapter 7

IDEALISM OR IDEOLOGY?

When Ron Hennessey slipped word of his military service in Korea into the exchange with the army patrol that had come to remove the EGP flag over San Mateo, it was the first time in years that he had mentioned that subject to anyone. Korea was not simply a place where he had spent eighteen months doing his duty for God and country. Korea was where he had experienced close up the consequences of war, its harvest of fear, cowardice, corruption, arrogance, hatred, and death, as well as its demonstrations of selflessness, courage, heroism, and at times, love and life. But the one far outweighed the other, as it was meant to. And he wondered why it turned some men into animals and others into heroes.

It was in January 1952 that the Buchanan County draft board notified Hennessey that his farmer's deferment had expired. The United States had been heavily involved in the Korean War for a year-and-a-half at that time and was then engaged in truce talks with North Korea and China. Nevertheless, lethal threats and ordnance continued to be hurled from all sides, while the killing and dying went unabated.

President Truman had dismissed General Douglas MacArthur, commander of UN forces in Korea, almost a year earlier for insubordination—the general had refused to remain silent regarding his insistence that all-out war be carried into mainland China, "unleashing Chiang Kai-shek," and using atomic weapons in both Korea and China, while Truman wanted to save the remainder of the U.S. atomic stockpile (approximately four hundred bombs) for what he considered would be an inevitable showdown with Russia in Europe.[1]

Ron accepted his government's call with a sense of inevitability, but also with a small degree of relief. Competing considerations of what he should do with his future could now be set aside for the time being. The army would merely provide an interlude. Still, the intense bonds of affection engendered by his family life and the pleasure of having worked the 165 acres of Hennessey-owned soil for the preceding six-plus years did not make his departure for the army's Aberdeen Proving Grounds in Aberdeen, Maryland, an appealing one.

Also, Ron had some unanswered questions resulting from family dinner discussions about the underlying causes of the Korean War that went beyond an unprovoked invasion of the democratic South by the communist North. After all, Korea was historically a single people with one language and culture, enslaved for the first four decades of the twentieth century by Japan, its postwar temporary partition agreed to in principle when President Truman insisted at Potsdam that Stalin bring Russia's military might into the war against the Japanese.

By January 1952 the division of Korea was six years old. Unification was keenly desired by both the North and the South, but based on conflicting premises. Neither side was democratic. Dean Acheson, Truman's secretary of state, had previously declared that what happened in Korea was of no interest to the United States. The North mistook the comment as a signal of U.S. intentions and the invasion of the South followed.

But since five older Hennessey brothers and a sister had all entered their country's military service during World War II or in the years preceding the Korean conflict with no moral or political doubts, Ron was inclined to do likewise. Putting his doubts aside, however, did not sweeten his departure.

Adjustment from life on the farm to that at the Aberdeen Proving Grounds was a bit more difficult than Ron had anticipated. He had never before been away from the intimate, supportive, and intellectually stimulating atmosphere of his large family. Furthermore, it had been in mid-1945 that Mom and Pop—with their children's help—had scraped together the last few dollars needed to escape the tenant-farmer syndrome and make a down payment on a farm in Monti, six miles outside Ryan, Iowa. Sowing, cultivating, and harvesting his family's own land during the preceding six years had given Ron a purpose in life . . . though not yet a vocation.

By June of 1945, Maurice Jr., "the family brain," had finished high school and was trying to decide whether to pursue an adolescent interest in the priesthood or follow brothers Tom and Jack into the military. Dave, the next in line, was still in high school, but his hay fever and enthusiastic descriptions of life in Dubuque had convinced Pop that his fourth son had no intention of remaining on the farm. It was Ron's work habits, his love of the creative aspects of farming, and his amazing patience that convinced Pop that his fifth son, though only a high school sophomore, would take over the family spread one day.

Ron's outgoing personality, his peacemaking instincts, and his singular sensitivity to a small number of socially marginal classmates made some of his close friends think that he would make an ideal politician, if not a priest. His younger sister Gwen had to warn him time and again that the friendliness he showed a few girls whom his male classmates referred to as "cows" had several mistakenly thinking he had a special affection for them. But Ron could not bring himself to do anything to persuade them otherwise. His smile, a throaty laughter that often slipped up into his nose, his jokes, and good humor were all infectious, and with his ability to charm potential antagonists, more than a few believed that he might some day make a good sheriff like two of his uncles.[2]

"It's hard to put your finger on what he has going for him," brother Maurice told Mom one day, trying to explain Ron's ability to calm troubled spirits. "A number of times, I've seen him get between two guys who were ready to slug it out, and three minutes later they're laughing together, slapping each other on the back, putting an arm on his shoulder. Maybe he cracks one of his silly jokes? I don't know!"

June of 1947 saw Ron Hennessey graduate from Ryan's Saint Patrick's High School with something less than a 4.0 grade point average, yet armed with a poetic salute to his joyfulness from his yearbook editor. For the following four-and-a-half years, he worked full-time at Pop's side running the family farm, while also doing odd plumbing, welding, electrical, and carpentry projects in and around the barns, bins, and house.

As a result of his work habits, Ron never seemed to have enough time to develop a balanced social life, though a few of Ryan's adolescent bobby-soxers tried to help him do so. When his sisters brought girlfriends around, he often found himself in the presence of bubbly individuals who did little to hide their fondness for his jokes and blinking, pale blue eyes. But when sister Gwen kidded him about some of his surreptitious, sidelong glances, he'd facetiously remark that none of the girls looked like they were ready to plump down on a tractor seat for eight hours or more, an answer aimed at exasperating Gwen and disguising his own hormonal urges.

Meanwhile, brothers Maurice and Dave had joined the military service. At least once a month, Ron would drive over to Dubuque with other members of the family to visit sisters Dorothy Marie and Miriam in the convent. His sisters' obvious love for the religious life and the joy they exhibited made Ron at times entertain the idea of the priesthood. But the thought never lingered with him once outside the convent walls, particularly when he thought of the years of study involved and the burden of priestly celibacy. All such speculation, however, ended when his name popped up in Buchanan County's monthly draft lottery.

It was something other than his farm-bred endurance and carefully cultivated country-boy image—"impression making"—that allowed Ron to adjust to army life and eventually learn to take advantage of it. He once counseled a barracks mate at the Aberdeen Proving Grounds that making do in the army was like getting along in a large family: "Keep your head down and never attract attention to yourself."

Like most post-World War II farmers, Ron was as familiar with the innards of an internal combustion engine as he was with those of a slaughtered pig. It was a skill that army officials had taken note of when they swore him in. By the time Ron had finished his eight weeks of basic training, his hands-on mechanical experience had earmarked him for a three-month course in vehicle repair and maintenance at the Army Ordnance Depot south of Atlanta. At the time, he was also told that he would be returning to Aberdeen after mechanics school to attend a two-month course in leadership. The army had spotted something it liked in the character of the 22-year-old farmer.

Once at the Army Ordnance Depot, Ron felt like "a pig in slop." The smell of grease and oil and the recognition accorded to intelligence and hard work provided a welcome change from the constant badgering at Aberdeen. Ron's first letter home after arriving in Georgia revealed a marked change in his attitude: "I'm ready to forgive the army for all its screw ups," he told his parents and siblings, "just so long as they let me be a mechanic and do a bit of thinking for myself."

Three months later, back in Maryland at leadership school, the Iowan was beginning to recognize that he might never make the grade as an army officer. The perception grew from a series of classes that he attended in what he facetiously called "military ethics and morality." A husky sergeant major from Alabama with an accent as broad as "a plow horse's ass" was the instructor for the classes.

One day, the sergeant major strode into the conference room and, after giving his oft-repeated five-minute pep talk with slight rhetorical variations about how leadership is based on personal courage and a firm demand for unquestioning obedience, he recounted an experience he had had during World War II: in 1944 he had received an order from a superior officer to drive a dozen German prisoners back to a U.S. base camp and to take a known "misfit" with him to ride shotgun. Each time the truck hit a pothole, the misfit's rifle discharged, killing one or more of the bound prisoners. "Them Heineys died of lead poisoning along the way," the Alabaman told the class, showing no sign of reproach and offering no explanation to put the story in context.

Hennessey left that class convinced that the sergeant major had told him and his classmates that a military leader could always find a "misfit" under his command to solve problems in ways not permitted by army regulations or the Geneva Conventions, let alone ethical considerations. It was a revelation that depressed the young farmer more than it shocked him. It had never occurred to him that he might face the dichotomy between the demands of American patriotism and his Catholic conscience, although it was a subject that he had debated with his parents and siblings from time to time in abstract family discussions.

After Ron finished the leadership course and had absorbed the principles and nuances of military command and the problems of unconscionable obedience, he was assigned as cadre to help whip a new platoon of recruits into physical condition. Recalling how abusive his own trainers had been, Ron wrote home that he was determined to treat his trainees like "fellow members of the human race," convinced that "degradation did not enhance the fighting ability of any recruit." He looked for unobtrusive ways to relieve the humiliation of new inductees unable to immediately perform up to the training sergeant's standards. Ron would count to twenty-five in a loud voice while only ten to fifteen pushups were actually executed by the weakest.

When the Iowan finally finished leadership training, his commanding officer (CO) encouraged him to attend Officer Candidate School (OCS) for six months to earn his lieutenant's bars. Apparently, Ron had confirmed his superior's earlier opinion when he assigned the Iowan to Aberdeen's leadership school. Whether his CO had noticed the Iowan's willingness to cut corners rather than religiously follow "the book," he did not say. But since OCS meant more authority and the possibility of ambiguous ethical decisions involving a sizable number of troops, Private Hennessey preferred to take his chances on an immediate assignment to the front lines in Korea. Thoughts of an incapacitating injury or his death in Korea never entered his mind.

South Korea was a whole new world for the young soldier from Monti: its architecture designed to ward off evil spirits, the multitiered roofs of Buddhist temples, the three-room, stone or mud-brick houses with thatched roofs, and floors heated underneath by channeled air from the kitchen fire; the lack of material and industrial development; and the people—their exaggeratedly polite manners, their sing-song language, and the way they walked with short, shuffling steps tailored by the loose fitting but limiting, heavily quilted clothing they wore, often with A-frames strapped to their backs for carrying heavy cargo. When he had a moment or two, Ron would unobtrusively watch Seoul's citizenry as they went about their daily tasks, asking himself what history had wrought in these fascinating people. Mom's charge of not judging a people without knowing their culture was never far from his mind.

Only Seoul's main thoroughfares were paved and wide enough for two vehicles to pass without constant jockeying. U.S. Army trucks and jeeps competed with ox-drawn carts on the unpaved roads in and around the city, with honking horns, shouted expletives, and clenched American fists answered by sullen Korean looks, murmured imprecations, and sometimes, a thrown stone. When an oxcart driver stopped to pick up the valuable fecal droppings of his animals for later use as fertilizer in his garden or fuel for his brazier, the impatient American drivers had all they could do to restrain themselves from pushing the offending cart aside—a struggle they too often lost.

Such encounters deeply offended Ron's sensibilities to the degree that on several occasions he was forced to explain in very personal terms the trouble that fellow Americans were creating for themselves by using their vehicles to shove slow-moving oxcarts off the road. He would begin his peroration by taking down the offending vehicle's ID number and then introducing himself to the angry but curious driver as head of one of Seoul's more important motor pools. He'd then detail the specifics of his imaginary duties, which he claimed included giving the driver's identity information to the "American Korean Traffic Court," which would then contact the driver who would be obliged to give oxcart driving lessons to his victim so that the latter could then be licensed to drive his cart on roads used by American military vehicles. Of course, the information could be discreetly disposed of, Ron would tell the offending soldier, if he would only cooperate by helping to return the Korean vehicle to its place on the road.

Each time, the offenders took note of Ron's amiable but stern demeanor, wiry build, and the staring blue eyes, as well as his calm explanation of the effects of their behavior on the war effort. The single stripe on his sleeve did not detract from his performance, delivered with the aplomb of a professional actor. On every occasion, the offender joined Ron and the victim in pushing his cart back onto the road, accompanied by the smiles and applause of Korean onlookers.

Within his first week in Korea, Hennessey had been assigned to one of Seoul's many motor pools, a mechanic's job to his liking. The pool's ten members were charged with keeping in good mechanical condition a given number of cars, jeeps, and trucks of various tonnage. Doing odd jobs like checking the vehicles' oil, cleaning them inside and out, changing tires, and sweeping up around the bays, fell to a number of hired Koreans.

The Iowan soon realized that the Korean people who worked around him did not fit the stereotypes fed to him by the majority of his war-seasoned countrymen who, in terms of personal regard and relationships, seemed to make no distinction between North and South Koreans.

The Koreans Ron knew, however, maintained a courageous dignity that came through whenever he or anyone else expended the patience to communicate and deal with them as "fellow human beings," rather than as "gooks." And as the Iowan spent his free moments trying to talk with them in depth, gesturing when words failed, provoking laughter on both sides, his appreciation for their quiet good humor, patience, and gratitude for simple signs of respect, grew proportionately. Later, he sometimes found himself unconsciously speaking to them in English as their facial features no longer signaled ethnic differences to his undiscriminating eyes, causing gales of laughter. In his letters home to his parents and siblings, he often remarked how much the Koreans wanted only what Americans wanted for themselves: peace, justice, freedom from foreign domination, and the opportunity to provide for their families.

How did this war ever start among such peace-loving people? Ron asked himself with sorrow and disgust. How does any war start? He knew some Korean history, how the country was caught between two behemoths, China and Japan, in a delicate balancing act that often enough failed. This would explain their passion for peace and for freedom from foreign invaders. But how was one to comprehend the brutality by both sides in this war, a brutality that seemed so at odds with the Korean people he had grown to know and with whom he had begun to feel some kinship?

For Hennessey, pictures of the North's assumed preference for Russian or Chinese communist slavery after being freed from four decades of a traumatic Japanese imperial slavery seemed like so much classical war propaganda. Yet, it was revealed truth as far as his superiors and comrades were concerned. The Iowan shook his head. There had to be another truth buried deep in the Korean national psyche, in Korean culture. But what was it?

As ambulances, trucks, and helicopters continued to ferry the broken bodies and shattered corpses of his countrymen to Seoul's militarized airport for flights to Japan, Hawaii, and the U.S. mainland, Hennessey began to put in extra hours at the motor pool to distract himself from the human wreckage of war, the sights that disturbed his nightly sleep. And as he labored at his job, he repeatedly asked himself what he would do if and when he caught in the sights of his carbine another human being—the father of three small children or an only son supporting his elderly parents—an individual defined by the macropoliticians and his superiors as his enemy. At such times, he gave thanks to God that his mechanic's job had so far prevented him from finding out.

Meanwhile, it was Ron's generous, unaffected manner of dealing with his comrades rather than his ability with engines or his off-and-on-again philosophizing, that set the Iowan apart. When he was advised that a "boy" from Alabama who was scheduled to relieve him on nighttime guard duty was too drunk to function, Ron said nothing and instead served the additional shift himself. He also refused to testify against a New Yorker, referred to as a "grease ball," whom the Iowan had seen shoot himself in the hand to avoid front-line duty, despite threats for maintaining silence from the investigating lieutenant. Such gestures did not go unnoticed by his platoon mates.

As the months wore on in Seoul, Private Hennessey's abilities with men and engines continued to attract the attention of his group commanding officer. When the sergeant in charge of the motor pool rotated home, he recommended Hennessey as his replacement. The company commander called in the Iowan and told him that he concurred with the sergeant's recommendation even though it meant granting Private First Class Hennessey in-shop authority over two corporals. It was a promotion the Iowan tried to decline.

"We'll get you another 'stripe' just as soon as we can," the commander told him. "Your predecessor says the men will accept you. I'm pushing for you."

Once settled into his new position, Ron acquired a stature above that called for by his corporal's—then sergeant's—stripes because of the company commander's habit of deferring to Hennessey's opinion on the serviceability of the pool's trucks, jeeps, and cars. And since many officers wanted to use those vehicles on dates with their Korean "girlfriends," they gave Hennessey access to the commissioned officers' PX.

At first, Ron said he felt like a pimp because without the vehicles the officers wouldn't get access to the women. Still, he felt no inclination to avoid cooperation with the practice since, as he remarked, Saint Augustine's misogynous theology had never appealed to him. Also, it would have been a fruitless crusade, one destined to bring into question both his sanity and his testosterone levels.

On the other hand, Ron could now play Robin Hood, using his opening to the officers' PX to help impoverished Korean friends obtain some scarce necessities of life, a practice forbidden by the army. Every road test he ran on a jeep or truck turned into an errand of mercy, or at least of friendship, down a narrow, twisting, dirt street, with the vehicle parked in front of one of a score of anonymous orphanages pointed out to the Iowan by his Korean coworkers. There, he would unload into the eager hands of his three-, four-, and five-year-old friends the remains of wooden shipping crates to serve as firewood, "throwaway" bedding that might require a bit of patching, K rations, canned goods, candy, and other "useless" items otherwise unobtainable by the powerless in war-torn Korea.

Eventually, the deep sense of satisfaction and friendship Hennessey felt during these visits to Seoul orphanages suggested that he might have a difficult time leaving his Korean friends to return to the sweet calm of Monti. When he first landed in Seoul, the demands of a new job and adjustments to an entirely new environment had largely consumed his mental and physical energy. Now, he had more time to himself and his thoughts often turned to questioning the nature of this war—and by proxy, all wars—its causes and goals, the human and ecological price paid, its untested alternatives, and the men who made life-and-death decisions with such destructive resolve.

Answers came slowly, sometimes to be rejected or refitted. It was like the discussions at the dinner table in Monti. Mom had always said to line up all the alternatives based on intense investigation and prayerful consideration and then knock them over one by one. The last one standing . . . .

War, conquest, arrogance, power, hatred, insecurity, even rape, the ultimate act of warped manhood, all seemed to go together, the primal cause buried deep in the human psyche. And not just the Korean psyche! Totalitarian communism is not an ideology that any sane person would give his life for, Ron told himself, . . . and the North Koreans are not insane. Individuals do not fight, kill, and die for ideologies, but to be or become who they and their loved ones want to be, bearers of the traditions handed to them by their forebears. Nor was the free-market, greed-driven capitalism of Iowa's banking elite that had brought his family to its knees—before FDR's "socialist" New Deal saved them—something a Hennessey would die for. What was he fighting for then? To worship the God who had created humankind with its capacity— no, with its love for—war against those who are different?

His first Christmas in Korea did nothing to resolve Ron's questions. On the contrary, they increased as a result of the visit to the front lines by Francis Cardinal Spellman, the Roman Catholic Archbishop of New York, unquestionably the most powerful Catholic church leader in the United States and a close personal friend of Eugenio Pacelli, Pope Pius XII.[3]

Ron had been looking forward for weeks to the visit of the cardinal, who intended to say Mass for and speak to the front-line troops. Spellman had done as much during the preceding two Christmas seasons. The Iowan hoped that his motor pool would be requisitioned for transporting his eminence's entourage, and that Hennessey himself might get to speak to the famous cardinal. But it was not to be. Ron's car pool was not called upon to serve the cardinal's needs, nor did he have the opportunity to see the famous prelate.

As the cardinal's sermons and comments were rebroadcast over the Armed Forces Radio Network, Hennessey felt that the prelate was going overboard with his bellicosity, sounding like a papal envoy out of the Middle Ages calling on the faithful to rise up in a new Christian crusade against a proxy Islamic scourge, godless communism. His eminence sounded more like he was peddling the very opiate that Marx had railed against a century earlier.

But even as these questions and the needs of Seoul's thousands of homeless and orphans persisted in invading his consciousness, he refused to allow himself to resolve his underlying problem: What could he do about it? What was he going to do with the rest of his life?

Then, in the spring of 1953, a warm letter from his younger sister Gwen back in Dubuque—she had entered the same religious order as her older sisters in 1950—telling Ron that she was going ahead to make her first vows as a nun, made him think that he should seriously consider the possibility of a religious vocation for himself . . . that of a missionary priest in Korea.

The thought did not come to him as a bolt out of the blue, however. The priesthood had always held for him a certain attraction, but even larger negatives. He had never considered himself an adequate public speaker nor professional student, both attributes of priests. Another drawback, the major one, one he was not sure his hormones and his need for intimacy could handle: lifelong celibacy. In Monti and Ryan, male and female virginity for the unmarried was an indispensable mark of social citizenship, where every shopkeeper and hairdresser could tell you who were the few (apparently!) who were not behaving properly. Respect for that tradition was an essential part of Hennessey family culture, and as such, lifelong celibacy did not seem to be an impossible goal. Nevertheless, the question remained, was the priesthood an attractive enough alternative to compensate for the sacrifice? Furthermore, a significant consideration in his musings was whether his efforts could make a difference in the landscape of suffering in Korea or anywhere else. Was he merely entertaining delusions of grandeur and self-importance? Better to go back to Monti and farming than to think that God had chosen him for something special.

With such thoughts he could laugh at himself, something he had learned to do early in life when his questioning had led him into a morass of ambiguous and ambivalent answers. And again, his laughter became a tonic, firing his imagination with thoughts of Iowa, of Monti, of a life he knew and loved, where he was known . . . and loved.

Ron wasn't home on the farm in Monti for more than twenty-four hours in December 1953—due to a pledge made by candidate Dwight Eisenhower during the 1952 presidential campaign—before he had put away his three Bronze Stars, donned his coveralls, and was back overhauling a tractor engine, getting ready for spring planting.

Pop was as happy as the family had seen him in some time, relieved to think that the army had not torn from his fifth-born son his love of the soil. And as the days turned into weeks, and then months, plowing, planting, and cultivating kept Ron busy enough so that future plans were never hammered out and alternatives never mentioned to parents or siblings.

By August 1954, however, Ron had decided it was time to move definitely one way or the other. He visited his two sisters, Dorothy Marie and Miriam, at their convent in Dubuque and confided his ideas for a missionary vocation in Korea. He wanted their advice. "You two make religious life seem to be an easy row to hoe. Is it always so pleasant as you make it seem to the rest of us?"

"Ron," answered Dorothy Marie, "you know us like the soil you love to plow. Of course it's a delightful life, the sense of satisfaction in doing something positive for others, . . . three healthy meals a day, no heavy lifting. What more could you ask for?"

Ron smiled. He loved his elder sister's straightforward assertiveness. "Don't you ever get lonely? Want a family of your own?"

"We have you guys," Miriam answered. "Who could want more family than that? . . . We also have each other, and Gwen, and all the other Sisters here. That's our family! We couldn't be happier! . . . But it's not for everybody."

"That's what bothers me most. It just may not be for me!"

"Look," Dorothy Marie came back, "you can always change your mind before ordination. You don't put your feet in concrete until ordination, probably eight years from now. Nobody gets hurt by trying."

"What about Pop? What do you think his reaction will be if I go ahead with this? . . . Just the thought of disappointing him . . . ."

Dorothy Marie laughed at her brother's concern. "Forget it, Ron! Pop will love the idea! His faith has always come before the farm! Don't worry about him. You'll see!"

Ron nodded, but not because he was fully convinced. "There's also the question of finding a missionary order that will take the likes of a rube like me and send me back to Korea. That's where I want to go."

"Maryknoll!" broke in Miriam, as if Ron should have known the answer. "Maryknoll is a great outfit, it has missionaries in Korea, it's all-American, and they love Iowans. Didn't you meet any of them over there?"

Ron stood looking from one to the other. His sisters' optimism was contagious. As he began to smile, the two women moved in and each planted a kiss on his cheek.

"Wait! Wait! You gals make it seem like there're no hurdles to be jumped here. It can't be this easy. I'll have to speak to Pop . . . very slowly . . . but you two have to back me up."

"Like I said, Ron, you're underestimating your father," replied Dorothy Marie. "He gave up two of his eldest daughters to the convent when he and Mom needed us most and never looked back. And now, Gwen. Forget it!"

"I wish I could be as optimistic as you two . . . . And no, I didn't meet any Maryknollers in Korea. But I heard about some American priests over there. I guess they were Maryknollers . . . . I'll send in an application but you two will have to serve as my character references . . . . Deal?"

"You've got it!" was the forceful reply from both.

The die was cast. Ron wrote to Maryknoll, "the all-American outfit," his sister Miriam had called it, and his application was accepted. It would be years before Hennessey would realize just how accurate his sister's description was. It was a point that would be brought home to him very forcefully by a patrol of EGP guerrillas in San Mateo Ixtatán one Sunday night in May 1981.

Chapter 8

David and Goliath

Sunday, 3 May 1981

Tap! Tap! Tap! Hennessey heard the far-off sound as he struggled to loosen the grip of sleep that held his brain in a state of semi-stupor. A few seconds later: Tap! Tap! Tap! Now he was coming awake, listening. What was it? He looked at the fluorescent hands on his watch. Only 8:50 p.m. He had gone to bed barely twenty minutes earlier but already it seemed like he had been asleep for hours.

Tap! Tap! Tap!

Someone's at the window, the priest told himself. Thinking that his visitor might be a parishioner in trouble, he slipped out of bed and crept to the casement. There, he stood with his back to the wall and peeked out into the moonless night. There was nothing to see but the bare outline of the long, descending pasture that backed up to the rectory. As the priest strained his eyes to capture any movement, a disembodied hand reached up from directly below the window and rapped again. The closeness of the movement startled him. He waited a few seconds more, but the hand's owner did not reveal himself.

What is this? A game of hide and seek?

Finally, while still standing to one side, the Iowan pushed the steel framed pane open an inch or two with just enough noise to signal his presence to the individual outside.

For some weeks now, Hennessey had been announcing in his catechetical meetings and at Sunday Masses that if anyone felt in danger from either the guerrillas or the army, they could come to the rectory at any hour for whatever assistance he could provide. By naming both sides as potential sources of danger, he felt he could ward off any misunderstandings of his position despite his ambiguity. His ultimate commitment was to life, whatever the political values of the victims, and he wanted that clearly understood, especially by himself.

The Iowan waited but still no sound came to him other than the chorus of several barking dogs. After a full minute, a man's muffled voice sifted up through the darkness, "Padre! Padre! Are you there? We have to talk to you!"

Hennessey waited, motionless and silent, realizing that the words were those of a ladino—highly unlikely that of a parishioner. He could be either a soldier or a guerrilla, the priest conjectured. He could be alone or with others. He may want to test my loyalties by representing himself to be other than he is. Or maybe he wants out . . . from either side . . . and needs my help to escape. The Iowan hesitated to answer.

Finally, seeing no movement nor shadow and recognizing that a waiting game would resolve nothing, the priest whispered, not without misgivings, "Go around to the front door."

Turning, Hennessey pulled on some pants and a sweater, grabbed a small flashlight from the bed stand and slowly made his way in the darkness across the bedroom and into the front room. There, he positioned himself behind the front door. When he felt the presence of his visitor outside, he gingerly cracked open the door.

"Don't be afraid, padre!" the same husky voice the priest had heard at his window whispered hoarsely. "We're EGP guerrillas. You're not in any danger! We're friends!"

God, the priest thought, *what if they're soldiers masquerading as guerrillas? Out to revenge the ambush of their elite patrol? Or trying a different tactic to see where I stand? The EGP flag is still flying over the town. Maybe they saw the graffiti on my wall? Got to push the neutral angle—I'm available to all in need!*

Slowly, he opened the door a bit wider—just enough to let one individual squeeze through. One, two, three, four, five pushed on past him. *How many more?* the priest thought, as he tried to swallow the dryness in his throat.

After the fifth man had slipped into the front room, the pressure on the door disappeared and the Iowan was able to close it. He turned on his flashlight, pointing it at the floor, and without turning to look at his visitors, proceeded to draw shut the curtains on the two front windows. He then went to the bookshelf against the back wall and lit a kerosene lamp, keeping the flame as low as possible. Meanwhile, no one had spoken a word.

Finally, the priest turned to face his guests. A quick appraisal of their dirty, khaki, fatigue uniforms, hair growing down over their ears and collars, emaciated looks, and the old carbines four of the five men held in their hands, indicated that the men were indeed what they said they were—EGP guerrillas.

The upright bearing of the six-foot-tall leader, his sense of self-assurance and lighter complexion identified him as an urban ladino. His companions' shorter builds, stooped postures—from years of performing traditional Mayan labor of carrying hundred-pound loads up and down mountain trails on their backs—darker skins and eyes and more self-effacing attitudes, signaled their Mayan ancestry. All five looked to be in their early to middle twenties.

The leader approached Hennessey, took off his cap, extended his hand and introduced himself: "With much pleasure, padre! *Me llamo Comandante Bernardo por el momento.* I call myself Commandant Bernardo for the time being."

"*Buenas noches, señor!*" the priest answered. "*Me llamo Padre Ronaldo para siempre.* I always call myself Padre Ronaldo."

The Iowan's greeting brought forth a chuckle from the leader's companions. One by one, the four Mayans came over to the priest. Each took off his cap and touched the priest's hand as he uttered a clipped Mayan version of the standard salutation, "*Buena noche, padre!*" Not one gave his nom de guerre.

The priest motioned to four rope armchairs circling the varnished, kidney-shaped, coffee table in the center of the small room. But the four Mayans preferred to squeeze together on the old green sofa against the wall in order to keep their dirty rubber boots from soiling the rug. Each carefully laid his ancient weapon on the floor in front of him, keeping the muzzle parallel to his feet. The old rifles looked like they might have been leftovers from World War I.

As Comandante Bernardo sat on one of the chairs fronting the coffee table, Hennessey sat down on another, across from him. The priest noticed immediately the man's long slender fingers resting lightly on the armrests, fingers better suited for the strings of a guitar than to opening a trail in the jungle with a machete.

After a few moments of silence, while waiting for one of the five to state the purpose of their visit, Hennessey decided to break the impasse. "Can I get you men some coffee?" he asked quietly.

Five faces lit up with evident pleasure. "That would be great, padre!" exclaimed the leader, rubbing his hands together. His four companions vigorously nodded their heads, adding a chorus of "*Sí, padrecito!*"

"We've been walking all day," Bernardo continued, "and are exhausted. We didn't stop to eat. Just a couple of cold tortillas along the trail. We had to keep pushing."

"I've got some cookies the nuns made today just in case any hungry guerrillas came through," the priest suggested with the trace of a smile. "I'll get them too."

The looks of simple pleasure told Hennessey that his visitors had missed his little joke.

When the Iowan returned with a thermos of hot water, cups, a jar of instant coffee, some brown sugar, and the cookies, he sensed a decrease in the room's tension. The four Mayans were busy thumbing through several copies of the Spanish-language edition of the *Maryknoll* magazine that Hennessey kept on the coffee table, commenting to each other on the pictures. The guerrilla leader, meanwhile, was sitting back in his chair, with legs stretched out and hands interlaced behind his head, a picture of unconcerned relaxation.

When each had served himself some coffee, Bernardo leaned forward and began what sounded like a practiced monologue: "Look, padre, we're EGP guerrillas! We're going to defeat the fucking Lucas García dictatorship and we're going to make a true agrarian reform. The land should belong to those who work it, not to thieves or the children of thieves! I'm sure you approve of that!"

The guerrilla leader fell silent, a questioning look on his face. This is my chance, the priest told himself.

"You folks," Hennessey began in his soft, hesitant way, "have hurt a lot of innocent people around here . . . . If the tactics you've been using are an indication of the kind of government you'd set up, . . . then, it seems that Guatemala won't have any more justice than it already has with Lucas García."

The priest had uttered the words softly in order to signal that it was not his intention to pick a fight, but to engage in a reflective dialogue. His remarks were not accepted as anything but an affront.

The five guerrillas stared at the Iowan in shocked silence. Finally, Bernardo, obviously stunned by Hennessey's remarks, asked, "What are you talking about? What have we done that could make you compare us to Lucas García and his fucking army? What about the massacres in the Ixcán, the Ixil Triangle, Quiché, Chimaltenango, Escuintla, Alta Verapaz? We have never done anything remotely like that!"

The guerrilla leader paused, breathing heavily, struggling for control. For a moment Hennessey did not reply. He recognized that he had unintentionally made it sound like he viewed the two sides as equally violent and abusive, but thought it unwise to back down in the face of Bernardo's anger.

"How about all the priests and catechists that have been kidnapped and murdered?" the guerrilla continued. "Even Padre Guillermo Woods, one of your own Maryknoll priests! The stealing of lands and forests? Generations of treating Mayans like animals? . . . We thought that you, after having worked at a colonization program in El Petén, would understand our struggle and be on our side."

Be careful, the priest told himself. *He's already checked me out.*

"Look," the priest countered, holding up his hand to calm the guerrilla's emotion, "I was not equating the EGP with the army . . . . I'll be specific. I was in Yacá and saw what your people did to Juan Silvestre. They suspended him by the neck for four hours because he was a *contratista* for the *finca* owners! . . . And another incident! The EGP killed Andrés Sebastián in Ixbajau simply because the people there taunted your troops . . . . And your *compañeros* killed several elders in Yolcultac without the semblance of a fair trial. Who's next?"

Hennessey knew that bringing up the murder in Ixbajau would especially antagonize his visitors. The murder had occurred a month earlier, during the first days of April, and had resulted in making the totality of Ixbajau's residents the sworn enemies of the EGP.

Ixbajau was an extremely conservative Mateano village about ten kilometers southwest of town where all the households practiced the *costumbre*. The approximately seventy-five families there were adamantly opposed to change of any kind, to the point that they even refused Hennessey entrance to their village to celebrate Mass or teach catechism. As San Mateo's staunchest traditionalists, they held to the ancient Mayan belief that the universe moves through 52-year cycles, renewing itself with each new age, but always in danger of falling into cosmic chaos. It was their job, accomplished by performance of *costumbre* rituals and prayers, to keep the universe in balance during each cycle. Any change in religious practices, or even in lifestyles, was a threat to cosmic equilibrium. With such a belief system, the whole idea of political and economic revolution was anathema.

When the EGP arrived in Ixbajau, the residents responded by taunting the guerrillas: "If you *cabrones* want to eat, put down your guns and get some hoes and till the land. There's no need to come to us like beggars looking for food."

The EGP quickly gave up on the Ixbajauans and decided to expend their efforts in more promising villages. But since their preferred footpath to the municipalities and villages south of San Mateo passed through Ixbajau, the guerrillas continued to face ridicule by the residents.

The guerrillas responded in kind, yelling at the Ixbajauans that they were "stupid mules content to bear the cargo of the blood-sucking landowners."

After a few weeks of exchanging insults, the guerrillas felt that by letting the Ixbajauans get away with their taunts, they were hurting EGP prestige in other nearby villages. So they sent a delegation to warn the Ixbajau elders of the consequences if the ridicule continued.

When the warning went unheeded, the guerrillas arrested Andrés Sebastián, the village's principal leader. Andrés was seen as the major cause of the Ixbajauans' antagonism, a gross oversimplification, since the roots of the animosity were broad-based and profoundly cultural. Nevertheless, Andrés was tried by a kangaroo court as an example to his neighbors, found guilty, sentenced to death, and shot. The Ixbajauans' taunts stopped but their hatred of the EGP became implacable.

The counterproductiveness of alienating practitioners of the sacred *costumbre* was a costly lesson that the Maryknollers themselves had learned only after many years of conflict with shamans, official prayer leaders, and elders over the issue of who would control church buildings, rituals, missals, and sacred vessels, abandoned a century earlier during a Liberal-sponsored persecution of the Church led by dictator General Justo Rufino Barrios.

Clearly, the moral compass of Hennessey's parishioners was now shifting slowly leftward, even for a people with a profound, traditional sense of social responsibility. For years—actually since feeling the impact of the teachings of the Second Vatican Council under Popes John XXIII and Paul VI (1961-65)—many priests throughout the country had been teaching parishioners the social and personal significance of their status as "children of God" and "the people as church," the dignity that flowed from such a status, and the rights and obligations that corresponded to it. These lessons were exercises in consciousness-raising that were bound to have revolutionary effects, although the priests and faithful never perceived them as anything other than a progressive orthodoxy.

The EGP and the three other guerrilla organizations, however, having perceived the revolutionary potential of these teachings, were tying the consciousness of one's God-given dignity to the right to employ explicit revolutionary activity. And in everyday conversations Hennessey's parishioners were using more and more terms such as rights, dignity, selfishness, social justice, and individuality. The old definitions of ritualistic right and wrong were becoming a bit blurred.

Now, talking to Comandante Bernardo and his companions, the priest's reference to the EGP murder of Andrés Sebastián in Ixbajau was enough to set five heads shaking. The leader leaned forward again in his chair even as Hennessey spoke, anxious for him to finish.

"Padre," the man said with a tone of exasperation, "I'm not going to justify everything our people do or everything that is done by those who say they belong to the EGP. We've spent eight years building this organization from nothing. Until recently, no one was allowed to join who wasn't well trained, or didn't know all our rules of conduct."

The guerrilla leader stood up, went behind his chair and leaned on it, facing Hennessey, his intensity burning like embers in his eyes. "Some of our people think this fight can be won with the same kind of popular uprising that occurred in Nicaragua. But we have a centuries-old ethnic problem here, something the Nicas didn't have. Most of us believe it will take years of slowly escalating armed struggle, training people as we go. We've got to be prepared to take on your Pentagon . . . . We have not forgotten 1954, even if you have! . . . Your country ended our Ten Years of Spring. The only sincere attempt at democracy we ever had! Ten Years of Spring! Ten years of democracy! Ten years of hope! . . . And your fucking government wouldn't let us have it. The fucking United Fruit Company meant more to your fucking government, *your* fucking government, than justice and democracy ever did, even now, for the Guatemalan people."

The speaker paused, his chin raised slightly, the muscles in his jaw tightening and relaxing, his breathing short and shallow.

Hennessey waited a few minutes, wondering if the atmosphere was conducive for understanding. When Bernardo finally sat down, the priest measured his words. "This is not 1954 . . . . Maryknoll has come a long way since then, as has the Church. We have Pope John XXIII to thank for that! . . . Maybe it's true that President Reagan and the current pope, John Paul II, see a communist conspiracy behind every cry for social justice, but that doesn't mean that all of us do . . . . But our sympathy for the Guatemalan people doesn't mean that we give carte blanche approval for all and any kind of revolutionary activity."

Bernardo was only half listening, his thoughts wandering. "The whole thing is like a mud slide! Entire villages are joining up all across Huehuetenango, El Quiché, and in Alta Verapaz. We have more untrained, nonpolitical people than we know what to do with. No one seems to know anymore who legitimately belongs to the EGP and who has decided on his own to claim to be EGP."

Hennessey nodded slightly. "I guess the things that bother me most," the priest replied softly, "are those incidents where not even a trace of the victims' guilt is present . . . . Like setting off the claymore against that truck beyond Momoxchecán, . . . if, in fact, your people did it."

"That's not what to think, padre," one of the Mayan peasants broke in. "We know that be mistake and we be sorry. The brothers wait in the cold for days to ambush soldiers. They be drinking a bit to be warm. The truck carry tarpaulin, hiding people inside. The brothers think they be soldiers. It be terrible mistake!"

Hennessey looked at the man in silence, unable to adequately verbalize his feelings. The four Mayans looked chastened.

"Look," Hennessey said, "saying you're sorry doesn't change anything. There's any number of ways to identify the occupants of a truck . . . . Why not put up a roadblock and force them to dismount? . . . And did any of your people go to the aid of the wounded once they knew who they were?"

Everyone looked at Bernardo while the leader stared steadily at the priest. "I guess all U.S. soldiers are geniuses and saints?" he answered in exasperation.

Again, the Iowan hesitated: "Even discounting the question of revolutionary morality, . . . you should know that blowing up truckloads of innocent victims and running out on potential supporters as in El Quetzal is not going to make you a potent political or military force . . . . And if you don't have the people with you, what do you have? . . . It doesn't make common sense!"

Just then a dog outside began to bark, then another and another. The noise sounded as if it might be coming from 100 to 150 meters away. The five guerrillas looked at each other.

"Someone's out there," Hennessey said, rising and moving toward the bookcase to douse the kerosene lamp.

No one answered. Bernardo picked up his Galil and moved behind the front door. The priest waited, listening for more barks closer by. No one else moved. In a minute, the barking died away.

"Probably just a coyote that spooked them," the Iowan sighed as he moved back to his chair. "Or maybe someone just went out to piss."

Bernardo waited a few seconds more before he returned to his seat.

All six maintained the silence for two or three minutes more and then Bernardo spoke up: "Look, Ronaldo, I like you! I want to come to an understanding with you. This revolution can't be successful unless we have all the exploited pulling together. But if the people think that we're cowards, or that we're capable of setting them up so that the survivors join us, then we've already lost . . . . But as you say, . . . it has happened, . . . and it must stop!"

Bernardo sighed, sat back in his chair, and waited, his anger having metamorphosed into what seemed to be sadness.

Hennessey allowed his eyes to close.

"Are you listening to me, padre?" the guerrilla asked in a disgusted tone.

Hennessey nodded, smiling slightly. "You'll have to excuse me, Bernardo. It's late and I heard everything you said."

"*Está bien!*" the guerrilla leader responded with a sigh. "But there is one major point I want you to understand: a revolution must be organized in secret. It has to be carried out on the hit-and-run because our enemies have limitless firepower, . . . thanks largely to the American and Israeli governments. And we may not be able to punish people for crimes in a way that reigning governments do, with staged trials, lawyers, and judges.

"If a crime is serious, we may impose the death penalty, which under other circumstances might only warrant fifteen or twenty years in prison. All armies execute traitors and criminals on the battlefield. That's even more of a necessity during a revolutionary war! You have to look at the tremendous imbalance of forces."

After a moment of silence, Bernardo continued, "A revolution is no fiesta, Ronaldo! We are like your biblical David, . . . and Lucas García and those who support him are Goliath."

Hennessey waited without changing his expression. Then he responded slowly: "What do you want me to say? That I'm 100 percent on your side? . . . I've never made a blanket statement that revolutionary war is always wrong. The last pope, Paul VI, gave the conditions under which revolutionary war can be considered moral . . . . But he also said that there's danger that such movements will bring on new disasters . . . . You must know the history of the Mexican Revolution! How many dead? Five million? Ten million? And for what? And the French Revolution, with Robespierre's Terror? . . . Russia had Stalin and China, Mao."

Bernardo continued as if he hadn't heard what the priest had said. "Let . me make one last effort. *De acuerdo?*"

The priest smiled. "You're going to anyway."

Lowering his voice, the *comandante* asked the question that must have been in the back of his mind all evening long. "Let's face it, padre! You're a North American and a priest! As a person, as an individual, is your primary loyalty to the U.S. government and its hypocritical support of fascism masquerading as emerging democracy, and with the bishops who dress in silk robes, drive around in BMWs, and tell us misery and oppression are God's will? Or are you really with the poor and oppressed of Guatemala?"

Hennessey sighed. He knew this question, this implicit accusation, would come up sooner or later. Disgusted, he was tempted to remain silent, to not answer. Finally, he responded: "My recognition of the role played by the United States, the Church, and Maryknoll in 1954, if anything, has made me more receptive to your perspective . . . . They promoted a revolution in favor of Guatemala's wealthy . . . and I'm not about to challenge your right to promote one to benefit Guatemala's poor . . . . But that doesn't mean I'll overlook the injustices your people commit in the name of the poor, . . . nor am I convinced that you will inevitably form a government that will bring a better life for most Guatemalans."

Bernardo shrugged his shoulders. Hennessey could see that his guests were as tired as he of the discussion, the dueling monologues. The conversation had been going back and forth for almost three hours and it was now midnight. The priest decided there was no reason to press his arguments any further.

Not so Bernardo. "Padre, I promise, this is my last point . . . . To put all that I've said in very blunt words, we will kill all those who would kill us or would have us killed. The Church has always permitted self-defense. Please remember that when you hear about some of our so-called injustices or crimes . . . . Anyway, let's leave this discussion for another day . . . . And despite the way our talk has gone tonight, I appreciate your frankness."

Ron fell silent. He was glad that Bernardo admitted that something had been gained by their discussion.

The guerrilla smiled, but only with his mouth.

Finally, the priest spoke: "Do you guys want more coffee and cookies, . . . or will it keep you awake?"

"We're not going to sleep for several hours yet so we'd appreciate anything that will keep us focused."

Hennessey rose and went into the kitchen. He could hear the men talking in subdued voices but made no attempt to listen. There was one other subject he wanted to discuss but was more anxious to end the visit. *But when will I get another chance?*

When everyone had a mouthful of cookie, the priest sucked in his breath and asked, "Why are you exposing your female recruits to sexual initiation rites in order to become full-fledged EGP members?"

Bernardo nearly choked. "Whaaaat?"

"The people tell me that one of the problems they have with you guys is that women recruits have to sleep once with all the top commanders before their commitment is accepted as sincere?"

"And you believe that shit?"

"It's not true?"

"Listen, padre, I was brought up a Catholic and taught to believe that every priest who performed a marriage slept with the bride on her wedding night. Is that true?"

"Of course it's not!"

"How do you know?"

"One, because I don't do it! Two, because I don't know any priest who does do it!"

"Bien! The same goes for me. I don't do it and I don't know of anybody who does."

Hennessey shook his head ever so slightly.

"You don't believe me?"

"Yes and no."

"Look, I didn't say there's no fucking going on . . . . Guerrillas have notoriously high levels of testosterone. At least, that's what we like to think . . . . We also have a *macho* culture . . . . All EGP sex is consensual. It has to be or it would ruin our organization! . . . In the next few days, you'll see what we think of nonconsensual sex."

Hennessey kept quiet, waiting for the guerrilla leader to explain his last remark. But Bernardo added nothing.

"Well, I got the information from two different fathers whose daughters are in the EGP and both girls told their mothers the same story. I believed them and still do!"

"Look, padre, forgive me for saying so. You are not a good one to discuss this subject. You're a celibate. You're as much of a sexual extremist as any EGP member, . . . just at the opposite end of the spectrum. Maybe you guys all have low testosterone levels? Or maybe there is some sacerdotal fucking going on that you don't know about? . . . Or haven't you heard that one of our members, a male *subcomandante,* was solicited by one of your priests in a parish not far from here?"

Hennessey grimaced. "I never said that some priests don't keep their vows. Only that brides are not obliged to sleep with their priest on their wedding night. What priestly sex there is, . . . I hope is consensual."

"Consensual? What about Padre Phil Gorley up in Todos Santos? The story up there is that he used to have his Todosantero altar boys suck him off after Mass. He let them think that was part of the program. Then his superiors shipped him off to Colombia to keep the whole matter a big, dark secret. Do you call that consensual? Did you complain about his sexual escapades?"

Hennessey sucked in his breath. It had never occurred to him that such information was out in the public forum. How much more does this guy know? Maybe more than I do!

"It happened before I ever got to Guatemala. Had I been here, I would have complained to our superiors."

"Hindsight? . . . Let's you and me not play games with each other, Ronaldo, trying to match each other as to whose membership plays by the fairest sexual rules . . . . Relations of equality between men and women are essential to any revolution worthy of the name. That includes how they relate sexually. Good healthy sex is of no interest to the Church *jefes,* but neither apparently is gender equality . . . . You guys will never understand . . . . So why don't we leave it at that?"

The Iowan fell silent. He knew he had lost a skirmish. *Better think through my side of the argument before bringing up that subject again!*

"Now, . . . we need a ride. We have to get to Momoxchecán. You'll take us there, won't you? We've been walking all day and have to be there tonight."

Hennessey felt a bit of relief that the meeting was over and the guerrillas didn't want anything other than a lift, though that was enough. He had thought during the evening that they might ask to use his rectory as a continuous source of food or money, or as a place to hide weapons, requests that he was prepared to refuse. Now he felt more at ease, even though the leader's request for a ride involved some risk and also seemed to contain an undertone of demand. And why would they want to go to Momoxchecán anyway, to the middle of the forest at this hour of night?

For a moment or two, the Iowan played with the idea of refusing the petition, to let his visitors know that he was not at their beck and command. But he was no more prepared for a confrontation than the bone-weary guerrillas seemed to be. Nor could he think of any moral reason to refuse them. *Had he not given plenty of rides to soldiers?* After waiting a moment or two to convey his hesitation, the priest nodded his head. *But why Momoxchecán? More punishment for Juan Silvestre in Yacá?*

"Are you going to Yacá?" the priest asked.

"No, padre, not Yacá! Don't worry about your friend there! Please, . . . no more questions!"

Again, Hennessey nodded. Yet, he had an uneasy feeling that the guerrillas were up to something that he preferred to know nothing about.

The risk for Hennessey in agreeing to the guerrillas' request for transportation lay in the possibility of being stopped by the military in those areas where the guerrillas were not active. Since the EGP had appeared in the town plaza back in November, the soldiers had been generally withdrawing after dark to the safety of their barracks in Barillas. But they sometimes made sorties into the night when they thought it safe to do so. Also, if some disgruntled *costumbrista* or antagonistic evangelical witnessed the priest giving a nocturnal ride to armed men and reported such to the army, his missionary tenure in San Mateo and Guatemala, at the very least, would be over.

"I know you have a rule about trucks with tarpaulins," the priest said, "but I'm not moving unless you let me put a tarpaulin on the pickup. Someone might see us and tell the soldiers I've been driving armed men around. Wait here while I go to the garage and get the truck ready."

As Hennessey moved toward the door, the leader rose and signaled his four companions to follow suit. "We'll go with you, padre," Bernardo stated firmly.

All five picked their weapons off the floor and held them at ready. Hennessey realized then with a touch of regret that whatever trust the guerrillas harbored toward him when they first arrived had been largely dissipated over the course of the evening's discussion.

"I have to put out this light before we go out the door," the priest told them with a note of authority. He moved toward the bookcase. "You can never tell who might be out there. Stay where you are for a few seconds until your eyes become accustomed to the dark . . . and then we'll move toward the door. I'll go out first and close the door behind me. If I don't see anything, I'll open the door and you can all follow."

Bernardo nodded his agreement.

As soon as Hennessey gave the all-clear signal, the five guerrillas came out the door. Without a word, they kept at his back as they passed the parish hospital and then cut behind the church, staying close to the buildings.

At the garage, the priest unlocked the big, double doors made of corrugated tin nailed to a reinforced frame of two-by-fours. As he eased one panel open, the old rusty hinges screamed for attention, louder than he had ever heard them before. His five companions held their breath. Finally, when all remained quiet, they slipped into the garage one by one and pulled the door gently shut behind them. Inside the darkened structure, lit only by the Iowan's small flashlight, the five men eagerly helped the priest arrange the tarpaulin over the metal frame on the back of the pickup. Their attempts to assist were actually more of a hindrance than an aid, but Hennessey said nothing.

"Get in the truck and I'll drive out. Once outside, I'll close these doors. You fellows stay in the truck."

When they had settled in, Hennessey doused his light and opened the garage doors slowly, lifting up on them to take some weight off the hinges and cut the noise.

Bernardo had entered the cab and held the Galil across his lap. "Put that weapon on the floor, Bernardo," the priest asked gently. "I don't want anyone to spot it."

The *comandante* did as he was told without a word. Hennessey then turned on the headlights and backed out of the garage. After shutting the doors, he turned the vehicle around and headed slowly up the twisting switchback above town toward Momoxchecán. He made the trip in about thirty minutes, careful to avoid potholes in case any of the four old carbines had less than adequate safeties. No one spoke during the ride.

Before the guerrillas left him at Momoxchecán, they insisted on helping to remove the tarpaulin. "If you run into any of our *compañeros*, padre, tell them you gave us a ride and they won't bother you," said the leader. "They know we're in the area."

Each man approached to shake hands with the priest and exchange a *buenas noches*. Then, as they disappeared into the darkness, he let out a sigh of relief, climbed into his pickup, and turned toward San Mateo.

Chapter 9

SIX YEARS OF SPRING AND COUNTING

"Ten Years of Spring! Ten Years of Spring!" Bernardo's words bounced back and forth inside Hennessey's head once he was back in the sack trying to will himself to sleep. How many times had he thought about the period demarcated by that expression? The Arévalo and Arbenz years, from 1945 to 1954, brought low and then to an ignominious end by the self-anointed ambassadors of the Divine Will sitting in council in Washington, New York, Boston, Managua, Tegucigalpa, and San Salvador. Learning the lesson of those ten years had been a long and painful process.

Juan José Arévalo Bermejo was inaugurated Guatemala's first popularly elected president on 15 March 1945, years before Hennessey had ever heard mentioned the man's name. In the United States, only academic and State Department specialists concerned with events in Central America noticed the transmission of power and took heart.

Two weeks earlier President Franklin D. Roosevelt had reported to both houses of Congress the results of his Yalta conference held with Stalin and Churchill regarding the postwar occupation of former German-held territories. Roosevelt's and Churchill's concessions to Stalin at Yalta, confirmed with some reluctance six months later by Truman's agreements with the Russian ruler at Potsdam, would lead to what can only be described as America's national paranoia, an irresolvable conviction that the Soviet Union possessed the preternatural ability to manipulate the intellects and psyches of philosophers, academics, workers, peasants, and the poor of the world, including those of loyal Americans, to its own anti-American, totalitarian, nationalistic ends. It was as close to mob hysteria that an entire modern nation could experience—

with the exception of Nazi Germany's obsession with "racial impurities"—a
psychosocial weakness that led to the so-called cold war, which, in turn,
claimed Guatemala's first attempt at popular democracy as its victim.

Juan José Arévalo Bermejo was in self-imposed exile in Argentina when
General Ubico resigned Guatemala's presidency in July 1944. Arévalo went
to Argentina as a young man to undertake postgraduate studies in education
and earn his doctorate. He returned to Guatemala City in 1934. Ubico,
always distrustful of educated men, appointed the young scholar to a minor
position in the ministry of education where the dictator could keep an eye
on him. But two years later, Arévalo went back to Argentina, disgusted with
the suffocating political and intellectual environment maintained by Ubico.

During his second sojourn in Buenos Aires, Arévalo published several
books on philosophy of education, works that he sent back to Guatemala to
his friends in the educational field. He was still in Argentina in July 1944
when he heard the news of Ubico's resignation.

With Ubico's political demise triggered by the capital city's teachers'
strike and talk of the possibility of democratic presidential elections heating
up, Arévalo's name became the principal one bandied about as that of a
potential candidate. A group of influential teachers fired off a telegram to
Argentina inviting the expatriate home to compete in the elections.[1] Arévalo
hesitated and then accepted, but not without some well-founded reservations.

When General Federico Ponce first heard the name of Juan José Arévalo
Bermejo mentioned as a candidate for Guatemala's presidency, he reportedly
laughed. And well he might! Nothing in Guatemala's history or culture
supported the idea of an educator as a political leader.

Ponce, however, was no longer laughing when *"el doctor"* arrived at Aurora
Airport in September 1944. The popularity of the candidate had spread
across the country in the intervening two months, a popularity magnified by
Arévalo's absence and inflated by the idea that Guatemala's future would be
in the hands of an intellectual, rather than in those of a single-minded militarist.

The concept of education taking priority over militarism had Guatemala's
middle class more than a little exhilarated. The land-owning class, meanwhile,
maintained an air of unconcern. Money could always make the political
system bend to its whims. Furthermore, the landowners knew that the poor,

especially the Maya, would do whatever was demanded of them, including vote the way they were told, should it ever come to popular elections. Otherwise, they would find themselves unemployed and starving.

For their part, the Maya remained indifferent to the possibility of elections. First, because 92 percent of them were disenfranchised as illiterates, and second—and more importantly—because their only concern was to possess enough land to feed their families, a concern that an urban intellectual could hardly appreciate. As for Ponce, he seethed.

The mostly middle-class crowd waiting to meet Arévalo at the airport was huge and festive. When their candidate stepped off his plane, a roar of welcome went up from thousands of throats.

At first, the new arrival looked startled. Then he smiled broadly and waved. An educator he might be, but Arévalo looked every inch a presidential candidate—except for the lack of a uniform and holstered pistol. His two hundred pounds spread in adequate proportions along a muscular, six-foot frame gave him the appearance of a true leader, well above the height and girth of the average Guatemalan. With his handsome wife at his side and his pointed references to the unsurpassed beauty of Guatemalan womanhood, he exuded a necessary self-conscious, self-confident heterosexuality. He might not have sat astride a white horse, but he came out of the blue on the silver wings of a Pan-Am bi-motor DC-4 to answer the call of his countrymen, and in 1944 that counted for something. He had white skin as testimony to his European genetic heritage and he spoke like a leader, with authority, wit, and vague ideas for Guatemala's future.

In short, Arévalo possessed the charisma and magnetism of a *caudillo* without the authoritarian tone and personality of one and seemed to embody all that the enraptured crowd could hope for in a civilian candidate for the presidency.

When Arévalo Bermejo finished his remarks and descended the mobile steps, he was quickly surrounded by supporters who whisked him away to plan his campaign, safe from Ponce's threats and plotting. There was no doubt in the mind of anyone present that more than a few members of Ponce's military clique were present in the audience dressed as civilians with orders to truncate Arévalo's candidacy. There were also three other soldiers who, if they weren't personally present at Aurora Airport that day, watched the day's proceedings through surrogates, each, for personal reasons, profoundly interested in the political fortunes of Juan José Arévalo Bermejo. They were Captain Jacobo Arbenz Guzmán (ret.), General Miguel Ydígoras Fuentes, and Private José Efraín Ríos Montt, recently enlisted.

Jacobo Arbenz Guzmán had been a young officer in good standing two months earlier when General Ponce marched into Ubico's parrot legislative assembly and demanded at the point of a gun to be appointed Ubico's heir. Arbenz was present in the gallery that day, recognized as the army's outstanding intellectual by his colleagues at the Politécnica, where he was an instructor. The young captain, a student of Guatemalan history and politics, had gone to the legislature to see how the pseudo-lawmakers would respond to the call for democracy from the capital's population. The legislature had assembled to put their seal of approval on Ubico's three choices—generals all—who would lead the country temporarily and supposedly draw up a timetable for elections. Ponce's action invalidated their first order of business and canceled the possibility of the second. Arbenz Guzmán, educated in the Politécnica under American directors and instructors and then appointed as an instructor himself, had become convinced that only popular democracy could pull Guatemala out of the sixteenth century and propel it into the twentieth. As he listened to Ponce tell the cowed legislators that he would carry on in the Ubico tradition, Arbenz's blood boiled.

The young captain left the gallery in a fury, resigned his commission that same day, and began to plot Ponce's downfall from across the border in El Salvador. Now, pushed by the same sense of history that led him to the legislative gallery in early July, Arbenz followed closely the public reception accorded to this revolutionary political phenomenon, one Juan José Arévalo Bermejo, D.Ed.

General Miguel Ydígoras Fuentes had other, more selfish motives for his interest in the arrival on Guatemala's political scene of Arévalo Bermejo. When Ubico named his three successors, Generals Ponce, Villagrán, and Pineda, "the Old Fox," as Ydígoras was known, had felt betrayed, believing that he should have been named to the ruling triumvirate. He had groomed himself for years to be Ubico's successor, cultivating the president's esteem.

This he had done, like many of his eighty brother generals, by engaging in competitive savagery, consisting of political murders at Ubico's request and Mayan massacres of his own initiative. On one documented occasion, Ydígoras had ordered his troops to rape a group of protesting Mayan women and imprison their children.[2]

Now, the Old Fox consoled himself with the thought that he was too strong a candidate to fit Ubico's obvious plan, namely, to appoint three relatively manageable generals (all three were stand-up alcoholics, a common weakness of the upper echelons of the officer corps), whom the dictator could manipulate from behind the scenes. Ponce's abrupt assumption of all power, however, had aborted not only Ubico's plans, but Ydígoras's plot to do something similar. He would now have to wait to see how the coming confrontation between Arévalo Bermejo and Ponce worked its way out, hoping for a power vacuum where he could insinuate himself.

Private José Efraín Ríos Montt was just a curious onlooker that day in September 1944 when Arévalo Bermejo was swept away by admirers determined to see his candidacy protected from the machinations of General Ponce. The young private had left Huehuetenango almost a year earlier in disgrace, determined to return someday as a soldier, an officer, perhaps even as a general, redeeming himself in the eyes of all those whom he felt had betrayed him.

Ríos Montt went to Guatemala City to sign up for the Politécnica, the only sure path to high military rank, from whence flowed all political power and ultimately, economic wealth and well-being. Rejected by the Politécnica because of his astigmatism, the young Huehueteco endured a severe, but temporary, depression. In a matter of weeks, his monumental pride and tenacity had reasserted themselves. He would join the army as a soldier, commit to memory the pertinent eye charts, and apply again to the academy after proving his mettle as an infantryman. With Arévalo's arrival, however, a new and obscure scenario seemed to be developing, with political power flowing into the hands of civilians. It was a time to watch, to wait, to plan, and react. God would be his guide, he would be God's servant. He knew that God had saved him as a young boy from a near fatal encounter with the hooves of an angry ox so that he could accomplish great feats for Guatemala.[3] But, he wondered, as a soldier or . . . as a civilian?

As *el doctor* crisscrossed the country from one campaign stop to the next, his gilded oratory, his promises of a new Guatemala guided by a philosophy he called "Spiritual Socialism," and the novelty of a civilian candidate not controlled by the military pushed his support ever higher. Then Ponce made his move. He sent his secret police to murder the most prominent of Arévalo's supporters, Alejandro Córdova, editor of the country's leading newspaper, *El Imparcial.*

Everyone knew that Ponce was responsible for the editor's death. They were supposed to know! Opposition leaders went into hiding, some into exile. Arévalo sought refuge in the Mexican embassy. The U.S. Embassy, out of touch with 99.8 percent of all Guatemalans, reported that by seeking such refuge, "many" thought that Arévalo was committing political suicide. The embassy theory was that a *caudillo,* even a civilian *protocaudillo,* had to show the Guatemalan electorate that "he had balls" by standing up to Ponce (and surely getting himself killed), and Arévalo had failed that test. It was an outdated mind-set on the part of American diplomats and their informants—American business expatriates and English-speaking members of Guatemala's land-owning class—who still believed that only militarist values had the power to inspire the Guatemalan people.

Ponce's crackdown on the opposition spurred Captain Jacobo Arbenz Guzmán to accelerate his timetable for a coup. He had already talked to a carefully selected handful of trusted colleagues and classmates, personal friends, younger officers in various positions of power. All assented to cooperate—once the plan was put in motion and a successful outcome looked probable.

The reaction of Arbenz's friends was one the captain expected. The Guatemalan Army is no monolith with a single chain of command. Like the society at large, it is based primarily on personal relationships, *personalismo,* and such relationships determine whether or not one gets the promise of support from fellow officers and the possible support of the men serving under them.

These personal relationships between officers are sacrosanct—up to a point—and institutionalized. Of the first order are those called "*de la promoción,*" the loyalties that all members of the same Politécnica graduating class owe to each other.[4] The second-order relationships are those of the *centenario* system, in which each Politécnica graduate gets a number that entitles him to a special relationship—and protection—with and from all those who hold a number with the same last two digits from previous graduating classes. The two systems make for a crosscutting set of loyalties for each officer. Not included in these systems are other, idiosyncratic relationships that may or may not override the loyalties of the *promoción* and *centenario* systems. Such would be blood and marriage relationships extending out two and three generations, as well as *compadrazgo* relationships, established by sponsoring a sacramental reception for a friend's offspring or some other religious or ritual event. Calculating the outcome of a coup on the basis of the strength and effectiveness of the many-stranded, interwoven, and often conflicting networks of personal military, family, and *compadre* relationships is much like playing a game of three-dimensional chess blindfolded. And Arbenz Guzmán was known as the best chess player the Guatemalan Army had seen in living memory.

On the night of 19 October 1944, at about 11:00 p.m., two Maryknoll priests, Arthur Allie—the Maryknoll superior in Guatemala, who had formerly served in Korea—and newly arrived Edmund McClear, looked out the windows of the archiepiscopal palace in Guatemala City to see tracer bullets being fired at and from the presidential palace across the city's main plaza. Although they did not realize it at the time, they watched the beginnings of an unprecedented, albeit short-lived, change of course in Guatemala's political and economic history. As far as their host, Archbishop Mariano Rossell y Arellano, was concerned, the firefight was merely a changing of the guard, one, he hoped, that would soon see the unruly public school teachers and other strikers put back in their place.

For his coup attempt, Captain Arbenz Guzmán had enlisted the support of, among others, his *compadre,* Major Carlos Aldana Sandoval, the commandant of crack infantrymen in the presidential Honor Guard. Aldana Sandoval had, in turn, brought into the plot another officer of equal rank, Major Francisco Javier Arana, the commandant of the Honor Guard's twelve tanks. Between the two men, they commanded the elite troops charged with protecting the president. At the last moment, however, Aldana Sandoval had second thoughts.[5] The termination of Ponce's reign would now be primarily in the hands of Captain Arbenz and Major Arana, seconded by a dozen or so other officers of middle-level rank brought into the plan by Arbenz, Arana, or Aldana Sandoval, as well as by any officers inspired by their initial successes, should these occur.

As he had promised, Arana led the entire tank corps of the Honor Guard, as well as Aldana Sandoval's troops, into the front ranks of the revolt. His participation was critical and would prove decisive. Arbenz, not having any troops at his command, took charge of arming and directing two thousand or more civilian volunteers who had previously demonstrated their militancy in support of Arévalo's candidacy.

The fighting lasted through the night and into the morning hours of 20 October. More and more civilians were volunteering to participate in the struggle. Major Francisco J. Arana, ever the proud soldier, was torn between allowing civilians to fight alongside his men and the need to win at all costs now that he had committed himself. Arbenz never wavered.

As the fight began to go the rebels' way, General Miguel Ydígoras Fuentes presented himself in civilian clothes at the U.S. Embassy to offer his services as a broker between Ponce and the rebels. He had no standing with the rebels to perform such a role but felt that if he could receive Ambassador Boas Long's blessing, then Arana and Arbenz would have to listen. And if they listened hard enough, he might still land himself in the presidency. But the Old Fox had misread his standing at the embassy and Ambassador Long ignored him.[6]

Ydígoras made the same offer to Major Francisco Arana, soldier to soldier. But Arana was not fooled as to the true nature of Ydígoras's objective. For the time being, the general's pretensions went nowhere. The Old Fox, however, had no intention of retiring to the background.

Just before noon, 20 October 1944, a white flag was hoisted above the presidential palace. By 2:00 p.m., Ponce's safe departure from the country had been negotiated and he was on his way to Mexico via the Mexican Embassy.

Arbenz and Arana asked Guillermo Toriello, a civilian leader in the battle and a well-known businessman, to join them in forming a ruling triumvirate to schedule presidential and congressional elections. That night, sporadic fighting broke out once again, led by officers who felt no loyalty to either Arbenz Guzmán or Arana—and probably not to Ponce— but they were quickly defeated and executed. About one hundred combatants died in the conflict.

The next day, the two Maryknollers ventured out of the archbishop's palace. They found the capital patrolled by armed, exuberant civilians. Father Allie remarked to his companion that strangers in the streets had never treated him with such friendliness since his arrival in Guatemala a year earlier.

On 22 October, the two priests left for Huehuetenango, traveling northwest. That same day, news reached Patzicía of the overthrow of Ponce and his retreat into exile. The Mayan community there and in its environs had been the source of many who had marched for Ponce in a staged parade on Independence Day, 15 September, armed with sticks, machetes, and the strongman's promise of land. Their reaction to the news of Ponce's political demise was to form a spontaneous public demonstration against the rebels, seeing the general's departure from power as another ladino plot to keep . them chained to the whims and exploitation of large landowners. Their cries of anguish, "General Ponce promised us land," were met with ladino derision.

Mayan response was immediate. They turned on their tormentors and began hacking away with their ever-present machetes. Before they came to their senses, a score of ladinos lay dead in the streets, many more wounded. Then, with typical Mayan fatalism, they waited for the response they knew would come.

Word of the killings was telegraphed to Guatemala City. Major Francisco J. Arana reacted swiftly and according to tradition, sending in troops with no restrictions as "a warning throughout the republic against any other disorders of this nature."[7] The soldiers slaughtered over nine hundred unarmed Mayan men, women, and children,[8] the kind of reaction ladino Guatemalans expected of their *caudillos* in response to Mayan provocations.

The two Maryknollers traveling through Patzicía the next day saw only a few wounded ladinos. They trembled at the suggestion of a pan-Mayan uprising, signs of which they thought they saw as they traveled northwest through overwhelmingly Mayan towns. They were relieved, however, to find armed ladinos patrolling the streets of Chichicastenango, where they were to spend the night.

Ambassador Boas Long reported that the junta's reaction was "the most drastic response of which the white and ladino population is capable."[9] He was grossly overstating the case, however.

The massacre at Patzicía was Major Francisco J. Arana's handiwork. Almost overnight, he had become a *caudillo*-in-waiting. After taking power and as the senior member of the new triumvirate, he began agitating to have the presidential elections postponed and then canceled altogether. In a letter more than two years later, dated 26 April 1947, he would write to Guillermo Toriello: "Don't forget what a hard time you had—the discussions, the arguments—convincing me to accept this situation which I never wanted because I knew that it meant handing the revolution over to civilians who would reap the benefits of what we, the military, had accomplished."[10]

Years later, President Arévalo would say of Arana, "In Guatemala, there are two presidents, and one of them has a machine-gun with which he is always threatening the other."[11]

Arbenz and Toriello managed to keep Arana in check, at least until the promised elections took place. The vote was extended to all adult males, including illiterate Mayan males and literate Mayan adult females. The junta retired all generals from the army—to erase any possible influence from Ubico, Ponce, Ydígoras Fuentes, and their cronies—and made colonel the highest military rank, one that both Arana and Arbenz accepted for themselves.

Arévalo Bermejo, despite Arana's opposition, remained a candidate, winning the December election with more than 80 percent of the vote. On 15 March 1945, Arévalo accepted the blue and white sash of the Guatemalan presidency, even while Colonel Francisco Arana continued pushing to nullify the election results.

Juan José Arévalo began his presidency by spelling out the four major principles of his Spiritual Socialism, which he likened to Roosevelt's New Deal "with a soul." He underlined his desire to preempt critics who, he knew, would charge him—as they had charged the American president—with being an "atheist communist materialist." His principles were these: the strengthening of popular democracy; the development of an education system that would meet the needs of all citizens, including the Maya; a labor code to protect industrial and agricultural workers; and an agrarian reform involving some sort of redistribution of unused agricultural lands.

The president also had a fifth, though unstated, goal: the assertion of his country's sovereignty, free from the political and economic manipulations by

THROUGH A GLASS DARKLY   171

U.S. business interests championed by the U.S. Embassy. It was Arévalo's movement toward this latter goal that was used in the U.S. Congress, principally by the United Fruit Company and the media, to paint Arévalo first as "a communist dupe," then as "a fellow-traveler," and finally, as "a communist." The singular event that accelerated the estrangement of the Arévalo Bermejo administration from the U.S. government was the passage in 1947 of a Labor Code that granted legal status to labor unions, allowed collective bargaining, gave workers the right to strike, formulated conciliation procedures to settle disputes, limited the regular workweek to forty-eight hours, outlawed arbitrary dismissals for labor union activity, set standards of health and safety in the work area, established a minimum wage that included agricultural workers, and restricted the use of female and child labor. Further, it established a series of Labor Courts to adjudicate accusations of infringements of the code, to force compliance, and to levy fines.[12]

Cries of "communism" from landowners who had never known anything but militarist support for their interests echoed throughout Guatemala and in Washington, D.C. In response, J. Edgar Hoover sent his G-men to find out exactly who these "communists" were—now that they had no need to look for Nazis—and to open a file on each. Juan José Arévalo Bermejo's name was the first on the FBI's list. Those of his cabinet ministers and labor leaders followed.

But it was not until the United Fruit Company weighed in with its accusations that the Labor Code was discriminatory and aimed directly at UFCO that official Washington decided to make a formal protest. The fruit company's discrimination claim was based on only four of the four hundred articles in the law that gave "special benefits" to workers on plantations employing more than five hundred individuals. UFCO's charge was made despite the fact that there were at least four Guatemalan family *fincas* that fell within the purview of the law, as well as several of the 192 government-owned plantations confiscated by the Ubico government in 1942 from German-Guatemalans at the insistence of the U.S. government.[13]

The United Fruit Company immediately pulled out all stops to undermine and rescind the Labor Code, utilizing its own economic and political power in Guatemala, and mobilizing its many supporters in the U.S. Congress, especially the Massachusetts delegation from the home-state of the Boston-based corporation, led by Senator Henry Cabot Lodge.

Assistant Secretary of State Spruille Braden answered UFCO's call for help by dressing down the Guatemalan ambassador to the United States without waiting for any evidence to buttress the company's discrimination claim. In July 1947, the State Department sent a representative to Guatemala at UFCO's request to warn the Arévalo administration that its treatment of UFCO "might have a serious effect upon relations between the two countries."[14]

Arévalo refused to budge. The "discriminating" articles remained in the law. UFCO responded, writing a memorandum to the State Department that could not be ignored, stating that the Arévalo administration "was subjected to communistic influences emanating from outside Guatemala."[15]

That accusation rang the panic alarm in Washington. From then on, economic issues, Guatemalan nationalism, and a small country's right to its sovereignty were never seen as underlying factors in the conflict. Rather, it was solely an issue of American free enterprise versus Moscow-directed tyranny. This, despite a report from an official in the U.S. Embassy stating in June 1947 that the Labor Code was based on that of Costa Rica, not on directives from Moscow, that it included considerations taken from all sectors affected by the code, and that it "cannot be considered radical or revolutionary in any sense, except that no coordinated labor legislation existed in this country previously."[16]

By this time, UFCO had decided that it would not recognize the Arévalo administration's right to legislate any matter affecting its relations with its workers. The fruit company peremptorily fired workers, ignored union wage demands, shut down Puerto Barríos—the country's only Atlantic seaport—and refused to negotiate.

It was about this same time that Archbishop Rossell y Arellano stepped up his antigovernment sermons and pastoral letters. The archbishop had proposed to Arévalo back in 1945 that he and the new congress safeguard the "preeminent right of the Church" when drawing up the nation's new constitution, requesting privileges that he had never asked of his friend, Jorge Ubico. These included the right to establish religious schools and to teach Catholic doctrine in public schools, to form and instruct labor unions in the duties of labor (a hitherto unclaimed right born of Arévalo's stated commitment to labor), to own property, to conduct public, outdoor demonstrations of faith, to outlaw divorce, and to preach the Church's unchallenged version of the public interest.

Arévalo received the archbishop with courtesy. The president was well aware of past attempts—some successful, others less so—made by earlier governments to control Church educational, political, and economic activities. Warily, he agreed to study the matter.

If Arévalo conducted such a study, nothing ever came of it. He made no attempt to influence the constitutional convention either for or against Rossell's position.

Members of the convention, noting that the archbishop had maintained a warm relationship with Ubico and harbored tendencies toward fascism, allowed to stand those restrictions on Church ownership of property, operation of schools, and political activity instituted by General Barrios in 1871. They also outlawed Church activities in reference to the establishment and formation of labor unions, noting the archbishop's traditional stand favoring the landed elite.

Formerly, Archbishop Rossell had damned such restrictions as "liberal," blaming Barríos, not Ubico. Now, however, the prelate used the inflammatory language in vogue among Guatemala's elite, declaring the new charter to be a "communist document."[17]

Two-and-a-half months after Arévalo's inauguration, almost before any serious civil labor organization could result from the freedom to organize granted workers by the new constitution, the archbishop orchestrated from behind the scenes the formation of his own labor federation, La Liga de Obreros Guatemaltecos (LOG), the League of Guatemalan Workers. LOG's focus was "to promote peace and tranquility among all members of the Guatemalan family," to avoid antagonisms between employers and workers lest it degenerate into "class warfare," and to seek social peace, "which is harmony, even in the midst of inequality,"[18] inequality that was preordained by God as a result of original sin.

As LOG floundered—perceived by most workers as a bulwark of the old order—and the membership of nonsectarian unions and peasant leagues multiplied, the archbishop declared that "the worst of all plagues has descended on Guatemala, . . . bourgeois wolves in sheep's clothing . . . wish to worsen even more the conditions of the laborers, so that on the shoulders of the workers they can impose the dictatorship ordered by international communism."[19]

Although it was true that the influence of Marxists in the formation of the labor movement was important, particularly in urban areas, their orientation was overwhelmingly nationalistic. Such was the ideology of Víctor Manuel Gutiérrez, the highly regarded head of the teachers' union. Gutiérrez, also known among Guatemalans as "the Franciscan" because of his ascetic lifestyle, had founded the Revolutionary Party of Guatemalan Workers (PRTG) in opposition to the Communist Party led by another labor organizer, José Manuel Fortuny, who was considered too much of an "internationalist." Gutiérrez held that it constituted a contradiction to be an enemy of the international operations and worldwide capitalistic ideology of UFCO, IRCA, La Empresa Electrica, and LOG, without also being a Marxist, or something close to it. He later joined Fortuny's party, however, as the U.S. government's support for UFCO solidified.

Rossell y Arellano chose to ignore the fact that President Arévalo in 1945 had closed down La Escuela Claridad, a school for training Marxist union organizers and had expelled El Salvadoran communists from the country.

The Maryknoll Fathers and Brothers, both as churchmen and Americans, were also being drawn inexorably into the fray. Political and cultural neophytes, they accepted the archbishop's counsel and influence from day one. As Americans, they quickly became friends with the on-site directors and managers of UFCO, IRCA, La Empresa Electrica, and Standard Oil, used the companies' swimming pools, golf course, chauffeur-driven cars, boats, and private railroad car, and they sometimes stayed in their homes. Dinners with the U.S. ambassador and consul general, as well as with U.S. military and FBI personnel were not uncommon. With such associations, the Maryknollers developed an American ghetto perspective of political and economic events in Guatemala.

Nor were the priests as sensitive to their own cultural biases as one might expect of men trained for years to work closely with, and influence the religious beliefs and practices of peoples among whom they lived. The diaries of the first Maryknollers in Guatemala were replete with references to "good old American know-how" and "American efficiency," as compared with

Guatemalan ignorance and backwardness. On one occasion, Father Arthur
Allie, the Maryknoll superior, called in the head of the Huehuetenango Men's
Society and dressed him down for his anticlerical behavior, telling him that if
it happened again he'd "send names to the American ambassador, to *Readers'
Digest* and to the diplomatic corps. You'll find out that dealing with an American
is like nothing you have ever experienced before," he declared.

By July 1948, the State Department's legal advisor had concluded that there
was no proof of discrimination against UFCO in the Labor Code. In response,
the secretary of state ordered the embassy in Guatemala to obtain such proof
"in as discreet a manner as possible."[20]

The ambassador, Richard C. Patterson, turned to UFCO when he found .
the request impossible to fulfill and asked the fruit company to provide
"clear and incontrovertible evidence" of discrimination. UFCO, too, found
that it could not provide such proof. The State Department then requested
"sufficient information" instead of proof in order to proceed against Arévalo.[21]

Finally, UFCO provided its "new information." On 10 December 1948,
the State Department telegraphed its ambassador to verify the new information,
and then, without waiting for such verification, "to renew representations in
protection of UFCO's interests."[22]

Patterson relished the order. He had told Arévalo at a formal dinner in
his honor, welcoming him to Guatemala, that his appointment was principally
"to protect and promote American interests in Guatemala." Later, to underline
his position, he reported to Washington that he had berated the president,
telling him that "these American interests have been persecuted, prosecuted,
and unmercifully kicked around over the past two years and that personally I
was fed up and that the patience of my government nearly exhausted."[23]

In early 1949, Patterson went to Arévalo and demanded that he fire
seventeen members of his government whom the ambassador named, accusing
each of communism. Arévalo refused. He then accused Patterson of interfering
in the internal affairs of Guatemala. The ambassador responded by meeting
with—and thereby encouraging—Guatemalans who were known publicly to
advocate the military overthrow of the Arévalo administration. The president,
in an aside to Samuel Guy Inman, a professor of international relations and
one of FDR's architects of the Good Neighbor policy, complained that "you

don't have an ambassador of the United States here, but a representative of United Fruit."[24]

It was inevitable! Arévalo finally declared Patterson persona non grata and asked the U.S. government to recall him. Before departing, however, almost as his final act, the ambassador wrote to the president of UFCO to suggest that his company launch an all-out barrage in the U.S. Senate on the treatment of U.S. capital in Guatemala, that "this takes the onus off UFCO and puts it on the basis of a demand by our senators."[25]

Senator Henry Cabot Lodge—whose family owned a substantial interest in UFCO—denounced the Arévalo government from the Senate floor for its discrimination against the fruit company and for forcing it into a "serious economic breakdown."[26] His sentiments were echoed in the House of Representatives by Congressmen Claude Pepper of Florida, Mike Mansfield of Montana, Alexander Wiley of Wisconsin, and especially John McCormack of Massachusetts.[27]

Despite all the rhetoric by the U.S. State Department and its ambassador regarding the "discrimination," "persecution," and "victimization" of UFCO by the Guatemalan government, a 1950 State Department review of the fate of American companies under Arévalo admitted that none had suffered any serious harm.[28] In fact, UFCO had ended up by paying the paltry sum of $690 in fines for all the infractions and outright flouting of the law that it had committed.[29] It was a small enough sum to pay to buttress its false claims and to give the State Department "proof" of Arévalo's "communism."

Now it was the closing weeks of 1950 in Guatemala and new elections for president and congress were coming up in December. It was incumbent upon the United Fruit Company to see that Arévalo was not followed into the presidential palace by a like-minded reformer. A suitable candidate had to be found, one "not manipulated by Moscow."

A powerful propaganda machine paid for by the CIA was cranked up to prove definitively that Arévalo was a communist beholden to the "International Communist Conspiracy," an assertion that would not rest on the accusations of UFCO alone. The proof: Arévalo, like all his Latin American presidential colleagues—with the exception of Colombia's Laureano Gómez—claimed that he could not meet U.S. requirements for sending troops to fight in

Korea. The requirements included a battalion-sized (or larger) commitment of well-trained, well-armed troops that would stay in Korea for at least ninety days. The commitment was largely symbolic—to give the appearance that the United States had the enthusiastic endorsement in the United Nations of a large majority of countries not controlled by Moscow.

Nevertheless, Guatemala's lack of a military response was falsely trumpeted as an exception to the UN mandate, proof of international communism's takeover of the Arévalo government. This was the first of several such decisions implemented by the Arévalo administration and that of his successor that Presidents Truman and then Eisenhower would claim to be symbolic opening shots in a hot episode of the cold war rather than a disagreement over how much control the Guatemalan government should exercise over its own foreign policy and economy.

One more time, Arévalo tried to invalidate the charge. He called to his office Samuel Guy Inman, who had written some supportive articles regarding Guatemala's social security system, the construction of hospitals and schools, the rights of labor, a free press and free elections, all benefits of the Arévalo revolution. The president asked Inman to tell the American people of his strong anticommunist views and actions, that Guatemala "has one and only one loyalty, geographically, politically, and militarily"—to the United States, and that his government is "in complete solidarity" with the United States regarding the Korean War.[30]

To no avail! When Inman returned to the States, he called a news conference to detail his interview with Arévalo. Although the news conference was well attended, little was published in the news media over the next several days about what Arévalo had to say, providing evidence that a "free press" is not always free from government influence.

As plans for the 1950 presidential election began to take shape, the names of Army Chief of Staff Colonel Francisco J. Arana, Minister of Defense Colonel Jacobo Arbenz Guzmán, and General Miguel Ydígoras Fuentes (ret.) bubbled to the surface of public and media attention as the most likely candidates. When the Guatemalan Congress asked Arana to step down from his army post as the country's constitution required political candidates to do, the chief of staff threatened to use his troops to close down the legislative branch. The U.S. Embassy had warned Washington back in 1948 of believable rumors that Arana had been waiting for the right opportunity to seize presidential power by the force of arms. Now, as talk of the election got underway, Arana's opportunities to realize his dream were becoming fewer by the day.

The inner circle of President Arévalo's consultors, including his minister of defense, Colonel Arbenz Guzmán, decided that it was time to end speculation that Arana was preparing a *golpe* by arresting him and having him tried before Congress. Whether the unspoken agenda of the plan was the possible (hoped for?) assassination of the resisting strongman, no one will ever know with certainty. An attempt was made to carry out the arrest in July of 1949 and Arana came out of his car shooting. He died in the exchange of gunfire, as did one of his intended captors.

The supporters of Arana and those of Ydígoras Fuentes accused both President Arévalo and Minister of Defense Arbenz Guzmán of murder. An armed uprising of troops loyal to Arana lasted three days but failed due in large part to the successful general strike organized by the members of the labor unions and peasant leagues. Plans for the election continued unabated, though the voting was still nineteen months away.

Now, the decision came down to a choice between Arbenz Guzmán and Ydígoras Fuentes. It was hardly any choice at all. Although Ydígoras could count on the support of the U.S. Embassy, the Catholic clergy, UFCO and the landed aristocracy, he did not stand a chance of being elected. During the campaign, Ydígoras tried to revive the accusation that Arbenz was guilty of the assassination of Colonel Arana. But he could not make it stick.

Finally, in November 1950, for only the second time in Guatemala's history, its voting population elected the country's president. Arbenz won the election with approximately 65 percent of the vote, a "landslide" in American political terms. The president-elect had campaigned on a platform of carrying forward the Arévalo Bermejo revolution, primarily the implementation of agrarian reform. The die had been cast and few Guatemalans had any doubts that the road they had chosen would become an even steeper climb.

In March 1951, when it was time to turn over the presidential sash to Colonel Jacobo Arbenz Guzmán, Arévalo made his final speech to the Guatemalan Congress. The president was no longer the handsome, self-confident individual who had returned from Argentina to greet his followers at La Aurora Airport six-and-a-half years earlier. Now, as he stood before Congress, his shoulders hunched in a permanent state of tension, his face

and forehead creased with furrows normal for a man much older, Arévalo
warned his nation of the dark clouds forming on the horizon:

> When I ascended to the presidency, . . . we had to combat a social
> system in which the culture, politics and economy were in the
> hands of three hundred families, heirs to colonial privileges, or
> rented to foreign interest . . . . The banana magnates, co-nationals
> of President Roosevelt, rebelled against . . . a Central American
> president who gave his fellow citizens legal equality with the
> honorable families of exporters . . . . It was then that this
> schoolteacher, . . . discovered how perishable, frail, and slippery
> the brilliant international doctrines of democracy and freedom
> really are.[31]

Sitting to the right and a little behind the outgoing president, Colonel
Jacobo Arbenz Guzmán, Arévalo's successor, evidenced no change of
expression as he listened to his predecessor's litany of charges against UFCO
and its uncompromising defender, the government of the United States. If
the president-elect did not fully realize before this moment the physical and
emotional consequences of the task before him, he now possessed a starkly
drawn outline to ponder. One can only guess what the Politécnica's all-time
number-one graduate, the initiator and hero of the 1944 revolution, was
feeling as Arévalo Bermejo suggested that "fascism was the real victor of
World War II,"[32] not democracy and freedom.

Doubt? Perhaps! Intimidation? Highly unlikely!

Chapter 10

REVOLUTIONARY JUSTICE

Monday, 4 May 1981

It was the day after the guerrillas' nocturnal visit to Hennessey's rectory. All morning long, the priest had been attempting to pull together a schedule of visits to outlying *aldeas* where he hadn't been in some weeks. Too often, he had caught himself reacting to fast-moving events provoked by advances and missteps orchestrated by the EGP, rather than taking charge of his moves. Now he was determined to be more proactive. But even as he worked, his mind returned repeatedly to the previous evening's conversation with Comandante Bernardo and thoughts of what might have been had Presidents Arévalo and Arbenz been left to engineer their own destinies. Close to noon, the parish sacristan appeared at the office door.

"Come in, *don* Santiago. Join me for a cup of coffee."

"Buen día, padrecito," the old man answered, holding his hat against his chest. *"Pues gracia, padre."*

The sacristan waited a respectful few seconds and then continued, "I don't bother you, padre. A delegation of Timacté elders be in church want you to pray *responsorios* in Timacté cemetery for three village *jóvenes* who die last night."

Hennessey nodded at the mention of three dead. Then in an attempt to prod more information without seeming pushy, he remarked, "The only time the Timacteanos seem to want a priest around is at baptism and for the *responsorios* . . . . How did they die?"

"They suffocate, *padrecito!* Ropes on their necks! *Los muchachos* come like night shadows and take them from bed."

The Iowan fell silent, looking out the window toward the church. "How many guerrillas were there, Santiago? Did anyone see them?" A cold feeling began creeping into the priest's stomach as he realized that he already knew the answers to his questions. "Many see them padre. Leader is ladino, with four *indígenas*. *Indígenas* not Mateanos. People say *los muchachos* go to Timacté to punish five *jóvenes* who rape a *compañera*. They find only three. They be buried today." Hennessey pursed his lips, nodding slowly. He knew *"los muchachos"* were the five guerrillas who had visited him the preceding evening. He also recognized that these killings were what Bernardo meant when he mentioned that the EGP's attitude toward nonconsensual sex would be evident in a few days.

Finally, the priest spoke, "What do you say, Santiago, should we go?"

"Well, this be the first invite to Timacté, *padrecito*. We be looking for this. Elders want you there."

"*Está bien!* Tell the elders we'll be at their cemetery right after midday."

Over the next two hours, several catechists who had spoken to the Timacteanos confirmed the priest's suspicions regarding the killers' identities. As far as Hennessey could piece together, the guerrillas had trekked to Timacté after he had left them at Momoxchecán, arriving there about 2:00 a.m. Forcing several residents to assist them, they located the village jail where two Q'anjob'al-speaking guerrillas were being held. After freeing the prisoners, the seven searched for five rapists, making no effort to hide their intentions. When they found three, they announced to onlookers that the EGP would not tolerate its troops, especially female members, being abused or betrayed.

The seven then hung the three rapists from a nearby tree and waited for them to die. The guerrilla leader repeated the warning as he and his companions marched off into the night.

The trouble at Timacté had started two days earlier when, unbeknownst to Hennessey, three EGP Q'anjob'al-speaking Mayans, two men and a woman, had gone to the village to do political education and organizational work there. Timacté was an eighty-family, traditionalist community, ninety minutes walking distance west of Momoxchecán. Not only were the Timacteanos, like the Ixbajauans, totally opposed to change, but they were also extremely resentful of the idea that Migueleños, and particularly a female, would presume to teach proud, Chuj-speaking Mateano men what life and social justice were all about. Folklore and ritual attested to the political and military superiority of the Mateanos over all surrounding Q'anjob'al towns and villages. It was a mutually accepted status with roots buried deep in the past, symbolically represented each year when Mateano aldermen effected the ritual capture and imprisonment of unsuspecting Q'anjob'ales visiting San Mateo during a February religious fiesta and then forcing them to drink themselves into a drunken stupor.

The Timacteanos' resentment manifested itself after the guerrillas had spent two hours imparting political education to over one hundred adolescent and adult males in the early evening of 1 May. Participation in the session was mandatory. After the session ended, the guerrillas rolled up in their blankets and bedded down for the night on the earthen floor of the meetinghouse.

As soon as the three were asleep a group of eight young men crept up on the visitors, disarmed them, and tied them up. They then gave the three a severe beating, threw them in the village jail, and retired to discuss their next move.

An animated discussion as to the possible negative consequences of their actions was followed by a drinking bout intended to calm ruffled nerves. For five of the participants, the *cuxa* produced an effect opposite to that sought. Inflamed by alcohol and angered by the untraditional presumption of the female guerrilla, the five goaded each other into making a rape-pact. The other three suggested that compounding their aggression was extremely dangerous. Nevertheless, the conspirators' cultural misogyny won out and they ignored the advice. The young woman was taken from jail to the house of one of the conspirators at the edge of the village, stripped, and tied to a typical wooden slat bed. As the five took turns raping her, their three more prudent companions slipped away.

Even after enduring several hours of abuse, the young woman retained enough courage and wits to escape. By taking advantage of the exhaustion into which her attackers had fallen, she managed to wiggle free, dress, and sneak out of the sleeping village without being detected, leaving behind her two male companions. She avoided all major trails, taking four hours to stumble to the home of an EGP contact east of San Mateo, arriving at daybreak. After hearing the details of the episode from the exhausted woman, the contact set out in the early morning to relay the information to her companions. He arrived that same night at their camp located some eight hours to the east of San Mateo, down in the hot country bordering the Ixcán.

Hennessey knew nothing of the three EGP guerrillas' political-education visit to Timacté nor of their capture, beatings, and gang rape when, two nights later, he received the unexpected visit from their five companions.

After hearing the story of the three Q'anjob'al guerrillas' visit to Timacté and the punishment dealt to the rapists by his nocturnal visitors, Hennessey chastised himself for not having insisted that Bernardo tell him what he and his companions were up to. Then, just as quickly, he was glad he hadn't asked.

The priest continued to mull over what Bernardo had said about not having the luxury to sentence people to jail for serious crimes, as well as the EGP's struggle to formulate some sexual parameters of equality between men and women. And he felt annoyance at the thought of how unprepared he had been to meet Bernardo's challenge to the Church's theology—or more accurately, its lack thereof—of sex and celibacy.

A week later, a second EGP patrol went to Timacté and shot the two remaining rapists. Hennessey received no request for transportation from the executioners on that occasion. He wondered whether the guerrillas had decided to avoid him as a result of the previous week's discussion

Over the next few weeks, as the season's rains turned mountain trails into streams of mud, and dyed the brown, barren fields a life-nourishing, corn-and-wheat green, the EGP grew progressively stronger among the rural, "barefoot ladinos" down in the Nentón region on the plains running up to the Mexican border. Nentón was now part of Hennessey's parish since the town's Catholic pastor there had been forced by the EGP to leave. The guerrillas burned down the Nentón town hall and other public buildings there and kept the army at bay.

As the EGP grew in numbers, Hennessey saw a possibility that it might only be a matter of time before the guerrillas took over the whole of

Huehuetenango Province, along with El Quiché, Alta Verapaz, Chimaltenango, Escuintla, and El Petén, and that this would be a prelude to opening other fronts and making a realistic assault on the government's forces all across the country. Meanwhile, the corruption among the top brass in the Lucas García government was alienating the younger members of the officer corps, sapping their morale.

I'll probably be irrelevant to the whole process, the priest thought with regret. *It's almost like trying to control the rain clouds coming across the Iowa plains. All we ever did was pray and hope for the best!*

But the Iowan's speculations were a needless exercise. A program was already in the process of formulation in Guatemala City, Washington, D.C., and Langley, Virginia, that would abort any scenarios being drawn up by the revolutionary forces. It would prove to be a more effective strategy in Guatemala than in the country where it had been conceived and brought to life—Vietnam—a program of state terrorism, assassinations, massacres in some cases, "scorched earth," and large-scale resettlement of surviving populations in "strategic hamlets," all monitored by one Craig Johnstone of the CIA, under the cover of the State Department. It was a strategy intended to dry up the civilian lakes in which revolutionary fish swam. And as Hennessey well understood, San Mateo Ixtatán was fast becoming an ever-expanding lake for revolutionary fish to swim in.

Chapter 11

Spring into Winter

Twenty-two months after the inauguration of Guatemala's second popularly elected president, Jacobo Arbenz Guzmán, the United States inaugurated its thirty-fourth, a 62-year-old retired army general and hero of the Allied victory over Nazism, Dwight David Eisenhower. Eisenhower entered the Oval Office with a popular mandate to bring the Korean War to an honorable end and to "clean up the mess in Washington." The "mess" was the result of what candidate Eisenhower had said was the Truman administration's "softness on communism" and what vice presidential candidate Richard Nixon had characterized as "twenty years of treason."

Two months after taking office, Eisenhower learned much to his disgust of a recently botched attempt funded by the United Fruit Company and supported by the Central Intelligence Agency to start a popular uprising in Guatemala by backing a group of one hundred counterrevolutionaries (terrorists or freedom fighters?) in an attack on government installations in Salamá, the capital of Baja Verapaz Province north of Guatemala City. It was the second time that UFCO and the CIA had unsuccessfully teamed up in hopes of triggering a popular uprising against Arbenz.

At some point during the summer months of 1953, Eisenhower decided that neither UFCO money and inspiration nor CIA weaponry and logistical efforts were sufficient to bring down Arbenz Guzmán. As a consequence, he ordered his National Security Council to formulate plans to overthrow Guatemala's government. "I want all of you to be damn good and sure you succeed . . . . When you commit the flag, you commit it to win."[1]

Approximately one year later, 27 June 1954, Arbenz took to the airwaves to announce to the Guatemalan people his resignation as president stating, "For fifteen days, a cruel war against Guatemala has been underway. The

United Fruit Company, in collaboration with the governing circles of the United States, is responsible for what is happening to us."[2]

Arbenz Guzmán believed that his personal departure from the presidential palace would be sufficient to placate the aggressive intentions of the U.S. government. He was wrong! Nothing but a pro-United States government, one willing to accept directives from Washington, would now placate the Republican administration that took power in 1952.

A few days later, trying to hide the involvement of the United States in the termination of the Arbenz government, as well as conceal the instrumental and motivational roles played by UFCO, President Eisenhower lied to the American electorate: "The people of Guatemala, in a magnificent effort, have liberated themselves from the shackles of international communist direction . . . ."[3]

Arbenz's predecessor, Juan José Arévalo Bermejo, had barely survived the final months of his six-year presidency, a term during which he had outmaneuvered more than a score of plots to overthrow him. In the center of most of the coup attempts had stood a favorite of the U.S. Embassy, the co-hero of the 1944 revolution, Colonel Francisco Javier Arana. After Arana's death, others were ready to move to the front of antirevolutionary elements in the army and among the oligarchy. They showed themselves during the 1950 presidential campaign in order to gain public recognition and a pseudo-legitimacy for later coup attempts.

Foremost among these would-be-*caudillos* was ex-general Miguel Ydígoras Fuentes, who in the throes of predestination theology, had run as "the Catholic candidate," claiming "God is on my side!"

Archbishop Rossell had angrily denounced such self-sanctifying tactics from his cathedral pulpit. The prelate, however, had no qualms about employing misleading rhetoric of his own, when he stated that the Church had always remained nonpartisan and would back no single candidate, and without his personal backing, there could be no such thing as a "Catholic candidate."

Archbishop Rossell gave his pastoral instructions to the faithful on their obligation to vote—even if they believed the elections to be fraudulent—and, more importantly, how not to vote: "avoiding the triumph of a Communist

or a communist sympathizer, . . . or Catholics who are contaminated with old and vicious habits of anti-Christian ideologies, or stained by a life notoriously immoral, . . . or anyone who formerly interfered with . . . the rights of the Church . . . ."[4]
The archbishop's strictures seemed to eliminate all the candidates from consideration.

Then, four days before the election, Colonel Carlos Castillo Armas, a brooding Charlie Chaplin look-alike, knowing that Arbenz Guzmán's paternity of the 1944 revolution assured him of an electoral victory, mounted a bumbling plot to thwart the vote. Backed by sixty men, most of whom were poorly armed civilians, he attacked the Aurora Air Force Base.

The colonel expected significant support from those within the base, an indispensable factor for the success of such an attack. However, his ineptly conducted, prior negotiations with the base commander resulted in just the opposite, a spirited resistance that quickly disposed of the attackers.

Castillo Armas was wounded, quickly captured, and jailed. Under most previous governments, such an individual would have been executed on the spot, or at least exiled. Seven months later, as a more practiced negotiator, the bumbling colonel received inside help to dig his way out of prison.

Castillo Armas emerged from the entire episode with a paradoxical reputation for ineptness and survivability, someone in possession of a *caudillo's* luck and *cojones,* the subject of a myth-making odyssey par excellence.

The immediate result of Castillo Armas's incursion into Aurora Air Base had been to heighten the citizenry's awareness of just how tenuous their hold was on democratic procedures. The popular turnout on 10 November 1950 resulted in Arbenz's landslide victory.

Born to a Swiss pharmacist father and a ladina mother in Guatemala's second largest city, Quezaltenango, in 1913, Jacobo Arbenz Guzmán was baptized into Xelajú's small but vibrant Presbyterian community. Of medium, muscular build, steady blue eyes, high forehead, blondish hair, a diffident smile, and fair complexion, Jacobo was a handsome boy by the standards of race-conscious Guatemalans. He was often compared in looks to Hollywood's Alan Ladd.

Arbenz's father was not a churchgoer, but he indoctrinated his son with the same self-conscious patriotism, self-discipline, and sympathy for the plight of society's most vulnerable that Ron Hennessey's Swiss mother had imbued in her offspring. While Jacobo was still an adolescent, his father suffered serious business losses that left the family destitute. At first, the senior Arbenz turned to what was nearest at hand, a druggist's inventory of psychological painkillers. But when these failed to alleviate his sense of stigma and loss, he resorted to a more drastic and decidedly un-Guatemalan solution—suicide.

The trauma triggered by the sudden loss of his beloved father had a lasting effect on young Jacobo, fostering in him a sense of meditative aloofness, an iron determination to succeed where his parent had failed, and a visceral empathy for Guatemala's exploited as a lifelong, filial requiem.

Unable to afford the university education his father had promised, Jacobo entered the Politécnica in 1931. There he went on to become an outstanding athlete in boxing and polo and to accumulate the highest academic and leadership score in the history of the military academy. He graduated as a sublieutenant in 1935, the most admired member of his *promoción,* despite— or because of—his self-contained, independent character.

Two years later, Jacobo Arbenz was brought back to the Politécnica to teach science and history, two subjects he loved. His new assignment allowed him to discuss at length with his American colleagues the military and political deficiencies of Guatemalan society, the nature of European and Asian fascism, and the probable consequences of Hitler's threats to the rest of Europe.

In 1939, Jacobo Arbenz Guzmán married Maria Cristina Vilanova, a beautiful, highly intelligent, twenty-four-year-old Salvadoran. Alienated from her wealthy parents because of her father's unapologetic participation in the 1932 massacre of thirty thousand Indians by the Salvadoran military government, Maria Cristina saw her marriage as an escape from the oppressive social milieu inhabited by her mother and father.

It is said that Arbenz Guzmán fell in love first with Maria Cristina's mind, and only later did he notice her beauty. Whether or not that observation is apocryphal, at some point in the year following, the Arbenz Guzmán residence in Guatemala City became the locus of animated political discussions involving both Salvadorans and Guatemalans, most of whom were invitees of Maria Cristina. Some of those who entered the young officer's home were homegrown, self-educated Marxists. Few of the invited, however, could match the analytical and questioning minds of their hosts when it came to discussing philosophies of social history.

Meanwhile, Arbenz Guzmán went on to become director of students at the Politécnica, a position that allowed him to discreetly share his social democratic ideas as these developed in tandem with the escalating crisis in Europe.

As the Allied armies continued to push back the Axis troops in late 1943 and Ubico fought to stamp out the budding ideals of democracy manifest in his countrymen, Captain Jacobo Arbenz Guzmán began to prepare himself to play a role in the nation's growing, restless, middle-class rebellion against Guatemala's nativistic fascism.

When Arbenz Guzmán took over the Guatemalan presidency in March 1951, he was determined to carry through on the reforms begun by his predecessor despite the formidable obstacles that confronted him. Not the least of these, of course, was the persistent opposition of the United Fruit Company and its deceptive media campaign run by a tough, pop psychologist by the name of Edward Bernays.

Edward Bernays had been hired in 1940 in order to combat the antediluvian reputation that UFCO possessed in many areas of the United States. In a 1928 book starkly entitled *Propaganda,* Bernays had outlined his manipulative view of the American political system, as well as what would become his future campaign against Arévalo Bermejo and Arbenz Guzmán:

> The conscious and intelligent manipulation of the organized habits and opinions of the masses is an important element in a democratic society. Those who manipulate this unseen mechanism of society constitute an invisible government that is the true ruling power of our county . . . it is the intelligent minority which needs to make use of propaganda continuously and systematically.[5]

Between early 1952 and mid-1954, Bernays, taking advantage of the unrestricted press policies of the Arbenz Guzmán government, organized five, all-expenses-paid, two-week trips to Guatemala for up to ten newsmen each. In Guatemala, the reporters and editors interviewed United Fruit directors, U.S. Embassy personnel, and other select, anti-Arbenz Guzmán sources to get a firsthand account of "the advances of communism" in the country. One of the "communist advances" that had not occurred but that went unacknowledged by these less-than-objective observers was state control of the media.

The trips accomplished what Bernays hoped for. The *New York Times* published a series of articles on the "Red advances" in Guatemala. *Newsweek, Time, United Press International,* the *Christian Science Monitor,* the *Miami Herald,* the Hearst organization, and the Scripps-Howard newspapers, all followed up Bernays's trips with lurid stories about the inroads of Marxism-Leninism in the country, zeroing in on Arbenz Guzmán's anti-UFCO agrarian reform.[6] Given the drumbeat of Bernays's propaganda, the anti-Arbenz Guzmán articles raised governmental and public anxieties across the American political spectrum and gave new meaning to the expression "freedom of the press."

The Guatemalan Congress, four of whose fifty-four members were communists, passed Arbenz Guzmán's agrarian reform law on 27 June 1952, after a year of expectation on the part of the peasantry and oppositional maneuvering by the landed oligarchy. The legislation gave the government authority to expropriate uncultivated segments of large plantations. A top FAO (Food and Agriculture Organization of the United Nations) official noted that the law "was constructive and democratic in its aims."[7] The Office of Intelligence Research of the State Department stated: "If the Agrarian Law is fully implemented, the impact upon private landholders would be borne chiefly by a minority."[8]

From January 1953, when the law went into effect, until June 1954, when Arbenz resigned, the Guatemalan government expropriated nearly 1.5 million acres and delivered them to one hundred thousand landless peasant families. It was a redistribution of national wealth like Guatemala had not experienced since the *conquistador* Pedro de Alvarado laid claim to all Central America in 1523 in the name of the royal houses of Aragón and Castile.

The United Fruit Company, the largest landowner in the country (550,000 acres) with the greatest percentage of uncultivated land (85 percent), became the law's principal target. The company lost nearly 387,000 acres. The government offered to pay UFCO the company's own recent assessment of its lands' value made during the Arévalo administration, that is, $2.86 per acre. It was a sum more substantial in real terms than that paid to dictators Estrada Cabrera and Ubico when the company acquired the lands. UFCO, however, demanded compensation of $75.50 per acre, an assessment with no relation to market reality.

On 20 April 1954, the U.S. State Department accepted UFCO's calculations at face value and filed a formal claim against the Guatemalan government in the name of the fruit company for $16 million for the first 210,000 acres. Arbenz Guzmán replied that he could not do for UFCO what the law would not allow him to do for Guatemala's own citizens. He also could have added that his government did not possess that kind of money.

The Church hierarchy in Guatemala had, in the meantime, marshaled its moral authority against Arbenz's agrarian reform. The bishops had long expressed their opposition to a serious change in land-owning patterns. Their episcopal lack of concern for Mayan land rights was due in part to their disdain for the Mayan belief that all lands were on loan from God (or the gods), giving humankind a usufruct interest only. More importantly, the hierarchy was caught up in its own attempts to recover Church property lost to the dictator Barrios in 1872. The thrust of their theological argument was that "private property"—in this case, Church private property—like the "sacred duty of work," was something written by the finger of God in the very nature of humankind. Any attempt to alter such concepts by state action could only be the work of atheistic communists under Satan's influence.

UFCO's lack of success in bringing Arbenz Guzmán to heel during the final years of the Truman presidency and the first months of the Eisenhower administration made the fruit company more determined than ever to convince Ike to personally intervene in stopping the Guatemalan agrarian reform. Sam "The Banana Man" Zemurray, UFCO's CEO, believed that it was Eisenhower, a man accustomed to the use of covert operations as commander in chief of Allied Forces in North Africa and Europe, who could and would sanction CIA front-line efforts to rid Guatemala for all time of Arbenz Guzmán and the revolutionary project begun in 1944. He was, of course, correct.

Although there were many actors in the counterrevolutionary drama, Dwight David Eisenhower played the pivotal role. And though he did not read the script or understand its full implications, by following the Dulles brothers' suggestions he must be awarded primary responsibility for the play's success.

Eisenhower was a complex man described as "at once ingenuous and shrewd, a proclaimed 'innocent' and an accomplished manipulator of men . . . firmly decisive yet apparently an amiable duffer."[9] putting on the cloak of whatever character attribute would serve his underlying purpose, the urgent need to excel. As a professional soldier, his was a determination to win a war at all costs without seeming to be so motivated.

All of these Eisenhower characteristics, especially his consuming desire to be admired and liked by his newly acquired capitalist friends, the conservative, wealthy captains of U.S. industry, filled the new president with a willingness to allow subordinates to make decisions with little or no input from him. And it was his fame for taking the advice of the last person to whom he spoke that led him into one of the more enduring failures of his illustrious career. If there is one man who can be singled out as the primary individual responsible for influencing Eisenhower's decision to eliminate President Jacobo Arbenz Guzmán, it was Secretary of State John Foster Dulles, a man well prepared to fight God's battles against Satan's communist hordes.

The oldest of five children born to the Reverend Allen M. Dulles, pastor of the First Presbyterian Church of Watertown, New York, and Edith Foster, John Foster Dulles let out his first cry of independence on 25 February 1888. Brought up in a rigidly religious household, the lad was expected to follow in the clerical footsteps of his father and paternal grandfather, the latter a missionary to India and later to Ceylon, where he died and was buried.

Upon graduation from Princeton summa cum laude in 1908, Foster revealed to his father his determination to become a "Christian lawyer," insisting that "my influence for good can be so much greater rubbing elbows with the powerful than preaching to the meek."[10]

After passing the New York State bar exam in 1911, the young lawyer gained a position with Wall Street's most prestigious law firm specializing in international trade, Sullivan and Cromwell—this with the help of his maternal grandfather, John Watson Foster, the secretary of state in the Benjamin Harrison administration, who pulled a few strings for him.

By 1926 Foster Dulles had become the senior partner of Sullivan and Cromwell. Using his new authority, he brought into the company his younger brother, Allen, also a lawyer, until then employed by the Foreign Service. One of Sullivan and Cromwell's more important clients in Central America was the United Fruit Company. Foster assigned Allen to the account and counseled his younger brother in helping UFCO draw up beneficial contracts with the dictator Ubico in 1931 and 1936.

During the middle 1930s, Foster Dulles was adamantly against U.S. involvement in any alignment against Hitler. His motivation was Sullivan and Cromwell's lucrative business in Germany. When Hitler's persecution of the Jews became undeniable in 1935, Dulles's junior partners demanded that he either close the firm's office in Berlin or they, as a group, would resign. Foster, according to his brother Allen, "was at first bewildered, then adamant, protesting among other things the loss of substantial profits. Finally, however, he capitulated in tears."[11] Later, Foster would deny, as he did after the overthrow of Arbenz Guzmán, that monetary considerations had anything to do with his stand.

John Foster Dulles's ability to reconcile the demands of doing Wall Street's dirtiest business with his Christian Presbyterian conscience never ceased to amaze many of those who knew him. Townsend Hoopes, his biographer, stated that in Dulles's speeches and writings, "there is rarely any reference to sin, no admission that political decisions are fraught with moral ambiguity, no evidence of any understanding that self-interest, self-preservation, and self-righteousness is implicit in every exercise of power."[12] A colleague in the Federal Council of Churches, theologian Reinhold Niebuhr, would write that "Mr. Dulles' moral universe makes everything quite clear, too clear . . . . Self-righteousness is the inevitable fruit of simple moral judgments."[13]

In the mid 1940s, Dulles became a student of Stalin's writings, particularly his book *Problems of Leninism,* and committed segments of it to memory, the same way he had memorized Bible verses as a child. As a result, Dulles had an unshakable faith in his own understanding of communism as an expansionist, political-military philosophy for global domination with the eradication of Christianity as its principal goal, "much like that of Islam 1000 years ago."[14]

It was Arbenz Guzmán's misfortune, then, that Foster Dulles answered to a somewhat disengaged president who allowed subordinates to do his homework and make critical decisions for him. To complicate matters, the Eisenhower administration and the CIA were in the grip of a triumphalist ethos induced by their recent overthrow of the nationalist premier of Iran, Muhammad Mossadegh, and the installation of the Shah Pahlavi to assure U.S. and British access to Iran's oil fields. The national anticommunist paranoia was brought to a white-hot heat by the likes of Senators McCarthy, Knowland, and Hickenlooper in conjunction with Pentagon brass's dreams of military heroics. They were followed by a long parade of congressional political entrepreneurs with an insatiable thirst for power. The drumbeat media campaign of Edward Bernays and the religious certitude of every major religious personality ably assisted these actors in all parts of the country. It was enough to make President Eisenhower the first victim of the CIA's "Operation PBSuccess."

Later, Eisenhower would characterize his "elimination of communism" from Guatemala as one of his "proudest accomplishments" as president.[15] One might be excused for wondering what Ike would have thought of the results of Operation PBSuccess had he been present in San Mateo Ixtatán with Ronald Hennessey on 30 May 1981 when the Guatemalan Army visited the town to continue the unfinished business begun by the Eisenhower administration in 1953.

Chapter 12

A Christian Lie

It would be comforting to exonerate President Eisenhower of any blame for the succession of terrorist regimes that have oppressed the Guatemalan people since the overthrow of President Arbenz Guzmán in 1954. America's patriotic mythology demands as much. But to do so, one has to ignore the fact that Ike remained in the Oval Office for six-and-one-half years after Arbenz's departure; he had ample time to assess the results of his crusade. There is no evidence that he ever did. Even if he had been present in San Mateo Ixtatán on the night of 30 May 1981, it seems unlikely that Eisenhower's professional military mind would have given second thought to the necessity of Operation PB Success and its aftermath.

In the two months following the ambush of the army patrol sent to remove the EGP flag flying over the town plaza, Ron Hennessey often wondered when and how the Barillas garrison would try to reestablish its control over San Mateo. Everyone in town, it seemed, was asking him/herself the same question. And would the EGP protect them? After the El Quetzal massacre, not a few doubted it could or would.

The army made its move on Saturday night, 30 May 1981, four weeks after the guerrillas' nocturnal visit to Hennessey's rectory. Ron had gone to bed early, about 8:00 p.m., and soon fell fast asleep. Shortly after midnight he awoke to the sounds of muffled explosions and the staccato bursts of machine-gun fire. For a moment, he thought the noises might have been part of a

Korean War-time dream. But the rapid succession of more gunfire and several more powerful detonations quickly erased that thought.

He sat up at the edge of his bed, straining to hear any shouting, hoping the sounds might be the result of fireworks. At the same time he knew the percussions were too loud to be pyrotechnics. *A shoot-out? No! There's no return fire! It's all coming from the same direction! No back-and-forth!*

The Iowan listened, but heard only the chattering sounds of guns and what he was now sure were grenade explosions slicing through the darkness. *Who's responsible? The army? The EGP?* He looked at the fluorescent hands on his watch. It was 12:33 a.m. The explosions and gunfire were closer now. *They wouldn't be coming here? Whoever they are, if they're killing, . . . they're not going to want any foreign witnesses.*

For a moment, the priest considered rolling onto the floor and under the bed, but quickly discarded the idea as senseless. He knew that if he were a target of the gunmen, no place in the small, adobe rectory would provide refuge. As he moved cautiously toward the front room door with the thought of rushing out and throwing himself down the bush-covered embankment at the side of the rectory, he strained to hear any screams. Not a one!

Then, as suddenly as it had begun, the shooting and explosions stopped. Only the barking and yapping of a hundred frightened dogs, like an uncoordinated choral salute blanketing the whole town, broke the silence.

Slowly, the priest crept to the front room window facing the plaza. There, he peered through the curtain, not touching it, his hands at his sides. But he could see only the plaza lights haloed by the moisture clinging to the windowpane.

Still crouching, he moved back to his bedroom on the east side of the house. Standing with his back to the adobe wall, he peered sideways out the curtainless window. After a few minutes, he caught sight of two pairs of headlights on the other side of the town's narrow valley slowly winding up the hill on the road to Barillas. *They're heading for Barillas . . . . They've got to be army!*

Hennessey stayed at the window for a few minutes, waiting for more departures, afflicted by the thought that many of the townspeople might need his assistance. But he also knew that outside his door lay a dangerous no-man's-land, where relatives and neighbors of the victims, having recovered somewhat from their first horrified surprise, would now react violently, using their machetes against anyone who approached in the dark. Also, a rear guard of gun-wielders might still be out there waiting to reward any show of curiosity with another series of blasts.

Finally, not detecting any movement outside, no anguished cries of despair or revenge, no moans, the priest convinced himself that his most prudent move was to wait until daylight. It was 12:55 a.m. He crawled back into bed, the sheets now cold, almost damp. The possibility of sleep was totally discounted as he lay staring into the darkness, his intellect trying to convince his conscience that there was no alternative but to wait.

At 5:00 a.m., just as the first signs of daylight touched his windows, he was out of bed, dressed in his work clothes and a heavy sweater, and on his way up the short cobblestone street to the mayor's office. A number of men, about twenty, had already gathered in front of the low, cucumber-green, cinderblock building that housed the municipal offices. Two new, spray-painted, revolutionary slogans traced across the building's facade caught his attention: *"Pueblo de San Mateo, Sos Traidores!* People of San Mateo, You are Traitors!" and *"Apoyás al Ejercito de los Ricos, y por eso, Van a Morir!* You Support the Army of the Rich, and for this, You Will Die!" Both statements, written in pidgin Spanish, were signed, "EGP." Several windows in the mayor's office had been broken.

The assembled men talked softly in groups of three and four, reporting what they knew of the night's violence. In one such group stood Abelardo Valenzuela, a ladino ex-soldier who had managed, it was rumored, to get himself discharged from the army some years earlier by shooting himself in the hand during an encounter with some guerrillas in the country's eastern provinces.

Abelardo was a barrel-chested bull of a man of medium height. He was light-skinned like most ladinos, with a round, wide-eyed face that looked like it was propped up by the massive black beard wedged against his chest. Abelardo's oversized ears, broad nose, and wide mouth gave the impression of an enormous head out of proportion even for an exceptionally large body. He breathed physical strength. The three bent fingers on his left hand lent stature to the rumor regarding his discharge from the army, a rumor that Abelardo never attempted to dispel.

A close friendship had developed between the priest and the ladino. Hennessey not only liked Abelardo for his personal qualities, his directness, and unaffected good humor, he also admired his courage as the only ladino in town willing to be seen socializing with Mayans. Furthermore, Abelardo volunteered to keep the priest abreast of all political information and rumors originating in and around the municipal offices, a significant contribution to Hennessey's sense of well-being. As a ladino, Abelardo's right to come and go in the municipal offices went unquestioned by the local authorities.

"It was the soldiers, padre," Abelardo muttered, as he came over and drew the priest aside, "They've killed a lot of people . . . maybe a hundred."

Hennessey stared at his friend, not wanting to believe him. "So many? . . . Are you sure?"

"Nobody's been out to count them. We're just guessing from all the reports coming in. It looks like they've cleaned out the west side of town!"

The priest stared at the burly man for a few seconds, hoping to force from him some sign of uncertainty, but without success. "Come on, let's talk to the mayor and see what he knows."

The two went over to where Mayor Diego Martinez was listening to a small group of Mayan men, several of whom were talking at once. Diego was also a friend of the new pastor, a former catechist who had given up the position when he became mayor.

Diego was half Mayan, half ladino, but he dressed and identified himself as a Mayan. He generally stood with his arms and hands tucked inside his brown, loose-fitting, woolen *capixay*-pullover, leaving the sleeves empty, a typical Mateano posture intended to conserve body heat. Only recently had he discarded the popular felt sombrero, exposing his thick mat of black hair to the weather in order to express his new social status as mayor. The felt sombrero, the most expensive item in the male Mateano's wardrobe, was not only meant to protect one's head from sun and rain, more importantly, it was to be worn as a symbol of Mateano identity, to be taken off in the presence of real or presumed social superiors, be they Mayan elders, or arrogant ladinos.

As the mayor turned toward the approaching men, Hennessey noticed a look of undisguised concern in his eyes. "Don't ask me what happened, padre! A lot of people apparently got killed last night. Their houses were broken into and riddled with machine-gun fire. Some were blown apart with grenades. I've got to go out now and verify their names and the cause of death, so their relatives can bury them."

"Who did it?" the priest asked.

The mayor looked the priest straight in the eye and shrugged his big shoulders. Turning partially around, he gestured with his chin toward the slogans on the front of the municipal building. Turning back to the priest, he looked at him silently. His eyes told Hennessey that such a question was to be neither asked nor answered in a public forum. The priest nodded and turned away.

After speaking to a few more men, the priest learned that some victims even then were being brought into the tiny, four-bed, parish clinic. Seeing that there was nothing more to learn at the mayor's office, the Iowan shook hands with everyone present and turned toward the parish compound to assist the Sisters with what he thought would be a tide of wounded.

Sister Justa met the priest at the hospital door. "We've got six children we're treating, padre," the young woman told him, "and they're all in pretty bad shape. The people say there are many more, badly hurt survivors, maybe as many as a hundred, mostly adults, but they've already gone into hiding. They're too afraid to come in. They think the soldiers might come back to finish them off. There are thirty or forty more who have already gone to God."

While Sister Justa rushed from bed to sink to bed to toilet to bed to medicine cabinet, Hennessey tried to console the children and the few adults who accompanied them. To make the situation more critical, the ladino student doctor was away for the weekend.

A malnourished little girl of three or four, Alicia Mateo, was seated on a bunk, alone and stunned, wrapped in a bloodstained shirt that was too big for her. She had spent the night seated among the seven dead bodies of her entire family. This graphic information had come from a neighbor who brought the child in, but didn't wait to hear the prognosis. When Sister Justa cut off the blood-drenched shirt, she discovered that the little girl had a bullet wound in her stomach. The priest wanted so much for her to cry, to give proof of the integrity of her nervous system and her desire to live. But crying was beyond her.

A little five-year-old girl with two black pigtails tied with a single ribbon in back at shoulder level whom Sister Justa knew only as Isabelita, her black eyes bright with fever, sat on the cement-tile floor against the receiving bench. A chunk of her calf muscle had been blown away. Her wound looked rouge-colored, not bloody, as if the intruding metal had cauterized the flesh even as it flew on its way. Her cry was only a whimper. When the priest placed her on a bunk, he didn't know that a mortal piece of grenade was lodged in her abdomen.

A gaunt-faced 13-year-old boy, Alfredo Sebastian, lay on his side on a bunk, a bloodstained pillow stuck between his knees. His inner thighs had been ripped away. He called softly to the priest, "Padre, . . . could you get me . . . some water?"

Hennessey walked over and noticed a huge opening in the boy's back near the base of the spine, presumably made by the same projectile that had torn away his thighs, passing through the intestines before exiting out the back.

"We have to take you to Huehuetenango . . . to be operated on," the priest answered gently, even while thinking the boy would never survive the five-hour trip. "It's best I don't give you anything until then . . . . Do you think you can hold out?"

The boy nodded.

While cutting away Alfredo's clothes, the padre had every expectation of getting nauseous as soon as he removed the bloodied shirt and witnessed the boy's exposed intestines. But Alfredo's stomach was whole.

"I have to shit, padre . . . . Can you help me?" the boy asked breathlessly.

The words were like a kick in the stomach. *How can this boy shit?* the priest thought. *More than shit will come out . . . and I don't think I can take that.* But when he helped Alfredo to his hands and knees and held the bedpan pressed against the boy's legs, waiting with half-closed eyes to see whether the intestines would appear, only his stools came out, without even a trace of blood on them. *Thank you, God!* the priest sighed, recognizing that the thigh and back wounds were unrelated, the products of two different projectiles, leaving the intestines intact.

"Maybe I can get you that glass of water after all, Alfredo . . . . Wait just a minute."

Sister Justa bandaged the head of seven-year-old Pablo Miguel, who had received a ricocheting bullet glancing off his scalp, saved by his grandmother's instinctive rise to a sitting position as the killers broke down her door. Her body had taken the several bullets that would have hit the sleeping boy beside her. She had sacrificed her life for his without

THROUGH A GLASS DARKLY

the satisfaction of knowing it. His six-year-old sister Carolina was not as lucky, taking a bullet to the head and two others in the arm. She now lay unconscious on the bunk next to his.

The one ladina patient, Dolores, the eight-year-old daughter of Felipe González and Marta Esperanza de González, sat crying on her mother's knee. A bullet had ripped through her upper arm, shattering the bone, fragments of which were protruding through the skin. Marta Esperanza magnified her daughter's cries by going into a spasm of weeping as Sister Justa taped a splint into place.

Hennessey spoke to the few adults who remained at the clinic after carrying in the children and, with what he had already learned at the mayor's office, was able to piece together a more complete account of what had happened during the night.

Several neighbors on the town's north side where the road from Barillas entered San Mateo had heard some vehicles around midnight coming from that direction. They crept outside to investigate. San Mateo is a relatively isolated town and Barillas, twenty or so kilometers to the east, was the last town on the road. Not many vehicles went through San Mateo in a single day, even fewer at night. Given the political situation, a vehicle coming to town in the middle of the night was a source of more than curious interest, more often consternation.

As the witnesses watched, they saw two pickups coming up the hill, transporting approximately thirty men. When the two vehicles got closer, they could see that the men in the first pickup were dressed in civilian clothing, while the occupants of the second wore camouflage. At the stream just below town, they stopped and some of those in the second pickup climbed into the first. The rest of the passengers remained at the stream while the driver of the first vehicle drove through town to the cemetery on the west end, turned around, and came back. At the bend in the road on the north side of the plaza, the men dismounted and split into two groups. The smaller group headed for the municipal building on the west side of the plaza, while the other, knowing what they were looking for, headed up the street to the house of Adán López, the ladino deacon of one of San Mateo's two evangelical chapels, a good friend of Hennessey, as well as his barber.

The men who went to the municipal buildings broke some windows and painted what they hoped would be interpreted as EGP slogans on the walls. The second group banged on Adán's door, demanding that he come out and point out the houses of those who supported the guerrillas.

Adán came to the door and protested: "Look, I'm an *evangélico* and I'm against violence. I can't tell you who the supporters of the guerrillas are."

The words had barely crossed the preacher's lips when they were punctuated with the exclamations of several machine guns that bounced the holy man up against the far wall of his small, adobe home. He hung there for a second or two as if nailed to the wall, dead before his body slipped to the dirt floor. Looking on in stupefied horror stood his wife and two small children. It took several seconds before anguished screams could burst from their constricted throats.

The killers then went to the nearby house of Felipe González, husband of Marta Esperanza de González and father of eight-year-old Dolores. Felipe himself was not at home at the time. The guerrillas had kidnapped him several days earlier. The soldiers demanded that Felipe's wife and his sister—who also lived with them—point out the households of guerrilla supporters. The two women, having been advised by the soldiers of what had happened to their deacon-pastor, were terrified. They obliged by accompanying the men and randomly indicated a series of houses, those of their closest Mayan neighbors. One or the other of the women was heard several times to say, "No, not that one. This one over here."

The men halted at Francisco Alonzo's house, broke down the door, and swept the interior with three blasts from their automatic rifles. Francisco never had time to get out of bed.

The soldiers then proceeded through the western section of town, apportioning houses along the way to this or that pair or trio. These would break down the doors, shine in a blinding light, and spray the interior with automatic weapons fire. The shooting was accompanied by shouts of, "You are all traitors. This is in retaliation for what your guerrillas did to our patrol, and in Nentón, and in the Ixcán," contradicting the intent of the slogans their companions were painting on the municipal buildings.

Sometimes they hurled hand grenades into a house. And the occupants, frightened out of their sleep, often met the onslaught in terrorized silence with almost supernatural stoicism.

Finally, their leader, recognized as the assistant commandant of the Barillas military base, took a small nucleus of men and, accompanied by Marta Esperanza and her sister-in-law, returned to Felipe Gonzalez' house. There, without explanation, the leader shot Marta's father-in-law and her eight-year-old daughter, Dolores. The daughter received only a bullet in the upper arm, but the old man was killed on the spot. Shortly thereafter, the two pickup trucks returned to Barillas with their full complement of passengers. Hennessey was watching them from his window as they crossed the valley and climbed the hill.

When the Iowan saw that the six wounded children would not fit into his jeep for the trip to the Huehuetenango hospital, he drove to Barillas to swap his vehicle for the large station wagon belonging to the nuns there. As he passed through the checkpoint at the entrance to Barillas, he knew that the soldiers who examined his papers were well aware of the previous night's hunting expedition, but neither he nor they mentioned the matter.

The Iowan returned to San Mateo with the larger vehicle and Sister Justa advised him that he would have only five passengers to take to Huehuetenango, "Little Isabelita, the feverish five-year-old who had part of her leg blown away, . . . she has died! We found a piece of metal in her stomach after you left. I'll get some men to help me load the others into the wagon. I'm sorry, padre!"

When Hennessey was ready to leave, Marta Esperanza de González, the mother of Dolores, was waiting for him. "You have to let me go with my daughter, padre!" cried the distraught woman. "They're going to kill me like they did my father-in-law! Oh my Jesus Christ! You can't leave me here! I beg of you, padre!"

Before the woman was through with her entreaty, the priest was already pushing her into the front passenger seat.

With a glance over his shoulder to check with Sister Justa, riding in back to care for the patients, Hennessey shifted into gear and eased out the clutch. As the station wagon crossed the plain above town, he noticed that the red and black flag announcing EGP hegemony that had been flying over San Mateo was no longer to be seen. Not even the pole had been left standing.

The priest squeezed the steering wheel to concentrate his attention on the dirt and gravel road in front of him, calling on all his skills to drive as fast as he dared while skirting potholes and rounding one hairpin turn after another, shifting from second to third and back to first with no loss of speed nor jerking motion. But even when the vehicle hit a hole in the road harder than the priest could avoid, no sound came from his passengers, except for the whimpering of Dolores's mother, Marta Esperanza.

Only in San Juan Ixcoy, where soldiers huddled together in the rain manning a checkpoint, did the priest slow his pace. But when no one stepped into the road in front of his vehicle, Hennessey pretended not to see them and drove on, holding his breath, knowing there would be endless questioning if they spotted the condition of his passengers. For a second, he thought he heard bullets exploding in his ears, but quickly realized it was his pounding heart. One hundred meters up the road, guessing he was beyond their marksmanship, he breathed a sigh of relief.

As they approached the mountain pass well above San Juan Ixcoy, reaching an altitude of better than 10,000 feet, the pungent smell of uncontrolled bowels, even with the windows rolled down, grew aggressively stronger. "Padre Ronaldo, you'll have to stop," Sister Justa told the priest. "Alfredo's bag of glucose is empty. I brought a spare."

They had just gone through the final pass before heading across the *cumbre,* an 11-mile, windswept plateau where small outcroppings of gray volcanic rock shaped like molten lead poured into a thousand jagged forms provided the only distraction. The pause provided the priest a welcome opportunity to get a breath of fresh, cold air and to relieve his burdened bladder. As he stood by the side of the road, looking across the barren plain, he wondered where the houses were that sheltered the three tiny shepherds in the distance.

In five minutes, the makeshift ambulance was on its way again. Hennessey hadn't driven more than ten feet when the glass container replacing the plastic bag threatened to break as it bounced against the back window. Again the priest pressed down on the brakes as gently as he could, bringing the vehicle to a smooth stop. After hunting under his seat for a rag and finding none, he removed his shirt and wrapped it around the bottle of precious fluid. Three minutes later, he shifted into gear and once more headed for Huehuetenango.

Little by little, as they drove along, Marta Esperanza divulged a series of critical events that helped explain to Hennessey the timing and targets of the previous night's murderous encounter, events in which she and her husband, Felipe Gonzalez, had played pivotal roles.

Hennessey already knew more about Marta Esperanza's husband than the woman realized. Felipe González was a wiry young ladino, sullen looking, in his early thirties. The priest had often seen him around town but Felipe always indicated that he was not interested in exchanging greetings, so Hennessey left him alone. Felipe had a lighter complexion than the average Mayan, giving what he and other ladinos considered incontrovertible proof that the socioeconomic differences between themselves and Mayans were the result of genetic inheritance rather than socialization and political power.

Felipe owned an aquamarine-colored uniform of the Border Patrol Police. Everyone in town knew that he'd never been a member of the Border Patrol. For years, he used the uniform to rob Mayan *contrabandistas* from more distant towns and villages, ignorant of his identity, as they walked across the unmarked border from Mexico into San Mateo territory.

Those not from San Mateo and who crossed the border to shop in Mexico were easy pickings for Felipe on their return. He would wait with his wrinkled uniform and phony badge to accost them with his very real gun. "You *indios* sons-of-whores will never learn to respect the laws of this country, will you?" he would ask them, laughing at his own monumental hypocrisy. "But I know you are ignorant, not bad. I should put you in jail, but then you wouldn't be able to support your families. So I'm going to be kind and let you go with only a fine."

Felipe would then strip his victims of some of their merchandise, such items as pants, sweaters, shoes, cigarettes, transistor radios, watches, and trinkets, before sending them on their way with a warning.

When the Guerrilla Army of the Poor began operating in and around San Mateo, Felipe Gonzalez got the not-so-bright idea of pretending that he represented the EGP, rather than the Border Patrol. Here again, his charade was practiced against those from outside San Mateo and its associated villages, people not likely to know him. "I've been appointed by the high command of the Guerrilla Army of the Poor to be their tax-collector for this area," he would tell his unsuspecting victims.

The game ended abruptly, however, when some Mayans from Soloma came through town and Felipe relieved them of their watches, transistor radios, and cash. He not only was a ladino performing a function reserved by the EGP for Mayans in Mayan towns and villages, but was also expropriating possessions that the guerrillas were not accustomed to levy. The Solomeros were not at all hesitant about checking with the EGP in their own area to see if Felipe's claims were true.

A few nights after he had relieved the Solomeros of their belongings, Felipe received a visit from a squad of guerrillas. They demanded that he turn over to them everything he had collected in their name. He denied that he had appropriated anything, only to be confronted by two of his victims. The guerrilla chief then ordered that Felipe be suspended from his house rafters by a rope tied with a nonslip knot around his neck—as they had done with Juan Silvestre. After satisfying themselves with an hour of this punishment, they marched Felipe off to the mountains.

This part of the story, Hennessey had learned only two days earlier from his sacristan, Santiago Quot. Now, without realizing the extent of the priest's background knowledge, Marta Esperanza, talking almost compulsively, brought him up to date.

"The guerrillas came after Felipe only because they know he supports the government. That's the only thing they had against him," Marta Esperanza lied. "As soon as they'd taken him away, I ran to the house of our deacon, Adán López. I was terrified! My father-in-law wasn't home at the time, nor were Felipe's sisters. Only myself and poor little Dolores!

"I told Adán what'd happened. He said that both of us would have to go the next day to the Barillas army base to report the kidnapping. It was his idea! This whole thing is his fault!"

Hennessey was curious as to what the woman meant by "this whole thing," but refrained from asking.

"Felipe's three sisters decided to go with us to Barillas. On the bus down, we talked about whether we'd get in trouble with the commandant. My sister-in-law, Elena, said she thought the commandant might think Felipe went with the guerrillas willingly and then we'd all be in danger. But Adán insisted that we had no choice but to make a report. He said that if we didn't report the kidnapping, the commandant would hear about it anyway and accuse us of trying to protect the guerrillas."

Between Hennessey's concern for his patients, the necessity to drive with utmost care on the hairpin curves bounded by precipitous drops of hundreds of feet, and Marta Esperanza's intermittent sobbing that caused her to swallow parts of her ladino colloquialisms, the priest's ability to catch all the nuances of the woman's story was pushed to the limit. He understood enough, however, to know that when Marta Esperanza, her three sisters-in-law, and Adán López were admitted to the Barillas commandant's office, she had a strong feeling she was doing the wrong thing.

"The commandant came from behind his desk and personally pulled out chairs for us. He acted like a gentleman. I told him exactly what had happened. I explained that the guerrillas' hatred of Felipe was because my husband always respected the military government and told others to do the same."

Hennessey glanced at his passenger. She was sobbing quietly, pressing her face in her handkerchief.

A few moments later, she again gained control and continued. "The commandant seemed to get angry when I said that. I didn't know then what he must have been thinking. 'We can help you, but you must also help us,'" he told us. He said we had to tell him who supported the guerrillas in San Mateo.

"But before I could answer, Adán spoke up. Oh, I could kill him now! He told me on our way home afterwards that he was afraid I might give out some names and the people would be killed. Now look what's happened! Instead of pointing out the guilty ones, he told the commandant that everyone in San Mateo supported the guerrillas! Can you imagine such a stupid thing to say? He called it 'a Christian lie.' I don't know why he said that! If he didn't want to give out names, why didn't he just say that no one supported the guerrillas? God knows that the ladinos don't support them! Who can tell about all those *indios?*"

Again, Hennessey remained silent. But Marta's account was beginning to throw much light on the previous night's happenings.

"The commandant got very angry when Adán told him that. I was tempted to tell him that Adán was wrong, to give him the names of the guerrilla supporters. But I knew he would kill Adán. So then he tells Adán that he had heard that same thing, that everybody in San Mateo supports the guerrillas, but that he didn't want to believe it. 'But since you say it's true, *reverendo,* it must be true!' he told Adán. "

As the woman repeated the commandant's words, Hennessey felt her shiver in the seat beside him.

The Iowan shook his head. He could understand Marta Esperanza's belief that the army was her only recourse for saving her kidnapped husband. But he found it hard to believe that a man of intelligence like Adán López would make the mistake of saying that "everybody" in San Mateo was a guerrilla supporter. *He should have said the opposite! Poor Adán.*

As they approached the Chiantla checkpoint eight kilometers north of Huehuetenango, Hennessey gave a little prayer of thanks for the drenching rain that kept the police confined to their small, two-man booth, letting the station wagon pass without a questioning glance in their direction.

As soon as they arrived at the hospital, the priest got the attention of the orderly through the emergency-entrance window and asked permission to drive through the gate to the inside patio to keep the victims from getting wet. "What's wrong with them?" the attendant asked.

"Gunshot wounds, . . ." the priest answered. "They're all children—five of them."

"I'd have to get permission from the officer on duty to let a vehicle into the patio if your passengers all have gunshot wounds. It's better we don't bring the police into this. Just park at the curb and I'll get some people to help carry them inside."

As soon as Hennessey had parked the vehicle and had begun to gingerly extract the first child, trying to protect her from the driving rain, a police officer in a yellow raincoat approached and suggested he drive his patients into the patio. Grateful, the priest did so. Two orderlies and two nurses had already been alerted by the gate attendant and were waiting to take charge of the children as he rolled to a stop in the small courtyard.

Meanwhile, the barely literate officer painstakingly wrote down the priest's personal data in a little notebook.

"I don't know who the authors of the attack were," the priest answered in response to the officer's question. "It was dark, . . . in the middle of the night."

The officer nodded his head. It was the answer he expected.

As soon as Marta Esperanza and all five patients were inside, Hennessey backed the station wagon out of the patio as fast as propriety allowed. He was afraid the police might want to impound the vehicle as "evidence" and charge him a small fortune to recover it.

Of the five children, three died within hours: Alicia Mateo, who sat all night with a bullet in her stomach among the seven corpses of her family members; Alfredo Sebastián, with his thighs torn away and gaping wound in his back; Carolina Miguel, sister of Pablo Miguel, saved by his grandmother, while his sister took a bullet in the head and two in her arm. Only Pablo Miguel and Dolores González survived.

That night was the last time the Iowan saw Marta Esperanza and her daughter. They never returned to San Mateo after their trip to Huehuetenango. As for Felipe González, Marta Esperanza's husband, Hennessey heard a few days after returning to San Mateo that the guerrillas had executed him in the mountains.

The final tally: thirty-seven unarmed, sleeping civilians murdered, untold scores wounded.

Chapter 13

LAYING THE GROUNDWORK

If the CIA-sponsored overthrow of the Arbenz Guzmán government was to look like the unsullied triumph of freedom-loving Guatemalans over communist tyranny, the Eisenhower administration had to line up a crew of willing Guatemalans to front for the agency. And although there was no dearth of Guatemalan wannabe *caudillos*-cum-liberators, not all of them could be trusted to do Washington's bidding. Furthermore, no one of them commanded sufficient respect from the Guatemalan people to trigger what could remotely be seen as a popular movement.

Among the self-selected candidates was an old soldier who refused to fade away, former *caudillo* and dictator General Federico Ponce (1944), who offered himself to the U.S. Embassy in Nicaragua, claiming to have one hundred thousand adherents in Guatemala City ready to rise up when he gave the word. All he needed were bombers, explosives, and weapons.[1] He was thanked for his patriotism and sent on his way.

A conspirator who placed himself at the service of the U.S. Embassy in Guatemala City was one José Luis Arenas, head of the Anti-Communist Unification Party. For the sum of $200,000, Arenas claimed that he and his party faithful would oust Arbenz from the presidential palace through "civic pressure," a claim, he said, that no other Guatemalan leader could make.[2] This, despite his dismal showing in the 1950 elections.

When embassy personnel turned Arenas down, he threatened to go to his good friend, Vice President Richard Nixon. Nothing came of his threat, but Arenas would reappear on the national scene two decades later as *"El Tigre de Ixcán"* and an antagonist of Ron Hennessey. The murder of Arenas at the hands of the EGP on 7 June 1975 would play a key role in triggering the Guatemalan government's escalation of the country's ongoing civil war that would then suck Hennessey into its vortex.

The CIA's choice to be the crown prince of their "liberation movement" spoke to the personal qualifications necessary to carry out the as yet unformulated plan of counterrevolution. Economic warfare had so far failed. The question was compounded by the insistence of Sam "The Banana Man" Zemurray that he play a major role in determining the choice of the *caudillo*. Allen Dulles wanted to continue to use UFCO as a conduit for the agency's plans and materiél. It was therefore necessary to listen to Zemurray.

Sam wanted the leader to be the Old Fox, ex-general Miguel Ydígoras Fuentes, an individual with whom the fruit company had worked closely when the dictator Ubico was in power, one who, he knew, had no qualms about using military and police firepower to keep unruly peasants and workers in line.

UFCO had the ear of J.C. King, the CIA's Latin American division chief (LADC), who went to bat with superiors in support of the Old Fox. But the bigwigs at headquarters, particularly Allen Dulles, the director (referred to as the DCI), and Frank Wisner, the deputy director of plans (DD/P), objected to Ydígoras for two reasons: he was his own man, and on many occasions had antagonized Archbishop Rossell y Arellano. Dulles and Wisner hoped to enlist the prelate in their crusade and an Ydígoras leadership role would be problematic.

Dulles and Wisner's first choice was an UFCO lawyer, Juan Córdova Cerna. Córdova Cerna had already been involved in the planning and execution of two unsuccessful attempts against the Guatemalan government sponsored by the United Fruit Company, one while Arévalo was still president (Operation Fortune), the second after Arbenz took power (Salamá). It was thought that "the distinguished and respected jurist" would make an attractive civilian president in contrast to the soldier, Arbenz.[3]

The discovery of Córdova Cerna's throat cancer as invasion preparations developed forced the lawyer's withdrawal. At the time of his elimination, he recommended his good friend, Colonel Carlos Castillo Armas (ret.), the leader of the inept attack on Aurora Air Base on the eve of the 1950 presidential election.

To help settle the disagreement, Wisner allowed King to send two CIA agents to accompany Walter Turnbull, a former UFCO executive and close friend of Ydígoras Fuentes to interview the Old Fox and evaluate the general's availability and probable level of cooperation. According to Ydígoras's own memory of the resulting interview, the CIA's conditions were "unfavorable" to Guatemala, conditions that included a promise to favor UFCO, destroy IRCA's railroad workers' union, establish an Ubico-style government, suspend his country's claim against Great Britain for the Belize territory (British Honduras), and to repay "every cent invested in the enterprise."[4]

Ydígoras claimed that the meeting ended when he told his visitors that he would have to be given time to prepare his own set of conditions. "I never saw them again."

The CIA interviewers were unimpressed with the Old Fox's responses, most probably with his lack of awe. They reported back to Frank Wisner their negative opinion and a green light was then given to interview Castillo Armas. The little colonel had been under consideration for the job for some months so the CIA's formal approach came as no surprise. Castillo Armas, while belittling Ydígoras Fuentes and pumping up the potential of American training and resources, reportedly waxed rhapsodic on the certainty of his success.

The overriding concern of the Eisenhower administration was to cover its symbolic privates with a fig leaf of global proportions, a declaration of multinational opposition to the Guatemalan government that would serve as quasi-legal cover for the planned intervention in case the CIA should get caught with its pants down and proverbial phallus erect. The occasion for Secretary of State Foster Dulles to accomplish this task presented itself at the Tenth Interamerican Conference of the Organization of American States (OAS) held in Caracas, Venezuela, in March 1954. Dulles spent two weeks in the Venezuelan capital pushing, shoving, and threatening—as Winston Churchill said of the man, "the only case I know of a bull who carries his china shop with him"—an indication of the meeting's importance.[5]

No one doubted that the United States had a large stake in having its way at the reunion. Its intention was to press for the support of two-thirds of the OAS foreign ministers to agree to a resolution that "the domination or control of the political institutions of any American state by the international communist movement . . . would constitute a threat to the entire hemisphere and require appropriate action according to existing treaties."[6]

Guatemala was not mentioned by name in the resolution. Every delegate present knew what country was the target of Uncle Sam's wrath. Guillermo Toriello, the Guatemalan foreign minister, did not play the patsy, however, when it came his turn to speak:

> What is the real and effective reason for describing our government as communist? . . . The answers are simple and evident . . . . With the construction of publicly owned ports and docks, we are putting an end to the monopoly of the United Fruit Company . . . . We feel this proposal was merely a pretext for intervention in our internal affairs . . . . cataloguing as "communism" every manifestation of nationalism or economic independence.[7]

Of all the pronouncements of the various foreign ministers, Toriello's speech received the most sustained applause. The sympathies of the Latin delegates were no secret. But in the end, such sympathies did not stand in the way of the recognition of power—not law, and certainly not justice—as the ultimate fulcrum of international relations. The United States was able to corner the votes it needed.

Sixteen nations signed on to the Dulles resolution. Guatemala was the only country to vote against it. Only Mexico and Argentina dared to abstain. Costa Rica had refused to attend the conference in the first instance because of its opposition to the dictatorship of the host government, Venezuela. One delegate, referring to the Guatemalan foreign minister's statement, remarked that "he said many of the things some of the rest of us would like to say if we dared."[8]

Secretary of State Foster Dulles closed out his participation in the meeting with a lie that contradicted the very reason for his resolution: "I believe there is not a single American state that would practice intervention against another American state."[9]

Now, all that remained for the secretary of state was to present "proof" that Guatemala's political institutions were under the dominion or control of the international communist movement. That would prove an easy task as

Arbenz tried to escape the corner into which the American administration had pushed him.

On 15 May 1954, a Swedish freighter, the *Alfhem,* steamed into Puerto Barrios, Guatemala's Caribbean port owned and operated by the United Fruit Company. UFCO employees were kept away from the ship. In her hold lay two thousand tons of small arms and artillery from Czechoslovakia labeled "Optical and Laboratory Equipment."

The shipment was meant to be a closely guarded secret, an attempt to circumvent the arms embargo that the United States had enforced against Guatemala since midway through the Arévalo Bermejo government. Previous arms deals with Denmark, Mexico, Cuba, Argentina, and Switzerland had all foundered on the rocks of U.S. diplomatic and economic pressure and Czechoslovakia was the source of last resort.[10]

That Czechoslovakia was a captive state of the Soviet Union was a fact not lost upon either Arbenz or his enemies. The Guatemalan president had been given no alternative by the U.S. administration. At the same time, he handed the Americans the excuse they sought to justify their intervention even while they denied that such was their intention. Had Arbenz Guzmán decided to run the risk of facing Castillo Armas and his backers with nothing more than the ancient pieces then in the hands of his army, he knew that the United States could find or invent any number of excuses for attacking him. Indeed, they had already been given several. So Arbenz gambled . . . and lost.

The Guatemalan president's need for weaponry had been anything but a secret since 29 January 1954, the day on which Guatemalan newspapers heralded the news of the CIA's invasion plans. They had done so by publishing photostat copies of correspondence between Castillo Armas, Ydígoras Fuentes, and Anastacio Somoza, the dictator of Nicaragua, letters turned over to them by a courier for Castillo Armas who had decided to betray the little colonel.[11] The plans detailed the invasion forces' training bases provided by Somoza on Nicaraguan soil, that the invasion itself would come through Honduras (with the approval of President Manuel Gálvez, formerly UFCO's lawyer in Honduras), and that assistance would be provided by El Salvador, the Dominican Republic, Venezuela, and "the government of the north."

The *Alfhem*'s arms were meant to be a response to those plans, plans the State Department had denied as "ridiculous and untrue," stating that "it would not comment further on Guatemala's accusations because it did not wish to give them a dignity they did not deserve."[12]

Long before the Swedish freighter put into port, the United States had marshaled a series of excuses to brand the regime as a captive of the "international communist conspiracy." Some of them were laughable, as the Guatemalans meant them to be, like flying the Puerto Rican flag for the island's athletic contingent instead of the Stars and Stripes in February 1950 during the Central American and Caribbean Games. Others were meant as a symbolic fist raised from a safe distance at a bully by a victim with no serious defense. Such was the congressional memorial service held for Stalin on the occasion of the Soviet dictator's death in March 1953, as was the congressional applause in July 1953 for a communist deputy who "extolled the victory of the peace-loving forces led by the Soviet Union over U.S. imperialism in Korea."[13]

Two days after the *Alfhem*'s arrival, the U.S. State Department issued a statement declaring the arms shipment a "development of gravity."[14] Foster Dulles was quoted as stating that the arms would establish a communist beachhead near the Panama Canal and indicated that they were probably destined for the invasion of Guatemala's neighbors, particularly Honduras, since the weapons exceeded Guatemala's "legitimate needs."[15]

Not to worry! Arbenz had been snookered by his Czech supplier: the weapons were a consignment of captured World War II arms in disrepair, largely useless. As far as the U.S. media was concerned, however, the Eisenhower accusation that the *Alfhem* cargo represented a communist dagger aimed at the heart of America was accepted at face value. Decree Number 900, the agrarian reform law that legalized the expropriation of unused UFCO land and was the real cause of American outrage, now slipped from the headlines.

Eisenhower, however, felt he now had all the excuse he needed to mount a more public offense against Arbenz. On 24 May, he gave orders to the U.S. Navy to board all "suspicious" ships bound for Guatemala to check their cargoes. The State Department's legal advisor protested that the action would violate international law. James Hagerty, Eisenhower's press secretary, noted in his diary that the United States had fought the War of 1812 for the specific purpose of defending the right of its ships to sail the high seas unmolested by the British crown. In what might be considered a poetic eye-for-an-eye of historical proportions, England now protested Eisenhower's order and said that it would not allow the United States to board its vessels.[16]

While the United States did board French, Swedish, and Dutch freighters with their captains' "cooperation" over the next few weeks, British ships were not searched.

When Arbenz received word of the American president's order, he recognized the seriousness of the U.S. threat. He immediately told his foreign minister to request a meeting between himself and Eisenhower. Arbenz Guzmán said that he was sure that any differences between his government and UFCO could be taken care of in a face-to-face session between the two presidents.

But it was too late. The request never got beyond Secretary of State Foster Dulles.

Up at Opa-Locka, Florida, the abandoned Marine air base requisitioned by the CIA as the nerve center for Operation PBSuccess, preparations for the overthrow of Arbenz Guzmán were moving forward. But tension was mounting. The lines of authority were not entirely clear and decisions were being made with little cross-fertilization by monumental egos in Washington, Florida, Guatemala, and Nicaragua. The elitist backgrounds and snobbish attitudes of the men involved tended to rub each other in ways that ordinary adults would find hard to understand (like Colonel Al Haney challenging Howard Hunt as to who between them had been driving Cadillacs the longest).[17] J.C. King, as chief of the Latin American Division, should have been in charge and thought that he was. Colonel Al Haney, however, had been brought in by Dulles to run things on the ground. Haney had been the CIA station chief in Seoul during the war there and had earned a reputation for tactics, organization, and bravery while training and leading South Korean saboteurs into the North on black-bag missions. Dulles did not consider King to be activist enough.[18]

J.C. King complained to Dulles that the gung ho Haney was about to begin "a Korean war right on our doorstep."[19] The DCI brushed aside the LADC's concern. Not so Frank Wisner, Dulles's number-two man and head of the clandestine "dirty tricks" division. Wisner, a paranoid, hands-on micromanager, sympathized with King's more cautious approach, ever afraid that the agency's involvement in the overthrow of a democratically elected president would blacken Uncle Sam's moral standing around the world and inevitably curtail the freedom of operation of the Central Intelligence Agency. Wisner wanted Arbenz out as much as anyone—even more so—but he preferred to bribe the president to resign, or failing that, to assassinate him, methods that the CIA could more easily disown.[20]

Wisner did not want Haney in Guatemala. Instead, the deputy director of plans recalled the CIA's Berlin station chief, Henry Heckscher, and sent him to Guatemala disguised as a coffee buyer. His job was to ingratiate himself with upper level officers in Arbenz's army and to bribe them to betray their chief. He was singularly unsuccessful.

An American mercenary, Rip Robertson, was put in charge of the 150 ragtag "soldiers" that the CIA had recruited and was now training in Nicaragua. Robertson considered his troops "tenth rate" and their designated leader, Castillo Armas, of sergeant's caliber.[21]

Finally, Dulles and Wisner sent Tracy Barnes, the CIA's chief of psychological and paramilitary warfare (CPP), and Richard Bissell, special assistant to Dulles (SA/D), to Opa-Locka to see if they could cultivate more cohesion between the various actors involved.

Haney was not happy with what he considered an intrusion by the two delegates. Barnes, however, was a self-contained individual and was not put off by Haney's braggadocio and complaints. He listened to Haney and listened some more. Soon Haney was doing some listening himself.

Barnes and Bissell returned to Washington with positive reports about the activity they had witnessed and assured Dulles and Wisner that all was proceeding in suitable fashion. Frank Wisner badly needed the assurance.

In December 1952 the linchpin of Allen Dulles's plans for Guatemala, Archbishop Rossell y Arellano, finally decided that he needed supernatural assistance to move the Guatemala people to violence in order to repudiate the results of their November 1950 presidential election. The archbishop was by then implacably opposed to the president not only because Arbenz had not warmed up to the prelate's idea of the Church's "preeminent rights," but also because he had betrayed the churchman's personal trust.

Leading up to the 1950 election, the archbishop had warned the faithful to refrain from voting for any candidate tainted with communism. That had seemed to some to be a warning against the candidacy of Arbenz Guzmán. But that was not what Rossell had in mind. The archbishop had thought that the colonel, as a professional soldier, would rule as a militarist, hopefully as a *caudillo,* not as a populist, and certainly not as a communist. After all, the prelate told his friends, Arbenz is "married to a woman from a very wealthy family, is a military officer, lives in a house in Zone 10 where the rich lived, and has the look of an aristocrat, white, distinguished."[22]

But Arbenz's land reform law, Decree Number 900, changed all that. It is said that hell hath no fury as a woman scorned. The same can be said of bishops.

Rossell y Arellano responded by enlisting Guatemala's most revered icon, the Black Christ of Esquipulas, in what became his passionate, anti-Arbenz crusade. In late December 1952, the archbishop announced that he would take *El Cristo Negro* from its sanctuary and parade "him" around the country, not letting him return to his resting place until communism had disappeared from the face of the fatherland.

But a problem arose: even archbishops are subject to the whims of saints, and *El Cristo Negro,* the saint of saints, did not want to move. At least that is what the *chimanes* maintained and what *chimanes* say is what the faithful often believe. After all, the *chimanes* talk directly with the saints and listen to them, while bishops and archbishops talk to each other and to God. And no one knows whom they listen to, other than someone called "the Holy Father" who lives in a far-off land and knows only what the bishops tell him about Guatemala.

Thus, as far as the *chimanes* were concerned, the expulsion from Guatemala of Arbenz Guzmán was not an acceptable reason to remove *El Cristo Negro* from his home, he who had come from heaven to Esquipulas to protect the health and welfare of his people. The outpouring of popular opposition to the archbishop's intention came close to becoming a full-blown riot. The prelate's life would certainly have been in danger had he persisted in his plan. Instead, a replica of the famous statue was constructed and carried to urban centers around the country where anti-Arbenz, anticommunist, and anti-Satan sermons were preached.

The Black Christ received exuberant expressions of devotion wherever "he" went. But only conservative political junkies and personnel of the U.S. Embassy associated the outpouring of affection with any anti-Arbenz sentiment. After all, every Guatemalan loves a procession, particularly one in honor of the Black Christ, "a saint" who, unlike the archbishop, was not a politician.

The men charged by President Eisenhower to bring down Arbenz Guzmán were well aware of Archbishop Rossell y Arellano's long trajectory of outspoken anticommunism and were determined to harness it—and him—to their cause. . They recognized that all wars at the infantry level need a divine patron—that "no atheists are found in foxholes"—and that the archbishop had the authority to invoke the blessing of orthodox Roman Catholicism's God on their side of the civil war they hoped to foment. But it was a tricky proposition. The prelate had spent half a lifetime excoriating American Protestant missionaries for their attempts to wean Guatemala's faithful away from their folk Catholicism, and he identified the United States as a "Protestant nation." Would he now agree to cooperate with the representatives of a "Protestant government"?

For help, the CIA turned to a New York churchman who had spent his entire adult life trying to prove to nativistic Americans and doubting Europeans that if Catholicism and Americanism were not ideological twins, they were at least stepsisters. Two Irish Catholic agents, Birch O'Neil, the CIA's station chief in Guatemala, and his deputy, John Doherty, were sent to visit a fellow ethnic Irishman, Francis Cardinal Spellman of the Archdiocese of New York, to ask the prelate to help arrange a clandestine contact with Rossell y Arellano. Spellman, in turn, contacted Maryknoll's superior general in Ossining, also of Irish descent, Bishop Raymond Lane. The cardinal knew of Maryknoll's decade-long, close relationship with Archbishop Rossell, as well as the treatment—including imprisonment and resulting death—some of the Society's key personnel had received at the hands of communist authorities in mainland China and North Korea after being accused of spying for the United States.

Maryknoll had already carried out a highly secret mission for Spellman and the CIA by hiding in its seminaries at Lakewood, New Jersey, and Ossining, New York, Ngo Dinh Diem, the man the agency was prepping to be the new anticommunist leader of South Vietnam. It was logical, therefore, that Spellman ask Maryknoll to help the CIA enlist Rossell in their crusade in Guatemala. The contact was duly initiated.

In early April 1954, Archbishop Rossell delivered a sermon in which he stated:

> Anti-Christian communism . . . is stalking our country under the cloak of social justice . . . . Everyone who loves his country must fight against those who—loyal to no country, the scum of the earth—have repaid Guatemala's generous hospitality by fomenting class hatred, in preparation for the day of destruction and slaughter that they anticipate with such enthusiasm.[23]

The archbishop sent copies of his sermon to every priest in his archdiocese and ordered that it be read at every Mass that day. Howard Hunt, in charge of PBSuccess's propaganda operation, then had thousands of copies of the prelate's pastoral printed, and dropped from the air across the Guatemalan countryside. The ideological impression made by the leaflets on the overwhelmingly illiterate population was never examined.

On 8 June, as political, economic, and religious tensions in Guatemala tightened almost to the breaking point, the Guatemalan Congress gave permission to Arbenz to suspend all constitutional guarantees for thirty days. Enno Hobbing, a former correspondent for *Time* magazine but now writing for Al Haney, had earlier suggested that the agency push Arbenz to the point where the president would have to employ more repression. He had his wish.

The police under the new decree picked up one hundred anti-Arbenz activists. Several unexplained deaths of individuals in custody gave Ambassador John E. Peurifoy the platform he needed to declare the Arbenz administration a "reign of terror,"[24] an expression that Foster Dulles gleefully echoed. An internal State Department memo noted that "the program of smearing Guatemalan maneuvers in advance was proceeding satisfactorily."[25]

One other loose end had to be tied up before the actual invasion could begin. The Guatemalan people had to be drawn into the preparations for the coming overthrow if there was to be any hope for triggering a significant popular uprising against Arbenz Guzmán, or at least of fomenting substantial loss of the president's political support among the electorate. This would be the role of Radio Liberación.

On 1 May 1954, the CIA's underground radio went on the air. David Atlee Phillips, a Spanish-speaking, part-time actor who had done previous recordings for the Voice of America, was hired by Tracy Barnes to head the operation. Phillips was not convinced that the United States had a right to overthrow a popularly elected government and questioned Barnes on the matter. Barnes replied that the Soviet Union was in the process of establishing an American beachhead in Guatemala. The part-time actor asked for proof. Barnes dodged the question by answering that President Eisenhower himself had given the CIA its marching orders.[26] Ike's stature was enough to placate Phillips's questioning conscience.

Phillips went to Opa-Locka to set up shop, forming a team with three Guatemalans who had already been hired for the purpose. The idea was to develop a "disinformation campaign" to sow confusion and panic inside Guatemala by exaggerating the number of "patriots" joining Castillo Armas's forces and lying about Arbenz's plans for the sovietization of the country. They called their network Radio Liberación and adopted the slogan, *"Trabajo, Pan, y Patria"*(Work, Bread, and Fatherland).

Powerful transmitters were set up in Nicaragua, Honduras, and the Dominican Republic, as well as inside the U.S. Embassy in Guatemala. All broadcasts claimed, however, to emanate from hidden sites within the Guatemalan countryside to give the impression of the government's impotence to control the nation's territory. The *New York Times* and other American media repeated these claims uncritically.

After the docking of the *Alfhem,* Phillips concentrated his broadcasts on the theme that Arbenz was smuggling in weapons to arm a peasant army that even at that moment was in the process of enlisting and training personnel. The aim, of course, was to frighten the professional officer corps and to sow dissension and mistrust in its ranks.

The words of Archbishop Rossell were repeated over and over: "Rise as a single man against this enemy of God and country."

The Liberación broadcasts were made on Guatemalan frequencies to ensure they were easily located, as well as to obliterate any government broadcasts that attempted to counter the CIA's propaganda. Dummy parachute drops were made from CIA planes in the countryside while listeners were asked to help locate drop sites to resupply the nonexistent "partisans."[27]

With each passing day, the radio campaign became ever more alarmist, causing broad-based unrest throughout Guatemala, particularly within the army's officer corps. And President Arbenz was unable to devise a strategy to stop it.

Chapter 14

THE INVASION

Colonel Carlos Castillo Armas knew he had a good six to eight hours of sunshine to get his 150 stalwarts into Guatemala before the daily weather pattern and mud would cause him problems. It was one month into the rainy season, 17 June 1954. The previous day, his men had been flown by Honduran Air Force DC-3s from Tegucigalpa, the Honduran capital, to a dirt strip in Nuevo Ocotopeque, eight miles south of the Guatemalan border. Before leaving Tegucigalpa, the "Liberator" had imparted marching orders to another four dozen *Liberacionistas* who would board a Honduran freighter to head for Puerto Barrios, the UFCO port on Guatemala's Caribbean coast. There, some fifty additional infiltrators who had been sneaking across the border in twos and threes would meet them. The latter had been given the mission of recruiting UFCO workers who might be tempted by the promise of lifelong employment and monetary rewards to help capture the port city.

Castillo Armas had passed the previous day in Nuevo Ocotopeque delivering pep talks, painting dreams of lottery-like financial windfalls, while reacquainting himself with the officers of his rag-tag army. Among the mercenary volunteers were Nicaraguans, Hondurans, and Salvadorans, more influenced by the promises of *Yanqui* largesse than by their anticommunist ideology. His CIA overlords had also informed Castillo Armas that his destination and target—Zacapa, site of the regional army headquarters and the major railroad link between Puerto Barrios and Guatemala City—had been cancelled as a too strongly fortified objective for his plebeian crew to handle. The peasant uprising that had been a major element in the agency's plans to capture Zacapa had failed to materialize, in spite of the best efforts of several score of *Liberacionistas* who had been enlisted to sabotage rail, phone, telegraph, and power lines in the Zacapa area and who then would support the invading troops. Furthermore, the command structure at the Zacapa base had remained intact, withstanding the best efforts of the CIA's Henry Heckscher, brought in from his station in Berlin, to bribe the senior officers. As a result, Castillo Armas was told that the revised plan called for him to proceed only as far as Esquipulas, the location of the miraculous Black Christ shrine, six miles inside Guatemala. There the Liberator was to sponsor a Mass of Thanksgiving—apparently in gratitude to the Divinity for his safe arrival—and there to await further instructions while the CIA's psyops (psychological operations) department pondered its next move.

Esquipulas had been chosen as the invasion force's holding pen for several reasons, primary among them the reasonable belief that Arbenz Guzmán would hesitate to send troops against the invaders while the latter remained encamped next to Guatemala's most sacred shrine. Furthermore, Esquipulas was close enough to the border to provide a fallback position and far enough from any military installation as to render unlikely an ambush by Arbenz's forces.

In order to keep the little colonel from demonstrating his incompetence and to rebut evidence that he was subservient to the orders of others, he was encouraged to look less like a paper *caudillo* by occupying and haranguing a few undefended peasant villages, Montecinos and Atulepa, encountered on the road to Esquipulas. He was also told to keep reporters at bay so that news of real events or nonevents would not contradict Radio Liberación's propaganda extolling the invaders' heroics. With an encouraging wave of his hand, the Liberator swung himself into the passenger seat of a salvaged Willys-Jeep station wagon, signaling to his men to board their convoy of pickups and light trucks and follow him.

Two uneventful days after crossing the border, the Liberator was getting itchy, feeling somewhat resentful that his CIA mentors had failed to pick a target of opportunity that could challenge his military skills without stretching them beyond a guaranteed victory. Motivated by the mutterings and questioning looks of his troops, Castillo Armas decided on his own to attack Gualán, a small town fifteen miles inside the border, guarded by a garrison of thirty troops. A real live victory would be grist for Radio Liberación's propagandists and would show his patrons that he had balls the size of their own, if not their material resources. He could then declare the town "liberated territory" and seat of a provisional government that the United States would immediately recognize.

The problem was that Gualán's thirty soldiers had not been listening to Radio Liberación's broadcasts and were therefore unaware of the attackers' inflated numbers and fierceness. After a day and a half of unsuccessfully exchanging shots from well-fortified positions, Castillo Armas gave the order for his men to fall back to Esquipulas. He had apparently learned the old saw that it is better to retreat and fight another day, a lesson that he had picked up from his bumbled attempt to take over Guatemala City's Aurora Air Base shortly before the 1950 presidential election.

The following day, 21 June, the small *Liberacionista* contingent coming by sea on a Honduran freighter moved in on Puerto Barrios and suffered an even more ignominious defeat. Met only by the city's police force and armed workers belonging to UFCO's labor union, the invaders were unable to sustain the attack for more than a few hours. By early afternoon, they were in confused retreat, leaving behind several dead as well as twenty prisoners, fewer than half of whom were Guatemalans.[1] It was the Liberation Army's first loss of blood.

The defeats of the two invading forces and their failure to inspire even token support among the peasantry and dock workers mandated that the CIA's psyops team of Richard Bissell, Tracy Barnes, David Atlee Philips, and E. Howard Hunt shift into overdrive. Their two-pronged plan was to make the populace, the president, and especially the army's high command think that uprisings were already in progress in those areas where government communications were sparse to nonexistent, and, more importantly, that the United States was prepared to make a massive frontal assault on Arbenz's army should a Castillo Armas victory ever seem in doubt.

The first of the two objectives was the updated mandate of Radio Liberación. The second belonged to Castillo Armas's air force, called *"los sulfatos"*—in Guatemala, the farts—by the capital's stand-up comics, referring to the noise of the planes as well as their effect on the army brass.

The CIA did not possess an operational air force. That had not yet been perceived as part and parcel of its modus operandi, as was intelligence gathering and misinformation dissemination. But the agency did possess an undercover airline, the Civil Air Transport Company (CAT), formerly General Claire Chennault's famous World War II Flying Tigers. And Chennault's former assistant, Whiting Willauer, was now installed as U.S. ambassador to Honduras, appropriately placed to give advice and support when and where needed.

Ten American pilots, all ex-servicemen, had unobtrusively entered Nicaragua under CAT aegis to train Guatemalan pilots for the Liberation Air Force. Contrary to CIA hopes, however, no Guatemalan Air Force personnel opted to fly for Castillo Armas despite several highly publicized desertions and offers of generous compensation. The ten Americans thus became the Liberation Air Force by default. They went to war on 18 June 1954 and would meet no competition from what little there was of Arbenz's air force, five 1935 trainers that had never been outfitted for anything other than to teach would-be pilots to fly. The United States had blocked all attempts since Arévalo Bermejo's midterm to upgrade his army, navy, and air force. Furthermore, in a gesture intended to reflect his government's vulnerability in the face of illegal foreign air power, as well as doubt about his pilots' loyalty, Arbenz had grounded all his planes after his former air force chief had deserted to the United States. In short, Guatemala had no functioning air force, a fact the CIA endeavored to exploit.

Jerry DeLarm, a former Navy pilot from San Francisco, owner of a car dealership and flying school in Guatemala City, put a new wrinkle in the CIA's psychological game plan by flying a C-47 over the capital city, dropping leaflets demanding that Arbenz Guzmán resign the presidency and leave the country. There was no doubt in the citizenry's mind that he was acting on behalf of the United States. His message had been implicit in everything the United States had done to Guatemala in the previous six months, but this was the first time the American government had admitted openly to the Guatemalan people that its intention was to permanently rid the country of Arbenz Guzmán. DeLarm's leaflets also warned the civilian population to flee to the countryside to avoid possible injury or death from the impending onslaught, or at least to steer clear of all military installations and government offices for the war's duration.

The leaflet drop proved successful, creating a pandemic atmosphere of confusion, fear, and anger among the city's population. The following day, 19 June, three CIA P-47 fighter-bombers flew over Guatemala City at treetop level to bomb and strafe. They knocked out a Protestant radio station thinking it belonged to the government and damaged some fuel tanks at Aurora Air Base. Two of the planes were crippled by ground fire and forced to limp back to Nicaragua. Meanwhile, DeLarm and Carlos Cheeseman, another ex-Navy pilot, flew a small single-engine Cessna dropping leaflets on Puerto Barrios's population, using grenades and dynamite on the port city's fuel storage facilities. Again, the intention was to confuse and frighten the inhabitants in preparation for the maritime invasion that was still two days away.

On the same day, 19 June, a 30-year-old from Tyler, Texas, William Beal, strafed Cobán, the capital of the northern state of Alta Verapaz, a center for Q'eq'chí Maya economic activity. But Beal failed to watch his fuel gauge, ran out of gas, and was forced to make a crash landing in Chiapas, Mexico. The State Department managed to pull a few strings and the Mexican Government quickly released the downed pilot.

On 20 June, Colonel Al Haney sent a top priority massage to Allen Dulles requesting an immediate replacement for his three damaged P-47 fighter-bombers, suggesting that the outcome of PBSuccess depended upon continuous aerial action. The DCI hesitated, fearing that the arrival of additional aircraft after the commencement of hostilities would broadcast to the world the executive role of the United States. His worry was well founded. James Reston had written in the *New York Times* that same day that the invasion had Dulles's handwriting all over it. The DCI cabled Haney that he would send two aircraft after he had obtained State Department approval.

Haney, upset by the delay, decided to force Dulles's hand by sending one of his still air-worthy planes to bomb a Honduran airstrip near the border. The idea was to have the Honduran government blame Arbenz, declare it an act of war, and call on the United States to honor its newly signed mutual security pact. The two 250-pound bombs failed to explode, however, and the Honduran government could not agree on where, and if in fact, the bombing had taken place.[2]

Dulles went straight to President Eisenhower with his request for the two planes. Henry Holland, the assistant secretary of state, argued that the planes should not be sent, that the entire enterprise was a serious violation of international law. Ike turned to Dulles and asked the DCI to assess the chances of PBSuccess without the planes.

"About zero," answered Dulles.

"Suppose we supply the aircraft?" asked the president.

"About 20 percent," responded the DCI.

Eisenhower smiled and approved the request, telling Dulles as he went out the door, "If you had said 90 percent, I would have said no."[3]

The two replacement planes arrived in Honduras on 23 June after a roundabout cover trip through the hands of the Nicaraguan dictator, General Anastacio Somoza, who had "purchased" the planes for $150,000 donated to him by the CIA.[4] The aircraft were immediately sent into action along with sister planes, conducting around-the-clock bombings of the Zacapa, Chiquimula, and Gualán military bases in preparation for Castillo Armas's long-awaited orders to advance.

The next day, four planes worked in tandem repeatedly strafed the town of Chiquimula, twenty-five miles northwest of Esquipulas. The town's commander, Lt. Colonel Jorge Hernández, had one hundred and fifty troops at his disposal. He knew that the four P-47s meant serious trouble, particularly since he had also received reports from friendly peasants that Castillo Armas's troops had left Esquipulas the evening before and were moving in his direction. He radioed a call for help to his superior, Colonel Victor M. León, commandant of two thousand troops at Zacapa, only twelve miles to the north. No response came from León. Mutiny was already brewing in Zacapa.[5]

Castillo Armas, dug in outside Chiquimula, nervously watched his CIA colleagues go through their aerial maneuvers. This was his big day, one that would go down in the annals of Guatemala's military history. Haney had sent the Liberator his coded attack message and Castillo Armas was determined to repair the damage to his flagging reputation inflicted by his poor showings at Aurora Air Base, Gualán, and Puerto Barrios.

After several hours of nail-biting observation and detecting only token resistance from several dozen peasants armed mostly with small-caliber pistols and single-shot rifles, Castillo Armas ordered his men to advance, slowly, house by house.

The invaders encountered no soldiers. Lt. Colonel Hernández and his 150 troops were carefully ensconced in their barracks, debating whether to defend themselves or surrender since Zacapa had not responded to their calls for support. The decision depended upon the attitude of the advancing Castillo Armas.

Without knowing each other's mind-set, both Castillo Armas and Hernández were locked in a potential death dance not unlike that of two trained fighting cocks, thrusting and parrying, trying to show macho courage while burying any evidence of fear. Both men preferred to avoid serious violence and arrive quickly at a gentlemen's agreement. Any false move on either side could initiate a deadly exchange. It was the battle plan repeatedly employed by officers of Guatemala's army for the past 130 years of political independence, while one tried to gauge the significance of quickly shifting loyalties as they occurred during failed coups, successful coups, and faltering countercoups.

The pieces fell into place exactly as both men had hoped. Shots were fired from both sides as the *Liberacionistas* approached the soldiers' barracks, but most were either going over the opposition's heads or thumping harmlessly into the walls of surrounding buildings. A few soldiers stationed on the perimeter were killed, as were several *Liberacionistas,* a face-saving result that officers on both sides neither sought nor avoided. Suffering casualties among foot soldiers, particularly Mayan recruits, was always an acceptable price to pay to keep the officers' pride, reputations, and health intact. Finally, the firing started to taper off, then halted entirely. The two commanders walked out into the neutral zone between their forces and shook hands as befitted officers and gentlemen. Castillo Armas had his liberated territory.

As they made their way through town, the *Liberacionistas* had captured some resisting peasants and killed others. Now that the contest was over, Castillo Armas ordered those captured be executed as a warning to the townspeople. These and other dead peasants would later be eulogized as "innocent victims of communist terror."[6]

Meanwhile, President Arbenz, believing that Castillo Armas was no match for his troops, had been concentrating all his efforts on the diplomatic front. He spent hour after hour on the phone to his foreign minister, Guillermo

Toriello, at the United Nations in New York. On 18 June, the day after Castillo Armas crossed the Honduran border, the foreign minister had filed a carefully worded emergency petition with the UN Security Council "to put a stop to the aggression," which he attributed to Nicaragua, Honduras, and "certain foreign monopolies whose interests have been affected by the progressive policy of my government."[7] The United States was not mentioned by name.

France responded to the Guatemalan petition by filing a motion demanding "the immediate termination of any action likely to cause bloodshed." The Security Council answered the French initiative by requesting "all members of the United Nations to abstain . . . from rendering assistance to any such action."[8]

But the bombings and strafing continued.

On 21 June and again the next day, Toriello renewed his appeals to the Security Council: "Acts of aggression against the republic continued last night and today, from bases in countries, members of the United Nations, in open contravention of the Security Council's resolution."[9]

As luck—or careful planning—would have it, the president of the Security Council for the month of June was the American ambassador to the United Nations and good friend of the United Fruit Company, Massachusetts's Henry Cabot Lodge. Cabot Lodge reported to Foster Dulles that the secretary general of the United Nations, Dag Hammarskjöld, wanted the Security Council to send a fact-finding mission to Guatemala to investigate the situation. He also reported that England was apt to side with France in approving the mission.

Dulles was furious. He told Cabot Lodge to recommend that the issue be referred to the Organization of American States (OAS)—knowing that the United States had a virtual stranglehold on that august body—and to block any Security Council action on Toriello's request. In the meantime, the secretary of state would call in the ambassadors of France and England to tell them that if their governments continued to insist on siding with Guatemala, the United States would not support England on the issues of Suez and Cyprus, nor France on Vietnam.

Dag Hammarskjöld was bitterly upset by the U.S. position. He argued that the UN Charter gave all members the right to bring any situation before the Security Council at any time, and further, that the Security Council had "primary responsibility for the maintenance of international peace and security."[10]

Lodge attempted to shut down the secretary general by appealing to a UN Charter article that stated that members "should make every effort to achieve pacific settlement of local disputes through such regional arrangements or by such regional agencies before referring them to the Security Council."[11]

At the same time, Foster Dulles issued a lengthy, mendacious statement on the situation in Guatemala, which noted in part:

> The department has been in touch with Ambassador John E. Peurifoy at Guatemala City . . . and he reports that all Americans are well and safe . . . . He also reports that during the past 24 hours serious uprisings were reported at Quezaltenango, Zacapa, and Puerto Barrios. He reports that there have been three overflights at Guatemala City . . . that there have been no bombings or strafings by planes in the Guatemala City area, and . . . that the department has no evidence that indicates that this is anything other than a revolt of Guatemalans against the government.[12]

In the meantime, the secretary of state was bringing pressure on the French and British ambassadors and his efforts were showing results.

Finally, on 25 June, Cabot Lodge, having been assured that England and France would not vote with Guatemala, allowed Toriello's petition to be brought before the Security Council. With Denmark, New Zealand, Lebanon, and the Soviet Union voting for the fact-finding mission, Britain and France abstaining, the United States carried the day, after having cornered four votes to match its own—including those of Colombia and Brazil—five votes against and four in favor of the resolution. There would be no investigation of Guatemala's charges.

Hammarskjöld later stated that the U.S. behavior vis-à-vis the United Nations "was the most serious blow so far aimed at the organization,"[13] and even considered resigning. After Arbenz's fall, the secretary general would write a letter to Cabot Lodge restating his position regarding UN jurisdiction. The United States then responded to Hammarskjöld that his position represented a "warped presentation" and requested that it not be circulated among the delegates.[14]

On the military front, word was beginning to trickle upward to Guatemala City that all was not well in Zacapa. Chief of the armed forces, Colonel Carlos Enrique Díaz, an Arbenz confidant, had sent his chief of staff, Colonel Enrique Parinello, to Zacapa on 23 June to see what his friend Colonel Victor M. León was doing to terminate Castillo Armas's badly led, undermanned, and inadequately planned skirmishes. The chief of the armed forces had only recently assigned Colonel León to Zacapa, along with two other personal friends, Colonels Pablo Díaz and Enrique Barzanallana, in the belief that the three men would quickly get rid of the Liberator and his followers.

However, friendships in the Guatemalan military are like the threads of a spider web, they hold together as long as the enemy's strengths do not match up to the web's weaknesses. Nor are friendships equal to familial, *compradrazgo, centenario,* and *promoción* relationships. Thus, before the three colonels departed for their new assignment in Zacapa, Colonel Pablo Díaz was heard to complain to associates, "I can't understand Carlos Enrique Díaz. Why is he sending his friends to fight against Castillo Armas? Why can't he send someone else?"[15]

Two days earlier Colonel Victor León had reported to the chief of the armed forces that he was then ready to take on Castillo Armas but was still waiting for needed materiél, delayed by a rebel bombing run on the supply train. Both Arbenz and the chief knew that León had more than enough men and supplies to take out the Liberator's forces in a matter of a couple of hours. Arbenz was anxious to know what was causing the delay. Was León falling for Radio Liberación's propaganda? "Send someone you trust down there to find out what's going on," the president told Díaz.

Colonel Parinello stayed only a few hours with Colonels León, Pablo Díaz, and Barzanallana. What he heard upset him deeply. The officers firmly believed that Eisenhower would send in the marines if Castillo Armas's mission to oust Arbenz Guzmán failed. León did not mention that Lt. Colonel Hernández had requested support for Chiquimula that very morning, a request that he, León, had decided to ignore.[16]

Parinello returned to the capital convinced that León would not mount an attack on Castillo Armas. And though Parinello remained loyal to Arbenz, his loyalty, embedded in his own complex web of personal relationships, had its limitations. He did not convey his suspicions of León to either Díaz or the president.[17]

Earlier in the month, on 5 June, at Arbenz's request, his senior staff had presented the president with a series of questions regarding their concerns. The questions all dealt with the communists in his administration and the tensions their presence was fomenting with the United States.

Arbenz had responded on that occasion that "I am not now, nor will I ever be a communist, but . . . neither am I nor will I ever be an anti-Communist . . . . There are communists in the agrarian reform department, but they are the best workers and the most honest."[18]

The officers had begun the 5 June meeting with protestations of loyalty to the president that they would obey him "absolutely and without reservation."[19] Now, on 23 June, with Washington's footprints all over Castillo Armas's back, no such protestations would be forthcoming from Zacapa.

On 25 June, Octavio Reyes, a member of Central Committee of the Guatemalan Workers Party (PGT, the communist party), returned to the capital from Zacapa, where he had gone two days earlier to investigate the military situation. He reported to Manuel Fortuny, the secretary general of the PGT, that the Zacapa officers were demoralized and unwilling to fight. When he argued with them, he said, they nearly shot him. Fortuny took Reyes to Arbenz to describe for the president the situation in Zacapa.

After Reyes left, the president called in one of his closest friends and allies, his *centenario*, Colonel Anselmo Getella, and asked him to go to Zacapa to confirm Reyes's information. Getella returned that same evening and reported to Arbenz: "*Centenario,* the high command asked me to tell you that you must resign . . . . They think that the Americans are threatening Guatemala just because of you and your communist friends. If you don't resign, the army will march on the capital to depose you. They have already begun to arrest peasants."[20]

Getella would later confess that he had "returned to the capital scared and depressed. Defeat was inevitable. There was no way to stop the gringos."[21]

As he left Arbenz, he advised, "You must move quickly, *centenario.* Otherwise the army will make a deal with Castillo Armas and move against the capital."[22]

Later that night, a bombing raid on the capital was carried out, accompanied by the sound effects of reverberating explosions blaring from loudspeakers atop the U.S. Embassy. It was impossible to distinguish between exploding bombs, their echoes, and the CIA's acoustic wizardry. The civilian population prayed. The army high command held its cowed, collective breath.

On 26 June, President Jacobo Arbenz Guzmán, the courageous leader of the 1944 October Revolution, the guarantor of Arévalo Bermejo's successful presidency, the determined initiator of the most profound agrarian reform Latin America had seen outside President Lázaro Cárdenas's Mexico, spent the day holed up in his office, drinking heavily, wracked by thoughts of self-doubt, trying to devise a strategy to save the social gains his country had won over the past ten years. More than once, he recalled his father's solution for handling career-ending pressures from out-of-control forces. That thought would trigger a new burst of redemptive determination, only to quickly fall victim to new evidence of treasonous desertions of additional members of his senior staff.

Finally, Jacobo Arbenz Guzmán made his decision: he would resign his presidency in favor of someone who would carry on the struggle. He could not expose the Guatemalan people to a bloodbath in order to maintain his own vocation.

That evening, the leaders of the PGT went to the presidential palace and met with Arbenz Guzmán in his office. They were shaken to see the man they held in such high regard being brought so low. They told the president that "resistance was still possible, that they could still win—if he armed the people."[23]

As Arbenz listened, he seemed to become energized once again. But even as he nodded assent, the president acknowledged that the situation was quite different from any they had ever faced before. On two previous occasions, when the army had cooperated in arming civilians, his enemies were Guatemala's homegrown counterrevolutionaries. Now, his principal enemy was one not of his choosing, the United States. Personal loyalties were not enough to motivate his officer corps to take on the U.S. Marines in the absence of any sense of militarist brotherhood or patriotism. If the army would not fight, its officers certainly would not allow him to arm civilians to do so. Only his own resignation would make the United States leave Guatemala to work out its own destiny. At least, that was Arbenz Guzmán's hope.

On Sunday morning, 27 June, word reached Arbenz that a CIA plane in Puerto San José had sunk a Norwegian freighter, the *Springfjord*, registered to a British company, on the Pacific Coast. If the president needed any more convincing evidence that Eisenhower would stop at nothing to rid Guatemala of his administration, the attack on a ship flying the British flag provided it.

The attack on the *Springfjord* was the handiwork of the CIA's Rip Robertson and Nicaragua's dictator, Anastacio Somoza. Somoza, long fed up with the slow progress of Castillo Armas—whom he referred to as "that little prick"[24]—had told Robertson to bomb the ship because it was carrying fuel . for Arbenz's army. Robertson asked permission from Opa-Locka. Haney and Barnes suggested he use frogmen to do the job so as to be in a position to deny responsibility for the attack.

Somoza was furious with Opa-Locka's answer. "If you use my airfields, you take my orders,"[25] he yelled at Robertson. Robertson complied, sending Ferdinand Shoup to execute the mission. One 500-pound bomb down the *Springfjord*'s smokestack did the job.

The freighter's cargo turned out to be cotton and coffee heading for British shores. Frank Wisner went that morning to the British embassy to apologize. Later, the CIA agreed to pay $1.5 million in damages to *Springfjord*'s insurers.

That same Sunday morning, Foreign Minister Guillermo Toriello went to the American ambassador without Arbenz's knowledge and asked the diplomat if the United States would be willing to accept a ruling military junta if the president resigned. Peurifoy was noncommittal.

A little later, the ambassador received a telephone call from Chief of the Army Colonel Carlos Enrique Díaz, inviting him to the officer's home. There, Peurifoy met with Díaz, Army Chief of Staff Colonel Enrique Parinello, Defense Minister Colonel José Angel Sánchez, Chief of the Air Force Colonel Luis Girón, and President of the Superior Defense Council Colonel Carlos Sartí, all close friends of the president, each of whom considered himself an *Arbenzcista* loyalist. Díaz told Peurifoy that he and his four colleagues had agreed that they should tell Arbenz he must resign. In return, the United

States had to give up on the incompetent, hated Castillo Armas. The officers told the ambassador that it was unthinkable that Castillo Armas could ever lead Guatemala.[26]

Peurifoy answered that he had little say in the matter, but that once Arbenz was gone, he was sure that all other issues would be open for discussion. Some minutes later, back in his office, the ambassador telegraphed Washington: "Situation appears to be breaking."[27]

As Sunday wore on, La Voz de la Liberación radio broadcasts became more triumphant. Guatemalans, a small jubilant minority made up of well-to-do landowners, bishops, priests, nuns, businessmen, religious devotees of the archbishop, and an organized group of the capital's market women, recited prayers of thanksgiving. Many others, a majority of the nation's citizens, including small and medium landowners, businessmen, merchants, teachers, workers, and peasants, all tense and fearful, listened as Liberación announcers predicted the imminent demise of President Jacobo Arbenz Guzmán. Two columns of citizen soldiers, God's Army, consisting of approximately 2,500 men each, were said to be marching on Guatemala City from Zacapa at that very moment. The announcer said that they expected to be in the capital within a day or so, when Guatemala would once more be "counted among the free nations of the globe." Fleeing urbanites and peasants were asked to stay off the roads so as not to complicate the advances of the surging insurgency forces.

The broadcasts, like much of the CIA's PBSuccess, were pure theater. But they worked their magic.

Up in Huehuetenango, the Maryknoll priests were ecstatic. They had been listening to the Voice of America English-language broadcasts for ten days. On 18 June, they heard one Morgan Bailey say, "The people are dancing in the streets tonight. Her own exiled sons have invaded Guatemala. Upwards of 5,000 well-armed and even better-trained soldiers are taking off in their transports—their landing fields, The Land of Eternal Spring."

In the archiepiscopal palace in Guatemala City, there was much joy as well. Archbishop Mariano Rossell y Arellano had played a singular role in the approaching collapse of the Arbenz Guzmán government and the Ten Years of Spring. After sponsoring the national procession of the imitation Black

Christ of Esquipulas—a fitting icon for the imitation freedom about to descend on his country—and issuing his pastoral letter calling on all Catholics to rise up against Arbenz Guzmán, he had personally gone to American Ambassador Peurifoy to beg the diplomat to bring U.S. forces into the country against the Guatemalan president. His efforts were now bearing fruit. He believed that Catholic Castillo Armas and Protestant Dwight Eisenhower would be God's instruments in restoring the Catholic Church to its pre-Independence power and glory.

Twenty-five hundred miles to the north, at the New York Catholic archdiocesan chancery office, a short, rotund cardinal, America's number one anticommunist religious personality, accepted congratulations from his chancellor for the successful play he had made in favor of Guatemala's Roman Catholic establishment and America's anticommunist foreign policy. Francis Cardinal Spellman's influence with the Maryknoll Society had been instrumental in bringing Archbishop Rossell and the CIA together.

President Jacobo Arbenz Guzmán, meanwhile, had accepted the inevitable, and had set himself, with the help of Manuel Fortuny, the secretary general of the PGT, to preparing an emotional speech of resignation addressed to the Guatemalan people.

Chapter 15

THE EDUCATION OF A CLERICAL CONSCIENCE

Two months after the overthrow of President Arbenz Guzmán, Ron Hennessey, vaguely aware of events in Guatemala, boarded a train in Marion, Iowa, immediate destination, Chicago. There, he would catch a Greyhound bus for Scranton, Pennsylvania, a few miles from Maryknoll's Junior Seminary at Clarks Summit.[1] As he settled into his coach seat and gazed out the dirty, double-paned, plexiglass window, a feeling of inadequacy invaded his thoughts. He drew a deep breath and exhaled slowly through pursed lips.

Five minutes later, hypnotized by the clackety-clack of steel against steel, the Iowan had put aside his vocational doubts and dozed off. It was late August 1954.

A day after arriving at the seminary, Ron was sitting on the edge of a two-tiered bunk in a large dormitory where a welcoming committee of three seminarians had left him after showing him around his new home. Although he had graduated from high school in 1947, Maryknoll's admissions committee felt that a repeat year of high school training with emphasis on Latin would retool his study habits to prepare him for a strenuous diet of college classes emphasizing scholastic philosophy, social studies, Church history, biblical analysis, and a foreign language.

Ron's clerical education began while he was still trying to digest the social and physical reality of his new surroundings. A few minutes after the welcoming committee had left him, the rector, Father John Elwood, a robust man with curly black hair and wearing a long black cassock, the clerical symbol of worldly renunciation, came by to extend his welcome. The priest was pleasant enough but no less authoritarian: "You'll have to get rid of that Hawaiian shirt, Brother Hennessey, and accustom yourself to wearing more conservative clothes."

Ron stood stiffly and nodded his agreement.

"Also, you are required to write a letter home every Sunday and leave it unsealed," Elwood said, folding his big arms across his chest as if to signal that he would tolerate no opposition. "It's one of the ways we have for checking your spiritual and emotional development."

Father Elwood paused and watched Hennessey for his reactions, but detected no change in the friendly smile the newcomer had retained since their greeting. Finally, Ron realized that the priest was waiting for a response.

"That's fine, father. I have a few rough edges from the army, but I'm sure I can adjust quickly."

"As a matter of fact, I think your army training will stand you in good stead here," the priest answered. "The discipline, following orders, the self-control, these are all important aspects of seminary and priestly life."

Again Ron nodded. It had not occurred to him that his new life might be anything like a replay of his old army days, but it made sense.

"Also," Fr. Elwood added, "you can have visitors once a month, on the first Sunday of each month. Only members of your immediate family. The regimen here is one of prayer, meditation, physical labor, and study. A stream of visitors would interfere."

"That's fine, father. I don't expect anyone to trek out here from Iowa to see me."

Elwood nodded, smiled, shook hands, and turned on his heel. "I think you'll do all right," he called as he went out the door.

The following day, the dormitory began to fill up with new and returning students. Many were Ron's age, several military veterans, others who had a couple of years of college, some who had left school and taken jobs before deciding to become priests. They were given "special student" status and separated out from the high school seminarians. Orientation sessions had already begun, where rules and regulations were explained. There was to be no talking at anytime anywhere in the building above the first floor. The

Magnum Silencium, the Great Silence, was mandated from 9:00 o'clock evening prayers until the end of breakfast the next morning, every day, on all floors, as well as outside the building. Also, there was to be no conversation at meals, during which a student lector would read from the monthly diaries sent in from Maryknoll missioners across the globe, or from some inspirational book.

On Saturday afternoons, the seminarians could obtain permission for walks off grounds into the surrounding Pennsylvania countryside in groups of three or more. A slip of paper had to be handed in with the names of those who made up each group, the purpose being to see that no cliques or "particular friendships" developed between students. Underlying the fear of such friendships, though never openly stated, was the number one bugaboo of sacerdotal sanctity, sex. Not so much sexual activity as such, though that was always a consideration, but sexual thoughts, sexual desires, sexual inclinations, where one could not be distinguished from the other, and the line between venial sin (punishment: purgatory) and mortal sin (punishment: hell) could be crossed in the blinking of an eye. Such was the beginning of a clerical regimen of physical and emotional isolation that in many cases—though not in Hennessey's—would undermine the very vocation it was meant to promote.

As the days turned into weeks, Ron adapted to the seminary regimen without any serious setbacks. As a farm and Korean veteran, he was the oldest of his classmates, giving him status as "senior student" with responsibility for serving as his classmates' spokesman in dealing with the faculty, particularly the seminary's rector. His natural self-control, appreciation of others' perspectives, and good humor all contributed to his fitting in with both faculty and classmates. They, in turn, gave him a level of respect that he found amusing. This, in spite of the fact that he sometimes played the role—as he had in the army—of a country bumpkin.

One aspect of seminary life that bothered Ron was the servile attitude that students were expected to show priests as a salute to their exalted status. Seminarians were assigned to make the priests' beds, clean their rooms, and wait on them in their refectory. And more often than not, gruff commands or complaints about service were the only recognition the seminarians could expect for their efforts. It reminded Hennessey of the demands that officers made on enlisted men, something the Iowan had not expected from the clergy. Father McElliott, pastor in his hometown, had always been so friendly and jovial that Hennessey thought that a pleasant disposition was a necessary personality trait for all priests. The personal power of some over others, whether it was political, economic, or religious, never appealed to the young Iowan's sense of self-worth or the value he placed on the autonomy of others.

On more than one occasion, a priestly criticism would be met with the Iowan's disarming humor. When the rector suggested that an increase in refectory cockroaches was due to Ron's lack of persistent cleanliness, Hennessey, as head refectorian, responded that he was meeting the challenge by building a small kitchen shrine to Francis of Assisi, hoping that the gentle saint would take a page from the book of Saint Patrick who is said to have charmed all the snakes out of the Emerald Isle.

The rector smiled appreciatively, then added that he thought Saint Francis might need the assistance of a little earthly elbow grease.

Ron replied that he would see what he could come up with.

In the academic sphere, Latin, a class taught by Father Francis "Torchy" Donnelly, was a challenge for Hennessey. Ron wasn't sure whether the name "Torchy" originated with the priest's red hair or his explosive Irish temper. Every morning's class became a battle of wills, with Torchy yelling at the ex-farmer for his inability to eliminate his Iowa nasal twang when reading the Latin text. Even when Ron finally did get the pronunciations right, he sometimes intentionally mispronounced the words in order, he maintained, to give the priest the opportunity to practice priestly patience. He also guaranteed that Torchy would immediately call on the next student to recite. The little ritual invariably elicited surreptitious smiles from Ron's classmates.

Early on, Father Elwood introduced the neophyte to some of the ramifications of sacerdotal celibacy. When a Jesuit priest, a Father Kelley, brought his 12-year-old niece dressed in shorts and tank top from Scranton to the seminary to watch his Jesuit high school track team compete against the Maryknoll seminarians, the red-faced rector hailed Ron, walking down the corridor nearby. "Brother Hennessey," the rector called in a voice reflecting a pronounced undertone of anger, "go tell Fr. Weiss, the athletic director, to come to my office immediately. He ought to have more sense than to allow young girls dressed like that onto our grounds."

As Ron nodded and turned away, the priest called after him, "And you tell him to knock on my door before entering."

Hmm, Ron thought, *that should show Fr. Weiss who's boss around here! But I should think the rector would recognize that anyone who gets excited by seeing a 12-year-old girl in shorts and tank top should be looking for another line of work.*

It was the first of many lessons the Iowan would learn as to the lengths some priests felt it necessary to go in order to preserve themselves, their colleagues, and their charges from the temptations of female flesh, fostering attitudes that were basically misogynistic. For a man coming from a close-knit family with eight sisters such sentiments were initially a source of wonder. Later, as Maryknoll superior in Guatemala, Ron would meet like attitudes in fellow priests with either an apology or a wisecrack, depending on the individual involved. When an aged, over-the-hill Father Bernie Murray complained to Hennessey that the Maryknoll Sisters were using a bathroom in the Guatemala priests' center house and that "fornication would be the likely result if the practice continues," Ron responded with a comic's straight face, "Whenever you feel the temptation coming on, Bernie, let me know and I'll get you the bucket of ice water I keep in my room for just such occasions." Father Murray walked off in a state of utter confusion, not knowing if Hennessey was "out of his gourd," or if ice-cold water was intended by the superior to be a realistic answer to temptations of the flesh.

Ron would later state after he had come to terms with—though not a happy acceptance of—such attitudes that he felt that of the three evangelical virtues, faith, hope, and charity, the most important of these for a seminarian or priest was chastity, followed closely by obedience.

Television was permitted the seminarians for sporting events that coincided with weekend free time, or to watch the televised philosophy lessons of America's most renowned Roman Catholic prelate, Monsignor Fulton J. Sheen.

Monsignor Sheen's favorite topic was to prove the existence of God and, by extension, to debunk Marxism/communism. One particular broadcast that made an impression on Hennessey was Monsignor Sheen's insistence that one of humanity's unique characteristics, its sense of humor, was incontrovertible evidence that God existed and that humankind had been created in His image and likeness. The argument rested on the human ability of abstraction. Ron read it differently. He wasn't sure whether the learned monsignor meant that God's preeminent creation was an expression of the divine sense of humor—which was a question he sometimes asked himself— or whether those who laughed at life were more like God than those who couldn't. *If sanctity means being funny,* the Iowan told himself, *then maybe there is some hope for the likes of me.*

It was Monsignor Sheen who reminded Hennessey that Guatemala was the only country in the world whose citizenry was able to rid itself of a communist government. This news item made a more favorable impression on the Iowa farmer than when he had first heard it through Foster Dulles's speech, since he had only recently learned that Maryknoll missioners were stationed there. But with no knowledge of Cardinal Spellman's brokerage via Maryknoll in the anti-Arbenz Guzmán crusade, he continued to wonder if Guatemala's Catholicism and Maryknoll's evangelizing efforts had played any role in motivating the people to stand up to communism.

Ron had his answer when, during breakfast one morning, the lector read a mission diary written by a Maryknoller serving in Guatemala. The author told how he and his pastor had encouraged a group of their young Mayan parishioners, drafted to fight for the presidency of Arbenz Guzmán by the local military commissioner, to "put their faith first."

"But how shall we know on whose side we should fight, padre?" many of the men had asked their pastor when they came to say good-bye.

"Just look for the ones with rosary beads around their necks," the priest had replied again and again. "They're the ones on our side."

With each admonition, the priest had slipped a string of beads into the hands of the departing man and sent him off with a sacerdotal blessing.

Most of the mission diaries tended to be anecdotal, with little information on the regional and national economic and political context within which the missioners labored. Ron found himself thirsting for a more complete exposition of the countries and cultures in which the Maryknollers worked. Diary authors generally limited themselves to telling humorous stories about the missionaries' cultural and linguistic missteps, or recounting touching demonstrations of faith in the face of grinding poverty, sickness, and death, or chronicles of deathbed conversions of public sinners. It was as if each missioner were isolated from the rest of the world, with important events ending at his parish boundaries. As far as the Maryknollers in Guatemala were concerned, the communists' atheism and consequent anticlericalism was sufficiently explained by their ideology.

Ron never heard any mention in the Guatemalan diaries of the historic struggle between the landless peasants and the landowning oligarchs for possession of the land. On the contrary, there were many references to Maryknoll's wealthy Guatemalan friends, large landowners among them, as well as the missioners' close relationships with the local directors of American companies and the spontaneous "social" visits by FBI agents, U.S. military attachés, and embassy personnel looking for political and cultural insights. No mention in the diaries was ever made of John Peurifoy, Foster Dulles, or President Eisenhower. What little was said about the fight between Castillo Armas and Arbenz Guzmán was portrayed, not as one to determine the distribution of the country's natural resources, but as a struggle between God and the devil.

Such was the perspective evoked by the missioners' diaries. Ron listened to these accounts with heightened interest. The Iowan's return from Korea ten months earlier meant that he still harbored vivid memories of the hatred, destruction, and death in a land where the people, though the majority were non-Christian, seemed to be of God's chosen ones. He had come to believe that the popular explanation for that war of brother against brother, that is, communism and evil leaders, left much to be desired. Yet, here were Maryknollers giving a similar explanation with a few novel wrinkles for events in Guatemala.

Ever ready to question his own fix on events, Hennessey decided that he'd have to pay close attention to what the Maryknollers had to say about Guatemala. Maybe his own ideas about the complexity of the Korean conflict were themselves simplistic? The obviously racist and gung ho attitudes of some of his former army buddies and superiors had rendered their explanation of the war suspect almost from the day of his induction. Priests with years of experience in Guatemala were giving a similar explanation for the country's civil conflict, while racism and gender insecurity could not be construed as sources of clerical bias. Or could they?

To follow up on the Guatemalan situation, Hennessey visited the seminary library where a smattering of secular magazines was available, among the more numerous religious publications. *Time* and *Newsweek* became his channel to the outside world. But Guatemala, once Arbenz Guzmán was gone, was of no concern to the editors of *Time* and *Newsweek*.

In the evening of 27 June 1954, the Guatemalan people listened to the taped address of Colonel Jacobo Arbenz Guzmán as he announced his resignation on the government radio transmitter, a transmission the CIA tried to block with only partial success. His voice burdened by emotion, the president told his countrymen that he was turning over his office to his loyal friend, Colonel Carlos Enrique Díaz, in order to preserve the gains of the October revolution and to avoid the bloodbath that the United States seemed determined to inflict on the Guatemalan people. With prophetic insight that underestimated by two decades the time frame of the scourge that would befall his country if the revolution were betrayed, he added, referring to his anointed successor's administration, "a government, although different from mine, that is still inspired by our October revolution is preferable to twenty years of bloody tyranny under the men whom Castillo Armas has brought into the country."[3]

There was reason for Arbenz's optimism, pale as it was. When Carlos Enrique Díaz spoke to the president earlier in the day to deliver the high command's demand for his resignation, the colonel told Arbenz that Ambassador Peurifoy had promised that the United States would allow him, Díaz, to assume the presidency and would withdraw support from Castillo Armas if only Arbenz resigned and he, again Díaz, rounded up all the communists.

Peurifoy, of course, had promised no such thing. It was wishful thinking on Díaz's part, reading into the ambassador's words that such issues as Arbenz's successor and support for Castillo Armas could be decided once Arbenz was gone. Peurifoy had intentionally misled Díaz by telling the colonel that "if he [Díaz] appointed reasonable men to his cabinet, I was sure all our secondary problems could be worked out, such as difficulties of American companies."[4]

Arbenz believed that Díaz knew what he was talking about. The president questioned his friend on the ambassador's state of mind, then reluctantly agreed that he would resign once Díaz swore that he would be faithful to the principles and spirit of the October revolution and promised to never negotiate with "that traitor," Castillo Armas.

After the president's farewell address, Colonel Díaz followed Arbenz on the air. He then repeated what he had told Arbenz: that he was taking over the government, that he would carry out the constitution and laws of the October revolution, and that "the struggle against the mercenary invaders of Guatemala will not abate."[5]

As John Doherty, the CIA station chief in Guatemala, and Enno Hobbing, the former correspondent of *Time* magazine brought aboard to help write the new government's constitution, listened to the Arbenz and Díaz broadcasts, they could hardly contain themselves. The two men immediately contacted Ambassador Peurifoy with the suggestion that they dump Díaz posthaste. The diplomat, having heard the two speeches, replied with a touch of anger, "Washington is happy enough that you've gotten rid of Arbenz. From now on, I don't care what the hell you do. Just leave me out of it."[6]

The two agents jumped in their car, picked up Colonel Elfegio Monzón, a nonideological, anti-Arbenz plotter possessed of a personal agenda with whom they had already negotiated, and headed for Díaz's office. Once there Doherty, inspired by the hubris and infallibility generally reserved for papal envoys, wasted no time launching an assault on Arbenz, the October revolution, the "communist" policies of the Arbenz regime, and its communist allies. When Díaz started to defend the advances made during the previous ten years, Hobbing cut him off: "Wait a minute, colonel. Let me explain something to you. You made a big mistake when you took over the government. Colonel, you are just not convenient for the requirements of American foreign policy."[7]

Colonel Díaz protested that he had an agreement with Ambassador Peurifoy to take over the presidency and had received the diplomat's okay for the tenor of his speech.

Doherty and Hobbing shook their heads.

"I want to hear it from the ambassador," Díaz replied.

An hour later, Peurifoy, accompanied by the two agents, was in Díaz's office. The ambassador expressed his outrage that Díaz would allow Arbenz to accuse the United States of sponsoring Castillo Armas's forces. "This being your first act, I do not see how we can work together to bring about a peace."[8] He then suggested that Díaz step down and designate Colonel Elfegio Monzón as president.

Díaz said he would have an answer for the ambassador later that same day. It was by now 6:00 a.m., 28 June, the back-and-forth, largely one-sided negotiations having proceeded during the entire night.

At noon, Peurifoy was again in Díaz's office. This time, Díaz was one step ahead of the American diplomat: "I have asked Colonel Monzón and Colonel Angel Sánchez to join me in forming a three-man junta to run the government."

Peurifoy seethed. Díaz still did not understand that the American government was not only determined to rid Guatemala of Arbenz, but of everyone and everything that had been part of the October revolution. As far as Peurifoy was concerned, the Ten Years of Spring had come to a dead end and Díaz with them. Who the hell did these Guatemalans think they were? The ambassador turned on his heel and left. He then contacted Doherty and Hobbing and asked them to send a telegram to Opa-Locka, "We have been double-crossed. BOMB!" [9]

Two hours later, Jerry DeLarm flew over Guatemala City in his P-47, accompanied by a pair of fighters. He bombed Fort Matamoros and the government's radio station then headed back to Honduras.

Díaz got the message. At 5:00 p.m., with discouragement bordering on despair, he met with Peurifoy and agreed to talk with Castillo Armas. He requested two conditions: that the ambassador order an immediate cease-fire and that the papal nuncio, Archbishop Genaro Verolino, be present at the talks as a neutral observer.

Peurifoy agreed, dropping the pretense that he did not control Castillo Armas. He also accepted the nuncio's participation even though Verolino had been sympathetic to the policies of the Arbenz government, particularly where the president, at the nuncio's request, had allowed foreign priests, including the Maryknollers, to enter the country to proselytize. Verolino had clashed with Archbishop Rossell y Arellano on more than one occasion due to the latter's public declarations of undisguised hatred for the president and his administration. But in recent days, acting like the representative of a world power in its own right and reading the writing on the wall, the nuncio had been expressing more sympathy toward the Liberator. Díaz then asked for more time to confer with his two junta colleagues regarding Peurifoy's suggestion that the talks take place in San Salvador, El Salvador's capital.

That night, about 2:00 a.m. on Tuesday, Peurifoy telephoned Díaz to tell him that he had spoken to the Salvadoran ambassador and had arranged that San Salvador would be the site for the talks. He then asked if he could meet with the colonel to settle the details.

Díaz, not knowing what Peurifoy had in mind, agreed.

At 4:00 a.m., Peurifoy was again at Díaz's office. Colonel Sánchez was also present, but Colonel Monzón was conspicuously absent. Díaz informed the ambassador that he and his two colleagues had agreed to talk with Castillo Armas and that the negotiations could be held in San Salvador.

Peurifoy nodded his approval. But just then the telephone rang. Díaz picked it up and spoke in a muffled voice, his back to the ambassador. When he hung up, the colonel, a concerned look on his face, signaled Sánchez to follow him out the door. While the two officers were gone, Peurifoy remained alone in the room. A minute later, Colonel Martin, the U.S. air attaché, burst in to tell Peurifoy that a plot was afoot to assassinate Díaz and Sánchez, and that he had better leave the building at once. The ambassador spent a moment wondering if he might be caught in the crossfire, but finally decided to remain,[10] sparking speculation that the plot had his approval.

A few moments later, a shaken Colonel Díaz returned. "Colonel Sánchez and I have decided to retire from the junta, Mr. Peurifoy. It seems that some of our colleagues think that neither of us would prove acceptable to Castillo Armas. So, in order to avoid any squabbling, the two of us . . . ." He shrugged his shoulders, turned and left the office.

At that very moment, Colonel Monzón entered the premises with a group of officers. Their apparent intention was to kill Díaz and Sánchez on the spot. When they saw that Peurifoy was present, however, they pretended only to want to confer with the two colonels. But Díaz and Sánchez had already been warned of the plot by someone in their personal networks and were then on their way out of the building. The ambassador's presence may have saved their lives.[11]

Minutes later, Colonel Monzón approached Peurifoy and remarked, "My colleague, Colonel Díaz, has decided to resign. I am replacing him."[12] Later, he told the ambassador that he was forming a new junta with Lt. Colonels Mauricio Dubois and José Luis Cruz Salazar as members. "We will negotiate with Castillo Armas but hope that you can stop his attacks in the meantime."[13]

Peurifoy smiled and said he would see what he could do. Neither man doubted that the ambassador need only say the word to stop the bombings. That same day, Colonel Elfegio Monzón flew to San Salvador with Papal Nuncio Verolino in Ambassador Peurifoy's plane. Colonel Martin, the U.S. air attaché, was at the controls. In the meantime, Assistant Secretary of State Henry Holland through the Honduran government had made contact with Castillo Armas. Castillo Armas was then flown to San Salvador via Nicaragua on Colonel Martin's second flight. Peurifoy remained in Guatemala on Foster Dulles's orders in order to keep a low profile and obscure the U.S. role in the whole sordid affair.

After some hours of unfruitful negotiations, Monzón and Castillo Armas had failed to reach an agreement regarding the Liberator's demands that he alone assume the presidency and be given total control of the army. The U.S. ambassador to El Salvador, Michael McDermott, then wired Foster Dulles that the talks were at an impasse, and needed Peurifoy's input. Washington passed the information to Peurifoy along with Dulles's authorization "to crack some heads together."[14] The ambassador then headed south.

At El Salvador's presidential palace, Peurifoy met first with Castillo Armas, but the colonel wanted nothing to do with Monzón. "I will have to talk to my men and see what they think about my participation in a junta headed by Monzón."

"Why do you have to ask anyone?" the ambassador responded, a feigned look of surprise on his face. "I thought you were the boss of your movement. If you're not the top man, bring in whoever is so I can talk to him!"[15]

The Liberator did a double take and had no answer to the ambassador's caustic remark.

While Castillo Armas pondered the ambassador's words, Peurifoy went off to speak to Monzón. He had no trouble convincing Monzón to accept Castillo Armas and Major Enrique Trinidad Oliva, the *Liberacionistas'* second-in-command, as members of his junta.[16] When Peurifoy returned, he found Castillo Armas willing to go along with Monzón for the time being, but still not happy with the arrangement.

Peurifoy, Castillo Armas, and Major Oliva walked together down the hall to a conference room where Colonel Monzón was waiting with Colonel Mauricio Dubois, the second member of his junta. Colonel José Luis Cruz

Salazar, the third member, was missing.[17] After all shook hands, it was quickly agreed that the new junta would have five members, the four officers present plus Colonel Cruz Salazar. It was also agreed that all hostilities would end immediately, that a new constitution would be formulated to replace that of 1945, and that all members of the Arbenz Guzmán administration and the leaders of the Partido Guatemalteco de Trabajo (PGT), the Communist Party, would be arrested and tried.[18] A photo showed Castillo Armas and Monzón giving each other a stiff *abrazo*, sealing the pact.

Archbishop Verolino then read a message from Archbishop Rossell y Arellano to Castillo Armas:

> I send you warm greetings and fervent congratulations in the name of the nation that awaits you with open arms, recognizing and admiring your sincere patriotism. May our Lord God guide you and your heroic companions in your liberating campaign against atheistic communism. You all have my pastoral benediction.[19]

With Arbenz Guzmán gone from the scene, Foster Dulles and President Eisenhower continued to deny to their fellow citizens any U.S. involvement in the overthrow of the Guatemalan president. Peurifoy knew, however, that such a charade was useless as far as the Guatemalan people were concerned. As a result, the ambassador decided to invite Castillo Armas to fly with him in his official plane from San Salvador to Guatemala City after completing the negotiations with Colonel Monzón.

The idea that the triumphant Liberator would return to his homeland in the plane of the U.S. ambassador did not appeal to the reluctant warrior. Castillo Armas wanted to go back to Chiquimula and march on the capital at the head of his ragtag troops, like a conquering *caudillo*. But Peurifoy prevailed once again, arguing that his return to Guatemala, accompanied by the other four junta members and by mediator Verolino on the U.S. ambassador's plane, would give a palpable demonstration of the cohesion existing between the principal power blocs in the country.

When the plane landed at La Aurora Airport, Peurifoy was the first to emerge, followed by the papal nuncio and the five junta members. The nuncio stepped up to the microphone and asked God's blessing on his fellow passengers and those gathered to greet them. Then Castillo Armas, not a good public speaker, stepped up and mumbled how happy he was to be back in his beloved Guatemala. Peurifoy was encouraged to speak but only answered with a *"qué viva Guatemala."* The Salvadoran ambassador Funes closed out the celebration with a few words on how delighted he and his government were to have contributed to the happiness of Guatemala.

The date was 3 July 1954.

Chapter 16

A Theological Dilemma

"Padre, we got big problems with *los muchachos*," sighed the lanky Mayan after settling uncomfortably into the large rope-weave chair offered him by the priest.

It was a month after the army's nocturnal attack on San Mateo and Milenario Pérez, the "health promotor" from San Francisco, had come in to consult with Hennessey.

"They make us kill the *patron*'s cows so they have meat. If the soldiers find out, they kill us . . . . You make the guerrillas stop!"

Hennessey swallowed, taken aback by the man's naive belief that his pastor had such authority with the EGP.

"What makes you think the EGP would listen to me, Milenario?"

The man shrugged. "*El pueblo dice* . . . . The people say . . . ."

The Iowan waited. But Milenario refused to continue.

"I've had nothing to do with the guerrillas other than talk with a few about the morality of what they're doing . . . . And I don't think they are paying much attention."

Milenario wasn't listening.

The priest nodded his head, took a deep breath. "Come on, Milenario, let's have some coffee."

Milenario Pérez lived with his wife and four children as a tenant farmer with sixty other Mateano families on Colonel Victor Bolaños's *finca,* San Francisco, a seven-hour walk north of town. Milenario was an old friend of previous pastors, having been a volunteer catechist for many years. When Bill Mullan turned over the parish to Hennessey, he told the Iowan that Milenario was one of the more reliable volunteers in the parish administration.

"The *muchachos* came to San Francisco two weeks ago," Milenario continued once he had politely tasted his thick, black coffee. "They make us go to a meeting. They say the *patrón* make us work for land stolen from our ancestors. That he live without working in Guatemala City. But they not know that the *patrón* is good to us, that he get us title to lands in Yulaurel."

"Did you tell them that?"

"They not listen! They butcher one cow and say we give one every time they come to the *finca*. They come again yesterday."

Milenario was in his late thirties, stood about five feet ten inches, tall for a Mayan, somewhat thin-faced, with deep-set, bright eyes, topped by thick, black eyebrows, and a turned-down mouth. He was a serious man, possessing little of the Mateanos' light sense of humor. "What are the other folks at San Francisco thinking? Do they believe the guerrillas can help them get back their lands?"

"No, padre! Everyone be angry! The guerrillas threaten us, say they kill us if we not give them a cow when they come. But we not want them to kill the *patrón*'s cows. We love those beasts . . . like our own children! I almost cry!"

Hennessey nodded. As a life-long farmer, he knew what it meant to form a particular feeling for each of the animals he cared for. "What makes you think they would listen to me?"

"Some *muchachos* are *de la doctrina*, Catholics, padre. We think the leaders are Catholics, some catechists. The people listen to you."

Hennessey hesitated. He had known almost from his arrival in the parish that some of his parishioners, even catechists, were supporting the EGP. But he had not considered it reason enough for anyone to look to him as having some sort of authoritative standing with them. He shook his head.

Then, changing the subject, he asked, "What does *don* Francisco say about this?"

Hennessey was referring to Francisco Paiz García, the wise old foreman and natural leader of the Mateanos on Colonel Bolaños's ranch. The priest had talked at length with Francisco on the three visits he had made to the *aldea*, spending several hours each time learning the ways and lore of San

Francisco and its environs from the mouth of an oracle. A strong bond of mutual friendship had quickly developed between the slow-moving, lanky Iowan and the slow moving, heavily built Mateano, based on a shared love of a good laugh and an insatiable curiosity regarding each other's background and culture.

Hennessey's affection and appreciation for the ranch foreman and his family was something that would later bring the priest great emotional pain. Even the death of his beloved father in early 1965 did not cause the distress that would soon envelop his soul.

"Francisco not know what to do, padre," the *promotor* answered. "The first time the guerrillas come, they hog-tie Francisco and tell us they kill him as the example. We tell them Francisco be a poor *indio* like us. They let him go. They say if he serve the *patrón* against us, they kill him. Poor Francisco! The guerrillas blame him if we not give them cows. The army blame him if we do . . . . He tell me go ask the padre."

Hennessey took a deep breath. Francisco had been the one man he had begun to think might provide some ideas as to how his parishioners should relate to the EGP. He sat looking at his visitor, saddened by his response. How many times had he heard variations on this fatalistic theme? He had spent the first couple of years in Guatemala trying to develop an appreciation in the Maya for the power of positive thinking. But by the time he had completed his first year in Petén's colonization project, he had concluded that Guatemala's social system guaranteed that all Mayan attempts to pick themselves up by their bootstraps were destined to provoke organized ladino opposition; that fatalism or rebellion were the only reasonable alternatives. It was a question of which alternative was God's will. Fatalism, after so many lost battles, was the traditional Mayan answer. But now it was losing its appeal among a growing segment of San Mateo's younger population.

Milenario stood up to leave. The Iowan reached out and grabbed the extended hand and pulled Milenario toward him, placing his other hand on the health promoter's shoulder. "Cheer up, Milenario! God will take care of us!" the priest said, forcing a note of animation into his voice to camouflage his lack of conviction.

Milenario looked away, but he returned the pressure of the Iowan's hand. Then, he turned toward the door and was gone.

Two days later, Sister Justa came by the rectory to say that a catechist from Bulej was waiting to see him.

"Ask him to come in and join me for a cup of coffee, *Hermana.* I get lonely here snacking by myself."

A few minutes later, Diego Pérez, the senior catechist from Bulej, a village about sixteen kilometers north of San Mateo and eight kilometers southwest of San Francisco, appeared at the rectory door. Diego held the position of *animador de la fé* (faith animator) in Bulej, allowing him to distribute holy communion in the padre's absence, and even administer infant baptism when the danger of death was imminent, a not uncommon occurrence. His principal occupation, however, was to teach Catholic doctrine. The expansion of his liturgical duties was of recent implementation, the result of the Maryknollers' eagerness—flowing from the spirit of the Second Vatican Council—to introduce lay people into . their evangelical and liturgical ministries.

Hennessey had passed the night in Diego's thatch-and-mud home on each of his visits to Bulej and had recognized an intelligence and determination that made him exceptionally willing to verbalize his resentment of ladino domination of Mayan society. At the same time, the *animador* had been noticeably silent about what he and others might do to challenge the situation, even when Hennessey tangentially brought up the subject of the guerrillas. The priest had looked upon Diego's reticence as an indication that he was probably more supportive of the EGP than he was willing to let on at the time.

As Diego settled into his chair, Hennessey hoped that their conversation was not going to be a repeat of the one he had had with Milenario two days earlier. The *animador* quickly disabused the Iowan of that notion.

"Padre, Milenario say he talk to you a few days ago. He say I should tell you what happen at El Campamento two days ago."

The priest nodded his encouragement but said nothing.

Diego waited. Then, slowly, he added, "Two days ago ten soldiers kill five *indios* in El Campamento. Those be the lands where your friend, *el señor* Widman, claims be his."

Again the *animador* paused, wanting the priest to react.

After several seconds of silence, the *animador* recognized that he had to try a different tack if he wanted Hennessey's input. "You remember we talk about the problems in El Campamento when you be in Bulej?"

"I remember you told me that those lands belonged to Bulej and that Widman has been trying to steal them for years . . . . I also remember telling you that I know Walter Widman, that he's a friend of some of the priests and nuns . . . . That does not make him a friend of mine, just an acquaintance."

Walter Widman was a wealthy landowner who lived in Guatemala City but whose principal lands were in the Pacific-coast region. He was a handsome man with light hair and an athletic build, the son of a German immigrant father who bequeathed to him the stern orderliness of Germanic culture, and a Colombian mother who taught him to take a personal interest in all who worked for and with him. He combined both attributes to turn his father's *finca* into a trampoline for floating bank loans to acquire more plantations, including a major interest in Guatemala's largest sugar refinery. In his ambitious climb to wealth and social status, he also acquired Mayan lands in San Mateo territory that had never been legally registered. Such lands included El Campamento, site of a small Mateano village located equidistant from Bulej and San Francisco, several kilometers from each.

Educated in the United States, Widman had sent his three oldest children to the United States for the same purpose. But when he decided not to send his two youngest daughters abroad, he lobbied long and hard in the late 1940s and early 1950s with Archbishop Rossell and a group of wealthy Guatemalans to get the Maryknoll Sisters to establish a Catholic school in Guatemala City to provide an English-language education for the daughters of the country's economic and political elite. The rationale for the Maryknoll Sisters to accept the plan was that they would have the opportunity to form the consciences of the daughters of the country's power brokers, girls who eventually would be the wives and mothers of Guatemala's leaders, thereby beginning, hopefully, a moral reform of the whole society.

Widman's success in using his political contacts with the Arévalo and Arbenz governments to obtain permits for the school's scholastic accreditation, his assistance in lining up qualified teachers to help staff the school, and his personal generosity in providing for the nuns' physical well-being, cemented a relationship of friendship with many Maryknollers. It was a relationship that lasted over the years, even after Widman's exploitative business practices became a concern to some of those Maryknollers whom he had assisted. Like many wealthy Guatemalan Catholics, Widman satisfied his religious longings by joining an elitist, quasi-secretive, clerically controlled organization called Opus Dei, an organization that indulges compulsive religious ritual with elitist social content, encouraging its members to accumulate political and economic power to use in favor of clerical interests disguised as charitable good works.

The Maryknollers had many friends such as Widman among Guatemala's wealthiest families. As Americans and professional religious, they were welcomed into the homes of people whose wealth put them in a social class that was well beyond the Maryknollers' reach in the United States. Most Maryknollers are from middle-class families. To sit at the tables of people who employed maids, housekeepers, gardeners, and security personnel at their two or three homes, including, sometimes, a residence in Europe or the United States, was heady stuff for the American priests, Brothers, and Sisters. To be treated as friends by people who possessed airplanes or helicopters—sometimes both—to fly from one estate to another, and who sent their children abroad to school and who often shopped abroad, made it difficult for some Maryknollers to be objective about the way people such as Widman amassed their considerable fortunes. It was an ideological distinction that separated those Maryknollers who were elitist-oriented from those who, like the Iowan, enjoyed living among and working closely with the Mayas.

"I know you not be a friend of a *cabrón* like Widman, padre," Diego continued. "He be liking to kill many Mateanos to steal our land! But he be not getting it! For the *cabrones* that work for him, their day be gone."

Hennessey waited for an explanation for this final remark.

Diego was content to let the priest wonder. "Two days ago Widman send ten soldiers to throw out the twenty-five *indio* families from lands he say be part of his ranch."

The priest knew that Widman had sent his ladino foreman on several occasions to warn the Mayans to vacate the lands or suffer the consequences. Hennessey had intended to talk to the *finquero*, but that had not yet occurred. Now he was beginning to regret his failure to act more proactively to locate the man.

The Mateanos disputed Widman's claim, stating that the contested lands belonged to their village, Bulej, "since the birth of our people." But, as was common with many Mayan communities, they lacked a legal title that could stand up to Widman's claim. In Guatemala, as far as the government is concerned, Mayan possession is not nine-tenths of the law.

On a previous visit to Bulej, Diego had told the priest that some of Widman's cattle had begun to disappear around August 1980, shortly before Hennessey's arrival in the parish. The *finquero's* foreman had told his *patrón* that the guerrillas were stealing the animals with the assistance of residents from El Campamento. The people living on the disputed lands denied they had anything to do with the thefts.

"Ten *pintos* [camouflaged ones] come in mid-afternoon," Diego recounted, "but they find only women and children. The *cabrones* tell the people they must get off the land or they kill them. Then they go to each house, kick pots and pans, break chairs and tables, steal radios and money. They make everybody leave their houses and they burn them."

The *animador* was watching the priest's reaction, but didn't pause to elicit comment. "The soldiers find two men in one house, a father and son. They stay home to fix their roof. They order the two to knock down their neighbors' houses . . . . The father, he refuse, his son, too. The *pintos* curse their seed, they beat and kill them. All before the eyes of the women and children.

"They catch three others coming from the cornfields, drag them in front of everybody and shoot them in the head. Then they torch the houses.

"A *cabrón* lookout come running to say he spot guerrillas only one kilometer away. So the *cabrones* run back to Widman's house. But the *muchachos* don't come until the next morning."

Hennessey remained silent for a few moments. Then, he spoke. "Do you think that Widman might have let the people stay in El Campamento lands if the guerrillas had not taken his cattle?"

Diego looked hurt. "Padre, why anyone think you be on the side of the *muchachos?* Widman be trying to steal our lands for years, long before anyone steal his cows. The guerrillas be trying to protect our land. They be our army!"

"Well, how does the EGP expect to win support by threatening men like Francisco Paíz García, the foreman on the Bolaños Ranch?" the priest asked quietly. "And killing the elders in Yolcultac and Yalanbajoch? Abandoning the people to the army at El Quetzal? Blowing up that truck at Momoxchecán, killing four of your people. Now five people are dead at El Campamento and the rest have lost their lands and their houses. What kind of poor people's army is that?"

"You be blaming the guerrillas for the killings in El Campamento and the loss of our lands, Padre? . . . Our fathers say that we have to fight, that only God and our *antepasados* help us get back what is ours . . . . Some say it must be done in peace. But that be what the landowners' say. They not be giving back what they steal. The soldiers kill when we protest . . . . Now you blame the guerrillas for the army murders!"

Diego looked at the priest reproachfully. Hennessey was feeling uncomfortable. *Here I go again, sounding like an apologist for this bloody army, just as I did with Bernardo.*

But Diego had not given up on his pastor. "These murders force the *muchachos* to face the *cabrones* now. After they help bury our five brothers, they attack the soldiers at Widman's ranch. People say they kill eight, Armando, the foreman, too. Now the *muchachos* show they can protect us. A lot of people be joining them. They be our army!"

Hennessey stared off into space, wistfully longing for the innocuous moral cases that he used to chuckle about in his theology courses in the seminary. All those mind-twisting, esoteric questions seemed so ivory-tower silly now: whether a priest could give a valid general absolution to the passengers of a ship sinking off on the horizon? Or whether he could licitly use banana oil instead of olive oil for the last rites? And if he tried, what kind of a sin would it be? It was like making God into a Divine Accountant, sitting up there with his ledgers, keeping score.

"We never had a course in the seminary on the ethics of revolution," the priest confessed with some regret. "But I can give you some principles that might help you decide what you can or shouldn't do . . . . Interested?"

Diego nodded and smiled.

"Bien! Here's what you have to figure out: what are your chances for success, because if they're slight, you shouldn't try; otherwise, you cause unnecessary bloodshed. Also, where nonviolent means, like strikes and marches, will get you what you want, you've got to use them. Third, you can only use force against those who threaten you with physical harm, not merely because someone is a landowner or a labor contractor for the *fincas.* "

"*Por Dios,* padre, how are we going to know how good our chances are unless we try? . . . You be in Guatemala long enough. You know marches and strikes get people shot! . . . And we not shoot anyone because he be a landowner or labor contractor. We give him a little beating. The *muchachos* kill those who kill our people."

Hennessey sat looking into Diego's eyes. The catechist held his gaze. *So, the priest thought, you are a member of the EGP. I only hope you can keep your Catholic faith and a clear conscience, . . . and that you win!*

Diego sat there, nodding. It was almost like he felt he had made a convert out of the priest, that Hennessey had understood nothing until Diego Pérez had come along. "You help me a lot, padre. I be glad you understand. It be important that our religion guide us. We not win if God not be on our side."

With that, Diego stood up, thanked the padre for his wisdom, asked permission to leave, shook the priest's hand, and left. The Iowan remained seated, watching the *animador* through the window as he trudged up the hill and disappeared into the plaza. Then he closed his eyes and thought: *How do I get myself into these predicaments? And how do I get myself out?*

During the first week of July, Milenario Pérez was back to see Hennessey. He looked even more depressed than on his previous visit. The Iowan was standing by the basketball court in front of the church encouraging some young men practicing their basketball skills as the *promotor* approached.

"My brothers, padre! Both of them be missing! . . . Colonel Bolaños send a telegram two weeks ago telling Francisco Paíz García send someone to Widman's *finca* to get three horses soldiers borrowed a month ago. Francisco say it be dangerous for one man to go. So he send five, two be my brothers. When they be at Widman's, the sergeant say he not have authority to give the horses, that they come back the next day to talk to the lieutenant."

"Diego Pérez," the Iowan responded, "was here a few days ago and he told me that the EGP had killed eight soldiers at Widman's ranch. Does that mean more soldiers have come in to replace them?"

"I not know if they be new, *padrecito,* or if they be there with the others before. But they be many still. And I think they do something to my brothers."

"What did they do, Diego?"

"All five men go to Nentón to pay their head tax. I know they go because I be in Nentón and the treasurer tell me they be there. He tell me what the sergeant at Widman's say. They spend the night in Nentón and start back the next day, but no one sees them since."

Hennessey sat down on the wall at the edge of the basketball court and patted the place beside him. "Have you checked the military posts in Nentón and Barillas to see if they're being held there? Or perhaps in Huehuetenango? The soldiers at Widman's have no place to hold prisoners. If they arrested the men, they'd have to hold them in some jail."

Milenario wasn't listening. "I be afraid to ask the *pintos* at Widman's if they know where the five go. When my bothers not show for a week, I must go. Six go with me and six stay nearby. The lieutenant say he not see the five since they visit. I think he lie, padre!"

Hennessey asked again: "Have you tried Barillas, Nentón, or Huehuetenango?"

Milenario shook his head. "I not go to the military in Nentón or Barillas, padre. Someone be seeing them if they be taken there and tell me."

"If they were taken to either base during the night, no one would know about it," the priest responded. "Why don't you go and ask? But take a group of witnesses with you."

Milenario left with a promise to visit the military base in Barillas the next day.

Late in the afternoon of the following day, the *promotor* returned to the rectory to tell Hennessey that the Barillas base commandant, a major, had suggested that his brothers had gone off to join the guerrillas. "He tell me because I look for my brothers, I be probably a guerrilla. I tell him I be against the guerrillas, I support the army. He say he going to investigate me. He say if he find out I support the guerrillas, he going to shoot me . . . . He not want me to look for my brothers, padre!"

Hennessey remained silent for some moments. He feared the worst. After a few moments, he uttered some words of encouragement, words that did not represent his true feelings.

Milenario did not respond. Finally, the *promotor* let out a long sigh, stood up, and shook the priest's hand. Without another word, he turned and left.

The Iowan ached inside. He sat for some moments wondering what he could do. *Visit the commandant in Barillas myself? After the 31 May massacre, that hardly seems like a promising thought. At times like this, I feel I'm standing in a pool of cold water up to my chest, watching as its level comes higher inch by inch.*

Milenario's predicament, that of the families of his two brothers and their three missing companions, and the grief of the five families who had lost members at El Campamento, prompted Hennessey to make an unscheduled trip to San Francisco during that first week of July. The trip over rocky, broken trails generally took from six to seven hours on foot during the dry season, eight during the rainy season, a bit more by horse. The rainy season had begun in May. Hennessey preferred to hike the distance because so few Mateanos could afford a horse and he felt that one way to break the traditionalists' antagonism toward him was to identify with their daily experience as much as possible.

As he walked, the Iowan wondered how much Widman knew of the activities of the army detachment stationed on his land, and whether a letter to him detailing the deaths at El Campamento and the disappearance of the five from San Francisco would prompt him to rein in the soldiers. But the priest guessed that if Widman didn't know, it was only because he didn't want to know, and a letter would hardly breach the protective shell around his conscience erected by ritualistic observation of his Opus Dei beliefs.

Hennessey climbed the trail above San Mateo that led to San Francisco, heading northwest through a plateau covered by pine trees, occasionally crossing savannas of natural grasslands, green and rocky, nibbled by herds of wild pigs, with bedraggled shepherds tending their scruffy sheep nearby. This was *costumbrista* country. Hostile and fearful looks were the only response he received for his cheerful waves.

The priest passed through the village of Chiquín Q'uen (the Rock's Ear) and then came out onto a spectacular view of a series of mountains, valleys, and rivers, a scene that looked more like a grandiose relief map stretched out at his feet than a geographical reality yet to be traversed by hours of leg-numbing descents and climbs. Off in the distance, he could see the sweltering lowlands of Mexico, waiting thirstily for the afternoon's promised rain. He stopped to rest and wonder at it all, forgetting for the moment the tens or possibly hundreds of hidden individuals moving among the trees, rocks, and crevices below, working on missions of mercy, support, and protection, or of destruction and terror. One moment, he supped on the breadth of God's magnificent creative power; the next, his nose crinkled up with what he thought might be the smell of the Evil One—except that he no longer attributed human failings and malevolence to the Evil One.

After several hours of ups and downs, climbing over the rocky, broken trail, the priest passed through Bulej. He waved his greetings to several friendly faces but indicated by his pace that he had no intention of stopping. From there, he ascended a few hundred feet before once again beginning his descent, continuing north, zigzagging toward Yalanbajoch. He could no longer see Bulej, nestled in a valley high above, off to one side. On the other side, the terrain, covered with pine trees, extended downward toward the crystal clear waters of idyllic Lake Bravo, called Yolmajab by the poetic Mateanos, "liquid of life."

As the Iowan plodded along, descending toward the ranch lands, the view began to change radically. Off far to the left spread the rolling, deforested hills and scrub-grass grazing lands belonging to *Finca* San Francisco, with heat waves shimmering across the plains. Not a blade of grass twitched in the scorching early afternoon sun. The priest thought to himself that this land didn't deserve to have its surface violated by hoe or digging stick. Still people had to eat of its barrenness, much as a hungry lamb continues to suck on its mother's drying teat. He was growing hungry now but took hidden pleasure in feeling what his parishioners experienced on a daily basis. *I'm a masochist!* He chided himself.

By three o'clock, he was approaching San Francisco, noting as he went how much thinner the people were here than those in Yalanbajoch.

Next to the small chapel in the center of the village stood the remains of an equally small, nearly complete, ancient Mayan temple, tastelessly rebuilt by Colonel Bolaños in a well-meaning attempt to render homage to his tenants' prehistoric past. It was about twenty feet high, with a 400-square-foot base, a series of increasingly smaller platforms, each about eighteen inches high, one on top of the other, the whole structure composing a flight of steps on all four sides. At the summit, where an altar once stood, there was now nothing, Colonel Bolaños's aesthetic sense having finally reasserted itself.

After exchanging polite greetings with each of the unusually solemn inhabitants gathered in front of the village chapel, Hennessey walked inside to hear confessions and prepare for Mass. The fresh pine needles spread over the dirt floor gave off a delicious forest aroma, nature's perfume fitting only for a place of worship, contrasting sharply with the sense of death that hung over the congregation. The Mass was offered for the five men killed by Widman's troops at El Campamento, and for the five *desaparecidos* (the disappeared ones) from the San Francisco community.

In his sermon, Hennessey dwelt on the people's need for strength and mutual support. "The very people who should be your protectors are doing evil things," he told them. "But is it their fault that they do not recognize their evil? We must continue to hope and pray that they will change. And if they do change, really change and ask forgiveness, we must be ready to forgive them, to allow them to make a fresh start, to become one with us again. But as long as they continue to torture and kill, they will not, they cannot, deserve our forgiveness."

In the second week of July, Milenario Pérez arrived at the rectory to tell Hennessey that he still had no word of his two brothers nor of their three companions. He had been to the Huehuetenango military base since his last visit without learning anything. Now he was on his way by bus to Guatemala City to see Colonel Bolaños and enlist his assistance. "The colonel has military friends to help me," he told the priest. "Francisco say he think the colonel be helping. He be my only hope."

The soldiers had abandoned the ranch a week earlier as evidence of the growing strength of the EGP spread. After the soldiers left, a guerrilla patrol burned down the Widman house, finding the five bodies at the same time. All five had been so disfigured by beatings and shotgun blasts, including one torso that was missing the head, that the bodies were unidentifiable. Their relatives were only able to identify them by means of the bedrolls buried nearby.

Chapter 17

SOLDIERS OF ANTICOMMUNISM

July 1954

"Throughout the period I have outlined, the Guatemalan
government and Communist agents throughout the world have
persistently attempted to obscure the real issue—that of Communist
imperialism—by claiming that the U.S. is only interested in
protecting American business. We regret that there have been
disputes between the Guatemalan government and the United
Fruit Company . . . . But this issue is relatively unimportant . . .
Led by Colonel Castillo Armas, patriots arose in Guatemala to
challenge the Communist leadership and to change it. Thus this
situation is being cured by the Guatemalans themselves."
(Nationwide address broadcast to the American people by Secretary
of State John Foster Dulles).[1]

26 July 1957

Three years after Castillo Armas took surrogate power in Guatemala, a
member of his elite presidential guard assassinated him. His presidency had
been short and controversial, marked by a greater degree of domestic conflict
than during the reign of either Arévalo Bermejo or Arbenz Guzmán. The
responsibility for many of Castillo Armas's problems, including to some degree
the atmosphere that led to his death, can be laid at the feet of Secretary of
State John Foster Dulles.

Dulles was a man obsessed. The secretary of state pressured Castillo
Armas from the moment the Little Colonel entered the presidential palace to

capture and imprison all "communists"—particularly the seven hundred *Arbencistas* who had sought asylum in foreign embassies. It was a task that Dulles felt Castillo Armas was not pursuing with sufficient zeal. The secretary of state was indifferent to the practice of political asylum and its long and sacred history in Latin America. The tradition had consistently been honored during periods of political upheaval and was a lifeline for all those who had chosen the wrong side at the wrong time, whether the right, left, or center. However, Latin American history and traditions were of no concern to Dulles. He demanded that Castillo Armas remove the "asylees" from the embassies and imprison them.[2]

The Liberator resisted. He himself had been granted asylum after his escape from prison in 1951. Dulles told Peurifoy to instruct Castillo Armas that the seven hundred had no right to asylum because "they were part of an international conspiracy," that criminal charges should be brought against them as covert Moscow agents.[3]

The Liberator stood firm. To do otherwise might have brought down his government. Dulles then insisted that the seven hundred be given safe conduct passes to nowhere but Russia, even though only two or three had ever been there.[4]

Castillo Armas ignored the secretary's demands and allowed the asylees to leave the country unmolested, most of them to Mexico. Arbenz Guzmán was among them. Determined to humiliate his predecessor, Castillo Armas ordered his agents to force Arbenz Guzmán to remove his pants and shirt in the airport before departing. The CIA's fingerprints were all over this insult. A photo showing the CIA's Tracy Barnes in Guatemala City gleefully showing off an effigy of Arbenz Guzmán draped over the mudguard of his jeep like a hunted deer demonstrated the American government's contempt.

The Liberator did respond, however, to Washington's pressures to go after the "communists" who had not sought or who had been unable to obtain diplomatic asylum, though he knew that most were simply *Arbencistas*. A threat to cut off economic aid was enough to frighten the Little Colonel into obedience. Lists of names of the accused had been shuffled back and forth between Washington and Ambassador Peurifoy. Peurifoy, it was said by Guillermo Toriello, had handed over just such a list to Colonel Enrique Diaz when the latter was still in control of the government. At the same time, the ambassador gave orders to shoot all those therein named within twenty-four hours.[5]

In his first public speech, Castillo Armas had declared 10 July "Anticommunism Day":

> Communism . . . has been completely destroyed by the force of arms. But communism still remains in the consciences of some bad sons of Guatemala. . . . The battle has begun, the hard battle that requires us to demand that each citizen be a soldier of anticommunism.[6]

The witch-hunt was on. Colonel Monzón told reporters that his biggest concern was to find enough jail cells to hold the thousands of communists he had successfully rounded up.[7]

Meanwhile, the Liberator appointed José Bernabé Linares as head of his secret police. It was a job that Linares had last held with morbid distinction under the dictator, Jorge Ubico.

Trying to fend off criticism, the U.S. State Department sent Richard Adams, a renowned American anthropologist acting under the aegis of the World Heath Organization, to Guatemala to document the communist sympathies of those held in the country's jails. Adams—not wanting his name associated with the enterprise, used the alias "Stokes Newbold" on his report—interviewed 250 prisoners in three jails and discovered that few of them knew anything about communism. Their crime seems to have been that they had all participated in Arbenz's agrarian reform.[8]

During the first week of July, 1954, acting at the insistence of Foster Dulles, Peurifoy pushed Castillo Armas to render the five-man junta more malleable. Colonels Cruz Salazar and Mauricio Dubois were each given what was rumored to be gifts of $100,000 to resign. The former also accepted a U.S. invitation to become Guatemala's ambassador to the United States, while the latter went to New York as Guatemala's consul general. The Old Fox, Ydígoras Fuentes, still lurked in the background, not an immediate challenge. After a few noises, he'd be sent off to represent Guatemala in Bogotá. That left Castillo Armas with only one competitor for power, Colonel Elfegio Monzón.

Peurifoy then proposed a vote among the three remaining members for the junta's "leadership." The idea was to move Castillo Armas toward an uncontested presidency, step by step. The ambassador knew in advance the outcome: the Liberator would vote for himself, while Major Trinidad Oliva would concur. Colonel Monzón would then read between the lines and decide that his best interests lay in making the vote unanimous. And so it happened.

The support of the American government for the Little Colonel did not waver when the Liberator closed down all opposition media—something Arbenz had never done—and made it a crime to speak disparagingly of himself. He also began a campaign to burn all communist literature, including novels by Victor Hugo, Dostoyevsky, and Miguel Angel Asturias, Guatemala's only Nobel Laureate whose principal literary subjects had been UFCO, "the Octopus," and the *caudillo* tradition.

Nor did the U.S. State Department voice any noticeable concern when seven UFCO workers—activists in the fruit company's labor union—were murdered in Guatemala City, while another seventeen—also UFCO employees—were butchered by "anticommunists" in Tiquisate, all within days of the Liberator's triumph. Unionized working men and women were now seen as enemies of the state. Acting on this presumption, the Liberator canceled the juridical personality of 533 unions, signed into law a prohibition against the formation of any new unions, and made most union activity a crime. Washington's silence, not to say its encouragement, could be heard around the world for those paying attention.[9]

The heart and soul of Arbenz's legislative agenda, the agrarian reform, was decimated as over 99 percent of the expropriated lands were returned to their former claimants. All peasant organizations and rural syndicates on farms with fewer than five hundred workers—98 percent—were dissolved. In the process, eight thousand peasants were murdered.[10]

The Liberator took the vote from illiterates and outlawed all political parties except his own.

Foster Dulles's response to these measures was to wire Peurifoy for information as to when it might be convenient for Serafino Romualdi, the professional anticommunist of George Meany's American Federation of Labor (AFL), to appear on the scene to help eliminate the "communists" from the few impotent labor unions left standing.

Romualdi arrived posthaste and set to work forming the National Committee for Union Reorganization. He was not Foster Dulles's nor the Liberator's man, however, soon expressing his misgivings that Castillo Armas had for all practical purposes annihilated the labor movement. He subsequently reported in the AFL's newspaper that "it is generally accepted that the decree dissolving the banana workers' and the railway workers' unions . . . was issued at the insistent request of the American companies."[11]

The only audible complaints issuing from Washington were John Foster Dulles's wailing that Castillo Armas was being too lenient to his "communist" enemies. The overthrow of Arbenz Guzmán had placed the United States in a political straightjacket. Since the trumpeted rationale for going after the Arbenz government was that it was communist, it was now imperative that many more communists be found and punished than had so far occurred. The stakes were high. U.S. prestige, not to say the country's honor, was on the line. American political leaders found it impossible to admit that errors had been committed, or were still being made. The line between denial and cynicism had disappeared like the wisp of a cloud. As Vice President Richard Nixon, the voice of American political fabrication, noted, "This is the first instance in history where a Communist government has been replaced by a free one."[12]

By August, the strain that had developed between Castillo Armas and Colonel Monzón had grown taut. The fulcrum was the open acknowledgement of a previously semi-contained hatred that existed between the *Liberacionista* forces—including latecomers who falsely claimed battle experience—and the regular army. The relationship between the two groups was paradoxical, totally Guatemalan, based on the rebels' undisguised contempt for an officer corps that had fled the field of battle without the semblance of a struggle, and the officer corps' contempt for the *Liberacionistas* who tended to preen as if they had defeated in battle an army that had never really fought.

Two-thirds of the 150 cadets at the Politécnica ignited the conflagration by attacking the *Liberacionistas* that had come from Zacapa for a victory parade and were lodged in the Roosevelt Hospital.

Although officers of the Politécnica's faculty did not side with the cadets, neither did they oppose the move. Two hundred soldiers from La Base Militar were sent to protect the cadets, while another contingent was sent to Aurora Air Base to keep the rebel air force on the ground after its initial run against the student warriors. No regular army units came to the *Liberacionistas'* aid.

Peurifoy moved fast. He went to Colonel Monzón and told him that he had better tell the cadets to back off, that the United States was prepared to support Castillo Armas all the way to the wall. Monzón reluctantly did as he was told. The cadets took his advice and called off their attack. But Colonel Monzón's resentment of the Liberator sprung ever-deeper roots. The Guatemalan press, now completely controlled by the government, made a statement that can be characterized as nothing short of farcical. It trumpeted the results as "another victory over communism."[13]

Three weeks later, Peurifoy insisted that Castillo Armas call together his two junta colleagues and propose that they elect a "president" from among their number, after which the other two members would resign. This was Guatemala's democracy in action, à la Washington. Again, the Liberator's election was a foregone conclusion. Once again Colonel Monzón's temperature rose.

In October, the Little Colonel held an unopposed national plebiscite wherein he asked a single question, "Are you in favor of Colonel Castillo Armas continuing in the presidency for a term to be fixed by the constituent assembly?" Voters answering in the affirmative numbered 485,531, while 393 said no and 655 refused to answer.[14] At the same time, sixty of the sixty-six seats in the Constituent Assembly were filled by members of the "official" National Anti-Communist Front (FAN), "[b]ut only"—as the CIA chief of special research noted—"through the use of concentrated government pressure and in the face of popular lack of interest."[15]

The assembly then turned around and gave the Liberator a six-year term to end in July 1960. Meanwhile, Castillo Armas ruled by presidential decree without any semblance of democratic procedure. It didn't matter. As far as Washington was concerned, Guatemala was a showcase of democracy.

In January 1955, the enmity between the *Liberacionistas* and the regular army escalated to the point where it could no longer be sidetracked by stern warnings from the U.S. Embassy. A powerful group of dissident officers had decided that Castillo Armas's incompetence, his obsequiousness when given U.S. directives, and the widespread public unrest with the faltering economy were reasons enough to mandate his departure.

The Liberator discovered the plot before it shifted into first gear and the Little Colonel ordered six of the lesser personalities executed on the spot. Colonel Elfegio Monzón and several senior officers were dismissed from the army. The government characterized the whole incident as a "pseudo-communist plot."[16]

The CIA concluded that "his [Castillo Armas's] support among the professional officers of the Army appears to have been weakened by the executions and dismissals, and some officers in key positions seemed to have joined the opposition."[17]

On May Day, 1955, labor dissatisfaction with Castillo Armas boiled over. When the minister of labor and other government officials took to the podium in front of the Palacio Nacional to explain the *Liberacionistas'* antilabor policies, they were booed off the stage by the angry crowd in what the U.S. Embassy characterized as "an apparently well-planned maneuver."[18] Five labor leaders, some of whom were prominent under Arbenz Guzmán, then took the microphone and criticized the government, much to the delight of the audience.

All such demonstrations of discontent with Castillo Armas's rule were labeled for public consumption as "communist" or "pseudo-communist" by both the U.S. and Guatemalan governments. Behind the scenes, however, reality was recognized as something quite different.

In June 1956, university students who had nicknamed the Liberator "the *Vendepatria*" (seller of the fatherland) planned a demonstration against the government for the twenty-fourth. The day before the planned demonstration, however, Castillo Armas decreed a "State of Alarm," suspending certain constitutional guarantees, including the right to demonstrate. Despite the suspension, three hundred persons paraded on the twenty-fourth, resulting in the arrest of "fifty, mostly students, but including leftist agitators."[19]

The following day, several hundred more students marched to protest the preceding day's arrests. A memorandum from Assistant Secretary of State Henry F. Holland described what followed:

> At one point three cars each containing six men, dressed in civilian clothes, met the procession. The men in the cars were armed with

machine guns and initially fired into air, probably to disperse the procession, but later fired into the marchers, killing at least six of them and wounding many more.[20]

No police action was taken against the occupants of the three vehicles. By 28 June, U.S. Embassy accounts of the confrontation had shifted 180 degrees. The Guatemalan government's claims were repeated: the students/ agitators had fired first on the police as part of a communist plot to incite repression and a backlash of public anger, ultimately destabilizing the administration. Ambassador Armour went to Castillo Armas and stressed to him "the importance of publicizing . . . the events as part of a communist plot. USIA [U.S. Information Agency] instructions along these lines have already been sent to our Latin American missions."[21]

Assistant Secretary Holland then called in the Guatemalan ambassador and instructed him to tell Castillo Armas to make a strong anticommunist speech as soon as possible:

> [I]n this case because of Moscow-directed agitators some innocent people were killed, . . . the speech should be a sober, serious one, possibly including a minute or two of silence in memory of those who lost their lives, . . . that those who died did so not because of government tyranny but because of cynical communist political maneuverings."[22]

Through all the ups and downs of the Castillo Armas tenure, the United States held its collective breath in view of the fact that the Liberator was "inexperienced in government and lacked the intellectual qualities to overcome this deficiency with ease," as noted in a secret memorandum of the Department of State entitled "National Intelligence Estimate."[23]

Weekly trips by State Department operatives to Capitol Hill to assure Congress of the continued need of economic aid was a foreign policy imperative. As articulated by Foggy Bottom's officer in charge of Guatemalan affairs: "We consider it vital that the Guatemala government be able to demonstrate to the people of Guatemala that they can have a better life under democracy than under communism, and this has been one of our major policy objectives in furnishing aid to Guatemala."[24]

That aid had gone from $600,000 during the Ten Years of Spring to $150 million during the three years Castillo Armas occupied the presidential palace.

Early on, Castillo Armas, encouraged by the U.S. ambassador and the promised assistance from the CIA's station chief, announced the formation of the National Committee for Defense against Communism (CNDCC) with power to declare anyone a communist, to arrest and hold such persons up to six months without right of defense or of appeal. In four months' time, the CNDCC had acquired seventy-two thousand names, many fed to it by the CIA, and had determined to expand its total list to two hundred thousand.[25] This, despite the fact that the State Department had known all along that the total number of communists in . Guatemala, even with its jaundiced definition of "communist," never exceeded four thousand, and the number was "perhaps substantially fewer."[26]

As a result, the CNDCC, the crown jewel of Foster Dulles's pressures, was described in the State Department's National Intelligence Estimate to be "incompetent, overzealous, and arbitrary and has aroused public disapproval and even ridicule,"[27] thereby creating strong pressures to dissolve and reorganize the entire government security system.

Organizing and reorganizing the government security system had become the most important priority for the U.S. government in Guatemala. It was now a question of whether the National Police—a force of thirty-nine hundred men whose officers were all active army personnel and who worked closely with and within the CNDCC—or the army itself would be the heart and soul of the intelligence and security systems. A letter from Deputy Under Secretary of State for Political Affairs Robert Murphy to the director of the Foreign Operations Administration, Harold Stassen, on 4 March 1955, opted for the army.

As a result, the ambassador of Guatemala to the United States was encouraged to make a formal request in the name of his government to the U.S. Army that an intelligence advisor be added to the U.S. Military Mission in Guatemala to train Guatemalan Army personnel in internal security and counterintelligence methods and techniques.

There were both pros and cons for the United States to undertake such an obligation. Among the pros was that "a qualified intelligence adviser might help establish closer relations with the military so that we could keep better informed of its activities."[28] On the other hand, "the Guatemalan military might consider such an intelligence adviser a threat to any plot it might be hatching against the government . . . and might be even less willing to take our military into its confidence."[29] Further, there was the danger that "his advice may be used to help control the noncommunist opposition rather than the communists or other [sic] actually dangerous subversives."[30]

None of these potential problems was thought to be important enough to outweigh the advisability of going ahead with the assignment, however. What was more troublesome for the State Department was the identification of the U.S. government with the arbitrary and incompetent CNDCC. It was thought that a "special emphasis on seeking to persuade the Guatemalan government to improve the organization and staffing of the security organization" was necessary.[31]

In a telegram to Foster Dulles, Ambassador Norman Armour expressed his misgivings about such a move::

> We agree with logic that local government should be encouraged look upon their regular forces primarily as instrument for dealing with subversion. We doubt, however, that it is realistic here at this time because of psychological factors. Guatemalan officer corps is deeply inculcated with ancient traditional and ethical concepts of profession of arms and any effort to regard them or make them regard themselves as policemen would be an outrage to their sense of honor. Our military missions have been working quietly to reduce pressure for combat material in favor of support but it has been impossible to go beyond this without causing resentment.[32]

Armour's opinion of the tradition and ethics of the Guatemalan military was decidedly ahistorical and his words of caution would be quickly disregarded. In the meantime, he recommended that the United States "continue supplying data on local Communist movement on case to case basis, and assistance towards improving CNDCC," as well as sending police officials for training in the United States, making available radio equipment and technicians for locating clandestine subversive stations, and the assignment of a U.S. intelligence officer to work with Guatemala military intelligence.[33]

The beginning date of Guatemala's civil war—which formally came to an end in December 1995—has been fixed at 28 June 1954, the date that Arbenz Guzmán left the presidency. Another date, that of 8 May 1955, might be considered more appropriate. That was the day that U.S. Ambassador Armour recommended that the United States throw its weight behind restructuring the CNDCC and slowly drawing in the army as the front line in ferreting out and eliminating "communists."

When Washington moved in this direction, the Guatemalan Army slowly, inexorably turned to terrorism as its first line of offense, a move that would turn two generations of military officers into homicidal maniacs beyond the reach of morality and law. It became the army that Father Ronald Hennessey and his parishioners in San Mateo Ixtatán would come to know so well in the early 1980s. When these "soldiers of anticommunism" found it inopportune to show their true khaki colors, they exchanged their uniforms for civilian clothes and functioned as murderous paramilitaries, allowing the government to claim they were outside official control. But on at least 444 occasions, by the army's own count, it was not deemed necessary to hide the soldiers' identity when they wiped out whole villages.

While all this anticommunist activity was proceeding, justified in the name of the perceived threat to Central American freedom from Russian ideological influence, the U.S. Embassy maintained a full head of steam down the very track that Arbenz Guzmán had repeatedly stated was the cause of U.S. intervention, and which Foster Dulles had just as vociferously denied: the preeminent right of American businesses to function as shadow governments in foreign lands where the United States claimed hegemony.

Early on in the Castillo Armas reign, Secretary Dulles had telegraphed Ambassador Peurifoy to pressure the Liberator to grant UFCO a generous contract, the sooner the better.[34] When the Little Colonel commented in a manner reminiscent of criticisms made by both Arévalo Bermejo and Arbenz Guzmán that UFCO seemed to be in charge of U.S. foreign policy, Under Secretary of State Henry Holland protested to the Liberator that "the United Fruit Company does not guide United States foreign policy decisions, and that, on the contrary, the United States Government from time to time found it necessary to guide and restrain the company in certain ways."[35]

What "ways" Holland did not say.

Another source of irritation between the two governments was the U.S. insistence that Guatemala continue to do business with the Empresa Eléctrica, owned and operated by a U.S. conglomerate, American and Foreign Power Company. The Empresa Eléctrica produced upwards of 75 percent of the country's electrical power, selling it at exorbitant rates. Castillo Armas wanted to accept French financing so that his government could build a new generating plant on the Usumacinta River and give American and Foreign Power Company a run for their money.

But the U.S. government would have none of it. Foster Dulles wanted any expansion of electrical generating capacity to be undertaken by private (Empresa Eléctrica) capital. When the Guatemalan ambassador protested to Assistant Secretary of State Holland that the managers of Empresa Eléctrica had "a 1920 attitude in 1956," Holland, offended once again by the Liberation government's lack of gratitude, answered that though "in the past some policies of American companies in Guatemala may have been short-sighted," he knew that Henry Sargent, president of American and Foreign Power Company, was "a man with 1956 and not 1920 ideas."[36]

Another of the U.S. Embassy's struggles to erase all vestiges of communism was to abrogate an Arévalo Bermejo law that reserved to the national government the right to exploit any petroleum deposits found within the nation's borders. For some years, it had been a belief of both the U.S. and Guatemalan governments that Guatemalan territory harbored some extensive oil deposits originating in the same fields developed by Mexico, fields from which U.S. companies had been expelled by Mexico's President Lázaro Cárdenas in 1938.[37] Now Castillo Armas was thought to be the key to getting back into those deposits.

Thomas C. Mann, a retired lawyer who had specialized in petroleum law, was named special assistant to Ambassador Armour in order to assist Castillo Armas in drawing up a new law. Mann immediately got on the wrong side of the Liberator by speaking up too strongly in support of the discredited UFCO and IRCA companies. Ambassador Armour saw the problem as basically a failing of Castillo Armas's intellect: "There are moments when he [Castillo Armas] seems almost pathetic. He must literally be led by the hand, step by step. It will be a difficult task to do this without arousing nationalistic reactions, but we intend expand scope of our efforts with Klein and Saks as one of [our] main vehicles."[38]

Counselor Mann, with the assistance of the Klein and Saks economic mission, was finally successful in overturning the Arévalo Bermejo legislation, replacing it with a U.S.-designed law, resulting in the fact that "twenty-two companies, mostly American, have been authorized to explore for petroleum; these are optimistic signs for the future."[39]

When destiny finally caught up with Castillo Armas, his death did not come as a surprise to the U.S. government. Only the hand on the murder weapon was a puzzle. Or was it?

The accused assassin was a member of the elite presidential guard. It was said that he had been discharged from the army for being a member of the Communist Party before joining the guard. After killing the Liberator, he turned the murder weapon, his rifle, on himself and committed suicide. Communist documents were found on his person.

A nationwide news blackout was put in place immediately; it lasted twelve hours.

It was all very neat! Too neat!

It was quickly noted that it is not easy to commit a nerve-wracked, hurried suicide with one's rifle, an awkward weapon at best. Nor do copies of printed communist declarations serve as unambiguous suicide notes. Why was the killer discharged from the army for being a communist and then allowed to join the elite presidential guard? Further, the on-the-spot news blackout showed a degree of organization that strongly implied prior planning. High-level planning!

Before long, yellow flags began flying in some quarters of Washington. A telegram from Acting Secretary of State Christian Herter on 31 July to the U.S. ambassador in London detailed plans to exploit the communist ties of the accused killer via the USIA. Herter added, however, that "we should proceed with caution . . . . Possibility cannot be overlooked that assassination was a rightist plot."[40]

The cautionary suggestions had come from none other than the DCI, Allen Dulles, during a meeting the previous day of the Intelligence Advisory Committee (IAC). Dulles had stated that "there is some feeling in the CIA that this action, the assassination, had been the trigger for a rightist coup."[41]

The DCI's caution was based on solid intelligence garnered time and again over the previous three years that Castillo Armas was in constant danger of suffering a coup from the right. In fact, "Castillo might have been deposed on any one of several occasions had his prospective opponents believed that the United States would not give him prompt support."[42] Even the names of the plotters were known to the U.S. government—not a communist, protocommunist, social democrat, or democrat among them.

Foster Dulles, however, would have no pussyfooting around the issue of who was responsible for Castillo Armas's murder. According to notes taken at the secretary of state's staff meeting of 7 August 1957, the secretary "took strong exception to this, the possibility of a rightist plot, . . . because Communists have a fundamental motivation which leads them to violent revolution; he, the secretary, did not think a direct tie to Moscow had to be demonstrated in order to show the Communist connection."[43]

Whispered rumors surfaced that Colonel Elfegio Monzón (ret.), and Colonel Carlos Enrique Díaz (Arbenz's handpicked successor) had now settled scores with the hated Castillo Armas as well as with the imperial U.S. government.

Two days after the Liberator's assassination, Archbishop Mariano Rossell y Arellano conducted a solemn funeral Mass for the fallen dictator in the national cathedral. A bevy of high-ranking military officers, leaders of the National Liberation Movement (Castillo Armas's official, and the only legal, political party), the presidential cabinet, members of the MLN Congress, and the diplomatic community were all present. President Eisenhower sent his son John to the service as his official representative.

The aging archbishop had maintained his high regard for the Liberator despite the fact that the prelate had been unable to obtain constitutional authorization to teach Catholic doctrine in the public schools and recognition of the "preeminent status" of the Catholic Church in public life. In their many tête-à-têtes, the Little Colonel assured Rossell that he was doing what he could to influence the constituent assembly in the Church's behalf but that anticlerical feelings ran wide and deep, not only in Congress but in society as a whole.

Archbishop Rossell was heartbroken to see his hero removed from the political arena in such cowardly fashion. He, at least, had no doubts that those responsible for the assassination were his lifelong enemies, the communists. In his funeral eulogy, this dignified churchman saluted his distinguished audience and declared with his accustomed authority that "Colonel Carlos Castillo Armas was more than just our liberator from atheistic communism; he was an authentic martyr of the Catholic Church."[44]

The Papal Nuncio Mons. G. Verolino, Salvadorean Ambassador Funes, and Col. Elfego Monzón flew from El Salvador to Guatemala on Ambassador Peurifoy's plane (see seal on door) after working out a peace treaty. (Credit: Rafael Morales)

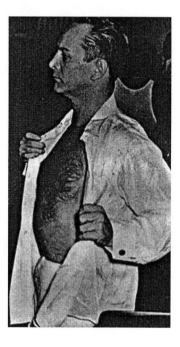

President Arbenz at the airport as he leaves Guatemala. (Courtesy: Rafael Morales)

Chapter 18

OH DEATH! WHERE IS THY STING?

The Guatemalan rainy season—referred to as "winter"—from mid-May to mid-November, is generally a time when everyone's spirits rise as water-laden clouds appear out of nowhere in the early afternoon, day after day, to dump their life-sustaining nectar on the waiting plant life below. The munificence of ancestors, patron saints, lesser gods, the Virgin, and *Tata Dios* is expressed in the greening of the fields across the length and breadth of the land.

But 1981 was different in San Mateo Ixtatán. Everyone's mood was somber. The random massacres by soldiers in El Quetzal, San Mateo, and El Campamento, and the macabre murders at the Widman ranch had sown a palpable fear and hatred of the army among many Mateanos. And even though most seemed ready to make excuses for the EGP's bumbling bombing of the stake truck near Momoxchecán and the more selective executions in Yolcultac, Ixbajau, and Timacté, they were also beginning to question the ability of the guerrillas to devise a coherent strategy against President Lucas García's troops, or even to protect the people from the military's seemingly senseless violence.

The rainy afternoons sometimes provided Hennessey with a couple of relatively uneventful hours during which he felt he should write to family and friends in Iowa. Still, he was finding it ever more difficult to do so. He had never found it easy to explain the world in which he lived to those who had never seen it, who had never been forced to understand it. But now, the complex struggles going on around him that tugged his mind, conscience, and heart in different directions made writing letters to blissfully unaware Iowans a troublesome experience. At times, it was easier to shove the notepaper aside and not write at all. On other occasions, he preferred to "balance" his letters by including references to violence perpetrated by both sides. Not that he felt both sides were equally brutal and guilty. His purpose was to avoid upsetting relatives and friends lest he sound like a wide-eyed revolutionary and cause them to lose any willingness to read, believe, and understand. The days became weeks as the tropical rains continued to soak the countryside and provide nourishment for the crops destined to alleviate Mayan hunger in the months to come. As a man of the earth, Hennessey loved the sound of rain-music on his rectory's zinc roof. Meanwhile, as incessant as the rains and not deterred by them, the guerrillas kept up their organizational campaign in the villages, as well as their oft-frustrated attempts to ambush army vehicles coming from Huehuetenango, heading for Barillas.

Then, late one evening in mid-July, Manuel Sánchez, the student doctor, advised Hennessey that a Mayan woman who had been in labor for three . days needed an immediate cesarean section and that the parish clinic facilities were not adequate for the operation. A tiring five-hour overnight trip to Huehuetenango was the only alternative. Still, the Iowan welcomed the thought of the trip as a small respite from the steady stream of insoluble moral problems that the Mateanos presented to him daily.

While Dr. Sánchez accommodated his groaning, semiconscious patient and her stoic but anxious husband in the back of the parish Jeep Wagoneer, Hennessey deflated his tire pressure to fifteen p.s.i. to cushion against the myriad potholes awaiting him on the road ahead. Then, after bidding good-bye to the visiting regional superior, Bill Mullan, he headed for the provincial capital. It was slightly past 7:30 p.m.

The four bumped along for two hours. When they passed the military checkpoint at San Juan Ixcoy without incident—what the priest hoped was their last major obstacle before Chiantla and Huehuetenango—he felt himself relax. Soon, his sustained tension gave way to drowsiness and Dr. Sánchez took the wheel.

They were just below the highest pass well above San Juan Ixcoy when the Iowan was jolted out of his slumber as the doctor jammed on the brakes and brought the jeep to a sliding halt, not two yards from a downed tree blocking the road. The priest and the doctor eased themselves out of the vehicle, keeping their hands away from their bodies and in front of them, within the glow of the headlights. Both men could feel the blockade's architects watching them from the surrounding darkness.

Working with care and not a little apprehension, the men rigged a tow-chain to the jeep and opened a path just wide enough for the vehicle to squeeze through. But once on the other side, with hardly enough time to shift gears and catch their breath, they ran up against another, even larger tree blocking further passage.

"There's no point in trying to move this one," Hennessey told his companions. "Too big! These are guerrilla blockades. They must be close by waiting to ambush an army vehicle. Let's hope they don't ambush us! . . . Call and see if they'll help us move this thing."

"That's foolhardy, padre," the student doctor answered excitedly. "Leave them alone! Let's go back to San Mateo and I'll try the operation in our hospital. I think I can do it."

"Look, Manuel, if they're nearby, they've already seen our headlights and may be waiting to see what we do. It's better that we identify ourselves before they make a mistake . . . . Anyway, we don't have enough gasoline to get back to San Mateo!"

Leaving the protesting doctor and his other passengers in the jeep, Hennessey slowly pulled his lanky frame onto the second downed tree, cupped his hands around his mouth and called to anyone who might be in the vicinity: *"Holaaaa! Buenas Noooches! Tenemos una mujer en peligro de muerte.* We have a sick woman with us."

He stopped and listened, but the only sound he heard was the rush of the river pounding through a ravine below him. He jumped down on the other side and proceeded slowly up the road, calling again, *"Soy el padre de* San Mateooo! We have a woman who needs an operation, to deliver her babyyy! *Holaaa, ayúdennos!* Help us throuuuugh!"

Again he listened, and again his only answer was from the river below, which seemed to laugh at him.

When he returned to the jeep, the priest told the frightened doctor and the anguished, silent husband that their only alternative was to await the arrival of help. "Either the guerrillas will come down and help us, or a bus out of Huehuetenango should be here by 5:00 a.m. Either way, we'll have enough help to cut and move that tree. We just don't have sufficient gasoline to make it back to San Mateo. And even if we did, Manuel, you've already said that our parish facilities aren't adequate for a cesarean."

"Listen, padre! That baby is not going to make it to 5:00 a.m., and we're taking a chance of losing the mother. I think we should go back. You could coast down all the downgrades and save enough gasoline to make it. We've got to attempt it!"

The Iowan tried to hold his ground knowing that the jeep lacked the fuel to make it back to San Mateo no matter how he negotiated the downgrades. Also, he knew that if either the mother or baby died under the doctor's knife in the parish hospital, the people's faith in "the padre's medicine" would be substantially—perhaps irrevocably—damaged.

In the end, however, the groans of his semiconscious patient and the pleadings of the anxious doctor became too much for Hennessey to ignore. Without another word, he started the engine, turned the jeep around on the narrow, mountain road, and headed back.

Seventeen kilometers outside San Mateo, the engine misfired and then coughed itself into silence.

"Wait here with these folks, Manuel," the priest suggested quietly, without a word of reproach. "I have to go for gas. It should take me three or four hours. Do what you can meanwhile to make them comfortable. I'll hitch a ride back from Padre Mullan."

Hennessey took a flashlight and set out on foot. He tried to accustom his eyes to the moonless darkness fearing that the beam of the flashlight might draw the attention of a guerrilla band or army patrol that would shoot before asking questions. For nearly four hours, the priest tripped, stumbled, and sloshed his way to San Mateo, sticking strictly to the main road. By 5:00 a.m., provisioned with a supply of gasoline, he was again leaving town, chauffeured by Bill Mullan.

When the two priests reached the jeep, Hennessey convinced Manuel Sanchez that a bus must have already cleared the roadblock and that they should again head for Huehuetenango. The doctor agreed. Just outside Soloma, an oncoming bus proved the Iowan's guess correct. Near the *cumbre,* above San Juan Ixcoy, they passed the scattered remains of the EGP blockades, a lot less formidable looking in the light of day. When their suffering patient finally fell into a fitful sleep, the student doctor announced that the baby imprisoned within her showed diminishing signs of life. Near Huehuetenango, Sánchez put his stethoscope in his pocket and whispered to the priest, "I'm pretty sure we've lost it, padre. I did all I could!"

Hennessey nodded.

The doctor's diagnosis of the baby's condition was confirmed at the hospital. The priest walked back to the jeep, wanting to be angry with someone. But when he realized that he felt no emotion, only a sense of emptiness, he wondered how long it had been since he had last experienced stomach contractions over such senseless deaths. The priest shook his head. *I really should be angry with the guerrillas. Sometimes . . . I think I'm becoming Mayan . . . too complacent in accepting these losses . . . . And worse, I don't know whether that's good or bad!*

In the week that followed the Iowan had two more unpleasant encounters with members of the EGP. At a Saturday evening dance in the parish hall, a drunken guerrilla used a knife on the face of a young Mayan girl who had refused to dance with him. When Hennessey heard the news, he rushed from his rectory to the scene to find an angry crowd of parishioners surrounding the frightened attacker, who continued to brandish his weapon. The sight of the priest moving to the center of the confrontation quieted the crowd, but did nothing to soothe the guerrilla. "Let me have your knife, son," the priest asked quietly, extending his hand. "No one will hurt you . . . . Not tonight, anyway."

The young man was breathing heavily, looking from the priest and then to the angry faces around him. "Come on, son, it's the only way out of this mess. Give me your knife and you can go home and think about the trouble you've caused . . . . Otherwise, we're all going to be in a peck of trouble."

Finally, the message penetrated and the assailant lowered his arm. Hennessey reached out and took the knife from the unresisting hand. He then took the man by the arm and led him to the door. Turning, he asked, "Are there any of this man's companions here tonight?"

No one answered.

"Look," the priest said, "if there are any EGP members or EGP sympathizers here tonight, it would be a great help if you would come forward and take your companion to wherever he's stationed and sober him up . . . . No one will make trouble for you . . . . If you don't, then I'm afraid something more unpleasant will happen here tonight and who can say what kind of violent retribution will ensue?"

Silence.

Then three young men stepped forward. "We'll take him, padre. There's no need for anyone here to punish him. We're sure his companions will punish him. You keep his knife."

The priest took the knife and went to a corner and sat down with a few friends. Sister Justa had already taken the young victim to the parish hospital where the nun had pulled together the woman's severed facial tissue by means of a few strategically placed butterfly bandages. On her way home, the victim came by with a group of relatives to thank the priest for his intervention.

"I'm happy I could contribute," Hennessey smiled as dance music again filled the hall.

A few days later, as the Iowan was returning after dark from a sick call in a nearby *aldea,* he was accosted on the path by an EGP member who had more than his quota of alcohol. "Who are you?" the guerrilla asked menacingly, pointing his unsteady rifle at the priest.

"Padre Ronaldo, priest of San Mateo," the Iowan replied.

"Where are you going, priest?" the *muchacho* asked curtly.

"To heaven!" Hennessey answered without a smile, the kind of response that often threw threatening antagonists off stride.

With that, a young woman stepped out of the shadows and placed herself between the rifle barrel and the priest. "Padre Ronaldo, how are you?" she asked pleasantly, ignoring the gun at her back.

Recognizing from her clothes that the woman was a companion of the unsteady gun-wielder, the priest answered, "I'm fine, *mi hija,* just a bit tired from making a sick call. Your friend is doing a good job guarding the road, I must say. I'll have to tell his *jefe* . . . . Got to be going now. And thanks for the greetings."

The young girl gave the priest a smile and a nod, wished him a *buenas noches,* and turned toward her companion. She pushed the rifle to one side, took the young man by the arm, and led him off into the bushes.

The Iowan let out a long breath and headed back to his rectory.

A month later, Hennessey was again forced to reflect on his diminished capacity to emotionally respond to what can only be described as mindless murders. In the forest clearing at Momoxchecán, he had left his jeep in the care of Manuel, a catechist, while he and Santiago Quot hiked to Yolquitac to celebrate Mass and perform a few baptisms. It was a cold, rainy day. The red and black EGP flag flapped in the breeze above several abandoned houses nearby, right where it had flown for over a year.

When the Iowan returned to his jeep several hours later, he found his catechist hiding in the bushes nearby. "What's the matter, Manuel?" he asked calmly.

In an eerie recitation that Hennessey seemed to recognize as having heard before, Manuel told his pastor that a loud explosion some two hours earlier had startled him. "It came from the direction of San Mateo, padre. A passerby told me that some people in a small truck have been injured, others killed."

Hennessey shook his head and climbed into his jeep. "Let's go, Santiago, . . . Manuel." He bit his tongue lest he make some unguarded remark that would later prove unfounded.

Only three kilometers back toward the parish center, they came across a group of people gathered around a new white Nissan pickup angled sharply into the embankment. As the priest grabbed the windshield and swung himself out of his seat, he spotted three men on the opposite side of the road, their coffee-colored *capixays* shredded, coated with dry, black-colored blood. The three lay face down, side by side, like rag dolls dropped neatly on a toy store floor.

As the priest turned toward the Nissan, the mayor of San Mateo approached. "Padre, we have several wounded here. Can you take them to the parish hospital?"

It took only a glance for Hennessey to see that the broken and twisted survivors sitting by the side of the road required more help than they could possibly receive in San Mateo, even if Dr. Sánchez and Sister Justa hadn't already gone to Huehuetenango on another mission of mercy. "How many are there, mayor?"

"Nine, altogether, but two have already been taken to San Mateo."

While counting what seemed like more than seven injured, the priest was brought up short to see that the three men sitting in the back of the pickup were staring at him with unusual intensity. As he stared back, it took him a moment or two to realize that the three were actually dead, jammed together in the same sitting position they held when the claymore exploded. Slowly, Hennessey brought his hand to his mouth, clenched it into a fist, and blew through it.

As he moved to the other side of the pickup, the Iowan almost stumbled over the battered bodies of two women laying face down on the ground nearby. One seemed to be in her late forties, the other not much older than a teenager, both with the neat, handwoven patterns of their Mateano *huipiles* violated by the random stains of dirt and blood. In all, there were eight dead and seven confirmed wounded.

As the priest rushed back to his rectory for an additional supply of gasoline and a few mattresses, he threaded his way mentally through this second claymore tragedy, again involving innocent, unarmed civilians. At first, there was no question in his mind that this was the work of the bumbling EGP. *What excuse,* he wondered, *would the guerrillas offer for this attack? The fog, the rain, alcohol? . . . This pickup wasn't even covered with a tarpaulin!*

Then, contemplating that the attack bore so close a resemblance to February's bombing, the priest considered another alternative: *A stupid coincidence or was it the army copying the February attack? . . . Hoping the EGP would get the blame? . . . Quién sabe? Who knows?*

As he started the engine for his return trip to the site of the killings, the Iowan whispered: "God, don't let the guerrillas block that road again!"

Then, thinking that God didn't always pay attention to his requests, Hennessey exited the jeep, grabbed an ax and a shovel from the garage, and tucked them in the back of his vehicle. He also picked up the two victims who had already been brought to the hospital, a father and son, insisting that they go with him to Huehuetenango. One of them, Alfonso, the father, went reluctantly, saying matter-of-factly that he had to arrange for the burials of three of the victims, his wife, another son, and his son's wife.

When Hennessey arrived back at the scene of the attack, a weather-beaten old pickup from Soloma was already there, taking on some of the dead. The priest tried to get the driver to pull to one side and let him pass on the narrow road, but the man's Mayan concern for the spirits of the dead excluded consideration of the priest's Western concern for the living. While Hennessey gently pleaded the cause of the wounded, bystanders loaded them one by one into his Jeep Wagoneer, three on the front seat, leaving scarce room for the priest, two sitting on a flat spare tire in the rear, the four more seriously injured laid out together on the mattresses. Finally, just as the driver of the old pickup decided to let Hennessey pass, a man gestured toward the crippled Nissan and asked, "What about Mateo, the *chofer,* padre? He's still alive!"

In his haste to get the wounded into his jeep, the priest had overlooked the driver of the fatal vehicle still clinging to a wisp of life with what looked like a death grip on the padded steering wheel. After seeing that the *chofer* was indeed still alive, Hennessey convinced Alfonso, whom he had picked up in San Mateo and who wasn't as seriously injured as the others, to relinquish his seat to the man. With the help of some onlookers, Mateo was wedged into Alfonzo's vacated front seat next to the Iowan.

They had not gone but a few kilometers when Hennessey guessed that the uncontrolled bobbings of the *chofer* beside him were those of a corpse. The priest leaned forward and looked questioningly at the stoic man sitting impassively to Mateo's right. Saúl had shrapnel lodged in both thighs. "Yes, he's dead, padre!" Saúl responded to the look. "It's not your fault! You couldn't see he wasn't going to last till Huehuetenango."

There was nothing for the priest to do but to drive on, keeping the dead man propped in a sitting position with an elbow against his chest.

Just before the priest reached Soloma, a fairly new, flaming red Toyota pickup bearing down on them along a straightaway braked to a stop in the middle of the road, throwing up a cloud of dust and leaving no room for the Iowan to pass. The vehicle's three occupants jumped out and rushed to the priest's window. They breathlessly identified themselves as the brothers of Mateo, the dead driver wedged in beside Hennessey. They had already received word of their brother's accident.

Hennessey groped for words, trying to break the news as gently as he could. But what he said didn't matter, since not one of the three was listening. Instead, they were staring as if transfixed at the corpse beside him. Suddenly, one of the brothers cried out, interrupting the priest in mid-sentence: "Arise and walk, brother Mateo! By the power of Jesus Christ, we command you to arise and walk with Jesus!"

Hennessey remained silent, his head bowed in deference to the men's beliefs. New sects, he knew, especially fundamentalist and charismatic sects, were springing up across Guatemala in response to the innumerable, wanton killings occurring daily. The Church's newfound emphasis on human rights, including the right to struggle to defend them, had bred a deep antagonism between the military and

Church authorities. Therefore many people had found some welcome safety in renouncing their Catholicism and joining a fundamentalist Evangelical sect. It was a response he understood and respected, a brutalized people experimenting with alternative religious rites aimed at controlling the forces, both human and supernatural, responsible for the dramatic increase in death and destruction which their traditional rites seemed unable to halt.

"They're *evangélicos,* padre," Saúl whispered. "They think they can bring the dead back to life. But they haven't been able to do it yet!"

The *chofer's* three brothers, nevertheless, persevered in repeating their prayer over and over, arms outstretched, swaying back and forth. "Arise and walk, brother. Arise and walk with Jesus."

Finally, thinking again of his wounded passengers and believing that he had demonstrated sufficient respect for the brothers' beliefs, Hennessey asked one of the three to squeeze in behind his seat so that he could resume the trip to Huehuetenango.

When the entourage arrived in Soloma, Mateo's brother asked the priest to take the *chofer's* body to the run-down, one-room government clinic, thinking there might still be some hope for a traditional medical remedy. The light was on inside the room but the priest's pounding on the door brought no response. "The ladina nurse doesn't answer night calls," someone remarked.

Already, a crowd of the victim's relatives had gathered, but there was no visible interest in the priest's struggle against time for those who still harbored some life.

Recognizing that the clinic was closed for the night and that the nurse wouldn't take Mateo's cadaver off his hands anyway, the priest turned to the *chofer's* brothers and, with empty hands open in a gesture of helplessness, told them, "I did what I could for your brother while he was alive. But now that he's dead, . . . you have to take him. I've got to try to save the living."

Meanwhile, the Iowan's mind was rushing ahead, envisioning the guerrillas felling trees and maneuvering rocks up at the godforsaken *cumbre,* crushing what hopes he might have to save the lives of those who had barely survived the claymore.

The protests of one of Mateo's brothers brought him back to the present. "But he's our brother, he's our brother! You can't just leave him here, *señor.*"

"I'm sorry, *hermano* [brother]!" Hennessey replied softly. "I've done all I can! I must get these people to the hospital."

"Padre," one of Mateo's brothers interrupted, employing the priest's title, which up till then the three brothers had conscientiously avoided, "you're a priest! You know what to do when a person dies. I know my brother's dead and he's not coming back! What should we do?"

Hennessey turned and put his hand on the young man's shoulder. "Look, *hermano,* all you can do now for your brother is pray for him. Take his body home, wash it, and dress him up as you've been accustomed to, invite in your neighbors to read the scriptures, to pray and sing with you. That's all that God expects. It will help both your brother and your family."

"Thank you, padre! Thank you! We'll do as you suggest."

And even as the two men were speaking, friends of Mateo's family began to transfer the *chofer's* lifeless body to his brother's pickup.

The priest turned and climbed back in his jeep. Then, just as he restarted his engine, the brother of Lucas Antonio, another victim, asked if he could go along to the hospital. Hennessey agreed, only to regret his decision a moment later when the brother insisted that the priest stop at his family's house.

Lucas, with his mangled leg, had already told Hennessey that he wanted to be let off at his home and not transported to Huehuetenango. He preferred to die in Soloma, he had said. And despite Lucas's whole family echoing his demand when the priest pulled up before their home, Hennessey didn't yield— even though he thought the battle for Lucas's life might already be lost. Instead, he refused to open either of the jeep's locked doors as the relatives crowded around, pressing their hands against the vehicle's windows, calling, "Lucas! Lucas! You must stay with us! Let him go, padre, let our Lucas go! He must die here in Soloma!"

Hennessey listened for a moment or two and then, opening his window just a bit, forcefully admonished the entire clan, "If you take your brother out of this vehicle, you will be guilty of killing him! He has suffered a lot of bleeding and doesn't have much time left! Now do your brother and yourselves a favor and let us go. I'm taking him to Huehuetenango!"

While Lucas's family discussed the priest's admonition in Q'anjob'al, Lucas's brother, still sitting behind Hennessey in the jeep and understanding the significance of what the priest had just said, changed his mind and whispered, *"Vámonos, padre, vámonos!* Let's go!"

With that faint encouragement, the Iowan nodded his head, raced the engine and jumped the jeep forward a foot or two. The roar of the motor and the jeep's movement were sufficient to scatter the crowd. With a clear path, Hennessey drove ahead, slowing a few meters beyond the group to lower the window further, stick his head out, and call, "If you want to talk more to Lucas or myself, take the bus to Huehuetenango in the morning."

It was a few minutes past midnight when the priest pulled up at the emergency door of Huehuetenango's gaudy-pink hospital, and roused the nurse and police. After showing the unusually polite officer his papers and explaining the cause of the victims' wounds, the priest spent the next hour helping to cut the bloody clothes off the victims, scrounge up some blankets, and get them onto cots. Then, he left his patients with the hospital staff and drove the short block to the bishop's house, hidden behind a ten-foot-high wall, for a fitful night's sleep.

While lying in bed for a sleepless half hour, the Iowan tried unsuccessfully to pull the pieces of this latest tragedy together, a nearly exact replication of what had happened eight months earlier. *A claymore exploding against a pickup carrying fifteen Mayans . . . . Even the number of victims is the same!*

Finally, exhausted, the priest fell asleep.

Chapter 19

THE OLD FOX LIVES UP TO HIS NAME

When word of the assassination of Castillo Armas reached Colombia, a wizened old militarist no sooner heard the news than he began planning how he would show the world—particularly the United States—what a real Guatemalan *caudillo* looked like. Miguel Ydígoras Fuentes knew that this was his last chance to grab the reins of presidential power and he was determined to make the most of it. The *gringos* would have to pay attention this time or blood would flow in the streets of Guatemala. Three times before he had come within a knife's edge of grabbing the prize, twice denied by the Americans (1944 and 1954) and once by the Guatemalan archbishop (1950). It wouldn't happen again!

As Ydígoras's Pan American flight approached Guatemalan airspace, a flight attendant approached the former Ubico executioner and told him that the pilot had just received a radio message from Aurora Airbase flight control that a rowdy lynch mob awaited the ex-general on the tarmac, making it too dangerous for him to deplane there. The captain, the young woman explained, had decided to detour to Ilopango Airport in San Salvador where his esteemed passenger could exit in safety.

The Old Fox nodded slightly, but said nothing. He had expected trouble somewhere along the line, but not so soon. He sat gripping the armrests for a moment while the flight attendant returned to her post and the plane banked to portside. A moment later, Ydígoras arose and walked slowly up the aisle toward the cockpit. He tried the door. It opened easily. He stepped inside and closed it behind him. He reached under his coat and with a quick movement he had practiced many times pulled out the .45 caliber revolver he carried at all times next to his stout heart. As he pressed the cold muzzle against the bone right behind the American pilot's right ear, he paused.

Then, slowly, he hissed in his best English: "You son of a bitch! We go to Guatemala or we all die!"[1]

Fifteen minutes later, the plane was descending on its final approach to Aurora Airport, the pilot trying to stay focused on his glide path lest an unnecessary bump at touchdown trigger a nervous index finger. Sure enough, there was a rowdy crowd on the tarmac, but the majority of them were Ydígoras supporters, rousted by the Old Fox's clique once its members knew the hour of their leader's return. The welcome wasn't nearly as large or as exuberant as that extended to Dr. Arévalo Bermejo thirteen years earlier, but it was a springboard the Old Fox knew he could exploit even as his rival had done before him.

Elections to name a new president had already been announced for 20 October 1957—the anniversary of the October Revolution—by the president pro-tem, Luis Arturo González López. At the time, the defense minister, Colonel Juan Francisco Oliva, a man the U.S. Embassy characterized as "having a good heart but no guts,"[2] was in actual control of the country. As far as Ydígoras Fuentes was concerned, both these men were merely bit players occupying the stage until the appearance of the star performer on the scene.

When the plane taxied to a stop one hundred yards from the small terminal, the crowd broke through the ring of restraining police like a surging Pacific tide against a small breakwater. The hatch door swung open even while the deplaning steps were being pushed into place. The ex-general stood framed by the doorway, a picture of historical inevitability, both arms raised over his head, hands clasped together, a huge smile on his weathered face. He was home and he knew it, as did many Guatemalans.

A six-week whirlwind campaign tour followed as the Old Fox crisscrossed the country promising to restore Guatemala's historical glory, its respect for God, the fatherland, its traditions, and laws. The seemingly unbounded energy the old man exhibited had his closest advisors looking on in wonderment.

The election took place on 20 October as scheduled. But even before the polls had closed, the *Ydígoristas* had already initiated an orchestrated cacophony of charges denouncing the stuffing of ballot boxes, acts of intimidation, and sundry other fraudulent activities, all allegedly indulged in by supporters of the candidate of the Movimiento de Liberación Nacional (MLN).

Two days later, the electoral commission announced that Miguel Ortiz Pasarelli, the MLN candidate and Castillo Armas's former interior minister (the top police official, for all formal purposes), had won a plurality of votes. At the same time, it discounted all Ydígoras's accusations of fraud.

A vote plurality was not enough to give the MLN candidate the presidency, but it would guarantee his selection in a secondary, follow-up election—if such occurred—mandated to be held in the MLN-controlled Constituent Assembly. That guarantee, however, depended upon Ydígoras Fuentes remaining quietly on the sidelines, a possibility everyone discounted.

The Old Fox would have none of the electoral tribunal's disclaimers. Ortiz Pasarelli was a nobody, a compromise candidate selected to avoid internal bleeding by the various MLN factions. His public stature could not raise a shadow, while Ydígoras Fuentes possessed a national reputation— albeit one besmirched in many quarters.

The ex-general called upon his supporters to take to the streets to protest the alleged fraud. It was part of a strategy the details of which the Old Fox had worked out with military precision several days before the election took place.

Organized rioting broke out across the capital. The next day, 23 October, pro-tem President González Gómez pronounced the election licit and valid; at the same time he declared a state of siege, suspending all constitutional rights and effectively placing the government in the hands of the army. The minister of defense waved González Gómez aside and announced that he was naming a three-man junta under Colonel Oscar Mendoza Azurdia to rule the country.

The following day, after consulting with the U.S. Embassy, the junta members invited Ydígoras Fuentes to a meeting in order to get the ex-general's cooperation to calm his supporters, who were still causing havoc in the streets. They also invited the U.S. ambassador, Edward J. Sparks, to attend, knowing that without U.S. approval, no agreement with the Old Fox could be made to stick.

Sparks sent Colonel Donald Cubbison, his military attaché, and Colonel Robert Hertzel, his air attaché, to the meeting, assuring that the dialogue would be soldier-to-soldier. The two attachés convinced the junta members to invalidate the 20 October elections and to schedule new elections for 19 January 1958 in which Ydígoras would participate against an MLN candidate to be named. Further, Second Vice President Guillermo Flores Avendaño would serve as provisional president in the interim to give the appearance of democratic procedure.

The freshly minted benediction of Ydígoras Fuentes by the U.S. Embassy was apparently triggered by Foster Dulles's diminished faith in the political trajectory of the MLN due to the revered Liberator's consistent unwillingness to move firmly—and illegally—against all *Arbencistas* qua "communists." The Old Fox, a man who had a history of singing the anticommunist tune like a virtuoso, would now become the second anointed savior of Guatemala's democracy, a successor to the Liberator preferable to any member of Castillo Armas's own political following.

The acceptance of Ydígoras Fuentes as the approved candidate of the U.S. Embassy mystified some political insiders. Had the Old Fox made his peace with the CIA? Or did the State Department have one candidate and the CIA another?

Assistant Secretary of State of Interamerican Affairs R.R. Rubottom, in reviewing the agreement, stated that he thought "the Commies had not gained and there was a reasonable chance of an orderly government emerging."[3]

Guillermo Flores Avendaño was sworn in as president pro tem on 27 October.

It was only a matter of days before Foster Dulles had second thoughts about allowing Flores Avendaño to function as president even if it were for only three months and in a ceremonial capacity. On 8 November, the secretary of state telegraphed Ambassador Sparks that "we feel strongly we should comply [with] request [of] Military Government [*sic*] that you assist identifying communists and undesirable political exiles who might be able to influence political situation in a way favorable to the communists."[4]

The junta's request for American help to identify "communists" and "undesirables" was not due to the colonels' ignorance of who was who among their countrymen and what political persuasions and activities they indulged in, but rather their recognition that the United States had different criteria for making such judgments, and it was those criteria and judgments that would prevail.

Dulles then underlined his determination to keep the "undesirables" out of the political fray and he hinted at the lengths to which he would go if he felt the need to exert pressure:

> In addition preventing entrance undesirable exiles, important GOG [Government of Guatemala] adopt firm attitude toward expulsion or firm control those who have already returned . . . . Should you encounter resistance or complacency from Guatemalan officials on taking effective action against these undesirables, Department wishes to be promptly informed with indication as to sources such resistance or complacency.[5]

Over the next two months, Secretary of State Dulles sent off telegram after telegram, each more hysterical than the preceding, ordering Ambassador Sparks to tell the Guatemalans, particularly Acting President Flores Avendaño (the junta had decided to let the president handle state affairs) that they were flirting with disaster and the possible loss of U.S. economic aid if they did not do a better job of controlling the upcoming election. Dulles was upset that some of the five hundred individuals named on the list his department had handed over to the junta were being allowed to return to Guatemala. Dulles took special aim at Guillermo Toriello, Arbenz's foreign minister, a businessman whom no reputable Guatemalan had ever accused of being a communist.

But Dulles was not to be deterred from exhibiting his pachydermal-style diplomacy, suggesting that President Flores Avendaño either did not understand communism or was possibly involved with the Partido Revolucionario (PR, a weak, moderately rightest party) and its presidential hopeful, Mario Méndez Montengro (MMM). He wired Sparks that:

> The Department considers the election of MMM and the PR would be most undesirable of possible eventualities now in prospect and that this would prove in the long run most harmful to Guatemala's interests, U.S. interests in Guatemala and U.S.-Guatemalan relations . . . . Méndez (M.M.M.) has been known as opponent of US companies in Guatemala and of GOG agreements with US companies. Department believes that troubles of U.S.

companies would multiply under regime headed by him, and believes this already indicated by PR backing of strike and intervening of IRCA [International Railroads of Central America, a UFCO subsidiary].[6]

Thus Dulles laid to rest any argument over whether the U.S. overthrow of Arbenz Guzmán was primarily a case of thwarting a communist government or protecting U.S. capital interests.

When Ambassador Sparks went to Flores Avendaño with Dulles's complaints, the president was reassuring. He told the American diplomat that the election was really between Ydígoras Fuentes and Colonel Cruz Salazar, the junta's straw MLN candidate and the Liberator's former ambassador to Washington. The president added that he thought Ydígoras Fuentes would win the election, indicating that he personally favored the Old Fox, and that Washington should stop worrying about Mario Méndez Montenegro.

As for letting exiled undesirables back into Guatemala, Flores Avendaño explained that many individuals blacklisted by the State Department had committed no crime, and that the Guatemalan Supreme Court had declared unconstitutional any attempt to keep them out of the country, a ruling he intended to abide by. On the other hand, the president added, he would block anyone proven to be a communist from reentering the country.

And so it was! On 19 January 1958, General Miguel Ydígoras Fuentes was said to have received a plurality of votes. Cries of fraud arose from the Cruz Salazar camp, but they were muted. Cruz Salazar placed second, having been paid a sizable sum—rumored to be the standard $50,000—by the CIA to make a credible run and then to drift quietly into obscurity. Méndez Montenegro placed an insignificant third. Two days later the Constituent Assembly voted to confirm Ydígoras's election, his term to begin 15 March 1958 and run for six years.

There is a single word in the minds of the vast majority of Guatemalans that best describes the years of the Ydígoras Fuentes government: *corruption*. There are other applicable terms, among them, anticommunist, antidemocratic, theatrical, duplicitous, inept, and conservative (in the true sense of that word), but "corrupt" remains alone at the pinnacle. And the government's corruption—or better, Ydígoras's—can best be seen in how the Old Fox disposed of Las Fincas Nacionales.

It wasn't long after Ydígoras Fuentes had donned the presidential sash that the Guatemalan economy went into a steep decline. Conditions had been bad enough under Castillo Armas despite huge investments from the World Bank and the U.S. government. The fratricidal infighting among the various self-seeking segments of the Liberator's ideologically diverse followers, the drop in world coffee prices, and several inadequate corn harvests had guaranteed a continuous, palpable level of popular unrest. But the unbridled thievery and adolescent incompetence of the Ydígoras Fuentes clique, the withdrawal of Castillo Armas-level economic aid by the United States and the World Bank, and the Old Fox's dead-end economic schemes, such as the development of a national maritime fleet, soon pushed the national economy into depression-like conditions.

Archbishop Rossell y Arellano stepped forward to pronounce his (and God's) take on the new administration and its policies—or lack thereof: "These are not anti-Communists who have sealed with their blood their conviction that Guatemala had to be freed from the ideology of atheistic Marxism. These are not anti-Communists faithful to the ideals of the *caudillo* of the Liberation . . . ."[7]

It was the aged prelate's response to the Old Fox's attempts—eventually successful—to manipulate the Vatican into refusing to allow Rossell y Arellano to name his own coadjutor bishop and probable successor, giving that privilege instead to Ydígoras Fuentes himself in exchange for the president's decree to allow the teaching of Catholic doctrine in public schools. The enmity between the two men went back a decade, born of Ydígoras Fuentes's political protestations of religious ideals of what in essence was his nonexistent Roman Catholicism.

As the corruption became more blatant, popular opposition coalesced, expressed in demonstrations, strikes, and bombings, the latter more sound than fury. The Old Fox responded like a scratched phonograph record, blaming time and again the communists and Fidel Castro's government—installed nine months after his own—for the unrest. Castro had opened himself to Ydígoras's criticism by granting a public platform to former president Arbenz

Guzmán and for urging disinherited Latin Americans across the continent to initiate revolutions of their own.

The evidence Ydígoras produced to back up his claims of Castroite culpability—explicit, subversive documents signed by Che Guevara and other luminaries of the Cuban government—were such obvious fabrications as to lead many to think they were CIA productions intended to scare the president into a closer embrace with the Agency. More knowledgeable observers felt, however, that the documents were too pedestrian to have come from either Washington or Havana and were actually the product of the Old Fox's own Machiavellian clique. In Guatemalan political parlance, the maneuver is known as an *auto-golpe,* a self-inflicted hit blamed on one's enemies and intended to gain sympathy for the target.

Ydígoras vacillated, blaming Castro one moment, the CIA the next.

As Castro continued to confiscate U.S.—owned properties, including sugar plantations, oil refineries, casinos, and bordellos, while using a firing squad to execute high-ranking, political and military supporters of the former Batista dictatorship, generally friends of the United States, Washington became ever more outraged. Allen Dulles and Richard Bissell began formulating plans on how to dispose of the Cuban dictator, focusing first on a Mafia-based assassination plan, and then, when that seemed unworkable, a campaign of guerrilla and psychological warfare that would result in a broad-based popular uprising. The CIA's 1954 success in Guatemala would be the template applied to the new situation in Cuba.

Once again, the whole operation had to be hidden from the American people. And once again President Eisenhower gave the CIA his soldierly blessing.

Meanwhile, the economic interests of Ydígoras Fuentes (read: greed) and the foreign policy interests of the United States (the desire for unchallenged hemispheric hegemony) began to converge, motivating the Old Fox to temper his anti-CIA rhetoric. Allen Dulles and Richard Bissell got the message.

Sometime in April 1960, the CIA station chief in Guatemala, Robert Kendall Davis, armed with the outline of a promising paramilitary enterprise, visited an old friend, Roberto Alejos, a dominant member of the Ydígoras clique and one of the wealthiest landowners in Guatemala. Davis asked Alejos to intercede with President Ydígoras to allow the CIA to train Cuban exiles on Guatemalan soil to be then infiltrated into their homeland as anti-Castro guerrillas. Davis hinted that there would be substantial monetary rewards for Guatemala/Ydígoras if cooperation were forthcoming. In the bargain, Guatemala could repay the United States in kind for its sponsorship of *La Liberación,* of which Ydígoras was an indirect beneficiary. Guatemala would thereby serve as the incubator of Cuban democracy in 1960 even as Honduras had performed this service for his country in 1954.

Alejos talked with the Old Fox and the meeting with Davis followed. A plan was quickly hatched. Helvetia, one of Alejos's plantations, with one hundred kilometers of private roads twisting through five thousand acres of remote piedmont lands in the province of coffee-growing Retalhuleu, much of it covered with subtropical flora, was chosen as the ideal site.

Four hundred Guatemalan Army troops under the orders of a cooperative colonel were sent to Helvetia in order to provide cover for the operation and to keep the *finca*'s thirteen hundred coffee workers at a safe distance. The army high command was never consulted. Ydígoras had no intention of sharing the CIA's payoff with any more individuals than necessary. Alejos, though, would have his place at the banquet table.

Then, with the monumental hypocrisy that only potentates and professional politicians dare muster, Ydígoras broke diplomatic relations with Castro, accusing the Cuban *caudillo* of training a guerrilla force in the Escambray Mountains of eastern Cuba with the intention of invading Guatemala.

By November of 1960, the CIA had finally decided that its efforts to resupply their infiltrated guerrillas in Cuba's Escambray Mountains with parachute drops from Nicaragua-based C-46s were largely unsuccessful. Castro, educated by his own guerrilla experience, had learned to contain the infiltrators and deny them effective contacts with the Cuban people. As a result, the CIA changed plans: an externally based invasion force—repeating the Guatemalan experience—would replace the guerrilla columns. Such an invasion force would hit the beaches of eastern Cuba accompanied by an air wing, capture and hold some land, then announce a provisional government that would ask for and receive U.S. recognition, facilitating resupply. Castro would then go the way of Arbenz Guzmán. It all seemed so academic.

But the secret plans were hardly secret anymore. On 30 October 1960, Clemente Marroquin Rojas, the right-wing owner and editor of one of Guatemala's principal dailies, *La Hora,* told his readers that an invasion of Cuba was being organized in Guatemala, "but not by Guatemalans." His revelations only served to confirm what had been rumored for months among knowledgeable Guatemalans. The same information was now beginning to appear in the *Miami Herald, Los Angeles Times,* and other news outlets in the United States.

Two weeks later, on 13 November, 120 Guatemalan Army officers and the troops they commanded, nearly one-third the entire army, rebelled. They seized Fort Matamoros, the army's major armory in Guatemala City, captured the Caribbean port city, Puerto Barrios, and took control of the Zacapa barracks, the central command base for the eastern provinces. As word of the revolt spread, eight hundred peasants presented themselves at the Zacapa base requesting arms, volunteering to fight at the side of the rebels. The officers refused, always distrustful of arming militant civilians.

The rebels' complaints focused on Ydígoras Fuentes' corruption, his manipulation of the October 1958 presidential election, but especially his permission to allow foreign military bases on national soil for the purpose of a sneak attack on a sovereign country—and what was even worse!—for personal monetary gain. The Old Fox's attempt to detour around the army high command had backfired.

Ydígoras reacted as if he had received an electric shock. He was shaking when he radioed the CIA at Alejos's ranch and demanded to speak to the head man. When he got Rip Robertson on the phone, he told the American in graphic terms that his military bases in Zacapa and Puerto Barrios were in the hands of mutinous troops. He also shouted that his cowardly air force had refused to fly against the rebels. If his government were to fall, he yelled at Robertson, a new military government would quickly expel the Cuban trainees and their American advisors, with unforeseeable international consequences for the United States. The Old Fox demanded that the United States use its Cuban air wing to put down the rebellion.

A radio call to Opa-Locka by an alarmed Robertson followed. The request was pushed upstairs to Washington. An affirmative answer came quickly from Richard Bissell. There was no question that President Eisenhower had been asked for and given his approval. Word then passed to Major General George Reid Doster, commander of the CIA air wing training in Nicaragua. Within hours, eight B-26s piloted by rebel Cubans were over Zacapa and Puerto Barrios, bombing and strafing the rebel positions.

The rebellion lost steam in a few days when the source of the attacking air power was identified and the U.S. aircraft carrier *Shangri-La* and five supporting destroyers were seen off the Puerto Barrios coast. The same psychological pressure that had been exerted on the Guatemalan officer corps by CIA planes and the threat of overwhelming U.S. firepower during Operation PBSuccess was again demonstrating its effectiveness.

As their efforts collapsed, a small group of the leaders chose to flee to the safety of the Sierra de las Minas Mountains, rather than accept traditional punishments—demotion, retirement, or assignment to embassies abroad. In the mountains, the rebels found substantial support for their action among the peasants who had lost their lands when Castillo Armas overturned Arbenz Guzmán's agrarian reform. They hid the rebellious officers, fed them, and then guided them over back trails into Honduras and El Salvador, promising them support should they ever try their luck again.

Ydígoras Fuentes blamed the uprising on his favorite scapegoats, the communists and Fidel Castro. Castro, for his part, went into stunning detail to describe the CIA's preparations in Guatemala and Nicaragua for its invasion of Cuba and its intervention in putting down the Guatemalan officers' rebellion. When Ydígoras later made a flight over a hunting site claimed by Roberto Alejos on the Pasión River in the remote northern jungle of El Petén to size it up as a containing pen for some disgruntled Cuban trainees, Castro denounced the president's trip the following day over Radio Habana. A group of angry trainees had been complaining about the leadership roles given to former supporters of Caudillo Fulgencio Batista and were on the verge of creating their own mutiny among the CIA enlistees.

Despite Castro's awareness of the potential for rebellion among the Cuban paramilitary recruits, he was not able to take advantage of the situation. The disgruntled trainees were nevertheless interned at Alejos's jungle fishing camp, a place called San Juan Acul. Eight years later, Ron Hennessey, while knowing nothing of the history of the site, took advantage of the half-dozen abandoned CIA constructions to house thirty-four landless Mayan families and begin a seven-year residency at San Juan Acul, where he guided his parishioners in what the government and Church hierarchy recognized as a successful colonization program.[8]

The Old Fox's attempts to blame all his ills on the communists even while he continued to plunder the national treasury abetted the forces of opposition on all sides. Even the U.S. Embassy was beginning to show signs of fatigue, making quasi-public statements to the effect that the government was abetting communism by its ineffective economic policies.

But as his difficulties multiplied, Ydígoras went to such lengths to distract his fellow citizens that many were questioning his sanity. The president ordered his air force to strafe some Mexican tuna boats purportedly fishing in Guatemalan waters, and then broke diplomatic relations with Mexico during the ensuing furor. He walked unannounced into British Honduras and planted the Guatemalan flag, claiming that the British colony really belonged to Guatemala, while threatening to go to war with England over the matter. He angered El Salvador by claiming that the waters of Lake Güija on their common border belonged to his government. And he promised to use the powers of his office with the pope to obtain the canonization of Brother Pedro Betancourt, a historical religious figure with a wide popular following in Guatemala.

Opposition mounted. High school and university students took to the streets demanding the president's resignation. Congress echoed the students' call. Bombs exploded across the city, giving Ydígoras a reason for calling out his army. In the resulting repression, scores were killed, hundreds wounded, and hundreds more jailed.[9]

Finally, the bishops issued a pastoral letter decrying the situation:

> On the plantations the peasant is frozen by customs hundreds of years old and submerged in conditions of blatant inferiority, receiving salaries that hardly permit him to avoid death by starvation . . . . Especially grave is the standard of living of thousands and thousands of workers on state and private plantations. Besides the conditions of their work, they live collectively in wooden shacks, without light, without windows, without interior walls for privacy, generally without sufficient and adequate sanitary systems, without the possibility of intimate family life nor morality.[10]

On 6 February 1962, three truckloads of armed men in camouflaged uniforms overpowered an army post in Mariscos, Izabal, took the resident soldiers' weapons and ammunition, destroyed their communications equipment, and retired down the dirt road toward the Atlantic Highway. A few hours later, these same men appeared at Bananera, headquarters for the Atlantic Coast operations of the United Fruit Company.

Driving up to Bananera's rows of banana yellow houses surrounded by expanses of well-trimmed lawns and colorful flower gardens kept fresh by a platoon of oscillating sprinklers, one feels an atmosphere of subtropical tranquility that only a Hollywood set might match. But appearances often deceive, and at Bananera appearances did deceive. The presence of a military post near the administration buildings was one indication that UFCO's directors did not view their surroundings as entirely idyllic. And located across the railroad tracks, both symbolic and real, where visitors were never welcomed, were the quarters where underpaid, overworked, disrespectful workers ate, drank, fought, slept, and organized.

A group of the intruders entered the company headquarters and there disabled the communications equipment and held management personnel at bay while a larger contingent headed straight for the military post where the executive officer awaited them. After assembling his puzzled troops, the officer introduced the visitors as his friends, telling his men that he—and they— were going to help the newcomers install a government of honorable men with the balls needed to stand up for what was right and just.

The visitors' leader was Comandante Marco Antonio Yon Sosa, a Chinese-Guatemalan trained as a ranger by the United States at Fort Gullick, Panama, and a participant in the abbreviated rebellion of 13 November 1960. He was one of the handful of officers who, after the attempted coup, had fled to the mountains of the Sierra de las Minas rather than cave in to CIA air power.

Yon Sosa took the floor to explain to the assembled troops that he was the point man for an entirely new movement, one based on the tactics and strategy of a guerrilla war modeled after that of Fidel Castro. It would be a war of the poor and landless against the thieving rich and powerful, aimed directly at an army whose officer corps was riddled with corrupt *vendenpatria* elements. A year of political work had already been done in Guatemala City and in the rural provinces of Zacapa, Izabal, El Progreso, Chiquimula, Jalapa, and Jutiapa. The nuclei of three guerrilla columns had been formed, one now led by himself, another by former lieutenant Luis Turcios Lima, a counterinsurgency expert trained at Fort Benning, Georgia, and a third by former colonel Carlos Paz Tejada, minister of defense in the Arbenz Guzmán government.

After spending a few more moments answering questions from the troops, Yon Sosa and his men crossed the yard to pay a visit to UFCO's directors and to let them know that they were being closely watched for behavior unbecoming foreigners in a poverty-stricken nation. They then retreated back down the road accompanied by the base's executive officer and a small group of his troops, heading back into the mountains.

News of the Bananera guerrilla operation had an immediate effect in Guatemala City where sympathetic demonstrations and strikes broke out. When the police killed twenty demonstrators, wounding hundreds more during the second week of March 1962, the Movimiento de Liberacion Nacional, the Democracia Cristiana, and the Partido Revolucionario all called for Ydígoras to resign in favor of a civilian-military junta. The Old Fox responded by replacing his entire cabinet, with the exception of his foreign minister, with military officers.

But Ydígoras's luck was beginning to run out. His opponents were . everywhere, including within the upper levels of his own administration. In the United States, a new president, John F. Kennedy, was growing exasperated, watching the expenditure of his political capital in support of an unpopular government that seemed intent on fueling a Marxist insurgency, while he tried to initiate a new, multilateral economic development plan for Latin America that he called his Alliance for Progress (La Alianza para El Progreso).

When Kennedy introduced *La Alianza,* he remarked, "those who make peaceful revolution impossible, make violent revolution inevitable." He had in mind Cuba. It was a pithy statement, but one that the young president refused to take to heart. On the contrary, his collateral creation, the Special Forces or Green Berets, was intended to prevent all violent revolutions from succeeding, even where peaceful revolution had been rendered impossible. This was especially true where the impossibility of peaceful revolution was a function of U.S. business interests.

Although Kennedy was not in the White House when planning for the overthrow of Castro began, Allen Dulles briefed him on it shortly after his election. After his inauguration, the invasion became the new president's kettle of crabs, though he personally never became enthusiastic. Three months later, the invasion at the Bay of Pigs took place minus Major General George Reid Doster's Nicaragua-based air wing, dooming the project before the Cuban troops set sail from Guatemala. Kennedy had nixed the additional use of air power after the CIA blew its cover by concocting an insupportable story to hide its sponsorship of a preemptive air strike on Castro's air force.

Camelot took a lot of political flack for the invasion's failure and the resultant loss of life.

So when Guatemala's fledging guerrilla movement began galvanizing support in the rural eastern provinces and gained respect in the urban centers, a chastened Kennedy did not hesitate to honor the requests of his military advisors to send help. The Pentagon established a counterinsurgency base staffed by Spanish-speaking Mexican-American and Puerto Rican Green Berets (with experience in Vietnam and Laos) at Mariscos, Izabal, the same site from which Comandante Yon Sosa had begun his guerrilla march on Bananera. The United States followed up by transferring to the Guatemalan Air Force several C-47 troop transports and four T-33 jet trainers outfitted for strafing and bombing runs.

As in the case of Castillo Armas where additional U.S. military training and hardware did nothing to strengthen a nonexistent unified army, merely increasing the ability of one military clique to threaten and control others, so too under Ydígoras Fuentes. In November 1962, using its newly acquired T-33s, the Guatemalan Air Force attempted to "terminate Ydígoras, with prejudice,"[11] strafing and bombing the Casa Crema (the Cream House), the luxurious, well-fortified home that Ydígoras had the government build for him and his family. But the army, recalling the air force's denial of support for its November 1960 coup attempt, refused to assist the rebellion.

The presidential honor guard, however, swung behind Ydígoras and mounted a spirited counterattack on the air base at La Aurora. The president marshaled his personal camera crew and had it film him as he left the Casa Crema on his way to La Aurora with a machine gun slung over his shoulder. That evening, the government TV channel broadcast its version of the day's events, showing footage of the country's *macho caudillo* on his way to settle another score with his favorite bête noire, Fidel Castro. For it was Castro, the Old Fox claimed, who was the brains and financier behind the uprising.

Ydígoras Fuentes made his final mistake in March 1963. After having repeatedly stated that he would not allow ex-president Juan José Arévalo Bermejo's return to Guatemala to run in the presidential elections slated for the end of the year, he changed his mind. He declared that Arévalo was now free to participate as a candidate for the presidency.

The Old Fox was intentionally baiting the United States when he invited Arévalo home. In November 1962, when the suggestion of Arévalo's new candidacy first surfaced, John D. Bell, Kennedy's ambassador to Guatemala, sent a three-page, telegraphic diatribe to Secretary of State Dean Rusk asking the secretary to clarify the U.S. position vis-à-vis Arévalo:

> Arévalo's accession to power would be completely adverse to U.S. interests. . . . Arévalo is an extremely dangerous man, pathologically anti-American . . . a man who invited into Guatemala and gave power to Communists from all over the hemisphere. . . . For the United States not to oppose him in every way is criminally stupid in my view. It is true that he enjoys a large popular support here; no doubt Castro did at one time in Cuba. . . . I think it is sheer and dangerous self-delusion to think that one could ever deal with him.[12]

On 24 January 1963, Dean Rusk cabled all U.S. ambassadors in Latin America to "avoid any association with Arévalo and where opportune to inform other governments and political leaders of our attitude." The secretary clarified what he meant by "where opportune," indicating that any anti-Arévalo talk should be undertaken in private, confidential conversations in order "to avoid the accusation of United States interference in the internal affairs of his county." It would be enough, Rusk counseled, to point to Arévalo's record and to cite his views, "which reveal the confused erratic and ill-balanced nature of his thinking."[13]

At a secret meeting chaired by President Kennedy during that same month, attended by his top Latin American advisors, Kennedy gave his approval for a coup against Ydígoras should the possibility of Arévalo's participation in the presidential elections materialize—recognizing that Arévalo would win handily should he run.[14] When the news broke that Arévalo had slipped across the border into Guatemala on 29 March, an immediate outbreak of popular enthusiasm was too much for the U.S. Embassy to abide. Word was passed to the minister of national defense, Colonel Enrique Peralta Azurdia, that he had the blessing of the U.S. government to escort the Old Fox out of the country and into oblivion.

At Maryknoll Seminary in New York, Ron Hennessey heard about the coup that terminated Ydígoras's presidency and was mystified. He knew Ydígoras to be an old Maryknoll admirer and an anticommunist who had assisted the CIA in training the Cuban exiles for the Bay of Pigs debacle. But the fact that the overthrow had been carried out by the Guatemala Army, itself a bastion of anticommunism, and the new government quickly recognized by the United States, puzzled the Iowan. He did not dwell on the matter for long, however. He had other more pressing issues to occupy his attention.

It was April 1963 and Hennessey was scheduled to receive the first of the three major Holy Orders, the subdeaconate, in little over two months. It was then that he would take his final oath of obedience to his Maryknoll superiors, as well as a papal-mandated oath against Modernism, and promise to remain celibate for the rest of his life. Naturally, questions of one's worthiness, commitment, and endurance would suggest themselves from time to time, more so as the weeks turned to days and the hour of no return approached.

Finally, during the first week of June 1963, Hennessey took the step he had been preparing himself for during the preceding nine years. He submitted himself to the rite of subdeaconate ordination, agreed to obey his Maryknoll superiors as long as such obedience did not conflict with the demands of his own conscience, consented to remain celibate for life to the degree that his free will was capable of mandating, but crossed his fingers when required to take the oath against Modernism. The joy he felt when he left the chapel a subdeacon, his sense of relief, could only be shared by his classmates. Everyone felt a sense of quiet excitement.

It would be years before some of them would decide that the celibate priesthood was not their vocation after all. Even the Iowan would at times have fleeting doubts regarding the decision he had made that day.

But not on this day!

PART V

Chapter 20

FROM THE HALLS OF TRANSCENDENTALISM
TO THE SHORES OF EXISTENTIALISM

The Delta Airlines flight out of New Orleans to Guatemala had a certain bicultural flavor that reminded Hennessey that this trip was like none other . he had ever taken, including those to and from Korea. The head flight attendant made all her announcements in both English and Spanish, rolling her "r's" with a facility the Iowan hoped he would soon be able to match.

Many of his fellow passengers had the looks and manners of international Latin American travelers, an elegance of dress that was unmistakable even in vacation clothes, an air of easy self-confidence not often found on public display in Anglo Americans. The pilot possessed an acceptable Spanish accent as he rattled off the exotic sounding names of Mexican cities and archeological sites, Mérida, Campeche, Chichén Itzá, Palenque, all accompanied by a pleasant southern drawl. Even the one stopover on the sunbaked limestone beds of Mérida, where Hennessey felt heat like none he had ever known, underscored the total transition that he was experiencing, a definitive break with his Iowa past. The date was 16 September 1964.

Suddenly, the Delta Airline's captain announced that below them lay Guatemala City. He ticked off the names of three surrounding volcanoes, Agua, Pacaya, and Fuego, the latter two very much alive. As more and more gingerbread tile roofs came into view, Ron was struck by the sense of a muted skyline, with few buildings of more than three or four stories, and the colonial churches with their telltale bell towers on the corner of every two or three blocks, mute testimony to a vigorous religious life of centuries past.

Father Frank Garvey, a veteran missioner who had worked in Guatemala for almost two decades, met Hennessey and fellow Maryknoller Larry Egan at the entrance to the international arrivals area as a welcoming committee of one. He was of medium build, outgoing and friendly, angelic looking, the quintessential stereotype of a priest. He laughed easily when Larry Egan suggested that they might have a long wait at customs due to the large amount of baggage they had brought with them. "Watch!" Garvey answered, shaking his head.

Frank went over to the agent who had taken charge of the priests' bags and, with a friendly smile, shook the man's hand. He then spoke to him, gesturing to the bags, putting a hand on the man's arm. The two then turned and looked at Hennessey and Egan. The agent smiled and nodded at the two priests. He then turned back to the luggage, slapped inspection stickers on each bag without opening a single one, and waved to a waiting handler to take them away.

"What did you say to him?" Ron asked once out of earshot.

"As soon as I greeted him, I asked about his family. That's always number one! Do that and you'll never go wrong!"

Once outside, Hennessey was stunned by the beauty that surrounded the airport, radiant subtropical flora, green grasses, flowers of every shape and color, especially red, white, and violet bougainvillea, palm trees swaying in the afternoon breeze, all irrigated by the cool waters of the late rainy season showers. As they left the airport in Garvey's ancient green Renault, Hennessey felt taken aback by the young, baby-faced soldiers in olive-green field uniforms with rifles and machine guns held in both hands, standing with backs against the walls at almost every street corner.

"Why all the guns, Frank?" the Iowan asked. "Those guys must be expecting trouble the way they're holding their weapons."

"You had better get used to the soldiers and guns, fellas, because we are in the middle of one of our frequent political crises. We've been hearing rumors for weeks about a coup attempt against Colonel Peralta Azurdia, the president. If it comes off, it probably won't be successful. He took power by way of a coup and should know how to handle it."

"Your calm in the face of a possible collapse of the government is to be admired, Frank," the Iowan remarked, half in jest.

Garvey shrugged. "It's nothing to concern us. It's a fight between soldiers about who gets what piece of the pie. Our only concern is what the winner thinks about American priests coming here to preach the gospel."

Fifteen minutes later, the three men arrived at the Maryknoll Center House in the wealthy southeastern suburbs of the capital city. Hennessey and

Egan spent the rest of the day looking around their new accommodations and neighborhood, trying out the few Spanish expressions they thought they had mastered, only to be greeted with amused smiles or looks of incomprehension.

On his third day in Guatemala, Hennessey flew with Egan in an ancient DC-3 bi-motor owned and operated by the national airline, Aviateca, to Huehuetenango, site of Maryknoll's Central American language school. During the forty-five minute flight, Ron tried to convince himself that the accommodations of the plane were in such poor shape because Aviateca was spending all its resources on keeping the engines, controls, and air surfaces in tip-top condition. His seat was not anchored tightly to the floor, missing two bolts. The luggage and cargo was piled haphazardly near the rear exit without benefit of secure tie-downs. And when the pilot made a close sweep of a mountain slope on the base leg of his landing pattern and then bounced the plane several times as he landed on the dirt strip, the Iowan was convinced he had come to live in a country of unrestrained serendipity.

Father Jim Curtin, the regional superior for Maryknoll's Central American region, stood his ground near the runway with his hat covering his face as the old DC-3 taxied up, turned, and blew a cloud of dust in his direction. "Welcome to Huehuetenango," Curtin smiled, opening his arms wide to give Hennessey and Egan a bear-hug *abrazo* as they came off the set of deplaning steps.

Curtin was a big man, almost six feet tall, well over two hundred pounds, much of it resting comfortably at his waistline. His thinning black hair belied his age, only forty-six years, mute testimony to his worrisome disposition. He walked flat-footed with a bouncy gate, arms hanging loosely at his sides, a study in uncoordinated movement. He greeted everyone with a friendly opener, masking the turmoil within. His thick, black eyebrows underscored the deep lines that never disappeared from his broad forehead.

The ten-minute trip from the airport into Huehuetenango City skirted a series of battered adobe homes with lime-based plaster peeling off and two or three small, windowless stores tattooed with beer and vegetable advertisements, all scattered along the unpaved, sparsely occupied road. When they reached the edge of the city center, the new arrivals found themselves traversing paved streets that signaled a sense of civic commitment that had not included the airport or its access road. Here, Curtin had to maneuver among buses, trucks, ox-carts, horses, and mules coming from several directions, all piled high with seemingly excessive cargoes of every description, from chickens and pigs to baskets of colorful fruits and vegetables, cases of soda and beer, shiny chrome truck rims and hood ornaments, all topped by unconcerned, precariously situated passengers.

On either side, cement block buildings of one and two stories stood side by side with single-storied, whitewashed, adobe constructions housing the destinations of the mountains of merchandise now making its way through the chaotic traffic that choked the streets. Most stores exhibited faded, pastel-colored façades stamped with incongruous pious names such as Santa Maria Shoe and Sandal, or All Saints Vegetables, with broad display windows packed with goods that had little relation to the entity's sobriquet. Curtin seemed to have internalized the nonlinear logic of the traffic patterns and store names by talking incessantly about subjects that had nothing to do with the scenes surrounding the newcomers. Hennessey wanted to interrupt several times with a question or two, but decided that it was more important for the time being to understand his superior than his surroundings.

"This is home, fellows," Curtin announced as they drove through the entrance of Huehuetenango's Maryknoll Center, a twenty-room, single story, adobe building spread out on a block-sized lot next to the city's cemetery. An eight-foot-high, cement wall topped off by thousands of pieces of broken glass embedded in a layer of concrete surrounded the compound, a symbol that all was not brotherhood and love in the neighborhood.

"This is where you'll live for the next five months studying Spanish and Mam, a regional Mayan language, and how to handle your relations with the ladino and Mayan people," the superior remarked. "Make the most of it."

By February 1965, Ron had finished his language and culture studies and Curtin had assigned him to Cabricán, one of four parishes staffed by Maryknollers in the neighboring province of Quezaltenango. Hennessey's laconic sense of humor and imperturbability in the face of cultural miscues and missed connections quickly endeared him to the Mam-speaking Mayans of Cabricán; his mechanical ability gave him the status of a quasi-saint for members of the parish cooperative whose two diesel trucks were forever refusing to perform the duties expected of them. The Iowan continued his studies in Spanish and Mam, all the while making trips to outlying villages to celebrate Mass and administer extreme unction to the dying, meeting with catechists, and checking on the results of their teaching efforts. He heard confessions and administered to the sick both spiritually and physically, rushing those who needed professional medical assistance to the public hospital in Xelajú, Quezaltenango's capital. In the evenings he composed diaries for Maryknoll superiors and reports for Quezaltenango's bishop. He also kept an eye on the national political scene, an interest he shared with only a few other Maryknollers. The political dispute that concerned him most was the continued threat of a coup d'état against Colonel Enrique Peralta Azurdia by unnamed fellow officers.

The Jefe Máximo—as Peralta Azurdia insisted he be called—was a gruff man, relatively honest, neither a womanizer nor an alcoholic, characteristics that made him a military anomaly. He was built like an adobe latrine, short—five foot seven or so—and stocky, a mask of anger frozen on his features, fire in his dark eyes, his orders given in good imitation of a canine bark. He looked and acted like a bull terrier and the U.S. Embassy personnel loved him.

The president's first act after expelling Ydígoras Fuentes from the presidency was to name a Constituent Assembly to draw up a new constitution—the third since 1945—mandated by his act of taking the government by force. He stacked the assembly with those whom he knew to be sufficiently intimidated. He ordered that the mere mention of agrarian reform be criminalized, and that only those political communications and activities that had received his prior permission be allowed. His purpose was to erase forever the very thought of land redistribution from the national marketplace of ideas and to make Guatemala a virtual one-party state, eliminating all electoral threat from the left and center, including that from the insignificant and moderate Partido Democracia Cristiana (PDC), an organization that the strongman labeled a "communist front."

As many of his military opponents hoped, Peralta Azurdia's frustration of the electoral process backfired, increasing centrist protests and pressures. He also provided a rallying cry for the liberal left and a motivational tool to the three-year-old guerrilla campaign in the eastern provinces of Izabal and Zacapa. The president, however, was not one to back down; he upped the ante by encouraging the growth of irregular, vigilante, paramilitary forces—death squads—led by off-duty police and military officers to hunt down and kill presumed guerrilla sympathizers.

The guerrillas responded by switching tactics, kidnapping wealthy landowners and industrialists to gain publicity and to finance their purchase of weapons for their new recruits. The step-by-step escalation of the attacks and counterattacks only generated further opposition to the Jefe Máximo.

On the tenuous basis of sketchy, misinterpreted information and his limited experience in Guatemala, Hennessey tried to pull the pieces of the puzzle together. He summed up his impressions in a letter home to his family toward the end of 1965: "We are expecting a coup d'état any day now, but so far it hasn't come off. No one knows to whom the army has its loyalty—if, indeed, they [sic] have any. I hope the present president holds out. He seems to be honest and fair. There are a lot of kidnappings of the rich. The Commies are short of money these days."

In one of Peralta Azurdia's first speeches to the nation, the president had stated his conviction that communist activity—which he defined as public disorder—was the only obstacle to Guatemala's economic and social progress. The primary tool he would use to stamp out public disorder—although he did not announce this at the time—was to revive and bring up to date the infamous "Lista Negra" of presumed subversives composed by the CIA in the months leading up to the overthrow of President Arbenz Guzmán in 1954. The list had fallen into disuse during the Castillo Armas and Ydígoras Fuentes administrations.

Another step was to take the rural Mobile National Police, whose primary function had been to capture small-time criminals—especially cattle rustlers—and convert it into the Policia Militar Ambulante (PMA). Peralta Azurdia then gave this Mobile Military Police the task of "observing all activity that tends to inflame passions among the peasant masses or in rural communities and, when necessary, repressing through licit means any disorder that should occur."[1] The PMA were to "lend assistance, in cases of emergency, to owners or administrators of estates, haciendas, agricultural lands, forests and all rural properties,"[2] though not to peasants and plantation workers, since they were the presumed authors of the "emergencies."

Peralta Azurdia's other paramilitary innovation was to take the *comisionados militares,* unpaid, unarmed civilians commissioned to draft local young men for military service—*"cazacabezas,"* head hunters—about three hundred strong under Ydígoras Fuentes, and turn them into a salaried, armed, 9,000-man intelligence gathering corps "to observe and report the presence of insurgents, political organizers and strangers; to accompany military patrols in seeking out insurgents and to question, detain and order the arrest of suspects."[3]

Peralta Azurdia's initial year as the country's chief executive had been the first year that funds from the Agency for International Development (USAID) went directly to the Guatemalan Army for the training of four elite infantry battalions in counterguerrilla operations, small unit tactics, and— importantly—"riot control." The fact that the USAID mission stood side by side with the president to suppress any expression of public unrest meant that AID officials working in downtown Guatemala City articulated their admiration for the Jefe Máximo throughout the American community, of which the Maryknollers were an integral part.

But perhaps the most effective—and seemingly innocuous— counterinsurgency tool put in place by the United States under Peralta Azurdia was the Regional Telecommunications Center. The RTC was set up by the USAID Public Safety Program to link up all police, local army commands, and security organizations with the presidential staff at the National Palace. These, in turn, were joined with other Central American security forces, as well as with U.S. facilities in the Canal Zone, operationalizing a broad informational network between military and paramilitary—death squad— forces, like nothing ever seen in Central America.

Many Americans in Guatemala, including a majority of Maryknollers, expressed their pleasure that their government had taken on the task of "professionalizing" the Guatemalan military in order to stop the threats of coups and countercoups and to firm up the anticommunist credentials of the army by underwriting and participating in its Civic Action Programs: erecting and staffing rural medical and dental clinics, building rural roads, constructing potable water projects. It was naïve in the extreme to think that a small group of foreigners—the eleven members of the MAP (Military Assistance Program) teams and personnel of AID's Public Safety Program, outsiders by definition—even though they had an excess of money and armaments to spread around, could change, simply by exhortation and example, a millennial culture based on personalized loyalties with roots that plunged deep into Guatemala's Latin soil. It remained an unanswered question in the minds of a few Maryknoller as to whether these U.S. advisors and teachers were really interested in substantive cultural change.

As the Guatemalan newspapers began reporting unidentified peasant bodies showing signs of torture and mutilation turning up along roadsides in Zacapa and Izabal, clearly intended to intimidate and terrorize, several Maryknollers began entertaining doubts about the nature of the Jefe Máximo's counterinsurgency program. Even some U.S. embassy personnel began noting that Peralta Azurdia's paramilitary troops were "a potent force, though one which was not worried about who is and who is not a communist" and whose success could be attributed to "the psychological impact of terror tactics."[4]

Ronald Hennessey, however, was still not numbered among such doubters. In early 1966, a letter home expressed his concern that the communists would create turmoil as the March rigged elections approached: "The commies will never forget that they securely had Guatemala until the United States armed the exiles in Honduras and Castillo Armas started his march north with his small army of liberation. He was not a real threat, but the U.S. commitment crushed the courage of the murderous clandestine communist regime and the survivors of the victims welcomed the liberators with open arms."

Some months after the Iowan's letter of support for Peralta Azurdia, Ron was assigned to take over the parish of San Carlos Sija, immediately south of Cabricán. The transfer threw the novice missioner into a parish whose center was located among an aggressive, anticlerical, ladino population that would quickly bring him face to face with Guatemala's major socioeconomic problem, the ubiquitous ladino-Maya conflict, a 470-year-old festering consequence of the Spanish Conquest.

For those priests who worked primarily with the Maya—as did Hennessey and the majority of Maryknollers—relations with the ladinos who lived among Mayan villagers were difficult at best, antagonistic and conflictive at worst. The ladinos would ask for special ceremonies at which they wanted no Mayans present. If they requested a funeral Mass, they might ask that all Mayans be kept to the back of the church. If they desired some service, they always pushed their request to the head of the line, and openly showed resentment if a Mayan was accorded equal respect.

Shortly after Ron's arrival in San Carlos Sija, a formal visit from the governor of Quezaltenango to the town gave the priest a rude encounter with Maya-ladino political realities. Governor Juan Baltazar Martínez, an army colonel, like the governors of all twenty-two provinces, made the journey in order to settle a land dispute between the Quiché-speaking Mayans of San Vicente Buenabaj—a neighboring village of some five thousand inhabitants situated just off the road to Cabricán—and the ladinos of San Carlos Sija.

The governor came at the invitation of the Mayan elders of San Vicente Buenabaj, a petition made at Hennessey's suggestion. Don Ramón, the ladino mayor of San Carlos Sija had illegally changed the descriptive markers of Sija's geographical boundaries vis-à-vis Buenabaj in the Sija municipal registry. When the residents of San Vicente Buenabaj protested the encroachment to . Sija's authorities, don Ramón demanded that the National Police back up his action by imprisoning the forty complainants. The police implemented the order, using their rifle butts on the heads, backs, and legs of the protesting Mayans, and issuing promises of more dire consequences if resistance to the land transfer continued.

Governor Martínez made the trip with a retinue of three jeeploads of assistants, bodyguards, and professional cheerleaders. After the customary, flowery, welcoming speeches, the governor, a dark-haired, florid-faced man with a developing paunch that constantly interfered with his attempts to maintain a stiff, military bearing, invited Sija's civil authorities and Buenabaj's elders into the mayor's office to settle the dispute. Hennessey, who had gone to the mayor's office to extend his personal greetings to the dignitary, did not stay for the meeting.

Some ninety minutes later, five Buenabaj elders presented themselves at the priest's house to give an account of the session's outcome. The Mayans marched through the doorway in single file according to seniority and, as they came into the room, removed their straw sombreros and held them against their chests, like shields against hostile projectiles. Meanwhile, Hennessey pushed six rope-weave chairs into a circle around a coffee table and invited his guests to sit.

As soon as Mauricio Cojti, the senior elder, sat down, his four companions followed suit. The Mayans looked from one to the other and then back to Hennessey.

"Están en su casa!" the priest said with a nod.

"Padre, con su permiso," Mauricio began. The priest nodded. Mauricio continued: "The governor praise us as loyal sons. He say our call to him to solve the problem be proof. He then ask the mayor to speak first."

Mauricio watched the Iowan to catch his reactions, but detecting none, continued. "Don Ramón praise the governor. He use important voice. Then he say too bad *indios* have no education. If we understand the law, the problem not be. Then he sit down."

Hennessey shifted in his chair and looked down at his large, freckled hands that he had placed on his knees. Then looking at Mauricio, he asked, "Did the mayor mention that he had jailed forty of you for ten days for insubordination and only let you out this morning?"

"Mire, padre," Mauricio answered, a note of exasperation creeping into his voice, "we be careful to not make governor angry. We speak carefully. When it be our turn, the governor point to me.

"I say I not speak good Spanish. I tell him I read and write but I not read law books. I tell him I be sure Guatemala have no law that lets one town steal lands from other town. I tell him these lands be given to our ancestors when God create all things. I tell him we feel honor that man of justice come to solve our problem . . . . *Fue una mentira!* I lied."

Again Hennessey waited to be sure that no one else wanted to add any details. No one did. The priest then asked, "Did you convince the governor?"

The old man let out a long sigh. "You know the *políticos,* padre! He try to show he be wise like King Solomon and order that stolen lands divide in two . . . . Do you think he read the Bible, padre?"

Hennessey smiled and raised his eyebrows. *"Quién sabe, don Mauricio?"*

"When the governor finish," Mauricio continued, "he shake hand of ladinos and leave. But some brothers shout the decision be unjust. The governor stop and want to know what *indio* know more law than he? He ask we not like his education or justice? Then, he say that we be good *indios* and be grateful that he give us half. If we not be careful, we lose all the land."

Hennessey took a deep breath, impressed by the calmness overlain with sadness in don Mauricio's voice, as if the only thing that he and his people could be certain of in their never-ending conflict with the ladinos was Mayan moral superiority. Ron felt offended by the governor's patently unjust decision, but recognized there was little he could do.

"What can we do, padre?" another elder interjected. "The *Sijeños* steal our lands and because they be ladinos, the governor support them. Someday we be without lands to nourish our children."

Hennessey shrugged, frustrated by his inability to provide any concrete encouragement. Finally, leaning forward in an unconscious attempt to emphasize his feelings of solidarity, he asked, "Have you thought of joining the land-resettlement program that the Cabricán cooperative has established in El Petén? They've got plenty of land up there and want people from other towns to join in."

"It be too far, padre," one of the elders protested.

"If our people go there, we never see them again," don Mauricio answered. "There be no roads there. This be where our ancestors be and this be where we be. The ladinos not push us off our land."

The Iowan sat silent, looking from one elder to the next, not knowing what to say, trying to gauge his visitors' expectations.

Finally, Mauricio Cojti, with a long sigh pushed through closed teeth, took the priest off the hook: "God see what be here. He punish the *cabrones* . . . someday! We see justice . . . someday!"

Hennessey nodded slightly doubting that Mauricio believed what he said. Finally, realizing there was nothing to add, the priest stood up and stretched his lanky frame. One by one the men approached to shake his hand and then head for the door. Ron limited himself to murmuring a soft "*gracias . . . adios*" to each.

The entire incident was a sobering one for the priest, beginning with the beating and imprisonment of the forty Mayans to the governor's final threat to take all the Buenabaj lands. Still, the Iowan saw the problem as a lack of personal moral integrity on the part of the mayor, his Sijeño neighbors, and the governor, rather than anything inherently wrong with the country's economic and political systems. He, like other Maryknollers, failed to see such problems as involving power status and economic control, buttressed by society-wide expectations that individuals—whether ladino or Maya—could violate only at great personal risk.

While Hennessey struggled with the everyday moral and health problems of San Carlos Sija's parishioners, Colonel Peralta Azurdia was slowly succumbing to the U.S. Embassy's pressure to hold presidential elections. The U.S. Congress had balked at giving continued military aid to the government-by-mailed-fist of the Jefe Máximo. Lyndon Johnson's State Department developed a two-pronged approach: push the strongman to hold elections in which at least two parties would participate that would result in the coronation of a figurehead civilian president, while continuing to encourage ever increasing political control by the antidemocratic military. Johnson, belligerent by nature, only recently had ordered the Marines into the Dominican Republic to restore an administration friendly to the United States. He did not want things to deteriorate so far in Guatemala that a similar undertaking might be necessary. Furthermore, the U.S. president was embarked on a strategy in Vietnam that was dicey, one that would shortly involve a half million troops.

Hennessey bought the embassy line, believing that elections would resolve the growing national debate over Peralta Azurdia's counterinsurgency tactics.

The president scheduled the voting for March 1966. Only three right-wing parties would be allowed to participate, the Partido Institucional Democrático (PID), Peralta Azurdia's personal party, the Movimiento de Liberación Nacional (MLN), the remnants of Castillo Armas's following now calling itself "the party of organized violence," and the Partido Revolucionario (Revolutionary Party, PR), an outgrowth of the Popular Liberator Front, a revolutionary party during the Arévalo years, but an opponent of Arbenz that had been drifting rightwards ever since. It now unabashedly supported Peralta Azurdia's authoritarian control of the country. All three parties had demonstrated to the strongman's satisfaction that their members numbered fifty thousand or more, the only qualification that the Jefe Máximo demanded. The largest political party in the country, however, the centrist Christian Democrats (PDC), surpassed the required number of members by a substantial margin only to see their signatures declared invalid by the electoral board. Peralta Azurdia had made it clear on numerous occasions that he considered the PDC and its emphasis on social responsibility to be a communist front and would not allow it to field a candidate. Then, on 3 March, a few days before the election, judicial police and army intelligence units surrounded several houses in Guatemala City and arrested the occupants. Among the detained were some members of the PGT's Central Committee, as well as prominent noncommunist labor leaders. These twenty-eight men disappeared into the bowels of the security system's undisclosed holding cells, never to be seen again. Their disappearance became known as the "Case of the 28," a calendrical marker of the government's turn to the use of permanent disappearance as a primary counterinsurgency tool.

Julio Cesar Méndez Montenegro (JCMM), the dean of San Carlos University's law school and candidate of the PR won a plurality of votes over his two opponents, both army colonels. Julio Cesar had replaced his brother Mario as the PR candidate a few weeks before the election when the latter's body was found with a bullet through the head. Mario Méndez Montenegro's unexpected death at a time when his campaign was picking up steam was labeled a suicide by government inspectors. The Jefe Máximo threatened to jail anyone who said anything to the contrary.

Although the newly elected Congress confirmed JCMM's plurality, he was not allowed to take office until he first signed a pact with the army that quickly became public. The pact included giving the high command exclusive control over military affairs (assignments, promotions, retirements, etc.), recognition of the traditional *fuero militar,* allowing the high command to name the minister of defense to veto any candidate deemed unacceptable for the minister of the interior portfolio, and carte blanche to wage the counterinsurgency war in any way the high command saw fit.

The Regional Telecommunications Center set up by USAID was then taken from JCMM's presidential jurisdiction and turned over to the minister of defense—another curtailment of the president's power and one made with the blessings of USAID—receiving a change in name to formalize the transfer, from "Presidential Intelligence Agency" to "Guatemalan National Security Service."[5] JCMM then made a tour of all major military command posts throughout the country with the explanation that "[my] first duty consists in presenting myself to all the military centers in the republic in order to present my cordial best wishes and express my personal regards."[6] He followed up his paean of praise for the men in olive green by presenting to each of the top twelve commanders a new house "in gratitude for the protection they have given the country."[7]

> The new government was civilian and democratic in name only, giving the U.S. government the cover it so desired. JCMM confirmed Colonel Rafael Arriaga Bosque, Peralta Azurdia's right arm, as his minister of defense.

Ambassador Gordon Mein and Peter Costello, USAID director for internal security matters, visited the new minister of the interior to offer their help in stabilizing the situation of the country.[8] This offer was followed up by the arrival from the State Department of Clare H. Timberlake and William L.S. Williams to "make an evaluation of the programs of internal security conducted with the collaboration of the U.S. Military Assistance Program and USAID.[9] Guatemala's military attaché in Washington, Colonel Carlos Arana Osorio, had been called home two weeks before JCMM's inauguration to head up the new antisubversion campaign.

As the United States pulled out all stops, American military advisors and materiél multiplied, and peasant disappearances and murders increased. Two of those advisors, Colonel John D. Webber and Lt. Commander Ernest A. Munro, would meet sudden, violent deaths a year later, an event that would change dramatically the trajectory of Ronald W. Hennessey's missionary career.

As Hennessey began to lift the curtain of military doublespeak and political legerdemain, his letters home started to reflect a change in attitude. In April 1967, he wrote to his sister Dorothy that "social justice is quite apart from religion [here], and the priest who dares expose this is often branded a Communist. I suppose this is partly why Padre Camilo Torres was killed with the guerrillas by the government forces in Colombia."

After three years in Guatemala, Hennessey went home to Monti/Ryan in September 1967 on a three-month leave to see his family and experience a change of scenery. Pop had died during his three-year absence and although Mom still demonstrated her spunk, a melancholy silence would overcome her from time to time.

Besides visiting relatives and friends, Hennessey spent his time explaining his work in Guatemala to church groups: his amateur medical and ambulance services, his distribution of USAID food donations to alleviate the Mayans' hunger and make friends for the United States, the attempts to mediate the ladino/Maya conflict, his spiritual ministrations to orthodox Catholics and the opposition to his proselytizing efforts by traditionalist Mayans, and his growing understanding of the "communist" threat and the government's bloody and indiscriminate means for combating it.

His descriptions and explanations to his Iowan audiences, however, proved to be a frustrating exercise. He found that almost everything he said needed several additional sentences of explanation, and yet he always had to leave his listeners with a hundred unanswered questions. "Isn't Guatemala a Catholic country?" he was asked again and again. "Why, then, is communism taking hold down there?" He tried to answer by explaining the differences between Anglo-American Catholicism and Latin Catholicism, and was met with, "Don't they have the same pope that we have here?" In response to his descriptions of the quasi-feudal economic system and racist culture that supported it, he was asked: "Isn't Guatemala an ally of ours? Don't they get our foreign aid? Can't we make them straighten up?"

"How does one explain Guatemala's poverty?" Ron asked his brother Maurice one day after such a talk. "There is nothing like it here in Iowa. . And how does one explain that Mayan misery is intentional, where large landowners deprive the people of their lands so that the poor will be forced to work for them for a pittance? And worst of all that the United States either doesn't understand the system, or has decided to support it along with its depredations for its own reasons . . . . You have to see it to believe it!"

Chapter 21

El Clavo

After three months of relative tranquility in Iowa, Ron Hennessey returned to Guatemala in mid-December to step into the middle of what soon would become a national conflagration of anti-Maryknoll emotion that threatened the very existence of the Society's missionary efforts in that country.

Ron deplaned in the capital and decided to remain there for a few days in order to write Christmas cards and do some needed shopping before heading to his parish up-country. In the afternoon of his second day at the Maryknoll Center House, he was at the writing desk in his room when a firm knock on the door announced the presence of someone determined to enter. Before he could rise from his chair, Father John Breen, the new Maryknoll regional superior, was striding across the room with a look on his face that told the Iowan to remain seated and not open his mouth. Now, Breen stood over Hennessey with clenched fists on hips, squinting like someone who had just come from a darkened movie theater into the bright light of day. The hurt expression on his face seemed to reflect an almost physical pain.

Breen was of medium build, wiry, athletic looking. He had sharp features, a jutting jaw, steely blue eyes, close-cropped light hair, a military cut. Among his colleagues, he cultivated the macho image of a cigar-smoking, tough-talking, no-nonsense cowboy, not afraid to be seen tossing down a jigger of Johnny Walker Black Label, always ready for a verbal confrontation with anyone who opposed his ideas or suggestions. At the same time, he was a very dedicated, disciplined priest who worked harder and longer at the tasks of proselytism than any of his colleagues. He started in without any pleasantries: "Don't go anywhere, Ron! Don't leave this room. I need to talk to you . . . bad! But I've got to round up Rudy first," referring to Father Rudy Kneuer, a former China missioner, his first assistant and friend.

"What's this about?" Hennessey asked tentatively. It was obvious that Breen was unusually agitated.

"You'll find out soon enough! We've got a couple of shitheads who think they're Pancho Villa and have gotten us into such a mess that we'll be lucky if we don't get our asses booted out of the country by morning. Just hold on and I'll get back to you."

He was gone almost as fast as he had appeared.

Fifteen minutes later, Breen was back. He knocked and this time waited for Hennessey's invitation to enter.

"We need to talk but not here. These walls have more ears than a field of corn. I've lined up Rudy and he's ready."

Breen had an oversized cigar in the corner of his mouth, hindering his enunciation but not his earnestness. "Come on! There's a coffee shop by the Trébol where we can talk." He put his hand under Hennessey's arm. "What are you waiting for?"

Seated in the Trébol Café at a table next to the window with a cup of hot Guatemalan coffee in front of him and no one but his two colleagues near by, Breen came quickly to the point: "We've got some serious problems with the government and that prick, Archbishop Casariego. I figure you're the only one who can help us out with the most important part of this mess. First, . . . tell me how friendly you are with Tom Melville? Are you two close friends?"

Hennessey hesitated a moment, wondering where Breen was leading. "Yeah, we're friends. I wouldn't say 'close friends,' but we get along well enough and I like him."

"That's okay as long as you do what I say! I don't want you to go near him or his brother Art until they're out of the country . . . maybe ever!" Then, lowering his voice and looking around to be sure that no one could overhear him, he almost hissed through his teeth, "Those jerks and Sister Marian Peter have been in touch with the guerrillas. When I heard about it, I confronted them. They didn't deny it! Said that if the Archbishop could be chaplain to the friggin army, they could do the same for the guerrillas. They also claim that the U.S. is behind the slaughter of peasants in Zacapa and they have to take a stand. Have you ever heard a bigger load of romantic bullshit in your life?"

Ron was tempted to say that it was something Padre Camilo Torres had recently done in Colombia, but the look in Breen's eyes advised against it.

"There are several others involved, about ten, I think, not all Maryknollers. But we don't know who they are yet. They had a meeting in Escuintla to map out their plans. A Spanish priest whom they trusted was there and he ratted on them to Jim Curtin. Curtin told the nuncio and Archbishop Casariego, and then he went to the U.S. ambassador, Gordon Mein. Someone told the president, Méndez Montenegro, and the minister of defense, Arriaga Bosque. Curtin let everyone know but me, the bastard. Now, they all want our three heroes and anyone associated with them out of the country and they want them out fast! As soon as they're gone, . . . they may want the rest of us out, too."

Hennessey sat in silence, hypnotized by Breen's outburst and information. The Iowan knew that the three culprits had been in Guatemala for many years and all three were heavily involved in projects of social development. Tom Melville had started the lime cooperative in Cabricán and the land distribution program in El Petén. His brother Art had organized a marketing cooperative for small-scale coffee growers in San Antonio Huista. Sister Marian Peter had founded a discussion and luncheon center in Guatemala City for students at San Carlos University. Ron had heard the two Melvilles on occasion express their distaste for the army's counterinsurgency program that seemed to be netting more bystanders than guerrillas. But siding with Marxist guerrillas?

"How could they be thinking of joining the guerrillas?" Ron finally asked. "The guerrillas don't want chaplains. They want bodies that can shoot! It sounds crazy!"

Breen, who was accustomed to out-staring people, watched Hennessey's eyes. The superior didn't blink. The silence lasted for a minute or two and then Breen continued: "That's exactly what I think! Bullshit crazy! . . . I'm sending the three of them back to Maryknoll but I doubt they'll ever get there . . . . Once they leave, though, they're no longer our responsibility . . . . Then I want you to go to the Petén to see if the resettlement project is worth saving . . . . What about it?"

Hennessey nodded slowly. "I'll go if that's what you want . . . . I know little about the project since I've been there only once, . . . though I'm acquainted with the Cabricán families there."

Breen shifted uneasily in his chair and leaned over the table, glancing once again over his shoulder. He was not accustomed to making paranoid gestures. "Look, this is really heavy shit," Breen went on. "When some hotheads in the army find out about this, those people in the resettlement project could be in real danger. Arriaga Bosque is liable to think they're all part of the guerrillas' supply network and fix their asses for good! What I need you to do is front for them, reassure them, make sure they don't start acting guilty! The only way we can save their necks and ours is to behave like the innocents we are."

Hennessey smiled. "I've played that role before."

Rudy Kneuer had remained silent during this entire exchange, arms folded across his big chest, tilted back slightly in his chair. Finally, he leaned forward, speaking slowly: "Look, we don't know what the archbishop and nuncio will do to the rest of us. They may figure we are all damaged goods. We want them to know we'll stick by our parishioners, that we're capable of carrying on. We're putting a hot potato in your hands and are depending on you to juggle it for us. Can you do it?"

"From what you say and the people involved," Hennessey replied, "it sounds like a complicated mess. I don't see how my going to the Petén will clear the air, . . . but if you want me to assist the folks in Tom's resettlement project, of course I'll go."

Breen broke in, "Look, if you run across any of those three shits before they leave, pretend you don't know what's going on. And if they later come back to the Petén with the guerrillas, I want you to promise you'll get word to me right away. I'll take care of them from there. It's the only way we'll save our asses and the people in the resettlement project . . . . Promise?"

"Listen, John," Hennessey answered, the trace of a smile playing at the corners of his mouth, "I know Tom Melville well enough to know he won't come back. He'll go home and write about this whole affair, what he thinks about the counterinsurgency tactics and U.S. involvement. But if it makes you feel better, . . . I promise to let you know if I ever see him or the others again."

Six days after the meeting at the Trébol Café and two days after the Melville brothers and Sister Marian Peter had boarded a plane for Miami, Hennessey was on an Aviateca flight to Sayaxché in El Petén. The date was 23 December 1967.

Ron's musings about what awaited him at the colonization project were brought up short by the noisy patter of small stones and dirt from Sayaxché's muddy landing strip thrown up against the underside of the wings by the landing gear. He stepped off the plane into what he felt was like a steam bath, though it was 10:00 a.m. late in the month of December.

The one-kilometer walk from the airstrip to the jumping off spot for San Juan Acul on the Pasión River left him sweating profusely, though he carried only a small athletic bag with a toothbrush, razor, and a change of clothing. At the river's edge, he spotted Pascual Méndez, one of the first colonizers from Cabricán, pulling his small dugout canoe loaded with corn onto the bank. Pascual hadn't seen the padre when the priest walked up behind him and whispered, "Pascual, how are you?"

The Mayan turned quickly, a look of fright in his squinting eyes. He stood a few seconds in a half-crouched stance, without moving, but seeming ready to spring. As an expression of recognition began to cross his face, he straightened up, allowing a shy smile to part his lips.

"Padre Ronaldo, . . . what you do here? . . . Don't you know we close down San Juan Acul?"

Hennessey hesitated, not sure what to answer. He hadn't expected the usual Mayan warmth, but Pascual's response caught him off guard. Best to pretend ignorance: "Why would you want to close down the project, Pascual? I've come to live at San Juan Acul and I sure don't want to live there alone."

"Have you heard? Padre Tomás be in trouble with government and that means we be in trouble, too. Everybody be going back to mountains. I sell corn and get money to take family to Cabricán."

"Okay, Pascual. Padre Tomás is gone but I'm here to work with whoever wants to stay. If Tomás is in trouble, that's his business! I'm not in trouble! So if you're going to sell your corn, sell it to me. And that means you'll have to take it back to San Juan Acul for me and give me a ride down there at the same time. How about it?"

The man stared at the priest without answering. Finally, he nodded. "Sure I give you ride to San Juan Acul, padre. If others stay with you, I stay. I don't sell you corn. I give you corn to eat! Okay?"

It was all the priest wanted to hear. He put one leg into the canoe, grabbed the bow and started to push off, calling, "Let's go, Pascual. We don't have all day!"

Pascual grabbed the gunwale, gave a push and hopped aboard. With one oar, he maneuvered the canoe out into the lazy current, turned it down stream, and began a slow, powerful rhythm with his paddle.

The three-hour trip to San Juan Acul was made in almost total silence, broken only by the high-pitched screams of parrots and macaws hidden among the foliage or by the occasional cry of a spider monkey signaling the passing of intruders to its distant mate. After two or three failed attempts to engage Pascual in conversation, the Iowan leaned back on a 100-pound bag of corn and, despite the impressive beauty of his surroundings, fell fast asleep.

Hours later, a tree branch brushed across the priest's face, waking him with a start. For a second, with his view blocked by a wall of shrubbery, Hennessey couldn't figure out where he was. Then, as the canoe pushed into the open, he remembered the hidden entrance from the river into the lagoon of San Juan Acul where, on the banks, sat the settlement project's dwellings. As they crossed the lagoon, he could see the colonists standing high on the 50-foot bank, waiting and watching, no waving arms, no young bodies tumbling down the embankment to meet the newcomer. Then, as they recognized Pascual's passenger, they hastened down to the water's edge to greet him. There were none of the usual Mayan smiles, no hugs, and warmth that one would have expected under different circumstances, however. Instead, he was the recipient of looks of despairing expectation and the perfunctory finger touchings that usually passed for handshakes among the *costumbristas*.

"Why all the long faces?" the Iowan asked. "I've never seen such a sad bunch of folks in my whole life! Why aren't you tending your animals and fields? Just because I'm the new pastor of San Juan Acul is no reason to take the day off to come and welcome me!"

A few tentative smiles began to appear. These people had known Hennessey back in Cabricán as a "*bromista*," one who liked jokes, to "pull people's hair." Then Mariano Ramírez, one of the leaders who had been whispering with Pascual, spoke up, "Isn't that right, Padre Ronaldo, you be here with us. We know God and the *Virgen* take care of us! *Qué viva Padre Ronaldo!*"

"I'm here to stay just so long as any one of you will stay with me. The bishop sent me here to take care of your needs. If you need me, that's what I'm here for. *Qué viva la gente de San Juan Acul!*"

A chorus of "*qué vivas*" told the priest that he had many takers.

As Hennessey and his friends made their way up the 50-foot embankment, one after another moved close to the priest to touch him and smile their welcome. More than a few needed to wipe tears from their eyes. As they approached the row of tin-walled, thatch-roofed houses that served as the cooperative headquarters, clinic, store, and school, a slender, sandy-haired American approached with extended hand. Brother Agustin Hogan came out to meet the Iowan. Hermano Gus, as everyone called him, was a Maryknoll Brother who had taken on the responsibility of oaths of obedience and chastity, but had not aspired to become a priest. Maryknoll had a lay brotherhood with many such members, sending one or more to each mission station to construct residences and keep the various physical plants operating, often under difficult conditions. Gus was a jack-of-all-trades: plumber, electrician, mechanic, carpenter, agronomist. He was Tom Melville's right arm and the fingers of his left hand.

Hennessey greeted Gus with as much aplomb as he dared. The Iowan did not want to overdo his carefree act, knowing Gus to be very perceptive and not overly patient with diplomatic exchanges. As they shook hands, Ron spoke matter-of-factly: "Breen has asked me to take over the project for Tom. You probably know that Tom is gone for good?"

Gus nodded. "He came up here a few days ago and told me he was leaving. He told a few other folks the same thing. He didn't tell everybody, though. I guess he didn't want to start a stampede. Some of the ones who got the word are already gone. More are planning to leave. We've gone from forty-two families down to twenty-eight. I don't know if we'll have anybody left here in a couple of days."

Gus was watching Hennessey closely for a reaction. Breen had told the Iowan that he thought Gus might be involved with the Melvilles' plans and that he should be told to hop the first plane back to the capital. Breen said he intended to send Gus back to the States whether he admitted guilt or not. But Ron hesitated. The moment was not right for such news. Hennessey's natural inclination was to be open with Gus, but not knowing what the Connecticut native had told the remaining colonists or how much he was involved with Tom Melville, he decided that silence was the best course for the time being. He would be evasive for the next several hours.

It was 23 December, two days before Christmas. Everyone should have been preparing for the holiday, but nothing was happening. No decorations had been hung, no procession planned. Without a priest, no Midnight Mass had been scheduled. It was a depressing atmosphere and Ron decided he had to turn things around fast.

His first stop was the quarters of the three Spanish señoritas who had come to San Juan Acul as lay missioners to staff the mission clinic and school. He knocked on their screen door and after a few searching glances shot in his direction from inside was invited to enter. They, like Pascual, as well as the welcoming committee on the beach, and Gus, seemed to reflect an ambiguous receptiveness to the Iowan's presence. None of the three stood up as he entered, though there were traces of forced smiles on their faces.

"*Buenas tardes, señoritas!*"

"*Buenas tardes,* padre!"

"Um, . . . I'm the new mechanic assigned here. I also do carpentry."

He waited for a reaction, but none was forthcoming. *No time for foolishness*, he thought. *Best to stick to what they want to hear.*

"I know the change in personnel must come as a shock to you, but I don't intend to make any changes from what Padre Tomás was doing . . . . You know your jobs better than I ever will so I have no suggestions. You have been here longer than most people could tolerate and I am in great admiration of your dedication. I'll give you all the support I can . . . . Let me know if you need anything."

Hennessey waited for a response. Silence. As he started out the door, a voice behind him said, "*Gracias,* padre." He turned, smiled, and left.

That evening, Ron and Brother Gus sat down at the card table to eat dinner in the thatch-roofed hut that the latter called home. It was better fare than the priest had expected, fried fresh bass, boiled black beans, corn tortillas, and cold Guatemalan beer.

"John Breen wants to see you in the capital, Gus. Told me to tell you it's urgent."

"What's it about? Something to do with Tom's *clavo?*"

"I guess. I think he wants to get your perspective on how Tom's departure will affect the people here."

Ron was fudging a bit. Breen had decided to expel all Maryknollers closely associated with the three culprits in order to remove any trace of suspicion from those remaining. Hennessey understood the logic but did not think it entirely fair to the unlucky ones Breen intended to finger. And he did not want to explain it or justify it to Gus. But Gus knew!

"When does he want me down there?"

"As soon as possible! Tomorrow! There's no plane out of Sayaxché, but you can get a lift to Flores and scrounge a ride on an air force flight to the city."

"Tomorrow's Christmas Eve. There may not be any flights. Maybe I should wait until after Christmas?"

Ron sympathized with Gus's plight. He knew how inspirational had been the pioneer efforts the Connecticut native had put in during the past year helping the colonizers get on their feet in their mosquito-infested, isolated jungle surroundings. He had witnessed his handiwork, helping to turn virgin forest into productive fields, and watched while hungry adults and malnourished children began to respond to a well-rounded diet, converting wild sources of jungle protein into pounds of healthy human flesh. Now it was all being taken from him and Hennessey wasn't sure Gus understood why or whether he deserved the harsh treatment.

Brother Agustin left San Juan Acul the next day, Christmas Eve. His goodbye to the three Spanish señoritas was short, with an air of emotion that none of the four wished to acknowledge. Gus wanted no fuss made over his departure, but he had let the three women know that it was almost certain he would not be back. He left the colonists with the impression that he was making a quick trip to Guatemala City and would return in a few days. Then he was gone, turning around once for a last quick look just as his dugout pushed into the underbrush at the edge of the lagoon leading out into the Río Pasión.

Over the next few weeks, the colony experienced no major incidents. No more families left the project, and the three Spanish señoritas began to warm up to the unassuming Iowan. Ron used the colony's shortwave radio to communicate with several colleagues, but no mention was made of the crisis that had necessitated his assignment to El Petén. As a result, he was pretty much in the dark as to what steps the nuncio, the archbishop, the government, or Breen were taking to deal with the crisis. No soldiers had shown up at the colony, contrary to the colonists' worst expectations, and so a degree of tranquility had returned to San Juan Acul. But it was not to last!

It was during the last week of January that things began to come unraveled. Ron was listening to the Voice of America's news broadcast as he did every night, when he heard the announcer mention the name "Maryknoll," bringing him fully awake. The news item focused on the Melville brothers and Sister

Marian Peter, stating that the three had been expelled from Guatemala a month earlier for sympathizing with the guerrillas but had failed to show up at Maryknoll, New York, as they had been expected to do. Father John McCormack, the superior general of Maryknoll, was quoted as saying that "no charges have been lodged against the three, . . . they remain in good standing within the Society, . . . and this announcement is made only to clarify their status."

Clarify their status? thought the Iowan. *For whom? Who was asking about them?* Hennessey had not heard mention of their names by Breen or anyone else since 21 December and figured that every Maryknoller in Guatemala wanted things to remain that way.

The next news item suggested an answer. The announcer was following up on a broadcast made two days earlier by giving details of an assassination of two American military advisors in Guatemala City by members of the Rebel Armed Forces (FAR). The FAR, the larger of two guerrilla groups operating in the western provinces of Zacapa and Izabal with about 150 members, was led by army officers who had failed in their attempt to overthrow President Ydígoras Fuentes in November 1960. It was also the guerrilla group that the Melvilles and Sister Marian Peter were supposedly thinking of joining. The Iowan reasoned that it must have occurred to the superior general that if he did not announce the trio's expulsion from Guatemala and the reason for same, Maryknoll might be accused of covering for the three, particularly if any connection could be made between them and the assassins of Colonel John D. Webber and Lt. Commander Ernest A. Munro.

The announcer revealed that the FAR had stated publicly that it was responsible for the killings, blaming the two—and other Americans—for five thousand to eight thousand innocent deaths in Zacapa at the hands of Guatemala's military. Webber, the broadcaster said, had made no bones about the tactical advice, arms, and helicopters he had given to Colonel Carlos Arana Osorio, "the Jackal of Zacapa." It was Webber's suggestion to Arana Osorio that he should arm local bands of "civilian collaborators" and license them to kill peasants whom they suspected of being "guerrillas or potential guerrillas." When questioned about the advisability of such tactics by a reporter from *Time* magazine, Webber had responded, "That's the way this country is. The Communists are using everything they have, including terror. And it must be met."[1]

Several years later, Major Vicente Collazo-Davila (USAF), would analyze the Guatemalan government's success in 1966-67 against the guerrillas in Zacapa and Izabel, stating, "While the contribution of U.S. aid to the counterinsurgent effort should not be underestimated, it would not have been decisive without a Guatemalan government totally dedicated to the task at hand. The government made good use of current counterinsurgency doctrine and in fact added a new twist with the widespread use of covert terror groups."[2]

As Hennessey sat and thought about the significance of these news items for the colonists, he began to raise for himself the curtain of misunderstanding that had shrouded the motivation of his three errant Maryknoll colleagues for siding with the FAR. He also began to speculate that his own position was now more deeply compromised, as well as that of the colonists, and that he had better begin considering what he could do to shelter them from any campaign of reprisal the army might feel the urge to implement.

The fallout from the superior general's announcement and the assassination of the American officers began almost immediately. Within two days, groups of reporters, editorialists and curious visitors—Guatemalans, Mexicans, Americans, Europeans, and others—began the trek to San Juan Acul to ask questions about "the guerrilla priests and nun." A French television crew came to film the colonists going about their daily tasks. A Canadian crew was close behind, followed by a U.S. outfit. Hennessey handled them all with the patience for which he was famous, answering all questions as honestly as he could—which quickly evidenced that his visitors often knew more than he did. A small group of self-identified American "university students" came with very pointed questions about the colonists' age, sex, and level of political sophistication, which made Ron doubt the innocuousness of their intentions, but he handled them with the same politeness and humor he extended to all comers.

Every day the Iowan arose thinking that the soldiers would appear on the lagoon that day. How should he respond? It depended on their intentions! There was no way to prepare for them except to hope that he alone was the object of their plans. Every night, as he went to bed, he'd thank God that they had all survived another day, while digesting the thought that a nocturnal visit might be on the army's agenda.

In early March, John Breen made his first trip to San Juan Acul to see how the Iowan was handling the pressure. Ron was delighted to have a guest

THROUGH A GLASS DARKLY 337

whose intentions he could trust without reservation. The regional superior gave Hennessey a rundown of the repercussions in the capital to the news of the Melvilles' and Sister Marian Peter's involvement with the FAR. The country's major newspapers were calling for the expulsion of all Maryknollers. Clemente Marroquín Rojas, inflammatory owner of the daily *La Hora*, was insisting in racist prose that all the American priests be allowed to mate with Mayan women—thus fulfilling their secret desires—in order to leave something of value to the country before their departure. Carroll Quinn, a fellow Maryknoller, was colluding with Archbishop Casariego, with whom he was friendly, to have Breen expelled from the country as the person responsible for the whole *clavo* for not having read the Melvilles' intentions months earlier. But the nuncio was resisting the pressure. The government, for its part, remained silent, hoping that public outrage would build to the point of forcing all the Maryknollers' departure.

An even larger issue revolved around the sudden disappearance of a dozen or so university students who had been members of Sister Marian Peter's discussion group. It was suspected that they had gone to Mexico to meet with the three errant religious to formulate plans for future involvement. The ten or twelve students came from some prestigious Guatemalan families and their parents were extremely agitated, demanding that Maryknoll return their offspring to Guatemala and reinstate them as law-abiding citizens of their social class. Breen felt helpless as to how to respond, but he heard that Archbishop Casariego planned a trip to Mexico to see if he could locate the young people and entice them home. "I don't know where that pompous ass will look," the regional superior remarked to Hennessey, referring to the archbishop, "but maybe he has contacts in Mexico that we don't have. If he's successful, it'll put him back on the front pages, and he'll feel like a pig in mud!"

Casariego would not be successful in locating any students, but he did manage to end up in the headlines for several weeks, proving Breen to be somewhat prescient.

The two men spent the rest of the day together discussing many other subjects besides *el clavo*. As evening approached, Breen decided to spend the night at San Juan Acul. The tranquility of the jungle, the sounds of animal life, had brought him a day of relaxation the like of which he had not felt in the preceding three months. "It's funny," remarked the superior, "that we can sit here and enjoy the peacefulness of a place built by the CIA even while they must be sweating bullets looking for the Melvilles. I bet they never thought Maryknoll and some peasants would be the beneficiaries of their generosity!"

A few days after Breen left San Juan Acul, Archbishop Casariego flew out of Aurora Airport for Mexico City, taking with him letters of reproach and hope from the parents of the missing university students addressed to their wayward offspring. Three days later, the prelate flew back to Aurora empty-handed. While driving to his chancery from the airport he was kidnapped.

The snatch took place in broad daylight in downtown Guatemala City, crawling with police and armed soldiers. It was an audacious act, well planned and executed, with no shots fired, no blood spilled. The government information office immediately denounced the kidnapping, blaming the FAR and calling for the total suppression of the guerrilla organization. The FAR denied the accusation, saying it had no motive for acting against the highest religious authority in the country. Further, it stated that such a "clean operation" could not have been carried out without the connivance of the national police and army, an observation that rang true to many.

The episcopal conference called for public calmness in the face of the outrageous deed. The country listened and remained calm. The pompous, self-promoting archbishop was hardly a popular personality. His effeminate mannerisms did not go over well in a *macho* culture. To make matters worse, Casariego had begun his episcopal reign in 1964 by creating a scene that had left the public questioning his sanity. At the funeral of his predecessor, Archbishop Rossell y Arellano, Casariego burst into a fit of pique at the demonstration of affection shown by thousands filing past the dead prelate's bier in the metropolitan cathedral. Some stunning remarks burst from the lips of this episcopal interloper to the effect that the dead should be left to the dead, and that he, the present occupant of the metropolitan see, should be the recipient of all the public's affection, respect, and obedience.

It was a dramatization of the man's character that none of those present would ever forget.

Now, with the kidnapping, some dared to think the unthinkable, and to say so: perhaps Archbishop Casariego had orchestrated his own kidnapping as an *autogolpe*, to garner the attention and sympathy he coveted so openly and unsuccessfully? Even the hierarchy began to downplay the whole incident, seeing it as an act of God.

When Hennessey heard the news of the archbishop's disappearance on his radio and the government's attribution of the crime to the FAR, he knew instinctively that it meant trouble for Maryknoll, and especially for himself. The very next day, a detachment of thirty soldiers dressed in jungle fatigues and heavily armed sped across the lagoon in three aluminum boats propelled by 45-h.p. Evinrude outboards. The captain was as nervous as he was curt. "Capitán Federico Gutiérrez, *señor,*" he announced with a half salute. "I am here on a routine check with my men. Do not interfere with us."

The captain had underlined the use of the term *señor* in order to demonstrate that the Iowan's sacerdotal standing was not a factor in the way they were to relate. He then sent his men from house to house looking for whomever or whatever they sought.

"Is it the archbishop you are looking for?" Hennessey asked with all the affectation of innocence he could muster.

The officer's eyes went wide with a look of surprise and then they quickly narrowed to reflect suspicion.

Seeing that he had gone too far, the priest added, "Well, he's not here! He'd be difficult to hide, . . . under a bed, I mean. We're here to grow corn and beans and to pray . . . . We know nothing about the archbishop's kidnapping."

The captain continued to stare silently at the Iowan. Meanwhile, the soldiers began returning, reporting that they had found nothing of interest. To relieve the tension, Ron offered the officer a cup of coffee, gesturing toward his hut to indicate the coffee would be served inside. Gutiérrez nodded his head, and strode for the door.

As the captain waited for the water to heat on the little kerosene burner, he tried to nonchalantly look into every corner, glancing under Ron's bed from a distance, as well as behind his freestanding clothes closet. Despite the Iowan's feelings of growing amusement, he began to feel sorry for the man. It was like a poorly scripted scene out of an old Charlie Chaplin movie. Did Gutiérrez really think that he would find the archbishop tied up in the priest's hut? Possibly garnering for himself the Guatemalan equivalent of a Bronze Star? Or was he just following orders, silly orders? The Iowan decided that he would not try to find out.

After gulping his coffee and muttering a formal *gracias*, the captain turned and walked out the door. Shouting orders to his men, he lined them up in parade formation to remind them they were soldiers and then marched them down the steep bank to their three boats pulled up on the muddy beach. Their outboard motors could still be heard long after they had passed out onto the Pasión River.

Down in Guatemala City, the political panorama was beginning to take recognizable shape. President Méndez Montenegro ordered Colonel Arriaga Bosque, the minister of defense, to cut short his visit to the United States and return home to head the search for the archbishop. Arriaga Bosque ignored the request and remained in Washington five more days.

The refusal of the minister of defense to effect an immediate return to Guatemala took on meaning when an informer revealed that the archbishop was being held prisoner on a plantation in Quezaltenango owned by a staunch member of the right-wing Movimiento de Liberación Nacional (MLN). Arriaga Bosque had connections to the MLN. He, like the "Jackal of Zacapa," Colonel Carlos Arana Osorio, supported the use of the MLN as a front for police and army personnel death-squad activity. It was only a question as to the motivation of Arriaga Bosque—and more likely Arana Osorio—for the archbishop's kidnapping.

A few days after Casariego's release, some of the pieces of the puzzle fell into place, appearing in a flier published by the White Hand (Movimiento Anticomunista Organizado, "Mano Blanca"), the country's premier death squad, a subgroup of the MLN. It stated that the prelate had gone to Mexico primarily at the request of President Méndez Montenegro to talk to the Guatemalan military attaché stationed in that country, a known antagonist of Arriaga Bosque and Arana Osorio, regarding his support for a putsch against the two aforementioned strongmen. Casariego also carried a message from the Guatemalan president for Mexican president Díaz Ordaz asking the latter to lend Mexico's weight against the two should they try a coup of their own. It was another round in the game of political chess, Guatemalan style, with President Méndez Montenegro making the penultimate move.

Although the flier did not say so, the archbishop's kidnapping was apparently a quick countermove by the two colonels to checkmate the president. Arriaga Bosque and Arana Osorio had obtained information from their sources on whom Casariego had visited in Mexico and intended to get a firsthand report from the messenger himself. Concurrently, Arriaga Bosque would remain in Washington during the caper, erroneously anticipating a popular outcry against the government for not having the power to prevent such a sacrilegious attack by suspected guerrillas on the person of the archbishop. The minister of defense intended to return home and take over the government as an excuse for solving the crime and punishing the perpetrators.

The plan fell apart when no public outrage manifested itself. Furthermore, when it became clear that the two strongmen were behind the kidnapping, Méndez Montenegro received the political support from the U.S. Embassy to move against them. Arriaga Bosque was removed from his ministerial post and sent as consul to Miami, while Arana Osorio lost control of the murderous counterinsurgency campaign in Zacapa and was sent to as ambassador to Somoza's Nicaragua. The president's victory, however, would be short-lived. The archbishop's odyssey, on the other hand, had more twists before it ended. Raúl Lorenzana, one of the leaders of the Mano Blanca death squad, was fingered by an inside source as the material author of the kidnapping. As a civilian, Lorenzana did not enjoy the protection of a military clique and was therefore offered up as a sacrificial lamb to take the heat off Arriaga Bosque and Arana Osorio. When Lorenzana realized he was the object of a police dragnet, he sought sanctuary in the metropolitan cathedral, a traditional Latin American refuge for political activists on the outs.

Archbishop Casariego went to Lorenzana as soon as he heard the kidnapper was hiding in his cathedral. After lengthy discussions, the prelate was able to convince the man that his only option was to give himself up and that he, Archbishop Casariego, would personally guarantee his safety. Lorenzana put his trust in the archbishop's standing with the police and military and accepted his proposal. When he exited the cathedral with his arms in the air, he was quickly apprehended and hustled into a nearby police cruiser. On his way to police headquarters, Lorenzana was shot in the head. A short time later, the kidnapper's death was announced in a police bulletin stating that the prisoner had been killed while attempting to escape, *la ley de fuga.*

As a result of his ordeal, Archbishop Casariego became somewhat of a cryptomartyr in the view of his friends in the Vatican. The idea circulated that an extraordinary step had to be taken to restore the prelate's reverential status and personal dignity. Pope Paul VI responded by announcing that Mario Casariego was to be elevated to the cardinalate, becoming the first "prince of the church" in Central America.

When the newly minted cardinal returned from his investiture in Rome, one of his first acts of theatrical magnanimity was meant to show that the prelate held no grudges and that he had forgiven all his putative enemies. Mario Cardinal Casariego held a very public ceremony in the cathedral wherein he presented a papal medallion blessed by the pope himself to the father of his kidnapper. After all, the public speculated, if it wasn't for Lorenzana, the prelate would still be Archbishop Casariego and not Su Eminencia, Mario Cardinal Casariego.

Chapter 22

WHOSE LAND IS THIS LAND?

The assassination of the two U.S. military advisors triggered a shift in Hennessey's assessment of Guatemala's political and military history and the role the United States played in formulating the rules of the game. It took some tough talk from two of his three Spanish colleagues to initiate the process with words that, had they been delivered to anyone but the Iowan, could easily have put an end to their relationship and the colonization project.

The binational duel began a week or so after the news of the killings had reached San Juan Acul. The four missioners were sitting around a card table in the women's thatch-roofed hut playing a few hands of rummy, the local version of which mandated that the winner clip a finger of hair from the head of the loser. Ron went along with the game despite the fact that he was the most vulnerable. The last rays of daylight played across the lagoon that lay spread out below them. Suddenly, their daily repartee regarding the dearth of hair on the Iowan's pate was cut short when Julia González let out a sigh and said, "Well, it's about time a *gringo* caught it from a Guatemalan. The *chapines* have been catching it from the *gringos* for decades. Simple justice demands some reciprocity."

Hennessey looked into Julia's blue eyes. He could see that her remark was aimed directly at him, probably intended to provoke. He had gotten to know this diminutive, somewhat tomboyish, tough-talking woman in the preceding weeks and had detected an unbending will under her carefree demeanor. If she wanted her statement to upset him, he intended to disappoint her.

"Are you talking about Webber and Munro?" Hennessey asked, trying to sound distracted.

"Who else?" the young woman responded, matching the priest's indifferent tone.

"Well, I can't agree with you. Those men came here to protect Guatemala from a terrorist movement . . . . Why do you say they got what they deserved?"

Even as he spoke, the priest felt that he sounded naïve. But there was no turning back.

"*Mierda!*" said Julia softly, folding her cards without a trace of rejection. "Webber admitted that he was involved in a terrorist campaign beyond anything tried by the guerrillas. He was sent here to carry on the destructive project your government began in 1954. Or don't you know what happened in 1954 or what's been happening since?"

Hennessey hesitated. The firmness that had crept into Julia's voice sent tiny electrical charges pulsating across warning synapses in his brain. He sensed this little discussion might quickly become a bit too personal with the danger of irreparably damaging their relationship. Finally, speaking in his usual soft voice, he countered, "Guatemala is now facing a strong communist underground movement, just as it faced the reality of a communist government in 1954. The United States helped overthrow that government in hopes of preserving democracy for the Guatemalan people. If the U.S. expectations went unfulfilled, I expect there is as much disappointment in Washington as there is in Madrid."

María Luisa Paláu could not contain herself as she began to shake her head, a look of disgust crossing her face. Her round, handsome face showcased a set of high cheekbones that set off a pair of dark, piercing eyes drawn tight with anger. She was several inches taller than Julia, possessed an emotional energy that made her at once appear attractive and threatening. She pushed back her chair, stood up and went to the screened partition facing the lagoon. "Are you trying to tell us," she whispered as she fought for control, her back turned, "that the U.S. government overthrew the only democratic government Guatemala ever had in order to preserve this country's democracy? You can't be serious, *padrecito!* . . . Do American priests take a vow of political naïveté?"

Hennessey sensed that the woman did not want an answer.

María Luisa drew in a deep breath and waited. Then, turning around and still speaking softly but with tension in her voice, she asked, "Are you going to tell us that the United States invaded Cuba, Puerto Rico, and the Philippines in 1898 to stop communism or to take colonies from Spain? The invasion of Colombia in 1900, was it to stop Marxism or to get land for a canal? How about grabbing one-third of Mexico's territory in 1850? What was your government's excuse then? . . . Or don't they teach imperial history in American schools?"

After a few seconds of silence, the young woman walked closer to the priest. She stood with her hands on her hips, almost like a schoolmarm demanding an answer from a boy she knows hasn't done his homework. For a moment Hennessey thought she might slap him, but his silence left her hanging.

"Why do we Spaniards seem to know more about U.S. history than most Americans?" María Luisa asked.

There was nothing subtle about the note of anger in the Spaniard's voice. Hennessey still felt his protagonist did not want an answer, nor was he inclined to give one. He didn't want to give María Luisa the lead in defining their dialogue, otherwise he would come off sounding defensive.

The silence continued. Now it seemed that the three Spaniards were demanding that he speak. He felt obliged to relieve the tension while not appearing apologetic. He pushed himself back from the table, crossed his legs, folded his hands across his knees and leaned forward. It was a typical Hennessey posture, one that conveyed sincerity, a desire for friendship, but self-control, as well.

"I admit there is much I have to learn about Guatemalan society and the role of the United States here. But if this country is a class-divided, racist society, are you forgetting Spain's role in forming it? If the United States has made mistakes here, what is the legacy of the Spanish conquest? Isn't it much more profound than anything the United States is guilty of?"

The Iowan watched the three women closely, trying to gauge their levels of antagonism.

After a minute or two, the priest continued: "So we have different versions of history! We have to recognize our own national biases. After all, we're out here in the middle of the jungle with no one to talk to but each other, the colonists, and the spider monkeys. And I wouldn't want you to prefer the monkeys to me, . . . though you may think them better looking . . . . Shall we call a truce?"

Julia reached over and put her hand on the priest's arm. "I agree to a truce, Padre Ronaldo, but you must give me the last word. Female prerogative, okay?"

Hennessey smiled his acquiescence and Julia continued: "It's important that we agree on what we are doing in this forsaken corner of God's creation. Let's admit that Spain invaded these lands, enslaved the Maya, taking their lands, freedom, and much of their culture. Four hundred years later, most Guatemalans joined together to overthrow that Spanish legacy and build 'The Ten Years of Spring,' the governments of Arévalo and Arbenz. Arbenz gave uncultivated land to 100,000 landless peasant families. Your country sent in Castillo Armas who threw the peasants off those lands. Now, here the four of us are trying to get legal title to jungle lands for fifty families, people who long ago would have had lands under Arbenz . . . . How many more landless families are there today than in 1954? Some in desperation have joined a guerrilla movement. Others, many others, are sympathetic to them . . . including me! . . . If you still want to defend what Webber and Munro's gang was—and still is—doing, it says to me that what you want is to help a handful of people so you can feel good about yourself, while to hell with the vast majority. If that's your take, *padrecito,* you can't expect us to hope that this project will last!"

María Luisa nodded her head as Julia held forth. María Jesús, the prim elder of the three by ten or more years, didn't move a muscle during the panegyric, her embarrassment shining through her wide-eyed stare.

Hennessey sat looking into Julia's steady gaze. She had spoken her piece quietly, attempting to convey sadness and psychic pain rather than anger. Her earnestness was evident in the way she leaned forward and continued to unconsciously squeeze the Iowan's arm. It was obvious she wasn't trying to bait him.

Hennessey didn't move, almost hypnotized by the young woman's simple eloquence, pinpointing a potential chink in his rhetorical armor. He mulled over her logic, not wanting to accept its validity, yet recognizing that what she had recounted fit the bits and pieces of Guatemala's history, as he knew it. He had grimaced at her question regarding his motivation. It was a question he had asked himself many times regarding his priesthood—to help the few while ignoring the many.

The Iowan shook his head and straightened up. "I don't get it, Julia . . . . If you feel as you do, why haven't you joined the guerrilla movement? Are you here—like me—to help a fistful of people so you can feel good about yourself?"

"I'm a coward, *padrecito!* A devout, Christian coward! Female prerogative, right?"

The elder María Jesús let out a long sigh, signaling her desire that the contest end. María Luisa was content to allow Julia's monologue be the finishing touch.

Julia picked up the deck of cards, flipped them expertly through her hands, and asked impishly, "Cards, anyone? Ronaldo still has plenty of hair that he's willing to give up and I for one would like to get some of it."

The four laughed uneasily, a signal that all four now ratified the truce. But each of them knew that this was only the first skirmish, though some unwritten ground rules had already been formulated.

Hennessey did not forget Julia's little speech. Nor María Luisa's! They motivated him to resort to an exercise his mother had insisted on whenever her children confronted their ignorance: to search authoritative books and other sources of information on the subject at issue.

"Once the Soviet Union falls on its face—and it must," María Luisa would say with a certitude that seemed to reflect more than female intuition, "you'll see your beloved United States come up with another series of excuses for kicking Latin America around!"

"You call it 'imperialism,'" the Iowan told the three Spaniards one evening. "I see it as a subtle, pervasive racism, or ethnocentrism. How else to explain the expression, 'the White Man's Burden'? Nineteenth-century America thought it was destiny's command to 'Go West'—and South—a twisted understanding of God and Christianity that is still deep in our national psyche. Racism was at the core of the Spanish Inquisition, the Crusades, and the Conquest of the Americas. It was also the foundation of the American economy built on the backs of African slaves. You and I continue to live with that heritage!"

"You're not very good at analysis, padre," responded Julia, "but you're getting there. Racism is just an excuse for imperialism, not its cause. You have to look at the desire for power, for natural resources, for cheap labor, best acquired through religion, colonialism, racism, and now capitalism."

And so it went, with periodic jousts, a growth of appreciation for different perspectives on all sides. Hennessey's understanding of himself, his vocation, his family, and country grew proportionately. It was not the first time that he had asked himself how much his self-identity was tied up with the image of moral rectitude that he projected onto the American government. Korea had opened up that train of thought. Yet, even as he found it easier to accept the conclusions of his readings and discussions, he sometimes experienced an uneasy feeling of betrayal toward his parents. These ruminations led slowly to the thought that his patriotism was more a reflection of his love for his mother and father and their values than a heartfelt intelligent appreciation for his country-of-birth, its racist history and imperial foreign policies.

A collateral idea also occurred in respect to the Church. In this, Cardinal Casariego's right-wing, narcissistic behavior played a significant part. As Hennessey thought back on his life, he recognized that the profound intimacy of his family and their love for and trust in the liturgies of the Church was his personal deposit of faith, and his loyalty to the hierarchy was in a real sense his determination to be true to his parents' beliefs. It was not an ironclad conclusion, since he was not easily given to introspection, nor did he demand of himself final resolution of his doubts. Many times he put such thoughts away by burying himself in repairing a tractor or welding a broken plow. But some new political maneuver on the cardinal's part would often bring them charging back to his conscience.

Ron was off in the fields fixing a chain saw when Monseñor Genaro Artazcos, Petén's prelate, put in an unscheduled appearance at San Juan Acul. It was a week after Cardinal Casariego's triumphant return from his medieval Roman coronation. "The bishop's here," announced a breathless colonist. "He wants to see you."

"What bishop?" the priest asked, hoping it wasn't the cardinal. "We have a slew of them!"

"The bishop! The bishop!" was the straightforward answer.

As Ron walked back along the path toward the landing beach, a short, balding, heavyset man in his early forties, dressed in a white *guayavera*, open a third of the way down the front, a tuft of black hair barely showing below the neckline, stained khaki pants and toeless sandals, came toward him. Judging by the clothes, Hennessey thought the stranger was the pilot for the nameless bishop's motorboat.

"Is this the famous Padre Ronaldo I've been hearing so much about?" smiled the visitor extending his hand.

The Iowan knew instinctively that although the man who held his hand in an assertive grip seemed anything but a presumptuous bishop, his steady gaze marked him as one secure in the knowledge that he was to be taken seriously.

"Monseñor Artazcos?" Ron asked tentatively, caught momentarily off guard. "How did you guess my identity?"

"You must be joking, *padrecito!* What other *gringo* might I expect to be living and working in the middle of this jungle? . . . Besides, the grease under your fingernails is a bona fide giveaway!"

"Well," Hennessey answered, recovering his equilibrium, "You only got part of it right, *Monseñor!* My name is Ronaldo, but as for the famous part, I hope for the sake of everyone in this colony that that's a misperception."

"Look, Ronaldo, you can thank Tomás for what fame you have, which is . exactly why I've come to see you . . . . Let's go back to your house so we can talk for a few moments."

After a few pleasantries that confirmed the bishop to be a jovial, unpretentious man, Genaro—as Ron's visitor insisted he call him—explained that he had come to warn the Iowan that he was being watched. "Petén's army commandant, a Colonel Mesquita, suspects you of leftist sympathies. Wants you to stay put here at San Juan Acul and not visit the other river cooperatives. Says he'd love for you to make one bad move. He wouldn't give you a second chance."

"It sounds like *el comandante* knows something that I don't," mused Hennessey. "We haven't met yet. Perhaps I should pay him a visit and show him I'm right-handed?"

The bishop smiled, "I'm glad you're not one to do a lot of worrying, Ronaldo. But don't take the advice lightly. Paranoia is an occupational disease in the army. There's one thing we have going for us, however. Mesquita's a confirmed alcoholic. I've covered for him several times when I've found him out cold on his office floor . . . . Still, if his bosses tell him they want you gone, or he thinks they are telling him that, he may do something rash . . . . Send word to me if you want to go to Guatemala City or come to Flores and I'll get his permission."

Hennessey nodded. "Gracias, *Monseñor.* Maybe you could take the colonel a bottle of scotch with my compliments?"

The bishop laughed. "I don't think he needs any additional suppliers. That's a major part of his problem . . . . I'll find a way to build you up in his eyes. For the time being, at least, Tomás's publicity is forcing the army to fake a moderate image."

"I figure that's what's happened . . . . Why they haven't visited us except when they were looking for the cardinal."

"Mesquita sent them," the bishop answered. "I don't think he was in on the kidnapping. By the way, do you have anything to eat? I've got a three-hour trip back to Flores ahead of me."

"*Mi mesa es tu mesa, Monseñor.*"

"You're learning fast," the prelate smiled.

The lunch was a simple one, including the meat of a wild turkey brought down with a slingshot in the bishop's honor by a young colonist. The three Spanish *señoritas* joined the two men at the table and Ron was soon at a loss to understand the rapid-fire Castilian that bounced back and forth amongst his four guests.

Before leaving, the bishop invited Ron and his three assistants to visit his rectory in Flores to stay for a few days any time they felt the need to get away from the jungle. Flores was the capital of Petén, a lovely haven sitting on an island in Lake Itzá, connected to the mainland by a recently built causeway. It was an invitation that Hennessey would accept periodically, particularly to listen to the bishop whose understanding of the country, the jungle, the army, and Guatemalan politics was profound, an understanding that he was more than willing to share with the Iowan. The bishop also possessed a library that continually responded to the priest's curiosity regarding the history of Latin America and the Latin American Church, while broadening his Iowa-formed horizons.

In August 1968, U.S. ambassador John Gordon Mein was murdered in downtown Guatemala City in what was said to be a kidnap attempt that went awry. The government immediately blamed the FAR (Fuerzas Armadas Rebeldes). Later the same day, the authorities claimed to have located the main culprit, Michele Firk, a Frenchwoman who had rented the car used by the kidnappers. When the police arrived at the house where she was hiding, she shot herself rather than surrender. Or so the minister of the interior stated. To many, the Mein scenario sounded like that surrounding the execution of Castillo Armas.

And well it might! Two years earlier, Mein had cabled the State Department that he had information that "the right wing" had formulated plans to assassinate both himself and the West German ambassador, Count Karl Von Spreti.[1] Although he minimized the threat, it was serious enough for National Security Advisor Walt Rostow to pass the information along to President Johnson. The motive for such action was enshrined in U.S. counterinsurgency doctrine: disruptive activities, including sabotage and murder, that could be blamed on the left and used to justify harsh countermeasures, wide-scale repression, and appeals for U.S. paramilitary and military assistance.[2] What the counterinsurgency deans at the Pentagon and in Langley did not envision was that such tactics might be used by the right-wingers against U.S. personnel, including an ambassador.

The ambassador's murder provided the stimulus—or excuse—for an upswing in police and army repressive actions. Armed men, some in official vehicles, others in unmarked cars, fanned out over the capital night after night, arresting suspected leftists. Some were released. Others were never seen again. Colonel Mesquita got in on the action by sending a contingent of seventy-five soldiers to San Juan Acul to look for evidence of subversive activities and literature. The Iowan brushed off several attempts to have him stand aside while the search was under way by claiming that good manners demanded that he act like an "educated host" as Guatemalan culture mandated. The priest wanted to stay close enough to the officer in charge to mitigate any desires he might have to rough up the colonists or allow his men to appropriate booty. Their search turned up nothing subversive and they left shortly thereafter showing signs of frustration.

Not a week had passed when ten men with M-1 rifles, dressed in civilian clothes and new straw hats, showed up at the project, having emerged from the jungle. When a colonist advised the Iowan of their presence, he went to meet them. "Anything I can do to assist you fellows?" he asked noncommittally after introducing himself.

"Yes, *señor*, you can," the leader answered nervously, pawing at the dirt like an anxious canine. "We're looking for the fucking soldiers. They think they run things around here, but we're going to show them that we're taking over. Have you seen them? Do you know where we can find them?"

Hennessey could tell from the visitors' dress that they had not walked very far through the jungle, nor did their weapons look like the kind a ragtag guerrilla band might possess. Their charade was so clearly a trap that the priest was tempted to play along with them. Fortunately, his good sense told him they were not to be toyed with. "I'm a foreigner here," he answered, "so there's a lot of things I don't understand. But I've been told that when one wants to contact the military, you go to the local mayor. Then, if he sees fit, he'll call them in."

The leader was obviously disappointed by the priest's answer. He looked down at the ground, then glanced at his comrades. They betrayed no reaction. "You're right, *señor*! I guess we'll have to talk to the mayor of Sayaxché." He turned, motioned his men to follow, and disappeared into the jungle.

Ten days later, Colonel Mesquita himself put in an appearance at the colony with a group of soldiers whom he claimed wanted to meet the priest. "This is Lieutenant del Valle, padre," the colonel said, beckoning a young soldier forward. "He's going to be the commandant of the new base we are establishing in Sayaxché. He and his men will be available to protect you and your settlers from the guerrillas, if there is ever any need. Feel free to visit him in Sayaxché."

"Ah, yes?" the Iowan responded with a quiet smile. "The lieutenant and I have already met, *mi coronel*. He was just here a little over a week ago but wore a new straw hat and civilian clothes on that occasion. Seems as if he and his men were lost."

The lieutenant blushed and the colonel laughed. "You're a good one, padre! Sharp! I like you!"

A week later, Colonel Mesquita denounced Hennessey to Monseñor Artazcos as "that communist priest."

"Don't worry about it," the bishop told the Iowan as he described the encounter on the occasion of the priest's next visit to Flores. "I doubt anyone down in the capital listens to him."

"Perhaps not," Hennessey answered. "But somebody down there appointed him commandant of El Petén and he still holds the job! And he doesn't need anyone's permission to use all those guns he's got!"

"I think you may be taking the good colonel a little too seriously, Ronaldo. If he really thought you were a communist, you wouldn't still be in San Juan Acul. I'm sure he wanted me to tell you what he said to keep you on your toes.

Maybe he had second thoughts about telling you he liked you. It made him look weak."

"Could be! I guess anybody living up here in the jungle to help peasants get land is, by definition, a communist. Maybe that was the real problem with Tomás and the others? . . . Too bad the powers-that-be don't define Christians and Christianity that way."

"Well, if Cardinal Casariego doesn't define Christianity that way, why should the colonels? And living here in the Petén was not Tomás's problem! He was indiscreet!"

Hennessey was puzzled by the bishop's last remark, but said nothing. In a few short years he would recall those words when it became his duty to bury Father Bill Woods, the "laughing Texan."

In November 1969, Colonel Carlos Arana Osorio, the Jackal of Zacapa, resigned his post as Méndez Montenegro's ambassador to Somoza's Nicaragua, where he had learned the lessons of Somozisation. He returned to Guatemala to initiate his political campaign for the presidency. Arana's candidacy was backed by the MLN and the misnamed Institutional Democratic Party (PID), founded by the former Jefe Máximo, Colonel Peralta Azurdia, to carry on his program of militarizing the country's political system. Arana Osorio then campaigned promising that he would turn the country into "a vast cemetery"[3] if such was necessary in order to pacify it for all time.

Arana Osorio had not been back from Managua for more than a week when he pressured President Méndez Montenegro to bring back from Madrid his old death-squad crony, the former chief of the National Police, Colonel Manuel Sosa Avila, and install him as minister of the interior. Sosa Avila's brother-in-law and understudy, Colonel José Efraín Rios Montt, was then brought back from temporary exile in Rome and made director of the Escuela Politécnica. Arana Osorio and four other top colonels were then promoted to the rank of brigadier general, the first officers to occupy that rank since the 1944 revolution. It would be President Méndez Montenegro's parting gift to the men who already controlled the country.

Despite the use of bribes, threats to burn down whole towns,[4] kidnappings, and murder during his electoral campaign, the Jackal of Zacapa failed to win 50.1 percent of the popular vote, throwing the choice into

Congress. Then, in order to assure his congressional support, his henchmen kidnapped thirteen Revolutionary Party congressmen, held them incommunicado for three days, and threatened to kill them if they did not vote in Arana's favor. The thirteen did as they were told and elected the Jackal of Zacapa president.[5] The public, thinking the thirteen had been off on a bribe-junket, remained ignorant of the real reason for their switch in loyalties. The public nicknamed them "the thirteen doves."[6]

One of the new president's first acts was to appoint Luis Arenas Barrera, the Tiger of Ixcán, to be chief executive of the Promotion and Development Institute of El Petén (Fomento y Desarrollo de El Petén, or FYDEP), replacing Colonel Oliverio Casasola, the organizer of the jungle's colonization program. El Tigre thus became the unsympathetic and ultimate arbitrator of the San Juan Acul colonists' struggles to obtain legal title to the lands they had spent four years of dawn-to-dusk labor clearing of trees, brush, and rocks.

On Hennessey's next visit to Flores, Monseñor Artazcos told the Iowan the significance of El Tigre's nickname. What he learned spelled trouble for the colonization project.

Back in November 1953, Arenas Barrera had proposed to the U.S. Embassy in Guatemala City that he be given the baton to orchestrate the CIA-sponsored movement against President Arbenz Guzmán. Fortunately, the CIA saw something in Arenas Barrera that made it turn its back on the man—perhaps his arrogance or sadism—choosing a more pliable Castillo Armas instead. El Tigre decided that his most promising move was to fall in line behind the Liberator, and to bring his tiny band of followers with him. As a reward, Castillo Armas, once in power, gave Arenas Barrera five thousand acres of unexploited land in the Ixcán jungle of El Quiché, to the southwest of El Petén.

Arenas Barrera's reputation for fraud, kidnapping, and even murder quickly spread across Guatemala as he flew landless Mayan peasants to his Ixcán property in military planes with promises of land tenancy, only to imprison them until they cleared sufficient land to win their release. He chained his less cooperative workers to trees, beat them, and killed more than a few of those who remained recalcitrant. But he was never indicted for any of his crimes. Luis Arenas Barrera, lord of the jungle in his own eyes, became "El Tigre de Ixcán," a national icon of ladino machismo for his admirers, an irrational terrorist for his opponents.

Arana Osorio was apparently impressed with how Arenas had turned his five thousand acres of Ixcán jungle into a profitable coffee plantation, La Perla, and hoped that he could work similar miracles for the colonel's friends in the Petén jungle as FYDEP's CEO.

It wasn't long after El Tigre took over FYDEP in July 1970 that Hennessey received word that the colonists' rights to the lands on the Subín River—their most fertile acquisition, one where they planned to start a rubber-tree plantation and for which they held a "letter of promise" from Colonel Casasola, FYDEP's previous CEO—had been revoked by Arenas Barrera. The Iowan's sources told him that title to the lands had been given to some wealthy landowners, personal friends of El Tigre.

"You've got to talk to Arenas," the priest told the colonists the following Sunday after Mass. "You've got to clarify the status of those lands. There is no point in continuing to clear them if you are not guaranteed their ownership."

"Why don't you be with us, padre?" asked Gilberto Xoyón, the cooperative's president. "Everyone knows what a *cabrón* El Tigre be. He say some law to take our land. He not do that if you be with us."

"I'm sorry, Gilberto, but I don't think it's wise for me to get involved in politics. I'm a foreigner and the authorities don't like foreigners, particularly priests, involving themselves in political matters."

The next day, Gilberto Xoyón, Anastacio Cucul, and Ambrosio Sec went to FYDEP headquarters in Santa Elena, across the lake from Flores, to talk with Arenas Barrera. El Tigre assured the settlers that their original claim was still valid, and that he wanted them to bring in their D-7 Caterpillar to continue clearing the Subín lands of all jungle growth. The earthmover—donated by a parish in Peoria, Illinois—had been growing rusty while stuck in customs at Puerto Santo Tomás, awaiting a substantial bribe that the cooperative could not afford.

The delegation returned to San Juan Acul with the good news late that afternoon.

The colonists gathered early that same evening to hear the delegation's report. Hennessey, standing off to the side as was his custom so as not to take a leadership role, attempted to dampen their upbeat mood. "I don't think you should trust Arenas Barrera. There are too many stories about deals he's arranged with political cronies. He may want you to clear the Subín lands before he gives final ownership of them to his friends."

After five months of continuous efforts of biweekly visits by one or more cooperative leaders to Puerto Santo Tomás and countless entreaties written in flawless and flowery Spanish by Julia González, a presidential order finally mandated the release of the D-7 Cat. In order to enlist President Arana Osorio's aid, however, the Iowan had to make his first incursion into the political arena—although he did not recognize it as such at the time—by visiting Arana Osorio's sister-in-law, a friend and supporter of Maryknoll and asking her to intervene with the president regarding the problem.

When the Iowan, accompanied by Gilberto Xoyón, passed through Santa Elena on his way to sign the papers for the release of the D-7 Cat, he once again heard the rumor that Arenas Barrera had given the cooperative's Subín lands to some personal friends. Back in San Juan Acul, the priest recounted the reports he had heard. A heated discussion ensued as to the value of again talking to Arenas Barrera. Finally, the colonists decided to send one last delegation—with no illusions—to speak with El Tigre.

This time, the director received the three colonists with a more aggressive attitude, telling them that "others have prior claim" to the Subín lands. He offered the cooperative a substitute, "more fertile" tract instead, which, if refused, would be interpreted as a rejection of any claim to Petén lands, including those at San Juan Acul. The delegation, believing that the personal decision of a major power broker was unappealable, investigated the new lands, only to discover that they were smaller, unsuitable for mechanized cultivation, and remained flooded by the Rio Subín during the rainy season.

The recognition of El Tigre's duplicity proved to be an influential factor in altering the Iowan's approach to his work. As he came to realize that all social interaction in Guatemala—including that of priests—was highly personalized, he felt compelled to take steps that he could only characterize as "political."

Furthermore, a sense of the political nature of his vocation had been slowly building in tandem with a growing awareness as to the significance of some of the currents that had been generated by Vatican Council II. Such was the meaning of a statement signed by many Latin American bishops during the council's final session, declaring their primary commitment to "the people of the Third World," whom they defined as the globe's "proletariat," battered by the "international imperialism of money."[7]

It wasn't until the Iowan got his hands on the "Medellín Manifesto" that he became a confirmed *político*, however. Such was the name given to the document issued by the Latin American Episcopate (CELAM) during their general conference in Medellín, Colombia, in September 1968. There he found expression of his basic values in terms that made his heart soar, such as "a social option for the poor," "justice is a prerequisite for peace," that the conditions of the overwhelming majority of the peoples of Latin America represented a situation of "institutionalized violence," and that governments "should not abuse the patience of a people . . . thereby provoking a temptation to violence."[8]

The turn to the left of Latin America's clergy and a significant proportion of the hierarchy were not only influencing young Maryknoll minds, but were causing some consternation in Washington. President Nixon sent Governor Nelson Rockefeller of New York on a fact-finding mission to assess what was going on south of the border. The governor returned to warn the president that the Catholic Church in Latin America was "ready to undertake a revolution, if necessary, to end injustice."[9] He also recommended U.S. support for military governments because of their efficiency and dedication, as distinct from "corrupt civilian governments."[10]

All of these currents—the Iowan's discussions with his Spanish associates and talks with Monseñor Genaro Artazcos, the suspicions and threats of Colonel Mesquita, the nefariousness of El Tigre, the reformulation of the Church's mission by Vatican Council II, the Latin American bishops' Medellín Manifesto, the Rockefeller Report—all contributed to Hennessey's growing politicization. Still, his was not a headlong rush into activism, nor a turn away from his natural openness to all sides and perspectives. He remained more reactive than proactive. His reactions, more liberal than radical, were still safely on the side he knew his father—if he were still alive—and his mother would understand and bless.

A week after El Tigre's threat to take away the cooperative's lands in San Juan Acul, the Iowan flew to Guatemala City and through a friend of Maryknoll arranged for a meeting with Arana Osorio's vice president, Eduardo Cáceres Lehnhoff.

The vice president was attentive to the priest's complaints about Arenas Barrera's activities, adding comments that revealed his awareness of El Tigre's pattern of abuses. Then, promising to look into the matter, Cáceres Lehnhoff excused himself to run off to a meeting with the president.

A few weeks later, El Tigre commandeered the cooperative's D-7 Cat as it was being transported from Puerto Santo Tomás to San Juan Acul. He then used the earthmover for several weeks to do work on lands controlled by his associates. When the cooperative's president protested, Arena Barrera threatened to crush the colony's further development if the settlers persisted in their complaints. Hennessey debated going to the vice president once again, but decided to try first to reason with El Tigre.

The next day, while preparing his trip to FYDEP headquarters in Santa Elena, the Iowan heard from the owner of a passing *cayuco* that President Arana Osorio was planning a five-day hunting trip to the Sayaxché region.

"This is your chance," the priest told the cooperative leaders. "I'll wager that Arenas Barrera drags him here to brag about all that he's done for your cooperative. You've got to figure out a way to tell the president the truth about El Tigre without cutting your own throats."

Two days later, the passenger in another passing *cayuco* dropped off a letter from El Tigre telling the priest in no uncertain terms that he was to prepare a reception committee, a meal, and a few "cultural events" in honor of the president, since Arana Osorio wanted to visit some of the colonization cooperatives. Vice President Cáceres Lehnhoff was listed among those who were to accompany the president.

"Maybe my visit to the vice president will pay off after all," the Iowan confided to several colonists. "It looks like we're going to get the opportunity to speak to the president."

Three days later, the priest waited on the muddy beach with the cooperative's officers as thirteen huge *cayucos,* filled with soldiers and a smattering of civilians, sped in V-formation like a flock of ducks across the placid lagoon, propelled by 40-h.p. outboard motors.

While one hundred or so soldiers disembarked, their M-16s poised to meet any subversive danger lurking in the colony or the jungle beyond, Hennessey searched the visitors' faces for the famous "Jackal of Zacapa." Not recognizing anyone who might be the president, the priest turned to one of the soldiers and inquired as to the whereabouts of the principal guest.

"He's right there," replied the young corporal with a look of perverse pleasure in his eyes, pointing with his chin to a solidly built, florid-faced man with a receding hairline trying to keep his balance in the back of one of the rocking *cayucos*. "He's the one who can hardly stand up. The one covered with mud."

Hennessey looked at the cussing, very drunk man in camouflaged fatigues shaking off the assistance of an aide, and decided that the situation contained a dangerous potential. Turning to the cooperative's reception committee, he whispered, "It's better that we wait to one side until the president disembarks. If he makes an embarrassing misstep, we could become the objects of his anger."

Finally, after one or two minutes of tortuous progress toward the bow, the famous Jackal of Zacapa stepped out onto the muddy beach and immediately inquired for the padre.

Hennessey moved forward and introduced himself. Arana Osorio noisily swallowing the thick dryness of his tongue, grinned and asked, "Sooo, you are the padre . . . the father of all these tykes?" motioning to the twenty or so children standing in the background.

Hennessey's acknowledgement that he was their padre was met with a look of feigned incredulity and a line that sounded like it was not the first time the president had sprung the question on an unsuspecting cleric: "You mean all these children . . . running around here . . . are yours? You must really be some machoooo!"

Boisterous laughter from the officers who accompanied the president greeted the remark.

Hennessey realized that Arana Osorio was determined to make him the butt of an embarrassing little joke. But Arana Osorio had misjudged the Iowan. "No, I'm not the father of *all* these children, *señor presidente*," the priest replied with a grin. "I've been here for less than three years. What do you expect? Even we *macho gringos* have our limitations."

Arana Osorio took a second or two to catch the significance of Hennessey's response, then threw back his head and laughed heartily.

Most of the soldiers had by now climbed the embankment and taken their positions throughout the colony. Hennessey led the president's party up the steep incline, pausing strategically so that the stumbling president wouldn't fall far behind. At the top, the group made their way to the colony's chapel/schoolhouse, where the day's events were scheduled to take place.

As host, it was the priest's duty to sit at the president's side, watching the children dance and recite poetry, "the cultural events," while listening to Arana Osorio boast of his political and sexual triumphs. An aide kept the president's glass filled from a bottle of Chivas Regal, egged on by a very sober Arenas Barrera, while Arana Osorio became more and more inebriated. And any thought Hennessey had to bring up the subject of El Tigre's autocratic treatment of the cooperative disappeared with the deteriorating mental capacity of the president.

Late that afternoon and into the next day, President Arana Osorio inspected other resettlement cooperatives, the new roads FYDEP was pushing through the jungle and the landholdings now claimed by Arenas Barrera and his friends.

Soon after returning to Guatemala City, word was out that despite his drunken escapades, the Jackal had seen enough to convince him to fire El Tigre.

The firing of Arenas Barrera did not mean that Arana Osorio had suddenly developed a social consciousness that included the needs of the colonization cooperatives, but only that the president now recognized that he had unwittingly given El Tigre a base from which to build a powerful, possibly independent, political following. On the contrary, the Jackal of Zacapa continued to demonstrate that his repressive instincts were as sharply honed as ever. During the first six months of his presidency, more than two thousand murders attributable to government-sanctioned death squads had taken place. When public complaints started to appear in the press, paid for by individuals and groups, Arana Osorio responded by declaring a state of siege, suspending all civil rights, and stated:

> You have elected Arana Osorio and Cáceres Lehnhoff and given
> them a mandate: pacify the country and end the wave of violence
> and crimes. You did not give them conditions or tell them how to

do this . . . . The government you elected made a promise and is going to keep it no matter what the cost, even though it might resort to very drastic measures to save the country.[11]

The resulting terror did exactly what the president intended. Fifteen thousand deaths attributed to Arana Osorio's government during the first three years of its existence eliminated all credible voices of protest. They included opposition politicians, lawyers, labor leaders, university professors and students, newspaper reporters and editors, broadcasters and station owners. Foreign diplomats privately admitted that for every death attributable to the revolutionary left, fifteen murders were committed by the government's death squads.[12] And during all this time, the Jackal of Zacapa was able to count on the U.S. government to stand shoulder to shoulder with him in his terrorist fight against subversion.

In 1971, complaints finally surfaced in the U.S. Congress. An investigation by the Senate Foreign Relations Committee concluded:

The argument in favor of the public safety program in Guatemala is that if we don't teach the cops to be good, who will? The argument against is that after 14 years, on all evidence, the teaching hasn't been absorbed. Furthermore, the U.S. is politically identified with police terrorism.[13]

But the U.S. public remained largely ignorant of the U.S. government's complicity in the crimes of the Arana Osorio administration. All eyes were still largely focused on Vietnam. Few Americans were paying attention to U.S. activities in Latin America. Even the Maryknollers working in Guatemala were, for the most part, unaware of what was going on in areas outside their parishes. And if it had not been for the insistence of his three Spanish associates, Hennessey himself might have avoided the distasteful effort needed to pull together the largely concealed pieces of an international political puzzle, an arrangement between U.S. and Guatemalan militarists and their supporters, the discovery of which had begun to dramatically alter the Iowan's worldview.

Julia González and some of the boys from Manos Unidas taking a bath in the San Juan Acul lagoon. (Credit: Marí Luisa Palau)

Ron and Fr. Cyril Schlarman check out a new pickup truck at Peten cooperative. Fr. Cy was a benefactor for Ron with several of his parishioners from Peoria, Illinois, who obtained his Caterpillar earth-movers and John Deere tractors. (Credit: Maryknoll)

Chapter 23

POLITICS, ECCLESIAL AND SECULAR

Arana Osorio ended his presidential administration much as he had initiated it, by foisting a massive electoral fraud on the Guatemalan people. But before he went, having completed Peralta Azurdia's project of militarizing the country's political system, the Jackal of Zacapa had begun making the army the heart and soul of the national economy. Arana's idea was not just to assure economic parity of the high command with the country's civil elite, but to actually outmuscle them in terms of how the nation would grow and who should profit from such growth. It was meant to be a program that he could control even after leaving office. His enemies called the plan "the Somozisation of Guatemala," modeled after the chokehold that the Somoza family held on Nicaragua.

Arana Osorio had implemented his economic plan by establishing the Army Bank (Banco del Ejercito) to facilitate fraudulent loans to cronies; a special social security system for the military (El Instituto de Previsión Militar) to insure command health and loyalty; a TV channel to keep the public abreast of military heroics; a cement factory and a construction company for the creation of military housing subdivisions, all maintained under his tight personal control. The success of the program depended on the malleability and follow-through of Arana Osorio's presidential successor. For this, the Jackal chose a mild-mannered general, Kjell Eugenio Laugerud García, his minister of national defense, a member of Arana's graduating class from the Politécnica (1947) and a member of his staff during the counterinsurgency campaign in Zacapa. The presidential election of Laugerud Garcia, however, did not go quite according to Arana's plan.

The Christian Democratic Party (DC) candidate, General José Efraín Ríos Montt, was far ahead in the voting on the evening of 7 March 1974 when suddenly all TV and radio coverage of the election results halted due to "technical difficulties." At 10:00 a.m. the following morning, when media coverage resumed, General Laugerud Garcia was declared the winner of the elections.

Ríos Montt should have expected as much. In July 1973, six months after Arana Osorio had appointed the Huehueteco chief of staff of the army, the two men had a falling out. Ríos Montt claims that the source of the disagreement was his persistent efforts to bring traces of morality to military affairs.[1] The claim seems exaggerated. Arana was not accustomed to surrounding himself with men who made judgments in terms of ethical considerations. Further, it is almost inconceivable that an individual of moral integrity could ever reach the rank of general in the Guatemalan Army. It had never been a positive factor in such promotions and would be a detriment in the execution of personal favors.

Whatever the cause of Arana's displeasure with the ambitious Huehueteco—more likely the latter's attempts to build a political base outside Arana's circle—the president called Ríos Montt to his office to tell him he was naming him to an important post at the Inter-American Defense College in Washington, D.C. Since it is not kosher even among militarists to directly insult a colleague, Arana Osorio painted a rosy hue to the proposed transfer. There was no way Ríos Montt could view the change as anything but a demotion.

The Huehueteco had no choice but to accept the job in Washington. But he did not go graciously. From the moment he left Arana's office, he went into an emotional funk.[2] Before he left, however, he made sure that everyone who would listen knew that his defeat was just one more step in Arana's "Somozisation plan."

For the next three months in the U.S. capital, Ríos Montt was withdrawn, brooding, depressed. Then, in early October, René de León Schlotter, chair of the Christian Democratic Party, showed up in Washington to invite him to be the DC's presidential candidate for the March 1974 elections.

Ríos Montt didn't have to be asked twice. But first he wanted to establish his authority to control his own campaign. Two days later, having brokered an agreement, he was on a plane back to the land of Eternal Spring.

Kjell Laugerud waged a dirty campaign. He depicted Ríos Montt as a Guatemalan Lenin aiding terrorist guerrillas. He stated that the Huehueteco's party, Christian Democracy, was a communist front organization. He also ticked off a decade of DC efforts to assist Mayan cooperatives, which, he claimed, were a façade "under which the Soviet Communist system is disguised."[3]

The accusations—like others—were seen by most as Laugerud's need to carry Arana's standard. The vitriolic anticooperative political rhetoric served notice on Ron Hennessey that a Laugerud presidency would probably make life much more difficult for himself and the San Juan Acul colonizers.

Ríos Montt ran a strong, populist campaign, generating much enthusiasm by promising land to the landless without land reform and hinting at taxes to fund education and health care that would not affect the incomes of landowners. There was no way Arana Osorio and his cronies were going to let the mouthpiece for such "communist ideas" become president. As far as the U.S. Embassy was concerned, the three months that Ríos Montt spent in Washington had earned him a reputation of emotional instability. Furthermore, suppression of the insurgency, not pie-in-the-sky schemes for development, was the number one U.S. priority.

When the fraudulent loss of the election became apparent, Ríos Montt's supporters took to the streets. The general slipped away to practice a lifelong habit, brooding. When the DC leaders arrived at his home to ask him to lead his followers in protest to the national palace, the Huehueteco demurred.

"There are army garrisons that will follow your lead," René de Leon Schlotter told the former army chief of staff. The example of Ydígoras Fuentes's successful refusal to accept his loss of the presidency in 1957 was thrown on the table.

"No," Ríos Montt responded. "There would be too much bloodshed."[4]

The cadets from the Politécnica sent a delegation promising to use their arms to uphold Ríos Montt's victory if he would just say the word. Students at the University of San Carlos also requested arms to defend the Huehueteco's triumph.

The general gave the same negative answer to all comers.

The end result was that Ríos Montt was sent off to Madrid with a substantial monetary reward for not prolonging the crisis. There he remained for three years as military attaché in the Guatemalan Embassy, distressed by the public attacks against his manhood coming from his former supporters.[5]

Up in San Juan Acul, Ron Hennessey monitored reports of Ríos Montt's campaign and its results on the Voice of America network. Guatemalan stations generally carried Arana Osorio's and then Laugerud García's version of events. Even though Ron was not an admirer of Ríos Montt, he had begun to root for the Huehueteco as his concern for Laugerud's anticooperative rhetoric increased.

But when Laugerud García finally took possession of the presidential palace, he surprised everyone by slowly moving away from Arana Osorio and toward the center. Among his measures were proposals facilitating the formation of new cooperatives and labor unions. The Iowan had never seen a more dramatic political about-face. Dared he hope that instead of being a threat to the colonists, Laugerud might be able to do something that Méndez Montenegro (1966-70) had not been able to do and that Arana Osorio (1970-74) had never thought of doing—grant legal titles to the settlers for the lands they had been working for eight long, arduous years?

What the Iowan didn't realize was that Arana Osorio had been able to construct an economic juggernaut that gave him considerable political weight to throw around!

As 1974's rainy season tapered off, Hennessey was unaware that some of his colleagues in the western highlands were thinking that his organizational talents and even-tempered disposition made him a viable candidate for the approaching election of a new Maryknoll regional superior. Two others, however, were considered stronger candidates because their supporters were organized.

Maryknoll headquarters in Ossining, New York, was not obliged by canon law to follow the democratic dictates of its members. However, unless the five members of the general council in New York had private information that would disqualify a candidate, they followed the wishes of a majority of members when naming a regional superior for a three-year term. If no one received a majority on the first ballot, a runoff election would be held between the two front-runners.

As time for the voting approached, some of the supporters of the two strong-minded frontrunners recognized that the election of either could divide the mission. Attention then swung to Hennessey, known for his imperturbability, thoughtfulness, jungle stamina, and administrative skills in holding together the colonization project under difficult circumstances. Furthermore, he was not seen as aligned with any power bloc. Having spent the seven previous years in the jungle, far removed from the give-and-take of Church and Maryknoll politics, Hennessey had become the favorite.

On 4 January 1975, little more than ten years after arriving in Guatemala, Ronald W. Hennessey moved to Guatemala City to take over as Maryknoll's regional superior for Central America. He left the colonization project with mixed emotions: sadness at having to sever the strong relationships he had built up over seven years; disappointment at leaving while the colonists still had not received legal title to their lands; and distaste for the idea of having to take a leadership role for Maryknoll throughout troubled Central America. He could not bring himself to say goodbye to his Mayan friends, leaving them instead with the impression that he would be gone for just a few days. As his *cayuco* headed out through the thicket to the Río Pasión, he turned for one final look at his beloved home. All of a sudden he felt a dryness in his throat as he recalled the image of Brother Gus seven years earlier turning for a farewell look, off on a similar trip not of his own choosing. Ron also did not wave.

The change of lifestyle could not have been more drastic. He had grown accustomed to a thatch-roofed hut, coveralls, grease, humidity, sweat, bugs, ants and snakes, egg omelets washed down with instant coffee made with lime-tainted lagoon water. And now he would live in a modern two-story, brick residence with electrical appliances and indoor plumbing, wear a black suit and Roman collar, have an automobile and paved streets, spring-like weather year-round, and three balanced meals at regularly scheduled hours. Within his new milieu, he would be expected to rub shoulders with, and try to accommodate, the dozen or so Central American episcopal power brokers in whose dioceses the Maryknollers worked. At the same time, he would be coordinating the efforts of forty-five priests and lay Brothers, some of whom worked tirelessly while others tired easily; all of whom harbored a variety of ideas, some conflicting, others unrealizable, about the nature of their evangelizing mission.

Upon arriving in Guatemala City, Hennessey went directly to the regional superior's office in the Maryknoll Center House and sat down with John Breen to receive the benefit of the retiring superior's almost nine years of leadership experience. Because the Iowan's official residence was to be in that same Center House, located in the Archdiocese of Guatemala City, Breen explained that two of the new regional superior's most immediate duties were to formally present himself to the reigning archbishop, Cardinal Mario Casariego, and to the papal nuncio, Archbishop Emmanuel Gerarda.

The following day, Hennessey accompanied John Breen and his first counselor, Father Charlie Huegelmeyer, to the *palacio arzobispal* to present himself to the cardinal.

Casariego was erroneously considered by most Guatemalans to have authority over all of Guatemala's bishops, an impression that he cultivated and the government manipulated, giving him substantial political clout. In theory, all bishops answer directly to the Vatican and the standing of a cardinal or archbishop among other bishops is one of prestige, or "first among equals." Often, however, cardinals and archbishops can more readily influence the curia officials in Rome than can mere bishops, and this gives them considerably more informal power.

The cardinal's residence was commonly called *el palacio arzobispal,* the archiepiscopal palace, but materially, it hardly deserved that designation. On the outside, *el palacio* looked more like scores of other colonial homes found throughout the central area of the city, except for its immense size and key location. It fronted the capital's main plaza, kitty-corner from the presidential palace and adjacent to the national cathedral. This location was highly symbolic, representing the very real colonial marriage of Church and State, when the viceroy and the archbishop fought over the boundaries of their respective temporal political powers. It was a tradition that Casariego, like his predecessor, had spent much time, effort, and moral capital trying to revive.

The three priests entered *el palacio* by a side door leading into a waiting room where a middle-aged man serving the cardinal as receptionist politely invited them to wait. After twenty uncomfortable minutes sitting in straight-backed, thinly padded, baroque-style chairs, the cardinal's priest-secretary beckoned them to follow him into the prelate's office.

As they entered, Casariego rose and bustled across the cut-stone floor to meet the three men, his arms outstretched like a victorious athlete. Hennessey's first impulse was to step aside to avoid the embrace, but decided to hold his ground.

The cardinal was a short man, two or three inches over five feet, rotund, with large ears and heavy jowls. It took only a few seconds for the Iowan to decide that the prelate's habit of pinching his small mouth and allowing his soft, brown eyes to dart from side to side gave him an aura of femininity. He wore a wide crimson cincture that came up under his armpits apparently intended to de-emphasize his girth but which accomplished the opposite effect.

As the prelate approached the three priests, he extended his hands palms-downward, fingers bent, offering his ring to the lips of his subjects. Each took his hand, shook it and let go, ignoring the ring-kissing ritual, much to Casariego's obvious displeasure. The cardinal, more so than his three guests, understood that in politics, symbolism is reality.

The cardinal looked at Breen; "Ah, padre superior, how good to see you again," he squealed, in his small, excited voice. "What is it today, my dear father superior? Some new priests for my archdiocese?"

Casariego had barely looked at Hennessey or Huegelmeyer since they had entered the room. Breen's answer, however, took the edge off the cardinal's thin smile and forced his quizzical gaze toward the two priests. "No, Eminence, I bring you no new priests; just a new padre superior. I am retiring from the superior's post."

The cardinal gave Hennessey and Huegelmeyer a quick once-over, sizing them both up. Then, recovering his thin smile, he stepped over to Huegelmeyer, a heavy-set man a few years older than the Iowan, grabbed his hand in both his own and squeezed tightly. He remarked that he was sorry to lose the dedicated assistance of Breen, but knew he could expect the same level of cooperation from his replacement.

The cardinal was still squeezing Huegelmeyer's hand while the three priests made unsuccessful efforts to hide their smiles. Then, recognizing that something was wrong, the prelate pushed Huegelmeyer's hand away and looked back at Breen, irritation showing in his narrowed eyes.

"Not him, Eminence! This one!" stammered Breen, coughing and shoving Hennessey forward.

This time, the cardinal didn't have the presence to easily recover his gracious manner. He stood there, looking Hennessey's gangly figure up and down, annoyance still showing in his eyes. Finally, the prelate slipped back into his customary expression of formal friendliness and went over to the Iowan. Taking Hennessey's hand as he had done with Huegelmeyer, Casariego exclaimed, "But, padre superior, you are so young! How was I to know that such a young man could take on so much responsibility?"

Then, the prelate quickly added, "If you ever need the advice of someone of much experience learned in the ways of God and the world, do not hesitate to call on me. My door and heart are always open to you."

Sensing that he was beginning to look and sound foolish, the cardinal suddenly gave a signal that the meeting was over by extending his ring finger toward the new superior, again seeking the ritual kiss of obsequiousness. Hennessey took hold of the prelate's hand, turned it and squeezed lightly. The mini-ritual was repeated with Breen and Huegelmeyer and then the three were on their way out.

Once on the street, the three priests had a good chuckle. "Well, you've had your first taste of dealing with His Eminence," Breen told Hennessey. "Just don't let him push you around. And don't tell him anything you don't want spread all over town. Gossip's his middle name, and I don't mean innocent gossip! He can be malicious, . . . all in God's service, of course!"

Hennessey smiled. "I've ridden bulls before."

"Not as slippery as this one, you haven't," Breen shot back.

A day after Hennessey's visit to Cardinal Casariego, Breen escorted the Iowan on his second pro forma courtesy call to another powerful Church figure, Archbishop Emmanuel Gerarda, the papal nuncio. As nuncio, Gerarda was the diplomatic representative of the Vatican to the Guatemalan and El Salvadoran governments, charged with negotiating Church privileges and safeguarding what the Vatican considered Church rights. His duties also included informing the Roman Curia as to how well local bishops were fulfilling their pastoral and doctrinal duties, recommending priest-candidates to the pope for vacant bishoprics.

"Father Breen and I have worked closely together over these last several years," the papal diplomat told Hennessey after the introductions. "He has been a good superior, not afraid of criticism. We have faced a number of troublesome situations together and I could always count on his wise counsel and firm support. I am sure I can depend upon you with equal confidence."

Hennessey nodded his agreement. "Don't expect me to measure up to Father Breen's standards, Your Excellency, but in time, I think you'll find me a dependable collaborator."

Five minutes later the two priests were back in their car heading for the Maryknoll Center House while Breen explained to Hennessey the meaning of the nuncio's appeal for the Iowan's cooperation. It meant that Emmanuel Gerarda was inviting Hennessey to play a role in the expulsion from Guatemala of Maryknoll's only bishop in Central America, the Most Reverend Mark Gerber.

Hennessey knew, as did all Maryknollers in Central America, that the Maryknoll bishop of Huehuetenango had problems of long standing due to his periodic immoderate consumption of alcohol. He had been a devoted missionary for decades, not blessed, however, with many social graces. He would spend months on end isolated in his parish, refusing to visit his colleagues, believing that such stamina was demanded of a self-sufficient missioner. It was a characteristic that he shared with John Breen, cementing a strong friendship based on mutual admiration. Like Breen, Gerber's dedication earned him the appreciation of many colleagues, resulting in his eventual election to the regional superiorship. In that position, Gerber had cooperated in the political intrigue of Nuncio Gerarda's predecessor by writing flattering letters to the Vatican praising the work of the ambitious hierarch. When the diplomat received a promotion to the nunciature of Colombia, he rewarded Gerber by recommending the Maryknoller for the episcopacy of Huehuetenango. Gerber's ascent to hierarchical status resulted in greater responsibilities and an increase in social isolation. His response was to increase his intake of alcohol, a habit that he had previously cultivated with some evidence of self-control. As bishop, he was then able to assign his friend, the pedophilic Padre Phil Gorley of Todos Santos, to the care of his Vatican mentor as a catechetical expert in Bogotá, Colombia.

Nuncio Gerarda had taken note of Bishop Gerber's drinking habits at diplomatic receptions, which sometimes led to public spectacles, such as the time Gerber put his fist through a glass water-dispenser at the nunciature in a show of anger, severely cutting his hand. Finally, the papal diplomat approached Breen to solicit his aid in having the prelate removed. The nuncio had already received verbal confirmation from the Vatican of Gerber's removal. Now, in the car together, the retiring regional superior was explaining the details of the case to his replacement. "Your job, Father Superior," Breen told the Iowan in a feigned sonorous voice, "is to carry out the Vatican's edict, once the document comes through. You will have the burden of breaking the news to Bishop Gerber and then of escorting him to the airport. He knows the end is coming. It will be an appropriate baptism of fire for you."

The Iowan gulped as he listened to the ramifications of the position that had been thrust upon him. "What do you think Maryknoll would say if I wrote to tell them that I don't want this job?"

"Chicken shit!" responded Breen.

In the days that followed, Ron had to sit through several sessions with Bishop Gerber while the prelate pleaded with the new superior to write to Maryknoll to contact the Vatican to assign him to the vacant see in Alta Verapaz. "This is all a personal vendetta of Breen's," the bishop claimed. "He has poisoned the nuncio against me. Please, Ron, you can save me."

Hennessey was embarrassed and saddened by the meetings. He had never foreseen that his priesthood would encompass such power, that a bishop would come to him seeking temporal redemption. The fact that it had only been a week since he had left the simple life of San Juan Acul contributed to his sense of suffocation.

This scene was repeated several times, each time with the same dialogue. Ron could not recall ever feeling more uncomfortable at not being able to fulfill someone's expectations of him. Finally, Rome's edict arrived at the nunciature. The nuncio called Hennessey and asked him to read the document. It was all in Latin so the Iowan pretended to read it, taking for granted that it said what the nuncio claimed it said. He then returned to the Center House and gave Gerber the bad news.

The bishop nodded, but said not a word.

The next day, Hennessey went to Aurora Airport to see the stricken man off. A few colleagues showed up to demonstrate their affection for Gerber and their feelings that the whole procedure had been a political football and grossly unfair. They also let Ron know that they held him as well as Breen responsible for the perceived injustice. It was, indeed, a baptism of fire.

Before Hennessey had time to catch his breath following Gerber's departure, another singular individual introduced the new regional superior to the burdens he had so innocently accepted. His name was Father William "Willie" Woods, also known as the "laughing Texan" by some of his close friends and admirers.

Woods had been a resident missioner in Guatemala for seventeen years by the time Hennessey took over the regional helm. He was now in charge of a colonization program with from 2,500 to 3,000 colonist families. They had been relocated in several distinct villages in the formerly uninhabited Ixcán area, in the northern Quiché province, east of Huehuetenango, not far from the lands farmed by the Tiger of Ixcán. There was nothing Woods loved more than a heated argument on the merits of his beloved Ixcán venture. He would spring to his feet and thrust a finger in the air to make a point, sometimes giving the impression that he was ready to defend his perspective with his fists, if logic should fail him. His blunt personality and easy laughter endeared him to some, antagonized as many others.

In mid-March 1975, Woods made one of his weekly flights to Guatemala City in his red and white Piper Cherokee 235. Hennessey, only two months in his new job as regional superior, decided to take advantage of the visit to lay out some ground rules for the Texan. The Iowan had always gotten along well with Woods, the two men having shared over the years the progress and problems of their respective resettlement projects. Still, Hennessey did not want to repeat Breen's ineffectual, strong-arm attempts to control Woods. Complicating matters were the persistent rumors that guerrillas were active in the Ixcán not far from Woods's project and that the Texan's name was on their hit list as "an enemy of the people."

It was late afternoon when Woods strode purposefully into Hennessey's office in the Center House, plunked himself onto an old, brown leather couch and, with a puckish grin, opened with a remark meant to maintain the same joking relationship of years past. "Ron, just because I led the voting for you as superior doesn't mean I expect you to go along with everything I do . . . . But it would be nice!"

The superior slipped his gangly frame into one of the rope chairs he had pulled around to better face his visitor. He told his friend that things between them were no longer the same. They had better come to some agreement in order to stop the rumors that periodically circulated among the Maryknollers regarding the Texan's escapades, especially his illegal flights—avoiding customs—to Belize, and his paternalistic manner of running the colonization project.

The quizzical look on Woods's face was quickly replaced by his customary impish grin as he admitted to the illegal flights, but defended himself by claiming that all private pilots in the country did the same. "Why give money to those thieves in customs who will just pocket it anyway?"

Hennessey shook his head. Patiently, he explained that a foreigner gets less leeway to bend the rules than a citizen does and that the Texan's activities put all Maryknollers in jeopardy of becoming objects of governmental wrath. "I'm prepared to leave you in the Ixcán, Bill, but only if you promise to keep me posted on everything you're doing . . . . I don't want to be surprised by any revelations coming from anybody but you. And no more flights to Belize without going through customs . . . . Do you agree?"

Woods sheepishly nodded his assent.

Hennessey waited a minute or two and then asked about reports he had heard regarding guerrilla bands being active in the Ixcán and the side rumor that the Texan's own name was on their hit list.

Woods explained that at one point, some colonists had told him that guerrillas were hiding near the Xalbal River, in a locale near one of the project's population centers. In response to the information, the Texan had called Guatemalan Army headquarters in the capital on his short-wave radio but couldn't raise anybody. Then, someone in Houston had answered the call and Woods asked the respondent to telephone the State Department in Washington to get word to the Guatemalan Army by way of the U.S. Embassy in Guatemala City. "I never saw any evidence that the message got through, nor have I seen anything to indicate guerrilla presence in our area," the Texan explained.

Hennessey had heard about the radio call—made before he had become regional superior—and had thought then that it had been a foolhardy, dangerous move. He said nothing to Woods about it at the time, not considering it his business. Now he decided to warn the Texan: "Do you think it smart to put yourself between the guerrillas and the army, Bill? . . . If the army goes up there looking for guerrillas, they won't come back empty-handed and you know that. They'll accuse the settlers of supporting the FAR or whomever, and that will be the end of the line for some colonists, probably for your project . . . . On the other hand, if there are guerrillas in the Ixcán and they hear that you're collaborating with the military, they're going to take you out for good and some of your close assistants with you!"

Woods shrugged his broad shoulders, seeming indifferent to the danger or unwilling to agree. "What do you expect me to do?"

"If you can't stay neutral, Bill, you had better at least be more discreet."

Then, promising to keep Hennessey abreast of any further developments, . the Texan stood up, stretched, and was gone.

Ron stayed sitting for a few moments, staring at the chair his colleague had just vacated. He knew that Woods would be trouble, but his affection for the Texan and his own instinctual rejection of heavy-handed authority kept him from pulling on the reins.

Over the next few months, Woods was in and out of the Center House several times but managed to avoid Hennessey. Not until mid-May did he feel the need to talk to the superior about a subject that was bothering him, the murder of a ladino colonist from the Xalbal Center where earlier reports had pinpointed a guerrilla presence.

"I can't believe that any of our colonists are involved in this," the Texan growled. "It has to be the guerrillas! If the army finds out about this, all hell will break loose."

Hennessey listened quietly while the Texan blew off steam. After some moments, he asked, "What did you tell me the last time we spoke? You said there were no guerrillas around the project. And how do you know that no colonists have helped them? Now, if the army hears about this, it will use the killing as an excuse to tear your project apart, . . . particularly if they think that some of the colonists are sympathetic to the guerrillas . . . or if their officers have designs on the colony's lands!"

Woods blew air through his closed lips, making a fluttering sound much like a tired horse, a gesture Hennessey was beginning to recognize as a sign of frustration and indecision. Further discussion did not provide a clear course of action to either man. The meeting broke up when the Texan agreed to refrain from speaking with any official about the ladino's murder, a man named Guillermo—like Woods himself—unless he had first consulted Hennessey. Meanwhile, the Iowan debated whether he should pull Woods out of the Ixcán altogether, a thought he quickly rejected.

Three weeks later, an incident occurred that spelled more trouble than Woods or Hennessey could have imagined. On 7 June 1975, a band of eight guerrillas from the then new revolutionary organization, the Guerrilla Army of the Poor (EGP), with both vengeance and revolutionary publicity on their minds, surreptitiously entered the fortified plantation of Luis Arenas Barrera, the legendary El Tigre de Ixcán, and shot the former director of FYDEP, Hennessey's old antagonist in El Petén. Unfortunately for Woods, El Tigre's plantation, La Perla, bordered the priest's resettlement project.

The EGP guerrillas had entered Arena Barrera's *finca* by mixing in with the hundreds of workers making their way to the plantation's central office to receive their biweekly pay. The eight revolutionaries burst in on El Tigre as he was distributing his workers' money and checking lists to see how much he should discount from each for debts incurred at the plantation's stores.

Arenas Barrera, according to reports later circulated by the EGP,[6] stared at his enemies for a few seconds and then, in a scene out of a Zane Grey novel, made a quick move for the pistol holstered on his right thigh. The terror of countless unnamed Mayans managed to get his gun waist high and aimlessly pull the trigger before being hit with a barrage of bullets and sliding lifelessly to the floor.

The guerrillas, who included five ladinos as well as a Q'anjob'al and two Ixil-speaking Mayans, identified themselves to the assembled workers and explained their motives. Even as they enumerated Arenas Barrera's offenses, onlookers began to recite other abuses and crimes committed by the *finquero,* which they had suffered or witnessed.

Later that same day, some of those present at the killing described El Tigre's last moments to some settlers in Woods's project. They, in turn, recounted the incident to the Texan.

The assassination of a nationally known landowner and right-wing political figure marked the beginning of a repeat phase of the broad-based terror tactics that Arana Osorio had used so effectively in Zacapa in 1966-67 and again when he took over the presidency in 1970-71. The government's reaction was swift and impressive. As soon as the news of Arenas Barrera's death reached Guatemala City, four C-47 transport planes—gifts of the U.S. government—loaded with army rangers, were dispatched to the Ixcán. Woods counted twenty-five men jumping from the first plane, estimating that one hundred paratroopers landed in and around his project. How many more dropped into the general area and nearer El Tigre's plantation, he couldn't guess. Later in the day, HU-IB helicopter gunships—Hueys, also donated by the "Behemoth of the North"—appeared in the sky firing machine guns and rockets to back up the paratroopers as they fanned out into the jungle, surrounding both the colonization project and El Tigre's plantation.

Within a day of the rangers' arrival, some of La Perla's workers and Woods's colonists were arrested and flown off in helicopters to Buenos Aires, a nearby jungle airstrip, where they were "processed" for three days. The torture techniques involved beatings, cigarette burnings, breaking fingers and toes, electric shocks on the testicles and tongue, food, water and sleep deprivation, hoodings, and near drownings. In the course of the interrogations, one or two of the victims attempted to save themselves by revealing the murder of the ladino colonist and blaming it on several Mayan settlers at the Xalbal Center, who supposedly supported the EGP guerrillas. The soldiers drew up a list of the accused while receiving unsolicited input from the spouse and son of the murdered settler regarding the alleged political sympathies of all colonists in the Xalbal area.

As Woods described these events to Hennessey, he became agitated, pacing back and forth, denying that settlers were involved in either killing or had any sympathies for the guerrillas. "It's all a *chingado* farce!"

The Texan stopped in front of Hennessey, his big fists perched on his hips, his legs spread, like a boxer waiting for the starting bell. "It's to the point where some of the colonists are so terrified that they're accusing each other of guerrilla sympathies to endear themselves to the goddamn army. This is going to tear the project apart."

Woods sat down and let out a long fluttering sigh. "I was thinking of going to the president. I've made friends with his personal secretary, Julio Maza, and he can get me in. The problem is that the president's brother is head of the Agrarian Institute [INTA] and hates my guts!"

"Just so long as you are aware of all the political implications," Hennessey responded. "Go to the president, tell him about the missing colonists, tell him you know they're innocent, and let him take it from there . . . . And don't ask him to remove the military from the Ixcán. From what I hear, he may not have the power to do so anyway."

Woods left, apparently relieved that Hennessey agreed with his approach. Two weeks later, when the kidnapped men had not reappeared and his efforts to see the president had proved unsuccessful, Woods went to see a lawyer friend in Quezaltenango. The lawyer advised the Texan to ask the wives of the missing men to make out writs of habeas corpus and send them via individual telegrams (the surest way of sending a verifiable message) to the judge of first instance in Santa Cruz del Quiché, the Ixcán's provincial capital.

On that advice, Woods flew to the Ixcán and helped the women, all of whom were illiterate, to compose and sign the telegrams—with thumb prints. He stuck the writs in his pocket and flew to Huehuetenango for a pastoral meeting, from where he intended to dispatch the telegrams. But, caught up in a thousand errands, the Texan forgot to do so.

A few hours later, as he was flying back to the Ixcán, Woods remembered the writs. Landing in Santa Cruz del Quiché, he asked a colonist who had accompanied him on the flight to take the telegrams to the telegraph office, while he sat on the dirt strip watching the plane. The Texan waited two hours, but the colonist never returned. At that point, deciding that something was wrong, Woods took off and flew to Guatemala City to see Hennessey. It was early August 1975.

"I've just sent off the writs," Woods told Hennessey with a nonchalance he did not feel, plopping himself into an easy chair, a glass of Scotch in his hand. "Now, all we can do is wait."

Hennessey came around his desk and sat on its edge. It was one of the rare instances that he did not sit down with his visitor, forgetting for the moment his usual habit of minimizing authority. "I've a feeling that you know that something's wrong, Bill. What aren't you telling me?"

Woods waited a few seconds before admitting that the colonist he had sent to the telegraph office in El Quiché with the writs had not returned after two hours.

Now it was Hennessey's turn to wait. Then, speaking gently, he explained that no telegraph operator in Guatemala would send a telegram accusing the commandant of the base next door of kidnapping innocent people. "The *telegrafista* took those writs to the base. The commandant had your messenger arrested to teach you a lesson. God knows what the poor guy's situation is now!"

Woods sat quietly, his chest heaving, acknowledging that his action was stupid. "I tried to convince myself that everything was all right. Now what do I do?"

The Iowan could see that the man in front of him was deeply shaken and there was no remedy for what had happened. "What about your visit to the president?"

Woods shook his head and remained silent.

"Have any of the disappeared returned?"

"Only one! A guy named Lupe Michu. He lost forty or fifty pounds. Looks like a skeleton. They broke two ribs and smashed his front teeth. They questioned him about me, asked if I was involved with the guerrillas . . . . I guess they decided to let him go so he could come back and tell his story and scare the shit out of the colonists, . . . and get at me."

Hennessey nodded, again debating within himself whether to pull the Texan out of the Ixcán hot spot. But he discarded the idea in the belief that an American priest with a lead to the president through his personal secretary was still the safest bet to get the colonists back, if they were still alive, and to protect others from further harm.

"You've got to continue pursuing this thing, Bill. But you should think through the consequences of your every move. Your first priority has to be to protect the colonists as best you can. I'll help, . . . but you've got let me know what you want me to do."

In the succeeding weeks, the army carried out additional kidnappings from the Ixcán resettlement project, totaling more that four dozen men in all. Woods, very dispirited now, was still trying to push the legal process forward for the first ten. The nation's judiciary was too terrified to initiate any case against a member of the "security forces." The Texan was now virtually certain that all the men were dead, their bodies thrown out on a road somewhere to intimidate passers-by. "Maybe I could speak to someone at the U.S. Embassy. With all the help we [*sic*] give the Guatemalan army, you'd think we'd have some influence over them."

"Bill, . . . you have to be kidding! You think the American government doesn't know what's going on here? . . . It probably wouldn't hurt for the folks at the embassy to realize that we hold them accountable, but I wouldn't get my hopes up thinking it would help."

The soldiers remained in the Ixcán, abusing the people, stealing grain and animals, raping women, pressing men into unpaid service as peons. The settlers cried and prayed a lot, feeling they had no recourse. Woods prayed and wept with them, resigned to the soldiers' presence for the time being, if not their crimes. Though he didn't realize it at the time, he himself was fast becoming the prime focus of the army's increased interest and developing wrath. He would soon discover just what that meant.

Woods's delicate situation was not the only one that was forcing the regional superior to think and act ever more politically with each passing day. It was probably the cooperation given by Breen for the removal of Bishop Gerber and Hennessey's follow-up that led the nuncio to believe that the Iowan would now assist him in the backdoor transfer of Bishop Arturo Rivera y Damas from San Salvador.

Several Maryknollers were working in the archdiocese under the supervision of both Hennessey and Bishop Rivera y Damas, and the regional superior's confirmation of a report to the Vatican of "unsuitability" of the San Salvadorean bishop could be very helpful to the nuncio. A telephone call from the papal diplomat's secretary had established the time for a meeting and the Iowan went to the nunciature without knowing its purpose.

"Cardinal Casariego and I are working to get Bishop Rivera y Damas removed from the archdiocese of San Salvador," the nuncio began, almost as soon as the two men had finished exchanging pleasantries. He went on to say that Rivera y Damas was not popular with the San Salvadorean laity. Yet the reigning archbishop—who would soon reach the mandatory retirement age of seventy-five years—had recommended to the Vatican, contrary to the nuncio's wishes, that the San Salvadorean auxiliary bishop, Rivera y Damas, replace him as archbishop. The nuncio explained to Hennessey that he and Cardinal Casariego had agreed that a letter from the Maryknoll superior to the nunciature critical of the way Bishop Rivera y Damas was handling the Maryknollers in San Salvador—which would then be forwarded to Rome— would be helpful to their cause.

For a moment, Hennessey was taken aback by the papal diplomat's proposal, but tried not to show it. He remained silent, wanting to give the impression of taking Archbishop Gerarda's suggestion under consideration. But in his mind, he had already rejected the plan as duplicitous and wrongheaded. As far as the Iowan was concerned, Bishop Rivera y Damas should have been the last of all El Salvadorean bishops whom the nuncio might have wanted removed. The Maryknollers working in San Salvador had repeatedly told Hennessey of their excellent relationship with Rivera y Damas.

Finally, the Iowan countered by asking the nuncio what segment of the El Salvadorean laity, according to Cardinal Casariego, opposed Rivera y Damas. The Iowan did not need to wait for the answer. He knew that both Archbishop Chávez y González, the reigning archbishop, and Bishop Rivera y Damas had been outspoken in their condemnation of the El Salvadorean military and police repression, the kidnappings, torture, and murders of student, labor, and peasant leaders. Casariego's wealthy San Salvadorean friends, the large coffee and cotton plantation owners whom the cardinal had escorted to Rome so many times, were imploring him to use his influence at the Vatican to keep the outspoken Rivera y Damas from succeeding the retiring Chávez y González. Their candidate for the position was Bishop Alvarez, an army chaplain with the rank of colonel, an apologist for the repressive military and police apparatus. Casariego, however, had already sounded out his patrons in Rome on Bishop Alvarez's chances and had found that the opposition to the colonel's militarism was too strong. His second choice, then, was Bishop Oscar Arnulfo Romero, a conservative, somewhat shy bishop from a tiny diocese in coffee—and cotton-growing country in eastern El Salvador. Romero had surrounded himself with members of the cultist, secretive Opus Dei Society. Opus Dei members embrace an ideology of sacramentalism and believe that the world's wealthy are God's chosen people.

The nuncio, with a note of hesitancy, responded to Hennessey's query that Casariego found opposition to Rivera y Damas strongest among the most ardent supporters of the El Salvadorean Church and that he had no reason to doubt the cardinal's judgment.

The Iowan was conscious of the fact that Archbishop Gerarda was already viewing him as an opponent to the cardinal's plan and that anything he might now say would only damage his relationship with the nuncio. Nevertheless, he blocked the small voice of caution and followed his instincts, noting that Cardinal Casariego had many wealthy friends in El Salvador and that they— not the most ardent supporters of the Church, the poor and the powerless— were the ones who opposed Rivera y Damas.

Hennessey waited while the nuncio digested his reply. The archbishop nodded, fixing his eyes on the priest's face, but made no response. Finally, he answered, obviously displeased. "Well, I'm glad you've been frank with me, padre superior. It is always helpful to get a variety of opinions before making a final judgment. Now, if you will excuse me . . . ."

On his way back to the Center House, Hennessey thought about his conversation with the papal diplomat, distressed by the prelate's willingness to play along with Casariego's backstage plans to obstruct the appointment of a progressive bishop to El Salvador's primary see. Furthermore, the Maryknoller's admiration for Rivera y Damas had quickly blossomed into a friendship between the two men, and now Hennessey felt burdened by the thought of the choice confronting him: either violating the nuncio's confidence or sidestepping the responsibility implicit in his friendship with the San Salvadorean bishop. By the time he reached the Center House, the Iowan had decided, not without some reservations, that his primary obligation was to Rivera y Damas and the bishop's pastoral values and not to the hierarchical power plays of the cardinal and the papal nuncio.

Two days later, Hennessey headed for San Salvador to visit Bishop Rivera y Damas. "Thank you, Padre Ronaldo," the bishop replied after hearing the Maryknoller's message. "I am happy that you have such confidence in me."

"Bishop," Hennessey responded, "what the cardinal and nuncio are trying to do is unfair to you and to the people of El Salvador. At the same time, I don't want to be sneaky about being on your side. If you choose to confront either of them with this information, please tell them that it was I who informed you. It is best that they know where I stand."

"You have a lot of courage, Padre Ronaldo," the bishop answered. "But you also must learn to play the political game and not reveal your hand so readily. Cardinal Casariego and his powerful friends are not forgiving people."

"I don't think it's a matter of courage, *monseñor.* I have nothing to lose. Furthermore, I just never learned to be sneaky. If that's a requirement for playing these political games, I guess I'll never be an insider!"

"I know what you mean, Ronaldo! But life often demands that we not reveal ourselves to our antagonists. What was it that Christ said about our being as wise as serpents?"

Later that same week, Bishop Rivera y Damas confronted the papal nuncio with Hennessey's information, much to Gerarda's consternation. After that, the Iowan found that he was no longer welcome at the nunciature. However, he was not bothered by the nuncio's attitude. On the contrary, he took satisfaction in being the object of the diplomat's displeasure, the same feeling he had experienced many times before, in the army, in the seminary, and in El Petén, when he had succeeded in putting a few grains of sand in the operational gears of self-important power brokers operating at the expense of the poor and powerless.

Cardinal Casariego, undeterred, continued his efforts in Rome to block Bishop Rivera y Damas's appointment. Finally, he saw his labors rewarded when Pope Paul VI named conservative Bishop Oscar Arnulfo Romero, the cardinal's second choice, to the archbishopric of San Salvador.

Cardinal Casariego was openly jubilant over the success of his efforts and made sure that everyone of any of significance was aware of his key involvement in the decision. His delight, however, at seeing Bishop Romero elevated to the archbishopric of San Salvador was short-lived, as was Hennessey's disappointment. Romero soon became the archbishop that Casariego had been afraid that Rivera y Damas might have been, with deadly consequences for the new archbishop and serious political consequences for Maryknoll's regional superior.

Chapter 24

A Warning and Then Some

During the night of 4 February 1976, Guatemala shook from head to toe. Sixteen of its twenty-two departments (provinces) felt the effects of a massive earthquake that rivaled those that leveled the country's ancient capital, Antigua, in 1717 and again in 1773. The modern version left thirty thousand dead, seventy-seven thousand injured and over one million homeless. The vast majority of those affected were the very poor, those who lived in dwellings with walls made of unstable mud adobe with heavy tile roofs, located on mountainsides and quake-prone ravines.

Cardinal Casariego led his countrymen in prayerful contrition, claiming the disaster was divine punishment inflicted by a disappointed Father on His disobedient children whose sins merited no less. Since the poor were the quake's main victims, they interpreted the churchman's prayer as a condemnation of their life ways, a thought that many Maya shared. Some, however, were puzzled by the seeming contradiction: the cardinal was wont to say in his Sunday homilies that God must love the poor very much since He had created so many of them. His was not an original concept!

The prelate also blamed the tragedy on those priests and nuns who had cast off their cassocks and religious garb to get more personally involved in responding to the social needs of Guatemala's poor, a current that had evolved from the Second Vatican Council. As far as the cardinal was concerned, one could leave the sanctuary only to evangelize and sacramentalize; all other undertakings were fraught with temptation, generally sexual. He, like his predecessor, believed that poverty, hunger, sickness, death, and its concomitant ills were part of a divine plan to give the oppressed a running start on gaining heaven, and as such, these burdens should be embraced, not contested. It was a theology he did not practice.

Ron Hennessey heard the cardinal's prayer and ignored its implications. He immediately wired Maryknoll for emergency funds and set about distributing whatever assets he could lay his hands on. He purchased a pair of front-end loaders and two dump trucks—all the mission could afford—to open roads to the most devastated areas. He assigned several Maryknoll Brothers to coordinate relief efforts and asked Bill Woods to fly in supplies to isolated communities, landing on whatever open stretch of real estate he could find. The Iowan threw open the doors of the Maryknoll Center House in Guatemala City to a score who had lost their dwellings, a charity that he undertook only after obtaining unanimous agreement from his housemates. Maryknoll answered his request for funds by appealing to its donor base and was able to send almost a half million dollars worth of corrugated metal roofing to be distributed to the homeless.

International aid began pouring into the country from around the globe, each country's embassy attempting to direct its assistance to projects that not only alleviated human suffering but presented a positive profile for Guatemalans and international observers to admire. President Kjell Laugerud set up the Committee for National Reconstruction (CRN) to coordinate the delivery of the foreign aid. Former president Carlos Arana Osorio, taking a page from the book of his mentor, Tacho Somoza of Nicaragua, tried to gain control of the CRN in order to siphon off for his own benefit whatever resources he could lay his hands on, much as the Nicaraguan had done after his country's 1972 devastating earthquake. Laugerud fought off Arana Osorio as best he could, naming Colonel Ricardo Peralta Méndez as head of the CRN. Peralta Méndez was a respected army officer with promising political ambitions, a nephew of the former Jefe Máximo, Colonel Enrique Peralta Azurdia (1963-66), a man who could call on his uncle's still powerful political base for backup when needed to out-muscle Arana Osorio.

Laugerud's lack of political gratitude fueled Arana Osorio's enmity and turned the Jackal of Zacapa into an implacable antagonist. Local reconstruction committees that had developed under Peralta Méndez's tutelage became the targets of a new wave of death-squad activities godfathered by Arana Osorio, one of which, the Secret anti-Communist Army (ESA), specialized in the kidnapping and assassination of union leaders, students, politicians, and professionals "who may have demonstrated the slightest interest in altering the status quo."[1]

At this point, Arana, feeling betrayed, turned to activities that heretofore had been taboo even for the army's most criminal element, kidnapping for ransom members of the nation's wealthy elite, smuggling arms for whomever could pay the price irrespective of their social ideology, and shepherding shipments of illegal Colombian drugs through Guatemala into Mexico for delivery to the United States. The anticommunist hero of U.S. Colonel John Webber's 1966-67 terrorist Zacapa campaign quickly fell out of favor with his former Pentagon sponsors.

Ron Hennessey wrote letters home praising Laugerud's attempts to see that the international aid got to the most needy sectors of the nation's poor. He also expressed disappointment that a new union federation, the National Committee for Trade Union Unity (CNUS), attempted to politicize the disaster by calling for strikes while criticizing the president for not providing adequate housing for the urban homeless, as well as for what it saw as ineffective attempts to punish those who speculated in basic commodities. When Laugerud responded by ordering the CNUS to call off the strike and get back to the task of rebuilding the country, the federation pointed out that the presidential order to shoot looters was being used as cover for the murderous death squads. As a result, the honeymoon between the new administration and the trade unions dissolved on the rocks of mutual recriminations.

The devastation wrought by the earthquake, as well as the social upheavals that resulted therefrom, meant that Laugerud would lose control over the government during the last two years of his presidency (1976-78). A cabal of hard-liners led by General Romeo Lucas García, Laugerud's minister of defense, took behind-the-scenes control of the army, the power fulcrum that Arana Osorio had so avariciously coveted but had forfeited by going beyond the recognized rules of the game. Antagonizing the U.S. government, whether from the left or the right, was a no-no that could not be sustained.

Two months after the earthquake, during the second week of April, Father Bill Woods received a note from U.S. ambassador Francis E. Meloy inviting him to talk about the Ixcán colonization project. The invitation excited Woods; he believed the ambassador's interest would translate into moral and financial support, as well as protection for the colonists from the military. The priest spent several hours pulling together a series of photographic slides he could show the ambassador to impress him with the effort already invested and the potential for further resettlement in the Ixcán. About 6:30 p.m., Woods headed for the ambassador's private residence.

Three hours later, as Hennessey was getting ready to retire, Woods returned. Coming through the door into the large parlor, the Texan attempted to sound unconcerned. He walked over to the liquor cabinet and poured himself a half glass of Scotch. Without turning around, he asked, "Ron, do you know what the ambassador wanted? What he really wanted?"

Hennessey remained silent. Woods sat down in a chair across from the Iowan and stared into his glass. After a few seconds, he looked up and sighed. "He wants me to get out of the country as soon as possible. He says my life is in danger from the five top military men in the government. He . also said that the U.S. government couldn't do a blessed thing about it . . . . Can you believe that?"

Hennessey watched the priest sitting across from him. The Texas bravado was gone and Woods actually looked smaller, his shoulders hunched forward, averting his gaze from the superior's eyes. Ron felt sorry for his friend.

"He told you that the suspicions of your collaborating with the guerrillas goes all the way to the top?" Hennessey asked.

"That's what he said. They told him that I don't obey Guatemalan laws, that I charge colonists too much for the airplane trips, and that I'm running arms from Cuba to the guerrillas."

Hennessey waited. "Who's 'they'?" He finally asked.

"General Romeo Lucas García, the minister of defense, is the most determined to get rid of me. Then there's General Rubio Coronado, the minister of agriculture, and Colonel Sandoval Torres, the commandant in Quiché. He included General Vassaux, the minister of *gobernación,* and President Kjell Laugerud himself, but he seemed to think the latter two were not as gung ho as the first three. But all five say I'm running stuff into the Ixcán from Cuba for the guerrillas. Can you believe that shit?"

"I can!" Hennessey replied. "You and I know the guerrillas are active in the Ixcán . . . . Your illegal flights into Belize must have been discovered— probably monitored . . . . What if one of your kidnapped colonists succumbed to torture and said you were involved with the guerrillas? . . . Maybe the ambassador is right?"

Woods was shaking his head before the superior had finished speaking. "Look, Ron, the settlers would get the impression that I was pulling out because things are too hot. Some would start to leave, the army would kill those who stayed behind, and we could kiss good-bye everything the people have worked for over the last six years. Please! Don't even think of asking me to leave!"

"Well, you'd better see what you can do about correcting this misunderstanding and do it quick. This whole thing is escalating too fast if the embassy is concerned . . . . Why don't you try to see all five and put your cards on the table? Tell them the truth. Belize! Your radio call to Washington! Everything! . . . It can't be worse than your present predicament!"

The Texan stared at his superior for a few moments. "Maybe I should ask Bishop Victor Hugo Martínez to go with me? It'd look good to have a bishop sticking up for me."

"Bill, . . . it would be easy for me to pull you out of the Ixcán. But I'm more worried about the colonists than I am about you. Since these guys have warned the embassy, it's not likely that they'll move against you, . . . at least, not for a while . . . . But the colonists are a different matter. The army could wipe them out tomorrow and we'd be the only ones to complain . . . . You have to stand with them, . . . be their witness!"

The two priests sat looking at each other in silence. Finally, Woods spoke up: "I'll go see those jerks right after Holy Week. I've got to be in the Ixcán for the Holy Week liturgies. As soon as I get back, I'll get Victor Hugo to come with me and we'll see all five.

Hennessey nodded. "Just don't approach them with a chip on your shoulder. You're not very good at hiding your feelings . . . . And by the way, I'm going with you to the Ixcán for the weekend. I want to hear what the settlers have to say."

Back in the capital on Easter Monday, Woods set about getting Bishop Victor Hugo Martínez to write to the five high-level accusers, requesting an appointment with each. Woods wrote a sample of the letter he wanted the bishop to sign. But the bishop refused. The prelate told the priest that his letter "was not political enough and smacked of breaking confidence," meaning that Woods had been too open about repeating the ambassador's message.

The Texan rewrote the letter in a more ladino tone and the bishop sent if off to the ministers of defense, agriculture, and the interior. Woods then wrote a letter to President Kjell Laugerud, telling him about the Ixcán project, denying any contact with the guerrillas, stating that he had no "political ideals," and asking for the president's support. He also wrote to the commandant in Quiché, but since he had already had a run-in with Colonel Sandoval, he knew the commandant wouldn't see him. His letter was short and to the point. No ladino niceties.

President Laugerud honored Woods's request and granted him an interview. The president listened attentively, the Texan told Hennessey later, but offered no help, suggested no solution. Woods went alone to see the minister of agriculture, General Rubio Coronado, but he met with the minister of *gobernación,* General Vassaux, in the company of Bishop Victor Hugo Martínez. The two cabinet members were noncommittal, however, and the visits nonproductive. The minister of defense, General Romeo Lucas García, never bothered to answer, while Colonel Sandoval Torres in El Quiché responded by asking the head of Civil Aeronautics to ground the priest's three planes because Woods continued "to fly in a manner that endangered innocent lives." The head of Civil Aeronautics complied with the colonel's request by canceling the airworthiness certificates of the three planes, even though volunteer pilots who assisted the Texan used two of the planes.

In August, after unsuccessfully appealing the grounding of his planes since May, Woods went home to Houston on vacation and to obtain some needed dental attention. He returned to Guatemala during the first week in October, but Hennessey did not see much of the Texan during the succeeding weeks. At one point, it occurred to the Iowan that he should ask Woods to come in to assess the status of his relationship with the government and the army. But when Hennessey learned that Woods had finally managed successfully to appeal the grounding of his planes to the president, he concluded that there was no need for immediate action. He was wrong!

During this same period the superior had several other matters that concerned him. The conflict in Nicaragua between Somoza's National Guard and the Sandinistas had been heating up and the Iowan was apprehensive for the safety of Maryknoll personnel stationed in areas where fighting was heaviest. The Maryknollers in El Salvador were pressing him to make a more spirited defense of Bishop Rivera y Damas in San Salvador against the intrigues of

Cardinal Casariego. As a result, Hennessey had hardly seen Woods since the Texan's return to Guatemala more than a month earlier.

Now it was 20 November and the Iowan lay in bed, unable to sleep, recalling the ins and outs of Woods's year-and-a-half odyssey, the visits to his colonists by the guerrillas, the murder of the ladino colonist, the assassination of El Tigre de Ixcán, the kidnapping of more than threescore settlers, their probable torture and deaths, Ambassador Meloy's warning, and now, earlier in the day, . . . the disappearance of the airplane Woods was flying with four American volunteers aboard.

As fatigue pressed in on him, the Iowan tried to convince himself that Woods and the others were safe. The Texan had survived so many close calls with undersized runways and prolific jungle undergrowth that had left him with only a single scar, a permanently twisted nose that Hennessey had come to believe that Woods was exactly what he claimed to be, indestructible. Finally, a fitful sleep gave the superior some relief.

At 5:10 a.m., on the morning of 21 November 1976, Hennessey woke with a start. He looked at his watch. What was it that was bothering him? Suddenly it all came back: Woods, his plane and passengers, all unaccounted for. He headed for the Center House radio room. He'd never forget that morning as long as he lived.

"TG5RW, calling TG5RW. Do you read me?" Hennessey called again and again, but received only crackles and hums for his pains. Finally, at 6:45, each of the ten Ixcán colonization centers began reporting in. None had any word of Woods or his passengers.

At 7:05 a.m., Charlie Huegelmeyer picked up the telephone in Hennessey's office. As he listened to the caller, his face blanched. He hung up the receiver and turned to Hennessey. "That was Aeronaútica Civil. The mayor of San Juan Cotzal in Quiché sent a telegram this morning advising that Woods's plane crashed yesterday. Everybody on board is dead."

The Iowan shook his head, took a deep breath and stood up. "Good God! How many times did Woods tell me that everything would be all right? . . . We both knew he'd be easy prey in his plane if they ever wanted to get him. It never occurred to me that he'd continue to fly others around . . . . How am I going to break the news to Phyllis Gauker . . . and to the families of the others?"

"I'll go out to the airport and talk to Phyllis, Ron." Huegelmeyer answered. "Richard Puig's wife was on that plane and he should be coming here soon to assist at Sunday Mass. You'll have to break the news to him. I'll try to dig up the U.S. addresses for the other two."

After Huegelmeyer left for Aurora Airport, Hennessey called Areonáutica Civil to find out what he could about the disposition of the bodies, only to be told that the air force had claimed jurisdiction over the matter. "What's the air force got to do with a private plane with private passengers aboard?" he inquired.

"You had better ask the air force commandant, padre. What he says is theirs is theirs. Maybe because the passengers were foreigners? *Quién sabe?*"

When Hennessey called air force headquarters, he was told that the air force was involved because a helicopter had been needed to extract the bodies from the remote area where the crash had occurred. "The remains of the dead are being flown to Santa Cruz del Quiché right now, padre, and should be there in fifteen minutes. We'll have them here in the capital about noontime."

About 11:45 a.m., Hennessey called the air force again and was told that the bodies were even then on their way to the capital, and that he would be informed of the time of arrival when it became definitive. Three subsequent calls received the same response. Finally, at 4:00 p.m., the answer was that the arrival would occur at 4:30 p.m.

Hennessey, accompanied by the director of Funerales Reforma, was at Aurora Airbase at 4:20 p.m. Colonel Roberto Salazar, commandant of the air force, presented himself on the tarmac and, showing much concern, informed the priest that he personally had been to the site of the crash and could verify what had happened: "Padre Woods was unqualified to fly in bad weather. He ran into some clouds and rain over San Juan Cotzal, got disoriented and flew into the side of a mountain. Neither he nor his passengers ever knew what happened. I'm sorry, padre!"

"*Gracias, mi coronel,*" responded Hennessey, wondering why the air force commandant would trouble himself to go to the remote crash scene of a small, private airplane with five civilians on board.

As soon as the five clear-plastic body bags with their contents were off-loaded from the transport plane and placed in two aging black Cadillac hearses, Hennessey accompanied the mortician to the funeral parlor to begin the identification process. The director advised him that the mortuary could do nothing with the corpses until he had the medical reports in hand and the names of the deceased were listed in San Juan Cotzal's civil register. He then suggested that Hennessey think about going to El Quiché to expedite matters.

Hennessey decided to act on the mortician's suggestion. He did not need to be reminded that Guatemalan bureaucracies tend to move slowly in the best of circumstances, and that an isolated rural town like San Juan Cotzal would more likely be at the less efficient end of the bureaucratic spectrum. At 8:00 p.m., two friends of Richard Puig and an employee of Funerales Reforma picked up Hennessey and Howard Gross, the U.S. consul general, and headed for El Quiché.

The two-hour drive out the Pan American Highway and then off onto a switchback mountain road into Santa Cruz del Quiché was a quiet one, with little being said among the vehicle's occupants. It was late, all were tired, and their errand had unpleasant implications for both the regional superior and the consul. Hennessey presumed that Gross was acquainted with Ambassador Meloy's warning to Woods seven months earlier, but felt that the diplomat's silence was an indication that he did not want to discuss the possibility of high-ranking Guatemalan officials being involved in the deaths of five U.S. citizens. Furthermore, the Iowan guessed that some of his Maryknoll colleagues would now accuse him of having made too little effort to control Woods or of having failed to assign the Texan outside the country.

When the five men arrived in Santa Cruz shortly after midnight, the coroner was waiting for them. A long discussion ensued regarding the doctor's mistaken belief that there was one more male and one less female passenger aboard the fatal plane than was actually the case. It took all of Hennessey's patience and diplomatic skill to maneuver the coroner into changing his report. The error was the result of having found two extra passports in the plane's wreckage belonging to volunteers who had not made the flight.

About 2:30 a.m., Monday morning, Hennessey and Gross, believing that the five-hour trip to San Juan Cotzal was too difficult to make at that hour, decided to return to Guatemala City and hire a helicopter to make a direct flight after sunrise.

By 10:00 a.m., the regional superior and the consul general, accompanied by the same two friends of the crash victims, were on their way to San Juan Cotzal in a rented civilian helicopter. Bad weather forced the pilot to land short of his destination and the last twenty kilometers were accomplished in the back of a pickup truck.

The four men arrived at the town during siesta time and were told to entertain themselves for the next two hours. The Mayan mayor, fearful of contradicting the military's version of events, had refused to write up a report. Instead he had been drinking heavily since the previous day and was now too drunk to inscribe the correct names of the deceased in the town's civil register and write up his version of the crash. Twenty-five quetzales worked customary bureaucratic miracle, however, and the ladino town secretary was soon busy preparing the official documents.

Hennessey took advantage of the five hours he was forced to wait for the documents to discuss the crash with the parish priest and several local Mayan residents. Padre Julio Méndez, the Guatemalan pastor of San Juan Cotzal, told the Maryknoller that he had left town for Nebaj at 11:00 a.m. the day of the crash. "There wasn't a cloud in the sky when I left here, Padre Ronaldo, nor had there been any all morning long. Padre Woods could not have flown into a cloud."

Several locals confirmed the pastor's observations. None of them were aware of the air force version of the accident that had Woods flying through clouds and into the mountainside at approximately 10:30 a.m. Some of the respondents claimed to have seen the plane go down, and although their accounts differed as to whether or not it was trailing smoke, all mentioned that the sky was clear. Several men stated they had seen the bodies transported in a pickup to Santa Cruz the day of the accident, and not the following day by helicopter as the air force had claimed.

Why did the air force need those extra hours? Hennessey asked himself. *What were they trying to hide . . . or find?*

On 25 November, the Civil Aeronautics Board issued its report over the signature of "Natzul René Méndez H., Aircraft Inspector." The report stated, among other things, that "the pilot's compartment and the passengers' section were completely destroyed by the impact and fire . . . . The accident was caused by bad weather . . . it was raining . . . . It is conjectured that when Mr. Wood [*sic*] saw the pass filled with clouds, he tried to go under them and ended up inside the clouds . . . he lost the artificial horizon . . . and crashed."[2]

On reading the report, Hennessey felt that his suspicions of foul play were vindicated. Not only was there the warning to Woods by Ambassador Meloy and the 24-hour delay by the air force in producing the bodies, while lying about their disposition, but now he had an official report diametrically opposed to accounts given him by numerous eyewitnesses. After dedicating some moments of meditation to the pros and cons of his next step, its dangers and benefits, the Iowan decided he could do no less than conduct his own private investigation of the crash.

In the week that followed, Hennessey spent three days at the accident's remote site examining the plane's wreckage. He knew the mountain setting was ideal for anyone interested in "disappearing" him to prevent discovery of incriminating evidence of wrongdoing. Nevertheless, he was able to salvage several important parts such as the broken propeller, engine rods, valves and pistons, and part of the landing gear, items that he felt might produce evidence as to the angle of impact, the speed of the plane at impact, and indications as to the cause of the crash. One thing that struck him as soon as he saw the wreckage, however, was that there was no sign of any fire at the scene.

Hennessey then returned to the capital and later to Huehuetenango to interview many close friends of Woods, his colleagues and assistants, trying to piece together the chronology of events that led up to his final flight. It was during these conversations that the Iowan heard of warnings against flying with Woods given by the air force commandant to several people, including to Dr. Joe Cain, head of the Direct Relief Foundation (a private U.S. charitable organization), to Ann Kerndt, an assistant to Woods and a passenger on the fatal flight, and to the governor of the department of Huehuetenango.

It was in late October, fully a month before the crash, that Colonel Roberto Salazar had advised the governor of Huehuetenango not to fly with Woods "because the priest is a careless pilot." Not a week later, Colonel Salazar told Dr. Joe Cain to disassociate his organization from Woods "because linking yourselves to that priest suggests that you may be party to his one-man rule in the Ixcán in opposition to this country's authorities."

In early November, Huehuetenango's governor, wanting to check on Woods and his project, obtained a ride on an air force helicopter to Centro Belén. But when the military left him stranded there for three days, he asked

Woods to fly him out. In the short flight to Huehuetenango, the governor told Woods of the colonel's advice. The Texan, either because he misread the warning or had decided to disregard it, continued his flights in and out of the Ixcán, but not before mentioning the governor's account of the commandant's words to one of his colleagues.

Then, just a few days later at the Huehuetenango airport, Colonel Salazar ran into Ann Kerndt and gave her much the same subtle advice. He told Ann it was all right for her to fly with Woods between Guatemala City and Huehuetenango, but not to accompany him to the Ixcán. Ann, not versed in the subtleties of ladino communications, did not grasp the intent of the colonel's warning and flew on the fatal flight.

Hennessey was disgusted that reports of these warnings had passed between several Maryknollers but none thought them important enough to advise the Iowan of their existence.

On 3 January 1977, Hennessey conferred with Howard Gross regarding the official Guatemalan report, which the consul now knew from the Iowan's investigation to be false. The following day, Gross told Hennessey that he had seen both Colonel Alvarez, the head of Aeronaútica Civil, and Natzul René Méndez H., the report's author. Méndez H. had admitted that he never set foot at the site of the plane's wreckage; he had only flown over it in a helicopter with the commandant of the air force. Colonel Alvarez told Gross that he would order a revised report to eliminate any mention of fire in the wreckage. He also stated that he would look into the discrepancies between the official weather report from Huehuetenango's airport (the closest weather station to the site of the crash) that stated that the skies were clear on the fatal day and that of Aeronaútica Civil, which described overcast, rainy conditions. A new report was then issued, backdated to the day of the original report, eliminating all mention of fire, but continuing to maintain that the weather over San Juan Cotzal on the morning of the crash was overcast and raining. The evidence offered for the claim was the testimony of unnamed witnesses. Consul Gross was satisfied with Colonel Alvarez's cooperation.

The families of the four passengers, along with several of their senators and congressional representatives, however, were not at all satisfied with the official report, amended or not. One after the other appealed to Hennessey for information, his observations and interpretations, and other reports. The Kerndt family of Lansing, Iowa, brought strong political pressure on the

U.S. State Department, the U.S. Embassy in Guatemala, and the National Transportation Safety Board to resolve some of the contradictory and false information coming from the Guatemalan government. But the State Department, not wanting to antagonize a friendly government and laboring through the last days of the lame-duck presidency of Gerald Ford, temporized. T.M. Kerndt, Ann's father, in a letter to Howard Gross, requested information on what Ambassador Meloy had told Woods back in April.

Gross, in his answer, dated 14 January 1977, replied: "I have learned that Father Woods knew several officers of the Embassy well . . . . I understand that on one occasion Father Woods was told that his life might be in danger. However, the embassy has no evidence . . . that the crash was anything but an accident."[3]

On learning of Consul Gross's answer to Mr. Kerndt, Hennessey understood immediately the significance of Ambassador Meloy's invitation to Woods to visit him at his private residence—rather than at the embassy— to hear of the Guatemalan government's threats: official deniability. There were no entries in the embassy logbook to testify to Woods's visit to the ambassador. There were larger things at stake here than the investigation into the possible murder of five American citizens.

In the succeeding weeks, Hennessey was finally able to convince the Kerndt family—the most persistent doubters of official U.S. sincerity—that the antagonistic, defensive attitude exhibited by the Guatemalan authorities and the unwillingness of the State Department and the National Transportation Safety Board to challenge the Guatemalan report made it virtually impossible to obtain further information regarding the cause of the crash and that any additional attempts to push the investigation would only lead to increased frustration. The Iowan wrote that "only time and a tongue loosened by braggadocio or alcohol could shed more light on what caused TG-TEX [Woods's plane] to dive into the mountainside."

While many of Hennessey's efforts during the weeks following Woods's death were devoted to responding to unanswerable questions from both Maryknoll and the families of the four deceased passengers of TG-TEX, polarizing developments among El Salvadorean Catholics, both clergy and laity, began to impinge upon his time and energies. The lobbying efforts of Cardinal

Casariego and Nuncio Gerarda in Rome in behalf of Bishop Oscar Arnulfo Romero had finally proven successful in February 1977 when Pope Paul VI named Romero to the archbishopric of San Salvador. The Vatican's cooperation in giving San Salvador a prelate who was judged to be a right-wing ideologue was seen by the government as a green light. They began a campaign of repression against Church clergy and catechists who had spoken openly in defense of Liberation Theology. The consequences for the Iowan were almost immediate.

Two Salvadorean priests were arrested and tortured, after which one was expelled from the country, the other dumped unconscious on a street corner. The rectory of a third priest was the target of a bombing, while that of a fourth was machine-gunned. Three foreign priests, an American Maryknoller, a Belgian, and a Spaniard, were arrested, stripped naked, and chained to bare bedsprings, where they were subjected to continuous mock executions by officers pretending to play Russian roulette. The first Hennessey heard of the arrests was when he received a phone call from Bernie Servil, the Maryknoller, incarcerated in the main police station in Guatemala City.

"Ron, this is Bernie Servil and I'm here in the police station on Sixth Avenue. I was picked up by the National Guard in San Salvador and expelled. I wasn't given the chance to go back for some clothing and now I'm freezing. Can you bring me a sweater? Make that three sweaters! There are two others here who need them besides me."

"Bernie, what's going on? Never mind! I'll go by the embassy and get the consul to go over with me. I'll be there as soon as I can."

When the Iowan and Consul Howard Gross showed up at the Sixth Avenue police station, the commandant was very courteous. "These men are being held for entering our country from El Salvador without the proper papers. When the legal questions are settled, they will be expelled to their native countries. We cannot allow anyone, including priests, to violate our immigration laws."

Hennessey and the consul were allowed to interview Servil and were told by the prisoner that he had his passport in his possession when he was received at the border by awaiting Guatemalan authorities. He had requested at the time that they stamp the document but they refused saying it was not necessary.

Unknown to Hennessey, Nuncio Gerarda had made a sub rosa agreement with the El Salvadorean authorities that they would expel "undisciplined priests" to Guatemala, rather than torture and publicly humiliate them—or worse, kill them—from whence they would be deported for lack of proper documentation. Servil was the Iowan's first experience with the new agreement, the details of which he would soon obtain from Archbishop Romero and Bishop Rivera y Damas.

A few days after Servil's deportation, Hennessey received a call from another Maryknoller stationed in El Salvador, Larry McCulloch, who recounted to the Iowan that he had been labeled a "troublemaker" by the El Salvadorean military and had been denied reentry into their country after a short visit to his cousin employed at the U.S. Embassy in Costa Rica.

Even as Hennessey discussed with his consultors what steps he should take in approaching the El Salvadorean government and Nuncio Gerarda regarding the Maryknollers' expulsions, fourteen El Salvadorean priests gathered at Apopa for an outdoor Mass. It was billed as a protest against the military and police repression of priests speaking out against the injustice of the country's social conditions. Six thousand people attended the Mass and listened to Father Rutilio Grande, chosen by his thirteen colleagues to give the sermon, declare, "It is practically illegal to be a Christian in this country . . . . Christians are branded traitors, communists, marking them for threats, kidnappings, torture, and possibly, the ultimate sacrifice."[4]

On 12 March 1977, Rutilio Grande was machine-gunned to death along with two catechists on a rural road outside San Salvador.

Back in Guatemala, Hennessey received an invitation to participate in a Mass for the repose of the soul of the El Salvadorean priest and his two assistants. When he arrived at the Sacred Heart church in downtown Guatemala City, the Iowan found that only four other priests were willing to disobey Cardinal Casariego's prohibition against the liturgy. The Mass was a moving experience for Hennessey as he felt the courageous spirit of Grande blend together with that of Bill Woods, and he wondered if the same kind of trial would be asked of others in El Salvador and Guatemala.

Not if Cardinal Casariego could help it! On Sunday, the prelate ascended the cathedral pulpit to denounce the five concelebrants, calling them "disrespectful priests," willing to challenge "legitimate authority." He asked, "What does the Guatemalan Church have to do with the El Salvadorean Church, that we should celebrate Mass for them."

Not in living memory had a prince of the Church uttered a more a-catholic statement.

The cardinal followed up his denunciation of the Iowan and his four colleagues by writing a pastoral letter to all the priests of his archdiocese. He cited "the recent case in El Salvador where several priests were expelled from the country for departing from their mission, getting mixed up in partisan and sectarian politics." He concluded his missive by advising his priests: "Stay out of politics or you will get what is coming to you, just like the priests in El Salvador."[5]

When Hennessey received a copy of the archbishop's letter, he could not believe that the cardinal was actually saying what it looked like he was saying. Because of the wording and juxtaposition of phrases, it seemed that the prelate was not only justifying torture and deportations, but also murder. "It can't be!" the Iowan told himself. He reread the letter. Then he read it again. Then he went to Charlie Huegelmeyer, his principal consultor and an excellent linguist, and asked him to translate the letter. "Tell me that the cardinal is not justifying the murder of Rutilio Grande for speaking out against social injustice," Hennessey begged.

Huegelmeyer read and reread the letter. "That's what he's doing, Ron. The guy is out of his gourd! This is going to have very serious consequences both in El Salvador and here in Guatemala." And so it would.

Chapter 25

BY WHOSE AUTHORITY?

After receiving Huegelmeyer's confirmation of his own reading of Casariego's letter, Hennessey went back to his office to figure out how he should respond. He had already made a decision to challenge the prelate, but he didn't want it to be a matter of just blowing off steam. It had to be public, straightforward, and impersonal. And no *ladinismos!*

The decision to publicly censure the cardinal marked more than a tactical shift for the Iowan, the man who—as far as his siblings and friends were concerned—was the master of the nonconfrontational approach to conflict resolution. Furthermore, to publicly rebuke a member of the hierarchy did not fit easily with his conservative conscience. But once he started to write, Ron wasted no words with filial pleasantries: "It does not surprise me that enemies of the Church twist the truth to suit their own purposes, but it worries me when the cardinal of Guatemala lends his support to those who kidnap, torture and assassinate the ministers of the Church . . . ."

Hennessey surprised himself. The letter was as harsh and uncompromising a statement as he had ever made against anybody. The man who seemed to see virtue and good intentions in everyone he met, or at least extenuating circumstances, could not find within himself a trace of explanation or excuse for the devious, self-important arrogance that possessed the soul of a "prince of the Church." But what distressed the Iowan more than Casariego's personal behavior was the recognition that immoral personalities like the cardinal and the papal nuncio could climb so high in the Church's hierarchy. The vestiges of that thought had been nagging at him for years, and it now left him feeling decidedly deceived, though not blindsided.

In addition to sending copies of his letter to the cardinal and to Nuncio Emmanuel Gerarda, Ron sent an additional copy to Bishop Juan Gerardi

Conedera, president of the Guatemalan Episcopal Conference. Gerardi himself was known to criticize Casariego on occasion and by sending him a duplicate, Hennessey knew that every bishop in Guatemala would soon be reading the bombshell and that many priests would see it as well.

Although Casariego and Gerarda seemed to ignore Ron's attempt to touch their consciences—days went by without any response forthcoming from either quarter—the Iowan's challenge to Cardinal Casariego quickly attracted attention in El Salvador. Archbishop Romero, who was beginning to move leftward as the murders of his priests continued, sent word to Hennessey that he would like to take a copy of the "Casariego letter" to Rome with him. The Vatican, in response to reports from Cardinal Casariego and Nuncio Gerarda questioning Romero's psychological stability, had called the San Salvadorean prelate on the carpet. Archbishop Romero felt that . Ron's letter would demonstrate to the pope that not everyone considered the two schemers to be doing the work of the Lord.

Hennessey knew that to comply with the archbishop's request would draw unwelcome Vatican attention to himself, nevertheless, he did not hesitate to send a signed copy of his original letter to Romero. Unfortunately, the date of the archbishop's curial appointment with Cardinal Cassaroli was moved up and he had to leave El Salvador for Rome before Ron's letter arrived.

When Archbishop Romero returned from the Vatican, a group of El Salvadorean businessmen and landowners published a full-page defamatory ad against their prelate in San Salvador's newspapers. They stated, among other things, that they had no obligation as Catholics to listen to Romero's moral admonitions since "Central American has a higher Church authority who is on our side [namely, Cardinal Casariego]."

Archbishop Romero was holding Hennessey's letter of rebuke to the cardinal as he read the businessmen's and landowners' ad extolling the Guatemalan prelate. The Salvadorean prelate responded by publishing the Iowan's anti-Casariego charges in his archdiocesan newspaper, *Orientación*. As a result of the exchange, Hennessey became a close friend of Romero, an instant celebrity among popular segments of the El Salvadorean people, and a target of vituperation of the El Salvadorean elite. As per his usual manner, Hennessey shrugged off the significance of both the acclaim and the enmity.

It was a full year after his Easter visit to the Ixcán with Bill Woods and almost six months after the Texan's death before Ron was able to return to the colonization project to see how the settlers were doing in the absence of their beloved pastor. As soon as he stepped out of the rented Cessna 185 and felt the oppressive jungle heat, memories of his last trip there came flooding back. The contrast was painful. Instead of the playful crowd of settlers who had clamored to touch and be touched by the exuberant Woods, a few hundred somber faces ranging from muted expectation through sadness to despair greeted the regional superior. "Reminds me of my first days at San Juan Acul," the Iowan mentioned to the puzzled pilot of the Cessna 185.

No sooner had the mandatory polite greetings been extended to all present than Hennessey began to hear accounts of deficiencies in the transportation service the air force had established to replace the one Bill Woods had set up. It was absent from the Ixcán for weeks at a time, often resulting in needless deaths. High tariffs were charged for moving patients and cargo. Constant verbal abuse from racist pilots questioned the colonists' patriotism and devotion to the army. As he listened to one depressing story after another, Ron grimaced at the thought of the high command's repeated accusations against Woods that he had been exploiting the settlers.

The Iowan set about hearing confessions and celebrating Mass in the large wattle-and-daub chapel for a prayerful but obviously intimidated congregation. He used his sermon to explain the circumstances surrounding Woods's final flight. He told them about the U.S. ambassador's warning to Woods of the high command's desire to have him out of the country or face fatal consequences; the air force commandant's advice to several people to avoid flying with Woods to the Ixcán shortly before the fatal trip; the deceptive nature of the official report of the crash; and, finally, the air force's unusual assumption of responsibility for removing and transporting the bodies of the dead from the crash site.

Ron also told his listeners of the give-and-take of his meeting with Woods during which he had suggested to the Texan that he go to another country for his own safety. When the Iowan described Woods's immediate rejection of the idea "because this is not an option available to the colonists," he evoked audible sobs from several listeners.

Finally, Hennessey exhorted the congregation to maintain their spirit of cooperation, not only for their mutual progress, "but for your own survival, so great is the greed of those who would add a few thousand more hectares to their disputed kingdoms."

Ron's remark was intended to underscore the powerful interests the colonists were facing in their struggle to obtain legal titles to their lands. A huge access road 350 kilometers long was even then being constructed across the country, starting on the Caribbean Coast in the northeast and reaching the western department of Huehuetenango. Its proposed trajectory looked like it had been made by a poisonous snake as it crawled along the northern edge of the settlement project, making the colonists' lands a prime target of its voracious appetite. The completion of the road would open up hundreds of thousands of hectares of jungle lands—called the Northern Transversal Strip (FTN)—in the departments of Izabal, Alta Verapaz, El Petén, El Quiché, and Huehuetenango. Large landowners, commercial lumber, nickel, and petroleum interests, and foreign investors would thus have access to lands that until now were of interest only to hardy, landless peasant families.

The Shenandoah Oil Company, the International Nickel Company, and the Guatemalan government were providing financing for the road. The National Institute for Agrarian Development (INTA), under the directorship of the president's brother, Hans Laugerud, was in charge of building the road and administering the finances.

In February, two months before this latest of Hennessey's visits to the Ixcán, President Laugerud had inaugurated the first fifty kilometers of the road in Alta Verapaz. At that time, the president had named his minister of defense, General Fernando Romeo Lucas García (Woods's main antagonist, according to Ambassador Meloy), to the newly created post of Overseer of FTN Development. It quickly became known that four generals, Carlos Arana Osorio, Kjell Laugerud García, Fernando Romeo Lucas García, and Otto Spiegler Noriega, had recently acquired over 700,000 acres of FTN lands. The public thereupon rebaptized the FTN as "the Zone of the Generals."

When it was time to leave the colonists, Ron told them that he was still looking for a priest to replace Woods. The qualifications, he reminded them, were stiff: an emotional and physical ability to live in the jungle, a pilot's license and sufficient cross-country (cross-jungle) flying experience, and a willingness to incur the enmity of the military authorities by standing with the settlers on coveted land.

"It's not easy! There are no idle priests walking around the countryside looking for work. But I've got a good lead. He's not one of ours—a German—so it will take a little negotiation. I'll let you know soon."

With many *abrazos* and handshakes, Hennessey climbed into the copilot's seat of the Cessna 185 while the pilot tested his brakes and magnetos. A few seconds later they were bumping down the grass runway. With a sudden extension of the flaps, the pilot jumped the plane over the small trees at the end of the strip and had them airborne, pushed the nose down slightly to gain airspeed while returning the flaps to their normal position, banked slowly left, and headed for Guatemala City.

Ron left the Ixcán with an uneasy feeling in his stomach. What most concerned the Iowan now was that with Woods gone the army would be free to continue its terror tactics without any outside, credible witness in a position to raise the alarm. Since Woods's death, more than eighty additional catechists and community leaders had been carried away by the soldiers and had not reappeared. The army was intentionally targeting those who had worked most closely with the Texan.

In response, the Guatemalan Bishops Conference (CEG) complained—more in defense of its august institution than standing up for the faithful: "It is shameful that there should be those who claim this work of the Church is a vehicle of international communism."

After some months of negotiations with the bishop of Quezaltenango, Hennessey was able to acquire the services of Father Karl Stetter, a German priest who had been working to form cooperatives in the Quezaltenango countryside. Stetter, a pilot, had been slowly radicalized by elitist opposition to his projects and was anxious to use his flying skills to pick up Woods's fallen mantle.

Slowly, the government's attacks against catechists, bilingual (Mayan/Spanish) teachers, and other community leaders associated with the Church pushed some members of the clergy and ever-greater numbers of nuns to share the radical, antigovernment position of their associates and students. They used their pulpits and classrooms to point fingers more clearly at the executioners and to detail their crimes. It was becoming customary in many communities to see strangers attending church services with tape recorders to record sermons and catechetical lessons. No one dared to accost the interlopers. Those who considered themselves prime targets of the repression, leaders of peasant and barrio communities, spoke cautiously about self-defense, about organizing early warning systems to announce the approach of police or army units, giving the targeted individuals time to hide.

Some bishops, almost half the total of sixteen in Guatemala, those who related in a personal way to their priests, nuns, and laity, were also moving toward more radical postures. The need for episcopal unity, however, to speak with one voice, insisted on by the isolated Vatican, created a constant obstacle to formulating a clear analysis of the national problems.

When the tortured bodies of two student leaders from a Catholic school were discovered in August 1977, over one thousand Christians, including representatives of several Protestant denominations, gathered in the capital's Don Bosco College to celebrate the funeral Mass. The following month, the 15 September Independence Day parade turned into an antigovernment demonstration. The army responded without hesitation, bayoneting fourteen people to death and arresting scores of others, most of whom were never seen again. The Confederation of Guatemalan Religious, a group that pulled together the socially committed members of the Church, protested, "It is truly hypocritical to celebrate freedom and sing the national anthem when the land that is sacred to us continues to be defiled by those who torture and murder."

National elections were only a few weeks away and many community leaders, as well as the guerrilla organizations, were encouraging people not to participate. They claimed that the election would be a charade organized by Arana Osorio and Laugerud García to give an aura of international legitimacy to the high command's chosen candidate, General Fernando Romeo Lucas García. The bishops responded through the CEG, insisting that "it is a serious obligation to participate in an election by voting."

In addition to the official candidate, Fernando Romeo Lucas García, a second military clique had a different standard bearer, the former Jefe Máximo, now wealthy industrialist, Colonel Enrique Peralta Azurdia (ret.). Peralta Azurdia had made a pact with Laugerud's outgoing vice president, Mario Sandoval Alarcón—secretary general of the MLN—that he (Peralta Azurdia) be the MLN's presidential candidate in the upcoming elections. The MLN had felt betrayed by both presidents Arana Osorio and Laugerud García (no relation to Lucas García), whom the party had previously supported. The MLN had provided many of the foot soldiers for the death squads during the

Arana and Laugerud administrations, at the same time agreeing to take upon itself public responsibility for all right-wing abductions and murders. They wanted to provide the illusion on the international scene that the government was caught between uncontrollable violence on the right and left and was not itself involved. The MLN's promised reward for such cooperation was supposed to be a certain number of lucrative governmental ministries—a promise that neither Arana nor Laugerud kept other than to give Sandoval Alarcón the ceremonial vice presidential post.

A third, wanna-be candidate was General José Efraín Ríos Montt. The general had recently returned from his forced exile to Madrid. While there he had dedicated himself to writing a political book in which "he cast himself as both a hero and a martyr" in order to prepare for a second run at the presidency.[1] Convinced that he still had a special political mission from God, he spoke with the leaders of the Christian Democratic Party, hoping to win their backing once again for his candidacy. But the DC, knowing that Arana Osorio remained the country's premier backstage power broker and remembering that Ríos Montt had been unwilling to challenge the fraudulent results of the 1974 election, had decided that it did not want to patronize a rerun of the Huehueteco's previous debacle.

Twice frustrated as a presidential candidate despite his putative divine mission, Ríos Montt turned inward once again.[2] As the crestfallen, would-be president fought the bitterness in his heart, a source of light, like a Bethlehem star appeared on his darkened horizon. In the guise of the Three Wise Men, the young elders of a new and obscure North American charismatic sect out of northern California called Gospel Outreach—a group that had arrived in Guatemala in the wake of the 1976 earthquake—came across the despondent "non-candidate" in the capital bringing news of great joy. The American visionaries prophesied that God had "special plans" for the unemployed general.[3]

For Ríos Montt, special plans emanating from the Divinity that included the Huehueteco's future could only mean political plans, and his eventual conversion to the newcomers' faith was all but assured. He had months of soul-searching and tears of bitterness and frustration ahead of him, but the prophecy was all the psychological balm his hitherto crushed spirit needed. The Catholic Church would betray him no more!

The election was held in March 1978. Sixty percent of the registered voters refused to go to the polls; another 20 percent invalidated their ballots in protest. With only 20 percent of potential voters participating, Colonel Enrique Peralta Azurdia garnered the most votes.[4]

When the government's electoral commission announced the results, General Fernando Romeo Lucas García was declared the winner. The former Jefe Máximo's followers, like those of Ríos Montt in 1974, begged the old warhorse to pick up the gauntlet and challenge Arana Osorio in the streets. But Peralta Azurdia had fought his last fight. Good tactician and strategist that he was, he knew he could not beat Arana Osorio in a dirty street brawl. He declined the challenge, not willing to jeopardize his newfound wealth or run the risk of losing the aura of a successful *caudillo* whose day had passed.

General Fernando Romeo Lucas García, a key aide to Arana Osorio in . the Zacapa state-terror campaign of 1966-67, graciously accepted his "election" as president of Guatemala.

In May 1978, one month before Lucas García was scheduled to take over the reigns of government and as President Laugerud scrambled to demonstrate to his army colleagues that he was as tough a *caudillo* as both his predecessor and successor, a pivotal event occurred that would serve as the definitive marker of the schizophrenic Laugerud administration. Several hundred Q'eq'chí Maya had assembled in the main plaza of Panzós, Alta Verapaz, at the invitation of the mayor. The stated purpose of the meeting was to hear the government's response to the Q'eq'chí protest that some powerful landowners, backed by the military, had forced the Mayans off their ancestral lands located in the FTN. The local army detachment was standing by, armed with their Israeli-manufactured Galil assault rifles.[5] The landowners were also present, backed by contingents of bodyguards and hired gunmen. A large ditch had been dug only a few days earlier on the outskirts of town, its significance unknown to the Mayans.

As soon as the Q'eq'chí had gathered in the square, the military and landowners staged a shoving match between a soldier and a Mayan as a pretext for opening fire on the unsuspecting peasants. More than one hundred men, women, and children were killed by the withering crossfire; an estimated additional one hundred and fifty were wounded. Others died by drowning as they tried to escape across the swollen Polochic River. Immediately, municipal trucks on standby were brought in to haul away the corpses, taking them to the recently dug ditch that served as a mass grave. Unfortunately for the government, a priest in civilian clothes was present at the scene with a small, unobtrusive camera. He captured aspects of the massacre on film, depriving the government of a credible denial.

The following day, the army press office gave its official version: "38 Kekchis [*sic*] died in a peasant uprising instigated by leftist guerrillas, Cuba's Fidel Castro and religious groups." [6] The newly named defense minister, General Otto Spiegler Noriega, added his own, more specific accusation: "The peasants were shouting threats as they attacked the military garrison at Panzós and the Catholic Church has been meddling in this whole question."

At first, Spiegler's finger-pointing was seen as the usual military attempt to shift responsibility from itself for its consistent, brutal, repressive tactics. But the specifics of his language made many think that a definite change of strategy had occurred, that a one-way bridge had been crossed and the Catholic Church was now to be officially labeled subversive. The government would now publicly link the Church to Castro's communist government and to the country's four guerrilla armies. It was remarked that Spiegler was starting his own presidential campaign four years early.

In response to the massacre at Panzós, sixty thousand people marched to the presidential palace a few days later where they screamed, "Cowards! Cowards!" at the president and his staff. The marchers included a core group of a newly formed Christian organization calling itself the Committee for Peace and Justice (CPJ), which embraced priests, nuns, catechists, and lay leaders. Ron Hennessey marched among their number.

The Guatemalan Episcopal Conference (CEG) felt obliged to issue a moderate statement "in a Christian manner" and "in the light of Christ's gospel" decrying the Panzós massacre.

An unidentified spokesperson for the U.S. State Department, quoted in a UPI dispatch that faithfully reflected the Guatemalan government's version of the massacre, hewed to the consistent U.S. foreign policy ethic of seeing no evil where allies were concerned. He compared the Panzós killings to those of the Ohio National Guard at Kent State University, "an overreaction of the troops." *Newsweek*'s Beth Nissen, however, was not satisfied to accept Guatemala's official line and she managed to negotiate with some unsuspecting army brass for permission to go to Panzós. As a consequence, the U.S. public was shown the priest's photo of a truck piled high with dead Q'eq'chí and received a verifiable version of the actual event.[7] When a liturgy was scheduled to honor and pray for the Panzós dead in a downtown Guatemala City church, Hennessey, as he had done in the case of the Mass for Father Rutilio Grande, decided that he should participate despite Cardinal Casariego's prohibition against the commemoration. Before the liturgy could begin, the cardinal, apprised of the disobedience and wanting to salvage some modicum of his tarnished authority, telephoned the pastor and gave an order: "You are not to allow any sermon at that Mass, nor should you permit the Prayer of the Faithful."

The prelate knew that both elements of the Mass would give ample opportunity for the outpouring of antigovernment sentiment.

The pastor assured the cardinal that his wishes would receive due consideration. He then conveyed the cardinal's words to his four concelebrants, one of whom was Hennessey, and asked what they wanted to do. All agreed that Casariego was overstepping the limits of his authority and should be ignored. And such they did.

When the five priests marched into the sanctuary and took their places behind the altar, the Iowan's disappointment at the small number of clerics involved turned to satisfaction as he looked out over the hundreds of dark, earnest faces of those willing to incur governmental and ecclesiastical wrath. The many nuns in the congregation, the backbone of the Church at all times and places of need, gave witness that they, more numerous than their male clerical colleagues, were not afraid to face down the cardinal and the generals.

At the moment of the offertory, dozens of fervent prayers, those that the cardinal had forbidden, arose spontaneously from the assembled congregation: "May our Q'eq'chí brothers and sisters rest in eternal peace." "May our memory of their struggle for justice and their sacrifice never be erased." "May God give us the fortitude to follow their brave example when the need arises." Each prayer was answered with a successively louder, collective "Amen!"

Some aggressive swipes were made at the army and the government: "May the soldiers understand that they do the work of the devil." "May God stay the hands of the ignorant and evil men who kill our brothers and sisters." "May God give us one day a government that understands the meaning of justice." The "amens" grew louder.

Then the name of each Panzós victim, inscribed in white letters on a black banner carried by a member of the congregation, was called out one by one. In answer to each name, the congregation shouted back an earnest *"presente!"*

Hennessey felt the tide of emotion building and feared for the safety of the participants if someone tried to take advantage of the passion. A young Guatemalan Jesuit and friend of the Iowan, Father Luis Pellecer, went to the pulpit to calm the crowd. He began slowly and the emotion subsided. But then a sense of guilt invaded the young priest as he felt he was betraying the spirit of the event. He ended with a look of sadness on his face, asking, "To whom shall our Mayan brothers and sisters turn for help to defend themselves from the army's exploitation and repression, if not to us? It is to us they turn, and we must respond."

As he listened to Pellecer, Hennessey felt a strange sense of victory married to defeat, a paradox of human perception that only deep religious faith could broker. The emotion of the prayers, the names and *"presentes,"* and the sermon was like a powerful garden perfume permeating the air around him, and he wondered how he could—or would—answer the Jesuit's question.

In a few short weeks, Pellecer's attempts to answer that question for himself would lead him into an incomprehensible tragedy. As he edited communiqués and position papers for the EGP, the author's identity became a poorly kept secret. Suddenly, four armed men in a white unmarked Bronco, the signature vehicle of the judicial (secret) police, kidnapped him off the streets of Guatemala City in broad daylight before several witnesses. Several weeks of torture followed, resulting in a trance-like, drug-induced psychosis. Pellecer was then driven from venue to venue where he publicly denounced his Jesuit colleagues as communist collaborators. Cardinal Casariego, as well as his closest U.S. congressional supporter and frequent visitor, Senator Jesse Helms of North Carolina, enthusiastically applauded these staged performances of a grossly violated personality by the Guatemalan government.

The first time the Iowan saw the young Jesuit wrapped in a robotic trance on television, he hardly recognized his old friend. Ron wanted to cry out to Pellecer but held his tongue. He didn't stay to watch the entire frightening spectacle, but instead went to the Center House chapel and meditated in the darkened environment on the plasticity for either good or evil of all human nature. *"But for the grace of God, go I . . . ."*

Two weeks after the Panzós massacre, the left wing of the PGT, now organized as a guerrilla organization, the FAR, blew up an army truck carrying military police in what the FAR said was an act of retaliation for the Panzós killings. Sixteen police were killed. The Guatemalan bishops committee (CEG) issued a harsh condemnation of the bombing, one that contrasted sharply with the "Christian" condemnation of the army's action at Panzós.

The following month, only a few days after the inauguration of General Fernando Romeo Lucas García, the new administration demonstrated that it intended to go beyond anything that the Laugerud government had ever done in breaking faith with the Church, while still keeping Cardinal Casariego as its symbol of legitimate religiosity. A death squad, using Israeli-made Uzi machine pistols, killed Padre Hermógenes López in full daylight on a street in San José Pinula, ten kilometers east of Guatemala City. Although elements of both the police and the army were nearby, no attempt was made to apprehend the killers. The priest had made the mistake that Hennessey had once warned Bill Woods against, writing a public letter to the president asking him to remove the army from his parish. Padre Hermógenes had previously spoken out against a company formed by large landowners and backed by the military, Compañía Aguas, S.A., for diverting the peasants' water supply to the irrigation needs of *finca* owners. It was the second of a string of murders of clerics whose blood stained the fingertips of Cardinal Casariego.

Meanwhile, the army's repression in the Ixcán, aimed at isolating and eliminating any vestige of support for the EGP, was having the opposite effect of that intended. The influence of the EGP had spread from the lowlands up into the El Quiché highlands, although not yet expressed overtly. Food supplies were made available for the revolutionary troops with expectation of payment, one that was consistently met.

The army was not slow in responding. For the first time, death lists began to appear with the names of priests and nuns. And in justification of this new offensive, Mario Sandoval Alarcón, the general secretary of the MLN, declared with some venom, "The Catholic Church has been one of the most important means by which communism has reached the people, the Indians, the humble." It was a declaration of war, one-sided though it might be.

Father Karl Stetter, Bill Woods's replacement in the Ixcán, was seen as an obstacle for the development of the military's plans to expel the area's colonizers from their lands. The German priest had continued Woods's practice of teaching the settlers their legal rights and he stood as a public witness to the army's continued terror tactics. Though he was a pilot and flew frequently over long stretches of uninhabited jungle, Stetter knew that he could not be removed as had Woods without thereby confirming what had become a national certitude. Nor could the high command eliminate a German national as it had a Guatemalan priest, Padre Hermógenes. The ploy the army selected, then, was to hide some automatic weapons in the priest's plane and to discover them at an appropriate moment. It would then accuse Stetter of smuggling arms for the guerrillas, arrest him—or kill him—with the evidence in hand.

The plan came unraveled when Stetter himself discovered the soldiers loading the weapons onto his plane. His protest resulted in the cleric's arrest with the claim that the weapons had been discovered in a "concealed area," namely, the plane's baggage compartment.

When Hennessey heard of the priest's detention from the colonists, he called the German Embassy. The Guatemalan authorities, however, denied to the German ambassador that they had detained Stetter. A few days later the Iowan happened to see the priest being pushed into a police van parked outside the immigration office. Ron followed the van to the airport while maintaining two vehicles between himself and the police. There he saw Stetter driven onto the tarmac and put aboard a flight to Europe. Again he called the German Embassy. The next day, in the face of prima facie evidence, the authorities admitted to having expelled the priest from the country "for endangering national security." Their original lies were brushed off as "doing politics."

In the face of ever more frequent and escalating atrocities, Cardinal Casariego continued to demonstrate his moral support for the military and police authorities. The government acknowledged his assistance by providing the prelate with a police motorcycle escort wherever he chose to go. At a festive meeting attended by the cardinal, at which Hennessey also assisted, the prelate told his listeners "in all humility" how blessed they were to have him as their archbishop, since he had been offered two other "attractive archbishoprics" before accepting that of Guatemala City. He also outlined how he had been at the center of the group of influential cardinals who, under the influence of the Holy Spirit, had selected Popes John Paul I and John Paul II to the papacy. As a result, the cardinal claimed, he had been rewarded with the personal friendship of both men.

Casariego's remarks made Ron's opinion of the College of Cardinals take a 45-degree slide south and made him question still further papal claims to be directly linked to the divinity.

At a subsequent diplomatic function, Hennessey heard the cardinal repeat much the same line. A little while later, Frank Ortiz, the U.S. ambassador, approached the Iowan and remarked "how fortunate we are to have a churchman like Cardinal Casariego heading up the Church here."

The Maryknoller swallowed to restrain his tongue while nodding his head with what he hoped was an expression of appropriate gravity.

Encouraged, Ortiz suggested that the political situation in the department of El Quiché was going from bad to worse and perhaps it was time to send in a team of U.S. Army doctors to bolster the Guatemalan Army's civic action program "to show the flag."

"The day has passed when the people of El Quiché will trust the Guatemalan Army or the U.S. government, Mr. Ambassador," the Iowan responded. "I would have thought that the help the United States gave Arana Osorio in Zacapa ten years ago and what that accomplished then would have cured you and the State Department of any such illusions by now."

"Maybe we should get out of the way and let the people and the army fight it out? Is that what you think, padre?"

"I don't think that's such a bad idea, Mr. Ambassador," was the regional superior's sardonic reply. "I'm not a good prognosticator regarding these kinds of conflicts, but I do know that without U.S. involvement there would be a lot fewer deaths."

Like the good soldier he was, Ortiz was undeterred by the frank exchange and he continued to engage the Iowan in conversation, trying in an offhand way to sound out Hennessey's estimation of the guerrillas' strength in different areas where the Maryknollers worked. But the regional superior understood the ambassador's interest and politely confessed his ignorance, explaining that his residence in the capital made it impossible for him to know anything more about the guerrillas than the ambassador himself already knew.

Having exhausted the intelligence potential of the Maryknoll regional superior, Ortiz moved on to other targets. Hennessey watched him go, wondering what, other than his family name and fluency in Spanish, had prompted President Carter to name the New Mexico native to such a delicate position. It would not be long before the Iowan would have his answer.

This clandestine photograph shows the victims of the Panzós massacre piled on top of one another in a truck bed. (Credit: anonymous/*Newsweek*)

Fr. Bill Woods readying a flight to his colonization program in the Ixcan.
(Credit: Maryknoll)

Chapter 26

DIPLOMATIC IMMUNITY REVOKED

Hennessey's cool remarks to Ambassador Frank Ortiz at the formal reception did not dissuade the hard-nosed diplomat from pursuing his quest for information on the guerrillas—real and imagined—from the Maryknoll superior and his colleagues. On Thanksgiving Day, November 1979, he went to the Maryknoll Center House in Guatemala City to celebrate this most civil of traditional U.S. holidays. He knew that many of the up-country Maryknollers would be together to partake of the feast and this would give him an opportunity to ask a few leading questions and to keep his ears open for offhand remarks. On this particular occasion, he got a bit more than he bargained for.

Father Bill Mullan had come to the city to report a murder by some soldiers in San Mateo Ixtatán in Huehuetenango where he was pastor. He had been sitting in his office a few days earlier, as he recounted to Hennessey, when he looked out the window to see a group of soldiers run by. He paid scant attention, thinking they were engaged in one of their periodic roundups of young Mayan inductees. A few seconds later, shots rang out, followed by a series of yells and more gunfire.

Mullan ran out to investigate. "They shot Gabriel, padre," one of the onlookers told him breathlessly. "All he did was run away when he saw them coming."

When the priest arrived at the shooting scene on a path below the rectory, two soldiers were about to pick up the lifeless body. Mullan stopped them to bless the corpse, recognizing the dead man as a recent convert. The commanding officer, a young lieutenant, walked over nonchalantly, stuck out his hand, and asked the priest if he were the pastor. Mullan, forearmed with more details of the bloody encounter by several parishioners on his way to the scene, ignored the officer's hand and, in a barely controlled voice, advised, "You and your men better get out of here before the people's anger gets out of hand."

The army patrol had executed its orders "to find some guerrillas" by killing the father of three small children, a simple man walking through town with a load of firewood on his back. The first shot hit him in the foot as he tried to run from them and they then finished him off with a pistol shot to the head at point-blank range. The lieutenant had just then ordered that the lifeless body be dumped in the town plaza for all to contemplate.

The milling, angry crowd was now screaming, "Killers!" "Assassins!" "*Afuera, afuera!* Out!"

The young, nervous soldiers began sweeping their Galil rifles across the crowd. Fearing an uncontrolled reaction and more bloodshed, Mullan turned and exhorted the gathering in their Mayan tongue: "Be quiet! Calm down! You'll get yourselves killed! . . . Remember Panzós! Let's get these soldiers out of here and then see what we can do."

The officer explained to Mullan in a somewhat chastened tone, "This man was a guerrilla. He ran when he spotted us. Why would he run if he weren't a guerrilla? Anyway, he shot at us. Go look. He has a grenade still in his hand."

Mullan refused to look. He was not about to play the lieutenant's face-saving game of symbolic virtue, a common military tactic meant to fool no one, but only to create the illusion at the heart of Guatemala's military culture, that fantasy is reality if you have the guns to back it up. The priest glared at the officer, hoping that the lieutenant could read the anger in his eyes. He then turned and trudged back to the rectory.

The following day, Mullan went to Huehuetenango to report the murder at the main army base. The priest was shown into the intelligence section and there, seated behind the desk, was the same officer who had been involved in the preceding day's shooting. "I want to speak to an official about a killing that took place yesterday in San Mateo Ixtatán," the New Yorker explained.

"I'm the one here who takes reports," the lieutenant answered with a mocking smile. "Tell me what happened."

Mullan stared for a minute or two trying to get a grip on his emotions. Then, without another word, turned and walked out.

"I could see that I was up against a stone wall in Huehuetenango," Mullan told Hennessey later in the day in Guatemala City. "My only recourse was to come here and hope you could put me in touch with somebody with the authority to discipline that guy."

It was two days before Thanksgiving.

"Ambassador Frank Ortiz is coming here for dinner the day after tomorrow," the Iowan responded. "Why don't you stay in town until then and tell him your story. Maybe he can do something. Then again, . . . maybe he can't—or won't."

On Thursday, Hennessey introduced Mullan to the ambassador and, after a polite exchange, the New Yorker proceeded to describe the killing in San Mateo. The diplomat pulled a small notebook from his pocket and began to write down the details. As Mullan spoke, evidencing some emotion, Ortiz would look up at the priest from time to time with a puzzled look on his face, as if wondering why the dead man provoked such feeling.

"Was the slain man someone important, someone close to you?" Ortiz asked.

"No! He was a fellow human being, Mr. Ambassador!"

"Now don't take offense, padre, but do you think he might actually have been a guerrilla? Is there a guerrilla presence in your area?"

Mullan took a deep breath and let it out slowly, making no effort to hide his emotion. "The man was not a guerrilla. The soldiers knew he was not a guerrilla. I know of no guerrilla presence in our area. This was an unprovoked murder, Mr. Ambassador, intended to intimidate."

Ortiz hesitated. Finally he answered. "I can ask my contacts in the Guatemalan Army to pay the man's window some kind of monthly pension, something to put food on the table for her children. What do you think of that, padre?"

"Is that all the justice we can expect?" asked Mullan, showing disbelief and not a little anger. "Is there no punishment for the killers?"

Ortiz shrugged his shoulders and looked quizzically at Hennessey, as if to say, "What does this guy expect me to do? Doesn't he know how things work around here?"

The conversation ended with Mullan showing signs of profound dissatisfaction on his face.

Some weeks later, back in San Mateo Ixtatán, Mullan checked with the dead man's father. He found that the commandant at the army base in Barillas had warned the man not to pursue compensation for his widowed daughter-in-law and grandchildren or he would suffer the same fate as his son.

When Hennessey later heard of the commandant's warning, he remarked to Mullan, "We should have expected as much. The executioners were only doing what their commander ordered, and any pension coming through army channels for a Mayan—if in fact it ever existed—had to stop in that commander's hands."

The army's murder of a simple man in San Mateo and its attempt to identify him as a guerrilla suggested to Hennessey that the authorities were becoming concerned about a potential guerrilla presence in San Mateo and the surrounding countryside, though Mullan had assured the Iowan that none such existed. Apparently the army figured that it was only a question of time before the EGP influence and organization moved out of El Quiché and the Ixcán immediately to the east and into the easternmost towns and villages of Huehuetenango. The show of force was meant to warn the Mateanos of the consequences of any such alliance. Its effect, however, would prove to be the exact opposite.

Nevertheless, the department of El Quiché remained the main object of concern for both the Guatemalan government and Frank Ortiz.

The army had established a small base in Chajul, El Quiché, a month after Karl Stetter's deportation in February 1979. Chajul had a parish cooperative that was very active in making legal attempts to protect its Ixil-Maya landholdings. The army's objective was to terminate the cooperative as well as to sow terror in surrounding villages in case anyone had ideas of aiding the EGP. A total curfew was established from 6:00 p.m. to 6:00 a.m. and anyone other than soldiers caught out during those hours was shot on the spot. While the peasants sat terrified in the dark of their homes, lightning raids were carried out accompanied by the victims' screams. No one ever knew who would be next. Over the next several months, more than fifty Ixils, cooperative leaders, teachers, catechists, health promoters, were "disappeared," some of their tortured mutilated bodies often appearing days later along nearby roadsides.

Finally, a small delegation of Ixil-Maya went to the capital to protest the army's brutality to the National Congress. They were denied an audience, however, denounced as "communists," and expelled from the congressional chambers. Disheartened, broke, and hungry, they returned to Chajul to report their treatment to the cooperative's membership and to their neighbors.

In November, the air force began bombing the *aldeas* around Chajul. In mid-November, nine leaders from San Miguel Uspantán were picked up and flown to Chajul by helicopter. Seven of their tortured bodies dressed in camouflaged uniforms together with two old, useless shotguns turned up in a mass grave near Chajul on 6 December. The Alice-in-Wonderland government claimed they were guerrillas killed in an armed confrontation with soldiers. .

After several Ixil-Maya clandestine meetings, a decision was made to send a larger delegation including Quiché and Q'eq'chí-Maya to the capital with a more creative plan for publicizing the Maya's plight. On 15 January 1980, approximately 130 Maya peasants arrived in the capital to break the information barrier erected by the government that held them practically incommunicado.

At first, the delegation held several press conferences, but nothing the participants said appeared in the capital's dailies. They then tried to purchase newspaper space to publicize their predicament, but none of the periodicals would accept their statements. They staged demonstrations in the city's streets, interrupting traffic, suffering beatings and arrests, but received no publicity regarding their motivation. At San Carlos University, the oldest university in the Western Hemisphere, they staged a rally among supportive students. Twenty of their number then marched to the office of the OAS in Guatemala City, where the director accepted a copy of their denunciations through a window.

The document, dated 24 January, was signed by leaders from the communities of Chajul, Nebaj, Cotzal, San Miguel Uspantán, San Pablo El Baldío, Chimel, and Chacamán, denouncing the army's repression and the "Civic Military Campaigns" that Ambassador Frank Ortiz was so fond of. The proclamation read in part: "We . . . can no longer support this repression, and we have decided to let all the people of Guatemala and all worldwide organizations know it. We want the army out of our communities. We do not want the army on our lands. We lived in peace before [the army] arrived . . . ."[1]

The following day, the demonstrators attempted to participate in the first anniversary memorial of the murder of Alberto Fuentes Mohr, the minister of foreign affairs under Méndez Montenegro (1966-70) and leader of the small Social Democratic Party. The police broke up the memorial gathering.

The Sisters of the Sagrada Familia, a Belgian Order, invited the demonstrators to their school for a Mass, followed by a strategy session. The minister of *gobernación,* Donaldo Alvarez Ruiz, went on television that evening to denounce the peasants as communists, accusing the Sagrada Familia nuns of having contacts with the guerrillas. He told his viewers not to be deceived by the simple peasant appearance of the protesters, that they were, in fact, highly trained guerrillas attempting to sow falsehoods and unrest.

Several of the Belgian nuns considered the accusation of Alvarez Ruiz as a less than subtle threat to their physical integrity and decided to leave the country for Mexico.

Finally, a decision was made to stage a sit-in at the Spanish Embassy. The date would be 31 January 1980. The delegation was made up of twenty-three self-selected peasants and six university students. They chose the Spanish Embassy because it was European, had no police presence guarding its doors, and its ambassador had made a recent visit to El Quiché where he had heard accounts of the army's atrocities from the Spanish priests working there. And with that decision, 31 January 1980 would become one of the more infamous dates among many of Guatemala's tortured modern history.

At 11:05 a.m., on the last day of January 1980, three upper-class Guatemalans of national prominence entered the second-floor office of the Spanish ambassador, Máximo Cajal, to discuss Spanish funding of an upcoming international conference on Procedural Law to be held in Guatemala City. The three were Eduardo Cáceres Lehnhoff, a former vice president under General Carlos Arana Osorio (1970-74) and friend of Ron Hennessey since El Petén days, Adolfo Molina Orantes, a former minister of foreign affairs, and Mario Aguirre Godoy, a well-known lawyer. The meeting had no sooner begun, when the Spanish consul, Jaime Ruiz del Arbol, appeared at the door to advise Cajal that three or four peasants from El Quiché had entered the embassy and had requested a session with the ambassador in order to give him some petitions. Cajal responded that he would meet with the new visitors as soon as he finished with the three jurists.

A few moments later, the consul came back, a bit breathless this time, to say that the three or four peasants were now about twenty or twenty-five, had closed the doors to the embassy and had declared that they were engaged in a peaceful occupation of the building.

The ambassador left the three Guatemalans and descended to the reception area on the first floor where he encountered twenty-nine people, five of them women, all dressed as peasants, wearing straw, broad-brimmed hats with the lower half of their faces covered with red and black bandanas. A young woman who spoke fluent Spanish—a university student it turned out—stepped forward. She told the ambassador that they were occupying the embassy as a peaceful demonstration in order to obtain the diplomat's help to transmit several demands to the Guatemalan government, since all previous attempts to do so had been frustrated. Their principal request was that the government open a grave in Chajul that she said contained seven bodies of neighbors whom the army had kidnapped from Uspantán in November. The seven had been tortured, dressed as guerrillas, and then executed, their corpses left for several days along the roadside before being buried. She added that her Mayan companions wanted to prove to the world that these men were not guerrillas by revealing the signs of torture they had suffered and the manner by which they had been killed. The Mayans went on to describe the general situation of repression and terror in which they and their neighbors lived.

The ambassador assured the visitors that he would honor their request. He stated that he had learned of their situation from the Spanish priests and the bishop of El Quiché, Juan Gerardi Conedera, during a recent visit. He intended to send a report of what he had learned to Madrid in hopes that his government would contact the Guatemalan government to express its concern. He then underlined the invaders' precarious situation should the police or army get word of their presence and encouraged them to leave immediately and peacefully. The three Guatemalans who had followed the ambassador down from his office echoed Cajal's fears.

The spokesperson, Sonia Magaly Welches Valdez, replied that she and her companions had come with the intention of staying until the Guatemalan government responded. If it took a week or two to carry out the negotiations, they had come prepared with sufficient food and bedding to last that long.

While this conversation was going on, some members of the group had begun to hang sheets out the embassy windows painted with lettering expressing their motives and demands. Ten minutes or so passed before several police cars pulled up in front of the building.

At this point, Ambassador Cajal asked permission of the intruders to telephone the Guatemalan authorities in order to avoid any unpleasant developments. The request was granted and Cajal began his calls. First, he called the minister of foreign relations, Castillo Valdez, but the official could not be located. Next, he attempted to reach the chief of protocol, Antonio Chocano, but was told that he was on vacation. Then he called the vice-minister of foreign relations, Alfonso Alonso Lima. Advised of the situation, Alonso Lima asked if the invaders were actually peasants and whether or not they were armed.

Cajal responded that he could not assure the vice-minister of the social status of the demonstrators but that the majority looked to be Mayan peasants judging from the homemade sandal footwear worn by most, the bare feet of others, and the short physical stature of almost all. Also, he had noticed that a few carried bottles filled with a rose colored liquid that he presumed to be gasoline—Molotov cocktails—but that the majority possessed only the ubiquitous peasant machete. He also emphasized that they had stated their intentions to be entirely peaceful, had claimed that they were unarmed, and had already agreed to allow all women present in the building to leave without difficulty.

The ambassador then requested that "you [Alonso Lima] must forward my request to the [foreign] minister and to the competent authorities that they pull back the police [who were then arriving in massive numbers] as a prudent gesture to calm tensions and to avoid greater problems."[1]

The vice-minister answered something to the effect that the ambassador's request would be rather difficult to fulfill.

After calling Madrid and explaining the situation to the Spanish foreign minister, Cajal telephoned the Guatemalan minister of government (*gobernación*, the government's highest police authority), Donaldo Alvarez Ruiz, but was told the minister was in a meeting and could not receive calls.

The Spanish ambassador responded that twenty-five to thirty-five demonstrators had created a delicate situation by occupying his embassy and it was urgent that he talk to the vice-minister. The answer was that the vice-minister was also unavailable, but that "the official" (highest-ranking individual on duty) would call right back.

"The official" never called. And, during the next two hours that the embassy telephones remained functional, no one from the offices of the president, the foreign minister, the minister of *gobernación*, or any other government office or agency called to inquire about the situation. As news of the occupation spread worldwide, however, calls from other sources continued to come in, including from news reporters in Madrid, from the ambassador's wife, also in Madrid, and from the Spanish ambassador in Costa Rica.

The total lack of communication from the Guatemalan authorities continued. About 1:00 p.m., when the police began their aggressive move on the building, all telephone connections were cut.

The ambassador, the consul, seven embassy employees, including five women, the three Guatemalan visitors, and the twenty-nine demonstrators, all retreated to the building's second floor as the police took control of the rooftop and balconies and moved against the building's main door. A metal gate sealed off the stairway leading from the first floor as the occupiers moved up the stairwell.

At that time, the police began cutting through the building's tile roof with an ear-piercing concrete saw, even as others moved in to occupy the embassy's bottom floor.

As the police force increased to approximately four hundred men—with a vanguard called "Comando Seis" consisting of several specialized units that doubled as kidnappers and death squads,[2] Cajal took to using a megaphone brought in by the invaders to appeal to the police to back off. He advised the security forces that the peasants were willing to come out two-by-two accompanied by all hostages and that he and the president of the Red Cross should be allowed to mediate the dispute. Both Cáceres Lehnhoff and Molina Orantes used the same speaker to make similar appeals.

At that moment, Odette Arzú, an official of the Red Cross and close relative of that organization's president, appeared on the scene. She had received a phone call from the Spanish consul, Jaime Ruiz del Arbol, a personal friend, appealing for help to negotiate with the police. When she identified herself and sought entrance to the embassy, permission was refused. When told that only reporters were allowed onto the first floor, Arzú produced press credentials and was given admittance.

As she approached the metal gate barring the stairway, the Red Cross official-qua-reporter recognized Máximo Cajal, Eduardo Cáceres Lehnhoff, and Adolfo Molina Orantes on the barrier's upper side. Molina Orantes appealed to the woman, "Odette, what these people want is to get out of here, but they need a guarantee to leave accompanied by the press, by the representatives of the University of San Carlos, and by the Red Cross."[3]

When the police heard the appeal, they asked Arzú to leave. But, being a well-known, upper-class woman with the mistaken idea that she was immune from any police indignities, Odette stood her ground. Again the police demanded she leave or suffer the consequences. For a second time, she refused to move. They then used rifle butts to shove her down the stairs and unceremoniously threw her onto the embassy patio. There, she dusted herself off and watched in horror as Comando Seis, machine guns in hand, continued to cut through the roof.

At that moment, the second in command of the Judicial Police (secret, plainclothes police) approached and asked, "Doña Odette, what are you doing getting yourself into such problems?"

"What are you talking about?" she answered with an unmistakable tone of offended dignity. "You know the Red Cross has to be where it's needed and I've been called here to do my duty."

"Well, just don't try to go in there again because we aren't going to let you."[4]

As Arzú stood there, a call came on the man's police radio. Arzú distinctly heard the individual on the other end of the transmission state: *"No quiero que salga ni uno vivo*; I don't want a single one to come out alive."[5]

"*Sí, mi coronel, sí, mi coronel*," the subcommandant answered as he turned his back.

Inside the embassy, the police had begun tearing a hole in the wall to bypass the metal gate barring access to the second floor. All occupants—the demonstrators, embassy personnel, and the three Guatemalan jurists began retreating along a short corridor toward the ambassador's office. At that moment Adolfo Molina Orantes, the Guatemalan lawyer, sensing the impending catastrophe, dashed toward the ruptured wall just as the police broke through. He was grabbed by two police, rushed down the stairs, and escorted to a police car. He was later driven to police headquarters where he was questioned by the head of the Judicial Police.

Retreating into the ambassador's private office, the occupiers locked the door and barred it with a sofa and a console. A few seconds later, Comando Seis personnel, having lost all trace of self-control, were hacking furiously at the door with axes. Others broke the window from the outside but were prevented from entering due to the burglar bars. As a hole was made in the door, the ambassador screamed through it that the situation could be settled without violence if the police would only negotiate.

"You have two minutes to negotiate," was the acid reply as the axe-wielders continued their battering.

"These people are at the limits of their desperation. They have Molotov cocktails. We are all going to die in here."

The police shouted back, not without irony, "If all of us die, all of us die."[6]

As Cajal pleaded once more for the president of the Red Cross or for some reporters to help negotiate a peaceful exit, his efforts were met with another axe blow that came perilously close to splitting his head. The intention was obvious. He jumped back, recognizing that he was dealing with "*energúmenos,* crazies," and made no further attempt to dialogue.

As the door began to come down, two or three of the occupiers, most probably the university students, took out pistols hidden under their clothes and pointed them at the door. One of them lobbed a Molotov cocktail at the entrance but it failed to ignite. Cajal quickly stamped out the wick. None of the demonstrators protested his act.

The sofa and console tumbled to the floor and the door came down. One of the demonstrators grabbed the ambassador by the arm and pulled him to the side of the transit. Cajal struggled to free himself and both fell to the floor. At that instant an enormous ball of fire erupted in the doorway followed by a muffled explosion. Shots were fired. Cajal struggled to his feet and ran through the wall of flames, through a reception room and the consul's office, down the stairs, and into the arms of the police below. It was 3:20 p.m.

Outside, onlookers witnessed a ball of flame bursting from the window that opened on the ambassador's office, accompanied at the same time by a muffled explosion. From inside the office, death screams poured forth, lasting a few moments. Firefighters were available but the police prevented their entrance. The ambassador, his clothes still burning, the hair on his head singed, and with severe burns on his hand and face, was quickly ushered toward a nearby police van despite the efforts of several Spanish nationals to move him toward an ambulance.

Odette Arzú witnessed the struggle from nearby and heard the subcommandant of the Judicial Police call to his men, "Kill him, kill him."[7] She ran instinctively toward the group screaming, "I'm a woman! I'm from the Red Cross!" She threw her arms around the ambassador and continued to scream, "He's the Spanish ambassador, he's the Spanish ambassador," while pulling him away toward the street looking for help.

The police regained control of the situation by pushing the two into their van, accompanied by the groans of Cajal and the screams of Arzú. "Quiet!" the lieutenant shouted. "We're going to take you where you have to go."

"Don't you understand? This man is the ambassador of Spain. Don't you know what it means to *disappear* an ambassador?"

"Nobody has said they are going to disappear him."

"*Hombre*, if you take us away from here, they will disappear us like two fleas with a squirt of flit."[8]

All the screaming attracted the president and vice-president of the Red Cross to the side of the van. "Don't let them keep us shut in here! Do something!" Odette pleaded.

The two men left but nothing happened. Arzú, afraid for both their lives, used a common tactic that over the last thirty-five years has become the virtual last hope of any unfortunate Guatemalan caught in such a situation: she began to scream through the window to all those standing around, giving her name, that she was the mother of six children, an official with the Red Cross, that she was being abducted with the Spanish ambassador, and they were going to be disappeared.

Finally, the emotional whirlwind that the woman's screams created around the van forced the lieutenant to let the two leave. Arzú immediately turned the ambassador over to the Red Cross personnel nearby and told them, "His life is in your hands. Take him to Dr. Herrera Llerandi's clinic [the best in Guatemala] and don't move from his side until I get there. I want two of you to stay with me and the rest of you, all of you, go with him and keep guard in his room."

The news of the Spanish Embassy disaster-in-progress finally penetrated the walls of the U.S. Embassy on Avenida La Reforma, almost four hours after it began. Ambassador Frank Ortiz listened to the news with consternation. He had established a close relationship with Máximo Cajal shortly after the latter's arrival in Guatemala the previous August, lunching with him every week, accompanied by the ambassadors of Costa Rica and Venezuela.

Ortiz decided he had to act. But despite the camaraderie that existed between the two men and the network of mutual support that is expected to exist among members of the diplomatic corps, Ortiz opted to keep himself out of the picture. He sent Mel Simms, the U.S. Embassy's first secretary, to the scene of the tragedy in the ambassador's personal armored limousine.[9]

Ortiz's version of what Mel Sims did when he arrived on the scene differs substantially from that of Odette Arzú. The American ambassador stated that "[Sims] found don Máximo wandering about, in a state of shock . . . . Nobody seemed to recognize the ambassador who was being taken to the police van. Mr. Sims occupied himself with getting the [Spanish ambassador] into an ambulance and taken to the best hospital for urgent care."[10]

Odette Arzú is not mentioned in Ortiz's account. Cajal's account makes no mention of Sims: "Señora Odette Arzú behaved in an extraordinary manner with me. She screamed that I was the Spanish ambassador, because it seems that one of the police had a cocked pistol pointing at my head and, according to her testimony which I invoke, if she hadn't been with me they would have shot me (there seems to be a tape on which voices are heard saying 'kill him, kill him')."[11]

The fire consumed thirty-eight people, including twenty-eight of the twenty-nine invaders, two of the Guatemalan jurists, the Spanish consul general, and seven employees of the embassy.

Besides Máximo Cajal, there was only one other survivor of the explosion and fire, an Ixil-Maya from Uspantán named Gregorio Yujá. He was discovered barely alive under a pile of incinerated bodies by Odette Arzú and her Red Cross coworkers and taken by ambulance to the Herrera Llerandi hospital on her orders. She and they had been allowed into the building once the fire had burned itself out.

No police personnel died in the fire, nor were any injured.

Despite this "miracle" of police good fortune, they continued to maintain that they were the targets of the fire and explosion, not the demonstrators. However, the facts at the scene belie their stance. The demonstrators were sitting when the fire began; their bodies were carbonized from the waist up; the direction of the explosive force had originated at the doorway and burst into and through the office. There was television evidence of a corpulent police officer entering the embassy with a large, strange-looking knapsack before the fireball explosion. Yet the official explanation for the conflagration would remain that it had resulted from one or more Molotov cocktails thrown by the demonstrators.

Spanish investigators found that the evidence indicated that one or more Molotov cocktails could not have caused such a unidirectional explosion and instantaneous fire.[12]

Hours later, Spain severed all diplomatic relations with Guatemala.

When the ambassadors of Venezuela and Costa Rica—like Ortiz, luncheon companions of Cajal—heard the news, they rushed to the Herrera Llerandi hospital fearing for the ambassador's life. Archbishop Gerarda, the Vatican representative and dean of the diplomatic corps, joined them shortly thereafter. A fourth person, a Guatemalan confidant[13] who remains unidentified for security reasons, received an urgent call from Madrid—more than likely from Cajal's wife—to rush immediately to the ambassador's bedside. Finally, a member of the Spanish Cooperative Technical Mission, Francisco Javier López, accompanied by his wife, drove up to the hospital.

By this time, the surrounding area was crawling with police, and the visitors spent a good amount of time showing their identifications and providing explanations before they were allowed to enter the building.

Cajal was in the intensive care unit; across the hall from him lay Gregorio Yujá. Both bedrooms had *antesalas* connecting the inner rooms to the hall. In both *antesalas* stood a pair of police guards blocking entrance to all but diplomatic personnel. Cajal begged his visitors to transfer Yujá to his room, fearing for the Mayan's life. His guests, however, vetoed the request, believing such a move would only jeopardize the ambassador's safety. They would live to regret their decision.

As night came on, a watch schedule was drawn up. Two friends were assigned to keep guard until early morning. The Costa Rican ambassador and the Guatemalan confidant drew the first shift, to be relieved by the Venezuelan ambassador and the Spanish technical expert.

At approximately 6:30 a.m. the following day, Francisco Javier López arrived at the hospital for his watch. Noticing that there was no police presence on the grounds outside, he remarked on this fact to his two companions. A few minutes later, the Costa Rican ambassador departed without drawing any conclusions.

Sometime before 7:30 a.m., the two police standing guard outside the ambassador's *antesala* disappeared. At the same time, four unidentified white Broncos sped up to the hospital's front door. The Guatemalan confidant looked out the window and announced to his colleague, "The kidnappers are here."[14]

Approximately fifteen men armed with machine guns and dressed in street clothes with handkerchiefs covering the bottom halves of their faces entered the hospital. They came down the corridor pushing the hospital personnel in front of them, nurses and doctors, whom they then shut in a room.

Several of the intruders stopped in front of the ambassador's door and swung their guns across the *antesala,* creating a heart-stopping panic among Cajal's two guardians. Others entered Gregorio Yujá's room, dragged the crying man from his bed and carried him outside. Cajal's two guardians took advantage of the distraction to retreat unceremoniously into the ambassador's bedroom, close the door, and lay down on the floor.

"What's the matter?" the ambassador shouted in a hoarse whisper. "What's going on?"

Both held their breath. Neither could respond.

After some minutes, when the noise outside had evaporated and not a sound could be heard, Francisco Javier López and the Guatemalan confidant slowly opened the door. Outside, in the *antesala,* stood two of the heavily armed plainclothes kidnappers.

"What's happening?" the Guatemalan asked. "What's going on out there?"

"What do you mean?" was the bland response. "We haven't seen anything. We've been standing out here keeping guard over the ambassador."[15]

Two minutes later, the Costa Rican ambassador returned to the hospital, having left earlier when relieved by Francisco Javier López. As he left the grounds, he had passed the four oncoming unmarked, speeding Broncos and became alarmed that the occupants were members of the Judicial Police arriving with the intention of disappearing the Spanish ambassador. When the Costa Rican ambassador discovered that Gregorio Yujá had been their victim, he decided to return to his embassy and call every ambassador he could reach to ask them to present themselves at the hospital to stand guard over Máximo Cajal.

About the same time, the uniformed police guards who had originally stood guard outside Cajal's ante-sala and had disappeared about an hour earlier, returned to relieve their plainclothes colleagues. After a few friendly words and what looked to be an exchange of ammunition, the kidnappers left.

Within a short time, the ambassadors from many Latin American and European nations began to arrive, among their number, the American ambassador, Frank Ortiz.

With the hospital now replete with faces sympathetic to the Spanish ambassador, an individual arrived escorted by a group of well-armed, husky "gorillas" with the intention of taking a statement from Cajal. He identified himself as the chief of the Judicial Police, Colonel Manuel de Jesús Valiente Tellez.

The ambassador's protectors refused to let the colonel enter Cajal's room despite the twisted faces and rumblings of dissatisfaction from the newcomers. Valiente Tellez made a gesture to quiet his men and remarked to no one in particular that he had been sent by President Lucas García to check on the Spanish ambassador. Lucas García, the colonel stated, had become worried when he learned from a radio broadcast of Yujá's abduction. The chief of the Judicial Police, a self-confessed murderer, then added, "If the decision had been mine, I would never have entered the embassy by force."[16] He then turned and, without another word, left the building followed by his henchmen.

As the various friendly ambassadors present at the scene discussed among themselves their next move, Frank Ortiz offered his private residence as a more secure setting for Cajal's recuperation. It was a proposal that was quickly accepted by his wife and the several Spanish authorities who had flown in from Spain, New York, and elsewhere in Central America during the previous twelve hours.

An hour later, the ambassador, wrapped in a blanket and sitting in a wheelchair, was whisked from his room by his shaking wife with an explanation to the police guards that he was being taken to the basement for

X-rays. The participants would later joke that they felt like bit players in a Hollywood movie, with survival the reward for a good performance. Once in the basement, the Spanish ambassador was spirited to the garage and into the Venezuelan ambassador's white Cadillac. The chauffeur, knowing the consequences of running from the Guatemalan police, streaked through the capital's streets pursued close behind by a carload of Judicial Police, taking Máximo Cajal to the fortified residence of Frank Ortiz.

Under the watchful eyes of Frank and Dolores Ortiz, the Spanish ambassador spent five days accompanied by his wife, Beatriz, in the American ambassador's residence. Carefully selected doctors and nurses attended him. He was sedated much of the time to relieve the effects of the physical and psychological trauma he had undergone.

Meanwhile, outside, the Guatemalan government had begun to cover its splattered derriere by igniting a firestorm of anti-Cajal feeling at home among its citizenry, and abroad by means of its ambassadors. In Mexico, Guatemala's ambassador, Jorge Palmieri, his country's combination of Walter Winchell and Hedda Hopper, trotted out the most adolescent of untruths. At the Organization of American States (OAS) and in New York at the United Nations, others tried unsuccessfully to best his fantasies. One press release after another followed radio and television interviews with high administration officials stating that Cajal had planned the embassy takeover in conjunction with the "terrorists" during a recent visit to El Quiché. The authorities claimed that the ambassador had suckered the three distinguished Guatemalans into the embassy in order to give the occupiers important hostages whom the government could not ignore. They said that he himself had called for police intervention. Further, that he was a "communist" with connections to Fidel Castro, Moscow, etc., etc. Cardinal Casariego not to be outdone in his anticommunist crusade jumped on the bandwagon by calling the demonstrators "trained terrorists," this despite the word from Bishop Juan Gerardi Conedera of El Quiché that the embassy occupiers were simple Mayan peasants.

President Fernando Romeo Lucas García went on television the evening of the tragedy to tell the world that in Guatemala there would be no more takeovers. "This is not El Salvador," the president protested, unintentionally giving the raison d'être of the uninhibited police riot. It was a statement by a man at the end of his wits, determined to end any and all sympathy for, or understanding of, the motives of the incinerated victims.

Gregorio Yujá's tortured body was one of two thrown from a moving vehicle at the steps of San Carlos University's rectory several hours after his abduction from the hospital. A cardboard sign was pinned to Yujá's chest: "Executed as a terrorist; the ambassador of Spain runs the same risk."

Yujá's life was disposed of without much fanfare. The ambassador would be a bit more troublesome to eliminate, however. Ortiz's home was machine-gunned from the street as a warning that there were some who were determined to make him pay. Making Cajal out to be a pathological liar was seen by others as a less complex solution than murder.

An attempt was made on the life of Odette Arzú on 15 February but the assailants only managed to nick her bosom with a knife thrust through a bag of cosmetics she carried, spilling a red liquid they believed to be her blood.

Nine days after the death of Cáceres Lehnhoff, Ronald Hennessey attended the novena Mass for the former vice president at Our Lady of Guadalupe church in zone 10, not far from the Maryknoll Center House. He had been in El Salvador during the massacre at the Spanish Embassy paying what he thought might be the final visit to an archbishop already targeted for death by friends and supporters of Cardinal Casariego. As the Maryknoller entered the vestibule, Padre Irwin García, the pastor, knowing the Iowan had been a friend of the deceased, invited Hennessey to preach the eulogy. Ron hesitated. He knew the assembled congregation would consist overwhelmingly of upper-class Guatemalans. He also knew that most of them would be supporters of the government's version of the Spanish ambassador's complicity in the death of two of their most prominent members. This was an accusation that the Iowan rejected unequivocally. He felt the former vice president would have given the lie to the government's version of events, had he lived to do so. Now, as the Iowan hesitated, he wondered how he would preach a eulogy honoring the memory of that man without offending his family and friends.

Undeterred by the suddenness of the request and the ambiguity of the theme, the regional superior accepted the pastor's invitation. Hennessey saw the request as an opportunity to pay homage to a friend and to speak out on the question of Mayan land rights without seeming to immerse himself in Guatemala's internal politics. The latter theme was the proverbial poisoned apple of all sermons that touched questions of social morality.

"Here in Guatemala City," Hennessey began, facing an audience of wealthy, politically active Guatemalans, "one does not dare to speak openly about the injustices perpetrated against the Mayan majority living in the countryside. Here in this twentieth-century metropolis, it is easy to forget our Mayan brothers and sisters living under feudalistic conditions, eking out a precarious livelihood from the few and eroded lands that have been left them."

As he progressed along this theme, Hennessey felt antagonism building up in the pews. Coughing became pronounced, feet shuffled, bodies were realigned stiffly in their seats, and faces took on looks of growing discomfort and anger, eyes riveted on the speaker, lips compressed. The Iowan knew that in any other venue, he could not have escaped unscathed when making such remarks. But he plunged on, hoping to diffuse the antagonism by holding up the memory of the deceased as an example to all: "Vice President Cáceres Lehnhoff was a rare man among men. I knew him personally to be an honorable man, a brave man, a man truly interested in the progress and future of this beautiful country. He tried vainly to assist me to obtain land rights for landless Mayan peasants years ago when I worked on a resettlement program in the Petén jungle. He was your government's vice president at the time. Those people had been denied the lands that had been promised them, refused legal titles to lands they had already cleared. When they tried to raise their voices in protest, they were threatened. The vice president courageously stood up for those people against great odds, against powerful interests, and tried to support them in their struggle for land rights. He was a great man!"

The tension seemed to ease somewhat as the Iowan tied the issue of Mayan land rights to the good character of the deceased. But then, in a moment of rare self-doubt brought on by the realization that he did not know what he might be tempted to say next, Hennessey reflected on a past that never was. He expressed some self-recrimination, an idea that he had never actually felt obliged to entertain. He continued, "Unfortunately, I interpreted the problem confronting the settlers as purely political, and as such, not being a politician nor Guatemalan, I decided to let the vice president speak out for the people while I remained silent. Had I raised my voice together with his at that time, if more committed people had spoken up, especially we churchmen who claim to follow in the footsteps of that peasant from Galilee, more of our Mayan brothers and sisters might today have land. There would be no marches on congress and foreign embassies, and señor Cáceres Lehnhoff might still be alive. I, for my part, want to express my apologies to his widow, his family, his friends, and admirers, and say I won't repeat my mistake."

Hennessey left the altar and walked toward the sacristy while the congregation's monumental silence rang in his ears. *Who did I reach with all that?* he asked himself, once inside the sacristy. *Do I really believe the vice president, myself, or any other who feel called upon to speak out is going to change 450 years of repression, or even survive? Did the vice president really put up such a fight that he could serve as an example to others? . . . It doesn't matter; . . . I got my licks in!*

The Iowan's ambiguous thoughts were interrupted by the tinkling of the altar bell as the celebrant intoned the words of consecration, "This is my body . . . . This is my blood."

After Mass, the vice president's widow came to Hennessey with tears in her eyes to thank him for his words: "My husband deserved that praise, *padrecito,* but no one has the courage to say so publicly. *Gracias, gracias!* You do not know what awful things some people are saying about him. May God forgive them because I cannot."

The regional superior smiled his acknowledgment of the woman's compliments, touched her on the elbow, and once again expressed his condolences for the untimely death of her husband, "The good we do dies with us, señora, while the evil . . ."

"*Perdón?* What did you say, *padrecito?*"

"*Nada, señora!* Nothing!"

Several months later, in mid-June 1980, Frank Ortiz lost his ambassadorial post "as a consequence of strong disagreements with [his] superiors in Washington regarding [his opposition to] a policy of direct confrontation" with the Guatemalan government.[17] He left Guatemala for a more fitting appointment in Panama where he was named the political attaché to the Pentagon's Southern Command. Hennessey heard at the time from several embassy staffers that Ortiz's dismissal was due in large part to the ambassador's benign views of the murderous policies of the Lucas García government, that he had never gotten behind the Carter administration's policy on human rights.[18]

The Spanish government administered an additional blow to the censured diplomat's ego when it decided to send Ortiz the Gran Cruz del Mérito Civil via parcel post rather than present the award in a public ceremony as they had done for the ambassadors of Costa Rica and Venezuela. Ortiz had been blind to the nature of Guatemala's conflict up until the very end, maintaining that the radical left and the ideological right were equally to blame for the violence. In a sense, Ortiz may have had a hand—slight though it may be—in provoking the tragedy in the Spanish Embassy if what Jorge Palmieri states is true. Palmieri, Lucas García's ambassador to Mexico at the time of the embassy massacre, claimed that Frank Ortiz had personally confided to him that Máximo Cajal was a communist even before the Spanish ambassador . ever arrived in Guatemala,[19] a confidence that Palmieri unselfishly shared whenever the opportunity arose.

If true, and there are plenty of reasons to doubt that Palmieri can distinguish between truth and falsehood, his statement throws a different light on Ortiz's desire to have weekly luncheons with the three "left-leaning" ambassadors from Spain, Costa Rica, and Venezuela. His visits to the Maryknoll Center House at Thanksgiving and on other occasions might not have been his only attempts to keep track of the barefooted, hungry "terrorists" who lived in fear of the government's threats to their lives.

Chapter 27

You Can Take This Job and . . .

Ron Hennessey had gone to El Petén on 29 January, two days before the Spanish Embassy massacre, to evaluate the medical program run by Maryknoll lay missioners and nuns and to warn them of the increased dangers they faced. The brother of the president and army chief of staff, General Benedicto Lucas García, had made some inflammatory accusations on national television that the Maryknoll nuns and lay missioners in the Petén were in reality guerrillas. Such accusations were often harbingers of anonymous physical attacks carried out against the accused, a high-level signal that those named were fair game for any officer who commanded a death squad looking for Brownie points. The basis for the general's statement was that the nuns and lay missioners traveled on foot to remote villages with knapsacks full of medicines strapped to their backs. "Who but a guerrilla would do such a thing?" the general asked incredulously, revealing the cold-war logic of the high command's mind-set.

The Iowan was determined to see what he could do to head off any such consequences. "Maintain as high a profile as you can," he counseled the women. "Let everyone you talk to know where you are going and why. Travel in threes or more whenever and wherever possible. Get your people to accompany you." It was plain common sense, but average American women, particularly trusting missionaries, have trouble sensing danger in every camouflage uniform they encounter, even in chaotic Guatemala.

Hennessey then headed to San Salvador to visit Archbishop Oscar Arnulfo Romero, prompted by the conviction that the threats to the San Salvadorean prelate's life were becoming more menacing and determined. A deep friendship had developed between the two men as a result of the Iowan's letter publicly challenging Cardinal Casariego's political theology. Since that time, Hennessey had tried to visit Romero every four to six weeks, or whenever he went to see how the Maryknollers stationed in El Salvador were holding up under the official suspicions and threats of the terrorist government's security forces.

As the days passed, Archbishop Romero had become more outspoken on the problems facing the "people of God," as he referred to his flock and the El Salvadorean people in general. His Sunday sermons invariably emptied the streets of San Salvador as rich and poor, right and left, tuned in to the archdiocesan radio station, YSAX, to listen, many with affection and gratitude, others with anger and hatred.

Hennessey followed closely the situation in El Salvador as four priests working with the poor in Romero's archdiocese were assassinated. The regional superior contemplated pulling out all Maryknollers from El Salvador, but rejected the idea as demoralizing to the El Salvadorean people. "Only if they request it, will I take them out," he told his counselors. "If the Salvadoreans ever needed us before, they surely need us now."

No Maryknoller in El Salvador asked Hennessey for a different assignment and, as a group, they stirred feelings of pride and gratitude in his Iowan heart.

Archbishop Romero, meanwhile, entertained no hesitancy when pointing his finger at the killers of his priests. He refused to assist at any government function until the murderers were caught and brought to justice for the whole country to see. But the president, Notre Dame University graduate Napoleón Duarte, merely turned to the papal legate, Archbishop Gerarda, any time he wanted an ecclesiastical presence at some public event. The Vatican's representative always obliged.

Romero wrote an open letter to President Jimmy Carter requesting that he halt all military assistance to the El Salvadorean government, which Carter had reinstituted a year earlier due to the growing strength of the Farabundo Martí National Liberation Front, the FMLN. The archbishop asked that Carter guarantee that the United States "would not intervene—by military, economic, or diplomatic means to influence the direction of the destiny of the Salvadorean people."[1]

That same afternoon, Archbishop Romero read his letter to the American president over the archdiocesan radio station.

Carter, however, was caught in a political chokehold that made it difficult to heed the archbishop's request. His political adversaries were holding him personally responsible for the ongoing humiliation of the United States by Iran's revolutionary guards who had imprisoned U.S. Embassy personnel. His adversaries accused Carter of not having fought hard enough to maintain the Shah Pahlavi in power.[2] Right-wing groups also pilloried the president for having "lost" Nicaragua to the Sandinistas in July of 1979 even though the president had already distanced himself from his much-heralded human rights policies by trying to keep Somoza's brutal National Guard in power. Reagan also made an issue of Carter's "giveaway" of the Panama Canal to the Panamanians. On top of all this negative political baggage, Carter felt that the El Salvadorean government ran a grave risk of being toppled by the FMLN. Facing a tough reelection bid, Carter was left with no viable political alternative but to ignore Romero's plea.

The day following the archbishop's radio appeal to President Carter, the archdiocesan transmitter was bombed out of existence. When Hennessey heard the news, he postponed a couple of minor appointments and headed for San Salvador to offer Romero Maryknoll funds for the purchase of a new, more powerful transmitter.

"Are you sure you want to be seen providing me with the means of awakening the consciences of the El Salvadorean people and our benighted security forces, Ronaldo?" asked the chuckling prelate on that occasion.

"I'm as sure of this as I can be, *monseñor* .... But I won't go around bragging about Maryknoll's generosity. We don't need more enemies than those who've already signed on."

The archbishop smiled. "Like one's relatives, Ronaldo, the Good Lord doesn't allow us to choose our bishops nor our enemies."

Hennessey had returned to Guatemala on that occasion deeply affected by Romero's courage, appreciative of his use of humor to deflect uncomfortable emotions. Two weeks later, a suitcase filled with dynamite was found in the church next to the altar where the archbishop was scheduled to celebrate Mass. His enemies were becoming more brazen. The following Sunday, he told his radio audience, "My life has been threatened many times. I have to confess that as a Christian, I do not believe in death without resurrection. If they kill me, I will rise again in the Salvadorean people. I am not boasting or saying this out of pride, but in all humility."[3]

Cardinal Casariego heard the sermon and expressed his anger to anyone who would listen. Among the cardinal's sympathetic listeners was Ambassador

Frank Ortiz, as well as the papal nuncio, and the entire El Salvadorean episcopal conference—with the exception of Bishop Arturo Rivera y Damas. Hennessey was privy to Casariego's wrath and decided that it was time to pay another visit to San Salvador. The next day, 3 February 1980, he made the four-hour drive to El Salvador's capital without joy. The Iowan had decided it was time to begin to say good-bye to the man who had become his inspiration and like a second father to him.

The customary block-long line of peasants, laborers, and housewives had formed at Romero's office door, as each waited a turn to ask for help in finding a job or a missing family member, in dealing with threats from the military or police, or just to pour out the fears and sadness that burdened their hearts. When the archbishop noticed Hennessey standing in line, he rose from his desk and came out to greet him. "Padre Ronaldo," the prelate exclaimed, opening his arms in a wide *abrazo*, "it is always such a joy to see you. But you were here just a short time ago. Are you in trouble? Come into my office."

"*Monseñor*, I am here only for a social visit. I am sure my time is no more precious than that of these people waiting to see you."

"No, *padrecito*! I know my people. They will feel bad if you stand here in line with them. Give them the pleasure of honoring you for all you do for them. Please! Come along."

The Iowan felt uncomfortable with all the attention the archbishop showed him but he accepted the prelate's invitation in order to avoid a scene.

"I only want to stay a few moments, *monseñor*," said the priest, accepting a metal folding chair that with the archbishop's small wooden desk, a matching chair, and the crucifix on the wall were the room's only furnishings. "I know how busy you are. I've come only to find out how you are holding up under all the threats and pressures."

"Everything is fine, Ronaldo. Don't worry about me! It is the soldiers, the police, and their officers that worry me. This war is destroying all trace of morality in them. I cannot reach them."

"I do worry about you, *monseñor*. Both the government and Church authorities are putting tremendous pressure on you . . . . An admirer of yours told me that you have suffered from nervous exhaustion before . . . . It's a story with special twists that Cardinal Casariego is spreading around his archdiocese and in the Vatican. I hope you don't think me impertinent for bringing this subject up . . . . But are you going to be able to continue to stand against the government, Cardinal Casariego, and his friends in Rome?"

"Look, Ronaldo," Romero answered, opening his arms and thumping his chest like a young boxer trying to demonstrate invulnerability to a cheering audience, "I've never felt better in my life! They are not going to break me. Of course," he continued, "I've had to take time off for periods of rest. That's something I think we should all do. Even you! But I feel that I am doing God's work now in a way I've never felt before. I know that what I am doing is right! I'm serving the poor of El Salvador. My opponents think they can break me, . . . but it is not going to happen!"

"*Monseñor,* I'm not very good at throwing verbal bouquets, but I want you to know that the majority of Maryknollers here in Central America look up to you as an example of what all churchmen should be, . . . and that especially includes me!"

"You don't know how much your words mean to me, Ronaldo. We will walk down this road together. We know where it will lead us."

The Iowan coughed his embarrassment and stood up. "I must be going. There must be a hundred people out there waiting to talk to you."

The archbishop stood and accompanied his visitor to the door. "You have a special vocation, Ronaldo. You must convince your fellow citizens that they have no stake in this conflict. They must learn what their government is doing here in El Salvador, . . . in Guatemala, Nicaragua, Honduras, . . . in their name . . . . But enough! I do not wish to become bitter!"

Hennessey drove back to Guatemala inspired by Romero's commitment, fearful that he would never see the archbishop again. In the days that followed, Archbishop Romero launched a direct radio attack on the government's power base by addressing himself to the people needed to staff its repressive organizations, the men whom the prelate called "uniformed peasants," the soldiers, national guardsmen, and police:

> Brothers, each one of you is one of us. We are the same people. The
> peasants you kill are your own brothers and sisters. When you hear
> the words of a man telling you to kill, remember instead the words
> of God, "Thou shalt not kill." God's law must prevail . . . . In the

name of God, in the name of our tormented people who have
suffered so much and whose lament cries out to heaven, I beseech
you, I beg you, I order you in the name of God, STOP THE
REPRESSION.[4]

This plea, spoken on the radio by the highest Catholic authority in an
overwhelmingly Catholic country, was seen by the government, the army, the
National Guard, and the landed oligarchy as an open declaration of war.

The archbishop saw it as such as well. In case there was any doubt as to his
meaning, he clarified: "When a dictatorship seriously violates human rights
and attacks the common good of a nation, when it becomes unbearable and
closes off all channels of dialogue, of understanding, of rationality—when
this happens, the Church speaks of the legitimate right of insurrectional
violence."[5]

Romero's break with El Salvador's oligarchic dictatorship, characterized
by the United States as one of incipient democracy, was now total. On 24
March 1980, with a feeling of impending finality, the archbishop drove to
Santa Tecla to make his last sacramental confession to his spiritual director.
When he returned, he celebrated Mass for the nuns of the Divine Providence
Hospital as he did almost daily. As he stood at the flower-bedecked altar, a
single Magnum bullet began its fatal trajectory at the back of the chapel, flew
over the bowed heads of the praying nuns, penetrated the archbishop's liturgical
vestments and tore open his chest. The prelate sagged, trying to support
himself by grabbing for the altar. Blood quickly stained the cross on his
chasuble as he sank to the floor in a heap, pulling the altar linens with him.
A nun screamed. Another ran to his side, knelt, and prayed. Outside, a
vehicle driven by an accomplice sped away with the assassin inside.

Cardinal Casariego saw the hand of God in the murder. Ron Hennessey,
recalling the archbishop's futile appeal to President Carter, saw the fingerprints
of the U.S. government all over the murder weapon. The American
ambassador, Robert White, echoed the refrain that one U.S. administration
after another employs to claim for itself the "democratic center"—while
distancing itself from the neofascist Latin right that the Pentagon supports.

He stated that the assassination "could have been the work of either the extreme left or the extreme right." No El Salvadorean had any such doubts as to the origin of that bullet. Ambassador White would subsequently demonstrate that despite his disclaimer, he had no such doubts himself.

Ron Hennessey went to San Salvador to pay his final respects to his murdered friend and hero. He marched in the funeral procession with over two hundred thousand mourners, wondering how long such a demonstration of affection for the government's number one antagonist would last without some sort of official retaliatory violence. On his drive into San Salvador that morning he had witnessed hundreds of soldiers out of uniform near an army base practicing crowd control tactics. All were heavily armed. Now there was not a uniform to be seen anywhere, despite the huge crowd and its potential for an antigovernment demonstration.

At the cathedral, a temporary altar had been set up in the portal so that the crowd outside in the plaza could participate in the Mass. To one side, a large four-by-ten foot banner spelled out the feelings of many in the procession: "*Afuera Nuncio Gerarda, Obispos Alvarez, Aparicio, y Revelo.*" Of all the El Salvadorean hierarchy, only Bishop Arturo Rivera y Damas attended the archbishop's funeral. Cardinal Corripio, one of Romero's severest Vatican critics, was sent by Pope John Paul II to represent the papacy, a slap in the face to the dead archbishop's stricken supporters.

During Corripio's nondiscriminating eulogy from the cathedral steps, someone detonated a small propaganda bomb in the street next to the cathedral, sending papers with an antigovernment message in all directions. The blast was immediately followed by an explosion, then automatic carbine fire from the rooftops of government buildings surrounding the plaza. Cardinal Corripio cut short his remarks and ducked back into the cathedral.

Panic ensued. Many of the mourners, believing that the clerics in attendance could function as miraculous talismans and protect them, grabbed for the sleeves, the habits, the hands of any religious within reach. Hennessey, who had earlier stationed himself behind the temporary altar, felt for a moment that the grasping hands would pull him to the ground, but he could not resist the comfort his contact provided. The crowd just outside the cathedral surged back inside the building for protection while those on the periphery sprinted for the side streets. Scores of mourners were shot in the process, while many more were trampled to death. Those who made it back into the cathedral struggled to shut the huge doors to protect themselves against the flying and ricocheting bullets. The Iowan was carried inside, caught in the middle of the surging mass of bodies.

At that moment, the excited rector of the cathedral managed to push his way over to Hennessey, attracted by his American head sticking out above the crowd. "Where is the Vatican representative, Cardinal Corripio? Have you seen him, *padrecito?*"

Hennessey, disturbed that the cardinal had slipped into the cathedral as soon as the first blast had sounded, instead of trying to calm the crowd, couldn't resist the temptation to allow his Irish humor to reflect his feelings, replied, "I saw him hiding under a bench up near the nave. Don't worry about him, padre, he's taking good care of himself."

"Oh, thank God, *padrecito!*" the cleric answered, as he pushed his way toward the front of the cathedral, a look of relief on his pious face.

Later, President Napoleón Duarte denied his government's involvement in the shootings, claiming that all security forces had been confined to their barracks. He maintained that the killings had been the work of leftist revolutionaries trying to blame the army. Scenes shot by Dutch cameramen, however, put the lie to the president's disclaimer; clearly showing armed soldiers stationed on rooftops of government buildings abutting the plaza as the funeral Mass began.

Thirteen bishops attending the funeral from Panama, Brazil, Honduras, Guatemala, Mexico, Peru, El Salvador, Ecuador, Spain, England, and Ireland publicly committed themselves to following in the slain archbishop's footsteps. They wrote a document that found its way to Rome and displeased Pope John Paul II. Bishop Martínez de Lejarza, Cardinal Casariego's right-hand man and representative at the funeral, refused to sign the pledge. Likewise, Cardinal Corripio. Hennessey would have liked to put his name on the document but since he lacked hierarchical status, he was not asked to sign it.

Before heading back to Guatemala City, he paid' one last visit to the cathedral where Archbishop Romero had so often raised his voice against the crimes of the El Salvadorean government and its American sponsor. There, he solemnly promised "Monseñor Oscar" and Pop that he would do all he could to introduce the U.S. public to the realities of its government's policies in Central America.

Archbishop Romero's death marked the beginning of a transition period for Ronald Hennessey. He had taken over the regional superior's responsibilities on 4 January 1975 and was now in the sixth and final year of his second three-year term. Maryknoll headquarters had scheduled a General Chapter for November 1980 to include all of the society's superiors and two elected delegates from each of its seven regions around the world. The Chapter's business was to elect a new superior general and governing council, as well as to examine the work of the Society's members, legislate new guidelines, revamp where necessary, open new missions or close old ones. Ron had participated in the previous General Chapter in November 1977 and had been able to make singular contributions due to his almost three years in the Central American regional superior's chair. In fact, during that assembly, he had acquired the reputation of being a "politician" and "king maker,"[6] due to his uncanny ability to bring opposing viewpoints together.

Now, as he received notice from Maryknoll to begin the election process for the region's delegates to the upcoming Chapter and to review suggestions for change coming in from all sides, the thought occurred to Ron that he should resign his position some months before the Chapter took place. That way, his successor, ordinarily due to take over in January 1981, could go to Maryknoll and play a more active role as a sitting superior rather than a groom-in-waiting.

The decision to request permission to withdraw from the superior's post was not a difficult one for the Iowan. The thought of being able to brush shoulders and rub elbows with his beloved Mayan friends was at times so overwhelming that he would almost salivate. Despite his colleagues' opinion that he was the best man for the job, he never really felt comfortable in calling the shots. As he told his family in a 1979 letter, "(t)he regional council and I dealt with some 60 projects and problems last week. I was glad to have it over with, as I don't like making decisions for other people's lives. One of the things I like less than the meetings is the many letters consequent to it."[7] And such meetings, decisions, letters, and reactions were what the superior's job was all about.

Ron had attended so many of these meetings over the years, not only for the Central American region, but others in Peru, Bolivia, Venezuela, Brazil, Mexico, and Hong Kong, as well as at Maryknoll, N.Y., that he began to feel that "most of the problems could be solved by a couple of competent

Maryknollers"—a category that he felt did not include himself—rather than spending a lot of time and money to gather too large a group to make common-sense decisions. Sometimes he had to be available to receive an official visit from a member of Maryknoll's general council. He also had to attend to the petitions, suggestions, and recriminations from the papal nuncio and ten bishops, four Guatemalans, three El Salvadoreans, and three Nicaraguans. He had to fend off pressure emanating from the Vatican and coming through the nuncio—but with support from Maryknoll—to remove Father Miguel D'Escoto as foreign minister of Nicaragua's Sandinista government. D'Escoto had begun his efforts as the Sandinistas' minister of foreign affairs with the unanimous support of Nicaragua's episcopal conference, but that support did not last.

In a reference to one regional meeting, Ron summed up his principal input as "measur[ing] our present works against the society's objectives and criteria, trying to demonstrate that in certain cases we have ceased to be missionary in favor of settling down to being pastors," that is, being satisfied with sacramentalizing the faithful rather than reaching out to nonbelievers. In preparation for a meeting at Maryknoll, he expressed his self-perceived deficiencies, stating, "I'm not sure I can adequately give [sic] the state of the region, let alone point out our strengths and weaknesses and show where we ought to be going."

When word began to circulate among Maryknollers and non-Maryknollers (Guatemalan, Spanish, and American) that Hennessey would soon be leaving his post, pressures on him began to build rather than decrease. Many had come to depend on the Iowan's steady demeanor in the face of nerve-racking situations, his willingness to stand up to hierarchs and militarists alike when he felt the occasion called for it or when asked for his intervention. Such was the case for Father Jim Hazelton, a Montana diocesan priest on loan to the bishop of Sololá. In June 1980 the young priest knocked on the open door of Hennessey's office in the Maryknoll Center House in Guatemala City and asked for permission to enter.

All the American non-Maryknollers in Guatemala—and there were a score of them—from time to time made the Maryknoll headquarters a retreat from their parish duties and pressures. There they swapped stories and received encouragement from compatriots. Some frequented the Center House more than others. Hazelton was a rare guest at the Maryknoll house so it was with some surprise that Hennessey looked up to see the obviously troubled countenance of the Montanan.

Hazelton took a minute or two to admire the colorful prints of Mayan women's *huipiles* hanging on the wall and to comment on a quotation from Winston Churchill, "The United Nations was set up not to get us to heaven, but to save us from hell." He then settled down on the couch and got to the point of his visit. The Montanan recounted with suppressed emotion how he felt that all he had gained from years of work in his parish was fast disappearing due to army and death-squad attacks against anyone who worked with him. He had started an agricultural program to teach the parishioners how and what to grow in order to maintain a healthy diet, only to have the official in charge of the local army detachment accuse him of growing food to feed the ORPA guerrillas (Revolutionary Organization of an Armed People). This was followed by a visit to the town of Santa María La Visitación from the leader of a contingent of the ESA (Secret Anticommunist Army), with a similar accusation.

Ron had heard of the ESA's visit from others and about how the group of gunmen had gathered everyone in the town square, including the Montana priest, for a public lecture on market day. They had made them sit for hours in the hot sun while they harangued the largely illiterate audience on the evils of communism and the "disaster" that was Cuban society. The pedagogics were punctuated with warnings that they would execute anyone suspected of being sympathetic to ORPA. The threats were not idle. They had already disappeared (and probably executed) nine of the town elders, including five of Hazelton's top catechists. "It's getting so I'm afraid to do anything knowing they will come after whomever cooperates with me. Maybe I'll be next?"

Since Santa María was not part of Hennessey's jurisdiction and Hazelton had not asked Ron to intervene before, he had taken no action when he had heard of the ESA threats. Now it was different.

"Ron, you must know some higher-ups in the government. Do you think you could get me an appointment with some army brass to let them know what's going on out there? Just a few days ago the air force bombed and strafed the other side of our mountain and I've been told they killed some *campesinos* and their kids, but no guerrillas. The army is still combing the area so they won't let me go out to help the wounded and bury the dead."

Hennessey was startled by the priest's naïve request. He thought everyone knew that the army had declared open war on the Church and on all Mayans anywhere in the country. The war was against the poor as well as on all who worked with them. He had forgotten how isolated some of the priests were, how easy to be ignorant of national events. "I'm not sure anyone in the government or army could or would help you, Jim. It's happening all over. It's the policy of the national government."

The Iowan went on to enumerate the number of priests and catechists murdered in the previous several weeks in Escuintla and El Quiché.

"How about our own government? Maybe a telephone call from someone in our embassy?"

Hennessey shrugged. It was not his custom to dash someone's hopes, but he did not like to encourage unrealistic expectations, either. "I used to think that Ambassador Ortiz could help. He claimed he could. But if he made any attempts to do so—I have reasons for believing he didn't—I've seen no evidence resulting from his efforts. However, if you wish, I think I can get you an appointment with the consul or vice consul. But don't get your hopes up."

The following evening, the Iowan accompanied Hazelton to the home of the U.S. vice consul in an upscale section of Guatemala City. Remembering Bill Woods's experience with Ambassador Meloy, Hennessey remarked, "This meeting is being held in a private home so there's no record of it in the embassy log."

Hazelton shot the Iowan a look of puzzlement.

The visit contained more than an element of the surreal. In the face of all arguments, the vice consul insisted to the contrary that she believed the problem was local to Santa María La Visitación, that if military authorities knew what was going on there, they would punish the local commander for harassing the priest and his parishioners.

"We'd like to believe that to be true," Hennessey responded, "but air force planes taking off from Aurora Airport and flying on bombing runs without high-level authorization or even command knowledge? We'd have to ignore reports coming in from across the country that demonstrate that what's happening in Santa María is no different from that in Nebaj, Comalapa, San Juan Cotzal, and a hundred other towns and villages throughout the mountains. Nebaj has been in the national news for months."

Nebaj was a small town in El Quiché Province, the scene of bloodletting three months earlier. The town had been occupied by an army contingent since the Spanish Embassy massacre in January. As soon as the soldiers arrived in Nebaj, anonymous death threats laboriously printed to feign peasant authorship began to arrive at the parish rectory, promising to send the pastor, a Spanish priest, to his Maker. After the threats became more insistent and gruesomely detailed, Padre Javier Gurriarán decided to continue his ministry from underground.

On the first Sunday of March, even though there was no Mass, many people came into town from surrounding villages to have a prayer service and attend the market. On the same day, the officer in charge of the military base decided that all men present in town would be forced to carry a new identification card signed by himself.

On their lieutenant's orders, soldiers surrounded approximately two thousand men in the town's center and herded them toward the marketplace. A single soldier with a barely serviceable typewriter was assigned to manufacture the cards.

When darkness fell, fewer than fifty people had their new identification carnets, and the typist was tired. As Sunday night blended into Monday morning, the corralled and hungry peasants began muttering curses at the soldiers, sparking confrontations that resulted in beatings and arrests.

At sunrise on Monday, a contingent of fifty women from a nearby village arrived in Nebaj to look for their missing husbands. On learning of their spouses' plight, they shouted curses at the soldiers. The soldiers responded with gunfire, killing six women, a child, and three men. At that point, the issuance of new identification cards was permanently suspended.

Two days after the Nebaj killings, the diocesan radio station carried news of the incident. A day later, the bullet-riddled body of the announcer was dumped at the station's doorstep. And to make sure the message was clearly understood, the mutilated body of the announcer's brother was left at the same spot a few days later. Bishop Gerardi Conedera needed no further warning to order the transmitter shut down.

The El Quiché diocese issued an unambiguous statement condemning "the arrogance of the military which is the cause of this massacre; the use of sophisticated weapons against defenseless peasants; . . . an arbitrary demand for new identification papers which discriminate against the citizens of Nebaj . . . ."

"I've heard stories about the killings in Nebaj, padre," the vice consul answered, nodding agreeably, "but who can tell who is responsible? The right blames the left and the left blames the right. Since our mission is government to government, when in doubt, we accept the government's word."

"Well, Ms. Graham," Hennessey replied, "even if you want to discount Bishop Gerardi's statement as to who was at fault in Nebaj, Father Hazelton here doesn't have to accept anyone's word on what is occurring in Santa María La Visitación. He is a witness! . . . I find it hard to explain the U.S. government's attitude. It is impossible to believe the persecution of those . working in Church-sponsored programs is anything but the national policy of the Lucas García administration and the U.S. government has decided to tolerate it—or perhaps agrees with it?"

The vice consul chose to ignore the Iowan's final remark, turning instead to Hazelton: "I'll set up a meeting tomorrow with the political officer, padre. I'm sure he will be interested in hearing your story."

"I don't think you'll get much satisfaction from the political attaché," Hennessey told his companion as soon as they were out the door. "His job is to assess the political prospects of off-scene actors to let Washington know who to back in the next coup attempt. He probably already knows everything you can tell him . . . . I sometimes wonder why these folks don't understand the anger of the Iranian revolutionaries against the embassy personnel in Teheran. If the EGP, ORPA, and FAR are ever successful here, I'm not sure these embassy folks will be safe from some kind of retribution. They remind me of Vatican bureaucrats."

Hazelton pushed some air through his closed lips. "How the devil can the United States be indifferent to what's going on here?"

"It's not!" was the Iowan's laconic reply.

During the next two weeks, several catechists and a Spanish priest working in Joyabaj, El Quiché, were assassinated. Two soldiers who arrived by motorcycle shot the priest in his office. They had come from the main army base in the provincial capital some fifty kilometers' distance for the sole purpose of ending the cleric's life. Their mission accomplished, they returned from whence they came.

Then, a detachment of soldiers used machine guns and grenades to attack the rectory and convent in San Miguel Uspantán, El Quiché, wrecking both buildings and destroying the parish vehicle. The pastor had been warned about his practice of giving aid to the widows and children of the Spanish Embassy massacre. Fortunately, all present were able to take cover and survive. A few days later, the same intimidating tactic was used on a convent in Morales, Izabal, on the east coast, forcing the nuns to give up their catechetical and social work and leave the area entirely.

Three unobserved catechists spotted an ambush-in-the-making set up by a group of heavily armed gunmen on the road between San Antonio Ilotenango and Santa Cruz del Quiché. The intended victim was Bishop Juan Gerardi Conedera, the prelate of El Quiché and the most outspoken member of the hierarchy in condemning official atrocities. Gerardi was scheduled to pass through the site in a matter of hours on his weekly pastoral trip to San Antonio. The catechists sent a runner to Santa Cruz in time to warn the bishop and avoid the killing.

Several of the El Quiché priests asked the bishop to convoke a meeting in Guatemala City to plan how they might continue to carry on their work without endangering more lives. After much discussion, Gerardi, with the support of a majority of his priests, chose to close all churches and pastoral works in El Quiché, and to allow those who so wished to go underground, to carry on a "church of the catacombs."

A majority of the nuns, showing remarkable courage, opposed the move as tantamount to abandoning the people. Bishop Gerardi however had the last word. Only four nuns were permitted to remain in the diocese, those who attended the sick in the provincial capital's hospital. Two priests decided to join the EGP, while several others went underground. A third group went to Costa Rica to establish an international information center called the Guatemalan Church in Exile to disseminate news to the international media regarding terrorist tactics and human rights violations by the Guatemalan government.

The exodus saved the bishop's life—for the time being—and those of most of his clergy, but their departure cost the people dearly, just as the nuns had feared. San Juan Cotzal, the town near where Woods's plane had gone down four years earlier, was the first parish to feel the consequences of the priests' departure. The problem had begun in mid-May. Four masked soldiers went door to door in the town demanding to see the identity carnet of every male who looked more than twelve years old. As they reviewed each document, the soldiers sent the bearer to the *comandancia* to get what they said would be a "special military stamp" on the carnet.

At the *comandancia*, four of the men, all catechists, were each executed by a single pistol shot to the face, as their terrified neighbors watched and trembled. The *comandante* offered neither accusations nor explanations for his action.

At noon, as two hundred townsmen lay face down in the dust of the central plaza, silently praying to God to spare their lives, a patrol of EGP guerrillas materialized out of the mountains. By firing their weapons from widely separated positions, the guerrillas managed to give the impression that their numbers were much greater than was actually the case, frightening off the soldiers in the process. After assuring the populace that they would continue to protect it from random army violence, the guerrillas disappeared back into the mountains.

At daybreak, on 28 July, approximately two hundred guerrillas surrounded San Juan Cotzal's military base and ordered the twenty-four soldiers to lay down their arms and come out, promising immunity if they did so. The troops, fearing retribution for the four killings of 12 May, decided to fight. The decision resulted in the deaths of sixteen soldiers and the wounding of eight. The EGP lost no one.

At 8:00 a.m., the guerrillas had drifted back into the mountains. By 9:00 a.m. the same day, the air force began bombing the town. A company of soldiers from Huehuetenango under Colonel Rodolfo Lobos Zamora's command, about four hundred men, appeared on the scene about 11:30 a.m., and proceeded to herd every man and boy from their homes to the town square. There, sixty of the assembled were chosen at random, lined up, and shot. The victims ranged from twelve to sixty-five years. The others were forced to dig a mass grave and bury the corpses.

Before leaving town, Colonel Lobos Zamora warned survivors: "Next time the guerrillas kill one of our soldiers anywhere near here, I will come back and kill every last man in this town. All you people do is bring us trouble."

The next day, the *El Gráfico* newspaper reported "thirty-four guerrillas were killed in an armed attack on San Juan Cotzal the 28th of this month, according to the official communiqué of the Army's Office of Public Relations. Only three soldiers were lost in the encounter."[8]

The Conference of Bishops, now outraged by the attacks on clerics and pastoral workers, published its reading of the situation. The prelates pointed no discriminating fingers, exhibiting a return to the pastoral ambiguities and journalistic neutrality of earlier statements:

> Armed factions of the extreme right and left maintain an undeclared war between them, dragging down our defenseless people with their criminal madness . . . . National problems cannot be solved by destroying the citizens' organizations . . . nor is it permissible to make attempts on the lives of those . . . charged with keeping public order and the security of the nation.

Meanwhile, Bishop Juan Gerardi Conedera, accompanied by the CEG's vice president, Bishop Próspero Penados, went to Rome to explain to Pope John Paul II the motives for closing the Quiché diocese and to inform him of the national situation. Upon Gerardi's return, the government denied him reentry into the country—although he was a Guatemalan citizen—"because," explained President Lucas García, "he is a Communist bishop and we cannot guarantee his safety. The leftists could kill him and blame it on the government."

Colonel Lobos Zamora was promoted to brigadier general shortly after the massacre at San Juan Cotzal.

On 24 August, soldiers raided Centro Emaús, a Church retreat center in the Escuintla diocese, and kidnapped seventeen union leaders holding a meeting there under the auspices of Bishop Mario Ríos Montt. The men disappeared, never to be seen again. The bishop denounced the crime in no uncertain terms: "If the army is responsible for these deaths, Guatemala is in terrible danger! If the army is not responsible, but is unable or unwilling to go after the killers, the situation is even worse."

In mid-August, as the feeling of inchoate fear among the clergy became more pronounced in many parts of the country, Hennessey received a visit from another non-Maryknoll U.S. diocesan priest from Spokane, Washington. Like Hazleton, the Washingtonian was on loan from his U.S. bishop to the "see-no-evil, hear-no-evil, speak-no-evil" prelate of Sololá. The Spokane priest had come to the regional's office, slipped himself onto the couch, and with a grim look on his face signaled the overwrought spirit within.

The taciturn farmer from Ryan had never felt the need to interrupt the quietude initiated by another. Finally, the visitor explained that a week earlier when returning from a trip to his *aldeas* in Santa Catarina Ixtahuacán, a group of catechists had hailed him on the road to tell him that there was a group of armed men waiting for him at his rectory. Instead of returning home, he drove to Sololá to tell Bishop Melotto. Melotto suggested that the Washingtonian stay with him until the whole thing blew over, . . . that the occurrence was probably just a misunderstanding on the part of the catechists.

"What do you say to a guy who shuts his eyes and ears like that, Ron?"

The priest wasn't expecting an answer, and Hennessey didn't venture one.

"Yesterday, some people from Santa Catarina arrived in Sololá to tell me that the air force had bombed the outskirts of town. No one seems to have been killed, but a lot of homes were destroyed, crops burned, some sheep killed . . . . I don't know if the army wants me out of there or what. Melotto is no help at all."

Hennessey waited, wondering what he could say that would be encouraging. "Have you talked to Jim Hazelton in Santa María? . . . He's had the same problem."

"I haven't seen Jim in weeks. I think he must be lying low."

"Well, if you're looking for my sage advice, I don't have any."

Then coming around from behind his desk in his usual supportive gesture, the Iowan settled his loose frame onto the couch beside his visitor. "But since I don't have anything special scheduled for tomorrow, why don't you and I drive out to Santa Catarina to see what's going on? I'd hate for the people to think that the ESA or the army can frighten us away . . . . If the two of us show up together, I doubt that they would want two dead gringo

priests on their hands. They seem to be avoiding us . . . at least for now . . . .
For small favors we can be thankful."

Early the next day, the two men headed out for Santa Catarina Ixtahuacán.
About one hundred kilometers outside Guatemala City, they ran into a bed
of nails strewn across the highway. Two tires quickly went flat. Hennessey
exited the vehicle and noticed ORPA literature scattered everywhere. The
nails were meant to halt buses and trucks and give ORPA the opportunity to
put their revolutionary message in the hands of any literate passengers riding
in the crippled vehicles.

"Whoever draws up these guys' marketing plan ought to find a new line
of work," the Iowan remarked, handing a couple of the papers to his
companion.

While the Spokane priest replaced one of the flats with the spare,
Hennessey hitched a ride on a truck whose driver had spotted the trap in
time to avoid it by driving through a nearby field. Only six kilometers down
the road, the Iowan, thanking the anonymous saintly patron of Guatemala's
troubled highways and byways, found a rare gas station with someone with
the materials and knowledge to repair the damaged tire. Three hours later,
the two men were again on their way to Santa Catarina.

As they arrived at the isolated mountain town, the priests were greeted
by a shouting, joyous throng that got larger as they drove down the main
street. Signs of the recent bombing runs were clearly evident, with piles of
adobe rubble of what were, until a few days earlier, Mayan homes, standing
in the middle of burnt-out corn and bean fields. From all sides they heard
cries of "*Padres! Padres! Bienvenidos!*"

The Maryknoller spent the next two hours talking to a number of
individuals about the events of the previous ten days. After assuring himself
that no gun-toting, unsavory types had been seen around town for over a
week, he encouraged his colleague to stay close to the rectory while cutting
back on parish social programs. "Your presence here is more important than
anything else you can do, Bill. The people have to see that you're standing
with them. This isn't the time to antagonize the army by involving yourself in
what they consider subversive activities. The smartest thing now is to play
dumb. That's something they understand."

"I don't have to playact, Ron. Haven't you noticed?"

Hennessey smiled and gave the priest an *abrazo*. Then, climbing into his jeep, he shook a score of outstretched hands before heading back to the capital.

Not all priests were of a pacifist philosophy in responding to the repression, however. Some openly joined the guerrillas. One of these was Fernando Hoyos, a Spanish Sacred Heart priest who had been working in El Quiché; he enlisted in the EGP after the bishop closed down the entire diocese and withdrew his priests. Another was Donald McKenna, also assigned to El Quiché. He joined Hoyos in the EGP and became a problem for Maryknoll's regional superior not long after.

McKenna was an enigma. He had studied for the priesthood in his native Ireland, had been ordained in Peru, but had somehow landed in Guatemala. Footloose priests often meant trouble for shorthanded bishops willing to accept them. McKenna was no exception.

The Irish priest, like the non-Maryknollers from Montana, Spokane, Wisconsin, and Oklahoma, quickly gravitated on his days off toward the Maryknoll Center House in Guatemala City as a source of English-speaking companionship. However, McKenna, as a result of not belonging to a particular congregation but seen frequenting the Maryknoll Center House, had earned for himself the status of a Maryknoller in the eyes of many Guatemalans who knew of him.

When the Irishman's picture appeared in a Mexican newspaper celebrating Mass for EGP guerrillas in the El Quiché mountains with a .45 caliber pistol placed antithetically on the altar next to his chalice, Hennessey was forced to deny to the Guatemalan press that McKenna was a Maryknoller. Public debate quickened on the role in Guatemala of foreign priests in general and Maryknollers in particular. President Lucas García railed against "subversive, foreign priests who have come here to destroy our country."

The Iowan was not thrilled the day he received a telephone call asking him to meet the hunted priest at a small unobtrusive restaurant on the outskirts of the capital. But Hennessey, responding to his habit of answering any need, went.

McKenna showed up accompanied by a Dutch nurse with whom, it soon became evident, he was romantically involved.

"I'm sorry Maryknoll is taking heat for my activities," the Irishman confessed to Hennessey. "I told that Mexican reporter to emphasize the fact that I was not with Maryknoll."

Hennessey remained silent as he watched the looks of affection passing between his two tablemates. "We've weathered worse storms than this," the Iowan finally commented. "I don't think the government will have any difficulty finding an excuse to move against us once they decide to do so. I expect that our nationality is the only thing that has protected us until now . . . . Right now I'm taking more heat from my colleagues for letting you use our residence than I am from Lucas García."

McKenna nodded. "I know. I shouldn't have added to your worries. I'm sorry."

The Iowan nodded. "I'm not going to argue that point. In fact, the reason I accepted your invitation to meet is to ask you not to come by our house again, and to suggest that you make a public statement of some kind that you are leaving the country. Later, you can come back, slip back in, or whatever—in a month or two. That way you will be seen as having made a definitive break with the Church, operating on your own, not as a guerrilla arm of the Church."

"Look, Ron, I want to be recognized as standing for the values the Church teaches. I . . ."

"Tell me, is that the Church of the Conquest or the Church of Vatican II?" the Iowan asked, deadpan.

"Come on, Ron, give me a fair hearing!" McKenna pleaded. "I'm only trying to apply the doctrines of a just war and the right of self-defense to the situation of the Mayans. I don't want to be seen as just another guerrilla! . . . Doesn't the U.S. Army have priest chaplains? What's the difference if they themselves use a gun or they limit themselves to blessing others' guns and those who use them?"

"I have never denied the right of the Mayans to take up arms to defend themselves," Hennessey answered quietly. "As much as I hate war, I do not deny your right to support them in doing so. But there are other types of support we can give the peasantry without giving the government the opening to accuse us of using guns against their administration, . . . such as it is. Furthermore, the just war doctrine demands a reasonable hope of success. My doubt revolves around your hope and that of the guerrillas to do something other than further antagonize the army and the U.S. government to bring down worse repression on the defenseless Mayans. Too often, it's those who have never seen war, its destruction, viciousness, and death, who jump first to its banner. If I thought for a moment that this would benefit them . . . ."

McKenna shrugged his shoulders. "I'm an Irishman!" he replied simply. "I've seen war! Sometimes, there is no alternative!"

Hennessey nodded. "I'm only half Irish. Maybe that's why I'm halfhearted about the alternative you've chosen?"

"Maybe!" McKenna laughed.

"Well, what was it you wanted to see me about?" the Iowan asked.

"I've said it," McKenna answered. "I figured I owed you an apology and I wanted to make it in person."

Hennessey nodded. "Just don't give me any more reasons to look for another apology."

"Don't worry, Ron. There will be no more public statements from me! No more sensational pictures!"

"I'd appreciate that! It'll make my job a bit easier!"

After a few more moments of subdued conversation, McKenna promised to abide by the Iowan's request to avoid going near the Maryknoll Center House. All three stood at the same time, shook hands, offered wishes of good luck, and parted company.

Later that same week, a letter from Sister Dorothy Marie in Dubuque made the protection of U.S. citizenship afforded to the Maryknollers look a lot less reliable. The 1980 U.S. presidential challenge of Ronald Reagan to Jimmy Carter had muddied the political waters as Central America became a pivotal campaign issue. Carter's emphasis on human rights as an aspect of his foreign policy was receiving ample criticism from candidate Reagan, who took quite a different tack, one that he expressed with growing frequency:

> I don't think you can turn away from some country because here and there they don't totally agree with our concept of human rights, and then at the same time maintain relations with other countries, or try to develop them where human rights are virtually non-existent.[9]

The reference was aimed at Guatemala-U.S. relations since Carter had already renewed military aid to El Salvador despite Archbishop Romero's plea to the contrary.

A week later, on 9 September 1980, the Carter administration announced that it had begun to investigate the relationship between the Guatemalan government and the Reagan campaign staff. The public relations firm of Deaver and Hannaford—Michael Deaver was a close friend and advisor to the Republican candidate—had signed a contract to represent an association of right-wing Guatemalan businessmen fronting for the Lucas García government. The company's efforts were directed at changing the image of the Guatemalan government in the U.S. media as a gross violator of human rights to one of an embattled, nascent democracy fighting for its life against Soviet-armed, trained, and directed terrorist hordes. The investigation was prompted by the fact that the Deaver and Hannaford firm had not registered as an agent of a foreign government as required by U.S. law.

As Reagan's popularity soared in the polls in tandem with Carter's decline, the Republican candidate's advisors on Latin American began a tour of Central America to build bridges. Premier members were Roger Fontaine, Pedro Sanjuan, James D. Theberge, Jeane Kirkpatrick, and General Daniel Graham. Fontaine was coauthor of the "Santa Fe Document," which described Central America as "the soft underbelly of the United States," where the United States "is engaged in World War III," and which called for increased military assistance programs for "friendly" Central American countries to help fight terrorism. Kirkpatrick had attracted Reagan's attention by writing an article recommending that the U.S. support right-wing, "authoritarian" governments as a frontline defense against left-wing, "totalitarian" governments. Graham's expertise extended to weapons systems and the World Anti-Communist League, an organization with strong Nazi and fascist connections, particularly in Argentina, Taiwan, and South Africa.

In Guatemala, the expectation of a Reagan victory brought a sense of euphoria to the landed gentry, the militarists, and the international business class. Mario Sandoval Alarcón, leader of the MLN, predicted that once Carter's defeat was assured, "the bloodletting would be quick, widespread and decisive." The Guatemalan Army admitted that it was planning "an offensive against the Marxist-led insurgents who have a large following among the country's Indians." Meanwhile wealthy Guatemalans made no attempt to hide the fact that they were contributing substantial sums to Reagan's election campaign—although the practice violated hypocritical U.S. laws—while some noted that what was good for the goose was a valid model for the gander's activities. It was also openly noted that the candidate's silence regarding what was being promoted in his name was encouragement enough for the ultra-right death squads.

By mid-September 1980, Hennessey had been in the regional superior's hot seat for almost six years and had only four months more to go on his second three-year term. A number of U.S. reporters, among them Alan Riding of the *New York Times,* Larry Rother of *Newsweek,* and Marlise Simons of the *Washington Post* had recently picked up his name as a source of information on the guerrillas, resulting in visits that did not appeal to him. He remarked to his family that "a lot of people think we know the mind of the peasants. And to many, the peasants are the equivalent of the guerrillas."

Ron by now had grown weary of the political pushing and shoving coming from on high associated with his position, and the idea coming from below that he could be an infallible factotum for every American priest and religious spinning dizzily in the chaos of Guatemala's environment of social, racial and religious antagonisms. He wanted out, much as he had when the U.S. Army tried to send him to OCS some thirty years earlier, essentially because any position of power did not sit easily on his egalitarian shoulders.

Maryknoll had accepted Ron's suggestion and had called for a new election. The majority of Maryknoll priests and brothers in the Central American region chose Father Bill Mullan, a New Yorker, a friend of Hennessey, a serious and appreciative student of Mayan culture and languages, to lead them into a very uncertain future.

Ron Hennessey agreed with their choice. He was also happy to be returning to his first love, pastoral work. Mullan assigned the Iowan to the parish he himself was vacating, San Mateo Ixtatán.

PART VI

Chapter 28

ELECTIONS, NOT LAND, NOT TORTILLAS

It was as nice a day as San Mateo Ixtatán ever experiences. The fog lifted about 8:30 a.m., allowing the sun to splash across the crowded plaza. Hundreds of men and women, the latter in their colorful Sunday best, the former a little less carefully attired, picked their way among the products and wares laid out in no recognizable pattern on the ground. It was the third Sunday of February 1982.

A successful harvest of corn and beans some weeks earlier had put a little money in the pockets of many. This allowed them to forget for the moment that in several months, shortages of basics would again occur, forcing the annual migration of entire families to the sometimes dangerous, always oppressive, living conditions found on the coffee, sugar, and cotton plantations down on the southern piedmont and Pacific coastal plain.

But even temporary tranquility was not in the heavens. Shortly after 9:00 a.m., an EGP patrol of some twenty-five men and women put in an appearance. The visitors walked purposefully among the merchants and their clients, dressed in their ragtag, khaki uniforms and rubber boots, with an odd assortment of rifles slung across their shoulders, machetes tucked away chastely in their scabbards. They stopped at each *puesto*, advising everyone to stay away from alcohol and to get what they needed from Huehuetenango before 1 March. That was the day, they said, that they intended to close down the road between Soloma and Huehuetenango for the duration of the war.

Ronald Hennessey had taken over the San Mateo parish some sixteen months earlier from Bill Mullan. Over those inaugural months Hennessey had watched the EGP hold its first mass rally in the town square; had seen the guerrillas politicize a sizable minority of Mateanos in a significant number of villages, a majority in a few more, and antagonize a majority in still others; had been party to attempts to resolve some deadly conflicts caused by such politicization; had witnessed the consequences of the army's savage, random attack on the town's sleeping population; was privy to the mortal effects of the EGP's bumbling attempts to ambush army transportation vehicles; and had a four-hour discussion with a middle-level ladino EGP commandant and his four Mayan troops. He was now a seasoned veteran observer of his parish's political conflicts and alliances, as well as of the violence they entailed, all of which he had learned to situate in the context of local, regional, national, and international relations and enmities. Now, after this Sunday's second Mass, Abelardo Valenzuela had come to the rectory to relay to Hennessey what he had heard in the plaza. "The guerrillas say they want to prevent the people from voting in the presidential election, that it's just another political charade."

"Do you think they can pull it off?"

"Padre, I'm not sure how the EGP makes decisions. They don't ask us what we think of their methods. They like to talk about 'the course of history,' but it's not our history. We're the ones who built those municipal buildings they've burned down and no matter who wins this war, we'll be the ones who'll have to rebuild them."

Abelardo's criticism of the EGP surprised Hennessey. The priest decided to try to keep the commentary going to get another insight into the *pueblo*'s feelings. "Well, intellectuals are noted for figuring out everyone else's mind-set but their own," the Iowan replied.

Abelardo nodded his agreement, missing the priest's little joke. "But the *muchachos* are right, padre. The elections are a charade! Why does the EGP think it has to prove that to us! They know that anybody who doesn't vote will be accused of subversive activities."

Over the next two weeks, preparations for the presidential elections proceeded on schedule, planned for the first Sunday of March. The EGP believed that the man who would "win" the election would be—as usual—the official government candidate, in this case, General Angel Aníbal Guevara, the minister of defense.

In order to counter the suspicion of impending fraud and lend international legitimacy to his candidacy, General Guevara had been running from one end of the country to the other giving pie-in-the-sky stump speeches. On one occasion, he had landed his official air force helicopter at a conference of Protestant pastors, donated notebooks and chalk to all attendees, and promised serious reconsideration of his almost nonexistent affiliation with the Catholic Church.

Down in the capital there was enough maneuvering among politically active groups to indicate that the election of General Guevara was not the foregone conclusion that the EGP cadres in and around San Mateo Ixtatán thought it to be. President Lucas García had generated many enemies across the political spectrum during his four-year reign, guaranteeing a plethora of plotters who did not want to see his handpicked heir succeed him in the presidency. They included leading members of the oligarchy, perhaps a majority of the army's young field officers, even some of the army's old guard, and the right-wing death squad of the MLN. Among them all was that persistent, would-be-president adamantly convinced of his divine destiny, General José Efraín Ríos Montt (ret.). In their shadows stood a self-designated, "neutral" observer, the U.S. Embassy, waiting for word from Washington as to whom it should give its whispered benediction.

The anger of the oligarchy focused on Lucas García's inability to grasp simple economic facts, the monumental—as opposed to the traditional—level of corruption in his administration, and his counterproductive, randomized, and heavy-handed prosecution of the war against the guerrillas.

When information broke in late 1981 that eight generals, including President Lucas García, had been involved in a deal whereby $175 million in U.S. arms had been sold to the army by the government for $425 million, many senior officials were angry simply because they had not been included in the scam. Outraged line officers, on the other hand, felt betrayed, claiming that their lives were being jeopardized and their sacrifices ignored.

The recently inaugurated Reagan administration had been frantically trying to find the right formula to convince Congress to reinitiate funding of Guatemala's counterinsurgency efforts, on the one hand, and to enlist the Guatemalans in attempts to overthrow the Sandinista government in Nicaragua, on the other. At the same time, Amnesty International was releasing its most devastating report to date on the human rights situation in Guatemala. The report documented that tortures and murders were part and parcel of a longstanding, official program of the Guatemalan government, with knowledge and support from the United States.[1] In 1981 alone, eleven thousand people had been murdered, including five Protestant missionaries and six Catholic priests, two of whom were U.S. citizens, Father Stan Rother, of Oklahoma, and John Troyer, a Mennonite missionary. Only when the State Department pushed the Guatemalan government to find Rother's killers did it come up with three rural Mayans, obviously innocent, whom it cynically blamed for the priest's death. As far as the killers of eleven thousand Guatemalans were concerned, no U.S. pressure was exerted to bring those responsible to even a minimum of justice. To do so would have revealed the nature of the counterinsurgency enterprise, something the U.S. government did not wish to see happen. Syndicated columnist Jack Anderson reported that officials of the State Department who had been sounding out key congresspersons on renewal of aid to Guatemala found that almost all of them, including conservative legislators, were against the initiative.

Finally, the Reagan administration recognized that it had little hope of pushing legislation through Congress favorable to their Guatemalan policy while Lucas García or a like-minded military successor remained in power. It then switched strategies and dodged congressional restrictions by reclassifying military equipment—such as army jeeps and trucks—as "regional stability controls." By following a precedent set during the Carter administration it allowed Bell Helicopter of Fort Worth to train Guatemalan air force pilots to fly their civilian 212 and 412 models, twenty-three of which were given export licenses by the Commerce Department. Once in Guatemala, the civilian helicopters were outfitted with .30 and .50 caliber machine guns.[2] With this show of goodwill toward Lucas García, the administration hoped to pressure the president to pick a civilian as his designated heir, preferably architect Anzueto Vielman or the moderate Christian Democratic representative Alejandro Maldonado Aguirre, the candidate who seemed to have the broadest public support.

All three alternate candidates to Guevara, including the MLN's murderous Sandoval Alarcón, were ideologically acceptable to the Reagan administration. The three had declared themselves firm anticommunists and had designated their first order of presidential business to be that of stamping out the "communist insurgency" for all time. All three could serve as did Méndez Montenegro (1966-70), a civilian figurehead ruling over an "emerging democracy."

This would allow the United States to support the Guatemalan Army's terrorist military option, free from sustainable congressional criticism.

The character with the most adroit moves in the anti-Lucas García/Guevara passion play was a "non-candidate," José Efraín Ríos Montt. Ríos Montt had continued to function since his 1978 religious conversion as an active member of the El Verbo evangelical church. However, he also attended services sponsored by several other fundamentalist congregations, keeping open a plethora of political options, a habit that concerned his politically naïve, North American mentors. This, in turn, made them rightly question his religious sincerity.[3] Little did they realize that Ríos Montt's piety was, among other things, a card in his political deck that he knew, if he played it right, would bring him the essential element for a successful presidential bid, namely, the backing of the U.S. Embassy. It wasn't a question of whether or not he needed a Guatemalan version of the White House prayer breakfast, the blessing of a Central American Billy Graham, it was merely an uncertainty as to which of the available denominations would impress Ronald Reagan the most.

When a three-party coalition approached Ríos Montt in the autumn of 1981 to propose that he run as their candidate in the presidential elections of March 1982, the general was flattered, even exhilarated. But first, he told his suitors, he would have to consult with El Verbo's elders and obtain their opinion.[4]

The elders decided that the general should spend three days of prayer and fasting in their company—four North Americans and three Guatemalans—to obtain God's perspective on this new political opportunity.

When the three-day retreat finished, the group of elders counseled the general against his candidacy, while promising to respect his decision should he decide to enter the fray. "I believe that now is not the time," Francisco Bianchi, one of the elders, told the general. "In fact, as we were praying here, I had a distinct impression—from the Lord, I believe—that another door will be opened to you. And it will be a sovereignly opened door."[5]

It was an impression that two of the North American elders, James Jankowiak and Jim DeGolyer, also shared, attributing the idea to the same divine source.

But before the general could make up his mind—or at least announce his decision—the three-party coalition became unraveled, much to the relief of the church elders.

A short time later, another political party invited Ríos Montt to serve as their vice presidential candidate. Again, when he sought their advice, the church elders told the general "to close that door." Ríos Montt had no hesitancy in accepting the advice this time. The vice presidency was, after all, a ceremonial post and had never shown itself to be a viable way station on the road to the presidency.

Unknown to the church elders, Ríos Montt had been plotting to challenge the minister of defense, not, however, through the ballot box, a route that he knew to be fatally flawed. Instead, he agreed to work for the candidacy of civilian Mario Sandoval Alarcón, of the MLN. But the Huehueteco's commitment to the MLN candidate was not entirely sincere.

The agreement was that Ríos Montt would help organize MLN civilian cadres into gangs of street provocateurs who would start riots throughout the capital when the government announced General Guevara's victory at the polls, forcing army officers sympathetic to the anti-Guevara forces to intervene. At meetings held weekly in his home, the general—actor that he was—told his agents that he was not going to let Sandoval Alarcón experience what he had endured in 1974. He also told them that under no circumstances were they to confront any army troops, that many young officers were being brought into the plot against Lucas García and Guevara by another route.[6]

Although some of these young officials were sympathetic to the MLN and had worked in the death squads that bore its signature, if not its influence, most had no intention of risking their lives and careers to put in the presidency a civilian who would then be charged with carrying on the war against the guerrillas and their sympathizers.

Knowing that military courtesy would not allow a captain, major, or even a colonel to properly demand and receive the resignation of General Romeo Lucas García, the young officers had sought out a general to involve in their plot. Several of the plotters had been cadets when Ríos Montt was director of the Politécnica and knew him well. Many liked and admired him. "Would the general consider accepting the presidency if we can bring enough troop commanders into the plan?" the principal schemers asked Ríos Montt.

"No one will know your name until the assault is virtually successful and you demand Lucas García's surrender. If we fail, you will not be named nor blamed."

Ríos Montt showed no hesitancy in accepting the young officers proposal. The "door" was being "sovereignly opened," just as the church elders had prophesied.

So, during the two weeks before the election, unknown to El Verbo church elders, nor to his MLN co-plotters, nor to the EGP troops in Hennessey's parish, Ríos Montt was planning with influential members of the young officer corps to lead a coup against Generals Lucas García and Guevara. Meanwhile he was plotting with the MLN civilian cadres to provoke the coup, supposedly in favor of Sandoval Alarcón.

Meanwhile, back in San Mateo, the EGP had participated a month earlier in the formation of a unified guerrilla front with the country's three other revolutionary organizations (ORPA, FAR, and PGT). As a result, the local EGP cadres had been instructed in the implementation of a national strategy, to threaten with death anyone who participated by voting in the government's election. Hennessey was not concerned by the warnings because he had never seen any evidence that the guerrillas would carry out such generalized threats. They preferred clearly defined, individual targets—especially army informants—where the political message of their actions would not be misunderstood.

The army, for its part, had stated that anyone who did not participate in the election would be regarded as "subversive" and would suffer the consequences. But even this threat was not the Mateanos' primary concern. What they professed to fear the most—and it was a topic on everyone's lips—was that the EGP would either ambush the soldiers coming to San Mateo to oversee the balloting, or shoot down the helicopter that was supposed to retrieve the ballot boxes after the vote.

Then, a week before the elections, someone had the bright idea of taking up a collection to pay off the guerrillas to dissuade them from attacking the soldiers and the helicopter. When Santiago Quot come to the rectory to tell Hennessey about the collection, the sacristan's anxiety was evident. "If *los muchachos* attack *los pintos* in San Mateo, padre," the old man whispered conspiratorially, "the army come and kill us. We have no way out. *Everyone* give to the collection."

The Iowan watched his sacristan closely. Santiago's emphasis on the word "everyone" suggested to Hennessey that his assistant might be dropping a subtle hint that the priest himself should also make a contribution.

"Don't you think that's dangerous, Santiago? If the army ever gets word that you're taking up a collection for the guerrillas, it will be just as bad as the attack on the soldiers that you're trying to prevent! The army will come in here with guns blazing, . . . no questions asked."

"We caught between them like always, padre! If *los muchachos* hit *los pintos* here, the soldiers strike us for sure! But if we pay *los muchachos*, maybe *los pintos* never hear it and we be safe."

Hennessey folded his hands in his lap and closed his eyes. Santiago kept silent, watching the priest. After a few moments, Hennessey shook his head, rubbed his eyes, and responded, "maybe you're right, Santiago. You've got to do it quietly—not collecting from everybody—just from those *de mucha confianza*, those you trust the most!"

The old sacristan nodded. "We be careful, padre. We not give support to *los muchachos*. We want they take the fight someplace else."

"Well, let's hope it turns out that way, Santiago," the priest replied. Then, as he walked the old man to the sala door, Hennessey explained that he preferred not to contribute to the collection because his attempts to maintain a balanced public neutrality might otherwise be compromised if word got out that he had contributed something.

The sacristan nodded his understanding.

The Iowan never found out how much was collected nor whether the offering was an effective tactic for dissuading the EGP from mounting an attack. He also felt it was better not to ask. One thing he was certain of, however: the gesture had undoubtedly sent a strong message to the guerrillas that any reprisals taken against the townspeople by the military would be blamed primarily on the EGP. He also knew that this was exactly what the army sought. In any event, the guerrillas remained out of sight on election day, and only two innocuous propaganda bombs were set off, their authors unidentified, their explosive effect more dramatic than political.

As the day wore on, many more people showed up to vote than Hennessey had anticipated. The large turnout was a good indication that few Mateanos believed that the EGP could protect them from the army if they didn't have their identification papers stamped by an election official. Hundreds of peasants stood for hours in long lines before each ballot box, waiting their turn to openly put an "x" next to the symbol of the party of their less-than-free choice.

Some Mateanos sought to avoid reprisals from both the army and the guerrillas by trying to obtain certified letters from the parish hospital stating that they were too sick to vote on election day. When Sister Justa hurried to the rectory to propose the idea, Hennessey dissuaded her: "If you do that for some, Sister, the idea will catch on and you'll have to do it for many. The army would quickly see through the subterfuge and hold us responsible."

"That's what I thought, *padrecito*," the nun replied, "but I was having a hard time saying no to our people."

The next afternoon, an air force helicopter came to retrieve the ballot boxes, landing on the soccer field without incident. A little later, several private commercial trucks commandeered in Barillas came to pick up the soldiers, but not before the troops had indiscriminately confiscated numerous *capixay* pullovers and felt hats from passing residents in order to make the thirty kilometer return journey disguised as Mateano peasants. The victims of the confiscation, having lost the most expensive items in their wardrobes admitted, however, that it was a small enough price to pay to have the soldiers leave town without bloodshed.

On election night, General José Efraín Ríos Montt, surrounded by a small select group of MLN coconspirators, sat in front of the television set in his Guatemala City home, waiting for the election results. Scene after scene showed long lines of citizens around the capital waiting four and five hours to cast their ballots. Many of those interviewed by reporters stated that they had waited patiently in the hot sun because "we are obliged to vote." And as Ríos Montt and his fellow plotters watched, TV news commentators began reporting that General Guevara was piling up a substantial lead across the country.

Monday, 8 March 1982, came and went with still no final announcement of the election results. But reports kept coming into the capital from around the nation of missing ballot boxes, of some polls closing early, others never having opened, of election officials destroying thousands of ballots. The Christian Democrats and the National Renovation Party screamed fraud. Telephone lines into the countryside went dead and only the army's radio communications network continued to function.

On Tuesday, General Guevara claimed that he had won the election. The three other candidates called on their supporters to protest in front of the national palace, but by this time General Ríos Montt wanted no part of street demonstrations. President Lucas García warned that any such gathering would be illegal and "repressed with appropriate force." The three defeated candidates, undeterred, marched on the presidential palace "with evidence of fraud." There they were arrested by the national police and held for an hour. Two hundred supporters who had answered their call to demonstrate in front of the palace were teargassed, clubbed, and arrested. Four U.S. journalists filming the scene, including ABC's theatrical Geraldo Rivera, were also detained. General Guevara, for his part, said he was prepared to defend his victory "in the streets" if necessary.

On Wednesday, the electoral commission announced the official results: with slightly less than 50 percent of the country's eligible voters casting valid ballots, General Guevara had won 37 percent. Having failed to obtain the necessary 50.01 percent meant that Guevara's election would have to be confirmed by Congress where the Lucas García administration held a majority of seats. Without Congress's blessing, a rerun was mandated. The outcome was a foregone conclusion.

Two days later, on Friday, Assistant Secretary of State Thomas O. Enders hinted at U.S. displeasure at Guevara's possible election. He stated that although the United States was not fully committed to supporting the election results, the Reagan administration could not ignore the fact that the Guatemalan regime was the target of a Cuban-backed revolution. The signal was a bit too ambiguous to block Guevara's election. On Saturday, Congress voted 39 to 13 to elect General Guevara to the presidency.

Though the fraudulent results of the election took no one by surprise, the Mateanos' disappointment was palpable. "This means the army keeps its license to go on massacring," a disgusted Abelardo told Hennessey, standing with a small group of catechists in front of the parish church.

"What did you expect, Abelardo?" the Iowan finally interjected. "The EGP told everyone that the election was going to be a charade. You yourself told me that everyone knew that to be so. So why do you act surprised?"

"I know, padre," Abelardo answered, "but you're the one who's always telling us not to lose hope. I keep praying that something will happen to bring a little peace."

As Hennessey, Abelardo, and the small group of men were talking together a savage slaughter was even then beginning at one of Woods's Ixcán cooperatives, a slaughter that would prove to be an omen of the fate many Mateanos would suffer in the months ahead. Eight days later the Iowan and his parishioners began to hear the outline of that Sunday's tragedy at Cooperativa Cuarto Pueblo as word seeped into San Mateo via the Mayan underground communication system.[7]

At approximately 9:00 a.m. on Sunday, 14 March 1982, a blue-and-white Bell helicopter flew into view and circled twice over Cuarto Pueblo's busy market plaza before flying away to coordinate an attack on Nueva Concepción, a subsidiary center of Cuarto Pueblo, a 90-minute walk to the north on the Mexican border. A few minutes later, the helicopter returned, landing on Cuarto Pueblo's nearby airstrip.

Buyers, sellers, onlookers, and their children had watched the "bird of death" descend, some curious, most hypnotized by fear. All were aware of a series of at least seven massacres carried out in neighboring centers by the soldiers during the previous month, killings that had resulted in the bizarre murders of between 100 and 150 men, women, and children. The killings included the disembowelment of a pregnant woman whose abdominal cavity was then stuffed with the severed head of someone else's child,[8] the beheading of several adults,[9] and the immolation of adults and children by locking them in their homes and burning these to the ground.[10] Several of the massacres had been preceded by the flight of a blue-and-white Bell helicopter, probably to warn of any ambush potential from EGP guerrillas.

On this Sunday, none of Cuarto Pueblo's leaders spoke up to encourage the people to flee into the jungle despite the fact that the EGP had warned them some days earlier that the army was on a savage rampage. Some of the cooperative's leaders possessed MLN party membership cards, making them think that their documents would protect them from military wrath. Others belonged to religious groups that they felt the soldiers viewed with sympathetic eyes. All would live a very short time, enough to regret their fatal errors of judgment. Little did they realize that the soldiers' purpose was not to kill potential enemies, but to sow terror in the surrounding countryside.

At the same time, the soldiers began to move toward the center from the north, splitting into two groups, one circling around to the east, the other to the west, then moving south to form a classic pincer maneuver intended to encircle the center and prevent any attempted escapes. As they moved, some shot their rifles into the air in celebratory fashion, but the majority turned their weapons on the crowded plaza.

Two religious services were in progress at the time, one in the Protestant evangelical chapel, the other in the community hall where charismatic (fundamentalist) Catholics were chanting, clapping, and dancing. The leaders of both services, inebriated with faith and fear, counseled their nervous members to remain calm, that the soldiers meant them no harm.

Perhaps as many as one hundred individuals in the plaza were caught in the first withering attack. They fell like so many magpies in a shooting gallery. Some of the targets managed to crawl into the nearby jungle and escape the barrage. The rest just sat on the ground, shivering and weeping quietly, trusting that their destiny had marked them for death. A small baby sat next to its murdered mother, crying plaintively. A soldier grabbed the child by a leg and slammed its head against the ground.[11]

When the soldiers had assembled all the survivors in the plaza, standing them among the bodies of their dead and dying relatives, friends, and neighbors, the commanding officer barked orders to separate the young men from older men, and both groups from the women and children. Mayan fatalism controlled the scene. The captain then ordered that a half-ton of cardamom—the cooperative's money crop—be loaded on the helicopter along with a group of about ten young men to be flown to the Playa Grande military base. Stealing from the dead, as well as from the living, was a sine qua non of Guatemalan military tactics. Everyone present also knew that the captain was consigning the ten to be processed at Playa Grande like so much cheese, to be ground up and crushed, more to terrorize them than to obtain useful military intelligence. The women and children were locked up in two separate buildings to contemplate their fates and to listen to the agonizing cries of their tortured loved ones.

Meanwhile, other soldiers, with much laughter and joking, attempting to assuage perhaps the last remnants of their humanity, hung the older men by their necks with nonslipknot nooses from crossbeams in the open corridors of buildings fronting the plaza. Still others set about rounding up chickens, turkeys, and pigs belonging to their captives and victims, butchering them in a parody of their colleagues' activities as they prepared the noontime repast.

During the afternoon, small groups of middle-aged men were taken aside, harangued with rhetorical questions about the blessings of patriotism and the evils of communism, then shot, their bodies doused with gasoline and burned. The program of systematic incineration of more than one hundred houses, cooperative installations, and the population's entire food supply would require three to four days to carry out.

As the afternoon sun descended in the western sky, mimicking the darkness that had begun to creep across their individual military souls, small groups of soldiers took turns entering the schoolhouse where the younger women were held. They began a ritualistic rape ceremony, one that represented a rite of passage rather than the mere satisfaction of a group sexual appetite. The violence continued throughout the night, accompanied by screams from the victims, with many soldiers returning for second and third violations, their boastful claims of multiple success clearly overheard by the few shivering escapees hiding in the undergrowth nearby. Slowly, inevitably, the blood lust, the sexual lust, the thrill of operationalizing the power of death, began to take their toll. Small groups of executioners broke away, one after another, to seek respite in fitful sleep.

The following day began with the commanding officer haranguing his troops: "We've got to kill all of them! They support the guerrillas. They say they don't, but they lie. Their lies are proof they support the guerrillas. Once we kill them all, things will be calm again. We'll finish off everyone here first, and then we'll go on to Centro Uno, Kaibil Balám, and Piedras Negras . . . . We'll finish everything here and then we'll move on to El Petén . . . . There's nothing to be afraid of; we're going to win. Planes are coming to help us, more helicopters are coming. The guerrillas don't have planes . . . . We must be thankful that the United States is helping us."[12]

The morning wore on and the children were separated from their mothers and locked up in the cooperative clinic. The health center now became the death center. The clinic was doused in diesel fuel and set on fire. The screams of the tiny victims scarred the hiding witnesses in ways they could not later adequately describe, but they agreed that this was the single act among the many brutalities they were forced to attend that they could never forget nor forgive.

Monday afternoon was given over to tearing down the Protestant chapel to build a pyre on which the bodies of the older women, jugular veins severed, were cremated. The younger women would remain alive for still another day, cooking meals and satisfying the soldiers' sexual appetites and their need to demonstrate to their companions their desire for misogynist recognition. When night came on, the soldiers marched the women into the cardamom drying shed where they again showed off the social construction of clinical sadism.

On Wednesday, the execution of both males and females, who, for one reason or another had been spared from the previous two days of slaughter, continued. One by one, they were taken out to be shot or have their throats slit. Sometimes a cry could be heard. Then suddenly, the place became eerily silent, . . . except for an occasional laugh coming like a bizarre announcement of temporary insanity from one or another soldier. The eradication of the entire village population, some 324 individuals—the final count made in terms of those known by name to have died—was now complete.

It was time for two catechists among those who had escaped the slaughter undetected in the jungle to take advantage of the lack of military vigilance. For three days they had huddled in terrified silence, eating leaves and drinking tainted water, stifling the urge to cry out when attacked by ants or mosquitoes, sleeping fitfully for only minutes at a time. Now moving only at night and accompanied by a small group of older children who had also managed to remain hidden, they headed for the Mexican border. En route they were joined by others fleeing from nearby cooperative centers, to whom they entrusted their wards. The two men then agreed to go to San Mateo to talk to Padre Ronaldo, the nearest priest whom they knew would sit and listen, to tell him what they had witnessed. They wanted a written record in the church archives with names and dates to accompany the parish baptismal records, so that generations yet unborn would never forget how their ancestors had lived and died. It would be the only decent burial and post mortem recognition that most of them would get for years to come.[13]

Yet unrecognized, the execution of Cuarto Pueblo's population would be the initiation of a new phase of the government's counterinsurgency program, whereby the army moved from selective—albeit indiscriminate—terror to wholesale eradication of entire towns and villages. It would be a scorched earth campaign that would sweep across northcentral and northwest Guatemala in the months and years to come and would eventually—according to the government's own subsequent count—result in the destruction and deaths of 444 *pueblos*, the barbaric murders of tens of thousands of innocent men, women, and children, driving hundreds of thousands into Mexican refugee camps, displacing at least a million people (one-sixth of the national population). This was a campaign against the Maya that the bishops' conference finally labeled "a program of genocide," like nothing seen since the 1520s when Pedro de Alvarado laid waste to the Land of Eternal Spring and its indigenous populations.

Hennessey sat listening to the witnesses' account without moving, his head in his hands, his eyes shut. The scenes that flashed before his eyes mirrored the descriptions whispered by the two catechists. Deep inside, he felt his stomach muscles tighten; he had an urge to cry, but no tears came. He had never been good at crying, even as a child. The priest stood up, walked to the window, and looked up at the hill leading to San Mateo's plaza, trying to stare away the images flashing before his eyes. His visitors fell silent.

Finally, realizing he owed the martyred dead a hearing of their final agonies, as well as an obligation to his visitors to allow them to relieve their burdened souls, Hennessey forced himself to return to his chair and encouraged the men to continue their graphic obituary.

After the two had fallen silent, their account complete, the priest said nothing. He reminded himself once again that he should struggle to maintain a capacity for anguish and grief. Was General Guevara determined to continue Lucas García's madness? But then madness seemed like such a breezy explanation, one that in the final analysis explained nothing, one that tended to excuse the culprits.

Chapter 29

The Second Coming of Ríos Montt

On the day following the visit of the two survivors of the El Cuarto Pueblo massacre, 23 March, Ron Hennessey thought for a few fleeting hours that change might at least be in the wind. Sister Justa hurried to the rectory in mid-morning to tell the priest that the radio had been broadcasting news of a coup attempt in Guatemala City. "It looks like it may already be successful, *padrecito*," the nun exclaimed. "Because they're announcing that Lucas García is under arrest and the army is now in charge."

"The army is now in charge?" Hennessey repeated as he turned toward his portable radio. "The army has been in charge for the last thirty years, *madrecita*, . . . and for the 130 years before that. For 450 years altogether! *Who* in the army is the question!"

The priest turned on his radio and heard Sister Justa's remarks confirmed. Between segments of martial music transmitted on all stations, a recorded voice repeated again and again that the army was in control of the situation and that "everyone should remain alert so as not to be deceived by the lies and rumors flying about."

The hypocrisy, the priest thought. *The monumental hypocrisy!*

About noontime, a call went out on the radio for General Ríos Montt and Lionel Sisniega Otero, the MLN's vice presidential candidate, to go to the presidential palace to meet with the officers controlling the coup. Ríos Montt, pretending to be oblivious to the significance of what was going on, was busy at the time in his office as academic director of El Verbo's day school. On hearing the news, he turned to the church elders and joined them in prayer.[1]

Sisniega Otero, however, made no pretense of ignorance nor did he stop to pray and ask advice, but went straight to the National Palace. He had no need to fool anyone. When Ríos Montt did not show up right away, the MLN vice presidential candidate went on the air to ask for the general's presence.

The Huehueteco finally presented himself at the coup's command headquarters in a store across the plaza from the National Palace. The palace itself was now rimmed with tanks and heavy artillery. "*Mi general*," the young officers in charge saluted, clicking their heels, "the president knows he is through but refuses to turn over his authority to anyone but a general. We told him one would be here shortly. He is waiting for you."

By 4:00 p.m., Ríos Montt had negotiated with General Romeo Lucas García the terms of the president's peaceful departure and had unceremoniously escorted the ex-chief executive to a side door of the palace where a group of middle-level officers and a contingent of guards met him. The Huehueteco then headed back into the palace to engage in strenuous political bargaining with the various elements involved in the coup. Successive radio broadcasts indicated that the negotiators were not having an easy time agreeing on the composition of the new government, since three different juntas made up of several different individuals were announced over the next five hours. The first included several young officers who had coordinated the rebellion. The second included the MLN's Sandoval Alarcón. The third would include only senior officers.

Meanwhile, out in the plaza in front of the palace, "a representative of the U.S. Embassy" received information from a series of young officers who exited the building to confer with him.[2] As the successive juntas were announced, each one contained one name in common—General José Efraín Ríos Montt.

Finally, shortly after 9:00 p.m., Ríos Montt, dressed in battle fatigues and in the company of two senior officers, a general and a colonel, announced on radio and television that the three men were forming an interim government of which he was the leader. In a 13-minute, rambling speech laced with biblical quotes and claiming divine inspiration and intervention, Ríos Montt demonstrated his independence of his coconspirators. At one point, he angered Sisniega Otero and his MLN faction by shouting that civilian politicians should "stay away" from his government, "and don't even come close." At another point, his two brothers-in-arms, hands locked behind their backs, legs spread wide, menacing looks on their faces, blinked uncomfortably when the new minister of defense—the position Ríos Montt had claimed for himself—declared: "I am trusting God, my Lord and King, to enlighten me. For He is the only one who gives or takes away this authority."[3]

It was a speech intended to impress President Ronald Reagan, American Fundamentalists, and Ríos Montt's own religious colleagues in El Verbo Church.

On the following day, Hennessey again listened as Ríos Montt came on the air to tell his countrymen that he would rule "in peace, with the help of God Our Lord and with your consideration." He assured his listeners that "no longer will corpses be thrown by the roadside or piled onto trucks. Anyone who acts against the law shall be executed. Let's have no more murders. We want to respect human rights and defend them."[4]

When the Mateanos first heard Ríos Montt's condemnations of government-sponsored murder, a sense of relief, like the first rains of May, washed over the town. But the Iowan was not so sure. He felt that the Huehueteco's claims to be in direct contact with God made him potentially the most rigid of the country's soldier-politicians, an affliction that often bedeviled popes and the Roman Curia's papal politicians. And Ríos Montt's statements seemed to confirm this view. "Neither votes nor bullets put me in this position of authority. God has placed me here . . . . Subversives, hear me well. We are able to communicate politically, but we also have the ability to defend ourselves with weapons, to employ weapons, to fulfill our duty with weapons."[5]

In Washington, D.C., the Reagan team watched developments closely, expressing some consternation, although U.S. embassy officials had confessed to "knowing" the coup plans since early January.[6] To know about a coup beforehand and make no attempt to stop it is in itself tacit approval, a game at which the U.S. government excelled. But now, Ambassador Frederic Chapin was avoiding Ríos Montt. Word began to circulate that the general's refusal to admit civilians into his junta, his suspension of the constitution and ban on all political parties, and his refusal to mention a timetable for elections were causing some second-guessing in Washington. This, despite the encouragement extended to the coup's leaders by the presence of the embassy's representative who had guaranteed Ríos Montt's inclusion in any junta suggested during the five hours of negotiation.

Meanwhile, prestigious U.S. personalities with close ties to the Reagan administration expressed pleasure with political developments in Guatemala. Among them was the Rev. Jerry Falwell, founder of the Moral Majority, and the charismatic televangelist of the Christian Broadcasting Company, the Rev. Pat Robertson. Robertson, five days after the coup, was in Guatemala City to see what he could do to help Ríos Montt gain visibility and support in Washington, D.C., and across the United States. The televangelist would later write that he found the general to be "a man of humility, simplicity, impeccable personal integrity, and a deep faith in Jesus Christ . . . [who] offered the people of his country—indeed the people of all Latin America— a true alternative other than the oppression of corrupt oligarchies and the tyranny of Russian-backed Communist totalitarianism."[7]

Despite the new leader's professed humility and deep faith in Jesus Christ, reports continued to leak out that massacres on an even larger scale than those under Lucas García were the order of the day in Mayan communities across the northern tier of predominantly Mayan departments: Alta Verapaz, Baja Verapaz, Chimaltenango, Sololá, Quiché, Huehuetenango, and San Marcos, but particularly in Quiché's Ixcán territory, the "zone of the generals." Refugees fleeing the Ixcán told Hennessey that military-sponsored burning, looting, and killings persisted in their resettlement cooperatives.

As the killings continued, Hennessey composed letter after wrenching letter to his family regarding the latest regional and Ixcán events. If nothing else, he thought, his three sister-nuns would see that the news got a wide distribution. As he sat struggling with one such letter trying to decide what to say, Santiago Quot knocked on the door. "Padre Ronaldo," the old man whispered, "there are three catechists from the Ixcán who want to speak to you."

The priest sucked in his breath. *More of the same?* He asked himself. "Ask them to come in, Santiago."

Weary and hungry from their two-and-a-half-day march, the three men gladly accepted Hennessey's offer of coffee and some hot tortillas laced with goat's cheese, a delicacy. Finally, their spokesman explained the purpose of the visit: "You come with us to Guatemala City, padre? We hear President

Ríos Montt talk on the radio as a holy man. But the soldiers continue to kill our people, to burn them alive in the fire in Xalbal, Kaibil. You come with us to talk to the president to tell him the soldiers not obey him. He force his will on them."

Hennessey's heart went out to the three exhausted men sitting before him, actors on a stage they had never before stepped on, with a script they were unable to read.

"*Miren, señores,*" the priest told them gently, "this is not Lucas García's army! . . . and it's not Ríos Montt's army! It's the Guatemalan Army! Its ladino officers are afraid of all Mayans, men, women, and children . . . . This is why they force Mayan soldiers to kill your own people, . . . to implicate your people in their crimes. They want to be able to claim that you are responsible for the disappearance of your *pueblo* . . . . Ríos Montt knows what's going on! . . . Do you think he became a general because other generals like the way he prays? No, *señores!*"

Pedro Supul, the eldest of the three, shook his head, not wanting to accept the priest's words. "If you speak truth, padre, we have no hope! We flee to Mexico, but why? . . . Some say we survive in Mexico, our children and grandchildren return someday to our lands. But the ladinos always be killing us and stealing our lands. This land is our Mother. The ladinos only rape her!"

The priest looked sadly into their eyes and saw more than a flicker of despair. "Maybe what life is all about is a never-ending struggle for justice? . . . We cannot give up! But appealing to General Ríos Montt for justice is not the answer! Ríos Montt did not become a general by seeking justice! Ríos Montt did not become head of the junta by working for justice . . . . I cannot tell you why God allows these things to happen to your people . . . I can only say that I ask your forgiveness for the part my government plays in these crimes."

The three men sat for some minutes, looking at their hands, picking up their hats and twisting them, only to set them back down on the floor. Hennessey remained silent. Finally, Pedro Supul rose, followed by his two companions. "Our brothers and sisters be sad to hear your words, padre. But we think you be right. It be best we not talk to Ríos Montt. Perhaps Mexico be our refuge for now."

The priest stared at the closed door for some long minutes after the three men had left. *Perhaps I should have gone to the capital with them?* He asked himself doubtfully . . . . *No! Ríos Montt's lower level of bloodshed in Guatemala City is just part of his strategy to improve his image.* Hennessey never saw the three men again, but as he listened to Ríos Montt's oft-repeated claims to divine inspiration and weighed his statements against stories of army depredations coming from the Ixcán, from across the western highlands, the Iowan became ever more convinced that his take on Ríos Montt had been correct.

After a week of shadow boxing intended to underline the Reagan administration's distaste for military governments, the United States responded positively to Ríos Montt's accession to power. It granted his government formal recognition and expressed a desire for close cooperation between the two countries. Assistant Secretary of State for Inter-American Affairs Thomas O. Enders explained that "a coup has installed a new leader who has improved the human rights situation and has opened the way for a more effective counterinsurgency effort." [8] Deputy Assistant Secretary of State Steven W. Bosworth stated that "political paralysis has ended." And U. S. Ambassador Chapin opined that Guatemala "has come out of the darkness and into the light." [9]

When Bosworth acknowledged that the administration hoped to establish a "more collaborative" relationship with the new military regime, the outlines of that collaboration came into focus by the end of April. The White House announced that it was preparing to approve a $4 million grant for helicopter spare parts, $50,000 for military training, and a request for another $250,000 in training funds for fiscal 1983. On 7 May, the prestigious *Latin American Regional Reports* (London) characterized the Ríos Montt regime as one of naked terror: "The army's strategy is to clear the population out of the guerrilla support areas. Troops and militias move into the villages, shoot, burn, or behead the inhabitants they catch; the survivors are machine-gunned from helicopters as they flee." [10]

On 12 May, with full understanding of the grave risk they were running, while banking on the government's hesitancy to move after the debacle in the Spanish Embassy, Mayan members of the CUC (Committee of Peasant Unity), largely from El Quiché, occupied the Brazilian Embassy and demanded that a statement they had composed be read over the government radio network. It said in part:

> Since 23 March we have seen how, far from ending the massacres, the army of the [Ríos Montt] junta has continued and increased them . . . . More than 3,000 people—men, women, children and old people—have been massacred in the most barbaric ways in this month and a half alone. They have been tortured, their throats cut, or burned alive in their homes . . . . We have seen how the army comes into our communities, burning all our houses, all the corn which sustains us, destroying or stealing our property, clothes and anything of value, and stealing and killing all our chickens and pigs.[11]

The Brazilian government warned Ríos Montt that it would not tolerate a police attack on its embassy like that executed against Spain. It negotiated the publication of the manifesto and obtained a safe departure of the occupiers into Mexican exile.

On 20 May, strong criticism of the new government came from a most unexpected quarter. Jorge Carpio Nicolle, the owner of the ultraconservative daily, *El Gráfico,* and a staunch supporter of right-wing military governments through the years, published a damning editorial over his own signature:

> To anyone who has any sympathy for his fellow man, the type of genocidal annihilation that is taking place in the Indian zones of the country is truly horrifying . . . . There has been much talk of improving our image abroad, but this image will continue to blacken itself more and more with this new resurgence of blind and absurd violence.[12]

By the end of May, the bishops, after much internal wrangling, were forced to issue a communiqué stating their perspective:

> Many families have been vilely murdered. Even the lives of the elderly, pregnant women, and innocent children have not been respected. The consequences of this irrational violence could not

be more dismal for the survivors: children orphaned, premature widowhood, insecurity, terror and hunger caused by the destruction of villages and the abandonment of croplands. These murders have reached levels of genocide.[13]

In a desire for the episcopal unity mandated by Pope John Paul II, the bishops again failed to buck Cardinal Casariego's insistence that responsibility for the massacres not be attributed to the government, but assigned to "sectors of the extreme right and left."

Then, as the massacres continued unabated, Ríos Montt issued a decree making June a month of amnesty for all who had fought against the "constitutional order" if they would but lay down their arms and turn themselves in to the army. The law also granted amnesty to all members of the state's security forces for acts committed in the counterinsurgency struggle. Although amnesty for the insurgents would last only thirty days and on the condition that they turn themselves in to the army, amnesty for the security forces was open-ended and mandated no acknowledgment of guilt.

The law was a puff of smoke and Hennessey warned many of his parishioners of the dangers of trying to take advantage of it. The U.S. Embassy, however, released a statement that the amnesty decree was proof of Ríos Montt's "conciliatory intentions."

Ríos Montt was pleased with the embassy's praise and responded that he would hold elections for a Constituent Assembly to formulate a new constitution at the end of 1982 and then conduct general elections, "probably in 1984." He also stated that since he had a commitment of "a billion dollars" from U.S. evangelicals, he would not file a request for either the economic or military aid promised by the U.S. government—a statement that seriously embarrassed the Reagan administration, making it look like the Guatemalans were being forced to militarize against their will.

Deputy Assistant Secretary of State Bosworth was immediately dispatched to Guatemala to talk to the junta members. He was rewarded with a contradictory statement from Colonel Gordillo, the lowest ranking member of the junta, that Guatemala did indeed want U.S. government economic and military assistance.

Although the promise of a "a billion dollars" was a gross exaggeration, political and monetary support from U.S. evangelicals was not. About this time, a meeting was held at the Washington, D.C., home of the U.S. ambassador to the OAS, William Middendorf, to discuss how the Reagan administration could utilize Ríos Montt's born-again religious beliefs and connections to the American religious right to develop congressional and popular U.S. support for rearming and retraining the Guatemalan Army. Present at the meeting were Ríos Montt's spiritual advisor and elder of the El Verbo Church, Francisco Bianchi, Ambassador Chapin, Reagan advisor Edwin Meese III, Secretary of the Interior James Watt, Moral Majority's Rev. Jerry Falwell, and televangelist Rev. Pat Robertson.[14]

At this meeting, the concept of a "Love Lift" from the United States to Guatemala originated. This was to be an effort to collect food and money to accompany teams of ministers who would go to Guatemala to "diffuse" the situation there. The State Department subsequently pushed the idea, as did Pat Robertson on his 700 Club television program. Congressman Jack Kemp sent out letters on his congressional stationary soliciting support for the effort. Although the drive managed to raise only $1.5 million, it did flood the White House and Congress with tens of thousands of letters in support of the Ríos Montt regime. And Robertson declared that his organization was sending agricultural and medical technicians to Guatemala to help design "model villages" to house the thousands of refugees fleeing "communist terrorism."

Meanwhile, Ríos Montt continued with his religio-political sermons, claiming he was acting in the name of God and that he would "kill people legally." "Whoever is against the instituted government, whoever doesn't surrender, I'm going to shoot. It is preferable that it be known that twenty people were shot, and not just that twenty bodies appeared beside the road."[15]

As reports of refugees numbering in the tens of thousands fleeing across the Mexican border continued to mount, six U.S. reporters returned from a trip to Guatemala to blast Ríos Montt for his suppression of news from the countryside, while some congresspersons began to question the reliability of the Reagan administration's claims of improvements in the Guatemalan human rights situation.

By the beginning of June, the amnesty month, soldiers from Barillas began periodic visits to San Mateo, more confident and aggressive than they had been in more than eighteen months. They used rifle butts against the arms, legs, and backs of anyone possessing a watch not adjusted to daylight-savings time—*caudillo* Ríos Montt's one claim to "social progress." Fortunately, only a small minority of Mateanos possessed watches.

In early June, Ríos Montt dissolved his three-man military junta, named himself president, and fired the nation's 324 elected mayors, replacing them with his own appointees. He left no doubt that he and his Lord would rule as a sacred duality. He then announced that beginning in July, he would declare a six-month, emergency "state of siege." During those six months, the army would conduct a sweep of the country, code-named "Victoria 82," aimed at permanently wiping out the four guerrilla organizations and their support networks. The state of siege would give Ríos Montt the power to suspend the . right of habeas corpus, ban all political activity, grant the army the right to enter homes and offices without search warrants to arrest and try delinquents and "subversives" in military courts without judicial review, and impose the death penalty in cases of "subversion." All union activity was to be proscribed, and the public media would be forbidden to broadcast any information regarding subversive or counterinsurgency activities that did not originate in the army's public relations office. In other words, the informal practice of the Guatemalan Army simply became declared policy of the new government. The only apparent change was the suggestion that instead of summary, chaotic extralegal executions, secret military "legality" would order the executions. Ríos Montt's justification for the suspension of all civil rights under the state of siege was a non sequitur: "In ten years without a state of siege, we have lost 150,000 people," the president explained to the nation. "With the state of siege, all executions will henceforth be legal."

Few guerrillas saw the new government's promise of amnesty as a solution to the historical problems that had motivated them to take up arms in the first place. Furthermore, most felt that the amnesty offer was only a ploy to get them to identify themselves to the army and thereby become easy targets for its death squads.

Hennessey agreed with the guerrillas' assessment but, unfortunately, he did not go out of his way to say so to Milenario Pérez, the solemn public health promoter on Colonel Bolaños's ranch, San Francisco. Milenario was not among those who doubted Ríos Montt's sincerity. He had gone from house to house in his little village, convincing his neighbors that the only way to protect themselves against army attacks was to request a grant of amnesty from the new government. Ever since the guerrillas had forced his neighbors to provide their troops with meat from Colonel Bolaños's herd, Milenario was convinced that he and his neighbors were suspected of being guerrilla supporters. It was an impression he was determined to erase before the army exacted retribution. He did not realize, however, that by asking for amnesty, he was admitting, as far as the army brass were concerned, that he and his neighbors were part of the EGP support network.

In late June, just one day before amnesty ended, Milenario took a list of names of all residents in San Francisco to Colonel Hernández Catalán, the commandant of the Huehuetenango military base, and applied for Ríos Montt's promised indulgence. Those named on the list had never been involved in any guerrilla activity. The officer who accepted the list from the health promoter, Chief of Intelligence Lt. Colonel Terraza Pinot, was most gracious, thanking Milenario as he perused the Mayan names, nodding his head.

When Colonel Terraza finished scanning the list, he made a photocopy, folded the duplicate, and slipped it into his shirt pocket. The original went into the office file as his secretary finished typing a report of the interview. Terraza Pinot read the report of the interview, nodded, and asked Milenario to sign it. The health promoter did so without reading the document. To have done otherwise would have demonstrated an unacceptable lack of trust in the officer and would certainly have been counterproductive. The chief of intelligence then reached out and shook Milenario's hand, looking the Maya squarely in the eye, a seemingly friendly smile on his sharply boned face. "You have done the right thing, sir, asking forgiveness for your treasonable behavior and that of your neighbors. I'll see that my executive officer gets this list."

The health promoter left the army base relieved that he had been the beneficiary of such a pleasant reception, convinced that he had done the right thing. But Milenario Pérez would soon regret his ill-placed trust in Ríos Montt, Hernández Catalán, and Terraza Pinot when the hypocrisy of June's "amnesty" was followed by the awful brutality of July's state of siege.

Gen. Ríos Montt at the first press conference after his coup. He is flanked by two members of his junta, Gen. Maldonado Schaad (left) and Col. Gordillo Martinez (right). (© Jean-Marie Simon 2003)

Mario Sandoval Alarcón, organizer of the White Hand Death Squad and President of the MLN (National Liberation Movement) shown here with photos of his two heroes. (© Jean-Marie Simon 2003)

Nuns carrying the corpse of Father Juan Alonzo, murdered by a death squad in Chichicastenango, Quiché. (© Jean-Marie Simon 2003)

Soldiers checking on their handiwork, Nebaj, Quiché. (© Jean-Marie Simon 2003)

Chapter 30

Subversive Bibles and Civil Patrols

"Padre Ronaldo, Padre Ronaldo, *espérame*, . . . way fore mee." The Iowan smiled at hearing the thick Spanish accent as he turned toward the caller coming up behind him. The date was 30 June 1982 and Hennessey had been lost in thought as he walked down the long, cement-tiled corridor of the bishop's residence-cum-retreat-center in the provincial capital. He had gone to Huehuetenango to assist at the annual diocesan retreat, a weeklong series of spiritual exercises, motivational talks, and planning meetings held with the bishop and other priests from the Huehuetenango diocese. The speaker was Mario Tzoj, a slightly built, young Mayan priest, one of nine Indian men from Huehuetenango Province whom Maryknoll had helped to the priesthood during its forty years in Guatemala. Padre Mario was pastor of San Idelfonso Ixtahuacán, one of the more staunchly orthodox Catholic parishes in the department.

"What's up, Padre Mario?" Hennessey responded in English, encouraging his companion to practice his linguistic skills. "You look like you've just eaten too many serrano chiles."

"Speeek slowwly, Padre Ronaldo, not so fass!" the young priest grinned. "Better I speek to yoo een Spaneesh." Then, taking the Iowan by the elbow, Mario led his colleague down a side corridor bordered by a succession of small bedrooms, away from the sala where other priests had gathered. Turning serious, he continued in Spanish, "I need your opinion on something, Ronaldo. I've heard that there's a lot of trouble in San Mateo, that the EGP is making a strong push to enroll your people in its ranks. The same thing is happening in San Idelfonso Ixtahuacán and I don't know what to do about it . . . . Because I'm indio, the guerrillas think I should be on their side. And because I'm a priest, the ladinos and the military are watching me like *zopilotes*, like

491

vultures waiting to swoop down on a sick horse. I don't want to tell the people they cannot fight . . . . It's their right! But I don't want to tell them they can join the EGP . . . because I don't trust those *universitarios,* those university types who think they have all the answers. And I'm afraid that many people will use the cover of rebellion to settle personal feuds . . . . What are you telling your people?"

Hennessey stopped and looked into the black, intelligent eyes of his young colleague, seeing the same uncritical trust he encountered in so many of his Mayan parishioners. Feelings of flattery and frustration invaded him. "I cannot answer those questions for you, Mario," the Iowan answered, shaking his head. "I try not to tell our parishioners to fight or to refrain from fighting. I leave it up to the conscience of each one. They know better than I what sacrifices they can afford and are willing to make . . . . I just ask them to keep in mind the moral principles involved by asking pointed questions . . . . If you come down on one side or the other, you will be associated with whatever that side does. I just let them know that self-defense and the fight for their rights is not a sin, . . . and that I am sympathetic to their struggle."

"But it is so hard to answer the parishioners' questions," Mario said after a few moments of silence, "and to advise them to get involved in a struggle that is just. But it is one I know they will lose, . . . in which many will be mutilated and killed—including women and children—and in which their side will commit injustices as well."

"Mario, . . . we're all asking those same questions. Maybe we'll have some answers before the retreat is over. For me, I'm not afraid to tell the people the army is their enemy, . . . carefully, . . . but that doesn't mean I tell them to join the EGP!"

Had Hennessey known that later that same afternoon, Milenario Pérez, the health promoter from San Francisco ranch, would be approaching the gates of Colonel Hernández Catalán's general headquarters to ask for Ríos Montt's amnesty for himself and his neighbors, the Iowan would have realized that some of his parishioners, at least, had not absorbed his distrust of the army. And if he had known—he would later tell himself—he would have tried to dissuade Milenario from going through with his plan. Unfortunately, however, neither the Iowan nor the health promoter knew of the other's presence in the provincial capital.

The bishop's house, the site of the retreat, lent itself to spiritual ruminations, located as it was next to Huehuetenango's main cemetery. After six days of conferences, meditation, and prayer, the retreatants still had no unified position as to how they should respond to the civil war taking place around them. Some thought that they should minister only to those who had not chosen one side or the other so that they could maintain their public stance of neutrality. Others agreed with Hennessey that to be totally neutral in the face of uneven conflict was in reality to side with the more powerful. However, the Iowan found himself unable to clearly articulate a course of action that would translate that concept into practical unambiguous guidelines.

There was little doubt that the priests were strongly opposed to the army's strategy and tactics, and deeply offended by U.S. support for the counterinsurgency program. Most felt that the situation fulfilled the conditions enunciated by Pope Paul VI acknowledging the people's moral right to rebel. Still, several raised objections to the guerrillas' tactics and their lack of discipline. Others feared that an atheistic Marxist philosophy held many of the revolutionary movement's leaders in a mental straightjacket. Still others, including Hennessey, argued that Christian idealism was at least as important a force in the guerrilla movement as Marxism, and that the guerrillas' Marxism in any case was an analytical tool for understanding Guatemala's ills, not necessarily a blueprint for fighting a war or setting up a government.

Finally, after much discussion, the priests and bishop agreed on a single course of action: they would refuse to bless any military base, weapons, or army personnel. This was more than a symbolic refusal. Guatemalans of all social classes have a strong cultural commitment to clerical blessings for every significant occasion, a custom that embraces superstition for many, proper social behavior for some. The military was no exception. For months, the commandant in Barillas had been pleading, threatening, and trying to trick Father Bill Donnelly, the Barillas pastor, into blessing his base. Colonel Hernández Catalán had done much the same in Huehuetenango with Bishop Víctor Hugo Martínez. But both Donnelly and the bishop had resisted the pressure, believing that such blessings would be interpreted as public sanction of army criminality. Some priests felt that the diocesan-wide agreement to follow this example was mere "pussyfooting," while others opined that it was getting "too close to politics." Hennessey felt that the agreement represented moral progress of sorts, a subtle way of withdrawing legitimacy from the government, a commodity that the Church had only too willingly bestowed on a succession of oppressive dictatorships in the past for scant return.

The retreat completed, the Iowan left Huehuetenango for San Mateo on Saturday, 3 July, the third working day of Ríos Montt's month-long state of siege. A health promoter employed in the San Mateo parish hospital accompanied the priest. Hennessey was driving a secondhand Ford pickup, recently purchased to short-circuit the progressive breakdown in Huehuetenango's transportation system. In the back he carried several boxes of medicines and twenty-four boxes of bibles. He also had fifteen Timex watches in the glove compartment that he was to deliver to the pastor of Barillas. They were to be gifts for the parish's volunteer catechists.

The two men approached Chiantla, a dusty little town a scant six kilometers north of Huehuetenango whose inhabitants had a reputation for more than the usual quota of ladino arrogance and not a little anticlericalism. There they encountered a roadblock manned by twelve men armed with four carbines, several clubs, and twelve machetes. One of their number approached the priest's window and demanded to see his papers and search his cargo.

"Stay in the truck," the priest whispered out of the side of his mouth to his companion. "Don't get out unless I tell you to!"

Hennessey carefully opened his door and moving slowly, slid out of the pickup, greeting the men with a pleasant, "*Buenos días, señores.*" Only a few of the men responded, and they with a noticeable lack of enthusiasm. Turning toward the man who had demanded his papers, the priest inquired with feigned indifference, "Whose side are you fellows on?"

"We're the civil patrol here," was the curt answer. The speaker was a man in his late twenties wearing an old, torn jumper, a misshapen straw hat and silvered sunglasses that hid his eyes. The glasses still had the price tag glued in the upper right-hand corner, like the sticker-price left on the window of a new BMW. "We've got orders from President Ríos Montt to stop everyone to see that their papers are in order and to check for subversive weapons and literature. No exceptions! We're in a state of siege, you know!"

"That's great!" the Iowan answered, sticking out his hand to shake that of the speaker, evoking a quizzical look in return. "I'm a good friend of

President Ríos Montt and I'll tell him what a fine job you guys are doing. I'm sure he'll be pleased!"

Hennessey's response was an old ploy the priest had used to wiggle out of tight circumstances on many occasions. He had found early on in his missionary career that it was much more effective to claim a personal relationship with a powerful person than to appeal to principles of Guatemalan justice and law. His claims to such relationships, coming as they did from a priest and an American, were generally accepted as fact rather than the fiction they often were.

Some of the Chiantla patrollers were already in the back of the pickup opening boxes with happy abandon when they heard the priest's little fib. As if by command, the four of them stopped what they were doing, straightened up, and stared at Hennessey. Then, again in unison, they looked at their leader who, by this time, had taken the priest's outstretched hand and was now watching the Iowan's face, searching for a clue as to whether he was telling the truth or not. In any ladino statement, lying was always a strong possibility when testifying to the abilities or connections of the speaker. But the leader couldn't decipher the priest's expressionless face. Finally, with a shrug of his shoulders and a sigh, the patrol leader responded, "Sorry, padre, but orders are orders! No exceptions! Even for friends of the president!"

At that, the patrollers went back to searching the priest's cargo, but with a noticeable lack of their previous enthusiasm. After a few minutes of half-hearted searching, still not sure of Hennessey's relationship to Ríos Montt, the leader called off his men, handed the priest his papers, and waved him on with a just-in-case apology.

As he maneuvered his pickup over the switchback above Chiantla, Hennessey quickly discovered that every little settlement he passed had its own civil patrol, the first phase of Ríos Montt's state of siege plans. Most of the participants were armed with clubs and machetes backed by one or two old carbines, except for residents of Todos Santos—one of the most ethnically secure of all Huehuetenango's Mayan communities—who had not been allowed to possess a single firearm. At each roadblock, the patrollers looked through the priest's papers and cargo as their most literate member tried to pronounce the priest's name as it appeared on his documents. Numerous complaints spilled forth that Hennessey's name was written "in gringo," making it impossible to pronounce. But by comparing his picture on the documents and asking him to recite from memory the official number of his residency permit, they were sufficiently convinced of his identity to allow him to proceed.

Time and again, the Iowan, with the timing and straight face of a stand-up comic, invoked Ríos Montt's name and friendship before an audience who took his claim at face value. Not that they believed everything uttered by a priest, just that they could not afford the consequences of disbelieving in case he was telling the truth. He thereby prevented the patrols at most stops from dumping his clothes onto the road for inspection purposes. At one barricade, a patroller pulled a rattail file from the glove compartment and announced proudly that he had discovered "a subversive weapon." The priest walked over to the proud discoverer and closely scrutinized the tightly held tool. "A subversive weapon?" he asked, scratching his head, an exaggeratedly puzzled expression on his face. "How did that get in there?"

At that, the leader strode over and grabbed the file, and, with a disgusted look on his face, asked, "Haven't you ever seen a file shaped like this before?" He then demonstrated its function on the knife-edge of his machete, accompanied by the laughter of the other patrollers and the embarrassment of the finder.

At another stop, a small cylinder of propane gas was identified as a bomb. This time, however, Hennessey reacted with an expression of feigned terror, telling the patrol leader that he thought the cylinder contained liquid gas for his stove. When the patroller who had made the discovery refused to demonstrate how he thought the cylinder could be used as a bomb, the priest took a match and gave a quick, tension-relieving demonstration on the firewood-saving properties of propane gas stoves.

All told, it took the priest's vaunted farmer's patience, jocular explanations, and claims of friendship with powerful people to get him unscathed past twenty-three check points before he completed the 168 tiring kilometers between Huehuetenango and the town of Soloma.

Situated in a centralized valley in the eastern Cuchumatán Mountains, Soloma had a moderate climate that made the town an attractive home for scores of hard-nosed ladinos whose main occupation was the political control and economic exploitation of the municipality's Mayan majority. As a result of their numerical minority status, the ladinos felt that if they allowed the *indios* the potential for power represented by membership in their central civil patrol, it would be equivalent to asking for trouble. Instead, the authorities chose to name only ladinos to the central patrol roster, while obliging the Mayans to fill the ranks of patrols at the town's outskirts and in outlying villages. It came as no surprise, then, when Hennessey ran into his first, all-ladino blockade below Soloma's town plaza, each man heavily armed with a carbine or shotgun. Nor was the Iowan caught off-guard by the gleam that appeared in each patroller's eye when their leader held up the watches he had pulled from the glove compartment and demanded in his sternest voice, "Whose watches are these?"

"They belong to the padre in Barillas, *señor*," Hennessey responded politely. "They're for his catechists, . . . in gratitude for their voluntary service to the Church!"

"Where is the bill of sale? How do we know they're not stolen or they're not meant for the guerrillas?" the leader asked aggressively.

"I don't have the bill of sale because it never occurred to me that I'd need it," Hennessey responded, feigning injured pride. "Who would have thought that the honorable people of Soloma would accuse me, the pastor of San Mateo Ixtatán, of stealing watches, or of running supplies for the guerrillas?"

A look of doubt crossed the patrol leader's face as he tried to interpret the priest's remarks. But the air of seriousness that the Iowan exuded obliged the patroller to give credit to his statements. "No, no, padre!" the man answered, reflecting a basic principle of ladino culture, that is, the avoidance of directly insulting another unless responding to a prior affront. "I would never accuse you of stealing watches or running goods for the guerrillas. But perhaps somebody else stole them, or led you to believe they were not meant for the guerrillas. The government insists that we check everyone, you know."

"Ah, if that is the case, . . . then I'll just take the watches and be going," the priest responded, holding out his hand.

The leader drew back, holding the watches close to himself, like a child not wanting to share his candy. The covetous looks on his companions' faces had told him that he would not be quickly forgiven should he relinquish this newly found treasure. After assessing for a few seconds the priest's calm reaction and the anxious attitude of his own colleagues, the leader dropped all pretense that his interest concerned national security. "Look," the man said, "if you don't give us the watches, you're going to get yourself in serious trouble. We'll have to turn you over to the military commandant."

It was a threat ladinos often used against Mayans, knowing that dragging someone before the military could mean imprisonment, abuse, and sometimes torture and death.

"Then let's go!" Hennessey answered with an air of abandon—one that he would soon regret—climbing into the pickup's cabin, dashing the patrollers' hopes for a quick take. A look of frustration spread over the leader's face as he ordered four armed patrollers to climb in the vehicle's carryall along with the hospital assistant and a young Mayan boy the Iowan had picked up along the road. He then slid into the seat beside the priest and angrily thumped the stock of what Hennessey hoped was an unloaded shotgun on the floor.

When the group arrived at the town hall, commandeered as the army HQ, the patrol leader jumped from the vehicle to give a good imitation of a military salute to the commandant, a lieutenant, just exiting the building. Responding to the officer's curt inquiry, the leader denounced the priest for possessing a bag of "suspicious" watches with no sales receipt. The lieutenant glanced at Hennessey, took the proffered bag and began examining the watches as though he might find some clue to their suspicious nature written on their faces. "You are very perceptive, *patrullero*," he praised the leader. Then, ignoring the priest, he turned back toward the town hall while shouting in a high-pitched, nasal voice to his soldiers lolling inside to come and search the pickup.

Hennessey followed the officer into the building and quickly decided that his narrow face, large, hooked nose that resembled a hawk's beak, his close-set, brown eyes, and three-day growth of beard, was not a visage to inspire confidence. Whether his appearance was nature's way of signaling the makeup of the character within, or the personality had molded the physiognomy without, it was obvious that one complemented the other. The officer's unwillingness to sit down even to sign a paper and his unsettling tendency to issue all orders as high-pitched shouts were interpreted by Hennessey as indications that the lieutenant lacked a secure sense of his authority.

After some minutes, a sergeant came back to report that the pickup was filled with boxes of medicines but failed to mention the more numerous boxes of bibles. The impression conveyed, intentional or otherwise, was that the Iowan was carrying materials that were considered subversive, that is, medicines for the guerrillas.

"Those medicines are for the parish hospital in San Mateo," the priest hastened to explain. "Didn't you see the twenty-four boxes of bibles? I'm the Catholic pastor of San Mateo and those things are for my ministry."

"We shall see what kind of ministry you have," Lieutenant Hawk-nose snapped with what sounded like a sneer. "*Sargento,* run over to the rectory and get the parish priest over here on the double," he shouted. "I want him to identify this foreigner."

Five minutes later, Padre Gabriel, a Guatemalan ladino priest, showed up to verify Hennessey's identity and then quickly return to his rectory. In the meantime, the lieutenant had again gone outside and ordered his soldiers to unload all the Iowan's cardboard boxes and to search them. This meant setting the boxes on the muddy road and opening them in a light rain just beginning to fall. Hennessey thought that the medicines were going to create . his biggest problem, but it quickly turned out that the lieutenant was more concerned with the bibles.

"Have you heard of Padre Luis Pellecer," the officer asked, traces of a smirk playing around his lips, "The guerrilla priest who used to write inflammatory garbage for the subversives but now works for the government?" The lieutenant was referring to the priest with whom Hennessey had concelebrated the anniversary Mass for the victims of the Panzós massacre two years earlier. Pellecer had been kidnapped later from a Guatemala City street by the police, then paraded before television cameras with a drug-and-torture-altered personality. He denounced certain Church leaders and several groups of religious (especially his own brother Jesuits) of pervasive communism.

When Hennessey answered the lieutenant's question by acknowledging that he was familiar with Pellecer, the officer continued: "He told us that the bible containing the picture of Martin Luther King is a subversive bible. All your bibles have Martin Luther King's picture in them. This bible has deformed the word of God! Are you a subversive?"

Hennessey leaned back against his pickup, folded his arms across his chest, and pinched his bottom lip between his teeth. He was very careful to keep a stoic look on his face. "I've read this bible from cover to cover," the priest replied after waiting a few tense moments, "and I've never found anything subversive in it. And furthermore, I know for a fact that General Ríos Montt uses one of these same bibles . . . . You would hardly call the president a subversive, . . . would you?"

The lieutenant stretched his neck and rubbed his three-day growth of beard, looking straight at Hennessey's chest. "Well," he replied doubtfully, "we'll have to look into this matter . . . . You can take your bibles with you but you'll have to leave one with me so I can have it checked out with military intelligence in Huehuetenango . . . . Also, if these medicines are not for the guerrillas, . . . why else would you have them?"

"I've already explained that we have a parish hospital in San Mateo . . . and all hospitals use medicines," the Iowan responded, unable to keep a slight note of sarcasm from his voice.

The lieutenant looked at the priest's eyes for the first time to see if the note of irony he thought he detected was an intended insult. "In the future, you'll not be allowed to bring medicines up here unless you have prior written approval from the chief of intelligence in Huehuetenango."

During the discussions and search of the pickup, Hennessey's two passengers had slipped away, fearing that the lieutenant might find an excuse to arrest them. When the officer noticed their absence, he launched into a tirade, stomping back and forth, waving his arms, and claiming that since the older one, the hospital assistant had run away, he must certainly be a guerrilla.

Hennessey tried to make the officer's accusation seem ridiculous without causing the man to lose face. "He works with me in the parish hospital, *mi teniente*," the Iowan responded calmly. "He's there every day all day long. If he had sympathies toward the guerrillas, I would know it and would not allow him to work for the Church!"

"Look," the lieutenant shouted back, mistaking the priest's quiet tone for weakness, "I don't need you or anyone else to tell me who is a guerrilla or a guerrilla-sympathizer, and who's not! You bring both of them back tomorrow morning and I'll question them and decide where their sympathies lie."

Even before the officer had finished, however, the priest felt anger building within him and decided that it might serve his purposes to let it show. At the same time, he realized that he shouldn't go too far. "I've had enough of this foolishness," he replied in a firm voice. "I'm not bringing those two fellows back tomorrow morning, nor tomorrow afternoon, nor tomorrow evening, nor the next day, nor the day after that. They are not guerrillas and I'm not going to cooperate in a witch hunt." The Iowan spoke loudly enough for the soldiers nearby to hear, but pretended to ignore their presence, even as he noticed flickering pleasure in several pairs of eyes.

The commandant, a surprised look on his face, quickly shifted tactics. "I'm only trying to do my job, padre," he answered in a mollified tone.

Hennessey felt a glow of satisfaction that his offensive had worked. He had been prepared to shift, even make an apology, if his estimation of the officer's character had been mistaken. But his usually perceptive judgment, honed by hundreds of microdecisions on whether a given tense situation demanded a silly joke, a white lie, or a firm stand, proved to be right on the mark.

When the soldiers, following the lieutenant's orders finally piled everything back in the carryall with the exception of one bible, Hennessey asked for the watches.

"They're in with the other stuff, in a box in back," one of the men replied, staring at the ground.

"There were fifteen watches in the glove compartment when I drove up here. What are they doing now in a box in back?"

The lieutenant listened to the priest's question and turned to his men. "Search those boxes until you find the fifteen watches," he commanded, his voice rising to its usual high pitch.

The watches were quickly "discovered" in the first box searched. "How many watches did you say you had, padre?" the officer asked, again using his polite tone.

"There were fifteen watches when I left Huehuetenango, *mi teniente*. None of them were touched between there and here."

The lieutenant counted the watches and found only eight. He then called the soldiers inside and asked Hennessey to wait until he found the others. A few minutes later, he came out to say he'd been unsuccessful in his interrogation. The priest could tell by the look in his eyes that the officer knew exactly where the missing watches were. "Don't worry, padre," the lieutenant said, "I'll find them!"

The commandant then ordered his men to unload all the priest's boxes once again and make a more thorough search. Hennessey knew the missing watches would not be found and, wanting to forget the charade and move on, told the officer he was going to leave.

"Just a few more minutes, padre. I know we can find them."

In the end, no more watches were found. The officer, smiling, apologized for their loss, as well as for the three hours spent haggling over the medicines, bibles, the priest's passengers, and watches.

After assuring the officer that in the future he'd abide by the army's new requirements to obtain permission in Huehuetenango to transport all medicines and catechetical literature, Hennessey climbed into his pickup and closed the door.

The lieutenant stood nearby and smiled, "We shall meet again soon, padre. I hope our next meeting will be more pleasant than this one."

The Iowan tried to think of an appropriate response, but decided that silence was his most fitting answer. Without looking back, he cranked the pickup's engine, shifted into first, and slowly drove out of the darkening town.

As he drove, the priest reflected on his unpleasant encounter with the beak-nosed lieutenant. *I'm glad I'm through with that guy*, he mistakenly told himself. *He's going to bring a lot of grief to the Solomeros!*

The Iowan did not know then that while he had been trying to get permission from Lieutenant Hawk-nose to proceed to his parish, a cousin of one of the nuns at San Mateo was lying unconscious in a back room of the Soloma town hall. Earlier in the day, after some public drinking in the town plaza, the cousin had made a drunken remark about army cowardice. The statement eventually reached the lieutenant's ears. He then ordered his men to arrest "the guerrilla" and torture him, under the pretext of obtaining subversive information that the victim did not possess.

The priest would prove to be right about the grief to come. What he did not know was that as many Mateanos as Solomeros would be among the lieutenant's victims. He would find out soon enough, however, and when he did, it would be in the context of a scene that would torture his soul

Hennessey passed through several settlements and roadblocks before arriving at the next town, Santa Eulalia. There, the civil patrol, shivering in the cold night air at 8,000 feet, attempted to make him spend the night. The priest responded that he had to be in San Mateo for Sunday Mass, scheduled for early the next morning. The patrollers were unmoved by his plea. But when the Iowan protested that he'd report them to Soloma's military commandant who had just given him permission to proceed to San Mateo, they allowed him to continue. In Pet Valley, just beyond Santa Eulalia, the priest found the all-Mayan civil patrol even more determined that he spend the night with them. "Beyond here is guerrilla territory," they insisted, "and no one goes in there without our permission."

Hennessey was resolved to return home that night and noticed that the patrollers were armed with nothing more than machetes. He then used a maneuver that had proved successful on other nonthreatening occasions: jamming the pickup into first gear, he revved the engine to a high whine and then jumped the vehicle ahead about two feet. As the patrollers scattered, he sped off, yelling out the window that the commandant in Soloma had told him he could go through. It was after 11:00 p.m. when the priest finally reached home feeling more than a little tired. He went straight to bed. His usual five-hour trip from Huehuetenango to San Mateo had taken more than fourteen hours.

At 5:30 a.m. the next morning, Sunday, Hennessey was already up, dressed, and hunched over the sala table preparing his weekly sermon. His attempts to formulate some of the thoughts that he had entertained during the just-terminated diocesan retreat were interrupted by a soft, persistent knocking on the door. *Who wants to see me at this blessed hour?* the priest asked himself, ambling across the room. *It's not going to be good news, that I know.*

Cracking the door a few inches as if to let the unpalatable news barely ease in, Hennessey confronted Sister Francisca, a native of neighboring Soloma. Francisca's epicanthic eyes squinted at the Iowan in the semidarkness, her lips tightly closed, reflecting something less than the buoyant mood that was her normal disposition.

"Come in, Sister," the priest said, pushing the door wide, bowing, and making an elaborate sweeping gesture toward the table in a futile attempt to resurrect the nun's good humor. "You're just in time to help me with my sermon .... In fact, ... maybe you could preach for me? I'm sure you could do a better job than a tongue-tied gringo!"

Sister Francisca allowed the trace of a smile to touch her lips as she shook her head. Her serious mien and hesitant gait across the room told the priest that something was decidedly wrong.

Sitting with an untouched cup of steaming coffee, the nun swallowed, looked down at her hands folded on the table and began softly, "Padre Ronaldo, the soldiers took ten men yesterday and killed them on the road near Nucá. The mayor was looking for you last night. He wants you to take an official letter to the commandant in Barillas requesting information on the men." She then looked up and stared into the priest's eyes.

Hennessey sat watching the young nun. Francisca was twenty-eight years old, with the pronounced cheekbones and strong chin so characteristic of her Mayan people. True to her convent training, she did nothing to emphasize her femininity, but this only enhanced her natural beauty. Her simple account of the possible murder of ten townsmen was vintage Francisca, her face almost a mask of seeming indifference, indicative of her Mayan self-control. The priest knew he'd have to pull the details out of her one by one. And though he was in the middle of preparing his sermon, he decided to let his preparation go until later. Leaning across the table, he laid his hand on hers and squeezed lightly, asking, "How did it happen, Francisca? . . . Do you know the names of the ten?"

The nun hesitated as she looked down at the priest's large, hairy hand covering her own . . . . "About fifty soldiers came yesterday morning in four pickups from Barillas, padre," she answered quietly. "They set up a loudspeaker in the plaza and told everyone to come to listen. Sister Justa and I went out and heard the commandant say he wanted to form a new civil patrol here in San Mateo. He read a list of forty names saying these were the people he had chosen."

Hennessey waited. He had withdrawn his hand and had settled back in his chair to wait for Francisca to continue. After a minute or two more, he decided to prod her again. "But a civil patrol had already been formed here! The mayor told me last week that he had been ordered by the Barillas commandant to do so and had already named several groups . . . . I went through twenty-seven civil patrol checkpoints coming up from Huehuetenango and it was obvious that none of them had any military training."

The nun nodded, again looking the priest straight in the eye. "Everyone knew that forming a new civil patrol was just a trick, *padrecito*. The names the commandant read included the men who've been leading the fight against the Cuchumadera. He also named one woman, Fermina Nolasco. There were no ladinos on that list."

Again, Hennessey waited. He was almost too afraid to ask the identities of those the commandant had selected. Then, pushing a small stream of air through his lips, he queried, "Were Agape Toltz and Tomás Acún on the list? Or Santiago, or any of the catechists?"

Francisca's eyes narrowed, as if to hide any feelings she might be experiencing, and then dropped her hands to her lap. "Agape and Tomás were both on the list. But they weren't here so they didn't go. Santiago wasn't on the list. Pascual Tomás, your catechist from Ocuyá was named. He's dead!"

Hennessey sucked in his breath. "Pascual Tomás? . . . But he didn't lead the fight against the Cuchumadera! . . . So where do you suppose the Barillas commandant got his list of names?" Then, swallowing loud enough to hear a popping sound in his inner ear, the priest added, "But what makes you think they've all been murdered, Francisca?"

The nun opened her hands, palms upward, in a gesture of certainty. "But of course they're dead, padre! The whole town knows it! Some people saw it happen! We've gotten word that the soldiers arrived back in Barillas and no Mateanos were with them . . . . But their families are still afraid to retrieve the bodies . . . . It is said that Nicanor Mauricio, the ladino landowner, must have provided the list. Everyone on that list had difficulties with him when he lived here. A number of catechists have seen him going into the Huehuetenango army base. The list must have come from him and the commandant in Huehuetenango!"

The priest sat with his eyes closed, his lips pursing and relaxing intermittently. The nun waited without moving. Finally, Hennessey opened his eyes and asked, "Tell me how it happened, Francisca. Who were the ten? Maybe you could make a list for me later with the names of the other thirty. We have to protect them!"

"When the commandant repeatedly called out the names, others would glance at them. But they didn't mean to do it. There were a lot of people in the plaza by this time, hundreds. The soldiers could see who the people were looking at and asked them to identify themselves . . . . The soldiers treated everyone nicely. They even offered each man on the list a can of fruit juice. The commandant seemed upset, though, that only ten of the forty were present . . . . He told the men they'd have to accompany him to Barillas for special training . . . . Some of the men knew this was bad news . . . . You could tell by the way they said goodbye to their wives. Then they got in the trucks and were gone . . . . Now they're dead!"

Hennessey watched the nun's expressionless face. *If I had only been here,* he thought. *I could have complicated their plan—maybe even stopped them altogether . . . . But while I was discussing bibles in Soloma, those men were being carted off for execution . . . . I wonder if old Beak-nose had orders to detain me a few hours?*

The Iowan knew enough about the efficiency of the Mayan grapevine to know that the men were almost certainly dead. Bill Mullan, Hennessey's predecessor, had warned the anti-Cuchumadera activists that they were apt to lose both their lives and their trees if they continued to oppose the army. The first part of his prophecy was now coming to pass.

After he had lost a few minutes engrossed in a kaleidoscope of brutal images, Hennessey shook his head and rose from his chair. "Thank you, Francisca! You've made my sermon easier and at the same time more difficult. If you could make out a list of the ten dead and the other thirty as best you can, I'd appreciate it."

Francisca nodded, rose, excused herself, and was gone. It was now 6:00 a.m.

The Iowan pulled on an old sweater and left a few minutes later to visit the mayor in his makeshift storehouse-office where he held court since the guerrillas had burned the municipal buildings. As the priest climbed the cobblestone hill, he met the official coming down toward him. "Just who I was looking for," the mayor greeted Hennessey.

"Likewise," the Iowan answered as the two men shook hands, turned, and headed together up the hill. At the mayor's office, filled with the pungent odor of cardamom, the two sat for several minutes and just looked at each other, neither sure how to begin.

"Padre, I want you to do me a favor," the mayor finally sighed. "You've heard about what happened yesterday? We've received word that the ten men who went to Barillas with the soldiers have been murdered near Nucá. I haven't gone down there to check things out because it's outside my jurisdiction . . . . But these are our people! I have to do something! . . . Would you take an official letter from me to the military commandant in Barillas requesting information on the status of the men they took yesterday?"

Hennessey waited a moment, thinking, nodding his head. "If you know they're dead, *don* Pascual, why do you want to ask the commandant about their status? Won't that antagonize him? . . . You might get your name on his next list!"

The mayor stared at the priest. "I have an obligation to the families of those men, padre. If the commandant took them to Barillas for training, he shouldn't mind if I check on them, do you think?"

"If the commandant took them to Barillas simply for training, he wouldn't mind if you inquired about their status . . . . But you know he took them for other reasons. That they never got to Barillas! I think he will be upset if you inquire about them."

Pascual's wrinkled brow evidenced the doubt building in his mind as he rethought his plan in light of the priest's remarks. But as the mayor headed in the direction of Hennessey's thinking, the Iowan was reconsidering his own position. He decided that a formal letter to the commandant would at least force the officer into the uncomfortable position of having to justify the murders or lie to cover them up, maybe making him think second thoughts before going after the other thirty. "On the other hand, *don* Pascual, an official letter from you might stay the commandant's hand from going after the other thirty still on his list. Maybe, . . . if we both wrote letters? . . . To answer your question, . . . yes! I'll take your letter to the commandant. Let's give him something to think about! I'll put gasoline in my pickup and be ready to go right after the second Mass. Send your letter over just as soon as the town secretary writes it up and I'll put it in the Barillas commandant's hands before noon."

Before the mayor had a chance to express his newly acquired reservations, Hennessey stood up, shook the official's hand, turned on his heel, and went back to the rectory.

When the Iowan returned to the sacristy after the eight o'clock Mass, an empty-handed messenger from the mayor was waiting for him. Hennessey knew instantly that the official had changed his mind, but he couldn't blame the mayor for trying to protect himself.

"The mayor told me to tell you," the messenger ventured softly, "that he's grateful for your offer to take a letter to Barillas. But he and the town secretary have decided against it. He sends his thanks."

Hennessey put his hand on the man's arm. "That's all right! Tell the mayor I'm going to Barillas anyway to inquire about the missing men. I'm leaving after the ten o'clock Mass. If he changes his mind and wants to send a letter with me, that's fine."

The messenger nodded, shook the priest's hand, and left.

Waiting for the church bells to announce the ten o'clock Mass, Hennessey tried to compose in his mind what he'd say to the Barillas commandant. The

Iowan had no doubt that it was no coincidence that many of the men on the commandant's list were the very ones the army brass had threatened for their opposition to the harvesting of the Mateano's rain forest. Nor had the members of civil patrols from other towns and villages been taken to any army base for military training. And now, there were said to be eyewitness accounts of the slayings at Nucá, accounts that Sister Francisca, the mayor, and presumably the rest of the townsfolk believed. What was there left to say to the commandant except to point an accusatory finger? And to what end?

By the time the priest finished the ten o'clock Mass, he had decided that it was a useless gesture to confront the commandant in Barillas. Instead, he would write a document, describing the incident, including the names of the ten men who had accompanied the soldiers, and send it to Bishop Víctor Hugo Martínez in Huehuetenango. He would ask the bishop to take it to Colonel Hernández Catalán at the Huehuetenango base, and then publicize the colonel's response. Hennessey decided that it was more important that the high command realize that their actions were the object of public scrutiny than for the Maryknoller to make a trip to Barillas only to listen to a mendacious army captain protest his innocence by claiming that the ten had been attacked by guerrillas.

That afternoon, Hennessey spoke to the wives of several of the dead men and promised special prayers and a Mass for the deceased. The Iowan then composed a document to the bishop with all that he knew of the killings. He added the parish seal to the paper to make the document look important and create more impact with Colonel Hernández Catalán. The document went out the next day on the bus to Huehuetenango with a personal cover letter to the bishop.

Colonel Hernández Catalán refused to see Bishop Martínez for several days though the bishop had stated that the interview was "a matter of life and death." When the commandant finally received the prelate, Bishop Martínez not only told the officer about the San Mateo killings, but he recounted several similar incidents reported to him by other priests. The colonel replied with the cynical politeness mandated by military culture that he would "look into the matter."

Bishop Martínez left the officer's presence convinced that because the killings had been carried out simultaneously in several municipalities and because of the commandant's indifference to the bishop's accounts of the murders, the killings had been carried out under Hernández Catalán's personal orders.

About a week after the incident, Hennessey, returning in his pickup from Barillas, offered a middle-aged man a ride into San Mateo. After his passenger had extended a few expressions of gratitude and the two had exchanged encouraging estimates of the nascent corn crop's potential harvest, the priest made a slightly derogatory remark regarding the army's new atrocity. After a few moments of heavy silence, during which Hennessey thought he might have misjudged his passenger, the man replied softly, "I see them do it, padre. I be on the road near Nucá when I hear the trucks. I hide in the bushes because I know it be the soldiers. They stop in front of me and I see the whole thing."

By this time, the ten bodies, all with slit throats, had been buried in a common grave at the base of the ravine where they had been thrown. The body of Pascual Tomás, one of Hennessey's catechists from Ocuyá, was missing an arm. The victims' families didn't dare go near the scene of the crime to perform their rituals until they were sure the soldiers were not watching the area. It was common army practice to kill anyone who ministered to the body of a murdered "*subversivo.*"

"How did it happen?" the Iowan prodded gently, not wanting to frighten his passenger by giving the impression of excessive interest.

"The four trucks stop and the commandant order ten brothers to get down," the man replied. "He tell the soldiers to tie the brothers' thumbs behind. Pascual Tomás hit the soldier who tie him and knock him down. Other soldiers knock Pascual down . . . . The commandant be angry and he tell a soldier to cut off Pascual's arm with machete, . . . Pascual make noises but he not cry. This make the commandant angry. The commandant put knife in Pascual's throat. The soldiers knife the throat of other brothers, but no one cry. The soldiers throw the bodies in the ravine . . . . I be in the bushes for an hour. Then I come out."

Hennessey's heart wept for the men. The thought of a soldier hacking off Pascual Tomás's arm made him shiver slightly. *If only I had been here,* he whispered to himself. A futile reaction he found himself experiencing almost daily, it seemed. *I know I could have stopped them! They would have had to let the ten go—or to have killed eleven.*

The priest was beginning to understand the nature of Ríos Montt's state of siege. He wondered at the sheer cynicism of the president's repetitious piety, his bible-quoting radio and TV sermons, his promise that "there will be no more murdered people on the roadsides; anyone who acts against the law shall be executed. Let's have no more murders. We want to respect human rights and defend them."

By this time, 10 July 1982, the army had murdered seven priests; eight if one includes the almost certain murder of Father Bill Woods in November 1976. The Iowan began to ponder the possibility that he, too, in the days ahead might face the same fate. He prayed that if that happened, he might have the grace to meet his Maker with the same courage shown by his parishioners, . . . and by his gentle friend, Archbishop Romero. And for a few moments, the thought of his own passing seemed to hypnotize and assuage his sorrow. But the rough road demanded his full attention and he quickly recognized the morbid thought for what it was: moral weakness, a longing for an easy exit from this personal purgatory.

"This is not the time for self-pity," the priest said half aloud.

"*Perdón, padre?*" his passenger answered.

Hennessey shrugged and remained silent.

Chapter 31

THE CIVIL PATROLS IN ACTION

It was four weeks into the Ríos Montt *golpista* government and the solitary figure standing in the portal of the old colonial church in Nebaj was totally alert, glancing from side to side, observing all that was going on in the dusty . plaza in front of him. His dissimulated concern for security was obvious. He had protected his back with the temple's huge, tightly shut, ancient doors directly behind him. No one could have opened the wooden monsters from the inside without their pivot-and-socket, cast iron hinges screaming a warning to everyone within a hundred feet. And it was doubtful that a bullet from anything other than a high-powered rifle in the hands of an enemy entering the building through the small sacristy side door could have breached their massive structure from the inside. Nevertheless, the bulletproof vest he wore and periodic, sideways shifts of a few feet in his position—ostensibly to obtain a better view of the quasi-festive events transpiring before him— provided additional security guarantees.

The man was dressed as a combat soldier in a baggy, camouflaged jungle uniform with black, laced, mid-calf field boots. He carried no visible weapons, but the bulges in the large thigh pockets signaled that he packed one or more prophylactic side arms either within or under his field jacket. The uniform wore no name, rank, or identification of any kind. A camouflaged cap had been pulled down over his dark eyebrows, its peak sitting on the rim of smoked sunglasses, protecting his eyes from the blazing tropical sun as it obscured the direction of his vigilant gaze. A swarthy complexion, field jacket sleeves rolled up above the elbows, his stance—fists on hips and legs spread wide like that affected by all Guatemalan commanders—further obscured his identity, while projecting an image of raw strength, perhaps a touch of arrogance, intended to intimidate.

Not more than three or four of the several thousand people in Nebaj's plaza that day knew that that solitary individual was not a Guatemalan officer, but Major George Maynes, military attaché at the U.S. Embassy and head of the U.S. Military Assistance Group (MAG) stationed in Guatemala. His job was to advise the Guatemalan Army in its ongoing program of developing, implementing, and analyzing "irregular warfare" tactics and strategies employed against revolutionary guerrillas, their supporters and suspected sympathizers.

The date was 22 April 1982 and Maynes was in Nebaj to observe the inauguration of the town's first Patrulla de Autodefensa Civil (Civil Defense Patrol, or PAC),[1] a strategy that the MAG had been pushing the Guatemalans for years to implement. And it was just as well that Maynes could pass as a Guatemalan. Nebaj was a center of EGP activity and influence, and if the guerrillas caught the U.S. military attaché overseeing the inauguration of a new phase in Guatemala's counterinsurgency campaign aimed primarily at the country's Mayan majority, the EGP would possess a propaganda bonanza of limitless possibilities, to say nothing of the risk to Maynes's health.

Maynes's presence at the ceremony was not an idle one. The PAC strategy was modeled on the pacification programs the United States had developed and employed with more than a little success during the Vietnam War. Both the Pentagon and President Reagan's State Department wanted Guatemalans to learn the lessons of Vietnam. William Colby, who would later become director of the Central Intelligence Agency, had developed the CIA's Phoenix Program in Vietnam, a strategy for eliminating the Viet Cong infrastructure by using civilian assassination teams, the Provincial Reconnaissance Units (PRU). The Civil Operations and Revolutionary Development Support Program (CORDS), financed and directed by USAID, had a broader pacification mandate than the CIA's. It relocated whole villages out of "free-fire zones" and into "strategic hamlets"; it also included the development of assassination squads, maintaining executive deniability by talking about "neutralization," and looking the other way while paid Vietnamese "employees" did the dirty work.[2] The axis of all these programs and tactics was that "those who are not with us, are against us. No neutrals allowed."

Assistant Secretary of State for Inter-American Affairs Thomas Enders agreed with his opposite numbers at the Pentagon that the Central American governments needed something akin to the Phoenix Program. So he appointed

L. Craig Johnstone, a man with no Latin American experience, as his director of Central American and Panamanian Affairs, with the rank of deputy assistant secretary of state. Johnstone had been director of evaluations for William Colby and the CIA in Vietnam. Ron Hennessey's and Craig Johnstone's paths would cross some months later in Guatemala, but neither one would accurately read the footprints of the other. Enders himself was adept at playing double-blind games, having been deputy chief of mission in the U.S. Embassy in Phnom Penh charged with overseeing Richard Nixon's secret illegal bombing of Cambodia during the Vietnam War.

Captain Jesse Garcia of Superior, Arizona, a Green Beret with Vietnam experience, was a member of Maynes's team. The Pentagon officially listed him as an English teacher at the Politécnica—in order to sidestep the continuing congressional ban on military aid to Guatemala. In reality he was teaching the cadets antiguerrilla warfare—"anything our army has," he told Alan Nairn, a stringer for the *New York Times* and *Washington Post*. Garcia confessed to Nairn that the Guatemalans were very interested in Vietnam, and "I tell them we had the firepower to win the war but were not allowed to use it politically." When Nairn asked Garcia if there were any limitations to what he could teach the Guatemalans, he answered, "Negative! The embassy doesn't tell me anything." The captain's instruction program included teaching the Guatemalans how to conduct "destruction patrols," wherein the troops would use "gunfire, artillery, explosives or aerial bombardment to destroy equipment, destroy bridges, destroy towns."[3]

Maynes's PAC strategy was simple: to force every male between the ages of sixteen and sixty to participate in a civil patrol for at least twenty-four hours each week. Their duty would be to maintain vigilance in their communities and denounce any strangers and/or unusual activities; to obligate PAC members to actively assist the army in hunting down guerrillas, their supporters, and their sympathizers; and to oblige PAC members to eliminate such people or be executed as subversives themselves. In other words, the PACs were to be a control strategy aimed at civilians rather than a strategy to fight the guerrillas. And the civilian population was to be forced to assist the army in its atrocities and thereby become accomplices in conscience and in fact.

The plan meant the militarization of the entire countryside, setting community against community, family against family, neighbor against neighbor. If one did not see suspicious persons and/or activities and take appropriate action in the area where the guerrillas were known to be active, it would be assumed that such individuals or communities were themselves involved in subversion. No law was passed to mandate the establishment of the PACs. By avoiding their legalization, the fiction could be maintained that the civil patrols were voluntary organizations. A lack of legal status also enabled military authorities to force the PACs into illegal and unconstitutional operations without any executive accountability. If guerrillas killed the patrollers, popular wrath against the revolutionaries could be expected. If PAC members themselves killed some guerrillas or their supporters, all the better, according to army strategists. If neither scenario developed, then those on the surrounding stage were left under the suspicion of being subversives and were fair game for "destruction patrols."

A secret five-page document called the "National Plan for Security and Development," elaborated a week after the Ríos Montt coup, and a subsequent addenda labeled "Appendix H" to the "Victoria 82 Campaign Plan" spelled out the military's plans for the PACs. Listed under "Strategy" is the following: ". . . to deny the subversives access to the population who constitute their social and political support base" and "to annihilate the Clandestine Local Committees (CCL, or guerrilla support networks) and the Permanent Military Units (UMP) of the enemy."[4]

Outlined under "Tactics to be employed" was a simple four-point program: (1) Trick them: A Plan of Disinformation must be in effect at all times. (2) Find them: Use local intelligence and saturate the area with patrols. (3) Attack them: When you have succeeded in locating a guerrilla force, maintain contact at all costs and immediately inform your command so that a larger unit can help you annihilate the enemy. (4) Annihilate them: Destruction of guerrilla forces is your mission."[5]

Major George Maynes went to Nebaj for several reasons, not the least of which was that Nebaj had been the place where two years earlier Colonel Lobos Zamora had executed sixty innocent men in reprisal for a guerrilla attack on the town's army base that resulted in the deaths of eighteen soldiers. Maynes came to witness and officially give Washington's blessing to the inauguration of the PACs. It was both a calculated risk and a signal of things to come. His presence clearly indicated that the executive branch of the U.S. government unconditionally supported the PAC strategy with all its unethical implications, and that counterinsurgency and human rights were considered to be two contradictory goals. For the time being, at least, human rights were to be honored only in denials of responsibility for violating them.

The inauguration ceremony provided the military attaché a few lighter moments, but he had dealt with Guatemalans long enough to know that to demonstrate any sign of amusement would be a terrible breach of proper decorum. After the Nebaj military commander had handed out some old Winchester rifles and a few hand grenades to the men in the first row of participants—for the benefit of the press photographers in the audience—a few uncoordinated thrusts and parries to the accompaniment of a chorus of uninspired grunts showed that the patrollers had little to no experience handling firearms, and even less enthusiasm for the drill. The rest of the participants were armed with nothing more than clubs and machetes, an admission of the army's recognition that more than a few patrollers were probably sympathetic to the revolutionary movement, and that some, perhaps, had even participated in its military units.

Next, one of the town's more energetic schoolteachers orchestrated an out-of-sync, interminable rendition of Guatemala's national anthem sung by a minority of the patrollers. Most of the Ixil-speaking Maya knew few of the ten stanzas, although the first grade of public schooling for Indians was generally devoted to teaching little else. Meanwhile, the commandant strode back and forth, shooting stern, reproachful looks at mumbling choristers, men who quickly responded with animated mouthings that had nothing to do with the anthem, but which pleased the officer.

"Miss Civil Patrol," a local ladina teenage beauty, then took center stage and followed with a motivational, cliché-riddled speech—probably written by the commandant—delivered in a soft, hesitant monotone. She encouraged her patroller-brothers to defend the motherland and to depend upon the support of their wives, sisters, and daughters in doing so. A ten-second silence followed the talk before anyone realized that Miss Civil Patrol had nothing more to say. Only then did her audience reward her with applause a little less enthusiastic than her own delivery.

A public admission of guilt and repentance was next on the program. A terrified group of "ex-guerrillas" apologized to the commandant and their fellow townspeople for allowing themselves "to be fooled by the lies of the subversives." They promised that they would not rest until they had helped rip "this foreign sickness" from the soil of the motherland.

The final act was a scene that seemed to have been lifted from an Albert Camus novel: the presentation to the commandant by a nervous patroller of a rifle and some blood-stained clothing said to have been taken from a dead guerrilla, the first casualty of the town's dramatic shift in loyalties. The ceremony ended with the ritual burning of an EGP flag and an orchestrated series of "*Qué Vivas*" for Guatemala, its army, and its civil patrols.

When the commandant went over to Major Maynes to escort his guest back to the local command post, the ceremony's participants began drifting out of the plaza. As the two men walked, the Guatemalan put his arm across the shoulders of the attaché, a *compadre*-like gesture of camaraderie and appreciation. The embrace was symbolic of the union between the two men's armies, even though its form of expression made the American uncomfortable.[6]

San Mateo Ixtatán, Huehuetenango.
Second week of July 1982

The rapping on the rectory door was firm and insistent, contrasting sharply with the nonchalant attitude affected by the burly visitor who greeted Hennessey when the Iowan answered the knock. It was early afternoon, only ten days into Ríos Montt's state of siege; rain clouds were pushing in from the northwest. "Padre Ronaldo," Abelardo Valenzuela murmured, trying to control the undertone of concern in his voice, "the Ixbajau civil patrol captured three guys from the east side of town this morning and they're accusing them of being guerrillas. The mayor has all three in jail now. The Ixbajauans want him to turn them over to the army!"

Hennessey nodded slightly, acknowledging the implied warning. "Are they really guerrillas, Abelardo?" the priest asked, leaning against the doorframe.

"You know the Ixbajauans, padre!" the ex-soldier replied with a grimace. "They said they found half a dozen dirty coffee cups on the table of the house where the three were talking. For them, six people drinking coffee together is proof that a guerrilla meeting was going on just before they arrived."

"Pfff! That's going to put a crimp in my style," the priest replied, nodding toward some dirty coffee cups on his sala table . . . . I'll go talk to the mayor.

If Pascual hangs on to those fellows for long, the soldiers are bound to pass through and that will be the end of them."

"Pascual trusts you, padre." Abelardo replied, a look of relief lighting up his face. "I don't think he wants to hang on to these guys on such flimsy evidence, but he's afraid to let them go."

"Is the Ixbajau PAC still up there?" the Iowan asked, nodding toward the plaza. "I don't want to appear on the scene while they're still there. The Ixbajauans are not very fond of me and their PAC will probably try to block anything I might suggest to Pascual."

"I'll go back and look, padre. But it's best that I not be seen coming down here again. I'll ask Santiago to keep an eye on the *juzgado*, and when he sees me come to the door, that's a signal that the PAC has left and he can let you know it's okay to come up."

Hennessey nodded his agreement and turned back toward his desk as Abelardo headed for the mayor's office. Five minutes later, Santiago Quot put in an appearance to tell the priest that the coast was clear.

On his way to the *juzgado*, Hennessey observed that the approaching clouds would dump plenty of rain on the town within the half-hour. *Thank God!* He breathed in gratitude. *Should keep the soldiers in Barillas for the afternoon.*

As the Iowan entered the makeshift, poorly lit office and stood just inside the door, he saw a group of five town elders already discussing with the mayor the consequences of turning over the three prisoners to the soldiers. One or two voiced concern that the mayor was setting a precedent whereby many others could be accused on equally flimsy or nonexistent evidence. Hennessey was pleased by the tone of the discussion as he waited to be acknowledged.

When the mayor stood and leaned across his desk, extending his hand, the priest approached, exchanged greetings, and took advantage of the opening: "Excuse me, *señor alcalde!* . . . I, too, am concerned with what will happen if these men are handed over to the soldiers. If they're guilty of feeding the guerrillas, and that's not been proven, . . . then so are many others . . . . Nobody can refuse them!"

The nodding heads around him reassured the priest that he had selected an appropriate line of argument. He went on: "And even had they willingly done what they're accused of, such an act is not deserving of death! . . . If we start to side with the army, everyone's grudge will turn San Mateo into one huge cemetery."

No one answered. No one wanted to step out in front of the others without being sure of consensus. Finally, one of the elders, gauging the looks of agreement on the faces of his colleagues, spoke up: "I agree with Padre Ronaldo. If we accuse our brothers that they be guerrillas, we have a mountain of killings that nobody stop . . . . We punish those who do wrong. We not need the army to punish our brothers. Remember what the soldiers do last year! . . . I say we give the prisoners ten strokes and send them home."

"Eso es! Está bien!" a chorus of voices chimed in as the mayor looked around, assuring the agreement of all those present.

"If that's what you want, I agree," the official responded slowly. "But if there be problems, . . . we all say that this be a decision made by the whole *pueblo.*"

"Está bien! Está bien!" the elders responded, each one nodding his agreement.

The mayor looked at Hennessey. "I keep them in jail until tomorrow, padre. The Ixbajau PAC be angry if I let the prisoners go now. It be starting to rain . . . . We not be seeing any soldiers this afternoon!"

"That's fine, *don* Pascual," the priest answered relieved. "Whatever you and the *principales* think . . . . Just make sure the three men are not in jail when the next truckload of soldiers comes through."

With that, Hennessey went around the room, offering words of encouragement. He knew, as well as they, that each one was taking a very serious risk—with life or death consequences. Then, grateful for their stoic courage, he turned on his heel and went back to the rectory.

The following day, about mid-morning, Santiago Quot arrived breathless at the rectory to tell Hennessey that the mayor had released the three detainees but that some Protestant townspeople were angry with the priest for having been instrumental in winning the prisoners' freedom. "Nobody think they should die, padre," the old man explained, twisting his felt hat in his hands as he stood by the sala table. "But some be afraid that when *el comandante* hear about them getting away, he be killing others in their place . . . . One of the prisoners be *un evangélico* and people from his church be afraid the soldiers kill all *evangélicos*. They say it be better that one guy be killed than their whole assembly be dead."

"Well, they can always blame me if it comes to that," the Iowan answered. "Anyway, maybe the Ixbajauans will think again before making any more unsubstantiated accusations. Anybody can do the same thing to them."

"I hope you be right, *padrecito!*" the old man answered. "Still, . . . you be careful. We not want anything bad happen to you!"

"Don't worry about me, Santiago," Hennessey replied with a smile, touched by the sacristan's concern. "The soldiers won't hurt a gringo," he continued, not sure that he believed it himself, "not while they want my government's help . . . . As for the *evangélicos* and Ixbajauans, they're good people! . . . None of us know what wrongs we are capable of until we are trapped by our own beliefs and fears!"

"We know, padre," sighed the old man, "but now we have another problem, . . . the same as yesterday. The mayor has three more brothers in jail that some say are guerrillas and he be afraid to let them go because of the *evangélicos'* anger. I think he already call the military base in Barillas to tell the *comandante* he has them."

Hennessey took a couple of deep breaths before replying. "So here we go again! . . . I wonder if Pascual called Barillas before talking to me in order to pre-empt my interference? I thought we had some kind of ongoing agreement firmed up yesterday . . . . I'd better talk to him again."

The sacristan did not reply as Hennessey rose, stretched himself, and headed for the door.

As he crossed the plaza, the Iowan had to thread his way through about seventy-five *capixay*-clad men standing around in seven or eight groups, all talking animatedly. He recognized immediately that some kind of important powwow was going on, that the town's consensus-building apparatus had been called into action. The priest's face reflected the surprise he felt that the process had developed to this stage without his having heard about it. As he passed each assemblage, one or two men, generally orthodox Catholics, would turn to shake his hand. And although curious as to the significance of their presence, the Iowan did not stop to ask.

In the mayor's office, eight men stood in front of the official's desk listening to Pascual discourse on some subject. As soon as he noticed the priest, the mayor stopped talking and stood to receive him. "This time it not be easy, padre!" Pascual told the Iowan after the two men exchanged greetings. "Two of these guys be recruiters for the guerrillas and everyone be knowing it. The other one be from Sebep. He be picked up this morning passing through Timacté and not have reason to be there. The Timacté PAC say he collect food for the EGP and they now get even with the EGP for the murder of the five guys for that rape crime. They not be letting him go."

Then, lifting his hands, palms up, the mayor spread his fingers wide to indicate he had nothing to give. "What can I do, padre? There be much anger for this morning's release. The Timacté PAC make me call the base in Barillas. Some soldiers be here shortly."

"Look, *don* Pascual," the priest answered softly, trying to calm the mayor, "I know you're in a difficult position and it's not fair to ask you to take sole responsibility for handing over these men to the soldiers, or letting them go free . . . . But you can always tell the commandant that I insisted that it was God's will to free the prisoners . . . . That way, he can blame God and me. What do you think?"

Pascual began to massage his chin, looking doubtfully first at Hennessey and then at the men around him. "I not know, padre," the mayor answered a bit plaintively. "I not think the commandant believe you speak to God, . . . the *pueblo* do."

Hennessey smiled at the mayor's polite little lie. "That's like something I'd say, Pascual . . . . Well, why don't we ask the men in the plaza what they think we should do? Then you would be acting in the name of the whole *pueblo*, God, me, the U.S. government—and the commandant would be left standing alone."

"Well, that's why we be here, padre," one of the men near the mayor interjected. The eight had been watching the priest and the mayor while the two men dialogued. The individual who had spoken was an orthodox Catholic, a friend of the Iowan's. "Those men in the plaza all be with us. The eight cantons of the town be present out there. We come together because of the blame and arrests . . . . We not know how to stop it, . . . but if we don't, we be going to have another massacre here in town, . . . like last year! . . . Maybe the soldiers be killing us all, anyway . . . . If so, we all go together with our ancestors."

Hennessey smiled at the speaker. "I should have known, *don* Pedro, that you would be right here with these other men looking for a way to put a stop to these accusations before everybody is pointing a finger at somebody else. We can't let *don* Pascual stand alone. You may think these prisoners deserve to be punished for helping the EGP," the priest went on, "but they certainly don't deserve to die! And if you turn them over to the army, we know we are sending them to their deaths . . . . The same thing could happen to any one of us tomorrow. Maybe it will anyway, like you say."

As he spoke, the priest looked methodically from one man to the next to emphasize that his remarks were meant for each of them, individually. "I suggest that if you think the prisoners deserve punishment, you should punish them according to your traditions . . . . But don't give them up to the army to be tortured and murdered! And when the soldiers arrive looking for the prisoners, just point to the cemetery. There are plenty of fresh graves there. Let them think the PACs have already killed them."

After some moments of thoughtful silence, *don* Pedro addressed the mayor. "I be agreeing with Padre Ronaldo! We each be speaking to men from our own canton and be hearing what they say. If everyone agree, we do it! That be closing the mouths of those who be wanting these men killed."

The speaker looked at each of his companions, urging an affirmative answer by nodding his head to each one, getting the answer he sought in return.

"What do you think about my going out and explaining to each group what we are thinking," the Iowan volunteered. "But only if you want me to, . . . if you think it would help."

"*Está bien*, padre!" a second man answered. "You do it! We be listening to what our neighbors say!" Six other heads nodded in agreement.

A minute later, Hennessey was out in the plaza, going from group to group, repeating the arguments he had made in the mayor's office. Each assemblage listened to him with silent respect, making no commitment until he had left to talk to the succeeding group. After speaking to the last gathering, the Iowan headed for the rectory to let the men deliberate without the weight of his presence causing interference.

Forty-five minutes later, Santiago Quot appeared again at the rectory door, a big smile deepening the creases on his very wrinkled face. "Well, you do it, *padrecito!* They like your idea! They let Gaspar from Sebep go, but they beat the two recruiters with hoses. They both be in the parish hospital now. When the soldiers came and ask where the prisoners be, everybody point to the cemetery, just like you say. The *pintos* laugh, climb in their trucks, and go to Barillas."

Hennessey was already heading for the hospital as Santiago finished his account of events in the plaza. When the priest saw the two ex-recruiters lying on their sides on the floor, their shirts and pants stained with fresh blood, he grimaced and swore to himself that he would not readily recommend traditional punishments again, at least not without some ironclad guarantee of limits. "Can you handle this, Sister Justa?" the priest asked the young nun as she began to cut away the two men's outer garments. "Do you need any help in lifting them into their beds?"

"No, *padrecito,*" the young woman replied. "I've got plenty of help here. Don't worry! . . . I don't think they're as badly off as they seem."

The Iowan took another look at the beaten men on the floor, glanced at the nun, and shook his head. He turned and went back to the rectory.

Later that same afternoon, Abelardo Valenzuela was again at the rectory door. Hennessey was sitting at a desk at the far end of the sala copying into the parish records the names of a dozen couples who had committed themselves to receiving the sacrament of matrimony during a parish fiesta to be celebrated in August. "You're not going to believe this, padre," the ex-soldier told the priest in an exasperated tone as Hennessey came over to greet him, "but those *hijos de su madre* . . . (sons of their mother—equivalent to sons of bitches) in Ixbajau went right back and arrested more people this noontime. Probably just to show everybody they're not going to allow anyone to interfere with their PAC activities."

The priest sat down at the table just inside the door and folded his hands, trying to hide his frustration. "Who did they arrest this time?" he answered slowly, trying to communicate calmness and take the edge off his friend's anger.

"They arrested that homely guy from Yacá who the guerrillas strung up last year. You remember, Juan Silvestre? He was Yacá's *contratista* for the plantation owners. They even got help from the Yacá PAC."

"Juan Silvestre?" the priest answered, startled, sucking in his breath. "Why Juan Silvestre? He's no supporter of the guerrillas! He could hardly talk when I went out to see him right after the hanging. Just two weeks ago I was in Yacá and celebrated Mass in his house. He told me then that he thinks the soldiers are bad because the government forces them to be that way, but that the guerrillas are bad because they want to be . . . . What do the PACs have against him?"

Abelardo's emotion made him ignore the priest's question. "They also got one of his sons, along with a guerrilla from San Sebastián Coatán. They caught the Sebastianero in Juan's house. Now it looks like they're going to kill all three. Juan's wife just came in to tell the mayor. Judging from the mayor's reaction, I'd say he's not going to do anything about it. I guess he doesn't want to risk the Ixbajauans going directly to the commandant."

"*Gracias,* Abelardo," the priest answered, stepping around his friend without waiting for more information and heading out the rectory door toward the mayor's office. Hennessey did not have to be a diviner to know that unless he continued to press the mayor, the town *principales*, and any leaders from the cantons and villages whom he could reach, the commitment to rein in the PACs that he thought he had negotiated would be quickly turned on its head.

A look of embarrassment crossed the mayor's face when the priest walked into his office. "Padre," the official protested before the two men had finished shaking hands, "I know why you be here. The civil patrols obey the army. I not have authority over them! I be taking a risk if I release prisoners here in the town jail. But I have no authority to be releasing captives held by a civil patrol out in a village. There be nothing I can do for Juan Silvestre and the others!"

Hennessey leaned on the edge of the mayor's desk, bringing his eyes down to the level of the official's. "Look," the priest answered calmly, but in a firm voice, "I don't know why the Ixbajau and Yacá PACs are going after Juan Silvestre and his son, but I do know that the Silvestres are not supporters of the guerrillas. You know that the EGP hung him for hours last year *because* he used to work as a *contratista* for the plantation owners and for the army as a *comisionado militar* . . . . This arrest is just to get even for personal reasons. If you leave him, his son, and the Sebastianero out in Ixbajau, the PACs will kill them. And . . . you . . . can't . . . allow . . . that!"

The mayor studied Hennessey's determined face for some moments, hoping to deflect the priest's moral intensity. After a few seconds, he answered,

"I not know how much of this *historia* you know, padre, but it not be easy to do what you say. Juan's wife tell me that this morning some folks from Ixbajau recognize an EGP guerrilla from San Sebastián Coatán when he walk the trail near their village. The Ixbajau PAC chase him to Yacá. The *muchacho* go to hide in Juan Silvestre's house. Juan's wife say that Juan try to get the *muchacho* out but the PAC get there before he be doing it. If Juan not support the EGP, why the guerrilla run to his house? You remember, Juan be the EGP tax collector in Yacá for a year.

"Come on, Pascual, you know that Juan didn't have any choice in the matter. The guerrillas threatened him! He didn't want to be on their side. And what does the PAC have against his son?"

"I not know why the PAC be against his son," the mayor answered, a little flustered. "But I know his daughter, Axul, be in the mountains with the EGP during three months. So maybe the son be with them, too! The PACs listen to the army, not to me! You be talking to the patrollers, . . . or to the soldiers!"

"Pascual," the priest responded, lowering his voice even further, "we've been friends since I came here. I've always admired you for the respect you've won from your people. You're a fine leader and the people of Ixbajau and Yacá respect you. They'll listen to you! Why don't you just send some *regidores* out to Yacá right now to bring in Juan and the other two, and tell the patrollers that you're going to turn their prisoners over to the army?"

Again the mayor studied Hennessey's face. He could tell by the upward thrust of the priest's angular chin that the Iowan was not going to back down. "*Está bien*, padre! I send some *regidores* to Yacá to bring the prisoners here. But I think the Ixbajauans not listen to me. They be hearing I release three men they bring in yesterday and three more this morning. And when they be here, I not be able to let their prisoners go!"

"Thank you, Pascual! Let me know when the prisoners get here. I'd like to talk to them. Also, if any patrollers from Yacá or Ixbajau come in, I'd like to speak to them as well, . . . if you don't mind."

The mayor nodded and stood up. Hennessey straightened, shook his hand, and returned to the rectory, knowing that the struggle to save the men's lives had just begun. The priest had already accepted the fact that in terms of the local picture, events were spiraling out of control and his most effective activity would be to try to save as many individual lives as possible. *Will the mayor again accept yesterday's suggestion to administer a lesser punishment and then set the men free? But what punishment? Another ten strokes with a rubber hose? Or twenty, or thirty? And how many times will the mayor be able to hide his action from the army, if he does cooperate again? . . . I've got to talk to the leaders of all the PACs.*

While Hennessey discussed his doubts with Abelardo, who was still waiting in the rectory sala, the mayor was only minimally executing the priest's plan. In the late afternoon, he dispatched a single *regidor* to Yacá to escort the three prisoners back to San Mateo. But apparently the mayor's instructions were not explicit enough—perhaps intentionally so—since they were not fully understood by the *regidor*, or else the *regidor* decided on his own authority that it was not in his best interest to try to exert any influence over the Ixbajauan and Yacá PACs. In either case, the mayor's delegate informed the leaders of the two civil patrols that they should take their prisoners to San Mateo the following day, but not before he had described for them the extent of Hennessey's intervention.

At about 8:00 a.m. the next day, just as the Iowan was preparing to leave the rectory to visit the mayor and inquire about the PACs' three captives, Santiago Quot walked unannounced into the sala. He gently advised the priest that three badly mutilated cadavers had been laid out in the town hall. Hennessey stopped and looked at his sacristan, sucked in his lower lip, and began nodding his head. He didn't need to ask the identity of the three deceased. After a few moments of silence, he thanked the old man, then turned and went out the door. A few minutes later, he arrived at the town hall, convinced that he already knew what he would find.

The hall was a large, one-room, three-sided, cement block structure built on an embankment on the eastern edge of the town plaza, twenty feet or so above it. An eight-foot-high, chain-link fence made up the façade of the building, ensuring that the atmosphere within the hall was always cold and often damp. During daylight hours, the plaza was generally the scene of much activity as citizens came and went, visiting the mayor, the military commissioner, and the town secretary, all located at the southern edge of the plaza. People congregated to discuss the resolution of their formal complaints or to accept neighborly courtesies as they registered family births, marriages, and deaths. But on this day, Hennessey found the plaza almost deserted, with only a few lonely individuals hurrying to complete private errands.

The priest pulled his leaden legs up the long flight of stairs that scaled the embankment, in no hurry to reach the top. Passing through the large double doors in the chain-link façade, he found a crowd of forty or so silent, immobile, *capixay*-clothed men standing together in the center of the room, their backs toward him, their felt hats held respectfully in their hands, a picture of corporate bereavement. An oppressive feeling of death's presence permeated the air.

As he approached the group, the priest's quiet request, *"Con permiso,"* opened a narrow passageway between the onlookers, allowing him to squeeze through and draw near the three cadavers laid out on the bare tile floor. And even though he knew beforehand what he would find, the sight made the Iowan suck in his breath and his heart pound. The face and head of the body nearest him had been severely battered, but that homely porcine nose and thick-lipped mouth were unmistakable.

The priest stood before the corpses for a few moments, his head bowed, trying to formulate an appropriate prayer, knowing he was expected to do so, a feeling of helplessness enveloping him. *"Dios Padre,* God, how can you let this happen? Aren't these your children? Is there no justice for them? Help their brothers . . . to recognize that they are playing into the hands of evil, . . . that by taking up machetes against each other they will quickly devour themselves."

A voice beside the priest responded softly, *"Así sea."*

Only then did Hennessey realize that the depth of his sorrow and disappointment had allowed the prayer to escape his heart and form on his tongue loud enough to be heard.

No one else said anything. No one else recited a prayer, no one lit a candle, no one displayed any emotions. All present realized that any demonstration of what could later be construed as sympathy toward the dead men was very dangerous. An army *oreja* could report them as closet supporters of the guerrillas, the equivalent of a death sentence.

As he looked at the stoic faces around him, Hennessey again recalled Juan telling him only two weeks earlier how he thought the soldiers were bad because they were ordered to be so, while the guerrillas chose that road for themselves. It was a simple analysis made by a simple man. Recalling those words, the priest's heart felt like a hand of ice was squeezing it. He turned to the silent crowd and said to no one in particular, "They have killed three innocent men."

Hennessey looked closely at the other cadavers. He didn't recognize Juan Silvestre's son—though he had known him well—nor the other man, so battered were their faces. Juan's son was dressed in a fatigue uniform, clothes that his captors had found under a bed in Juan's house and had forced the son to don before beginning the trek to town, meant as clinching evidence that the man was a committed guerrilla. It was an unnecessary, even silly, gesture since the army requested no proof. An unfounded, even patently false, accusation of guerrilla sympathies was sufficient to merit a death sentence.

The Iowan, without a word, made his way from the hall. He trudged kitty-corner across the plaza to the mayor's office, lost in thought, gripped by feelings of impending disaster. The *alcalde* was deep in conversation with his *regidores* when the priest entered. Pascual looked up, caught the priest's eye, and looked quickly back at his assistants. Hennessey waited, saying nothing, while the official continued his earnest, whispered conversation. Finally, the mayor came over. "I be sorry, padre. I try to save those men. Juan be a good man. Those people from Ixbajau be brutes. On the trail they tell the Yacatecos that you make me free the prisoners. They say the army blame them for the guerrillas' escape. That they themselves be killed. So they *machetear* the three there on the trail. I be sorry, padre! Not be my fault!"

"I know, Pascual! I don't blame you! But we've got to work together to see how we can control the PACs. I'm afraid there's going to be a lot more false accusations made against innocent people merely to resolve old land disputes and personal vendettas. This really could get out of hand, if it hasn't already! These three murders are not the end of this thing!"

The mayor looked at the priest with a startled expression and hesitated. "What is it, Pascual?"

"You not hear, padre? Not three deaths! . . . Eight! . . . They kill Juan's daughter, the one who go in the mountains with the guerrillas, his grandson, and three other men from Yacá who be feeding the guerrillas. The five bodies be back in Yacá. I be going out there to make my report when you walk in."

Hennessey stiffened. His worst fears were being realized even before he had time to catch his breath. "Not Juan's grandson, . . . the little twelve-year-old? . . . My Lord! They're destroying their own hope for the future! This is exactly what the army wants!"

The mayor shrugged. "There not be anything we can do, padre. The people have their way of settling arguments. Now the army give orders to kill each other. There not be any way to stop it."

The priest stared at the mayor, nodded, and turned distractedly toward the rectory. Then, coming back again, he took a step toward the official, extended his hand, and touched the mayor's outstretched fingers. "Thank you, Pascual. I'll talk to you later. We've got to do something! Quickly!"

Back in the rectory, Abelardo had returned and was waiting for the priest. "You've probably heard about the other murders in Yacá, padre? This is a bad situation! . . . I think the mayor could have prevented some of those killings, . . . but he would have had to risk his own neck to do so."

"Why do you say that, Abelardo?" Hennessey asked, a slight edge to his voice. "Pascual did what he could!" Then, more tentatively, "Don't you think?"

"Well, from what I've heard," the burly ex-soldier went on, "Pascual sent only one *regidor* to confront both PACs. He knew they wouldn't listen to one *regidor*. He should have sent five, or ten, to show he meant business. And for the *regidor* to tell the PACs that he had been sent at your request was sure to cause trouble. And that's what happened!"

The priest said nothing, squeezing his bottom lip between his thumb and index finger, pondering his friend's words. "You may be right, Abelardo, . . . but I want to believe that Pascual thought that one *regidor* would be enough . . . . And how did Juan's daughter and grandson get involved, anyway? The boy was only twelve-years-old! They couldn't have suspected him of guerrilla activities!"

"After the *regidor* left, a lot of drinking went on," Abelardo responded. "The two PACs argued about whether they should pass sentence themselves, or bring the prisoners to town to be held for the army. They knew the army would kill the three, so it was a question of who would do it.

"The Ixbajauans wanted to do the punishing. But the Yacatecos—many of them are related to the families of Juan and his wife—wanted to deliver the three to the army, to keep their hands clean!

"The Yacatecos won out. But the Ixbajau PAC said they were willing to bring Juan, his son, and the Sebastianero to town only if they were allowed to punish some others who they thought were also guilty of helping the EGP.

They named three Yacatecos, as well as Juan Silvestre's daughter, Axul. The Yacatecos didn't like the idea, but they never stopped drinking. All four were dragged in and beaten. Maybe the Ixbajauans didn't intend to kill them. But somebody grabbed a machete and started hitting. Others joined in. Juan Silvestre Paiz, Juan's grandson, was killed when he tried to rescue his aunt, Axul."

Abelardo was used to the Iowan's silence, but waited a few moments out of respect. "This morning, the two PACs were bringing the three prisoners to town. When they got near the edge of town, the Ixbajau PAC convinced the Yacatecos that if they turned the three over to the mayor, you'd use your influence to have them released and they would be blamed. The Ixbajauans won the argument and the three prisoners were *macheteados* on the trail."

Abelardo finished his description of the gruesome details and waited for Hennessey to respond. But the priest merely sat back in the huge hemp chair, looking at the floor, his legs stretched out, crossed at the ankles, the tips of his long, thick fingers pressed together, the left hand seeming to struggle against the right. Finally, he stood up, thanked his distressed informant, and went into the church to meditate.

Sitting in a straight-backed, wooden bench, the priest found that he couldn't pray. Juan's laughing, homely face flashed before his eyes again and again, sometimes punctuated by the pretty face of Axul, at other moments, by the bright-eyed image of Juan's grandson. Finally, the priest looked up at the gaudy crucifix hanging over the altar with its gaping wounds dripping painted, crimson blood, and whispered, "If you know what comes next, Lord, give me a clue as to what you want me to do."

But just as he expected, no inspiration came crashing through his gloom. At that, the Iowan stood up and walked out into the cool mountain air.

Guatemala City. Mid-July 1982

The U.S. ambassador to Guatemala, Frederic L. Chapin, sat in his spacious, wood-paneled office in Guatemala City with two advisors, Consul General Philip Taylor and Political Attaché Harold Baum. On the ambassador's desk sat a just-published Amnesty International (AI) report detailing the massacres that had taken place in the Guatemalan countryside since Ríos Montt had come to power. Names, places, and dates of army-perpetrated attacks in which over twenty-six hundred peasants had been killed were given in minute detail, accusing the government of "massive extrajudicial executions." In 1981, a similar AI report entitled *Guatemala: A Government Program of Political Murder* had described how the Regional Communications Center financed by USAID in the sixties and seventies and housed in the Presidential Palace, was the nerve center of all death-squad activities throughout the country. It answered directly to the president himself and maintained contact with the command center of U.S. forces in Panama. Now, Ambassador Chapin was visibly upset by AI's latest accusations. Since 30 March, he and his staff had been engaged almost daily in word-to-word combat with Amnesty International, Americas Watch, the church-sponsored Washington Office on Latin America, and a phalanx of international reporters, mostly European. The embassy's assignment was to delegitimize all chronicles of Ríos Montt's depredations. The ambassador's first order of the day, every day, was to develop information and issue statements that would refute defamatory accusations against Ríos Montt and protect his born-again Christian image across the United States.

Now, on this pleasant July morning in Guatemala City, Chapin issued marching orders to his two underlings: Amnesty International had to be branded as part of a communist disinformation campaign, whether acting wittingly or not, and supporting evidence had to be sent on to the State Department for publication in the U.S. press.

Taylor and Baum quickly set about carrying out the ambassador's orders. Within the week Assistant Secretary of State Thomas O. Enders had a five-page embassy memo in his hands, which he released to the press in Washington. It accused the respected human rights organization of "lacking professionalism" and utilizing "biased sources." The Guatemalan government issued a supporting statement claiming that the report was a "horror story conceived by an insane author," while the embassy itself went public in Guatemala by declaring AI to be part of a "communist-backed disinformation campaign."[7]

Two months later, a letter to his family in Iowa from Ronald Hennessey describing the counterinsurgency tactics of Ríos Montt's government would cause more consternation for the embattled Chapin than AI's own report. In Hennessey's case, however, an accusation of "biased sources" and participation in "a communist disinformation campaign" just wouldn't stick. A more creative approach would be needed, and Chapin, Taylor, and Baum would be up to the challenge.

Col. George Maynes (USMAP), military attaché, in Nebaj to inaugurate civil patrols. (© Jean-Marie Simon)

Fr. Ron dons liturgical vestments to celebrate Mass in San Mateo Aldea. (Credit: Maryknoll)

Ejercito Guerrrillero de los Pobres (EGP) volunteers practicing maneuvers in the Northwestern Highlands. (© Jean-Marie Simon 2003)

Civil patrol shows off for Col. Maynes (USMAP). Ten thousand Ixil men from Nebaj, Cotzal, and Chajul were ordered to attend this army rally at the inauguration of the local civil patrol. Note: only the men in the first row were given rifles, and the weapons were collected as soon as the rally finished. (© Jean-Marie Simon 2003)

Civil patrol searching bus passengers in Huehuetenango. (Credit: Maryknoll)

Civil patrollers turn over the accused to the army in Chichicastenango, Quiché. This activity means a certain death sentence without trial for the accused. (© Jean-Marie Simon 2003)

Suspected guerrillas, victims of army "justice." "They dragged them out and killed them. They stabbed and cut them like they were animals, laughing as they killed them." (© Jean-Marie Simon 2003)

Chapter 32

PROBLEMS OF CONSCIENCE

Hennessey sat alone at the small, neatly set table next to the dew-tinged front window of the Sisters' convent in San Mateo Ixtatán. He had not touched his egg, tortilla, and coffee breakfast that the nuns had prepared for him. He had no desire to eat. It was Monday, 19 July 1982, and the cold, overcast weather outside reflected his gloomy mood. Shifting in his chair, he watched distractedly a small group of men talking animatedly in the far corner of the parish basketball court directly in front of the church. *What a crazy place to build a basketball court,* the priest thought to himself. *Whatever possessed Ed McClear to build it there? Probably thought he could talk the players and onlookers into church once their game was over.* As he watched, the Iowan saw Santiago Quot break away from the group and walk purposefully toward the convent.

"Come on in, Santiago," the priest welcomed his sacristan, forcing a smile to his lips. He had risen from his chair and opened the door before the old man had a chance to knock.

Santiago entered and stood to one side refusing the chair Hennessey offered him. The old man had never seen his normally jovial pastor as subdued as during the last three days. The sacristan was clearly worried.

"Would you like a cup of hot coffee to warm your stomach, Santiago?"

"Not now, padre!" the old man answered, bowing slightly. "*Gracia,* but my stomach be already warm. How did you dawn this morning?"

The priest hesitated a few moments, took some deep breaths, and debated whether he should try to answer honestly. "I dawned with a very heavy heart, Santiago," he sighed as he sat down, shaking his head. "The heaviest of my priesthood, I would think. At this stage of my life, I am having trouble trying to understand what it means to be a priest, . . . to be a human being! . . . And now, San Francisco! . . . It's incredible! And I just sit here like a fool trying to figure out what I'm supposed to do about it! . . . And God be hiding from me."

The old man watched the priest, a worried frown deepening the creases on his normally furrowed face. "What be done, be done, padre! You can do nothing to stop it! Only God can! But He not be wanting to!"

"Santiago," Hennessey responded in a voice barely above a whisper, "that's a question I keep asking myself . . . and I don't have the answer. Why doesn't He stop it? Why doesn't He want to stop it? If He ever sent the Virgin with a message before, this is the time to do it again . . . . I have to be careful. I don't want to blaspheme . . . or despair. Who can understand God's mind?"

The sacristan remained standing, silent.

"Well, *don* Santiago, you came here to tell me something. Judging from the way you walked across that basketball court, I'd say you have something weighing on your mind. If it's more bad news, sit down and tell me slowly. I'm not sure how much more I can take!"

"Excuse me, Padre, but I be thinking it be good news," the old man answered softly, still standing. "Angelina, widow of Diego Pérez, be in church. She bring thirty-two men from the Bulej PAC to confession. They be the ones who kill the four brothers in Bulej on Thursday, not Diego. Some be out on the basketball court now."

The Iowan sat looking at his venerable old friend without moving, and the sacristan responded in kind. A lot of unspoken understanding flowed between the two men. Over the previous three days, Hennessey, with Santiago at his side, had remained riveted to his chair while he transcribed one account after another of hundreds of burlesque-like murders committed earlier in the week in the Mateano villages of Sebep, Yolcultac, Petenac, and Bulej. The priest was in Huehuetenango when the killings took place, attending the meetings of the diocesan senate. He had spent most of his time since his return listening to descriptions of the terrible violence from a steady stream of survivors, catechists, and bereaved relatives. The priest speculated that the attacks, like others before them, had been purposely planned to take place during his absence from the parish.

Even as recently as the preceding day, Sunday, Hennessey had heard new accounts of still another massacre, perpetrated on Saturday, 17 July, at Colonel Bolaños's ranch, San Francisco. According to the first, confused descriptions from the scene, it had been a debauchery of death that claimed well over three hundred lives and made the killings at the other four villages seem almost like dress rehearsals before the main production.[1] The petition that Milenario Pérez, the San Francisco health promotor, had submitted to Colonel Terraza Pinot requesting a grant of Ríos Montt's promised amnesty for himself and his neighbors had apparently brought high-level military attention to the village and had unwittingly occasioned the death of virtually every man, woman, and child present in San Francisco on that day.

As the reports came in, Hennessey painstakingly wrote a detailed description and chronology of the killings, compiled a list of the dead, identified the perpetrators, and noted the rationale they used to justify their acts. He knew there were many interests, especially in the United States, who would challenge his accounts as soon as he made them public—something . he was determined to do if he survived long enough.

Now, seated at the breakfast table in the nun's convent, undisturbed before Santiago's entrance except by his own troubled conscience, he again tried to interpret his motivation for the recurring urge to go out to the targeted villages. He knew there was nothing he could do to stop any further slaughter—even should he encounter the marauding executioners. Rather, a confrontational face-off would provide the possibility, perhaps the probability of his own death. Such a consequence would end his agony, but it would also leave the Mateanos without sacraments, without his moral direction (as ambiguous as it often was), and without their principal conduit to the outside world.

If my intervention would stop the killings, Hennessey told himself, *I'd gladly go! . . . What greater love doth anyone have, . . .* he paraphrased the biblical verse . . . . *But the government would blame my demise on the EGP! The killings would go on! . . . My first obligation is to get this news out. It isn't much, . . . but it's the most—the least I can do!*

During his chronicling of the week's traumatic events, Hennessey had been told that many Catholics had participated in the brutal slayings. At first, he had been shocked and dismayed. But as he learned of the circumstances and weighed the alternatives presented to the participants, he wondered about the degree of their responsibility. Still, he had been apprehensive that the involvement of Catholics, although unwilling, might serve them as an unintended rite of passage, that by seeming to reject that Church's moral prescriptions, they would now feel obliged to sever all association with him. As a consequence, Santiago's statement that many of the participants now wanted to receive the sacrament of reconciliation pleased the Iowan.

"Excuse me, padre," the sacristan coughed, "but what shall I be telling Angelina?"

Hennessey shook his head and rubbed his eyes. "That's good news, Santiago! If the men want to go to confession, that's good news! Tell Angelina and the civil patrollers that I want to talk to them before I hear their confessions. I want to get some issues out in the open first and I want everyone to know that my knowledge of these events is not coming from anything heard in the confessional. If they are willing to talk to me publicly, tell them to go to the parish hall . . . . And by the way, thank Angelina . . . . She's strong, . . . a good woman."

"I talk to them, *padrecito,*" the sacristan answered with some animation. Outside the door, Santiago put on his hat and headed in the direction of a small group of men waiting for him on the basketball court. Hennessey meanwhile remained at the breakfast table ignoring his food, chin cupped in his right hand, eyes closed, as he tried to make some sense of the goings-on around him.

On Monday, 12 July, a week earlier—though it now seemed as if a year had already passed—Hennessey had climbed into his pickup and headed for the provincial capital. He was oblivious of the orders that Colonel Hernández Catalán in Huehuetenango had issued over the weekend to his executive officer and chief of intelligence, Colonel Byron Lima Estrada,[2] and to the *comandantes* of the nearby military bases in Barillas, Soloma, and Jacaltenango. Bishop Victor Hugo Martínez had invited all the diocesan priests to Huehuetenango to discuss the recent increase in threats made against the lives of several nuns and clerics, and to plan coordinated steps for the evacuation of some parishes should that prove necessary.

Father Ray Furbish, a Dominican priest from Chicago, was pastor of Nentón, the parish directly to the west of San Mateo. His superiors had pulled him from his post after they decided that the army might try to eliminate him because the EGP had been so successful in politicizing his congregation— even though Furbish had done everything he could to stop it. After Furbish's departure, Nentón became part of Hennessey's domain, more than doubling the area and population under the Iowan's jurisdiction.

In February a military death squad had murdered James Miller, a nonpolitical Wisconsin native and Christian Brother teaching in the regional Catholic high school in Huehuetenango. It had been debated ever since whether he was the intended target or whether this was just a warning shot across the bow of the Huehuetenango Church. More recently, the Mayan priest in neighboring San Miguel Acatán and the American nuns there, had been warned by the EGP that they had either to support the revolutionary struggle among their parishioners or leave the area entirely. Padre Andrés Lainez and the nuns had chosen to close down the parish. Now, with more reports surfacing in Huehuetenango that other diocesan clerics were targets of assassination squads, including Hennessey, the bishop wanted to discuss security plans for the entire diocese.

At first light on the day following Hennessey's departure for Huehuetenango, 150 soldiers in camouflaged uniforms, their faces painted black, intended, perhaps, to terrorize as much as deceive, crept through the cornfields surrounding the Mateano village of Sebep. Sebep was a community of one hundred families, a four-hour walk northwest of San Mateo. Some fifty or so families were evangelicals, thirty-five practiced the traditional Mayan rites, and another fifteen were orthodox Catholics. The advancing soldiers were Mayans, none of them from the local area, their officers, ladinos. Before noon, the soldiers had swept the community's entire male population— with the exception of small children—into the village center. A nervous, fidgety individual dressed in a camouflaged uniform identical to that of the soldiers, a ski mask covering his face—a man who quickly proved to be a defector from the EGP—accompanied the troops. The people, not knowing who he was, would later ruefully nickname the defector "Miguel de San Miguel," having identified his language as Q'anjob'al, with verbal variations and accent they recognized as those of the Migueleños of San Miguel Acatán.

Hennessey was unaware of what was occurring in Sebep as he conferred with his colleagues in the provincial capital. On that same day, Tuesday, 13 July, he had met with Ray Bonner, the Central American correspondent for the *New York Times*. Bonner had arranged during the previous week to travel by rented helicopter to San Mateo to talk to the Iowan about the abuses of the newly established civil patrols. The correspondent had first gone to Bill Mullan in Guatemala City for information on what was happening in the countryside and Mullan had directed Bonner to Hennessey. But after the bishop issued his call for a meeting of the diocesan senate, Hennessey had suggested that he and Bonner meet in Huehuetenango rather than in San Mateo Ixtatán. Later, Hennessey would remember that change of venue with a sense of chagrin. *If we had met in San Mateo where we had originally planned,* the Iowan chided himself, *Bonner's helicopter ride would have given him a firsthand view of the Guatemalan Army in action, and a chance to break the news much earlier and with more credibility.*

Back in Sebep, the fidgeting Miguel de San Miguel stood in the doorway of the old adobe courthouse while the soldiers made their captives march slowly before him. When the nervous defector jerked his right hand to shoulder level in a gesture that looked like a swearing-in ceremony, several shouting soldiers would grab the person parading directly in front of the accuser, throw the unfortunate designee to the muddy ground, face down, and hog-tie his hands and feet. A total of twenty-seven individuals—including four terrified boys, the youngest only ten-years-old, the oldest fifteen—were singled out and bound in less than an hour.

For the next twenty minutes, a light-skinned, agitated ladino commander, a slightly built captain perhaps twenty-five years of age, strode back and forth, sidestepping puddles and mud, haranguing his audience on the evils of communism, calling those on the ground "*indios* sons of whores" and "traitors to their *patria.*" Those who had not been singled out stood to one side, two and three deep, hardly daring to breathe, their eyes fixed on the ground lest the least movement or even eye contact attract the officer's attention and make them objects of his wrath.

Finally, the officer commanded his men to release five of the bound prisoners. Telling the five they had but one chance to redeem themselves, he ordered his men to give each a club, a heavy piece of firewood. "Separate out another five from those *indio cabrones,*" the captain told his men. "Now, you patriots, you who want to show us how much you love Guatemala and support its army, crush the fucking skulls of these traitors . . . . If you hesitate, your wives and children will be next."

The five men stood paralyzed. A few soldiers moved up behind them and pushed. "NOW!" the officer screamed.

As if hypnotized, the men took their clubs and approached their five relatives, friends, neighbors. First one struck a glancing blow, intending to do little harm. Others followed the first man's example. "Harder!" the captain yelled. "I want to see their fucking brains on the ground. I want to see their fucking blood and hair on your fucking clubs. HARDER!"

The five executioners, muttering to themselves, praying perhaps, hit harder and harder, some of them trembling in anguish at what their bodies were doing, their minds rejecting the implications of their actions. Low moans came from several of the victims. Onlookers closed their eyes, others stifled gasps, tears ran down several faces. Finally, well after the five heads resembled nothing human, the commander yelled, "*Basta! Stop!*"

For a moment, there was complete silence in the square. The five unwilling executioners stood with heads bowed, shoulders hunched forward, holding their clubs loosely, breathing heavily. Then, with a flick of his head, the officer ordered, "Tie them up. They are good patriots! *Felicidades!* Congratulations!" he told them, laughing nervously. "You've done your duty! You've saved the lives of your wives and children! But now you must pay the penalty for your treasonous behavior. We must give an example to everyone that the Guatemalan Army administers justice to all the *patria's* citizens! *Justicia para todos!* Tie them up!"

The five executioners, now praying audibly, were like rag dolls, exhibiting no resistance as the soldiers threw them in the mud and bound them. The captain then ordered five other prisoners released. They were given the same bloodied clubs and made to crush the heads of those who moments before had served as executioners. Again, they were told that their cooperation was the only way to save their wives and children. And again, the debauchery of patriotism and death was reenacted.

The exercise was repeated twice more, with each successive group barely motivated by the thought that they were saving the lives of their families, while knowing that their own similar deaths were only minutes away.

Finally, the local PAC, acting under the same threat, was forced to club the last seven victims, including the four boys. As the officer went from one body to the next, kicking each in turn, he called out to his captive audience, "You see what happens to those who love Russia and Cuba and Nicaragua more than they love Guatemala? Let there be no more fucking Communists among you! The same punishment will be meted out to anyone suspected of assisting the fucking subversives."

The men and youngsters who had escaped the purge turned and began shuffling homeward in stunned silence, many thinking that their own deaths would have been a preferred alternative. Suddenly, Miguel de San Miguel sidled up to the captain and informed him that "the most important communist" in Sebep, Felipe Lucas, a local merchant who had sold food and flashlight batteries to the guerrillas, had not been picked up in the original roundup.

Felipe Lucas ran a small store out of his home down the road about three hundred meters from the courthouse. He was the owner of the village's only *nixtamal*, a gasoline-powered, corn-grinding machine for producing *masa*, the raw material of what made up 75 percent of the Mayans' diet, corn tortillas. Felipe's *nixtamal* was the first introduction of modern technology into the village and it had already initiated a slow process of social differentiation based on wealth. Felipe and his family were on top, those who could afford to use his machine next, and those who continued to grind their corn in the traditional way—by hand, using a stone *metate*—at the bottom. Felipe had been accustomed to sell canned sausages, crackers, tortillas, beans, and other foodstuffs to the guerrillas when they occasionally passed through Sebep. As the richest man in the village, he was a target of EGP wrath and could hardly have refused the guerrillas anything they wanted. But that didn't seem to matter to the captain as he called to his stunned audience, "Wait! Don't anybody leave until I find that *hijo de puta*, Felipe Lucas, the most important fucking communist in Sebep. I haven't finished giving you a lesson on what happens to *indio* traitors." And then, turning to his men, "Go find Felipe Lucas and any members of his fucking family and bring them here."

Twenty minutes later, a sullen Felipe, his clearly fearful wife and their four children—a husky son and a pretty daughter, both in their twenties, an asthmatic fourteen-year-old boy, and a one-year-old girl strapped to her mother's back—were brought before the commander.

"*Cómo están ustedes?*" the smiling officer cynically greeted his six new prisoners as they stood before him.

Felipe muttered a barely audible, "*Bien,*" in the name of his family.

"Now tell me," the captain continued, sitting down on a chair that one of his men had taken from the courthouse, the back of the chair between his legs, "You must have a lot of money from cheating these poor people here and from selling supplies to the guerrillas. That money is not legitimately yours, you know! So it's best that you turn it over to me and I'll see that it's spent for the good of all. Where is your money hidden?"

Felipe remained silent, his eyes focused on the ground in front of him.

"Now let's be reasonable," the commandant continued, his voice a low growl. "We'll walk over to your house and you can show me where your money is hidden. If you refuse to cooperate, you and your family will get what your neighbors got."

The officer stood up, swung his leg over the back of the chair, and led Felipe Lucas, his wife, children, and a small group of soldiers to the family's house. The remaining troops stayed with Sebep's male population in the muddy courthouse patio.

Through the evening hours to well past midnight, Felipe's moans and the officer's screams told the women huddling with their terrified children in nearby homes that the officer was having no success in making his prisoner talk. Before morning, however, the captain became convinced that the battered man on the ground before him was probably capable of going to his Maker without divulging his secret hiding place. Realizing that the opportunity to get his hands on the merchant's savings was fast slipping away, the young officer ordered his men to revive the prisoner and turn their interrogation skills toward his family.

The soldiers had hardly begun to use their knives and cigarettes on Felipe's wife and children when the merchant's resistance broke and he revealed the spot where his treasure was buried. Soldiers searched the indicated area and found more than three thousand quetzales, a sizable fortune.

Then, telling his men to take anything of value they could find in and around the residence, the captain, flushed by his success, ordered the six family members tied together inside their house. Bidding them farewell, he closed the door. "Torch it!' he yelled to his men, making a backhanded wave toward the structure. As soon as the first match was applied, the flames leapt up from the cedar shake roof, soaked with gasoline taken from Felipe's *nixtamal* engine. Ten minutes later, with only the muffled cries of the one-year-old baby indicating any signs of life within, the roof and its underlying support structure went crashing in on the six prisoners below, throwing off a shower of sparks and embers.

During the evening, while the captain was occupied with Felipe and his family, Miguel de San Miguel had remembered another "communist" who so far had escaped detection and capture. When the captain returned from Felipe's house, Miguel told the officer that Gaspar Andrés Sebastián, a leading Sebep Catholic in whose home Hennessey often celebrated Mass, had collected food for the guerrillas—something Hennessey knew Gaspar had done willingly. It was an activity that the commandant, as soon as he had heard the defector's accusation, attributed to the man's "fucking Catholic communism." When the soldiers could not locate Gaspar by daybreak, the captain ordered the execution of his wife, his twenty-two-year-old daughter-in-law, and his three-year-old grandson. The soldiers tied the three together in their home and set it ablaze. All three, like Felipe Lucas's family, perished in their wattle and daub oven.

Several of Sebep's Catholic families became frightened by the captain's furious denunciation of the Catholic Church's "communist propaganda mouthed by that fucking communist priest in San Mateo." Right then they promised the officer to sever all ties with the Church the same day, renounce their Catholicism, and join the local evangelical congregation. The captain congratulated the new converts by telling them they were "good Christians" and "were doing God's will."

By 8:00 a.m. the next day, Wednesday, 14 July 1982, half the soldiers, led by a ladino lieutenant who was later described as having a "hawk-like nose," set out for Yolcultac, a small village one hour's walk to the west. Miguel de San Miguel accompanied them. The other half, under the command of the captain, left Sebep a short time later for Petenac, another small village of some twenty homes one hour's walk to the south. Before leaving, the captain forbade the villagers to bury their dead until he returned. "It will be a good reminder of what happens to fucking *indio* communists," he told the grieving, terrified crowd.

In Yolcultac, the lieutenant's troops corralled all teenaged and adult males and marched them to the village center. Again, the masked Miguel repeated the same accusatory ritual he had performed in Sebep.

At the first go-around, the informer pointed out four men who had supplied the guerrillas with food. Each was thrown to the ground and bound hand and foot. But the lieutenant was not satisfied with the fingering of only four collaborators, so he ran the prisoners by Miguel once more. On the second pass, the informer, wanting desperately to please the officer, picked out two more purported guerrilla-supporters, including Diego Torres.

Diego became extremely agitated and thought he might escape the fate of his companions by accusing another neighbor, Juan Hernández, of supporting the EGP. The lieutenant thanked Diego for his information and quickly included Juan Hernández in the group of bound detainees. But that act of betrayal didn't save Diego. The officer ordered the Yolcultac PAC to club all seven men to death under the same threat the captain had used in Sebep.

The patrollers slowly picked up the clubs that had been thrown to them and stared nervously at each other. No one wanted to initiate the bloodletting. The lieutenant, again taking his lead from the captain's example, screamed, "NOW! . . . or we begin going for your wives and children!"

The PAC members gingerly approached their victims to begin the sacrifice. Once the initial blows were administered, however, their sense of guilt seemed to diminish and their blows increased in intensity. In a few short minutes, all seven accused were dead—and Lieutenant Hawk-nose was parading around the corpses with a foolish grin on his whiskered face that reflected the sense of power he felt, conferred on him by the bodies at his feet.

Meanwhile, the contingent of soldiers that had left Sebep under the command of the young captain arrived in Petenac. There, the officer wasted no time ordering his men to round up every man, woman, and child in the village and bring them to the center. Apparently, the decision to treat everyone in Petenac from the oldest to the youngest as a subversive—or a potential subversive—had been made before arriving in the village.

"I've been told," the captain explained to his captive audience, "that there's a secret EGP arms factory in a cave nearby. That means that every fucking man, woman, and child in this *aldea* knew about it and did nothing to inform the authorities. That means that you are all guilty of subversion! You must all pay! We cannot allow treason to go unpunished! . . . Tie them all up."

The soldiers bound the men first and pushed them into a nearby adobe house. The women and children were left unbound but were herded into an adjacent structure. Many of the women were carrying babies in *rebozos* on their backs. Half the troops, quickly driven to a frenzy by the captain's screaming claims of what Guatemala would become should the "fucking communist EGP" ever take power, began to shoot and stab the men trussed up in the first house. The exercise went on for a full fifteen minutes and ended only when the executioners became tired of their efforts, some several minutes after all the prisoners were apparently dead. The soldiers then piled the bodies in the center of the house, stacked furniture and clothing and bedclothes around and on top of the heap, doused it with gasoline and set it on fire. Unbeknownst to them, two men at the bottom of the pile were still barely alive.

Meanwhile, a second group of soldiers had turned its attention to the women, children, and babies. Unlike their companions, however, they expended no emotion as they set about their task. They first doused the captives, along with the furniture, bedding, and cedar shake roof with gasoline. The captain himself then lit a torch and handed it to a soldier. The chosen individual marched to the front of the structure, turned, saluted his leader, then lobbed the flame through the front door. A vacuum whoosh from the exploding fire quickly extinguished the screams and cries inside, followed by the snapping and crackling of tinder, and the celebratory laughter of troops.

Dorotea Marcos, wife of Petenac's public health promoter, was able to save herself and her three small children by hiding in a gully until sundown. She had been washing clothes when the soldiers arrived. During the day she listened to the shouts, cries, and shootings as the soldiers went about their grizzly business. She would later provide Hennessey with the first description of the Petenac massacre. A man working in his cornfield in another small gully a short distance away was also overlooked. He, too, would come forward to describe the slaughter to the Iowan. Several others, all men on business outside the village, escaped the captain's plans for them.

After supper, the tired soldiers loaded their booty, consisting of squealing pigs, frightened chickens, radios, tape recorders, watches, and whatever else of value they could find, onto "requisitioned" pack animals and set out for Bulej, stopping in Patalcal to spend the night.

Late that same night, well past midnight, some strangers from nearby villages, armed only with machetes, snuck into Petenac to investigate what they knew to have been a savage massacre. Among the ruins, they found the remains of eighty-nine charred bodies and a pervasive, overpowering smell of burnt flesh. After they recovered from the first shock, the visitors, fearing punishment from the souls of the dead if they left the bodies exposed, interred the men in a mass grave in front of the house where they had died. The effort occasioned much difficulty and nausea as many bodies fell apart when carried to the pit. They struggled to finish the task as quickly as possible since all knew that to be caught burying the dead was to be considered *subversivos*. They would be branded as sympathizers and bring down on their heads a similar fate. When they recovered the last two victims at the bottom of the pile, they discovered that both were still barely alive. A small group was sent to make a quick check on the women, children, and babies, only to find that all were dead.

The two survivors were each tied to a separate litter fashioned from a chair—a common device used by the Maya for transporting their sick over the mountains. Each chair was then strapped to the back of a volunteer, who, accompanied by relief help, spirited the two away. En route, one of the victims died. The other, 65-year-old Pascual Gómez, shot, stabbed, and burned, survived to reach a friendly hideaway. There, he was cared for with medicines sent by Hennessey from the San Mateo parochial hospital. It was not enough to save him, however; he died several weeks later.

After interring the men with little margin of darkness left to protect them, the strangers decided that they had no time to dig a grave for the women, children, and babies. Instead, they created a tomb by pushing in the adobe walls of the makeshift crematorium to cover the charred bodies. They then crept back to their own villages.

When Hennessey was first informed of Pascual Gómez's almost miraculous survival, he made plans to go to him with medicines and the sacraments. Santiago Quot, however, dissuaded him. The sacristan warned the priest that he, Hennessey, was being closely watched and that going to the old man would reveal Pascual's hideaway to the soldiers and thereby guarantee that the murderers would return to finish their task. Hennessey reluctantly acquiesced.

Around noon on Thursday, 15 July, the two contingents of soldiers returned from Yolcultac and Petenac. They met outside Bulej and surrounded the village. Once again, they herded all teenaged and adult males into the village center and began the same accusatory ritual employed at Sebep and Yolcultac by the masked Miguel. Five men were accused, thrown to the ground, and bound. Among them were two who were actually opposed to the guerrillas. Another of the accused was Diego Pérez, Bulej's "animator of the faith," husband of Angelina. Diego was the man who had gone to Hennessey shortly after the Iowan's arrival in San Mateo to denounce the PMA soldiers' murder of five Mayans on the *finca* of Walter Widman, a leader of Maryknoll's wealthiest supporters in Guatemala. On that occasion, Diego had told the priest, "Now the guerrillas will protect us and a lot of people are going to join them. It's the only way, padre! They're our army! That's why they call themselves the Guerrilla Army of the Poor!" It was a statement that the Iowan would recall with sadness many times during the next several months.

Diego supported the EGP but he never actually joined the ranks of the organization. He considered his work as faith-animator too important to sacrifice in order to fight at the side of the guerrillas. Part of his duties involved teaching catechism classes to any *costumbre* traditionalist who wished to be accepted as a baptismal godparent, a regulation mandated by the diocesan senate. He also had been in charge of building a Catholic chapel in Bulej with volunteer labor. But since only half the households in the village were Catholic, Diego had been hard-pressed to find enough willing hands to carry his pet project to fruition. Without Hennessey's knowledge, the faith-animator began granting dispensations from catechism class to any traditionalist who would work for a day or two on the chapel, making adobes, or cutting and trimming wood for the roof. When Hennessey found out about the practice and gently chided the catechist for preferring a visible religious structure to an educated congregation, Diego replied, "Padre, their work be their prayer. and once we have a church, they'll be wanting to study and join us. I think God be pleased with the people's efforts."

But as Diego lay on the ground, accused by four neighbors of being an EGP member, traditionalist antipathy toward the faith-animator bubbled to the surface. "This man, Diego Pérez, be the principal Catholic in our village," a practitioner of the *costumbre* called out to the captain. "He be in charge of building the church and he be teaching the people the padre's religion."

"His brother be off fighting with the guerrillas," another shouted.

The officer paused for a moment to digest this new information and then walked over to where Diego lay. "So you are the Catholic teacher in this *aldea*," the captain sneered, kicking the prone man in the stomach.

Diego grunted but said nothing.

"What do you teach? . . . Communist shit like the fucking communist priest in San Mateo? All you *catequistas* teach the same communist shit. That's enough to convince me that you are this village's principal fucking communist!"

Each interrogatory was accompanied by a stiff kick in the ribs meant to serve as emphasis. After one final kick that seemed to lift Diego off the ground, the officer turned to the onlookers. "We will make an example of this fucking communist scum!" he yelled, his adrenaline pushing a note of triumph into his voice. "Where is the head of the civil patrol?"

When the Bulej PAC leader appeared before the captain and did his best at imitating a military salute, the officer demanded, "Bring me the dullest old machete you can find and do it on the double. I don't want this shit to live any longer than he has to!"

Diego knew what was coming. His lips moved in prayer.

When the machete was handed to the captain, he ran his finger along the blade's rusty edge to test that it was indeed dull. Satisfied, the officer turned over the prone man, using only his foot to do so, as if he wished to avoid contaminating himself. Looking around, he shouted, "I will teach all of you *sinvergüenzas* what a real man and patriot does when he confronts treason." .

The captain placed his foot on the faith-animator's chest. "Open your eyes, pig. I want to see your fear. Open your eyes!"

When Diego refused to open his eyes, the officer raised his machete and brought it down with a thud on the catechist's throat. The blow was not meant to kill, but the prone man's eyes flew open and blood spurted from a severed carotid artery. The captain wiped his boot against Diego's convulsing body, then he struck again, cutting through his victim's windpipe and larynx, bringing bubbles of blood and air to the man's mouth as he struggled for air, accompanied by gurgling sounds. The captain struck again and again determined to see the catechist's head roll from his body.

Finally, tired and breathing heavily, the officer stopped to wipe his brow. Again, he took up his machete and using both hands, struck furiously, trying to cut through Diego's spinal column. Angry that his victim's anatomy was stronger that his biceps, the commander kicked Diego's head and hit the neck with one last blow. The head rolled free.

"Soccer, anyone?" the captain sneered, looking around. No one looked at him. "Dogs deserve to be treated like dogs!"

"It took many, many strokes," witnesses would later tell Hennessey.

Persuaded that he had demonstrated his patriotic resolve, the captain ordered the eighty PAC members to form a line and walk slowly past the four remaining accused, taking turns beating each on the head with a club. A light blow was met with a threat that the club-wielder and his family would undergo the same fate unless he struck harder. The captain watched carefully to insure that each patrol member participated fully, continuing the pounding until all eighty men had wielded several blows each and the four heads were crushed beyond any recognizable form. Of those who had taken part in the clubbing, thirty-four were practicing Catholics.

The five bodies were left out in the plaza overnight while the soldiers bivouacked in Diego's nearly completed chapel.

On Friday morning, after ordering the residents to bury their five dead, the soldiers left Bulej for other villages, visiting Patalcal and Ocanté, checking for guerrillas and their supporters. They found none. Early Saturday morning, they departed in the direction of San Francisco, to be joined there by other troops coming from their base in Jacaltenango.

At the very moment that the captain was denouncing Hennessey as a "fucking communist" to the people of Bulej, the Iowan, tired and totally ignorant of the traumatic string of events that even then continued to unfold in his parish, was driving back to San Mateo from the diocesan senate meetings in Huehuetenango. The priest smiled ironically as he drove, thinking about his role at the meetings. He had been prompted to speak out by the current of unrest that had surfaced during the diocesan assembly. Some priests, frightened by the increased repression since the beginning of the state of siege, had suggested to Bishop Martínez that he close down the Huehuetenango diocese, just as the bishop of Quiché had done two years earlier. But the bishop, with the support of Hennessey and several other priests, had rejected the idea with the comment, "Quiché has become one mass graveyard since the priests and nuns left. We must stay!"

At the time of the diocesan senate meetings, Hennessey had no inkling just how dangerous his parish had become.

When the Iowan arrived back in San Mateo about 8:30 p.m. on Thursday, 15 July, Sisters Francisca and Justa had been waiting for several hours—knowing he had scheduled his return for this day—to tell him what they had learned about the soldiers' rampage out in the northern villages. Seated stiffly on the edge of the couch in the rectory sala, the two nuns waited patiently while Hennessey took his time to build a small fire in the brick fireplace situated in a corner of the room. Even though it was the middle of July, San Mateo's rainy season and evening mountain air combined to make the prevailing weather much like that of Ryan in late October. Finally, the priest joined the two women by the kidney-shaped coffee table, knowing that their presence at such an hour signaled more trouble.

"You should be in bed by now, or you're going to have saddlebags under your eyes bigger than mine," Hennessey joked, trying to lighten the nuns' normal reticence.

Francisca smiled, waited a decent interval, and then began to relate what they had heard about the killings in Sebep, Yolcultac, and Petenac. No word had arrived in town at this point about what had happened during the day in Bulej. The nuns' information was sketchy: "The soldiers made the PACs kill about forty people in Sebep, mostly men, including Felipe Lucas and his whole family, and the wife, daughter-in-law, and grandson of Gaspar Andrés Sebastián. They killed fewer than ten in Yolcultac but more than a hundred in Petenac, mostly women and children. Many witnesses and relatives are still too terrified to come to town, so we don't have the whole story. But it seems that some Catholics took part in the killings. The commandant was very explicit in expressing his anger at both you and the church catechists, *padrecito* . . . . You have to be more careful! It sounds like he would like to kill you."

"I don't think he is really worried about me," the priest answered, trying to dismiss the nuns' concern. "Nobody pays any attention to me except you two anyway!" The two women smiled wanly. "It had to happen here sooner or later!" He shook his head and sighed, "After what has been happening in the Ixcán, in San Miguel, San Rafael, and Barillas, they had to come here next."

Then, since it was already late and the nuns' knowledge of the murders was limited, the priest decided to bid the two women goodnight and go to bed, angry with himself for having been in Huehuetenango during those terror-ridden days. *Why is it that I'm always away when they commit their worst atrocities?* he fretted. *It must be planned . . . . And what good would I have accomplished had I been here?*

Now, four days later, as the Iowan waited in the sisters' convent for Santiago Quot to return and tell him if the Bulej patrollers were ready to publicly discuss the murders in their village, Hennessey's thoughts again turned to Ray Bonner. *I should try to get him up here to look at this San Francisco massacre. Publishing that story would give lie to this talk coming from the embassy and the White House about the human rights situation here . . . . Who can believe that the U.S. Embassy doesn't know what is going on? Are they so hypnotized by the administration's anticommunist rhetoric, . . . or are they simply trying to protect Reagan's nearsighted version of "American interests?" Probably neither! . . . Just suckered in by the prevailing political winds, . . . with a desire for job security, without the courage to stand apart! . . . Would that a replay of the Nuremberg Trials could include some of my patriotic countrymen!*

When Santiago Quot returned, Hennessey was still sitting at the breakfast table, eyes closed, fist under his chin supporting his head, debating the difficulties of generating some meaningful, effective publicity in the international media about recent events in his parish.

"*Perdón*, padre," the sacristan interrupted, "the Bulej patrollers be wanting to speak to you. A few go to Angelina after the officer cut off her husband's head to say sorry they be for helping kill the others. She tell them they must confess to you. They ask her to come in case you be angry. Others heard they be coming and want to come too."

Hennessey shook his head, "I'm not angry, Santiago. Sad, yes! Terrified of what is happening to us, yes! . . . Tell them I'll be right over."

When Hennessey entered the large adobe hall some five minutes later, the men were all kneeling along the far wall, their heads bowed, reciting the rosary together. Some had tears rolling down their faces, a few were shaking, almost convulsively. The priest waited in the doorway until the men finished their prayers, deeply touched by the obvious show of distress that burdened them. When they fell silent, they remained kneeling, thinking that the pastor's intent was to have them make a public confession together.[3]

"There's no need to kneel now," Hennessey told them gently. You can sit on the benches. I just want to talk to you for a few moments before you confess privately, in order to let you know that I am aware of what happened in Bulej and in the other villages . . . . I doubt that you can give me any new information in your confessions. But if you should, it will remain with me in secret . . . . I do not intend to discuss individual guilt. We'll leave all judgments to God. All you need to say is that you're sorry you've offended God and your brothers and sisters by your actions . . . . Personally, I don't think there's much guilt in what you did. The real sin is with those who planned these killings and forced you to take part. You, like your dead brothers, are victims of the madness that surrounds us."

Someone spoke up, "*Sí*, padre, we be sorry! Very sorry! We not want to do this terrible thing! . . . These soldiers be our brothers. What be happening to them?"

Another chimed in, "The soldiers make us do it, padre! They be killing our families if we not obey . . . . Perhaps it be better if they kill us all, . . . like in Petenac and San Francisco! Can God be forgiving us? May our dead brothers be forgiving us!"

"Listen," Hennessey replied in a firmer voice, walking closer to emphasize his point, "we all do things we regret. But God is a loving, forgiving parent. He forgives us when we recognize our guilt and profess our sorrow, just as you pardon your children . . . . Angelina here," the priest gestured toward Diego's widow, "is a fine example of the kind of forgiveness God asks of all of us and is Himself willing to grant . . . . Let's go into church to confess and pray for the grace to resist this evil and ask God to make this insanity pass away . . . . And let's pray for the soldiers, too! They also are our brothers. They have lost the ability to think and judge for themselves . . . . It is so easy to hate! So difficult to love!"

The men blessed themselves, stood up, and one by one followed Hennessey out of the hall and into the church. Since the church did not have a formal confessional, Santiago Quot had already arranged a chair for the priest at the edge of the sanctuary, facing the side wall, a kneeler to its left, facing the altar.

The priest's main concern was to assuage the tremendous guilt the men felt. He told each one that what they had done occurred only because they had been confronted by a terrible threat and God understood that and took it into consideration. The priest then assigned a recital of the rosary as penance and asked each to recite the Act of Contrition. As Hennessey repeated the prayer of absolution, "*Yo te absuelvo de tus pecados, en el nombre del Padre, del Hijo, y del Espíritu Santo,*" raising his right hand in benediction, more than one penitent pounded his breast loud enough for the priest to hear the blow. Others sobbed quietly and one unconsciously laid his hand on the priest's left arm and squeezed nervously, as if the depth of sorrow had flowed to his fingertips, sending spasms of pain into the priest's arm. "*Vaya con Dios,*" the Iowan told each one gently.

After the last penitent had finished his confession and returned to sit among his neighbors in the pews, Hennessey remained sitting in the confessional chair. His legs were crossed at the knees, his right hand under his chin, eyes closed, wondering if, in his concern to give them moral support, he had downplayed the patrollers' guilt a bit too much. *After all*, he thought, *the soldiers behave under the same threat, kill or be killed. Even the officers are prisoners of the system, of their own tradition and propaganda. Presumably, anyone who refuses to participate courts execution. But are their families also threatened? . . . So where does the guilt start? . . . or stop? . . . with Ríos Montt? . . . with the U.S. Embassy? . . . with the Reagan administration and its coterie of ideologues?*

At that moment, Santiago stood beside the priest and coughed. Hennessey looked up at the old man. "That be all, padre," the sacristan whispered, his voice coming out louder than he intended. "There not be more. Everyone confessed! Everyone be forgiven!"

Hennessey smiled weakly and looked about him. The Bulej men had all gone back to the pews and were waiting for his signal of dismissal so that they could return to their village together. Angelina sat in the first row looking straight at the priest, the men spread out behind her. Hennessey went over to her pew and slid in beside her. Putting his arm around her shoulders, he bent over and looked into her black eyes. "Angelina," he told her, "you know that I am very sorry about what happened to Diego. He was like a brother to me, a good man, one who gave much of his energy to the work of God, to teach the people to love. I'm sure he's with God now and will look after you and your children . . . . Thank you for encouraging the men to come in and confess. You have done much to heal some terrible wounds . . . . If you need help, come and talk to me and I'll do what I can."

Angelina smiled at the priest. "I know, padre. Diego be a good husband, a good father. He not beat us and not drink. But his son be taking his place and his grandsons, too. We be surviving!"

Hennessey nodded, squeezed Angelina's shoulder, got up, and went to the rectory.

Two minutes later, Angelina left the church for Bulej, followed by a parade of thirty-two repentant civil patrollers.

On 21 July 1982, one of Guatemala's most conservative daily paper, *El Imparcial* (The Impartial One), reported recent occurrences in San Mateo as detailed by the army's office of information:

On the sixteenth of this month, San Mateo Ixtatán's PAC, stationed in the vicinity of the town, discovered a group of subversives moving toward town. An armed conflict resulted and three rebels were killed. The PAC found armaments of various calibers, claymore mines and binoculars abandoned by the rest of the delinquents when they fled.

El Imparcial, 24 July 1982:

The Civil Defense Patrols from the villages of Chontala [*sic*], Chichi [*sic*], Quiché [*sic*] and Puley [*sic*] of San Mateo Ixtatán, Huehuetenango, confronted rebel groups [intending] to capture said villages, with the result that three rebels were killed.

No other reports in the Guatemalan newspapers mentioned anything other than the above happening during the month of July in San Mateo Ixtatán. There were, however, references to massacres in other parts of the country and national news items relating to the conflict.

HEADLINES

El Imparcial, 26 July 1982:

Guatemala has broken its isolation. Senator [*sic*] Charles Wilson[4] of Texas will ask the Reagan Administration to renew arm sales to Guatemala.

El Imparcial, 28 July 1982:

Minister of Foreign Relations Eduardo Castillo Arriola said that the government knows all about the families along the border fleeing into Mexico which is the result of subversive actions. He told of cases of deaths of villagers of Huehuetenango right in front of their families, murdered by guerrillas.

Chapter 33

AN ANTISUBVERSION MASS

"In the name of the Father," Hennessey prayed, blessing himself with the sign of the cross, "and of the Son," echoed by the congregation, "and of the Holy Spirit," he finished in unison with the faithful, and then together with a thousand pious, shouting voices, "*Así sea! Amén!*"

"Brothers and sisters," he began, looking out at a sea of upturned faces of a larger than normal audience. They were standing on the parish basketball court in front of the church. A half hour earlier, he had set up two small loudspeakers to broadcast his voice across the plaza, using a handheld microphone. "This is a special Mass that we celebrate today! It is a special Mass because it is an antisubversion Mass! And it is an antisubversion Mass because it has been requested by the authorities!"

The day was Sunday, 1 August 1982. The sky was clear and sunny, not unusual weather for this time of year in San Mateo. It was a short break in the usual winter season rains, called a *canícula*. Hennessey paused for a moment, looked down at his large, stained hands reposing lightly on the edge of the improvised altar before him, as he waited for his words to sink in. A few seconds later, he looked up again, surveying his ever-patient parishioners and the curious onlookers who had come to witness this unusual public display of officially requested religiosity.

San Mateo's mayor had solicited the Mass of Hennessey the preceding day. The mayor was a Protestant evangelical appointed by Ríos Montt. He, like mayors across the country had been named by the born-again militarist to replace his elected predecessor. The new official, Fernando Supul, had made the petition in such a way that Hennessey knew the order for the service had come from the Barillas commandant, although the mayor did not openly say so. He had used the ladino custom of employing barely concealed insinuation to get his point across while maintaining a margin of ambiguity to claim misunderstanding should later developments demand it. Apparently, the commandant wanted the mayor to pretend the suggestion was made on his own initiative.

The priest and the mayor sat opposite each other across the coffee table in the rectory making small talk. Hennessey had offered the mayor a cup of coffee when they first sat down together, but his guest's refusal of the invitation, a violation of Mayan protocol, was a strong indication that this was a painful call for the official to make. Yet, the Iowan had been content to comment on the weather and the state of the season's crops until his guest felt enough at ease to bring up the real purpose of his visit.

The man was obviously nervous, continually wiping his nose with the back of his hand and then squeezing the fingers of one hand with those of the other.

"Excuse me, padre," the mayor had finally said, clearing his throat while using a title not favored by the evangelicals, "but you be praying your Mass here in town tomorrow, no?"

"Of course, *don* Fernando," the priest responded cautiously. "Sunday is the day everyone comes to town for market and Catholics expect to be able to go to Mass at the same time. I celebrate Mass here every Sunday. You know that! Why do you ask?"

"Well, I talk it over with my assistants and we think it be nice if you and the evangelical pastors here in town each have a public antisubversion service tomorrow morning on the basketball court while everyone be here for market. We think it best you pray your Mass first, then the evangelicals follow you . . . . I already talk to the pastors and they be willing. I think it be easier and safer for all of us. I hope you agree!"

Hennessey did not respond to the mayor's request right away. It was Fernando's emphasis on the word "safer" that told the Iowan that the suggestion, or more likely, the order, to hold the service had come from the military. He knew that the mayor and his advisers would not have come up with such a brazen idea. Only the military would attempt to use the priest and other pastors to bolster their authority after employing a terror campaign that violated every principle of religious morality. Hennessey also knew, judging from the mayor's final remark, that any hesitation on his part to do what was asked would be interpreted by the military as a sign of the priest's support for the "subversives." And remembering the accusations recently made against him by the captain in Sebep and Bulej, Hennessey knew that to do anything that would lend credence to this charge could be dangerous.

"Of course I'll celebrate the Mass tomorrow, *don* Fernando," the priest finally answered. "And it will be an antisubversion Mass, as you request. I welcome the opportunity to speak out publicly against subversion . . . . I live with the nightmare of what happened to Francisco Paiz García, a good friend killed in the most barbarous way in San Francisco, Bartolomé Matzún in Bulej, Felipe Lucas and his family in Sebep, and the hundreds of others. I've been frustrated by my inability to do anything about these murders . . . . But your invitation will allow me to speak my mind beyond the confines of our church walls. We'll set up the altar tomorrow on the basketball court and I'll leave out our portable loudspeakers for the evangelicals to use."

Once Hennessey expressed his willingness to go along with the mayor's request, the official remained silent, trying to interpret what the priest meant by "subversion." The mayor knew, as did everyone in San Mateo Ixtatán, that the army was responsible for the crimes in the *aldeas* that Hennessey alluded to, although on the national and international levels the government was continuously attributing all such atrocities to the guerrillas. Did this foreigner misunderstand the word subversion? Or did he merely intend to talk about the massacres that were themselves public knowledge and pretend that they were the work of the EGP? The mayor knew, as should the priest, that the word "subversion" was employed only to refer to guerrilla activities, not those of the army. An antisubversion Mass, by definition, therefore, had to be in the context of condemning the guerrillas.

"*Está bien, padre,*" the official had finally responded. Then, to be sure he relieved himself of all responsibility for what the priest might say, added, "I communicate to you our request. Only you be knowing how to pray your Mass."

After a few more minutes of conversation that scrupulously avoided any mention of the army's terrorist activities, the mayor stood up to leave. As the two men walked to the door, Hennessey remarked in an offhand way that he intended to offer the Mass especially for Francisco Paiz García, the foreman on Finca San Francisco, and his more then 360 neighbors. The mayor hesitated briefly, looked at the priest with a puzzled expression—a squint of the eyes, shrugged his shoulders, nodded his head, and bid him, *"Hasta luego, padre."*

After watching the mayor, head down, shoulders hunched, climb the cobblestone street toward his office, Hennessey shut the rectory door and turned distractedly toward his writing table. He was already crafting the next day's sermon in his mind, determined to clearly condemn the army's subversion, as well as its leaders, without any equivocation. At the same time, he recognized that he had to do it within the framework of ladino culture, allowing himself maneuverability to later claim misunderstanding or misinterpretation if he were accused of a direct attack on the *"dignidad de las fuerzas armadas,"* a crime under Guatemalan law. The priest was well aware of his propensity to make spontaneous remarks and it was essential that he make no explicit mention of "the army," "the military," or "the armed forces." He had to balance that with the deep emotional need he felt within him to make as strong a public statement as possible regarding his personal perspective, in order at the same time to strengthen the resolve of his congregation. This, while giving testimony of his affection for those friends and parishioners victimized by the army's "unconventional warfare."

As Hennessey sat at the table trying to compose his sermon, pencil in hand, he discovered the meaning of writer's block. A kaleidoscope of pulsating images of crushed and severed body parts and disembodied faces, those that had been tormenting him for almost two weeks now, flashed once again through his mind like a video loop, repeating over and over again. His loss of composure made it impossible to decide where or how to begin. After several minutes of troubled indecision, the Iowan pushed his chair back from the table, linked his fingers behind his head, closed his eyes, and forced himself to sort out the scenes. Almost immediately, the vision of the scant details of the sacrificial ritual of blood and violence gleaned from those who had secretly visited the scene at San Francisco expelled all competing images from his mind. A feeling of physical revulsion passed over him as he visualized a U.S.-made helicopter coming in from the departmental capital transporting a top military *comandante* to oversee the slaughter.

As the Iowan imagined laughing men in blood-splattered, camouflaged uniforms leading a parade of crying children, some literally babes-in-arms, from the San Francisco chapel where they had been imprisoned, he shivered noticeably. With his breathing coming in short, powerful bursts, the priest could see the soldiers leading men from the courthouse, ten at a time, tying each group together, then mercifully cutting them to ribbons with Israeli-made Uzi machine-guns.

The tragic figure of his good friend Francisco Paiz continued to break through the Iowan's efforts to block it. Hennessey shuddered, feeling his anal and stomach muscles tighten. He could see the ranch foreman, barely able to walk, held up by a soldier on either side, a wooden stake driven in his anus and out through his abdomen. How many times had that scene come back to him during the past ten days, ever since it had been painted by some parishioners from Yalambojoch who had witnessed the demise of the foreman on the trail from San Francisco near their village.

Oh Lord, the priest moaned. *Whatever made Milenario trust Ríos Montt's promise of amnesty? . . . I can't just talk about these atrocities in a sermon! . . . I've got to drag this insanity into the open . . . in Guatemala City and . . . in the United States! . . . We've got to try to understand, . . . for Guatemala, . . . especially for the United States!*

Finally, Hennessey settled down and decided that he would make his sermon short and to the point, holding up Francisco Paiz García and his San Francisco neighbors as exemplars of biblical fidelity. He would not go into any detail regarding the killings. Every one of his listeners already knew at least as much as he.

"I am happy to comply with that request of the authorities," Hennessey's voice boomed across the basketball court and up into the plaza beyond. "I, too, am opposed to subversion, as are all of you! . . . But, . . . we should ask, . . . whose subversion is this that we oppose?"

Again, the priest paused for effect before continuing. "What some call subversion, . . . others call defense of their God-given rights! And what some refer to as patriotism or national defense, . . . others consider subversion, . . . exploitation, . . . slavery, . . . and yes, as the bishops themselves have said, . . . even genocide!"

Hennessey drew in a deep breath and exhaled it slowly, as total silence engulfed the congregation. Even the children seemed to sense a tension in their parents, and they stopped fidgeting and fell silent. The Iowan could feel his respiration pick up in anticipation of what he was about to say.

The priest shifted the microphone to his left hand, wiped the perspiration from his right palm on his vestments, and continued his sermon: "As you know, we have had the worst kind of subversion here in San Mateo these last few weeks, subversion of the laws of God; subversion of the laws of Guatemala; subversion of all moral principles; subversion of our very humanity!"

The priest paused as little beads of sweat trickled down his back. "I am talking about the raping, the burning, and the disemboweling of men, women, and children in San Francisco . . . . I am talking about forcing innocent victims to club their neighbors to death in order to save the lives of their loved ones, in Sebep, Yolcultac, and Bulej . . . . I am talking about the stabbing, shooting, and burning of all the inhabitants of Petenac, young and old, male and female, without any regard for their guilt or innocence . . . . Thousands of innocent people are now fleeing for their lives to the safety of Mexico, emptying many of our northern *aldeas*, to escape the wanton death and destruction being sown with impunity by insane killers."

Again Hennessey stopped to catch his breath, leaning heavily on the altar . . . . "If these heinous crimes are not subversion, . . . then there is no such thing as subversion."

The Iowan experienced a rush of adrenaline as he watched a sea of chocolate brown and black eyes open wide, staring at him, almost unblinking. Both he and his audience knew that he was accepting a much larger risk than ever before by confronting the government so clearly during an open-air public service. It was one thing to condemn the government with barely disguised language in what might be considered the relative privacy of the church during a service in which the military had no particular interest. It was quite another to do so in public before an audience of Catholics, evangelicals, and traditionalists, Mayans and ladinos, friends and non-sympathizers, in a public service almost assuredly requested by the military authorities.

Now, suppressing a small inner voice of caution, the Iowan continued his sermon. "Some participated in those killings against their will, to save the lives of their loved ones. Others participated in order to save their own lives because they wanted to demonstrate their loyalty to an institution that merits no loyalty. The men who ordered those murders are the ones who committed the worst of crimes—against God, against humanity, against all Guatemala!"

A few people, walking along the street above the steep bank bordering the basketball court, stopped to listen to the priest condemn deeds and their authors that only the foolhardy dared mention, and then only within the circle of one's closest, most trusted relatives.

"But we must also recognize that each of us is guilty to the degree that he or she went along with the murders. Even if we acquiesced only in our hearts, we have committed a grave sin . . . . Now we must begin to heal the deep, ragged wounds opened by this godless subversion . . . . And we must also ask God to forgive those who committed these terrible deeds once they have acknowledged their guilt . . . . Although, in our hearts, we are sometimes tempted to hope that He never does."

The Iowan again surveyed the basketball court looking to see if any soldiers were present. He hadn't noticed any earlier and did not expect any now—at least, not in uniform. They could hardly accuse the Church of spreading communism and then attend Mass in any capacity other than to spy. He presumed that someone or ones were present to make such a report, but he had no idea who they might be. Yet he saw no contradiction between the officers accusing the Church of communism and then asking him to celebrate an antisubversion Mass. Confusion, fear, disorientation, lack of faith in any power except that of the army were their goal. They hoped to drive a wedge between the people and the Church, between himself and his terrorized parishioners, to isolate guerrilla sympathizers, to stop all talk of human and God-given rights.

"This Mass today," the Iowan continued, "this antisubversion Mass, is offered for all those who have undergone suffering and death as a result of the subversion about which I speak. Although Pope John Paul II may never officially recognize their sacrifices, all of us here know that we now have our own legion of martyrs in heaven. We can rejoice that their suffering is now over, but we must condemn with all our moral energy those who are responsible for their deaths."

Now, as some of those scenes flashed once again through his mind, Hennessey looked out over the congregation and shook his head, trying to concentrate on the faces before him. "And who are those responsible for these terrible crimes?" he asked . . . . "We know who they are! . . . We may not know their names, but we know what they look like, how they dress, where they come from! . . . But, . . . there are still others, those who hide behind the killers, who are not so visible, who are more difficult to recognize . . . . I speak of those who support this repressive system and the activities it spawns in the name of God, with claims of Christian legitimacy, . . . some of whom hold high positions in the Catholic Church . . . . They are not free of responsibility for these murderous acts. Perhaps their guilt is greater than that of the soldiers who wield the knives and guns that sever the chords of human lives and human relationships."

He stopped, realizing that he had used the word "soldiers," something he had told himself not to do. Well, there was no turning back.

The crowds on the edge of the bank overlooking the basketball court . had now become quite numerous, as many people left their buying and selling in the plaza to hear this priest, bereft of his senses, challenge the army to shut him up for good. Did he think he was immune from government anger? Did he believe that his priestly robes would work a miracle, restrain military vengeance?

But these were not Hennessey's thoughts. He had invested too much of his life in his Guatemalan mission, too much of his moral energy, to curb his tongue now in the face of army atrocities and army threats.

"Finally," the Iowan continued, "I must also mention another group of individuals, . . . hidden, . . . faceless, . . . but nonetheless responsible for what is happening here, and of whom I am equally ashamed . . . . They are the ones who live in Guatemala City and work in a building with the flag of the United States flying above it . . . . They are the ones who live and work in Washington, D.C., President Ronald Reagan, as well as members of the U.S. Congress . . . . They supply the money, the guns, the training, and the twisted ideology for the men who butcher your brothers and sisters and children and babies . . . . Both as a priest and as a citizen of the United States, I stand before you to tell you I am ashamed to be associated with such men and to apologize for them . . . . It is for these reasons that I am happy to have this opportunity to offer this antisubversion Mass, . . . to plead with God to send His grace, a spark of humanity, a flash of understanding, to help them see and renounce the terrible subversive crimes in which they participate."

564 THOMAS R. MELVILLE

Hennessey stopped. He could tell by the silence and lack of movement that he had shocked his congregation. He looked from one wide-eyed expression to another and knew that they had gotten his message. But he felt none of the happiness that he had just claimed that offering the antisubversion Mass had given him. It was a gut-wrenching experience to stand before these people and point his finger at members of the Church's hierarchy and at the U.S. government and its diplomatic apologists. In a strange, ambivalent way, a vague feeling of disloyalty had lodged in his stomach. He shook his head. *No! Disloyal to what? To lies, murders, and massacres?* He pulled his eyes from those of the congregation and looked down at the altar to catch his breath. His hands held his attention. *Have I said too much? No! No! No!*

The priest raised his head and forced himself to continue: "One more thing! I ask you to join with me in offering this Mass that this subversive psychosis cease! . . . May God touch the hearts of the cruel and blind men who have commanded this unnatural, inhuman subversion of His laws . . . that they recognize the full evil of their actions . . . . And in order to help them do so, I tell you that I will make every effort to see that the full story of the crimes committed against you, your families, and your neighbors, be broadcast to all corners of the world . . . . My voice is small, but the pulpit in which I stand is large. I will focus my energies to see that the world acknowledges these evils, . . . so that these holocausts stop, . . . these hatreds wither away, and the rivers of tears run dry . . . . May these power and prestige games be seen for the meaningless fantasies they are, . . . and may the spirits of your dead live on in the memories not only of us here, but of all humankind as testimony to our hope . . . that such crimes never be repeated."

Hennessey waited a few moments, looking out over his frozen congregation and the crowds of silent bystanders on the bank above, reaffirming within himself this commitment to tell the story of San Mateo's "Julio Negro," its Black July, to all who would listen. Then, slowly, he stepped back from the altar, spread his arms wide as if to embrace all who stood before him, and after pausing, intoned: *"El Señor . . . esté . . . con vosotros.* May the Lord . . . be . . . with you."

For a second or two, his stunned audience did not respond. But then, Santiago Quot, standing to one side of the altar, called out the proper liturgical reply: *"Y con tu espíritu!* And with your spirit!" Then two or three others answered hesitatingly with the same response. Finally, in a burst of Mayan emotion, the whole congregation called out: *"Y con tu espíritu!"*

When he finished the antisubversion Mass and took off his liturgical vestments, Hennessey approached the two evangelical ministers standing beyond the shadow of the altar. The priest had noticed toward the end of his Mass that the evangelical faithful were beginning to assemble at the edges of the basketball court in anticipation of their own antisubversion service. As the three men talked about making changes in the altar configuration, including placement of a temporary lectern to support a bible, Catholics began moving off the basketball court to allow the evangelicals to move in. Then, suddenly, a hush fell over the crowd and all movement ceased. Hennessey and his two colleagues looked up together, struck by the abrupt change in the noise level. All eyes were turned toward the embankment overlooking the court. Slowly, by twos and threes, soldiers in muddy, stained camouflaged uniforms began to congregate there, pushing their way through the silent bystanders. The effect was electric. No one said a word. All knew that running for cover was on everyone's mind, but not a soul dared move, except to make room for the new arrivals.

"So this is why they wanted the services today," Hennessey whispered to his two colleagues.

The two ministers turned and looked at the priest with questioning expressions.

The priest continued: "They held those guys out in the *aldeas* until today so that they could make a triumphant entrance on market day in front of everybody, on a Sunday, blessed by the town's religious authorities."

The two men nodded.

Finally, the Catholics moved slowly to the outskirts of the court and the evangelicals took their place. Someone brought in a lectern and a large bible while Hennessey and Santiago Quot removed the Mass vestments, crucifix, and candles from the altar. More soldiers gathered on the bank. The ministers conducted their services distractedly, their eyes on the troops above them. No mention was made of subversion or antisubversion. Faith in the Lord's holy word, love of Guatemala, and respect for authority were the themes of their services. Everyone tried to keep the soldiers in view without seeming to look at them. The soldiers, for their part, stood talking and laughing, overlooking the service, surveying everyone and everything with an undisguised arrogance, as if they were the conquering legions of Caesar, having just won a glorious battle.

That afternoon, Hennessey watched as more dirty, blood-stained soldiers, led by Lieutenant Hawk-nose from Soloma, straggled in with their victory booty: turkeys and chickens, tied by the feet and slung over the shoulders of their new owners; radios, tape recorders, and guitars for the musically inclined; clothes, shoes, and blankets to send home to families, much of it piled on the backs of fourteen horses and a single donkey. The Iowan drew a deep breath when he saw the donkey. He recognized it as the same animal that Francisco Paiz García loved so much, the one about which he and Hennessey had made so many "subversive," antimilitary jokes.

The soldiers drank a lot of *aguardiente* that afternoon. At 3:00 p.m., several mortars were shot off, apparently in celebration of having killed so many "guerrillas." The priest worried what a couple of hundred drunken soldiers might do to the town and its inhabitants, even though the market had closed early and the villagers had all slipped away as unobtrusively as possible. But the officers managed to keep the soldiers in their makeshift barracks in the town hall.

At nightfall, a messenger from the mayor's office arrived at the rectory to tell Hennessey to report to one of the lieutenants because the officer wanted to use the priest's pickup.

The Iowan nodded. "The lieutenant wants to use my pickup? And does he know that I celebrated an antisubversion Mass this morning? Does the lieutenant have a hawk nose? . . . Never mind! If the lieutenant wants to talk to me, he should come here. I have no desire to talk to him!"

The messenger shot a startled look at Hennessey. "Do you really want me to tell him that, padre?" the man asked.

The Iowan thought it over, "Just tell him that I have no interest in talking to him, and that if he wants to talk to me, he'll have to come here."

Not one, but two lieutenants, neither one Hawk-nose, put in an appearance shortly thereafter, both decidedly drunk. "Open up, priest," one of them called, as he banged on the rectory door.

When Hennessey opened the door, the two officers pushed past him with no attempt at asking for permission to enter. Once inside the sala, they turned to face the priest. "We need your vehicle . . . to go to Barillas," the more aggressive of the two demanded with slurred speech. "We are commandeering your vehicle in the name of the Guatemalan Army, . . . for official army business . . . . We need to recharge our radio batteries in Barillas."

Hennessey waited, wondering if the two officers before him were more dangerous drunk or sober. A staring contest was on. Suddenly, one of the lieutenants lurched to one side. The priest froze, ready to dive for the floor. But then, he recognized the officer's movement as simply an attempt to maintain balance and prevent falling.

Still standing by the partially open door with his hand on the knob, the Iowan decided to try to placate his two visitors by offering to let them borrow his spare twelve-volt battery. The gesture proved counterproductive. The two men tried to out shout each other, protesting that theirs was a unique Israeli-made unit that needed a special adapter from the Barillas base.

"Well, I'm sorry, but I can't let you have the pickup," the Iowan replied. "You've both been drinking too much to drive. It's nighttime and you could easily hit a rock in the road and tear out the crankcase. You'll have to figure out something else for your radio!"

The two drunken officers stared at the priest, not wanting to believe their ears. As their anger built noticeably, the Iowan recognized the need to quickly terminate the interview. He took a step back, opened the door wide, stood at stiff attention, and said, "Good evening, gentlemen."

Furious, the two officers pushed past the Iowan on their way out the door. Outside, the first speaker turned and glared at the Iowan for a moment, then muttered, "Your time is coming, priest! The captain will make you obey . . . or pay! Just because you're a gringo, you think you can defy the Guatemalan Army. But you can't! . . . We know what you said at Mass this morning. Your time is coming, *cura!* Just wait!"

The two turned and stumbled up the street, yelling, *"Cura, gringo, chingado,* fucking gringo priest!"

Hennessey remained at the door for a few moments, watching the two retreating shadows until they disappeared into the plaza. Then he went to his chair and sat down, trying to think of what he should say when and if the captain showed up. *If he's drunk, I'll tell him the crankshaft is broken. If he's sober, I'll tell him the engine overheats. Or maybe I'll just tell him that I refuse to cooperate with ghoulish murderers.*

But Hennessey need not have concerned himself. Neither the lieutenants nor the captain came back.

The following day, the captain and his men auctioned off the animals they had stolen. It was like an old-fashioned farm sale similar to many the

Iowan had attended back in Independence. One of his parishioners paid forty quetzales for Francisco Paiz's donkey, hoping to return it to one of the murdered foreman's relatives. Hennessey thought to himself that he would have gladly given all the money he could lay his hands on to have saved the dozens of butchered children from their executioners.

Later that evening, the soldiers' celebration became noticeably noisier as they shot off their weapons and fired mortars into the air, lighting up the evening sky. One soldier, according to what Abelardo Valenzuela later told Hennessey, demonstrated that he still harbored a spark of conscious humanity, if not the needed dexterity, by tying the trigger of his rifle to his big toe in a failed suicide attempt. It was an awkward mechanism and the guilt-ridden man only managed to crease his skull. The captain, furious at this sign of weakness, ordered the man's comrades-in-arms to pummel the "coward." The beating lasted three hours and almost accomplished what the unfortunate soldier had failed to do for himself.

On the following day, nine truckloads of new soldiers came from Guatemala City. Those who had brought "Black July" to the people of San Mateo Ixtatán boarded the trucks, laughing and shouting like heroes. As he watched the trucks roll out of town with singing, waving soldiers, Hennessey wondered if he shared a common human nature with them. *If it's the last thing I do, I'll see that the world knows what bastards you are and what you've done here.*

It was a promise that Hennessey would not find easy to keep.

Chapter 34

THE EMPEROR EXPOSES HIMSELF

The day following the antisubversion Mass, Hennessey asked a colleague passing through San Mateo to hand deliver his written account of the Sebep, Yolcultac, Petenac, Bulej, and San Francisco massacres to Maryknoll's regional superior in Guatemala City. The Iowan included a cover letter asking Bill Mullan to pass along a copy of the report to the U.S. Embassy and find someone to deposit the original, addressed to his family, safely in the U.S. mails. Ten days earlier, the priest had asked a local Mayan merchant/smuggler, thought to be trustworthy, to drop a similar account of the massacres into the Mexican postal system on his next trip across the border.

Hennessey had been sending out "subversive" mail in this manner for eighteen months—ever since someone began opening his letters shortly after his arrival in San Mateo. He never knew whether the sloppy work the inspectors performed resealing his envelopes was due to normal incompetence or to their desire to give him a touch of paranoia by letting him know that he was being watched. At the time he sent his report to Mullan in Guatemala City, the Iowan did not know that the military commandant in a border town, Gracias a Dios, had discovered an earlier letter on the person of his merchant/ smuggler/courier. The commander had demanded that all the priest's subsequent letters be turned over to him or the man would forfeit his life. By the middle of August, then, Colonel Hernández Catalán already knew that Hennessey was trying to send a full report of the July massacres in his parish to the United States.

For years, Hennessey had been explaining to his family, friends, and sponsors the repressive nature of the Guatemalan economy and politics, underpinned by the army's guns and U.S. government aid, and legitimized by Cardinal Casariego. But during this time, he had never asked anyone to publicize the facts beyond their own circle of acquaintances. He had often met with U.S. and European reporters, especially while serving as Maryknoll's regional superior, to give details of the army's murderous activities. But he had always asked for anonymity, knowing that if his remarks were publicly attributed, the government would expel him from the country and curtail the work of Maryknoll.

On 16 August 1982, Hennessey went to the capital to take a young parishioner with a tumor on the side of his face to the cancer hospital. There, he discovered that Mullan had not yet been able to put his July report into the hands of a trustworthy U.S.-bound visitor. Fortunately, on that very day, a willing courier passed through on his way from El Salvador to Illinois. The Iowan wrote a cover letter for the report and sent both off to his sister Dorothy Marie, stationed at a convent in Dubuque. After detailing his inability to aid the Petenac massacre survivor who had been spirited away to a distant village, Hennessey ended his missive by exhorting his sister to help divulge the news: "Please use this and anything else I sent to try to get others to stop the madness. I suspect the U.S.'s dirtiest hand is coming through Israel."

The priest's speculation about Israeli involvement was not off the mark. Such involvement had been openly recognized by President Lucas García, Ríos Montt's predecessor, who had extended effusive, public thanks to Israel for setting up the computer system used to track down guerrillas and their supporters in Guatemala City by identifying houses where above-average usage of electricity and water revealed the presence of unregistered occupants. In December, four months after Hennessey's letter, a high-ranking U.S. State Department official would confirm the Iowan's suspicion. The official acknowledged in typical government catachresis that Israel was providing arms and ammunition to the contras in Nicaragua, as well as to the Guatemalan government: "We've indicated that we are not unhappy that they [the Israelis] are helping out. But I wouldn't say that we and the Israelis have figured out together what to do."[1] An Israeli government spokesperson was more straightforward in admitting his government's involvement in Central America: "When a country friendly to Israel asks for help, we don't ask whether it's democratic or non-democratic, and we don't ask about its motives."[2]

Representatives of the fundamentalist Campus Crusade for Christ, the Christian Broadcasting Network, and Maranatha Campus Ministries had attended a briefing at the State Department on 27 July, ten days after the San Francisco massacre.[3] The session was arranged to follow up on the June meeting of Protestant evangelical leaders with Ambassador Chapin and Ríos Montt's spiritual advisor, Francisco Bianchi, at the home of OAS ambassador William Mittendorf. The evangelical participants in the July meeting stated that they were well on their way to sending to Guatemala a convoy of one thousand trucks from all over the United States loaded with supplies for displaced families. A State Department official had responded that "a convoy of the scale being proposed might be the vehicle that could get U.S. recognition for the Ríos Montt government."

The no-nonsense head of the Southern Command in Panama, General Wallace Nutting, sat ramrod straight in the witness chair before the Senate Armed Services Committee on 18 August 1982. He was there to demand that the senators send military aid to Guatemala because "the implications of a Marxist takeover in Guatemala are a lot more serious than in El Salvador."[4] The general, bedecked in his splendid uniform and campaign ribbons, maintained that the confrontation between the guerrillas and the Guatemalan Army had been planned in Moscow and carried out with support from Cuba and Nicaragua. Although Nutting admitted that there would have to be an acceptable political situation before military aid could resume, he added, "It is unfortunate up to this point that those [in Congress] responsible for making that judgment have felt that that kind of political situation did not exist."

By 1 September, Ambassador Chapin was able to announce that the United States would soon renew military aid to the Guatemalan Army, "in view of the government's improved human rights record." But Hennessey's report of the massacres in his parish still had not reached his sister's hands in Dubuque.

Finally, on 10 September, the priest's denunciation arrived in Iowa and Sister Dorothy Marie Hennessey turned it over to the *Des Moines Register*. On Sunday, 12 September 1982, the *Register* published the report in its entirety on the front page. Over the next few days, Sister Dorothy Marie received calls from newspapers across the country trying to get a slant on the story not contained in the *Register* account. Editorials began appearing saying that Father Ron Hennessey's description of the situation flatly contradicted the State Department's contention that human rights abuses had decreased under the Ríos Montt government. Some expressed fear for the Maryknoller's safety. The ensuing congressional uproar resulted in Ambassador Chapin receiving instructions from Washington requesting that he do everything possible to eliminate the possibility that the Guatemalan Army might take drastic action against the priest. An invitation that Hennessey received from the embassy's political officer, Harold Baum, to visit with him posthaste, was the result of this congressional concern.

On 29 September 1982, Hennessey and the regional superior met at the U.S. Embassy with Harold Baum and the consul general, Philip Taylor. The two diplomats tried to convince Hennessey that his life was in danger from the guerrillas. They strongly advised Hennessey to leave the country. They also tried to convince the Iowan that the massacres he had described were almost certainly the work of the EGP, almost as if he had never been to San Mateo.

The following day, Joe McClain, a man representing himself as a State Department investigator on the status of refugees, visited Hennessey at the Maryknoll Center House in Guatemala City. He quickly showed that he was not really interested in refugees. When the Iowan tried to tell McClain that Guatemalan soldiers moved with impunity across the Mexican border from his parish's territory to kill Guatemalans in the refugee camps, McClain maintained that it was probably the guerrillas doing the killing. The priest told him that he had verifiable information that the army had brought back refugees from Mexico to their newly established airbase at Ixquisís,[5] located in the northern sector of San Mateo parish, and had tortured and killed them there. McClain answered by asking Hennessey what he thought might be the strength of the guerrillas in the San Mateo area. With that non sequitur, Hennessey decided to cut short the interview; he stood up and bade McClain goodbye.

Back in the States, especially in Iowa, Hennessey's many siblings, relatives, and friends petitioned their elected officials to block military aid to the Guatemalan Army. Iowa Republican congressman Tom Tauke, a member of the pastoral council of the Catholic Archdiocese of Dubuque, said that he would vote against the administration's military aid package and would attempt to convince his colleagues to do likewise. But Senator Charles Grassley (R-IA), in answer to complaints from some of his constituents, wrote, "In contrast to its predecessor, the Ríos Montt government seems to recognize that it cannot win the war against the guerrillas by exclusive reliance on military action . . . . I cannot support total abandonment of Guatemala because the evidence suggests that a revolutionary government, patterned after Nicaragua's State, would not provide a legitimate alternative."

In a letter to Sister Gwen Hennessey, Senator Charles Percy (R-IL) wrote, "Various reports were presented to us [by the State Department] demonstrating that much of the violence has been the responsibility of the guerrillas in recent months and that serious measures are being taken by the government to curtail violence by its own forces and to work with the rural and indigenous populations in the country."

Congressional ignorance of the situation in Guatemala was largely self-inflicted, although not entirely, since Ambassador Chapin had taken the lead in feeding disinformation to Congress that they, in turn, might utilize to pacify any inquiring constituents. Deputy Assistant Secretary of State for Interamerican Affairs Steven Bosworth supported Chapin's claims. In a letter to Representative Michael Barnes (D-MD), chairman of the House Committee on Interamerican Affairs, Bosworth demonstrated the administration's contempt for the truth by using Hennessey's own words against him, taking them out of context and dropping a few key phrases. He said that "Hennessey now asserts that more people are being killed by the guerrillas than by the army," when in reality what the priest had said was, "If someone were to ask me who killed the most people in San Mateo Ixtatán during the past week, I would have to say that the guerrillas did, since they killed three people, while the army, fortunately, has killed none that I know of over the same period."

The *Des Moines Register* finally contacted Melvyn Levitsky, himself an Iowa native, and asked him to clarify the discrepancy between State Department claims and Hennessey's testimony. The subsecretary responded that he had helicoptered over the burned-out villages named in the priest's report but that it was impossible to tell who had destroyed them, the guerrillas or the army. He then implied that Hennessey's testimony had to be taken with a grain of salt since "the priests are always on the side of the guerrillas."

574   Thomas R. Melville

On the very day—29 September 1982—that Hennessey went to the U.S. Embassy to discuss the charges he had made in the Iowa press, the White House removed Guatemala from its list of human rights violators.

In early October, the results of eliminating Guatemala's name from the blacklist became evident: the White House announced it would support the Guatemalan government's applications to the Inter-American Development Bank (IADB) and the World Bank for $170 million in loans "because of improvements in the human rights situation." The first request in the package was for an $18-million-dollar loan from the IADB for a rural telephone network. Two key congresspersons, Tom Harkin (D-IA) and Jerry Patterson (D-CA), said they would introduce legislation to block the loans. Patterson explained: "The improvement of communications in zones where the government is committing atrocities is a form of indirect military aid." Ambassador Chapin, seeing Hennessey's report as the focus of congressional opposition to his embassy's attempt to rehabilitate the Guatemalan government's image, dispatched Harold Baum to talk to the Iowan to see if the priest would make a positive statement regarding the telephone network's developmental potential. Hennessey refused, being careful not to make any sarcastic remarks, though the temptation was appealing.

On 5 December 1982, President Reagan met with Ríos Montt in Honduras. After the meeting, Reagan told reporters that the Guatemalan head of state had provided evidence that widespread charges of human rights violations were a "bum rap," and that he, Reagan, recognized that Guatemala was facing a brutal challenge from guerrillas armed and supported by others outside the country. "I am leaning toward approval of a military aid package for the Ríos Montt government," the president assured the reporters. He might as well have confessed that the decision had been made long before he had left Washington.

Two months after President Reagan's spirited defense of General Efraín Ríos Montt's human rights record, Sister Francisca went to the church sacristy before Sunday Mass. She was there to ask Hennessey if in his sermon he would encourage their parishioners to participate in Pope John Paul II's upcoming visit to Quezaltenango, scheduled for the first week of March. Quezaltenango, Guatemala's second largest city, was the center of the country's most urbanized Mayan population. It was 6 February 1983 and Francisca was in charge of lining up transportation for those who expressed an interest in making the eight-hour trip.

"Sister Francisca," answered Hennessey, letting out a long sigh and massaging his chin between his thumb and index finger, "I think you and Sister Justa should line up whomever you can to go to see the pope . . . . I'm sorry, but I've decided not to attend and I don't feel comfortable encouraging others to do so."

Sister Francisca stood staring at the priest, a faint smile on her lips as she waited for the usual Hennessey one-liner, but the Iowan added nothing. Then, disbelieving her ears, the nun, with some hesitation, prodded him, "But . . . *padrecito* . . . . you're not going to see . . . the Holy Father? . . . But why?"

"Francisca, . . . don't take it so hard! No one will miss me in Quezaltenango! . . . You know, . . . at times I think the pope doesn't understand the conflict in this country any more than President Reagan does . . . . John Paul pays attention to Cardinal Casariego and the cardinal's political friends in the Vatican bureaucracy. And in both the pope's and Reagan's case, I don't think . . . their ignorance is excusable . . . . If I thought that John Paul would speak out clearly to condemn these atrocities and the friends of Cardinal Casariego who continue to commit them, . . . then I'd go! But he won't, . . . and I won't."

The look of disappointment in the nun's eyes bordered on hurt. She knew Hennessey was not a fan of Cardinal Casariego, but she had never heard him say anything pro or con about Pope John Paul II. For a few moments more, Francisca stood waiting, as if trying to find something appropriate to say. Finally, she turned and left the sacristy.

Hennessey's decision to refrain from participating in the celebration of the pope's visit had not been made in a moment of pique. The Iowan's ambivalence toward John Paul II had been building since the first days of the Polish pope's reign three years earlier, an attitude fostered in the priest by the affection and respect he felt for the memory of Pope John XXIII. Ever since the initiation of the Second Vatican Council, called by Pope John XXIII to "throw open a window" of the Church to allow the workings of the Spirit in the modern world to penetrate, Ronald Hennessey had rejoiced with his seminary classmates in the climate of reform that had begun to penetrate Roman Catholicism. John extended an ecumenical hand to the world's religious leaders and insisted that all cultures and all religions reflected the working of the Spirit and contained the availability of salvific graces. He wanted to promote the catholic spirit of his Church at the expense of its Roman (European) character.

Pope John Paul II had imbued little of the spirit of the Second Vatican Council. He ordained a series of right-wing bishops for Latin America, particularly those of the elitist congregation Opus Dei to replace the left-leaning bishops who had championed "the preferential option for the poor," an orientation that John Paul II—educated under the Polish communist system—considered a stepsister of liberation theology and a bridge to communism.

It was the inspiration of the Second Vatican Council's deliberations that motivated Hennessey to back away from trying to replace traditional Mayan religious beliefs with those of "orthodox" Catholicism. He no longer saw one as the antithesis of the other, but complementary approaches to the Divine. Now, as the Guatemalan Church prepared for John Paul II's triumphal visit to their troubled land, the Iowan refused to see it as the blessing that so many of his colleagues and faithful did. John Paul II could triumph his own infallibility and power in order to weaken or break the more pastoral members of the Church's hierarchy but try as he might he could not erase the effect of John XXIII's legacy on Ronald W. Hennessey nor on a sizeable proportion of the Catholic faithful.

Unknown to Hennessey, Pope John Paul II had met for fifty minutes with President Reagan in the Vatican library on 7 June 1982, just six weeks prior to the San Francisco massacre. It was the first meeting between the two men, and according to Richard Allen, later the president's national security advisor, they formed between them "one of the great secret alliances of all time,"[6] one that was intended to bring about the collapse of communism in Eastern Europe. To think that Latin America's search for social justice was also on the minds of the two men would be to underestimate the ideological commitment of these two professed anticommunist leaders.

A month after Hennessey's conversation with Sister Francisca, during the first week of March, Pope John Paul II began his visit to Central America.

Before arriving in Guatemala, he stopped in Nicaragua and El Salvador. On the tarmac after landing in Managua, the white-robed pontiff carefully knelt to kiss the pavement. It was a purely theatrical ritual that John Paul employed every time the papal aircraft landed in a new country, intending to show his affection for the land and its people.

When he approached the welcoming dignitaries in the Managua receiving line, the pontiff publicly rebuked Father Ernesto Cardenal, a Trappist monk and the government's minister of culture. John Paul accused the priest of involving himself in partisan politics, a field that the pontiff reserved for himself and his appointed legates. While in Nicaragua, however, the pope paid special homage to Cardinal Obando y Bravo, the most outspoken opponent of the Sandinista revolutionary government and a supporter of President Reagan's terrorist contras. Obando y Bravo had been honored in Rome by Pope John Paul II with the cardinalate. Father Miguel D'Escoto, a Maryknoll priest and the Sandinista foreign minister, stayed away from the receiving line. The Maryknoller's entrance into the Sandinista government while Hennessey was still regional superior had met with the Iowan's silent approval.

In El Salvador, the Roman pontiff agreed to abide by the government's request that he not pay public honor to the memory of assassinated Archbishop Oscar Romero, making only a private visit to the prelate's grave. John Paul had taken Casariego's side in the cardinal's dispute with the slain archbishop some years earlier, although the U.S. government had played an important role in influencing the pope. President Carter had sent to Rome a prominent Catholic layman, former New York City mayor Robert Wagner, on two separate occasions to request that the pope silence Archbishop Romero. John Paul was sympathetic to the U.S. request and had called Romero to the Vatican and cautioned him to be careful of "false ideologies," implying that the archbishop was a communist dupe. Now, as the pontiff tried to put a damper on revolutionary currents sweeping through the Salvadorean Catholic peasantry, he made sure not to signal ecclesiastical support for the dead archbishop's outspoken opposition to U.S. aid for the Salvadorean government's counterinsurgency terrorism.

Four days before John Paul II's arrival in Guatemala, Ríos Montt ordered the summary executions of six individuals convicted of subversion by secret military tribunals. The pope had previously issued a public plea for the men's lives. Ríos Montt's disregard for that appeal just days before the pontiff's arrival in Guatemala was universally interpreted as an intentional rebuke of John Paul by the evangelical fundamentalist president.

Hennessey felt that the papal visit to Guatemala was anticlimactic. The Guatemalan episcopate had spent a full year preparing for the event, utilizing newspaper, television, and radio ads in a long-term, determined effort to make the visit an epic occurrence, a ritualistic expression of solidarity and triumphalism that would revitalize the nation's conservative Catholicism to its core. The bishops' principal hope was to stay the flow of large numbers of Guatemalans who had been fleeing to the safety and emotionalism of fundamentalist and charismatic Protestantism, a stream that had turned into a virtual river since Ríos Montt's accession to power.

Some months before the papal visit, Guatemalan Protestant fundamentalist leaders had gathered to plan their own public demonstration of triumphal solidarity to occur just before John Paul's arrival in order to counter the effects of the pontiff's pilgrimage. A week before the pope landed at Aurora Airport, the evangelicals brought together a huge crowd for a prayer meeting at a military field in Guatemala City. They claimed one million people—fully one-eighth of the nation's population—in attendance, an exaggeration by a factor of anywhere from two to five, but an impressive turnout, nonetheless.

Such a gathering put the bishops in a bind: how to produce a significantly larger outpouring of Catholic sentiment for the pope than the fundamentalists had had for their prayer meeting? Every parish in the country, including San Mateo Ixtatán, received a letter from its respective bishop exhorting all priests, nuns, and laity to go see the pope in person, either assisting at his Mass in Guatemala City or attending his sermon directed specifically to the nation's Maya in Quezaltenango.

Only five of Hennessey's parishioners accompanied Sisters Francisca and Justa to Quezaltenango. Many truckloads of faithful from surrounding parishes—Barillas, Santa Eulalia, Soloma, Jacaltenango, San Sebastián, San Rafael, and San Miguel Acatán—made the journey to see and hear the pope.

Hennessey welcomed the Mateanos back from their trip to Quezaltenango. As they descended from the bus, they shouted their excitement to him: "*Padre, vimos al papa!* We have seen the pope!" But the Iowan knew that the pope had not seen them, nor had he listened to them. In fact, the pope had listened to only a few of the hundred thousand Mayans who attended the Quezaltenango event. Anyone who talked to the pontiff—and they were mostly the elite of Quezaltenango's ladino citizenry, with a sprinkling of wealthy Mayans—had to be chosen beforehand by the bishops, and their remarks had to be given prior approval by Vatican bureaucrats. This ensured that the pope did not hear what Vatican officials did not want him to hear. This, of course, was done with John Paul's approval in order to foster the appearance of total Church unity, an image that might be tainted if someone were to state a position that did not correspond to the pope's own conservative beliefs.

But much to Hennessey's surprise and delight, John Paul II did one great service for the Church while in Guatemala: he reversed his former uninformed support for Cardinal Casariego and put the cardinal-archbishop of Guatemala City firmly on notice that he was no longer the pope's fair-haired boy. In a private meeting with the entire Episcopal Conference, the pope made it clear that he did not approve of Cardinal Casariego's underhanded maneuvers intended to inflate his personal power by creating disunity among the bishops, an unforgivable public sin as far as the pope was concerned. As a consequence, the papal putdown was a severe blow to Casariego's inflated ego and ecclesiastical power. When John Paul II left Guatemala, the cardinal retired to his episcopal palace to pout, much like his civil counterpart did in similar circumstances. Three months later, Mario Casariego, the darling of Guatemala's oligarchs and militarists, suffered a fatal heart attack. "Sic transit gloria mundi," Hennessey remarked to a puzzled Santiago Quot when the Iowan heard the news.

During Casariego's reign, government forces had killed thirteen priests and one nun, intentionally pushed another priest into insanity with torture and drugs, closed religious schools, clinics, hospitals, radio stations, convents, and rectories, drove priests and nuns from their parishes, murdered thousands of catechists and leaders, and tens of thousands of laity. And all this was done without a word of protest from the cardinal, in exchange for the pomp and circumstance supplied to the prelate by one illegitimate administration after another.

Cardinal Casariego was, fittingly enough, buried with full military honors. General Héctor López Fuentes, head of the army general staff, eulogized the dead prelate, stating, "Until his death, he [Casariego] was the spiritual guide of many army officers and confessor to the majority. He was considered the religious guide of the military institution with which he was always identified."

Guatemala's mighty and powerful were sorry to see the cardinal go. Although his influence had waned considerably during those three final months, high-ranking military officers, large landowners, and wealthy business leaders continued to use the prelate's name to buttress their concepts of a Christian social order: "Slaves, be subject to your masters." But by this time, the cardinal's ability to influence events both within and outside the Church was minimal.

Though Hennessey and many colleagues concelebrated Mass together that the cardinal's soul might rest in heavenly peace, the Iowan did not bemoan the prelate's passing. At communion time, he wondered wistfully whether Archbishop Romero was being given an opportunity to speak to Cardinal Casariego on the other side?

Cardinal Casariego had been gone from the national scene for only two months when a military upheaval swept away another power broker, one who, like the cardinal, had made it to the top by utilizing spiritual sloganeering to manipulate the temporal order. When Hennessey turned on his short-wave radio at breakfast on 8 August 1983, the newscaster for the U.S. Armed Forces Network announced that a coup d'état was in progress in Guatemala City. Some minutes later, the same newscaster told the world that Brigadier General Oscar Mejía Víctores, Ríos Montt's minister of national defense and the man with direct responsibility for overseeing the tactics and strategy of the counterinsurgency war, was the new head of state. Ríos Montt was finished!

The coup took no one by surprise. Displeasure with Ríos Montt had been brewing in powerful sectors of the military, the business community, and the Church since two or three months after the Huehueteco had taken power. During his sixteen months in the presidential palace, Ríos Montt had already survived four coup attempts, none of which had the approval of the most important player in the game of presidential musical chairs, the U.S. Embassy. Rumors had begun to spread more recently, however, that the U.S. government had become weary of the Huehueteco's continued stubborn refusal to enlist Guatemala in the U.S.-organized coalition pursuing the overthrow of the Sandinista government in Nicaragua. It was suggested to top military confidants that the Reagan administration was no longer opposed to a coup. Two months earlier, in June, General José Guillermo Echeverría Vielman (ret.), the former chief of army intelligence and éminence grise of the death squads, published an open letter to Ríos Montt in which he demanded that the president fire the group of young officers who served him as advisers, that he get rid of the religious counselors who allowed him to think he had a direct line to God, and that he return Guatemala to "constitutional rule." The general's letter was a call to arms, the meaning of which nobody could ignore. Other indications of crumbling authority quickly appeared when word began to circulate publicly that the commanders of the Huehuetenango, San Marcos, and El Quiché garrisons, as well as the air force, had all refused to carry out presidential orders.

Two weeks after General Echeverría Vielman's broadside, Colonel Francisco Gordillo—one of the original three members of the Ríos Montt junta, whom the Huehueteco had fired in a grab for total power, but who still remained on active duty—appeared on television to call for the president's overthrow. The colonel thundered that "Ríos Montt thinks God made him president, but it was we who appointed him." Leonel Sisniega, the MLN leader who had been a primary coconspirator with Ríos Montt, a man betrayed by the Huehueteco on the day of the coup, appeared with Gordillo to add his voice to the mounting public call for the Huehueteco's ouster, denouncing him as "a traitor and a religious fanatic."

Hennessey had heard for months from well-connected friends in Guatemala City that Ríos Montt's bible-quoting piety was angering many of his senior officers, forcing them to question the president's institutional loyalty and predictability. The fact that the Huehueteco had appointed several civilian North American *fanáticos* as close advisors was more than unconventional; it was an insult to national pride. And more than once, the Iowan had heard that Ríos Montt was considered "a religious psycho" by major personalities on the business-political scene.

Nor was General Mejía Víctores an unknown quantity for the Iowan. The general's reputation had it that he was a close ally of former presidents Arana Osorio and Lucas García, having participated with them in the army's first broad-scale terror campaign in Zacapa in 1966-67. Mejía Víctores had also made a name for himself as Ríos Montt's minister of defense by publicly expressing his opinion from time to time on the progress and goals of the ongoing counterinsurgency war. On one occasion, he acknowledged the underlying racist philosophy that fueled the army's vicious attacks on Mayan villages, stating that "we must do away with the words 'indigenous' and 'Indian' Our mission requires the integration of all Guatemalans."

When Representative Clarence Long (D-LA), chair of the powerful U.S. House Appropriations Subcommittee on Foreign Operations, went to Guatemala to verify U.S. State Department reports on the "improving" human rights situation, Mejía Víctores accused the congressman of "sounding like an emissary of the EGP and Amnesty International." Long responded that he thought "the general's collar was going to catch fire every time the subject of human rights came up." Back in Washington, Long stated, "If [my] committee does anything for El Salvador, it would be on the condition that Guatemala doesn't get a penny."[7]

Hennessey digested those first radio reports of the Mejía Víctores coup and had made an intuitive judgment that things could be no worse for the Mateanos and their countrymen than they had been under Ríos Montt. He then went to the front window to scan the hill above the rectory for any sign of unusual military activity. Everything appeared normal. Only two young ladino soldiers were engaged in animated discussion, sitting on the retaining wall at the edge of the basketball court. Thinking they might be arguing the pros and cons of events in the capital, the priest went out to speak to them. As he approached, the two men stopped talking to look at him with sullen anticipation.

"You fellows heard anything from the capital about General Mejía Víctores taking over the government from General Ríos Montt?" he asked after the customary salutations.

"What do you mean, padre?" the sublieutenant growled as he stood up. "Are you saying there's been a *golpe de estado*? Where did you hear that? I don't believe it!"

The sublieutenant's eyes were like two burning coals, not the most pleasant aspect of a face contorted with anger. Like the bearer of unpleasant news that he was, the priest recognized that he had made himself the object of the officer's emotion.

"I heard it on the radio from the United States, . . . but they're often wrong!" Hennessey replied, making a lame attempt to calm the officer's temper. "I'll check a little later and see what subsequent reports say. Things are still pretty confused right now."

"Maybe we could go with the padre and listen to his radio," broke in the other soldier, a sergeant, trying to bridge the gap between his colleague and the priest. "Is that OK with you, padre?"

"The broadcasts I'm listening to are in English," the Iowan replied, "so I don't think it would be of much help to you. But if I hear anything more, I'll let you know."

"Well, we've got to tell our *compañeros* about this anyway!" affirmed the sublieutenant. Then, more thoughtfully, "I wonder if the commandant knows?"

The officer stood looking at Hennessey for a moment, nodding his head. Then, abruptly, he threw back his shoulders, stamped his feet together, stuck out his hand and recited a carefully enunciated, *"Buenos días, padre!"* almost like he had just learned it at Guatemala's Military Academy of Good Manners. The priest shook the two soldiers' hands and turned back toward the rectory, while the sublieutenant and sergeant headed up the hill toward the municipal buildings.

During the afternoon, Hennessey walked past the parish basketball court where a team of soldiers was engaged in a volleyball game against a group of public school teachers. The soldiers had left their carbines leaning against the retaining wall within easy reach, guarded there by a few of their comrades-in-arms serving as cheer leaders. No bystanders dared to cheer for the teachers. As the Iowan passed by the net, he could not resist the temptation to poke a little fun at the soldiers: "Which team represents Mejía Víctores and which one is for Ríos Montt?" he asked, feigning an innocent look.

The Iowan's question was met with more than a few military scowls and several audible growls. The teachers, on the other hand, remained guardedly expressionless. Hennessey coughed, shrugged his shoulders, and moved on.

That evening, while writing home to relate news of the coup, the priest heard sounds of gunfire coming from the plaza and thought the soldiers might be having a minicoup of their own, Mejía Víctores insurgents against Ríos Montt supporters. Again, wanting to give expression to his penchant for ribald humor, he told his family, "Well, we're rid of what is known down here as the 'brassiere'—Ríos Montt—that which suppresses those within in order to impress those without."

On the following morning, Sublieutenat Julio Calderón and two privates brought a colleague to the parish hospital on a stretcher. At first, Hennessey thought the patient was the victim of the previous evening's shooting. However, the student doctor advised him that the man suffered from an advanced case of typhoid fever and needed emergency surgery in Huehuetenango to stop internal bleeding.

The surly sublieutenant overheard the doctor's remarks. "We've already sent for a helicopter," he said. "His uncle is head of the Honor Guard at the Presidential Palace. We'll have him in Huehuetenango in an hour-and-a-half to two hours."

Hennessey shook his head. "I doubt that you'll get a helicopter up here today, even if his uncle is an important man. The change of government is still shaky and no one with authority will want to trust a helicopter in the sky just yet."

"But Walters might die if we don't take him down in a hurry. His uncle has a temper and we don't want Walters dying on our hands. I better try to contact someone with authority in Huehuetenango."

"Do what you have to do," the priest answered, "but if you don't have any luck, I can drive Walters to Huehuetenango."

Hennessey could see the animosity subsiding in the sublieutenant's eyes as he spoke.

Ten minutes later, the Iowan and the three soldiers gingerly put the moaning Private Walters into the back of the parish jeep and set out for Huehuetenango.

The five men had not arrived at Santa Eulalia when Sublieutenant Calderón began to open up. "Have you heard any more on your radio, padre? We're not getting much information from the stations in Guatemala City, and the authorities in Huehuetenango aren't telling us anything. Who went in on this with General Mejía Víctores? What did they do to General Ríos Montt?"

"As far as I know, Ríos Montt is under house arrest. He resisted the coup for a couple of hours but finally gave up. Only one soldier was killed. A couple of civilians, too! . . . General Fuentes López is still army chief of staff so that means that he supported Mejía Víctores . . . . Only two or three days ago, Mejía Víctores met with General Fred Woerner of the U.S. Army's Southern Command on the U.S. aircraft carrier *Ranger,* off the Pacific Coast. That means that Woerner conveyed the U.S.'s okay for the coup. Ríos Montt is finished."

"Well, that's just too bad if the United States is in on this one," the sublieutenant replied. "Ríos Montt was a good man! . . . Mejía Víctores *no tiene cabeza,* he doesn't have a brain. He'll get us back in the same trouble as Lucas García . . . . Now I understand why we were transferred to San Mateo a couple of months ago. We were the Honor Guard at the Presidential Palace and they knew we'd stick with Ríos Montt . . . . I wonder if Walter's uncle was in on this *golpe*? If not, . . . all our worry over this guy is for nothing!"

As Hennessey listened to the sublieutenant's frank remarks, he decided to take advantage of the moment to ask what rationale the officer could offer for the army's atrocities. "*Subteniente,* why do your *compañeros* kill so many innocent men, women, and children? Many Mateanos were not on the guerrillas' side. But when the soldiers slaughter innocent people indiscriminately, everyone turns against the army . . . . It seems to have been a very counterproductive strategy."

"Well, padre, . . . it's probably hard for you foreigners to understand what this war is like. Before I was assigned to the Honor Guard, I was stationed in Sololá. At one place near a village there, guerrillas killed a number of our men. We didn't know who or where the guerrillas were and the people wouldn't tell us. So I took my men in there and we killed everyone in the village. It was the only thing I could do! Most people don't understand what this war is like."

"No," the priest answered, "you're wrong, *subteniente!* The only solution is to let these people have a piece of land to grow their corn and beans, and to guarantee that they'll be treated like human beings on the plantations . . . . As long as the army insists that these people live the way they do, there'll be trouble."

"No, padre, . . . *you're* wrong! I think we've scared these *indios* so much they'll never dare take up arms against us again. Not in a hundred years!"

When the four men and the patient drove through Santa Eulalia, there were no soldiers stationed at the guard posts. The same non-reception awaited them in Soloma and San Juan Ixcoy. Nor could any soldiers be seen on the streets of the three towns. "Everybody's got orders to stay in the barracks until Mejía Víctores is sure of his control," mused the sublieutenant. "I hope we don't get in any trouble when we arrive at the base in Huehuetenango."

After a long silence, the priest asked, "What was all that gunfire at the municipal buildings last night? It sounded like you guys were having a miniwar of your own up there."

"Some of our men went to Barillas yesterday to play soccer against the base team there. The commandant, Teniente de León Custodio, stayed in San Mateo drinking, and he got himself drunk. He became very angry when we told him our team lost. He ordered the other *compañeros* to discipline the players, to keep punching them in the stomach. When Walters here said he was too sick to participate, the lieutenant began to punch him. Walters started bleeding from the mouth and some of the men protested. That angered the lieutenant all the more. At one point, he started shooting in the air, threatening us. Some of us jumped him from behind and tied him up. When he fell asleep, we released him. He didn't remember anything this morning, so no one said anything about it."

Hennessey looked over at the sublieutenant and was rewarded with a smile that seemed to demand understanding. When the Iowan looked ahead again without having altered his expression, the officer shrugged his shoulders and fell silent.

When they arrived at the base in Huehuetenango, the two privates carried Walters into the military hospital while Calderón conferred with the garrison commander in order to arrange an interview with the priest. The interview was the sublieutenant's idea, one that did not appeal to Hennessey. The Iowan knew that the commandant did not appreciate the notoriety the priest had gained as a result of his reports to the U.S. press. Also, Hennessey believed that the colonel might still be angry because of a telegram the Iowan had fired off two weeks earlier asking the base commandant about three Mateanos who had returned from a Mexican refugee camp only to be imprisoned without charge. The men had been set free two days after he had dispatched his telegram, but Hennessey heard later that the commandant was furious at "that fucking gringo priest's repeated interference in our mission." The colonel refused Calderón's request for the interview and the Iowan breathed a sigh of relief.

The next day, Hennessey returned to San Mateo, while Private Walters underwent surgery for a perforated intestine. Back in his rectory, the priest heard the Armed Forces Radio admit that Major William Mercado of the U.S. Army had been photographed talking on his walkie-talkie in the portal of the Presidential Palace while the coup against Ríos Montt was in progress. The purpose of the admission seemed to be the intention of showing the U.S. Armed Forces' objectivity, if not its integrity, by acknowledging a news item prejudicial to their claim of political neutrality, a news item, nevertheless, that was already common knowledge in Guatemala and reported in the U.S. press. A State Department spokesperson replied to a query, however, that Major Mercado was merely carrying out a routine investigation and that the United States did not favor a coup. "We had no prior knowledge of a coup and we reject these allegations." John Hughes, also speaking for the State Department, added, "General Mejía Víctores has promised Ambassador Chapin that he will terminate the state of siege, abolish Ríos Montt's secret courts, and continue the process of returning the government to democratic leadership."

Chapter 35

A Dios, Guatemala

General Oscar Humberto Mejía Víctores made a gesture toward Ambassador Chapin and the U.S. government: he dissolved the secret military tribunals. These had become a bone of contention for General Ríos Montt, the Reagan administration, and Pope John Paul II. A principal effect of the gesture was the release of sixty individuals who had been imprisoned under the tribunals' jurisdiction. Three hundred detainees, who had already been tried before the tribunals, could not be found—their bodies buried in some clandestine cemetery. They were now numbered among the sixty to eighty thousand Guatemalans who had "disappeared" since 1954.

Mejía Víctores, however, did not change the scorched earth policies of the Ríos Montt government, although he discarded the legal nicety of calling it a state of siege. The army's rationale for continuing the practice—as had been explained by Ríos Montt and his spiritual adviser Francisco Bianchi—remained operational. Ríos Montt had answered reporters' questions about the killings of unarmed civilians, stating: "Look, the problem of war is not just a question of who is doing the shooting. For each one who shoots, there are ten working behind him."[1]

Bianchi, however, stated the government's case even more explicitly: "The guerrillas won over many Indian collaborators. Therefore, the Indians were subversives, right? And how do you fight subversion? Clearly, you had to kill the Indians because they were collaborating with subversion. And then they would say, 'You are massacring innocent people.' But they weren't innocent. They had sold out to subversion."[2]

And so the kidnappings, tortures, disappearances, murders, and massacres continued. And even as the Reagan administration had claimed that Ríos Montt had bettered the human rights situation that existed during the Lucas

588

García regime, now the party line focused on Mejía Víctores as a marked improvement over Ríos Montt. And it looked like Ambassador Chapin would not miss a step in waltzing with his new partner, Mejía Víctores, because Ronald Reagan's tune remained the same. But appearances were deceiving and Chapin was just beginning to hear a discordant note coming from his reawakening moral conscience. It was a note he would begin to whistle to Mejía Víctores that would make impossible the pas de deux the two were engaged in.

In a roundabout way, Hennessey became aware of ambassador's ambivalence toward the lies and misrepresentations he was forced to generate and repeat in defense of President Reagan's Central American policies. The awareness began in January 1984 on a trip to Huehuetenango when the Iowan ran into his young Mayan friend, Padre Mario Tzoj, pastor of Ixtahuacán. Padre Mario was visibly upset when the two priests met in the corridor of the bishop's house in the provincial capital. A shared understanding of the alternatives facing their parishioners served as a bond between the two men, as did the younger priest's appreciation of Hennessey's years of experience and serenity in the face of almost daily dangers. The Mayan needed no circumlocutions to speak of the problem bothering him.

"The soldiers came to Ixtahuacán in mid-December and picked up three men from town, Ronaldo, two ladinos and a Mayan. Two days before Christmas, the *pintos* came back with the same three men dressed in army uniforms and wearing masks. Everyone knew who they were! The soldiers made them point out supporters of the guerrillas. They fingered ninety men from six different villages."

"During Christmas week," Mario continued, his words tumbling out so fast that the Iowan was having trouble picking up every expression. "They arrested all ninety men, some of them our best catechists. I heard they brought them here to Huehuetenango. Their families are begging for help. I came to see the base commander but he won't talk to me. His executive officer told me they weren't holding the men and that I should mind my own business. I don't know what to do, Ronaldo! You've had a lot of success with the military! Can you help me? . . . Maybe if you went to see the base commander?" the priest asked, a bit more hesitantly. Then, stepping ahead and turning toward Hennessey with a little laugh, added, "The army always listens to you gringos."

The two men stopped walking at the end of the corridor and stood facing each other. Hennessey smiled at the Mayan's little verbal jab. "I'll try to help, Mario. But I don't want you to think I can do much for them. I haven't had a lot of success in San Mateo . . . . I'm on my way to the capital now. It might be beneficial if I were to talk to the new papal nuncio, Monseñor Quilici. He seems like a decent fellow. I can also talk to some people at the U.S. Embassy. They've gotten some bad publicity from me in the past and I just might be able to use the threat of more if they don't give us a hand. Can you get me a list of the men and their villages?

"Yes! Yes! I have the list right here," Mario almost shouted, forgetting for the moment the confidential nature of their conversation and shoving a wad of wrinkled papers into the Iowan's hand. "I knew you would help!" Then, squeezing Hennessey's hand, he continued, "Do what you can, Ronaldo! *Y Dios te lo pague!*"

When the Iowan arrived in Guatemala City, Father Bill Mullan, the regional superior, accompanied him to the residence of the papal nuncio. The prelate was sympathetic. "But, Padre Hennessey, you must realize that I have little influence with this government. I can't be of much help except in protecting our priests and religious personnel. And even there, my influence is limited. I wish I could help those poor men."

"But, if you get the chance, Excellency, do what you can. Any time the government realizes the world is watching, they all become more cautious. It's the only lever we have."

Hennessey and Mullan followed up the visit to the nuncio with a stop at the U.S. Embassy. There, they were ushered into Harold Baum's cluttered, dingy office in the political section. Baum was not overjoyed to see them.

The Iowan began without any verbal niceties. "Ninety men were kidnapped in one of our parishes in Huehuetenango by the army during Christmas week. We think they are being held at the base in Huehuetenango, but the commandant refuses to see the pastor and his subaltern denies any knowledge of the men. We're hoping you will use your influence to find out where they are before they are murdered and buried off somewhere . . . . That is, . . . if they haven't already been interrogated and processed."

Baum sat looking at Hennessey, almost as if he wanted to outstare the priest. "It's not the policy of the Guatemalan government to do this sort of thing," the attaché answered without blinking, obviously aware that Hennessey recognized his deception to be nothing more than a diplomatic nicety. "Now, if it's the policy of a local commander, bringing it to the attention of the national authorities might be of some help."

"I intend to go to the foreign press with this story right away if we can't find out what is happening to these men any other way. The U.S. government, based on your statements and those of Ambassador Chapin, is now claiming that President Mejía Víctores is cleaning up the human rights situation left by Ríos Montt, . . . just as Ríos Montt was said to be curbing the excesses of the Lucas García administration. It wouldn't look good for your claims of blossoming democracy and human rights progress if the *New York Times* gets the Ixtahuacán story."

Baum stiffened. "There's no need to drag the press into this, Father Hennessey. That might hurt the men you're trying to help . . . . You seem to have a tendency to go at these problems in a counterproductive way . . . . Now I can make some inquiries with contacts I have in the military. I can't guarantee anything. Just let me make a few phone calls before you do anything. I'll get back to you in a day or two."

"That's fine, Mr. Baum. I think your efforts will be much more productive than anything I can do. I'll go to the newspapers only when I don't have any other alternative. I'm convinced that if we don't do something soon, the men will be dead, . . . if they aren't already. I'll wait one or two days to see what you can do."

Then, trying to keep all traces of sarcasm out of his voice, Hennessey added, "I appreciate your help and concern, sir."

The next day, the Iowan called the attaché at the embassy. Baum's tone indicated he wasn't happy to hear from the priest, but Hennessey felt the need to keep the pressure on.

"I haven't been able to get through to my contacts yet," the political officer answered. "I've called around and left several messages. I'll let you know as soon as I hear anything. If you need to return to Huehuetenango, feel free to do so. I'll let Father Mullan know when anything develops and he can relay word to you."

"That's all right, Mr. Baum. This is an extremely important matter. I'll stay right here in the capital until you have word for me."

The next day, the attaché telephoned to say he had contacted "his man," but was skeptical that he could do anything about the imprisoned men.

Hennessey thanked the diplomat for his good-faith effort and hung up. He then wrote a letter to the U.S. Catholic Bishops' Conference with all the details of the case, and sent it by personal messenger to Bishop James Malone of Youngstown, Ohio, the conference president. Before the Iowan left for Huehuetenango the next day, Baum called to say that he had been in contact with the commandant of the Huehuetenango base and had made arrangements to visit him during the following week, on Wednesday, 11 January. The attaché mentioned that although the colonel was not happy with the purpose of the visit, he admitted that he had the Ixtahuacán men at his base but intended to do nothing with them for the time being. Hennessey thanked Baum once again and headed for Huehuetenango.

The Iowan was convinced that Baum, as the embassy's political officer, was closely tied to the CIA and that his personal contacts were with G-2, the Guatemalan Intelligence Service. Hennessey had come to that conclusion years before due, in part, to his contacts with other embassy political attachés.

Back in the late sixties, Lawrence Pezzullo had been in charge of the political desk. He had made a virtual pest of himself by asking so many questions about the Melvilles after their expulsion, and about their contacts, that Sean Holly, the embassy's labor attaché, felt obliged to apologize to John Breen, the Maryknoll superior at the time, for Pezzullo's behavior.

A later occupant of the same position, Ray González, had been very helpful in using his influence to assist a witness to the death-squad murder of Father Stan Rother to leave the country before another death squad could kill the man. It saved the man's life, but effectively buried his testimony in the silence of Mexico. The government was trying at the time to pin the blame for Rother's death on three innocent Mayan bystanders. Like Baum, González had close contacts within the Guatemalan G-2. He told Bill Mullan on one occasion that the army had been responsible for "processing" Padre Juan Alonzo to death, the kind of information only a trusted insider would have.

On Friday, Hennessey began his two-day drive back to San Mateo, arriving late Saturday afternoon in time for weekend services. On the following Tuesday, he headed back to Huehuetenango to be on hand for Baum's visit to the commandant the next day. When Baum didn't show up on Wednesday, the priest sent him a telegram requesting information on the status of the investigation. Hennessey made the telegram as explicit as possible, knowing that all telegraphers had strict orders to take copies of all "suspicious" telegrams to the intelligence officer at the closest army base.

On Thursday, 12 January, Baum arrived on the Aviateca flight from Guatemala City. By early afternoon, he was in the bishop's residence looking for Hennessey. "I received your telegram," he volunteered before the priest could say anything. "I had every intention of coming yesterday, but I got a call Monday from the commandant asking me to put off my trip until today. He said he had to go to the capital yesterday and couldn't meet with me until today. So here I am!"

"Well, what did you find out? I presume you've already seen the commandant? Are the men alive?"

Baum lit up with a smile that signaled success. "Certainly they're alive! Furthermore, . . . they're all free! The commandant released the last sixty- . two yesterday, after he had finished his investigation. He said they will remain under suspicion but he doesn't have enough evidence to hold them at this time. He was surprised that you were so concerned. He told me to tell you that the next time you want information, all you have to do is go to the base yourself. His door is always open to you."

A glassy look had once more passed over Baum's eyes. It was the attaché's little technique for keeping himself from smiling and winking.

Hennessey thanked Baum for his efforts. The priest knew that the threat of a newspaper story on the kidnappings was what had moved the diplomat to act, but that didn't detract from his gratitude. The Iowan returned to San Mateo relieved that his efforts had been successful.

On Monday, 23 January, Hennessey had to go to Huehuetenango for consultations with the bishop and several other priests. He knew something was wrong as soon as he saw Padre Mario Tzoj approach him with a puzzled look on his broad features. "*Cómo estás,* Ronaldo?" the Mayan said softly, holding out his hand. "I didn't get a chance to thank you for everything you did for our parishioners. Most of them are home now and recuperating . . . . But we have no word from ten of them. Did you find out what they are going to do with them?"

A sickening feeling hit Hennessey in the stomach. "You mean they didn't release everyone?" he asked hesitatingly. "I was told by the political officer of the U.S. Embassy that all were set free. He even came to Huehuetenango to talk to the commandant personally. He must have thought all the men were released."

"Well, they're still holding ten men," Mario answered. "If what happened to the ones they released is any indication of what they're doing to the ones they still hold, they probably won't survive! The others came back with their hands and feet burned with cigarettes, electric shock burns on their tongues and testicles, finger and toenails missing, and some of them incoherent. They kept many of them standing in cold water up to their necks for days and no one got more than one tortilla and a bit of water each day. If they're still holding the other ten, who knows how long they'll last? Maybe they're dead already!"

Hennessey was stunned! Here he'd been back in San Mateo for two weeks, thinking that all was well with the Ixtahuacanecos, congratulating himself on the success of his efforts. He hadn't thought to check on the condition of the men when they were released, nor to verify the freedom of all. "*Ay, Dios*, Mario, I'm truly sorry! I should have checked on them. Now, I don't know what to do! If the U.S. Embassy can't get them released, well . . . ." He didn't want to finish his thought.

"I know what you're thinking," whispered Mario.

"The fact that they kept ten and released eighty doesn't look good!" Hennessey answered. "I've written to the U.S. Bishops' Conference and know the incident has already received some publicity in the United States. I can follow up with a letter to Maryknoll. They have ways of making the media pay attention. It's not much, but I can't think of anything else to do."

"I know you've tried and we certainly appreciate all you've done for us, Ronaldo. I know you take a risk every time you confront the military with their crimes. We're not unmindful of the risks you take for us."

Hennessey smiled, a bit embarrassed. "Look, Mario, all I did was talk to our embassy. I haven't done anything that anyone else wouldn't have done . . . . We still have to work to get the other ten free."

"I know!" Mario said. "It's just that I have another favor to ask of you and I hate to do it. I don't want you to think I'm not conscious of the risks you take. So forgive me if I embarrass you!"

"Mario, Guatemala wouldn't be the place for me if I were worried about risks and dangers. I decided years ago that my life, just like yours and everyone else's here, was on the line all day, every day."

"It's Felipe Ortiz, the principal of our parochial school in Ixtahuacán. The army is out to kill him and he's hiding out here in Huehuetenango. He's the cousin of Patricio Ortiz Maldonado, the teacher in the USAID bilingual program whom they killed last year. You remember? Your embassy raised quite a fuss about it. They recently killed four more teachers in the same bilingual program. So now we have to get Felipe to Guatemala City where he'll have a better chance to go underground. The padres here at La Inmaculada want to send him on a bus, but I don't think he'd get past Malacatancito. What do you think?"

Hennessey shuddered at the thought of a wanted man going on a public bus to the capital and was surprised that the priests would even suggest it. "I agree, Mario. He'd never get past Malacatancito. For him to get on a public bus would be suicidal . . . . How do you know the army is after him?"

"A death squad tried to kidnap him Friday night during the fiesta in Ixtahuacán. It was about 11:00 p.m. There were five of them, driving one of the government's red and white Toyota wagons, with the dark glass and no license plates. There were people around and Felipe screamed. He was able to tear himself away in the confusion. He ran down some alleys and escaped. It took him two nights to walk in here over the mountains. I guess they want him because he's an educated *indio*."

"I'll tell you what," the Iowan said. "I'll drive him to Guatemala City myself. We can leave right away. There's more traffic on the roads during the day and the soldiers and civil patrols aren't as apt to challenge us as at night. Tell Felipe to get ready and I'll pick him up in an hour behind the church."

An hour later, Felipe and Hennessey were on their way in the Iowan's jeep. The Pan American highway runs past Huehuetenango from the Mexican border on its way to Guatemala City and beyond. They picked up the two-lane highway seven kilometers outside of Huehuetenango and headed south. Just as the priest had anticipated, the Malacatancito civil patrol was on duty right where the highway swings past Huehuetenango's nearest southern neighbor. A single patroller signaled him to stop as he tried to drive slowly past the dust-covered, blue-and-white GMC bus other civil patrollers were poking through at the side of the road. All the passengers were standing behind the bus in a line, while their baggage, persons, and papers were examined in minute detail.

Before the patroller could say anything, Hennessey handed over his identification carnet, volunteering that he was the pastor of San Mateo Ixtatán and his passenger, the sacristan. The patroller looked at the papers, obviously unable to read, stared at the priest's companion for a second or two, handed back the carnet, then signaled the two men to proceed.

Six hours later, after passing eight more checkpoints, Hennessey and Ortiz were in Guatemala City. The priest dropped his companion off at a run-down hotel where merchants from up-country often stayed in the capital. "Stay off the streets, Felipe, and I'll see what I can do," Hennessey told the young man as he stuck his hand through the window. "It's too late to go to the U.S. Embassy today. I'll come by tomorrow to let you know what the ambassador says."

The following day, the Iowan was able to get an appointment with Ambassador Chapin by telling the ambassador's secretary that he had a matter to talk over with the ambassador relating to the murder of Patricio Ortiz Maldonado, the USAID bilingual teacher from Huehuetenango. "You remember," the priest said, "there was a big fuss in the *New York Times* and in Congress some months back over the incident." The secretary came back a few moments later with an appointment with the ambassador for 2:30 that afternoon.

Hennessey knew the ambassador would be touchy about anything relating to the bilingual program established to teach Spanish to rural Mayans. The project had been financed by a $3 million grant from USAID. But in February 1983 it had become public knowledge that the program's Mayan teachers, like all educated Mayans, had been singled out as subversives bent on raising Indian consciousness, when soldiers killed four of them in Ixtahuacán— including an AID employee, one of the directors of the program, Patricio Ortiz Maldonado. At first, the army had denied culpability. But when it became evident that dozens of witnesses had last seen the victims taken away by uniformed soldiers, the Huehuetenango commandant claimed, "They were shot by the soldiers for trying to escape while being questioned about subversive activities." It was later revealed that the commandant himself had given the order by radio to execute the four.

When four more teachers, including two linguists, were kidnapped and murdered in October and November 1983, the embassy had asked the Guatemalan government for protection for "our linguists," presumably recognizing some special moral obligation toward people employed by a U.S. government-financed program. An official of the Guatemalan Education Ministry, when questioned about the possible motivation of the killers, had said, "there are powerful groups in this country that label as communist anyone trying to improve the lives of Indians." An official in the Ministry of Defense had promised "to look into the deaths."

Up in Washington, Congress had voted to cut $13.5 million from Guatemala's most recent appropriations, leaving more than $50 million in military sales credits and economic aid untouched. The State Department recalled Ambassador Chapin "for consultations" over the Christmas holidays, an action intended to signal disapproval to the Guatemalan authorities for the negative publicity. Chapin had returned from Washington only a few weeks earlier and Hennessey knew that mention of Patricio Ortiz Maldonado and the bilingual program was sure to get Chapin's attention.

The Iowan was not expecting much help from Frederic Chapin. At the time of the murders of Father Stan Rother of Oklahoma in Santiago Atitlán and Brother Jim Miller of Wisconsin in Huehuetenango, Chapin had met two different delegations from the United States that had come to protest Guatemalan government involvement in the killings. On that occasion, the ambassador told the delegates: "The murders were not something to be surprised at. Violence exists all over the world. Why, my own mother-in-law was murdered in her apartment in New Jersey not so very long ago."

Chapin's attempts to imply that the kidnappings, tortures, dismemberments, murders, and massacres that plagued the country were somehow the work of common criminals were ludicrous. Hennessey was prepared to say some such thing to Chapin if the ambassador tried that approach again.

After the priest finished explaining Felipe Ortiz's predicament, the ambassador asked what the case had to do with the United States. "I thought you said you wanted to talk about the murder of Patricio Ortiz Maldonado and his colleagues? This man, Felipe Ortiz, doesn't work for the AID program."

"He's a cousin of Patricio Ortiz Maldonado," Hennessey replied. "He's a bilingual teacher, just like Patricio. The army wants to kill him because he's a leader among his people. He's director of the parochial school in Ixtahuacán. If anything happens to him, I'm going to bring it to the U.S. media and I'm going to draw the obvious parallels between Felipe's case and Patricio's. It will put what is happening here back on the front pages."

"But the United States government has no responsibility for this man," the ambassador responded. "We can't take care of every Guatemalan that the government considers subversive. Why don't you go to the Mexican Embassy? Mexico takes in a lot of political refugees."

"Well, first of all, Mr. Ambassador, I'm not a Mexican citizen. Furthermore, I don't agree with you that the U.S. government has no responsibility for these people. We don't have to look back to 1954 to point a finger at the United States. And you, Mr. Ambassador, have been quite straightforward in your support of this government."

The ambassador looked at the priest for a few moments, breathing deeply, and then suddenly put his head in his hands. "What can I do? What can I do?" he repeated. "The Guatemalan military is a bunch of animals! They're just animals, and that's all they are! They're not human! You cannot deal with them as rational human beings! What am I supposed to do?"

Hennessey, mesmerized by what he was seeing and hearing, sat staring at the ambassador. Chapin, his shoulders rising and falling with his heavy breathing, was still holding his head in his hands. The priest knew that this was not a scene he was meant to witness: an ambassador giving in to his emotion and to ethical considerations he had tried so long to bury in his professional soul. The Iowan felt sorry for the man before him. For a second, he experienced an impulse to put a hand on the shaken diplomat's shoulder. But he knew that to do so would break the spell and cause the ambassador not a little embarrassment. He was pleased to see that Frederic Chapin was neither ignorant of, nor indifferent to what was going on around him. Here was the highest official of the U.S. government in Guatemala admitting that the Reagan administration had been propping up a series of killers—those whom the White House and State Department had continuously insisted were "advocates of human rights" and "leading Guatemala down the road to democracy"—who were, in reality, animals and irrational beings. At this, Hennessey knew implicitly that Mr. Chapin was not going to last long as the front man for the Reagan administration in Guatemala.

After a few moments of silence and noticing that the ambassador's shoulders had steadied, the priest asked, "What if I'm able to get a visa for Felipe Ortiz from some other embassy and am caught driving him to the airport? Can I expect protection from this embassy?"

Chapin had now regained his composure and was again fixing the Iowan with a steady gaze. "It's best that you don't do that, Father Hennessey. Such an act will make you an accomplice in hiding a suspected subversive. In such a case, we would try to see that you get a fair trial. But Guatemala law is very severe in punishing subversion. I wouldn't do that if I were you."

The priest decided then that there was no benefit in prolonging the conversation. When he stood up to shake the ambassador's hand, Chapin insisted on accompanying him to the main foyer where he bid the Iowan goodbye.

A visit to the Canadian Embassy got the priest the visa he sought the following day. He then picked up Felipe Ortiz and drove the young man to the airport, wondering all the way what Chapin would do if he were picked up. A military guard unit stopped them as they entered the airport, but the Iowan's carnet and his companion's Canadian visa got them through the barrier without any problem. Hennessey waited until Felipe Ortiz's jet was a speck in the late afternoon sky before he turned and headed back to the Maryknoll Center House. The priest received word some months later that Felipe was able to meet his wife and children in Mexico City and the entire family then emigrated to Canada.

During the first week of April, the final ten prisoners of the ninety kidnapped Ixtahuacanecos were released. Five of the ten were mute, having lost either their physical or psychic capacity to communicate. The families of all ten then moved out of Ixtahuacán and took up residence among the anonymous masses of seasonal plantation workers on the south (Pacific) coast.

Six months after Chapin's tête-à-tête with Hennessey, Alberto Piedra, a naturalized Cuban exile and outspoken supporter of Senator Jesse Helms, replaced Chapin as ambassador. It was common gossip in Guatemala City that Chapin had become a persona non grata as far as the Mejía Víctores government was concerned because of his ever-increasing vocal accusations against senior military officers for their human rights violations. Mejía Víctores, having agreed to forge documents on arms acquisitions that were then secretly transshipped to the Nicaragua contras, asked Washington to remove Chapin from his post. The White House was happy to oblige. Frederic Chapin, a man who had given his life—and for many years his integrity—to the foreign service, was the first U.S. ambassador in living memory to leave Guatemala without having been awarded that government's highest civilian honor, the Order of the Quetzal. Mejía Víctores explained the snub by saying that the ambassador "had done nothing" for Guatemala. Washington responded by assigning the former ambassador to a do-nothing job in the State Department, a post he held until his death a few years later, a broken and bitter man.

It was August 1985 and General Mejía Víctores was responding to pressure from the U.S. government to move the country toward elections that would improve its international image without forcing the army to give up political power. The political situation was relatively stable, despite pockets of guerrilla resistance across the western highlands and in the Petén. The scorched earth policies of the Ríos Montt and Mejía Víctores governments had accomplished their goal by "drying up the water in which the guerrilla 'fish' swim." In a little more than three short years, they had destroyed 440 peasant villages (the army's own count), killed or disappeared up to 75,000 individuals, and sent another 250,000 fleeing for their lives into Mexico. Air force bombings of unprotected, suspect villages continued, while nomad populations hid in the Ixcán and Petén jungles, trying to avoid contact with Mejía Víctores's troops. Displaced individuals and groups who were captured or forced to surrender because of sickness or hunger were settled in "model villages" and "development poles," quasi-concentration camps controlled by the army to "reeducate" the inhabitants in the duties of "patriotism."

Between fifty thousand and seventy-five thousand people were relocated to the model villages, which were patterned on the strategic hamlets that the U.S. Army introduced in Vietnam (with much less success than in Guatemala). This program was a major component of the Mejía Víctores government strategy for pacification, along with the PACs and the Inter-Institutional Coordination Committees (CICs) that established military control over all local and regional governmental entities and activities. The model villages, PACs, and CICs effectively militarized every aspect—political, economic, and social—of Mayan life in the western highlands. It was a program intended to destroy Mayan culture and Mayan social relationships. The program was amply underwritten by USAID, as was the strategic hamlet program in

Vietnam, and by major U.S. fundamentalist Protestant groups such as the Christian Broadcasting Network and the Full Gospel Businessmen's Fellowship.

Local army commanders in Nentón, Gracias a Dios, and Ixquisís continually attempted to block Hennessey from visiting many of his parish's decimated villages by threatening him and refusing to issue safe-conduct passes to him. Yet, he found that going over local commanders' heads to appeal their actions to the Huehuetenango provincial commandant generally brought favorable results. The Iowan knew that his earlier access to the U.S. media and Congress was the deciding factor in obtaining the commandant's acquiescence.

Then, in mid-August 1985, the Iowan received a telegram from Guatemala City saying that the Maryknoll regional superior was coming to San Mateo for a talk. Hennessey knew the visit had serious implications since the ten- . hour drive—under the best of road conditions—from Guatemala City was too much for the conscientious Bill Mullan to undertake for a mere courtesy call.

Mullan was not one to spend much time on irrelevant circumlocutions. He waited a few seconds after the last of several groups of Mateanos who had come to greet him had left—the superior was still well regarded in San Mateo from his tenure there as Hennessey's predecessor. Mullan then leaned toward the Iowan, fixing his friend with his steady, blue eyes, which, with the bushy, black eyebrows that dominated them, spelled quiet determination, even stubbornness. The superior began: "Ron, I've been discussing moving Maryknoll back into El Salvador with my consultors. Archbishop Rivera y Damas has been pushing me on it and various other factors are making it imperative that we get back in soon. Your name came up in that context at our last council meeting. You've been here in San Mateo for five years now under extremely trying circumstances. You've stood up under the pressure better than any of us could ever have hoped. El Salvador is a hot spot, . . . but maybe not as bad as here. It won't be easy, . . . but what do you think of going down there?"

Mullan had pulled out all Maryknoll priests and Brothers—Maryknoll Sisters weren't under his jurisdiction—from El Salvador a year earlier after Father Roy Bourgeois had created a lot of governmental anti-Maryknoll animosity by going on his own initiative into territory controlled by the guerrillas (FMLN). On assignment to accompany a U.S.-based TV crew in

El Salvador, Bourgeois had disappeared, leaving a letter to be delivered after his departure explaining that he wanted "to walk with the poor." But the people who were supposed to deliver the letter, guerrillas in charge of escorting him into their stronghold, held the letter back to gain maximum exposure for their cause.

When Bourgeois's disappearance was noted, it was presumed that Salvadorean paramilitary or military forces had kidnapped him for his alleged guerrilla sympathies. As a result, the government was publicly denounced for its presumed culpability in the disappearance. When Bourgeois showed up some days later, right after his letter had been released, and none the worse for the experience, government spokespersons expressed outrage. The resulting threats made against all Maryknollers and the demands coming from powerful personages that the American priests be expelled from the country, had prompted Mullan to act. But now, the regional superior wanted to begin moving missioners back in, ever so slowly, without fanfare or commotion. And Hennessey had been chosen as the point man.

Mullan's request was straightforward, no embellishments. Hennessey was not prepared for the superior's proposal, but it did not come as a shock, either. He had lived day to day for the preceding five years, knowing that any day could be his last on earth, let alone in San Mateo. But he had never considered the possibility that the decision to end his tenure in San Mateo would be his own.

"Look, Bill," the Iowan answered, stretching his arms and legs and then lacing his fingers behind his head, "I've got no problem going to El Salvador . . . . But what happens to the Mateanos? We've neglected these people more than any other in Huehuetenango . . . . They've been hit as hard or harder by the army as those in any other parish in the province . . . . They're always the first to lose their priest any time we need a man some place else."

Mullan waited a moment, accustomed to Hennessey's habit of pausing between sentences. When he saw the Iowan was not going to continue, he answered, "I've thought of that. I certainly don't want to see this place abandoned any more than you do. I've already talked to Fern Gosselin about replacing you. He's willing to come up from Nicaragua, especially since he's not very fond of the Sandinistas. Besides, you've only got one more year on your second three-year term in this place. If Gosselin comes in now, that means the Mateanos will have a pastor for at least three more years."

Hennessey nodded and yawned. "My concern," the Iowan replied, "is whether Gosselin would be too hard on the *costumbre* traditionalists, whether he'd allow them to perform their rituals in the church . . . . You know as well as I that too many of our guys have been hard-nosed with them in the past . . . . If Fern doesn't work with them, there could be lots of trouble . . . . And if there's one thing the Mateanos don't need at a time like this, . . . it's trouble coming from the Church."

"I don't think you need to worry about Gosselin, Ron. I know he's on the conservative side. But he did learn the Q'eq'chí Mayan language before he went to Nicaragua and he worked well with the Mayans. I'm sure he'll do fine here."

"Well," the Iowan responded, scratching his head and running his fingers through his hair, "I guess that settles it! . . . But do me a favor, Bill? Just keep this thing under your hat and don't tell anyone here. La Cuchumadera lumber company is moving very slowly . . . . Still the army and some PAC leaders will try to take advantage of a situation like this if they know I'm leaving."

Hennessey's willingness to accept an assignment to El Salvador didn't mean that he was ready to leave San Mateo without looking back. San Mateo had become too much a part of him for that. He had lived moments of great joy there, had seen evidence of heroic generosity and self-sacrifice. He had also experienced despair and wonder as he witnessed that capacity of some to take perverse pleasure in making others suffer unbearable pain. Life in San Mateo had been a cradle of unresolved contradictions: peaceful acceptance beside wrath and frustration; unscrupulous betrayal with trusting acquiescence; love beyond measure coexisting with implacable hate. The Iowan's response was also contradictory, wanting to be out of San Mateo in the worst way, and desiring to remain there forever.

A few days after Mullan's visit, Hennessey began fielding hesitant questions from Sisters Francisca and Justa, as well as from several catechists, regarding rumors that he might be leaving San Mateo. "Where did you get that information, Justa?" he inquired blandly, when the young nun first broached the subject. "Rumors like that have been flying around here for years and you've never paid any attention to them before."

When Justa looked down at the floor, her serious expression unchanged, the Iowan sensed that the nun knew. And if Justa knew—which she did—Francisca knew, as well as several of the catechists. And if several catechists knew, so did the whole parish—but possibly not the army! But no one would come out and contradict his denials. Mayan culture dictates that one seldom, if ever, confronts another's lack of frankness—that everyone has valid reasons for dissimulating, which maintains a degree of social peace.

Hennessey had good reasons for not wanting anyone to know he was moving on. If the soldiers got word of his departure, they might strike at those who had been close to him even before Fern Gosselin had time to take over. As it was, whenever he left San Mateo, the commandants in the surrounding bases never knew when he'd be back. And even if he was gone for a week, they knew he would find out about any atrocities committed in his absence as soon as he returned and would quickly get the news out. But if they understood that a replacement was coming in, the commandants might take advantage of the new pastor's inexperience to settle old scores.

Word of Hennessey's departure spread throughout the parish. He assumed that the pastor in Santa Eulalia or in some other neighboring parish had heard the news from the bishop of Huehuetenango and had let it slip unwittingly to one or more catechists. That guaranteed that word would quickly filter into the Mayan communication system and that all Mateanos would soon be privy to it. And so it was!

The effect of the news was almost immediate. Six leaders in the fight against La Cuchumadera's plan to harvest the Mateanos' rain forest, men whom Hennessey had again convinced to maintain their firm stand only a few months earlier, arrived at the rectory. They wanted to inform the priest that they would no longer try to block the company or its local representative, the town's ladino treasurer, if the Iowan were not going to be there to support them.

Hennessey's first reaction was to give the six men another pep talk. But he quickly decided against it, realizing that he might be leading them like the proverbial lambs to the meatpacking plant. Instead, he reluctantly accepted their decision as the wisest course of action in view of the circumstances. The anti-Cuchumadera fighters had come full circle, from reluctant acceptance of the army brass's intention to exploit their forest, to determined resistance, to militant defiance supported by the guerrillas, to hesitant opposition supported by Hennessey, and now, to discouraged acceptance of the return to Guatemala's historical, political reality.

The next-to-last chapter of the Cuchumadera story had begun months before the Iowan had any idea that he'd soon be leaving San Mateo. It was late 1984, when it had finally become apparent to even the most committed of the guerrillas' supporters that the EGP was no longer a serious threat to army control of the area. A telegram or two had crossed the mayor's desk from the army high command in Huehuetenango, once again renewing its demands that those opposed to harvesting the Mateanos' arboreal patrimony present themselves at the Huehuetenango military base to explain their opposition.

Agape Toltz, the principal leader of the anti-Cuchumadera opposition, had warned the priest about the telegrams at the time. Agape had gone to the rectory and sat toying with his cup of coffee for some minutes. Hennessey knew that the man's hesitancy to get to the point spelled bad news.

"Padre, La Cuchumadera is coming back in," the old man sighed. "We've just received word that they want us at the base in Huehuetenango. We've been discussing it and have decided to ignore the order. If they're going to cut down our rain forest, they'll do it whether we make these expensive trips to Huehuetenango or not. What do you think?"

"If they didn't specify your names in the telegram, Agape, . . . I think you should ignore the summons. They may have lost your names or maybe they're just trying to gauge the depth of the town's resistance . . . . I'll support you on this. If they try to harvest your forest, . . . we'll go to the newspapers and we'll go back to court . . . . At least we'll let plenty of people know who's stealing your patrimony."

Agape nodded, smiled, stood up and gave the priest an *abrazo*. "Everyone said you would stand by us, padre. *Gracias a Dios!*" The old man turned and left.

In late May 1985, another telegram came from the base commander in Huehuetenango demanding the presence of the Cuchumadera opponents on the following Monday. Hennessey was out of town at the time. The town's ladino treasurer, Octavio Hernández Gómez, emboldened by the telegram, sent the civil patrol to arrest Agape Toltz. Once Hernández Gómez had Agape in his office, he pressed a small caliber pistol to the old man's chest and dared him to move, all the while debating vocally with himself whether to kill

Agape on the spot. Fortunately Abelardo Valenzuela walked in at that moment and convinced the treasurer to spare Agape's life, but only after the old man had agreed to make a 200-quetzal extortion payment to the official and refrain from future opposition to La Cuchumadera's plans. The civil patrol then escorted Agape to his house where he dug up 165 quetzals, his life savings, and turned them over to Hernández Gómez with a promise to borrow the other 35 quetzals within three days.

When the Iowan heard the news, he called the other five leaders together to encourage them to testify against the treasurer. The five men sat in a circle with Hennessey in the rectory, sipping coffee and smoking cigarettes.

"The treasurer is taking advantage of Agape today," the priest told them, watching each one closely to assess their commitment, "but your turns will come soon unless you stand together . . . . He's way out of line with this extortion and threat of murder. Let's see if La Cuchumadera stands behind him . . . . If you men will testify against Hernández Gómez, I'll help you. I think we can beat him in the courts and maybe hold off La Cuchumadera in the process . . . . If the army high command gets insistent, we'll have to think of something else . . . . But let's give it a try!"

The agreement, though not enthusiastic, was unanimous.

Now, three months after that scene, the Iowan's six friends had come to inform him that if what they had heard about his departure were true, they intended to stop all opposition to La Cuchumadera's plans.

Hennessey looked at the six men with sadness. He put his head in his hands and massaged his forehead with the tips of his fingers. *I've got to be Mayan to handle this,* he told himself solemnly. Then, looking up, he nodded. "If I were to leave, . . . and I'm not saying that I am, . . . I agree that your struggle with La Cuchumadera will be more difficult . . . . And if I leave, . . . and I'm not saying that I will, . . . another priest might come in whom you could place your confidence . . . and from whom you could seek help . . . . You and your ancestors have fought for five hundred years against these kinds of abuses . . . . You have to look for a way to continue the struggle, . . . but never forget the lessons you have learned during these last five years."

Two weeks later, in early September 1985, Hennessey left San Mateo much as he had left San Juan Acul ten years earlier, and Cabricán seven years before that—with no good-byes. He preferred to avoid the emotion—the silent tears and moist eyes—that he knew such a scene would create. One week later, after twenty-one years, the Iowan left Guatemala, no longer the secure, idealistic Roman Catholic priest who had gone there in 1964 to play his part in saving the world from itself. He left as a Catholic, even more as a catholic, and in a very radical sense as a priest, that is, an advocate of the Maya before humankind, before history, and before the Almighty. He departed Guatemala chastened by the knowledge of his own ignorance of God's plan for humankind, an understanding assimilated over two decades of living with and loving the Maya and their cultures, feeling in his bones the cosmic betrayal they have been allowed to suffer by a seemingly indifferent creator.

Chapter 36

Guatemala Revisited

After leaving San Mateo Ixtatán in late 1985, Ron spent seven frustrating, dangerous years (1986-92) in El Salvador, assigned to Zacamil, a parish in the capital in which the FMLN, the Salvadorean guerrilla umbrella group, exercised a strong influence. Even before the murders of Archbishop Romero, Padre Rutilio Grande, and several other priests, Liberation Theology, as far as the army high command was concerned, had thrown a subversive stole over the shoulders of all clerics, nuns, and catechists throughout the country. Exceptions were made for those who expressed vocal support for the army's repressive tactics and its human rights abuses. As a result, ambitious military killers took ideological aim at Ron's predecessors in the parish of Zacamil and bombed their rectory into rubble, while the two priests barely escaped with their lives. Archbishop Rivera y Damas thereupon closed down the parish and left its eighty thousand parishioners without clerical support for five years.

When Bill Mullan decided to send Maryknoll priests back into that abused, godforsaken Central American nation, he chose Ron Hennessey appropriately enough as his point man. The archbishop, for his part, selected Zacamil as a fitting place for the Iowan to begin his work. Ron and his two associates inherited the reputation of their predecessors as soon as they began making inquiries of the military authorities as to the whereabouts of arrested (kidnapped!) parishioners. Every day relatives of the disappeared presented themselves at the rectory door requesting the priests' assistance in locating their sons, brothers, fathers, wives, sisters, and daughters. The families of the disappeared knew that for them to make such inquiries was to risk their own freedom, health, and often, their lives. They believed that the Americans' nationality and their sacerdotal status might provide them with a shield of immunity denied to all others. At one point, Ron and his associate, Fr. Bill Schmidt, along with several Spanish Jesuits teaching at the Central American University, were singled out in a radio broadcast as particularly effective supporters of the FMLN guerrillas. Such public recognition generally telegraphed a warning to the accused as well as a "go" signal to a designated hit squad. The choice presented to the targets was to either run or suffer the consequences.

A few days after the warning, the fingered Spanish Jesuits, their housekeeper and her daughter were lined up in the middle of the night and dispatched like so many head of cattle by a squad of National Guardsmen acting on orders from the top of the military hierarchy. Hennessey and Schmidt recognized that their nationality had saved them once again from their wanna-be-killers, at least for the time being. The Spanish Jesuits' deaths were nothing more than a flyspeck on the reputation of the United States, the patron of El Salvador's National Guard and army, as far as the Reagan administration was concerned.

Hennessey left El Salvador to return to the Land of Eternal Spring in October 1992 to once again don the mantle of Maryknoll's Central American regional superior, elected to that post for a third and then a fourth term by his appreciative colleagues. The third election was not a landslide, however, resulting in two ties, one resolved by flipping a coin, the second by picking the high card from a deck of playing cards. The second vote had been necessitated because one of the voters was absent during the first, busy taking care of his stomach cramps. Ron, commenting on the election with his signature sense of humor, wrote home, "While kings and bishops claim office 'by the grace of God,' in my case I can only claim the regional superiorship by the caprice of the coin, the cut of the cards, and a call of nature."

But Guatemala's political atmosphere had changed in some important respects since Hennessey's departure in December 1985. For one thing, Guatemala was again listed by the State Department as "an emerging democracy," a category the principal characteristic of which was its elasticity, that is, its ability to hold elections while preventing large segments of the population from voting, by stopping representative candidates from running, or merely by making sure that the selected president would accept the army's executive role. President Reagan had been pumping to have Guatemala included in just such a category since his pounding of President Carter in the 1980 elections. Reagan not only wanted to resurrect the Guatemalan Army from its global pariah status in order to provide it with continued counterinsurgency training, arms, and political support, but also to enlist Guatemala's assistance in the overthrow of Nicaragua's Sandinista government. The Great Communicator had accused the Sandinistas of having established a "Soviet beachhead" in Central America, echoing Dwight Eisenhower's 1954 fraudulent claim against Guatemala.

Reagan's Washington had sent a mandate to General Mejía Víctores to dump Ríos Montt and schedule presidential elections through the good offices of Brigadier General Fred Woerner, a brigade commander with the U.S. Southern Command in Panama. On 8 August 1985, Mejía Víctores seized the helm of Guatemala's military and political establishments from the hands of the genocidal Ríos Montt. Mejía Víctores proceeded to patch the army's chain of command, such as it was, by expelling from the National Palace the young officers who had helped engineer the Ríos Montt coup fourteen months earlier and to prepare the ground for constituent, congressional, and presidential elections. A few weeks after Hennessey left Guatemala, a civilian, Christian Democrat Vinicio Cerezo Arévalo, was elected to the presidency by a majority of the 44.2 percent of the eligible voters who actually voted.

Cerezo quickly demonstrated his political acumen by agreeing to an inaugural pact with the army high command not to interfere with the generals' prosecution of their counterinsurgency war. A corollary of that promise was Cerezo's commitment to make no attempt to repeal his predecessor's amnesty of all military personnel accused of crimes perpetrated in prosecution of the dirty war. To explain his docility, the president confessed to an American journalist that he possessed no more than 25 percent of the government's executive power, probably an exaggeration. As if to demonstrate the inflation of the president's estimate of his influence, a marked increase in the political kidnappings, disappearances, and assassinations accompanied Cerezo's entrance into the National Palace. The Washington-based Council on Hemispheric Affairs cited the Guatemalan government as the worst human rights violator in Latin America for the years 1989 and 1990. The Inter-American Commission On Human Rights of the OAS, Amnesty International, and America's Watch all echoed these findings.

Among the many atrocities of this period were the kidnapping in Antigua of an American nun, Sister Dianna Ortiz, who was then repeatedly raped, pushed into a pit of tortured, dying men and women, then forced to participate in the murder of a fellow female prisoner, an act that was videotaped by her captors for purposes unknown, probably for later attempts at blackmail.[1] There was the stabbing death on a Guatemala City street of an internationally respected Chinese Guatemalan anthropologist, Myrna Mack, known for her research on the plight of displaced, hunted, bombed peasant populations. Finally the revelation of two more murders with U.S. connections blew the lid off the kettle of fish that the U.S. government had been cooking for years to maintain its innocence of responsibility in such deaths. One was the execution of an American hotel owner, Michael DeVine, in El Peten by a CIA "asset," apparently because of DeVine's discovery of the asset's agency in a drug smuggling enterprise. The second was revealed through the persistent, courageous efforts of an American lawyer, Jennifer Harbury, to find her captured husband, a URNG commander known by the CIA to have been tortured over a period of months and finally executed, but of which the agency had consistently denied knowledge. The Guatemalan government, for its part, refused to carry out any investigation, let alone prosecution, of these and multiple other crimes. Still, the U.S. embassy heralded the Cerezo administration as "the final step in the reestablishment of democracy in Guatemala."[2] President Ronald Reagan had his cover.

In 1987, the five Central American presidents, led by the more legitimately democratic president of Costa Rica, Oscar Arias, met at Esquipulas in Guatemala to hammer out and sign the Central American Peace Accords, an agreement that encouraged the warring parties in Nicaragua, Honduras, El Salvador, and Guatemala to come together for peace negotiations. Although Cerezo's defense minister, General Héctor Gramajo, claimed that the accords did not bind his army, and no member of the Cerezo administration joined the Committee of National Reconciliation (CNR) established by the accords, a momentous first step had been taken on the road to peace. Almost immediately, individuals representing a wide range of groups, including labor leaders, members of political parties, religious and indigenous leaders, and members of the URNG joined the informal discussions under the auspices of the CNR chaired by Bishop Rodolfo Quezada Toruño.

The hard-liners in the army, upset by what they perceived to be the beginnings of a public grant of a quasi-legal standing to the URNG, attempted several unsuccessful coups. Their primary targets were President Cerezo and his minister of defense, General Héctor Gramajo, the leading light of a group of officers known as the "developmentalists." The latter were as gung-ho on the extralegal nature of counterinsurgency warfare as any of their colleagues, but they saw that eventual military victory also resided in "national stability," a heretical doctrine that mandated some response to the basic needs of the population. The leader of more than one such attempt against Gramajo and Cerezo was a sociopath, Colonel Byron Disrael Lima Estrada.[3]

Lima Estrada had been closely monitored over the years by the U.S. military mission in Guatemala as a comer, "a very competent officer . . . who could have extremely good political potential."[4] As a result, Lima Estrada was sent to one training course after another conducted by the U.S. Army, the objective being to find the "best ways of gaining subject's confidence and exerting influence on him."[5] Much of Lima's training was in counterintelligence conducted under the Pentagon's Military Assistance Program (MAP), a specialty that propelled him into many important posts. One such position was that of deputy director of the Regional Telecommunications Center (CRT), set up by the United States to hunt down would-be communists during the administration of dictator Colonel Peralta Azurdia (1963-65). The CRT had proven itself in the years since to have become a high-level coordinating center for death-squad decisions, commands, members, and activities. Another important post held by Lima Estrada was that of deputy executive officer of the Huehuetenango garrison before and during the Ríos Montt years, the period when most of the San Mateo massacres occurred.[6]

Although the coup attempts by Lima Estrada had the backing of several key factions of conservative officers, Gramajo held his ground and sent Lima Estrada off to Peru as military attaché in the Guatemalan embassy. Perhaps emboldened by the success of his minister of defense in standing up to the *golpistas,* President Cerezo finally authorized the CNR to participate in meetings with the URNG in Oslo and later encouraged representatives of legalized political parties to follow up with dialogues in Madrid that included the URNG.

When Ron Hennessey returned to Guatemala in October 1992, Jorge Serrano Elías occupied the presidential palace. Serrano, a Protestant fundamentalist, had been elected in a runoff election in January 1991 in which he obtained only 24.8 percent of the vote, rendering him politically weaker even than Cerezo. Serrano's election had been more a repudiation of the corruption and ineffectiveness of the Christian Democratic administration than a choice for Serrano. Nevertheless, during his first month in office, the new president proposed what he called his "Comprehensive Peace Plan," including a ceasefire that embraced the surrender of the URNG to be followed . by the guerrillas' participation in the negotiation process. The army brass agreed to formal negotiations with the URNG, seeing it as a tool to disarm the guerrillas and gain the upper hand.

The guerrillas refused to disarm but instead pursued their political goals. They focused the country's attention on the five hundredth anniversary of the Spanish invasion of the Americas with its subsequent subjugation of the continent's indigenous populations. As a result, international pressures built for an end to the conflict, calling for a gradual demilitarization of the country, putting the army once again on the defensive. The high command responded with increased attacks on guerrilla strongholds on the south coast, while the human rights situation deteriorated dramatically. The URNG-Guatemalan Army dialogue, such as it was, folded completely.

In January 1993, Serrano appeared before the United Nations in New York and proposed that the United Nations verify the Peace Accords and that the URNG withdraw into predetermined areas free of conflict. Although the president's intention was to isolate the guerrillas and to manipulate the United Nations to control and weaken the URNG, the opposite occurred. The army's continued insistence on its impunity, backed by threats and murders to stifle the judiciary, inflamed public outrage. Attacks continued against returning refugees. CACIF (Coordinating Committee of Agricultural, Commercial, Industrial, and Financial Associations) recognized that the potential financial rewards accruing to Guatemala's businessmen for participating in the growing globalization process would pass them by if the civilian government did not control the army. The United States indirectly assisted the current for demilitarization by beginning to make barely audible noises regarding high-level military drug connections.

Serrano, on 25 May 1993, attempted to remedy his political weakness and make a comeback with army support by engineering "an autogolpe," a self-inflicted move against his own administration in order to garner sympathy. He dissolved congress, fired the members of the Supreme Court of Justice, suspended constitutional rights, and cancelled the human rights ombudsman's authority. But Serrano had picked a hard-line segment of the army to back him up, one that was unable to garner the broad military support needed to make the moves stick. While the Presidential Military Guard (EMP—the death squads' high command), the minister of defense, and army chief of staff all supported the president in his unconstitutional moves, the powerful Council of Commanders did not. Meanwhile, the "Institutionalists" (those who favored a civilian president controlled by the military), including the head of the D-2 (intelligence), likewise opposed the coup and freed the human rights ombudsman, Ramiro de León Carpio. In a decisive move, the president of the Constitutional Court refused to recognize Serrano's authority to make such decisions, thereby sealing the president's fate. Both Germany and the United States threw their considerable weight behind the opposition, saying they would withhold all aid until a constitutional regime was reinstated. As a result, the influence of international oversight of the peace process increased. On 6 June, Congress elected as president the ex-human rights ombudsman, Ramiro de León Carpio.

By late 1993, de León Carpio had proven himself a cipher, aligning himself with the "Institutional Wing" of the army and making straightforward efforts to drown the peace process. As a result, both international and domestic pressures built to give the United Nations a more active role in monitoring the peace process. The government (the army), for its part, was fed up with the chairmanship of Bishop Quezada Toruño, viewing him as partial to the URNG. It therefore felt that the United Nations might be the lesser of two evils.

In January 1994, an Acuerdo Marco, a framework agreement, was signed, formalizing international oversight of the peace process, recognizing the key role of the "Group of Friends," Mexico, Norway, Spain, the United States,

Venezuela, and Colombia. The agreement also instituted the manner by which popular segments of the population would have active participation in the negotiations, forming the Asamblea de la Sociedad Civil (ASC). In April, in response to the Marco, a Comprehensive Agreement on Human Rights was signed calling for UN verification of all human rights accords. The response of the right-wing hard-liners to the agreement was to assassinate the head of the Constitutional Court. Two months later, two more agreements were signed under considerable pressure from the Group of Friends. One accord dealt with the resettlement of populations displaced by the war, the second establishing a Truth Commission, called the Historical Clarification Commission (CEH), empowered to investigate the responsibility and whereabouts of the civil disappearances and deaths that had occurred over the previous thirty-five years.

The signing of these two accords created a severe backlash in the government and army, the government refusing to comply with the documents, the army going on the warpath against the civilian population organized in the ASC. By August, the URNG stated it would no longer bargain with the army while the hard-liners were in control. Consequently, the UN mission (MINUGUA) did not arrive in country until November 1994, though it had been scheduled to appear on the scene back in March. When the crisis was finally resolved, an historical agreement was signed under strong pressure from the United Nations. This agreement, called the Accord on the Identity and Rights of Indigenous Peoples, included a constitutional statement declaring the country to be "multiethnic, multicultural, and multilingual."[7] Meanwhile, the new American administration, under Democratic President Bill Clinton, responding to the demands of Dianna Ortiz, Jennifer Harbury, and the relatives of sundry other victims to make public the U.S. role in Guatemala's tragedy, agreed to an airing of the CIA's and State Department's files on Guatemala to discover, *not* the "who," but the "what" and the "when" of U.S. sub-rosa activities in that benighted country.

It seemed that Guatemala might finally be coming out of the dark night of its national civic soul, imposed on it four decades earlier in June of 1954 by an ignorant and arrogant American administration. But there were yet many slips and stumbles on the road to peace and democracy. The effects of four decades of impunity for the sociopathic behavior of Guatemalan and United States personalities and institutions would probably take several generations to erase.

Former FMLN amputees demand that the Salvadorean government comply with Geneva Conventions during a sit-in at the national cathedral. Ron, at left, sits with them in solidarity. (Credit: Maryknoll)

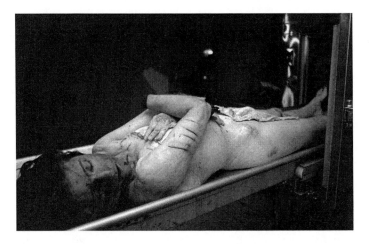

Eugenia Beatriz Barrios Marroquín in the morgue in Escuintla. The 26-year-old mother of two small children and a school teacher had been kidnapped by a death squad related to the Honor Guard G-D Intelligence Office. Her hacked body, hands amputated, face gouged, was found the following day with a cardboard sign on it saying "more to come." (© Jean-Marie Simon 2003)

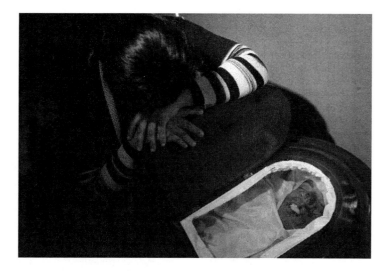

Mercedes Gómez, leader of GAM (Grupo de Apoyo Mutuo/Group of Mutual Support), mourns her tortured husband's corpse. GAM was formed to support the relatives of the "disappeared." (© Jean-Marie Simon 2003)

Partial view of massacre victims of army incursion in Salacuim, Quiché, 13 April 1982 (Credit: *El Periódico*, Guatemala)

Epilogue

In 1989, the archbishop of Guatemala City, Próspero Penados, spurred by his activist auxiliary bishop Juan Gerardi Conedera, established the Archdiocesan Office on Human Rights (ODHAG). The purpose of this office was to bring together dedicated lawyers under the aegis of the Church to connect with the families of kidnapped and disappeared individuals in an effort to tear away at the armor of decades-long impunity with which the "security forces" had managed to clothe themselves. The office was also meant to provide a forum where the bereaved could pour out their sorrows, their frustrations, and their desperations in hopes of finding some modicum of closure, and know that someone would listen, would care, and would try to protect them from retribution for speaking out. The effort was successful in providing an element of psychic balm to some of the victims' families who dared to come forward, while it managed to keep an international focus on Guatemala's dismal human rights situation for those who paid attention. But in itself the work of the ODHAG did little to stop the uniformed criminals and their surrogates, nor was it able to strip away their immunity.

The cause of human rights was a special vocation for Bishop Gerardi. Back in 1980, in a spirit of collegiality, he had accepted the vote of his clergy to close down the entire diocese of El Quiché after several of his priests had been murdered and an assassination attempt had been made against the prelate's own life. Prior to this move, the bishop, on several occasions, had publicly accused the military of being responsible for the priests' deaths and those of more than a score of catechists, as well as other acts of brutality and terrorism committed against the Mayan population in general.

ODHAG's lack of success was due in large part to the terrorization of the country's legal system. Any judge or lawyer who persisted in following criminal trails that potentially led to senior military officers would quickly receive anonymous phone calls and letters threatening death to the individual concerned, or more often, against her/his family members. After several years of frustration, Bishop Gerardi decided that at the very least the nation needed a record of the names and circumstances of all officially sanctioned, extrajudicial deaths that had occurred since the first appearances of guerrilla activity in 1960. The bishop understood that the task would be monumental and that many killings would never be catalogued due to time elapsed and the fear of reprisal against those with something to tell. By 1994, Gerardi was again able to convince the archbishop and a majority of members of the Episcopal Conference to undertake the task. The effort was baptized "The Project for the Recovery of Historical Memory" (REMHI).

Four years later, on 24 April 1998, REMHI issued its final report consisting of four volumes under the title *¡Guatemala, Nunca Más!* (Guatemala, Never Again!).[1] Bishop Gerardi presented the report to the public during a solemn Mass, advertised as an unveiling ceremony, held in the Metropolitan Cathedral. In his homily, the bishop said, among much else, "To open ourselves to the truth and to bring ourselves face to face with our personal and collective reality is not an option that can be accepted or rejected . . . . It is a truth that challenges each one of us to recognize our individual and collective responsibility and to commit ourselves to action so that these abominable acts never happen again."

The verifiable statistics of the REMHI report, based on personal, individual accounts made by family members risking their own lives, came as a shock to much of Guatemala's see-no-evil ladino population, as well as to any international audience paying attention; but not to the Maya. The numbers included fifty-five thousand human rights violations that had resulted in twenty-five thousand plus deaths, with more than fifty thousand of the violations (89.7 percent) attributed to the military and their surrogates (death squads, civil patrols, police, military commissioners); only 4.8 percent were ascribed to the guerrillas. Two days after the report's appearance and even though no names of those responsible had been cited, killers bent on revenge and terrorism followed Bishop Juan Gerardi into his garage in the early evening and crushed his skull with a cement block.

The authorities accused Father Mario Orantes, the bishop's assistant and a friend of eight years, and Orantes's German shepherd pet, Baloo, of a "crime of [homosexual] passion." The dog's role in the crime was said to have been to attack the bishop when the tryst went sour. In any judicial system other than that of Guatemala, the public outcry would have stayed the system's risible antics. Church authorities and the faithful were outraged at this latest and most blatant miscarriage of justice. Ron Hennessey, Gerardi's good friend, was quoted in an Iowan newspaper as saying that the bishop "was a person who did not seek the limelight . . . he continued to talk about the truth, what really happened in the war, rather than sweeping things under the rug. The army would like to keep it covered up . . . . The guy who did it was certainly a hired killer. That's the way they do it here." [2]

Finally, information began to bubble up through the cracks that pointed to Hennessey's old acquaintance from Huehuetenango, Colonel Byron Lima Estrada, and his son, First Infantry Captain Byron Lima Oliva. Six months after the murder, Gerardi's body was exhumed and no dog bites were found on what remained of the corpse. But Orantes and Baloo remained under arrest, while the priest's physical and psychological condition deteriorated. As evidence built against the Limas, father and son, as well as against a third army officer, evidence that included the testimony of eyewitnesses, an unbelievable breech of military impunity occurred: the three men were brought to court to answer the accusations against them. After a trial that had many starts and stops due to threats against—and the resulting resignations and flight of—witnesses, lawyers, prosecutors, and judges, the court finally handed down a judgment of guilty and the three accused went to jail. The verdicts are now under appeal, but at this writing the two Limas are still incarcerated (the younger Lima is said to run the prison in which he is confined), while the third accused was murdered during a jailhouse "disturbance."

In February 1999, almost a year after the appearance of the REMHI document, a UN commission, La Comision para el Esclarecimiento Histórico (The Historical Clarification Commission, or CEH), issued its own report under the title *Guatemala: A Memory of Silence*. The report was the result of an agreement made by the Guatemalan government and the URNG (Unidad Revolucionaria Nacional Guatemalteca) in Oslo in 1994. The statistics marshaled in the CEH document are even more damaging to the Guatemalan government than those in the REMHI publication: 93 percent of the atrocities are attributed to Guatemala's "security forces," while only 3 percent are laid at the feet of the URNG. The nine-volume CEH account accuses the

Guatemalan military of "acts of genocide" against the country's Mayan people and states that the American training of the officer corps in counterinsurgency techniques "played a significant role in the torture, kidnapping and execution of thousands of civilians."[3]

One month after the CEH report appeared, President Bill Clinton visited Central America and while in Guatemala remarked in somewhat prophylactic prose at an informal forum of Mayan leaders, widows, government officials, and representatives of the truth commission that "for the United States, it is important that I state clearly that support for military forces and intelligence units which engaged in violence and widespread repression was wrong, and the United States must not repeat that mistake."[4]

Whether Clinton's muted apology was prompted by the CEH report or was the belated reaction to the published, fifteen-month investigation of his own administration's panel, the Intelligence Oversight Board (IOB), should be noted, but indicates that the president's words were more political than a statement of moral outrage. The IOB report is more critical of U.S. behavior in Guatemala than either those of the REMHI Commission or the CEB, though the IOB strove to walk a tightrope between blame and excuse. A synopsis of the IOB report made by the Marin Interfaith Task Force (California) (MITFCA) notes that the IOB acknowledged that the CIA station in Guatemala was not a rogue operation; that its actions can be viewed as approved government policy; that the funds provided to the Guatemalan D-2 and Archivos, the two most notorious intelligence operations directing assassinations and massacres, were vital to their operations; that the Department of Defense's School of the Americas at Fort Benning, Georgia, and the U.S. Southern Command used instructional materials in training Latin American officers, including Guatemalans, that "appeared to condone" practices such as the execution of guerrillas, extortion, physical abuse, coercion, and false imprisonment. The MITFCA assessment ends by pointing out that "(m)ost significantly, the IOB report accepts at face value the U.S. relationship with the Guatemalan military and intelligence services. The IOB discounts any inconsistency to promote human rights and democracy . . . that any negative aspects of association with the Guatemalan intelligence services were outweighed by the positive benefits of the intelligence received."[5]

In a telling response to the IOB's comparison of the CIA's relationship with the murderous Guatemalan intelligence services to the FBI's practice of placing undercover agents inside the KKK and the Mafia, Sr. Dianna Ortiz remarks that the FBI agents in the Ku Klux Klan and the Mafia are seeking information on the practices and individuals that belong to the penetrated organizations and not on their enemies, mostly innocent civilians. The comparison lacks credibility in the sense that it is tantamount to saying the FBI infiltrates the KKK in order to get information on African American organizations attempting to change discriminatory U.S. laws and practices.[6] The CIA, however, supports the dirty work of "penetrated" organizations— the Guatemalan Army, the police, the intelligence units—and even trains them in torture methods to obtain useful information from their mutual enemies.

Back in 1968, Viron Vaky, the second-ranking official in the U.S. Embassy in Guatemala wrote a very telling and prescient memo to his superiors in the State Department. It bears quoting at length because it goes to the heart of this book:

> [The Guatemalan security forces] are guilty of atrocities. Interrogations are brutal, torture is used and bodies are mutilated. Many believe that the very brutal way the ex-beauty queen was killed, obviously tortured and mutilated, provoked the FAR [Rebel Armed Forces] to murder [U.S.] Colonel Webber in retaliation. If true, how tragic that the tactics of "our side" would in any way be responsible for that event! But the point is that this is a serious practical political problem as well as a moral one: Because of the evidence of this brutality, the government is, in the eyes of many Guatemalans, a cruel government, and therefore, righteous outrage, emotion and viciousness have been sucked into the whole political situation . . . . In the minds of many Latin Americans, and tragically, especially in the sensitive, articulate youth, we are believed to have condoned these tactics, if not actually have encouraged them . . . . This leads to the aspect that I find most disturbing of all—that we have not been honest with ourselves. We *have* condoned counterterror; we may even in effect have encouraged or blessed it. We have been so obsessed with the fear of insurgency that we have rationalized away our qualms and uneasiness. This is not only because we have concluded that we cannot do anything about it,

for we never really tried. Rather we suspected that maybe it is a good tactic, and that as long as Communists are being killed it is all right. Murder, torture and mutilation are all right if our side is doing it and the victims are Communists. After all, hasn't man been a savage from the beginning of time so let us not be too queasy about terror. I have literally heard these arguments from our people.

Have our values been so twisted by our adversary concept of politics in the hemisphere? Is it conceivable that we are so obsessed with insurgency that we are prepared to rationalize murder as an acceptable counterinsurgency weapon? Is it possible that a nation that so reveres the principle of due process of law has so easily acquiesced in this sort of terror tactic?

The record must be made clearer that the United States Government opposes the concept and questions the wisdom of counterterror; the record must be made clearer that we have made this known unambiguously to the Guatemalans; otherwise we will stand before history unable to answer the accusations that we encouraged the Guatemalan Army to do these things.[7]

When a journalist questioned Vaky about the effect of what he had written three decades earlier, he answered, "No one read what I wrote." He continued, "My deepest regret is that I did not fight harder within the embassy councils when I was there to press these views."[8]

Now we, the people of the United States, stand convicted, as a nation, before the world. There exists no verifiable witness, no evidence to present that can question the facts that we (or rather, our representatives) encouraged the Guatemalan Army, police, and paramilitaries to use terror as a tactic and a strategy to prevent the Guatemalan people from controlling their own destiny. Hundreds of thousands of innocents suffered terrible, unspeakable deaths over the 40-year span of the Guatemalan civil war. Neither in war nor peace have American civilians experienced anything comparable. The forces who waged this war were our surrogates, so it was our war.

Reviewing the legal and moral basis for the postwar trials of German and Japanese war criminals, General Telford Taylor, the chief U.S. prosecuting attorney at the Nuremberg trials, stated in 1971 that if the planners and executioners of the American war in Vietnam were to be judged by the same standards "there would be a strong possibility that they would come to the same end he [General Tomoyuki Yamashita] did," that is, public execution.[9]

The same can be said of those who oversaw and excused the slaughter in Guatemala. There is enough blame to go around. If General Taylor can point the finger of guilt at the likes of Richard Nixon, Henry Kissinger, Robert McNamara, Generals Westmoreland and Abrams, surely we can list Ronald W. Reagan, George "Out of the Loop" Bush, CIA director William Casey, John Negroponte (the U.S. ambassador to Honduras, who oversaw Reagan's terrorist war against Honduran and Nicaraguan civilians[10] and is now George W's ambassador to the United Nations), Elliott Abrams, Philip Taylor, Harold Baum, and many, many others on a list of criminals guilty of war crimes in Central America. Is it too much to hope that these men will some day stand before the bar of justice and face a world court? More than likely! since the United States has excused a priori all its representatives, uniformed or not, from the jurisdiction of the World Court. I can only hope that history, at least, and those who document it will some day acknowledge the extent of their and out culpability.

Notes

Introduction

1. Lawrence E. Walsh, *Firewall: The Iran-Contra Conspiracy and Cover-up* (New York: W.W. Norton, 1997).
2. For an account of the experiences that led to our decision, see Thomas Melville and Marjorie Melville, *Whose Heaven, Whose Earth?* (New York: Knopf, 1971).
3. In January 2002, two of Ron Hennessey's sisters, Dorothy (88) and Gwen (68), were sentenced to five months in federal prison for trespassing on the grounds of the U.S. Army's School of the Americas at Fort Benning, Georgia. The occasion for their disobedience was a public demonstration attended by four to five thousand participants to protest the school's mandate to train Latin American military leaders in the techniques of counterinsurgency. Many of the school's graduates, including the leaders of Guatemala's army, have become infamous as torturers, assassins, and unindicted war criminals for which the institution's sponsors (both houses of the U. S. Congress) refuse to accept any responsibility.

Chapter 1

1. The figures of 150,000 murdered and 40,000 disappeared have been used for over a decade, even while the killings and kidnappings have continued. While no one has any way of making an accurate estimate, these guesses may be short by another 100 percent.
2. Colonel Byron Disrael Lima Estrada was a rising star with "extremely good political potential," according to a Department of Defense Intelligence Information Report dated 20 January 1971. His relationship with the U.S. Army, which had begun in the early 1960s, was cemented when he went to

Fort Benning, Georgia, for training in 1965, and then on to the U.S. Army School of the Americas at Ft. Gulick, Panama in 1968. By 1970, Lima Estrada's intellect and dedication had distinguished him sufficiently enough that he was selected for instruction in counterintelligence by the U.S. Mobile Training Team in Guatemala, an education that resulted in his being named deputy of the Regional Telecommunications Center (RTC), the heart and soul of the U.S.-established Central American counterinsurgency network that quickly became a center for death-squad activity. In 1981, Lima Estrada was promoted to the rank of colonel and became the second in command of the Huehuetenango Military Zone, the position he held at the time of the San Francisco massacre. Lima Estrada left Huehuetenango to become chief of intelligence on the National Defense Staff. Lima Estrada's role at the San Francisco massacre was revealed to Hennessey some months later when the priest was summoned by the colonel to the Huehuetenango base to discuss Hennessey's complaints of army kidnappings. The colonel was serving as the temporary replacement of the base's intelligence officer when he and the Iowan met.

3. Ricardo Falla, S.J., *Massacre de la Finca San Francisco Huehuetenango, Guatemala (17 Julio 1982)* (Copenhagen: IWGIA, 1983). Jesuit Falla is a Guatemalan anthropologist (Ph.D., University of Texas at Austin, 1975) who has chronicled many massacres of Mayans by the Guatemalan Army. His account of the San Francisco massacre is a faithful reproduction of the testimony of two survivors, recorded on tape by Falla in Chiapas, Mexico, on 4 September 1982.

4. Jonathan L. Fried et al., eds., *Guatemala in Rebellion: Unfinished History* (New York: Grove Press, 1983), 146-47.

5. Ibid.

6. George Black, *Garrison Guatemala* (New York: Monthly Review Press, 1984), 159.

Chapter 2

1. The information regarding the content of the meeting between Hennessey, Mullan, Taylor, and Baum is taken from several letters Hennessey wrote to his family as well as his memory refreshed by notes from his diary describing the meeting. Bill Mullan has confirmed Hennessey's account. A letter was sent to Consul Philip Taylor asking for his version of the

meeting, but Taylor refused to answer. Taylor's father, a Ph.D. in political science, of the same name, was an acquaintance of the author at the University of Houston in the mid-1980s. When I requested his help in contacting his son, telling him of my purpose, he responded with an angry letter, telling me I was "sanctimonious" for the position I was taking in regards to his son's responsibility in covering for Ríos Montt. A not dissimilar meeting with Consul General Philip Taylor experienced by Chilean-born anthropologist Beatriz Manz is detailed in an Americas Watch Report, *Guatemala: A Nation of Prisoners* (New York and Washington, D.C.: Americas Watch, January 1984), 246.

2. *New York Times,* 24 March 1982.
3. Unclassified telegram HCR462, dated 22 October 1982, from Embassy Guatemala to SecState WashDC Priority 1577. State Department files, . FOIA request by the Hennessey family, no date.

Chapter 3

1. Pope Paul VI, *On the Development of Peoples (Populorum Progressio)* (Washington, D.C., U.S. Catholic Conference, 26 March 1967). "We know, however, that a revolutionary uprising—save where there is manifest, long-standing tyranny which would do great damage to fundamental personal rights and dangerous harm to the common good of the country—produces new injustices, throws more elements out of balance and brings on new disasters."
2. John Cornwell, *Hitler's Pope: The Secret History of Pius XII* (New York: Penguin Books, 1999).
3. The value of a quetzal in 1980 was US$0.25.

Chapter 4

1. Pop's quote is from the *Cedar Rapids Gazette,* 12 May 1957, on the occasion of his reception of an award from the National Fathers' Day Committee for having eight daughters attending college.
2. Victoria Reifler Bricker, *The Indian Christ, The Indian King* (Austin: University of Texas Press, 1981), 33. Citing Sedley J. Mackie, *An Account of the Conquest of Guatemala in 1524* (by Pedro de Alvarado) (The Cortes Society, New York).

3. Ibid.

4. Helen Rand Parish, *El Redescubrimiento de Las Casas* (Berkeley, Calif.: Library of the University of California at Berkeley, 1987), 6.

5. Bricker, *The Indian Christ,* 20.

6. Frederick P. Bowser, "The Church in Colonial Middle America," *Latin America Research Review* 25, no. 1 (January 1990): 139. Citing Inga Clendinnen, *Ambivalent Conquests: Maya and Spaniards in Yucatan, 1517-1570* (Cambridge: Cambridge University Press, 1987). Also, H. McKennie Goodpasture, *Cross and Sword* (Maryknoll, N.Y.: Orbis Books, 1989), 36-40.

7. Today, Pope John Paul II "silences" Catholic theologians who dare to differ with Vatican interpretations of Catholic traditions wherever he has the power to do so. Cardinal Josef Ratzinger, head of the Vatican Curia's Congregation for the Doctrine of the Faith, was quoted in the *National Catholic Reporter,* 18 October 1996, as saying "the [Roman Catholic] church can never accept putting one's faith on the same level as the conviction of others."

8. This belief in the "rights" of the Sword to enforce the "rights" of the Cross explains why so many Latin American churchmen have supported the dictatorial "dirty wars" of the 1970s and 80s. Prime examples: Argentina, El Salvador, Guatemala, and the "contra" war against Nicaragua.

9. Mary W. Helms, *Middle America: A Culture History of Heartland and Frontiers* (Washington, D.C.: University Press of America, 1982), 165.

10. Kenneth Grieb, *Guatemalan Caudillo: The Regime of Jorge Ubico* (Athens: Ohio University Press, 1979).

11. Anita Frankel, *Political Development in Guatemala, 1944-54: The Impact of Foreign, Military and Religious Elites* (Ann Arbor, Mich.: University Microfilms International, 1969), 173.

12. Ibid.

13. Ibid., 175

14. Ibid. In another such letter, the prelate exclaimed that "the disorganized tribes which inhabited our America would have caused themselves to become extinct had not the Spanish conquest arrived so providentially which united them and gave them their triple gifts of religion, blood, and language."

15. Walter LaFeber, *Inevitable Revolutions: The United States in Central America* (New York: W.W. Norton, 1983), 33, quoting Secretary of State James G. Blaine, 1881.

Chapter 5

1. The former Maryknoller and friend is the author of the present volume.
2. Luis Olmedo Requeña, *Fé Cristiana y Violencia Revolucionaria* (Buenos Aires: Tierra Nueva, 1982).

Chapter 7

1. Michio Kaku and Daniel Axelrod, *To Win a Nuclear War* (Boston: South End Press, 1987), 87.
2. Ron, of course, never became Buchanan County's sheriff, but his brother Maurice did. And Mom and her shotgun once served Maurice as backup when some roughnecks tried to tip over his pickup.
3. John Cooney, *The American Pope: The Life and Times of Francis Cardinal Spellman* (New York: Times Books, 1984).

Chapter 9

1. Piero Gleijeses, *Shattered Hope: The Guatemalan Revolution and the United States* (Princeton: Princeton University Press, 1991), 32-33.
2. Richard H. Immerman, *The CIA in Guatemala: The Foreign Policy of Intervention* (Austin: University of Texas Press, 1982), 61 (quoting Samuel G. Inman, *A New Day in Guatemala*, 13).
3. Joseph Anfuso and David Sczepanski, *He Gives—He Takes Away: The True Story of Guatemala's Controversial Former President Efraín Ríos Montt* (Eureka, Calif.: Radiance Publications, 1983), 34.
4. In 1962, Luis Turcios Lima, a former army lieutenant turned guerrilla leader, was considered public enemy number one by the Guatemalan high command, the U.S. embassy, the U.S. Agency for International Development Mission (USAID), the U.S. Military Assistance Program, and the CIA. During the implementation of the Guatemalan Army's

scorched earth strategy to capture Turcios Lima in 1963, he was smuggled into Guatemala City from his stronghold in the mountains of Zacapa by his Politécnica classmates to participate in their yearly graduation anniversary celebration. After two days of carousing under the noses of his mortal enemies, he was escorted in a borrowed uniform back to his mountain hideout by four classmates. This author was witness to the fury and disbelief that invaded the AID Mission when its principals discovered that the millions of dollars they were spending on "Public Safety Programs" were so ineffective as to allow army officers to party with the man whom the U.S. government felt most threatened Guatemala's "democracy."

5. Gleijeses, *Shattered Hope,* 28.
6. Ibid., 75
7. Ibid., 52.
8. Ibid., 31.
9. Ibid.
10. Ibid., 52.
11. Stephen Schlesinger and Stephen Kinzer, *Bitter Fruit: The Untold Story of the American Coup in Guatemala* (New York: Anchor Press/Doubleday, 1982), 43.
12. Ibid., 39-40.
13. Ibid., 26-27.
14. Gleijeses, *Shattered Hope,* 96.
15. Ibid.
16. Ibid., 97.
17. Anita Frankel, *Political Development in Guatemala, 1944-1954: The Impact of Foreign, Military and Religious Elites* (Ann Arbor, Mich.: University Microfilms International, 1991), 205.
18. Ibid., 209.
19. Ibid., 203.
20. Gleijeses, *Shattered Hope,* 103.
21. Ibid., 104.
22. Ibid.
23. Immerman, *The CIA in Guatemala,* 99.
24. Ibid.
25. Schlesinger and Kinzer, *Bitter Fruit,* 86.

26. Immerman, *The CIA in Guatemala*, 117.
27. Schlesinger and Kinzer, *Bitter Fruit*, 72.
28. Gleijeses, *Shattered Hope*, 105-6
29. Ibid., 103
30. Schlesinger and Kinzer, *Bitter Fruit*, 85.
31. Ibid., 47.
32. Ibid.

Chapter 11

1. Schlesinger and Kinzer, *Bitter Fruit*, 170.
2. Ibid., 199.
3. Immerman, *The CIA in Guatemala*, 178.
4. Frankel, *Political Development*, 198.
5. Schlesinger and Kinzer, *Bitter Fruit*, 80.
6. Ibid., 87.
7. Gleijeses, *Shattered Hope*, 150.
8. Ibid., 152.
9. Peter Lyon, *Eisenhower, Portrait of the Hero* (Boston: Little Brown, 1974), book jacket.
10. Townsend Hoopes, *The Devil and John Foster Dulles* (Boston: Little Brown, 1973), 47.
11. Ibid.
12. Ibid., 37.
13. Ibid.
14. Ibid.
15. Immerman, *The CIA in Guatemala*, 5.

Chapter 13

1. Schlesinger and Kinzer, *Bitter Fruit*, 122.
2. Ibid., 127.
3. Ibid.
4. Miguel Ydígoras Fuentes, *My War with Communism* (Englewood, N.J.: Prentice-Hall, 1963), 124.
5. Schlesinger and Kinzer, *Bitter Fruit*, 142.

6. Ibid.
7. Ibid., 143.
8. Ibid., 144.
9. Ibid.
10. Ibid., 148.
11. Gleijeses, *Shattered Hope,* 258.
12. Schlesinger and Kinzer, *Bitter Fruit,* 129.
13. Gleijeses, *Shattered Hope,* 181.
14. Schlesinger and Kinzer, *Bitter Fruit,* 151.
15. Ibid., 152.
16. Ibid., 162.
17. Evan Thomas, *The Very Best Men, Four Who Dared: The Early Years of the CIA* (New York: Simon and Schuster, 1995), 115.
18. Schlesinger and Kinzer, *Bitter Fruit,* 112.
19. Ibid.
20. Ibid., 111.
21. Thomas, *The Very Best Men,* 115.
22. Gleijeses, *Shattered Hope,* 210.
23. Ibid., 287.
24. Schlesinger and Kinzer, *Bitter Fruit,* 166.
25. Ibid., 167.
26. Thomas, *The Very Best Men,* 115.
27. Schlesinger and Kinzer, *Bitter Fruit,* 169.

Chapter 14

1. Gleijeses, *Shattered Hope,* 327.
2. Schlesinger and Kinzer, *Bitter Fruit,* 175.
3. Ibid., 177.
4. Ibid., 178.
5. Gleijeses, *Shattered Hope,* 333.
6. Ibid., 334.
7. Ibid., 329.
8. Ibid.
9. Ibid.

10. Schlesinger and Kinzer, *Bitter Fruit*, 180.
11. Ibid.
12. Ibid., 18.
13. Gleijeses, *Shattered Hope*, p. 331.
14. Schlesinger and Kinzer, *Bitter Fruit*, 182.
15. Gleijeses, *Shattered Hope*, 338.
16. Ibid., 327-8.
17. Ibid.
18. Ibid., 307.
19. Ibid.
20. Ibid., 332-3.
21. Ibid., 333.
22. Ibid.
23. Ibid., 343.
24. Schlesinger and Kinzer, *Bitter Fruit*, 176.
25. Ibid., 193.
26. Gleijeses, *Shattered Hope*, 345.
27. Schlesinger and Kinzer, *Bitter Fruit*, 195.

Chapter 15

1. A junior seminary is equivalent to a high school, a minor seminary to a college, and a major seminary to a postgraduate institution.
2. Diary of Father Albert Reymann, Maryknoll, September, 1954.
3. Schlesinger and Kinzer, *Bitter Fruit*, 200.
4. Gleijeses, *Shattered Hope*, 245.
5. Schlesinger and Kinzer, *Bitter Fruit*, 205.
6. Ibid., 206.
7. Ibid.
8. Ibid., 207.
9. Ibid., 209.
10. Ibid., 210.
11. Ibid., 211.
12. Ibid.
13. Ibid.

14. Ibid., 213.
15. Ibid.
16. The fact that the second-in-command of the *Liberacionistas* was a lieutenant rather than a colonel is an indication of the paucity of support among the officer corps for Castillo Armas.
17. Lt. Colonel Cruz Salazar was not a supporter of Castillo Armas but merely someone jockeying for his own position, much as Colonel Monzón.
18. Schlesinger and Kinzer, *Bitter Fruit*, 213.
19. Ibid., 214.

Chapter 17

1. Schlesinger and Kinzer, *Bitter Fruit*, 216-7.
2. Ibid., 222.
3. Ibid.
4. Ibid.
5. The *San Francisco Chronicle*, 24 May 1997, reports that fifty-eight members of the Arbenz government were on a secret CIA assassination list, part of 1,400 pages of details released under orders by President Clinton. "The CIA now stresses that it does not believe any Guatemalan officials were assassinated on CIA orders during the coup." The term "orders" does not include "suggestions," a procedure used to maintain deniability.
6. Ibid., 216.
7. Ibid.
8. Ibid., 220.
9. Thomas Melville and Marjorie Melville, *Guatemala: The Politics of Land Ownership* (New York: The Free Press, 1971), 87.
10. Susanne Jonas, *The Battle for Guatemala: Rebels, Death Squads and U.S. Power* (Boulder, Colo.: Westview Press, 1991), 41.
11. Schlesinger and Kinzer, *Bitter Fruit*, 223.
12. Ibid., 234.
13. Gleijeses, *Shattered Hope*, 360.
14. Schlesinger and Kinzer, *Bitter Fruit*, 224.

15. U.S. State Department, *Foreign Relations of the United States, 1955-1957,* vol. 7 (Washington, D.C.: U.S. Government Printing Office, 1987), 120.
16. Ibid., 93.
17, Ibid., 120.
18. Ibid., 121.
19. Ibid., 123.
20. Ibid.
21. Ibid., 124.
22. Ibid.
23. Ibid., 94.
24. Ibid., 131.
25. Schlesinger and Kinzer, *Bitter Fruit,* 221.
26. U.S. State Department, *Foreign Relations,* vol. 7, 96.
27. Ibid., 97.
28. Ibid., 70.
29. Ibid.
30. Ibid.
31. Ibid., 77.
32. Ibid., 78.
33. Ibid.
34. Schlesinger and Kinzer, *Bitter Fruit,* 218.
35. U.S. State Department, *Foreign Relations,* vol. 7, 57.
36. Ibid., 129.
37. President Lázaro Cárdenas had the good fortune to coexist with the Good Neighbor policy of the Franklin D. Roosevelt administration. Otherwise, he might have befallen the bad luck of Premier Mohammed Mossadegh of Iran who suffered the fate of Arbenz Guzmán when Eisenhower gave the CIA orders to topple him in 1953 as he tried to nationalize his country's oil reserves.
38. Klein and Saks's public relations stated that it provided "a private enterprise prescription for sick national economies." Since the Agency for International Development (AID) had not yet come into existence, the U.S. government depended upon the World Bank and private consulting firms to oversee its grants and loans to foreign governments. Klein and

Saks, according to Susanne Jonas, "promoted orthodox I.M.F.-type policies" and functioned out of Guatemala's National Palace as a "shadow government," insuring American private interests a firm ideological justification for its activities. Jonas, *The Battle for Guatemala*, 58.

39. U.S. State Department, *Foreign Relations*, vol. 7, 132.
40. Ibid., 143.
41. Ibid., 144.
42. Ibid., 94.
43. Ibid., 146.
44. Melville and Melville, *Guatemala*, 119.

Chapter 19

1. Schlesinger and Kinzer, *Bitter Fruit*, 237.
2. U.S. States Department, *Foreign Relations*, vol. 7, 145.
3. Ibid., 147.
4. Ibid.
5. Ibid., 148.
6. Ibid., 151-2.
7. *El Imparcial*, 8 July 1958.
8. Carlos Enrique Centeño Cordón, *Las Cooperativas de El Petén*, vol. 1 (Guatemala: Universidad de San Carlos, 1973), 141-4. The most successful colonization program, though one not mentioned in Centeño's book, was the Ixcán Colonization Project founded by Father William Woods, a Maryknoller. In November 1976 Woods was killed in a plane accident that was most likely engineered by the Guatemalan Army. Many of the colonizers were murdered or driven from their lands by the army in the early 1980s.
9. *El Imparcial*, 25 January 1962.
10. Ibid., pp. 21-28 January 1962.
11. "To terminate with extreme prejudice" is a CIA euphemism for assassination.
12. U.S. State Department, telegram marked "Secret" to the Secretary of State from the U.S. Embassy in Guatemala #262, 1 November 1962.
13. U.S. State Department, airgram marked "Secret" from the Secretary of State to all ARA Diplomatic Posts #CA-7769, 5 January 1963.
14. Ydígoras Fuentes, *My War*, 2; and Schlesinger and Kinzer, *Bitter Fruit*, 243-4.

Chapter 20

1. Michael McClintock, Vol. II, *The American Connection: State Terror and Popular Resistance in Guatemala,* (London: Zed Books, 1985), 65. Volume I concerns El Salvador. All McClintock references below are understood to be to the second volume.
2. Ibid.
3. Ibid., 66.
4. Ibid., 60.
5. Ibid., 72.
6. *El Imparcial,* 1 August 1966.
7. Ibid., 22 November 1966.
8. Ibid., 6 July 1966.
9. Ibid., 22 November 1966.

Chapter 21

1. *Time,* 26 January 1968, 23.
2. Vicente Collazo-Dávila, USAF, "The Guatemalan Insurrection," in *Insurgency in the Modern World,* ed. Bard O'Neill, William Hinton, and Donald Alberts (Boulder, Colo.: Westview Press, 1980), 120.

Chapter 22

1. McClintock, *The American Connection,* 97.
2. Ibid. See also *The Nation,* 16 June 1997, 5; *National Catholic Reporter,* 4 October 1996, 3; *National Catholic Reporter,* 18 July 1997, 10.
3. Collazo-Dávila, "The Guatemalan Insurrection," 114.
4. Norman Gall, "Guatemalan Slaughter," *New York Review of Books* 17, no. 9 (20 May 1971).
5. J.C. Cambranes, *Agrarismo en Guatemala* (Guatemala/Madrid: Centro de Estudios Rurales Centroamericanos, 1986), 60.
6. Ibid.
7. Dom Helder Cámara et al., *Declaracion de 15 Obispos,* Doc. 67/35 (Cuernavaca, México: Centro Intercultural de Documentación, 10 September 1967). See also *Boston Archdiocesan Pilot,* 23 September 1976.

8. Latin American Bureau, *The Medellín Documents* (Washington, D.C.: U.S. Catholic Conference, September 1969).
9. "The Rockefeller Report," *Washington Post,* 9 November 1969; "The Rockefeller Report," *New York Times,* 10 November 1969.
10. Ibid.
11. McClintock, *The American Connection,* 99.
12. Roger Plant, *Guatemala: Unnatural Disaster* (London: The Trade Printing Company, 1978; Washington, D.C.: Latin America Bureau, 1978), 22.
13. U.S. Congress, Senate Committee on Foreign Relations, Subcommittee on Western Hemisphere Affairs, *Guatemala and the Dominican Republic* (Staff Memorandum, Pat Holt. p. 121, no. 149. [Washington, D.C.: Government Printing Office, 1971]). (Quoted in McClintock, *The American Connection.*)

Chapter 23

1. Anfuso and Sczepanski, *He Gives—He Takes Away,* 51ff.
2. Ibid., 58.
3. McClintock, *The American Connection,* 133
4. Anfuso and Sczepanski, *He Gives—He Takes Away,* 67.
5. Ibid., 74.
6. Mario Payeras, *Los Días de la Selva* (México, D.F.: Editorial Nuestro Tiempo, 1981), 90.

Chapter 24

1. Richard F. Nyrop, ed., *Guatemala: A Country Study* (Washington, D.C.: The American University Foreign Area Studies, 1983), 37.
2. *Dirección General de Aeronáutica Civil,* Aircraft Cessna 185, Registration TG-TEX. Property of William Wood. Accident occurring in the Jurisdiction of San Juan Cotzal in the Department of El Quiché on 20 November 1976. Guatemala, 25 November 1976.
3. Embassy of the United States of America. Guatemala City, Guatemala. Letter addressed to Mr. T.M. Kerndt of Lansing, Iowa, from Howard R. Gross, American consul, dated 14 January 1977. Besides Bill Woods,

those killed in the crash of his Cessna 185 were John Gauker of Auburn, Alabama, Ann Kerndt of Lansing, Iowa, Dr. Michael Okada of Minneapolis, Minnesota, and Selwyn Puig of Corpus Christi, Texas. Four years later, a Guatemalan air force captain was reported to have told his girlfriend that he had participated in the murder of two priests, Padre Juan Alonzo, in El Quiché, and Padre Bill Woods, in San Juan Cotzal. The captain was said to have helped install a remote controlled bomb on Woods's plane that was detonated by another air force officer sent to the army base in San Juan Cotzal. The girl gave the information to her priest in a nonsacramental form, allowing the priest to pass it on to Bishop Victor Hugo Martínez of Huehuetenango. When Hennessey tried to follow up on the report and obtain the name of the officer, the bishop, afraid of the consequences, blocked his efforts.

4. Plácido Erdozaín, *Archbishop Romero: Martyr of El Salvador,* John McFadden and Ruth Warner, trans. (Maryknoll, N.Y.: Orbis Books, 1990), 11.

5. Jon Sobrino, *Archbishop Romero: Memories and Reflections,* Robert Barr, trans. (Maryknoll, N.Y.: Orbis Books, 1990), 11.

Chapter 25

1. Anfuso and Sczepanski, *He Gives—He Takes Away,* 80.
2. Ibid., 85-86, 90-91.
3. Ibid., 99.
4. Nyrop, *Guatemala,* 37.
5. The make of Guatemalan weaponry will be noted at appropriate intervals to underscore their provenience. The repression of the Mayan Indians during the late 1970s and early 1980s could not have taken place to the degree achieved without the full knowledge and assistance of several Israeli governments. They filled the role of advisors and providers after President Jimmy Carter cut off all military aid to Guatemala in 1977 because of human rights abuses. The assistance continued after Carter left office with President Reagan's encouragement.
6. *Newsweek Magazine,* 19 June 1978, 55.
7. Ibid.

Chapter 26

1. Máximo Cajal, *¡Saber quién, puso fuego ahí!* (Madrid: Siddharth Mehta Ediciones, 2000), 47. Most of the information on the assault on the Spanish Embassy has been taken from Cajal's book. The book contains verbatim statements of many eyewitnesses to the events at the embassy, including those of Frank Ortiz, Odette Arzú, Jaime López, Cajal's wife, and a Guatemalan confidant.
2. McClintock, *The American Connection,* 159.
3. Arzú in Cajal, *¡Saber quién, puso fuego ahí!* 102.
4. Ibid., 102.
5. Ibid., 103.
6. Ibid., 36.
7. Ibid., 103
8. Ibid., 104.
9. Ibid., 105.
10. Ortiz in ibid., 114.
11. Cajal, 38.
12. Ibid., 37.
13. Ibid., 70.
14. Ibid., 68.
15. López in ibid., 78.
16. Ibid., 79.
17. Ortiz in ibid., 117.
18. *Washington Post,* 6 July 1980.
19. Cajal, *¡Saber quién, puso fuego ahí!* 216.

Chapter 27

1. Erdozaín, *Archbishop Romero,* 77.
2. The fact that a Republican president, Eisenhower, had foisted the Shah and his terrorist secret police, the Savak, on the Iranian people in a CIA-sponsored coup two decades earlier, did not prevent the Republican presidential candidate, Ronald Reagan, from blaming Carter for the embassy takeover.
3. Erdozaín, *Archbishop Romero,* 75.

4. Ibid., 79.
5. Ibid., 81.
6. Letter from Father Robert Carleton to Sister Dorothy Marie Hennessey, dated 11 December 1978.
7. Letter from Ron Hennessey to his family, dated 8 October 1979.
8. *El Gráfico*, 29 July 1980.
9. *New York Times*, 7 November 1980.

Chapter 28

1. Amnesty International, *Guatemala: A Government Program of Political Murder* (London: Amnesty International, February 1981).
2. McClintock, *American Connection*, 189.
3. Anfuso and Sczepanski, *He Gives—He Takes*, 94.
4. Ibid., 105.
5. Ibid., 106.
6. Nyrop, *Guatemala*, 135. See also Raymond Bonner, "A Guatemalan General's Rise to Power," reprinted from the *New York Times*, 21 July 1982, in Fried et al., *Guatemala in Rebellion*, 126ff.
7. The information regarding the attack on Cuarto Pueblo was taken from three sources: a letter that Ron Hennessey wrote in late April, 1982; Hennessey's own verbal account given to the author; and Ricardo Falla's book, *Masacres de la Selva, Ixcán, Guatemala (1975-1982)* (Guatemala City: Editorial Universitaria, 1992). Hennessey's Spanish was above average North American; his informers' Spanish was adequate for native Chuj speakers. Neither he nor they spoke fluent Spanish, the language in which the conversation took place. Falla is a Guatemalan native speaker of Spanish, a trained anthropologist, and a Jesuit priest. Where the three accounts differ, I have chosen to go with Falla's very careful reporting style and the fact that he had more eye and ear witnesses to the massacre than Hennessey. The two catechists that served as Hennessey's informants were apparently not the same two witnesses interviewed by Falla.
8. Falla, *Masacres de la Selva, Ixcán, Guatemala*, 52.
9. Ibid., 56.
10. Ibid., 69.
11. Ibid., 94.

12. Ibid., 98ff.
13. Falla's book gives the names, gender, age, and native village of the individuals massacred at Cuarto Pueblo (324) as well as those massacred elsewhere in El Ixcán. He collected his data during a five-month stay at the end of 1983 and the beginning of 1984 in the refugee camps in Chiapas, Mexico, where the majority of the refugees had fled.

Chapter 29

1. Anfuso and Sczepanski, *He Gives—He Takes Away*, 113.
2. *New York Times*, 24 March 1982.
3. Anfuso and Sczepanski, *He Gives—He Takes Away*, 117.
4. José Efraín Ríos Montt, "A Pacification Program for Guatemala," in Fried et al., *Guatemala in Rebellion*, 146.
5. Ibid., 147.
6. McClintock, *The American Connection*, 227. Also in the *New York Times*. 25 March 1982.
7. Anfuso and Sczepanski, *He Gives—He Takes Away*, ix
8. *Miami Herald*, 7 April 1982. Cited in Black, *Garrison Guatemala*, 150. Also in McClintock, *The American Connection*, 228.
9. Black, *Garrison Guatemala*, 150.
10. *Latin American Regional Reports* (London), 7 May 1982. Cited in McClintock, *The American Connection*, 233.
11. Ibid.
12. Ibid., 232.
13. Comité Episcopal de Guatemala, *Carta Pastoral*, May 1982.
14. CBS Television, *Guatemala, Special Report*, 1 September 1982. McClintock, *The American Connection*, 230.
15. McClintock, *The American Connection*, 230.

Chapter 31

1. Americas Watch Committee, *Civil Patrols in Guatemala* (Washington, D.C.: Americas Watch, 1985), 23ff.
2. Neil Sheehan, *A Bright Shining Lie: John Paul Vann and America in Vietnam* (New York: Random House, 1988), 731ff.

3. *Washington Post,* 21 October 1982, A1.
4. Americas Watch Committee, *Civil Patrols,* 20.
5. Ibid.
6. Ibid., 23-24.
7. Black, *Garrison Guatemala,* 159.

Chapter 32

1. Falla, *Masacres de la Selva, Ixcán, Guatemala.*
2. Col. Lima Estrada. See chapter 1, note 2, above.
3. Hennessey's request that the men listen to a public airing of what had occurred was intended to demonstrate to all that any knowledge learned exclusively by sacramental confession could never be used in any communication, either public or private, written or oral.
4. Charles Wilson was a right-wing congressman from Texas in the U.S. House of Representatives, a fervent defender of Nicaragua's Somoza-family dictatorship during his years in Congress.

Chapter 34

1. *New York Times,* 17 December 1982.
2. Ibid.
3. Maranatha Campus Ministries, *The Forerunner,* August, 1982.
4. *New York Times,* 22 August 1982.
5. The Ixquisís Air Base was a new addition to San Mateo's municipality. It was constructed to handle Israeli-made Araba STOL (short takeoff and landing) aircraft, particularly suitable for strafing mountain villages and suspected guerrilla hideouts.
6. *Time,* 24 February 1992, 28-35.
7. Council on Hemispheric Affairs, *Washington Report on the Hemisphere,* 19 April 1983. Cited in Black, *Garrison Guatemala,* 174.

Chapter 35

1. Amnesty International, *Guatemala: The Human Rights Record, 1987,* 96.
2. Ibid.

Chapter 36

1. When Sister Ortiz stated that her escape had been facilitated by a blond, English-speaking associate of the torturers (CIA?), the American ambassador at the time, Wyoming businessman Thomas Strook, incensed by the implied accusation, used a tactic often employed by the former ambassador, Fredrick Chapin, to explain such crimes, claiming that "the attack was not politically motivated; it was a case of Latin men getting excited over North American women." See Sister Dianna Ortiz, with Patricia Davis, *The Blindfold's Eyes: My Journey from Torture to Truth* (New York: Orbis Books, 2002).

2. International Human Rights Law Group/Washington Office on Latin America, quoted in Susanne Jonas, *Of Centaurs and Doves: Guatemala's Peace Process* (Boulder, Colo.: Westview Press, 2002).

3. The lowdown on Lima Estrada was that he had thrown a grenade into a bread oven in Ixtahuacán, Huehuetenango where three frightened children were hiding from him, killing the three. The colonel maintained that the three must have had connections with the guerrillas or they would not have feared him, an oft-cited excuse to explain many such unprovoked murders.

4. Department of Defense Intelligence Information Report, *Capitán de Infantería Byron Disrael Lima Estrada.* Prepared by the 610th Military Intelligence Detachment, Special Forces Group, 20 January 1971.

5. Ibid.

6. When General Mejía Víctores toppled Ríos Montt, he named Lima Estrada to the prestigious post of Chief of Army Intelligence. In May 1984, Lima Estrada was back in Huehuetenango, filling in for the vacationing provincial intelligence chief, at which time he had a visit from Ron Hennessey who was seeking the whereabouts of a group of kidnapped parishioners. From this encounter and judging from some asides that the colonel made at the time, the Iowan concluded that Lima Estrada had been in command of the troops that slaughtered the 362 (302?) peasants at Colonel Bolaños's ranch, San Francisco, 17 July 1982.

7. Jonas, *Of Centaurs and Doves.*

Epilogue

1. The institutions that assisted in producing the REMHI report, both financially and through moral and political support for those giving testimony, deserve mention and include the Swedish International Development Cooperation Agency (SIDA), the Norwegian Agency for Development Assistance (NORAD), the European Union (EU), the Protestant Association for Development Cooperation (EZE), Misereor of Germany, the Danish International Development Agency (DANIDA), OXFAM UK, the Project Counseling Service, the Heinrich Böll Foundation, the German Development Service (DED), the German Society for Technical Cooperation (GTZ), the Swedish Government, INKOTA-Medical International of Germany, and the Robert F. Kennedy Memorial Center for Human Rights. The thousands of individuals who contributed to the report, heroes in the truest sense of the word, are too numerous to mention here, but their names appear throughout the original four-volume report. Note: Except for the Robert F. Kennedy Memorial Center for Human Rights, no help for the project came from the United States.
2. *Cedar Rapids Gazette,* 29 April 1998.
3. *New York Times,* 11 March 1999, A12.
4. Ibid., 11 March 1999.
5. *MITF Central America Report,* August 1996, 1.
6. Ortiz, *The Blindfold's Eyes,* 431.
7. Quoted in Daniel Wilkinson, *Silence on the Mountain: Stories of Terror, Betrayal, and Forgetting in Guatemala* (Boston and New York: Houghton Mifflin, 2002), 324-25.
8. Ibid.
9. Quoted in Christopher Hitchens, *The Trial of Henry Kissinger* (New York: Verso, 2001), 25.
10. Walsh, *Firewall: The Iran-Contra Conspiracy,* 313. Also in Holly Sklar, *Washington's War on Nicaragua* (Boston: South End Press, 1988), 89.

Postscript

On 9 November 2003, the Guatemalan electorate went to the polls to elect a new president, vice president, 158 national legislators, and 331 local mayors from around the country, all for four-year terms. Seventeen political parties contested the elections, but only eight fielded presidential and vice presidential candidates, none of whom obtained 50 percent of the vote. The results necessitated a runoff election between the two front-runners, Oscar Berger of the Gran Alianza Nacional (GANA) and Alvaro Colom of the Unidad Nacional de Esperanza (UNE). In third place ran ex-dictator José Efraín Ríos Montt whose electoral participation was the result of some clever legal legerdemain since he had been prevented from running in 1990 and 1995 by Article 186 of the Guatemalan Constitution, which prohibited the candidacy of anyone who had previously taken power by force of arms. Ríos Montt, secretary general of the Frente Republicano de Guatemala (FRG) and president of the National Congress (1996-2000) had managed to get his front man, Alfonso Portillo, elected in 1995, giving the ex-general the power to rule the roost from behind the scenes. One of Portillo's slight-of-hand moves was to appoint close friends of Ríos Montt to the Constitutional Court. The Court then voted four to three to overrule Article 186 and allow Ríos Montt to run in the 2003 elections. Although the Supreme Court subsequently ruled the Constitutional Court's decision invalid in July 2003, provoking two full days of rioting in the capital by followers of the general, the Constitutional Court responded by declaring that its decisions were unappealable. The Constitutional Court won the battle of wills and the verdict of supremacy, allowing Ríos Montt to run in the November elections.

On 28 December 2003, Oscar Berger of GANA was elected president. He took office on 16 January 2004. What his election means for the future of Guatemala is difficult to predict since politicians and political parties all have to contend with agitators, assassins (in uniform and in street clothes), as well as traditional money interests and "new money," some of it from an illegal entrepreneurial class of drug brokers serving Colombian interests. Berger and his GANA party, for example, are considered to represent the traditional large landowners and business enterprises, but his vice presidential running mate, Eddie Stein, was foreign minister under Alvaro Arzú (1991-95) and carried forward a leftist foreign policy, opening relations with Cuba, an unheard of shift in direction. Berger's wife, Wendy Widman, a graduate of the Maryknoll Sisters' school, Monte María, has spent many years organizing destitute women who pass their waking hours looking for food, clothing, and recyclables in the country's garbage dumps.

On the other hand, Alvaro Colom (UNE), who ran in 1995 with the backing of the URNG, a self-confessed "champion of the poor" who accused Ríos Montt of "having blood under his fingernails" and stated during the campaign that he would back those human rights organizations working to bring the ex-dictator to trial for crimes against humanity, chose as his running mate Fernando Andrade Díaz-Durán. Andrade Díaz-Durán has been counselor to dictators Romeo Lucas García, Efraín Ríos Montt, and Humberto Mejía Víctores, serving as chancellor to the latter. Further, during the run-up to the 28 December election, Colom went all out to gain support from the backers of Ríos Montt by promising to continue payments begun by the FRG government to former civil patrollers, those guilty of many massacres committed doing Ríos Montt's 1982-83 tenure, men who acted as shock troops for the ex-general by breaking up GANA and UNE electoral rallies during the campaign.

With the distribution of the 158 deputies to the National Congress divided between GANA/Berger (47 seats), FRG/Ríos Montt (43), UNE/Colom (32), PAN/Arzú (17), and seven also-rans dividing the remaining nineteen seats, the backroom deals are going to be difficult to monitor. But, who knows, maybe Berger, with help from his wife, Wendy Widman, can start something that could bring Guatemala back to where it was in 1945 before the United States decided that it could not tolerate a nationalist democracy in its own "backyard." Not, however, while George W. Bush and his cronies control U.S. foreign policy.